HISTORY
OF THE
WAR IN THE PENINSULA
AND IN THE
SOUTH OF FRANCE
FROM THE YEAR 1807 TO THE YEAR 1814
Vol. I

By

W. F. P. NAPIER

HISTORY
OF THE
WAR IN THE PENINSULA
AND IN THE
SOUTH OF FRANCE

FROM THE YEAR 1807 TO THE YEAR 1814
Vol. I

by **W. F. P. NAPIER**

ISBN: 978-93-59396-27-9

Published by

DOUBLE 9 BOOKS

2/13-B, Ansari Road, Daryaganj
New Delhi – 110002
info@double9books.com
www.double9books.com
Tel. 011-40042856

This book is under public domain

ABOUT THE AUTHOR

William Francis Patrick Napier was a well-known British military commander and historian who lived from 1785 to 1860. His massive book, "History of the War in the Peninsula and in the South of France from the Year 1807 to the Year 1814," which is regarded as the canonical account of the Napoleonic Wars in the Iberian Peninsula, is what made him most famous. Napier, who was raised in a military household, enlisted in the British Army at an early age and participated in a number of conflicts during the course of his career. He had outstanding leadership qualities and was admired for his fearlessness and tactical prowess. Napier gained important insights from his first-hand experiences in the conflict, which he subsequently included in his historical books. He became well-known as a historian due to his thorough study and attention to detail. Napier's research on the Peninsular War continues to make an important addition to military history by providing an in-depth and interesting account of the fight. Napier worked in the military for numerous years and also wrote historical works in addition to his writings. His commitment to academic pursuits as well as military duty established his standing as a renowned figure in British history.

CONTENTS

BOOK IV

PREFACE

For six years the Peninsula was devastated by the war of independence. The blood of France, Germany, England, Portugal, and Spain, was shed in the contest; and in each of those countries, authors, desirous of recording the sufferings, or celebrating the valour of their countrymen, have written largely touching that fierce struggle. It may therefore happen that some will demand, why I should again relate "a thrice-told tale?" I answer, that two men observing the same object, will describe it diversely, following the point of view from which either beholds it. That which in the eyes of one is a fair prospect, to the other shall appear a barren waste, and yet neither may see aright! Wherefore, truth being the legitimate object of history, I hold it better that she should be sought for by many than by few, lest, for want of seekers, amongst the mists of prejudice and the false lights of interest, she be lost altogether.

That much injustice has been done, and much justice left undone, by those authors who have hitherto written concerning this war, I can assert from personal knowledge of the facts. That I have been able to remedy this without falling into similar errors, is more than I will venture to assume; but I have endeavoured to render as impartial an account of the campaigns in the Peninsula as the feelings which must warp the judgment of a contemporary historian will permit.

I was an eye-witness to many of the transactions that I relate; and a wide acquaintance with military men has enabled me to consult distinguished officers, both French and English, and to correct my own recollections and opinions by their superior knowledge. Thus assisted, I was encouraged to undertake the work, and I offer it to the world with the less fear because it contains original documents, which will suffice to give it interest, although it should have no other merit. Many of those documents I owe to the liberality of marshal Soult, who, disdaining national prejudices, with the confidence of a great mind, placed them at my disposal, without even a remark to check the freedom of my pen. I take this opportunity to declare that respect which I believe every British officer who has had the honour to serve against him feels for his military talents. By those talents the French cause in Spain was long upheld, and after the battle of Salamanca, if his counsel had been followed by the intrusive monarch, the fate of the war might have been changed.

Military operations are so dependent upon accidental circumstances, that to justify censure it should always be shown that an unsuccessful general has violated the received maxims and established principles of war. By that rule I have been guided; but to preserve the narratives unbroken, my own observations are placed at the end of certain transactions of magnitude, where their real source being known they will pass for as much as they are worth, and no more: when they are not well supported by argument, I freely surrender them to the judgment of abler men.

Of those transactions which, commencing with "the secret treaty of Fontainebleau" ended with "the Assembly of Notables" at Bayonne, little is known except through the exculpatory and contradictory publications of men interested to conceal the truth; and to me it appears that the passions of the present generation must subside, and the ultimate fate of Spain be known, before that part of the subject can be justly and usefully handled. I have, therefore, related no more of those political affairs than would suffice to introduce the military events that followed, neither have I treated largely of the disjointed and ineffectual operations of the native armies; for I cared not to swell my work with apocryphal matter, and neglected the thousand narrow winding currents of Spanish warfare; to follow that mighty stream of battle which, bearing the glory of England in its course, burst the barriers of the Pyrenees, and left deep traces of its fury in the soil of France.

The Spaniards have boldly asserted, and the world has believed, that the deliverance of the Peninsula was the work of their hands: this assertion so contrary to the truth I combat. It is unjust to the fame of the British general, injurious to the glory of the British arms. Military virtue is not the growth of a day, nor is there any nation so rich and populous, that, despising it, can rest secure. The imbecility of Charles IV., the vileness of Ferdinand, and the corruption of Godoy, were undoubtedly the proximate causes of the calamities that overwhelmed Spain; but the primary cause, that which belongs to history, was the despotism arising from the union of a superstitious court and a sanguinary priesthood, which, repressing knowledge and contracting the public mind, sapped the foundation of all military as well as civil virtues, and prepared the way for invasion. No foreign potentate would have attempted to steal into the fortresses of a great kingdom, if the prying eyes, and the thousand clamorous tongues belonging to a free press, were ready to expose his projects, and a well-disciplined army present to avenge the insult; but Spain being destitute of both, was first circumvented by the wiles, and then ravaged by the arms, of Napoleon. She was deceived and fettered because the public voice was stifled, but she was scourged and torn because her military institutions were decayed.

From the moment that an English force took the field, the Spaniards ceased to act as principals in a contest carried on in the heart of their country, and involving their existence as an independent nation; they were self-sufficient, and their pride was wounded by insult; they were superstitious, and their religious feelings were roused to fanatic fury by an all-powerful clergy, who feared to lose their own rich endowments; but after the first burst of indignation the cause of independence created little enthusiasm. Horrible barbarities were exercised on those French soldiers that sickness or the fortune of war exposed to the rage of the invaded, and a dreadful spirit of personal hatred was kept alive by the exactions and severe retaliations of the invaders, but no great and general exertion to drive the latter from the soil was made, or at least none was sustained with steadfast courage in the field. Manifestoes, decrees, and lofty boasts, like a cloud of canvas covering a rotten hull, made a gallant appearance, but real strength and firmness were nowhere to be found.

The Spanish insurrection presented indeed a strange spectacle; patriotism was seen supporting a vile system of government; a popular assembly working for the restoration of a despotic monarch; the higher classes seeking a foreign master; the lower armed in the cause of bigotry and misrule. The upstart leaders secretly abhorring freedom, yet governing in her name, trembled at the democratic activity they had themselves excited. They called forth all the bad passions of the multitude, but repressed the patriotism that would regenerate as well as save. The country suffered the evils, without enjoying the benefits, of a revolution! Tumults and assassinations terrified and disgusted the sensible part of the community; a corrupt administration of the resources extinguished patriotism, and neglect ruined the armies: the peasant-soldier, usually flying at the first onset, threw away his arms and returned to his home, or, attracted by the license of the *partidas*, joined the banners of men who, for the most part originally robbers, were as oppressive to the people as the enemy. The *guerilla* chiefs would, in their turn, have been quickly exterminated, but that the French, pressed by lord Wellington's battalions, were obliged to keep in large masses. This was the secret of Spanish constancy! Copious supplies from England, and the valour of the Anglo-Portuguese troops, these were the supports of the war! and it was the gigantic vigour with which the duke of Wellington resisted the fierceness of France, and sustained the weakness of three inefficient cabinets, that delivered the Peninsula. Faults he committed, and who in war has not? but his reputation stands upon a sure foundation, a simple majestic structure, that envy cannot undermine, nor the meretricious ornaments of party panegyric deform. The exploits of his army were great in themselves, and great in their consequences: abounding with signal examples of heroic courage and devoted zeal, they should neither be disfigured nor forgotten, being worthy of more fame than the world has yet accorded them—worthy also of a better historian.

BOOK I

CHAPTER I

Introduction.

The hostility of the European aristocracy caused the enthusiasm of republican France to take a military direction, and forced that powerful nation into a course of policy which, however outrageous it might appear, was in reality one of necessity. Up to the treaty of Tilsit, the wars of France were essentially defensive; for the bloody contest that wasted the continent so many years was not a struggle for pre-eminence between ambitious powers, not a dispute for some accession of territory, nor for the political ascendancy of one or other nation, but a deadly conflict to determine whether aristocracy or democracy should predominate; whether equality or privilege should henceforth be the principle of European governments.

The French revolution was pushed into existence before the hour of its natural birth. The power of the aristocratic principle was too vigorous and too much identified with that of the monarchical principle, to be successfully resisted by a virtuous democratic effort, much less could it be overthrown by a democracy rioting in innocent blood, and menacing destruction to political and religious establishments, the growth of centuries, somewhat decayed indeed, yet scarcely showing their grey hairs. The first military events of the revolution, the disaffection of Toulon and Lyons, the civil war of La Vendee, the feeble, although successful resistance made to the duke of Brunswick's invasion, and the frequent and violent change of rulers whose fall none regretted, were all proofs that the French revolution, intrinsically too feeble to sustain the physical and moral force pressing it down, was fast sinking when the wonderful genius of Buonaparte, baffling all reasonable calculation, raised and fixed it on the basis of victory, the only one capable of supporting the crude production.

Sensible, however, that the cause he upheld was not sufficiently in unison with the feelings of the age, Napoleon's first care was to disarm or neutralize monarchical and sacerdotal enmity, by restoring a church establishment, and by becoming a monarch himself. Once a sovereign, his vigorous character, his pursuits, his talents, and the critical nature of the times, inevitably rendered him a despotic one; yet while he sacrificed political liberty, which to the great bulk of mankind has never been more than a pleasing sound, he cherished with the utmost care political equality, a sensible good, that produces increasing satisfaction as it descends in the scale of society; but this, the real principle of his government, the secret of his popularity, made him the people's monarch, not the sovereign of the aristocracy; hence, Mr. Pitt called him, "the child and the champion of democracy," a truth as evident as that Mr. Pitt and his successors were the children and the champions of aristocracy; hence also the privileged classes of Europe consistently transferred their natural and implacable hatred of the French revolution to his person, for they saw that in him innovation had found a protector; that he alone had given pre-eminence to a system so hateful to them, and that he really was what he called himself, "the State."

The treaty of Tilsit, therefore, although it placed Napoleon in a commanding situation with regard to the potentates of Europe, unmasked the real nature of the war, and brought him and England, the respective champions of equality and privilege, into more direct contact; peace could not be between them while both were strong, and all that the French emperor had hitherto gained only enabled him to choose his future field of battle.

When the catastrophe of Trafalgar forbade him to think of invading England, his fertile genius conceived the plan of sapping her naval and commercial strength, by depriving her of the continental market for her manufactured goods; he prohibited the reception of English wares in any part of the continent, and he exacted from allies and dependants the most rigid compliance with his orders; but this "continental system," as it was called, became inoperative when French troops were not present to enforce his commands. It was thus in Portugal, where British influence was really paramount, although the terror inspired by the French arms seemed at times to render this doubtful; fear however is momentary, self-interest lasting, and Portugal was but an unguarded province of England.

Monsieur de Champagny's Report, 21st Oct. 1807.

From Portugal and Gibraltar, English goods freely passed into Spain; and to check this traffic by force was not easy, and otherwise impossible. Spain stood nearly in the same position with regard to France that Portugal did to England; a warm feeling of friendship for the enemy of Great Britain was the natural consequence of the unjust seizure of the Spanish frigates in a time of peace; but although this rendered the French cause popular in Spain, and that the court of Madrid was from weakness subservient to the French Emperor, nothing could induce the people to refrain from a profitable contraband trade; they would not pay that respect to the wishes of a foreign power, which they refused to the regulations of their own government; neither was the aristocratical enmity to Napoleon asleep in Spain. A proclamation issued by the Prince of Peace previous to the battle of Jena, although hastily recalled when the result of that conflict was known, sufficiently indicated the tenure upon which the friendship of the Spanish court was to be held.

Napoleon, in Las Casas, vol. ii. 4th part.

This state of affairs drew the French Emperor's attention towards the Peninsula; a chain of remarkable circumstances fixed it there, and induced him to remove the reigning family, and to place his brother Joseph on the throne of Spain. He thought that the people of that country, sick of an effete government, would be quiescent under such a change; and although it should prove otherwise, the confidence he reposed in his own fortune, unrivalled talents, and vast power, made him disregard the consequences, while the cravings of his military and political system, the danger to be apprehended from the vicinity of a Bourbon dynasty, and above all the temptations offered by a miraculous folly which outrun even his desires, urged him to a deed, that well accepted by the people of the Peninsula, would have proved beneficial; but being enforced contrary to their wishes, was unhallowed either by justice or benevolence.

In an evil hour, for his own greatness and the happiness of others, he commenced this fatal project; founded in violence, executed with fraud and cruelty, it spread desolation through the fairest portions of the Peninsula; it was calamitous to France and destructive to himself. The conflict between his hardy veterans and the bloody vindictive race he insulted, assumed a character of unmitigated ferocity disgraceful to human nature; for the Spaniards did not fail to defend their just cause with hereditary cruelty, and the French army struck a terrible balance of barbarous actions.

Napoleon observed with surprise the unexpected energy of the people, and bent his whole force to the attainment of his object; while England coming to the assistance of the Peninsula employed all her resources to frustrate his efforts. Thus the two leading nations of the world were brought into contact at a moment when both were disturbed by angry passions, eager for great events, and possessed of surprising power.

The extent and population of the French empire, including the kingdom of Italy, the confederation of the Rhine, the Swiss Cantons, the Duchy of Warsaw, and the dependent states of Holland and Naples, enabled Buonaparte through the medium of the conscription to array an army, in number nearly equal to the great host that followed the Persian of old against Greece; like that multitude also his troops were gathered from many nations, but they were trained in a Roman discipline, and ruled by a Carthaginian genius. The organization[1] of Napoleon's army was simple, the administration vigorous, the manipulations well contrived. The French officers, accustomed to success, were bold, enterprising, of great reputation, and feared accordingly. By a combination of discipline and moral excitement, admirably adapted to the mixed nature of his troops, the Emperor had created a power that appeared to be resistless, and, in truth, it would have been so, if applied to one great object at a time; but this the ambition of the man, or rather the force of circumstances, would not permit.

Exposé de l'Empire, 1807-8-9-13.
Napoleon's Memoirs, Las Casas, 7th part.
Lord Collingwood's letters, vide Appendix.

The ships of France were chained up in her harbours, and her naval strength was rebuked, but not destroyed; inexhaustible resources for building vessels, vast marine establishments, a coast line of many thousand miles, and the creative genius of Napoleon were nursing up a navy, formidable as a secondary arm; and the war then pending between the United States and Great Britain promised to nurture its growth, and to increase its efficacy.

Exposé, 1808-9. Napoleon, in Las Casas, vol. ii. 4th part.

Ibid. 6th part.

Maritime commerce was indeed fainting in France, but her internal and continental traffic was robust; her manufactures were rapidly improving; her debt was small; her financial operations conducted on a prudent plan, and with exact economy. The supplies were all raised within the year without any very great pressure of taxation, and from a sound metallic currency; thus there seemed to be no reasonable doubt, that any war undertaken by Napoleon might be by him brought to a favourable termination.

On the other hand, England, omnipotent at sea, was little regarded as a military power. Her enormous debt was yearly increasing in an accelerated ratio; and this necessary consequence of anticipating the resources of the country, and dealing in a factitious currency, was fast eating into the vital strength of the state; for although the merchants and great manufacturers were thriving from the accidental circumstances of the times, the labourers were suffering and degenerating in character; pauperism and its sure attendant crime were spreading over the land, and the population was fast splitting into distinct classes, — the one rich and arbitrary, the other poor and discontented: the former composed of those who profited, the latter of those who suffered by the war. Of Ireland it is unnecessary to speak; her wrongs and her misery, peculiar and unparalleled, are too well known, and too little regarded, to call for remark.

This general comparative statement, so favourable to France, would however be a false criterion of the relative strength of the belligerents, with regard to the approaching struggle in the Peninsula. A cause manifestly unjust is a heavy weight upon the operations of a general: it reconciles men to desertion—it sanctifies want of zeal—is a pretext for cowardice—renders hardships more irksome, dangers more obnoxious, and glory less satisfactory to the mind of the soldier. Now the invasion of the Peninsula, whatever might have been its real original, was an act of violence on the part of Napoleon repugnant to the feelings of mankind. The French armies were burthened with a sense of its iniquity, the British troops exhilarated by a contrary sentiment. All the continental nations had smarted under the sword of Napoleon, but, with the exception of Prussia, none were crushed; a common feeling of humiliation, the hope of revenge, and the ready subsidies of England, were bonds of union among their governments stronger than the most solemn treaties. France could only calculate on their fears, England was secure in their self-love.

The hatred to what were called French principles was at this period in full activity. The privileged classes of every country hated Napoleon, because his genius had given stability to the institutions that grew out of the revolution, because his victories had baffled their calculations, and shaken their hold of power. As the chief of revolutionary France he was constrained to continue his career until the final accomplishment of her destiny, and this necessity, overlooked by the great bulk of mankind, afforded plausible ground for imputing insatiable ambition to the French government and to the French nation, of which ample use was made. Rapacity, insolence, injustice, cruelty, even cowardice, were said to be inseparable from the character of a Frenchman; and, as if such vices were nowhere else to be found, it was more than insinuated that all the enemies of France were inherently virtuous and disinterested. Unhappily history is but a record of crimes, and it is not wonderful that the arrogance of men, buoyed up by a spring-tide of military glory, should, as well among allies, as among vanquished enemies, have produced sufficient disgust to ensure a ready belief in any accusation, however false and absurd.

Napoleon was the contriver and the sole support of a political system that required time and victory to consolidate; he was the connecting link between the new interests of mankind and what of the old were left in a state of vigour; he held them together strongly, but he was no favourite with either, and consequently in danger from both. His power, unsanctified by time, depended not less upon delicate management than upon vigorous exercise; he had to fix the foundations of, as well as to defend, an empire, and he may be said to have been rather peremptory than despotic. There were points of administration with which he durst not meddle even wisely, much less arbitrarily; customs, prejudices, and the dregs of the revolutionary licence interfered with his policy, and rendered it complicated and difficult. It was not so with his inveterate adversaries; the delusion of parliamentary representation enabled the English government safely to exercise an unlimited power over the persons and the property of the nation, and through the influence of an active and corrupt press they exercised nearly the same power over the public mind.

The vast commerce of England, penetrating by a thousand channels (open or secret) as it were into every house on the face of the globe, supplied unequalled sources of intelligence. The spirit of traffic, which seldom acknowledges the ties of country, was universally on the side of Great Britain, and those twin curses, paper-money and public credit, so truly described as "strength in the beginning but weakness in the end," were recklessly used by statesmen whose policy regarded not the interests of posterity. Such were the adventitious causes of England's power; and her natural, legitimate resources were many and great.

If any credit is to be given to the census, the increasing population of the United Kingdom, amounted at this period to nearly twenty millions: France reckoned but twenty-seven millions when Frederick the Great declared that if he were her king, "not a gun should be fired in Europe without his leave."

The French army was undoubtedly very formidable from numbers, discipline, skill, and bravery; but contrary to the general opinion, the British army was inferior to it in none of these points save the first, and in discipline it was superior, because a national army will always bear a sterner code than a mixed force will suffer. With the latter, the military not the moral crimes can be punished; men will submit to death for a breach of great regulations which they know by experience to be useful, but the constant restraint of petty though wholesome rules they will escape from by desertion, or resist by mutiny, when the ties of custom and country are removed; for the disgrace of bad conduct attaches not to them, but to the nation under whose colours they serve; great indeed is that genius that can keep men of different nations firm to their colours, and preserve a rigid discipline at the same time. Napoleon's military system was, from this cause, inferior to the British, which, if it be purely administered, combines the solidity of the Germans with the rapidity of the French, excluding the mechanical dulness of the one, and the dangerous vivacity of the other; yet, before the campaign in the Peninsula had proved its excellence in every branch of war, the English army was absurdly under-rated in foreign countries, and absolutely despised in its own. It was reasonable to suppose that it did not possess that facility of moving in large bodies which long practice had given to the French; but the individual soldier was (and is still) most falsely stigmatized as deficient in intelligence and activity, the officers ridiculed, and the idea that a British could cope with a French army, even for a single campaign, considered chimerical.

The English are a people very subject to receive and to cherish false impressions; proud of their credulity as if it were a virtue, the majority will adopt any fallacy, and cling to it with a tenacity proportioned to its grossness. Thus an ignorant contempt for the British soldiery had been long entertained, before the ill success of the expeditions in 1794 and 1799 appeared to justify the general prejudice. The true cause of those failures was not traced, and the excellent discipline afterwards introduced and perfected by the duke of York was despised. England, both at home and abroad, was, in 1808, scorned as a military power, when she possessed, without a frontier to swallow up large armies in expensive fortresses, at least two hundred thousand[2] of the best equipped and best disciplined soldiers in the universe, together with an immense recruiting establishment, and through the medium of the militia, the power of drawing upon the population without limit. It is true that of this number many were necessarily employed in the defence of the colonies, but enough remained to compose a disposable force greater than that with which Napoleon won the battle of Austerlitz, and double that with which he conquered Italy. In all the materials of war, the superior ingenuity and skill of the English mechanics were visible, and that intellectual power that distinguishes Great Britain amongst the nations, in science, arts, and literature, was not wanting to her generals in the hour of danger.

CHAPTER II

Nellerto.[3]

Vide Doblado's Letters.

For many years antecedent to the French invasion, the royal family of Spain was distracted with domestic quarrels; the son's hand was against his mother, the father's against his son, and the court was a scene of continual broils, under cover of which artful men, as is usual in such cases, pushed their own interest forward, while they seemed to act only for the sake of the party whose cause they espoused. Charles IV. attributed this unhappy state of his house to the intrigues of his sister-in-law, the queen of the Two Sicilies. He himself, a weak and inefficient old man, was governed by his wife, and she again by don Manuel Godoy, of whose person she was enamoured even to folly. From the rank of a simple gentleman of the Royal Guards, this person had, through her influence, been raised to the highest dignities; and the title of Prince of the Peace was conferred upon a man whose name must be for ever connected with one of the bloodiest wars that fill the page of history.

Ferdinand prince of the Asturias, naturally hated this favourite, and the miserable death of his young wife, his own youth and apparently forlorn condition created such an interest in his favour, that the people partook of his feelings; and the disunion of the royal family extending its effects beyond the precincts of the court, involved the nation in ruin. Those who know how a Spaniard hates, will readily comprehend why Godoy, who was really a mild, good-natured man, although a sensual and corrupt one, has been so overloaded with imprecations, as if he, and he alone, had been the cause of the disasters of Spain.

Napoleon in Las Casas.

Nellerto.

The canon, Escoiquiz, a daring and subtile politician, appears to have been the chief of Ferdinand's party; finding the influence of the Prince of the Peace too strong, he looked for support in a powerful quarter; and under his tuition, Ferdinand wrote upon the 11th of October, 1807, to the emperor Napoleon; in this letter he complained of the influence which bad men had obtained over his father, prayed for the interference of the "hero destined by Providence," so run the text, "to save Europe and to support thrones;" asked an alliance by marriage with the Buonaparte family, and finally desired that his communication might be kept secret from his father, lest it should be taken as a proof of disrespect. To this letter he received no answer, and fresh matter of quarrel being found by his enemies at home, he was placed in arrest, and upon the 29th of October, Charles denounced him to the Emperor as guilty of treason, and of having projected the assassination of his own mother. Napoleon caught eagerly at this pretext for interfering in the domestic policy of Spain, and thus the honour and independence of a great people were placed in jeopardy by the squabbles of two of the most worthless persons in the nation.

Some short time before this, Godoy, either instigated by an ambition to found a dynasty, or fearing that the death of the king would expose him to the vengeance of Ferdinand, had made proposals to the French court to concert a plan for the conquest and division of Portugal, promising the assistance of Spain, on condition that a principality for himself should be set apart from the spoil. At least such is the turn given by Napoleon to this affair; but the article which provided an indemnification for the king of Etruria a minor, who had just been obliged to surrender his Italian dominions to France, renders it very doubtful if the first offer came from Godoy. That, however, is a point of small interest, for Napoleon eagerly adopted the project if he did not propose it; and the advantages were all on his side. Under the pretext of supporting his army in Portugal, he might fill Spain with his troops; the dispute between the father and the son, now referred to his arbitration, placed the golden apples within his reach, and he resolved to gather the fruit if he had not planted the tree.

A secret treaty was immediately concluded at Fontainebleau, between marshal Duroc on the part of France, and Eugenio Izquerdo on the part of Spain. This treaty, together with a convention dependant on it, was signed the 27th, and ratified by Napoleon on the 29th of October; the contracting parties agreeing to the following conditions.

The house of Braganza to be driven forth of Portugal, and that kingdom divided into three portions, of which the province of Entre Minho e Duero and the town of Oporto, forming one, was to be given as an indemnification to the dispossessed king of Etruria, and to be called the kingdom of North Lusitania.

The Alemtejo and the Algarves to be erected into a principality for Godoy, who taking the title of prince of the Algarves, was still to be in some respects dependant upon the Spanish crown.

The central provinces of Estremadura, Beira, and the Tras os Montes, together with the town of Lisbon, to be held in deposit until a general peace, and then to be exchanged under certain conditions for English conquests.

The ultra-marine dominions of the exiled family to be equally divided between the contracting parties, and in three years at the longest, the king of Spain to be gratified with the title of Emperor of the Two Americas. Thus much for the treaty. The terms of the convention were:

That France should employ 25,000 infantry and 3,000 cavalry. Spain 24,000 infantry, 30 guns, and 3,000 cavalry.

The French contingent to be joined at Alcantara by the Spanish cavalry, artillery, and one-third of the infantry, and from thence to march at once to Lisbon. Of the remaining Spanish infantry 10,000 were to take possession of the Entre Minho e Duero and Oporto, and 6,000 were to invade Estremadura and the Algarves. In the mean time a reserve of 40,000 men was to be assembled at Bayonne, ready to take the field by the 20th of November, if England should interfere, or the Portuguese people resist.

If the king of Spain or any of his family joined the troops, the chief command was to be vested in the person so joining, but with that exception, the French general was to be obeyed whenever the armies of the two nations came into contact, and during the march through Spain the French soldiers were to be fed by that country, but paid by their own government.

The revenues of the conquered provinces were to be administered by the general actually in possession, and for the benefit of the nation in whose name the province was held.

Although it is evident that this treaty and convention favoured Napoleon's ulterior operations in Spain, by enabling him to mask his views, and introduce large bodies of men into that country without creating much suspicion of his real intention; it does not follow, as some authors have asserted, that they were contrived by the emperor for the sole purpose of rendering the Spanish royal family odious to the world, and by this far-fetched expedient to prevent other nations from taking an interest in their fate when he should find it convenient to apply the same measure of injustice to his associates that they had accorded to the family of Braganza.

Voice from St. Helena, vol. ii.

To say nothing of the weakness of such a policy, founded as it must be on the error that governments acknowledge the dictates of justice at the expense of their supposed interests; it must be observed that Portugal was intrinsically a great object. History does not speak of the time when the inhabitants of that country were deficient in spirit; the natural obstacles to an invasion had more than once frustrated the efforts of large armies, and the long line of communication between Bayonne and the Portuguese frontier could only be supported by Spanish co-operation. Add to this, the facility with which England could, and the probability that she would, succour her ancient ally, and the reasonable conclusion is, that Napoleon's first intentions were in accordance with the literal meaning of the treaty of Fontainebleau, and that his subsequent proceedings were the result of new projects conceived as the wondrous imbecility of the Spanish Bourbons became manifest.

Again, the convention provided for the organization of a large Spanish force, to be stationed in the north and south of Portugal, that is, in precisely the two places from whence they could most readily march to the assistance of their country, if it was invaded; and in fact the division of the marquis of Solano in the south, and that of general Taranco in the north of Portugal, did afterwards (when the Spanish insurrection broke out) form the strength of the Andalusian and Gallician armies, the former of which gained the victory at Baylen, while the latter contended for it, although ineffectually, at Rio Seco.

The French force destined to invade Portugal was already assembled at Bayonne, under the title of the first army of the Garonne. It was commanded by general Junot, a young man of a bold ambitious disposition, but of greater reputation for military talent than he was able to support. The men were principally conscripts, and ill fitted to endure the hardships which awaited them.

Thiebault, Exp. du Portugal.

At first, by easy marches and in small divisions, Junot led his army through Spain; the inhabitants were by no means friendly to their guests; but whether from any latent fear of what was to follow, or from a dislike of foreign soldiers common to all secluded people, does not clearly appear. When the head of the columns reached Salamanca, Junot halted, intending to complete the organization of his troops in that rich country, and there to await the most favourable moment for penetrating the sterile frontier which guarded his destined prey; but political events marched faster than his calculations, and fresh instructions from the emperor prescribed an immediate advance upon Lisbon. Junot obeyed, and the family of Braganza, at his approach, fled to the Brazils. The series of interesting transactions which attended this invasion will be treated of hereafter; at present I must return to Spain already bending to the first gusts of that hurricane, which was soon to sweep over her with such destructive violence.

Nellerto.

Historia de la Guerra contra Nap.

The accusation of treason and intended parricide, preferred by Charles IV. against his son Ferdinand, gave rise to some judicial proceedings which ended in the submission of the latter; and Ferdinand being absolved of the imputed crime, wrote a letter to his father and mother, acknowledging his own faults, but accusing the persons who surrounded him of being the instigators of deeds which he abhorred. The intrigues of his advisers, however, continued, and the plans of Napoleon advanced as a necessary consequence of the divisions in the Spanish court.

> Return of the French army.Appendix.
> Journal of Dupont's Operations MSS.

By the terms of the convention of Fontainebleau, forty thousand men were to be held in reserve at Bayonne; but a greater number were assembled on different points of the frontier; and in the course of December, two corps had entered the Spanish territory, and were quartered in Vittoria, Miranda, Briviesca, and the neighbourhood. The one, commanded by general Dupont, was called the second army of observation of the "Gironde." The other, commanded by marshal Moncey, took the title of the army of observation of the "Côte d'Ocean." In the gross they amounted to fifty-three thousand men, of which above forty thousand were fit for duty; and in the course of the month of December, Dupont advanced to Valladolid, while a reinforcement for Junot, four thousand seven hundred in number, took up their quarters at Salamanca.

> Notes of Napoleon. Appendix, No. 2.

It thus appeared as if the French troops were quietly following the natural line of communication between France and Portugal; but in reality Dupont's position cut off the capital from all intercourse with the northern provinces, while Moncey secured the direct road from Bayonne to Madrid. Small divisions under different pretexts continually reinforced these two bodies, and through the Eastern Pyrenees twelve thousand men, commanded by general Duhesme, penetrated into Catalonia, and established themselves in Barcelona.

In the mean time the dispute between the king and his son, or rather between the Prince of the Peace and the advisers of Ferdinand, was brought to a crisis by insurrections at Aranjuez and Madrid, which took place upon the 17th, 18th, and 19th of March, 1808. The old king, deceived by intrigues, or frightened at the difficulties which surrounded him, had determined, as it is supposed by some, to quit Spain, and, in imitation of his brother of Portugal, to retire from the turmoil of European politics, and take refuge in his American dominions. Certain it is that every thing was prepared for a flight to Seville, when the prince's grooms commenced a tumult, in which the populace of Aranjuez joined, and were only pacified by the assurance that no journey was in contemplation.

Upon the 18th the people of Madrid, following the example of Aranjuez, sacked the house of the obnoxious favourite, Manuel Godoy. Upon the 19th the riots recommenced in Aranjuez: the Prince of the Peace secreted himself from the fury of the mob; but his retreat being discovered, he was maltreated, and on the point of being killed, when the soldiers of the royal guard rescued him. Upon the 18th Charles IV., terrified by the violent proceedings of his subjects, abdicated. This event was proclaimed at Madrid on the 20th, and Ferdinand was declared king, to the great joy of the nation at large: little did the people know what they rejoiced at, time has since taught them that the fable of the frogs and their monarch had its meaning.

During these transactions, Murat, grand duke of Berg, who had taken the command of all the French troops in Spain, quitted his quarters at Aranda de Duero, passed the Somosierra, and entered Madrid the 23d, with Moncey's corps and a fine body of cavalry, Dupont at the same time deviating from the road to Portugal, crossed the Duero and occupied Segovia, the Escurial, and Aranjuez.

Napoleon in Las Casas.

Ferdinand arrived at Madrid on the 24th, but was not recognised by Murat as king; nevertheless, at the demand of that powerful guest, he surrendered the sword of Francis I., which was delivered with much ceremony to the French general. Charles, who had sent a paper to Murat, declaring that his abdication had been the result of force, wrote also to Napoleon in the same strain; and this state of affairs being unexpected by the emperor, he employed general Savary to conduct his plans, which appear to have been considerably deranged by the vehemence of the people, and the precipitation of Murat in taking possession of the capital.

Before Savary's arrival, don Carlos the brother of Ferdinand, departed from Madrid hoping to meet the emperor Napoleon, whose presence in that city was confidently expected; and upon the 10th of April, Ferdinand, having first appointed a supreme junta, of which his uncle, don Antonio, was president, and Murat a member, commenced his own remarkable journey to Bayonne, the true causes of which certainly have not yet been developed; and perhaps when they shall be known, some petty personal intrigue may be found to have had a greater share in producing it, than the grand machinations attributed to Napoleon, who could not have anticipated, much less have calculated, a great political measure upon such a surprising example of weakness.

The people everywhere manifested their repugnance to this journey; at Vittoria they cut the traces of Ferdinand's carriage, and at different times several gallant men offered, at the risk of their lives, to carry him off, in defiance of the French troops quartered along the road. But Ferdinand, unmoved by their entreaties and zeal, and regardless of the warning contained in a letter that he received at this period from Napoleon (who, withholding the title of majesty, sharply reproved him for his past conduct, and scarcely expressed a wish to meet him), continued his progress, and on the 20th of April, 1808, found himself a prisoner in Bayonne. In the mean time Charles, who, under the protection of Murat, had resumed his rights, and obtained the liberty of Godoy, quitted Spain, and also threw himself, his cause, and kingdom, into the hands of the emperor.

These events were in themselves quite enough to urge a more cautious people than the Spaniards into action; but other measures had been pursued, which proved beyond the possibility of doubt, that the country was destined to be the spoil of the French. The troops of that nation had been admitted without reserve or precaution into the different fortresses upon the Spanish frontier, and, taking advantage of this hospitality to forward the views of their chief, they got possession, by various artifices, of the citadels of St. Sebastian in Guipuscoa, of Pampeluna in Navarre, and of that of Figueras, and the forts of Monjuik, and citadel of Barcelona in Catalonia; and thus, under the pretence of mediating between the father and the son, in a time of profound peace, a foreign force was suddenly established in the capital — on the communications — and in the principal frontier fortresses; its chief was admitted to a share of the government, and a fiery, proud, and jealous nation was laid prostrate at the feet of a stranger, without a blow being struck, without one warning voice being raised, without a suspicion being excited in sufficient time to guard against those acts, upon which all were gazing in stupid amazement.

It is idle to attribute this surprising event to the subtlety of Napoleon's policy, to the depth of his deceit, or to the treachery of Godoy. Such a fatal calamity could only be the result of bad government, and a consequent degradation of public feeling; and it matters but little to those who wish to derive a lesson from experience, whether it be a Godoy or a Savary that strikes the last bargain of corruption, the silly father or the rebellious son that signs the final act of degradation and infamy. Fortunately, it is easier to oppress the people of all countries, than to destroy their generous feelings; when all patriotism is lost among the upper classes, it may still be found among the lower. In the Peninsula it was not found, but started into life, and with a fervour and energy that ennobled even the wild and savage form in which it appeared; nor was it the less admirable that it burst forth attended by many evils. The good feeling displayed was the people's own; their cruelty, folly, and perverseness, were the effects of bad government.

There are many reasons why Napoleon should have meddled with the interior affairs of Spain; there seems to be no good one for his manner of doing it. It is true that the Spanish Bourbons could never have been sincere friends to France while Buonaparte held the sceptre, and the moment that the fear of his power ceased to operate, it was quite certain that their apparent friendship would change to active hostility; the proclamation issued by the Spanish cabinet just before the battle of Jena, is evidence of this feeling; but if the Bourbons were his enemies, it did not follow that the people sympathised with their rulers. The resources of the country were, it is said, already at his disposal; but that availed him little, as the corruption and weakness of the administration had reduced those resources to the lowest ebb. His great error was, that he looked only to the court, and treated the nation with contempt. Had Napoleon taken care to bring the people and their government into hostile contact first, — and how many points of contact would not such a government have afforded! — instead of appearing as the treacherous arbitrator in a domestic quarrel, he would have been hailed as the deliverer of a great people.

Journal of Dupont's Operations. MSS

The journey of Ferdinand, the liberation of Godoy, and the flight of Charles, the appointing Murat to be a member of the governing Junta, and the movements of the French troops, who were advancing from all parts towards Madrid, roused the indignation of the Spanish people; tumults and assassinations had .taken place in various parts; and at Toledo a serious riot occurred on the 23d of April; the peasants joined the inhabitants of the town, and it was only by the advance of a division of infantry and some cavalry of Dupont's corps (then quartered at Aranjuez) that order was restored. The agitation of the public mind, however, increased, the French troops were all young men, or rather boys, taken from the last conscription, and disciplined after they had entered Spain, their youth and apparent feebleness excited the contempt of the Spaniards, who pride themselves much upon individual prowess; and the swelling indignation at last broke out.

Memoir of Azanza and O'Farril.

Upon the 2d of May, a carriage being prepared (as the people supposed) to convey don Antonio, the uncle of Ferdinand, to France, a crowd collected about it, and their language indicated a determination not to permit the last of the royal family to be spirited away: the traces of the carriage were cut, and loud imprecations against the French burst forth on every side. At that moment, colonel La Grange, an aide-de-camp of Murat's, appearing amongst them, was assailed and maltreated; in an instant the whole city was in commotion, and the French soldiers expecting no violence, were taken unawares and killed in every quarter: above seven hundred fell. The hospital was attacked by the populace; but the attendants and the sick beat them off; and the alarm having spread to the camp outside the town, the French cavalry came to the assistance of their countrymen by the gate of Alcala; while general Lanfranc, with a column of three thousand infantry, descending from the heights on the north-west quarter, entered the Calle Ancha de Bernardo. As this column crossed the street of Maravelles, in which the arsenal was situated, two Spanish officers, named Daois and Velarde, who were in a state of great excitement, discharged some guns upon the passing troops, and were immediately put to death by the voltigeurs; meanwhile, the column, continuing its march, released, as it advanced, several superior French officers, who were in a manner besieged in the houses by the mob. The cavalry at the other end of the town, treating the affair as a tumult, and not as an action, made some hundred prisoners; and by the exertions of marshal Moncey, general Harispe, Gonzalvo O'Farril, and some others, order was soon restored.

After night-fall, the peasantry of the neighbourhood came armed and in considerable numbers towards the city, and the French guards at the different gates firing upon them, killed twenty or thirty, and wounded others, some few were also crushed to death or lamed by the cavalry in the morning.

In the first moment of irritation, Murat ordered all the prisoners to be tried by a military commission, which condemned them to death; but the municipality interfered, and represented to that prince the extreme cruelty of visiting this angry ebullition of an injured and insulted people with such severity. Murat admitted the weight of their arguments, and forbade any executions on the sentence; but it is said that general Grouchy, in whose immediate power the prisoners remained, exclaiming that his own life had been attempted! that the blood of the French soldiers was not to be spilt with impunity! and that the prisoners having been condemned by a council of war, ought and should be executed! proceeded to shoot them in the Prado; and forty were thus slain before Murat could cause his orders to be effectually obeyed. The next day some of the Spanish authorities having discovered that a colonel commanding the imperial guards still retained a number of prisoners in the barracks, applied to the duke of Berg to have them released. Murat consented to have those prisoners also enlarged: but the colonel getting intelligence of what was passing, and being enraged at the loss of so many choice soldiers, put forty-five of the captives to death before the order could arrive to stay his bloody proceedings[4].

Such were nearly the circumstances that attended this celebrated tumult, in which the wild cry of Spanish warfare was first heard; but as many authors, adopting without hesitation all the reports of the day, have represented it sometimes as a wanton and extensive massacre on the part of the French, at another as a barbarous political stroke to impress a dread of their power, I think it necessary to make the following observations.

Manifesto of the council of Castile. Page 28.

Surgical Campaigns of Baron Larrey.

That it was commenced by the Spaniards is undoubted: their fiery tempers, the irritation produced by passing events, and the habits of violence which they had acquired by their late successful insurrection against Godoy, rendered an explosion inevitable. But if the French had secretly stimulated this disposition, and had prepared in cold blood to make a terrible example, undoubtedly they would have prepared some check on the Spanish soldiers of the garrison, and they would scarcely have left their hospital unguarded; still less have arranged the plan so that their own loss should far exceed that of the Spaniards; and surely nothing would have induced them to relinquish the profit of such policy after having suffered all the injury. Yet marshal Moncey and general Harispe were actively engaged in restoring order; and it is certain that, including the peasants shot outside the gates, the executions on the Prado and in the barracks of the imperial guards, the whole number of Spaniards slain did not amount to one hundred and twenty persons, while more than seven hundred French fell. Of the imperial guards seventy men were wounded, and this fact alone would suffice to prove that there was no premeditation on the part of Murat; for if he was base enough to sacrifice his own men with such unconcern, he would not have exposed the select soldiers of the French empire in preference to the conscripts who abounded in his army. The affair itself was certainly accidental, and not very bloody for the patriots, but policy induced both sides to attribute secret motives, and to exaggerate the slaughter. The Spaniards in the provinces, impressed with an opinion of French atrocity, were thereby excited to insurrection on the one hand; and, on the other, the French, well aware that such an impression could not be effaced by an accurate relation of what did happen, seized the occasion to convey a terrible idea of their power and severity; but, while it is the part of history to reduce such amplifications, it is impossible to remain unmoved in recording the gallantry and devotion of a populace that could thus dare to assail the force commanded by Murat, rather than abandon one of their princes; such, however, was the character of the lower classes of Spain throughout this war; fierce, confident, and prone to sudden and rash actions, they had an intuitive perception of all that was great and noble, but were miserably weak in execution.

The commotion of the 2d of May was the forerunner of insurrections in every part of Spain, few of which were so honourable to the actors as that of Madrid. Unprincipled villains hailed this opportunity of directing the passions of the multitude, and, under the mask of patriotism, turned the unthinking fury of the people against whoever it pleased them to rob or to destroy: pillage, massacres, assassinations, cruelties of the most revolting kind were everywhere perpetrated; and the intrinsic goodness of the cause was disfigured by the enormities committed at Cadiz, Seville, Badajos, and other places, but chiefly at Valencia, pre-eminent in barbarity at a moment when all were barbarous! The first burst of popular feeling being thus misdirected, and the energy of the people wasted in assassinations; lassitude and fear succeeded to the insolence of tumult at the approach of real danger; for it is one thing to shine in the work of butchery, and another to establish that discipline which can alone sustain the courage of the multitude in the hour of trial.

To cover the suspicious measure of introducing more troops than the terms of the convention warranted, a variety of reports relative to the ultimate intentions of the French emperor had been propagated: at one time Gibraltar was to be besieged, and officers were despatched to examine the Mediterranean coasts of Spain and Barbary; at another, Portugal was to become the theatre of great events, and a mysterious importance was attached to all the movements of the French armies, with a view to deceive a court that fear and sloth disposed to the belief of any thing but the truth, and to impose upon a people whose unsuspicious ignorance was at first mistaken for tameness.

In the mean time, active agents were employed to form a French party at the capital; but as the insurrections of Aranjuez and Madrid discovered the fierceness of the Spanish character, Napoleon enjoined more caution and prudence upon his lieutenants than the latter were disposed to practise. In fact, Murat's precipitation was the cause of hastening the discovery of his master's real views before they were ripe for execution; for Dupont's first division and cavalry crossed the Duero as early as the 14th of March, and upon the 10th of April occupied Aranjuez, while his second and third divisions took post at the Escurial and at Segovia; thus encircling the capital while Moncey's corps occupied it. Hence an intention to control the provincial government left by Ferdinand became manifest, and the riot at Toledo, although promptly quelled by the interference of the French troops, indicated the state of the public mind before the explosion at Madrid had placed the parties in a state of direct hostility.

Murat seems to have been intrusted with only a half confidence, and as his natural impetuosity urged him to play a rash rather than a timid part, he appeared with the air of a conqueror before a ground of quarrel was laid; not that he acted entirely without grounds, for a letter addressed to him about this time by Napoleon, contained the following instructions: "*The duke of Infantado has a party in Madrid; they will attack you; dissipate them, and seize the government.*" But Murat's policy, as his after life proved, was too coarse and open for such difficult affairs.

At Bayonne the political events kept pace with those of Madrid. Charles IV. having reclaimed his rights in presence of Napoleon, sent orders to the infant, don Antonio, to resign his office, the presidency of the governing junta, to Murat, who, at the same time, received the title of lieutenant-general of the kingdom: this appointment, and the restoration of Charles to the regal dignity, were proclaimed in Madrid, with the acquiescence of the council of Castile, on the 10th of May; but five days previous to that period, the old monarch had again resigned his sceptre into the hands of Napoleon, and Ferdinand and himself were consigned, with large pensions, to the tranquillity of private life.

The throne of Spain being now vacant, the right to fill it was assumed by the French emperor, in virtue of the cession made by Charles IV. He desired that a king might be chosen from his own family, and after some hesitation upon the part of the council of Castile, that body, in concert with the municipality of Madrid, and the governing junta, declared that their choice had fallen upon Joseph Buonaparte, at that time king of Naples. Cardinal Bourbon, primate of Spain, first cousin of Charles IV., and archbishop of Toledo, not only acceded to this arrangement, but actually wrote to Napoleon a letter testifying his adhesion to the new order of things.

As it was easy to foretel the result of the election, the king of Naples was already journeying towards Bayonne, and arrived there on the 7th of June. The principal men of Spain were also invited to meet in that town upon the 15th, with a view to obtain their assent to a constitution prepared by Napoleon. At this meeting, called "the Assembly of Notables," ninety-one Spaniards of eminence appeared, and, first accepting Joseph as their king, proceeded to discuss the constitution in detail, and after several sittings adopted it, and swore to maintain its provisions. Thus finished the first part of this eventful drama.

The new constitution was calculated to draw forth the resources of Spain: compared to the old system it was a blessing, and it would have been received as such under different circumstances; but now arms were to decide its fate, for in every province of Spain the cry of war had been raised. In Catalonia, in Valencia, in Andalusia, Estremadura, Gallicia, and the Asturias, the people were gathering, and fiercely declaring their determination to resist French intrusion.

But Joseph, apparently contented with the acquiescence of the ninety-one notables, and trusting to the powerful support of his brother, crossed the frontier on the 9th of July; and on the 12th arrived at Vittoria. The inhabitants still nourishing the discontent caused by Ferdinand's journey to Bayonne, seemed disposed to hinder Joseph's entrance; but their opposition did not break out into actual violence, and the next morning he continued his progress by Miranda del Ebro, Breviesca, Burgos, and Buitrago. The 20th of July he entered Madrid, and upon the 24th he was proclaimed king of Spain and the Indies, with all the solemnities usual upon such occasions; not hesitating to declare himself the enemy of eleven millions of people, the object of a whole nation's hatred; calling, with a strange accent, from the midst of foreign bands, upon that fierce and haughty race, to accept of a constitution which they did not understand, and which few of them had ever heard of; his only hope of success resting on the strength of his brother's arms; his claims upon the consent of an imbecile monarch, and the weakness of a few pusillanimous nobles, in contempt of the rights of millions now arming to oppose him. This was the unhallowed part of the enterprise; this it was that rendered his offered constitution odious, covered it with a leprous skin, and drove the noble-minded far from the pollution of its touch!

CHAPTER III

Memoir of O'Farril, and Azanza.

Joseph being proclaimed king, required the council of Castile to take the oath of allegiance prescribed by the constitution; but with unexpected boldness, that body, hitherto obedient, met his orders with a remonstrance. War, virtually declared on the 2d of May, was at this time raging in all parts of the peninsula, and the council was secretly apprized that a great misfortune had befallen the French arms. It was no longer a question between Joseph and some reluctant public bodies, but an awful struggle between great nations; and how the spirit of insurrection breaking forth simultaneously in every province was nourished in each, until it acquired the consistence of regular warfare, I shall now relate.

Just before the tumult of Aranjuez, the marquis of Solano y Socoro, commanding the Spanish auxiliary force in the Alentejo, received orders from Godoy to withdraw from that country with his division, and to post it on the frontier of Andalusia, to cover the projected journey of Charles IV. Napoleon was aware of these orders, but would not interrupt their execution. Solano quitted Portugal without difficulty, and in the latter end of May, observing the general agitation, repaired to his government of Cadiz, where a French squadron[5], under admiral Rossily, had just before taken refuge from the English fleet. As Solano passed through Seville (that city being in a state of great ferment), he was required to put himself at the head of an insurrection in favour of Ferdinand VII. He refused, and passed on to his own government; but there also the people were ripe for a declaration against the French; and a local government having been in the mean time established at Seville, the members at once assumed the title of the "Supreme Junta of Spain and the Indies," declared war in form against the intrusive monarch, commanded all men between the ages of sixteen and forty-five to take arms, called upon the troops of the camp of St. Roch to acknowledge their authority, and ordered Solano to attack the French squadron. That unfortunate man hesitated to commit his country in a war with a power whose strength and means he was better acquainted with than the temper of his own countrymen, and was instantly murdered: he died with a courage worthy of his amiable and unblemished character. There is too much reason to believe that his death was coolly projected, and that the junta at Seville sent an agent to Cadiz for the express purpose of exciting the populace to commit this odious assassination.

This foul stain upon the cause was intensely deepened by the perpetration of similar or worse deeds in every part of the kingdom. At Seville the conde d'Aguilar was dragged from his carriage, and, without even the imputation of guilt, inhumanly butchered; and here again it is said that the mob were instigated by a leading member of the junta, count Gusman de Tilly, a man described as "capable of dishonouring a whole nation by his crimes," while his victim was universally admitted to be virtuous and accomplished.

Sir Hew Dalrymple's correspondence.

As early as April, general Castaños (then commanding the camp of St. Roch) had entered into communication with sir Hew Dalrymple, the governor of Gibraltar; he was resolved to seize any opportunity that offered to resist the French, and he appears to have been the first, if not the only Spaniard, who united patriotism with prudent calculation, readily acknowledging the authority of the junta of Seville, and stifling the workings of self-interest with a virtue by no means common to his countrymen at that period. When the insurrection first broke out, admiral Purvis, commanded the British squadron off Cadiz, and in concert with general Spencer (who happened to be in that part of the world with five thousand men), offered to co-operate with Solano, if he would assail the French ships of war in the harbour: upon the death of that unfortunate man, this offer was renewed and pressed upon don Thomas Morla, his successor; but he, for reasons hereafter to be mentioned, refused all assistance, and reduced the hostile ships himself. Castaños, on the contrary, united closely with all the British commanders, and obtained from them supplies of arms, ammunition, and money; and at the insistence of sir Hew Dalrymple, the merchants of Gibraltar advanced a loan for the service of the Spanish patriots[6].

Moniteur. Azanza an O'Farril. Nellerto.

Meanwhile the assassinations at Cadiz and Seville were imitated in every part of Spain; hardly can a town be named in which some innocent and worthy persons were not slain. Grenada had its murders; Carthagena rivalled Cadiz in ruthless cruelty; and Valencia was foul with slaughter. Don Miguel de Saavedra, the governor of that city, was killed, not in the fury of the moment, for he escaped the first danger and fled, but being pursued and captured, was brought back and deliberately sacrificed. Balthazar Calvo, a canon of the church of St. Isidro, then commenced a massacre of the French residents. For twelve days unchecked he traversed the streets of Valencia, followed by a band of fanatics, brandishing their knives, and filling all places with blood: many hundred helpless people fell the victims of his thirst for murder; and at last, emboldened by the impunity he enjoyed, Calvo proceeded to threaten the junta itself; but there his career was checked. Those worthy personages, who (with the exception of Mr. Tupper, the English consul, then a member), had calmly witnessed his previous violence, at once found the means to crush his power when their own safety was concerned. The canon, being in the act of braving their authority, was seized by stratagem, imprisoned, and soon afterwards strangled, together with two hundred of his band.

The conde de Serbelloni, captain-general of the province, placed himself at the head of the insurrection, and proceeded to organise an army; and at the same time the old count Florida Blanca assumed the direction of the Murcian patriots, and those two kingdoms acted cordially together.

In Catalonia the occupation of Barcelona impeded the development of the popular effervescence, but the feeling was the same, and the insurrection breaking out at the town of Manresa, soon spread to all the unfettered parts of the province.

In Aragon the arrival of don Joseph Palafox kindled the fire of patriotism; he had escaped from Bayonne, and his family were greatly esteemed in a country where it was of the noblest among a people absurdly vain of their ancient descent. The captain-general, fearful of a tumult, ordered Palafox to quit the province. This circumstance, joined to some appearance of mystery in his escape, inflamed the passions of the multitude; they surrounded his abode, and forced him to put himself at their head: the captain-general was displaced and confined, some persons were murdered, and a junta was formed. Palafox was considered by his companions as a man of slender capacity and great vanity, and there is nothing in his exploits to create a doubt of the justness of this opinion. It was not Palafox that upheld the glory of Aragon, it was the spirit of the people, which he had not excited, and could so little direct, that for a long time after the commencement of the first siege, he was kept a sort of prisoner in Zaragoza; and evident distrust of his courage and fidelity was displayed by the population which he is supposed to have ruled.

The example of Aragon aroused the Navarrese, and Logroño became the focus of an insurrection which extended along most of the valleys of that kingdom. In the northern and western provinces the spirit of independence was equally fierce, and as decidedly pronounced, accompanied also by the same brutal excesses. In Badajos the conde de la Torre del Frenio was butchered by the populace, and his mangled carcass dragged through the streets in triumph. At Talavera de la Reyna, the corregidor with difficulty escaped a similar fate by a hasty flight. Leon presented a wide, unbroken scene of anarchy. In Valladolid, and all the great towns, the insurgent patriots laid violent hands upon every person who did not instantly concur in their wishes, and pillage was added to murder.

Gallicia seemed to hold back for a moment; but the example of Leon, and the arrival of an agent from the Asturias, where the insurrection was in full force, produced a general movement. Filanghieri, the governor of Coruña, an Italian by birth, was by a tumultuous crowd called upon to exercise the rights of sovereignty, and to declare war in form against the French: like every man of sense in Spain, he was unwilling to commence such an important revolution upon such uncertain grounds; the impatient populace instantly attempted his life, which was then saved by the courage of an officer of his staff; but his horrible fate was only deferred. He was a man of talent, sincerely attached to Spain, and he exerted himself with success in establishing a force in the province: no suspicion of guilt seems to have attached to his conduct, and his death marks the temper of the times and the inherent ferocity of the people. A part of the regiment of Navarre seized him at Villa Franca del Bierzo, planted the ground with their bayonets, and then tossing him in a blanket, let him fall on the points thus disposed, and there leaving him to struggle, they dispersed and retired to their own homes.

The Asturians were the first who proclaimed their indefeasible right of choosing a new government when the old one ceased to afford them protection. Having established a local junta, and invested it with all the functions of royalty, they declared war against the French, and despatched deputies to England to solicit assistance.

In Biscay and the Castiles, fifty thousand bayonets overawed the great towns; but the peasantry commenced a war in their own manner against the stragglers and the sick, and thus a hostile chain surrounding the French army was completed in every link.

This universal and nearly simultaneous effort of the Spanish people was beheld by the rest of Europe with astonishment and admiration: astonishment at the energy thus suddenly put forth by a nation hitherto deemed unnerved and debased; admiration at the devoted courage of an act, which, seen at a distance, and its odious parts unknown, appeared with all the ideal beauty of Numantian patriotism. In England the enthusiasm was unbounded; dazzled at first with the splendour of such an agreeable, unlooked-for spectacle, men of all classes gave way to the impulse of a generous sympathy, and forgot, or felt disinclined to analyse, the real causes of this apparently magnanimous exertion. But without wishing to detract from the merit of the Spanish people, and certainly that merit was very great, it may be fairly doubted if the disinterested vigour of their character was the true source of their resistance. Constituted as modern states are, with little in their systems of government or education which conduces to nourish intense feelings of patriotism, it would be miraculous indeed if such a result was obtained from the pure virtue of a nation, which for two centuries had groaned under the pressure of civil and religious despotism. It was, in fact, produced by several co-operating causes, many of which were any thing but commendable.

The Spanish character, with relation to public affairs, is distinguished by inordinate pride and arrogance. Dilatory and improvident, the individual as well as the mass, all possess an absurd confidence that every thing is practicable which their heated imagination suggests; once excited, they can see no difficulty in the execution of a project, and the obstacles they encounter are attributed to treachery; hence the sudden murder of so many virtuous men at the commencement of this commotion. Kind and warm in his attachments, but bitter in his anger, the Spaniard is patient under privations, firm in bodily suffering, prone to sudden passion, vindictive, bloody, remembering insult longer than injury, and cruel in his revenge. With a strong natural perception of what is noble, his promise is lofty, but as he invariably permits his passions to get the mastery of his reason, his performance is mean.

In the progress of this war the tenacity of vengeance peculiar to the nation supplied the want of cool, persevering intrepidity; but it was a poor substitute for that essential quality, and led rather to deeds of craft and cruelty than to daring acts of patriotism. Now the abstraction of the royal family, and the unexpected pretension to the crown, so insultingly put forth by Napoleon, aroused all the Spanish pride. The tumults of Madrid and Aranjuez had agitated the public mind, and prepared it for a violent movement, and the protection afforded by the French to the obnoxious Godoy increased the ferment of popular feeling: a dearly cherished vengeance was thus frustrated at the moment of its expected accomplishment, and the disappointment excited all that fierceness of anger which with Spaniards is, for the moment, uncontrollable. Just then the tumult of Madrid, swollen and distorted, wrought the people to frenzy, and they arose with one accord, not to meet a danger the extent of which they had calculated, and were prepared, for the sake of independence, to confront, but to gratify the fury of their hearts, and to slake their thirst of blood.

Napoleon's Memoires, Campagne d'Italie, Venise.

During Godoy's administration the property of the church had been trenched upon, and it was evident, from the example of France and Italy, that, under the new system, that operation would be repeated. This was a matter that involved the interests, and, of course, stimulated the activity of a multitude of monks and priests, who found no difficulty in persuading an ignorant and bigoted people that the aggressive stranger was also the enemy of religion and accursed of God; hence processions, miracles, prophecies, distribution of reliques, and the appointment of saints to the command of the armies, were freely employed to fanaticize the mass of the patriots. In every part of the peninsula the clergy were distinguished for their active zeal, and monks or friars were leaders in the tumults, or at the side of those who were instigating them to barbarous actions. Buonaparte found the same cause produce similar effects during his early campaigns in Italy; and if the shape of that country had been as favourable for protracted resistance, and that a like support had been afforded to them by Great Britain, the heroes of Spain would have been rivalled by modern Romans!

Appendix, No. 9.

The continental system of mercantile exclusion was another spring of this complicated machinery. It threatened to lessen the already decayed commerce of the maritime towns; but the contraband trade, which has always been carried on in Spain to an incredible extent, was certain of destruction; and with that trade the fate of one hundred thousand excise and custom-house officers was involved. It required but a small share of penetration to perceive, that a system of armed revenue officers, organized after the French manner, and stimulated by a vigorous administration, would quickly put an end to the smuggling, which was, in truth, only a consequence of the monopolies and internal restrictions upon the trade of one province with another — vexations abolished by the constitution of Bayonne: hence all the activity and intelligence of the merchants engaged in foreign trade, and all the numbers and lawless violence of the smugglers, were enlisted in the cause of the country, and swelled the ranks of the insurgent patriots; and hence also the readiness of the Gibraltar merchants to advance the loan before spoken of.

The state of civilisation in Spain was likewise exactly suited to an insurrection: if the people had been a little more enlightened, they would have joined the French; if very enlightened, the invasion could not have happened at all; but, in a country where the comforts of civilized society are less needed, and therefore less attended to than in any other part of Europe, where the warmth and dryness of the climate render it no sort of privation or even inconvenience to sleep for the greatest part of the year in the open air, and where the universal custom is to go armed, it was not difficult for any energetic man to assemble and keep together large masses of the credulous peasantry. No story could be too gross for their belief, if it agreed with their wishes. "Es verdad, los dicen," "It is true, they say it," is the invariable answer of a Spaniard if a doubt is expressed of the truth of an absurd report. Of temperate habits, possessing little furniture, and generally hoarding all the gold he can get, the Spanish peasant is less concerned for the loss of his house than the inhabitant of another country would be: the effort that he makes in relinquishing his abode must not be measured by the scale of an Englishman's exertion in a like case; and once engaged in an adventure, the lightness of his spirits, and the brilliancy of his sky, make it a matter of indifference to the angry Spanish peasant whither he wanders.

Historia de la Guerra contra Napoleon.

The evils which had afflicted the country previous to the period of the French interference was another cause which tended to prepare the Spaniards for violence, and aided in turning that violence against the intruders. Famine, oppression, poverty, and disease, the loss of commerce, and unequal taxation, had pressed sorely upon them; for such a system the people could not be enthusiastic; but they were taught to believe, that Godoy was the sole author of the misery they suffered, and that Ferdinand would redress their grievances; and as the French were the strenuous protectors of the former, and the oppressors of the latter, it was easy to add this bitterness to their natural hatred of the domination of a stranger; and it was so done.

Such were the principal causes which combined to produce this surprising revolution, from which so many great events flowed, without one man of eminent talent being cast up to control or direct the spirit which was thus accidentally excited. Nothing proves more directly the heterogeneous nature of the feelings and interests which were united together than this last fact, which cannot be attributed to a deficiency of natural talent, for the genius of the Spanish people is notoriously ardent, subtle, and vigorous; but there was no common bond of feeling which a great man could lay hold of to influence large masses. Persons of sagacity perceived very early that the Spanish revolution, like a leafy shrub in a violent gale of wind, greatly agitated but disclosing only slight unconnected stems, afforded no sure hold for the ambition of a master-spirit, if such there were. It was clear that the cause would fail unless supported by England, and then England would direct all, and not suffer her resources to be wielded for the glory of an individual, whose views and policy might hereafter thwart her own; nor was it difficult to perceive that the downfall of Napoleon, not the regeneration of Spain, was the object of her cabinet.

The explosion of public feeling was fierce in its expression, because political passions will always be vehement at the first moment of their appearance among a people new to civil commotion, and unused to permit their heat to evaporate in public discussions. The result was certainly a wonderful change in the affairs of Europe; it seems yet undecided whether that change has been for the better or for the worse. In the progress of their struggle, the Spaniards developed more cruelty than courage, more violence than intrepidity, more personal hatred of the French than enthusiasm for their own cause. They opened indeed a wide field for the exertions of others; they presented a fulcrum upon which a lever was rested that moved the civilised world; but assuredly the presiding genius, the impelling power, came from another quarter. Useful accessories they were, but as principals they displayed neither wisdom, spirit, nor skill sufficient to resist the prodigious force by which they were assailed. If they appeared at first heedless of danger, it was not because they were prepared to perish rather than submit, but that they were reckless of provoking a power whose terrors they could not estimate, and in their ignorance despised.

It is, however, not surprising that great expectations were at first formed of the heroism of the Spaniards, and those expectations were greatly augmented by their agreeable qualities. There is not upon the face of the earth a people so attractive in the friendly intercourse of society: their majestic language, fine persons, imposing dress and lively imaginations, the inexpressible beauty of the women, and the air of romance which they throw over every action, and infuse into every feeling, all combine to delude the senses and to impose upon the judgment. As companions they are incomparably the most agreeable of mankind; but danger and disappointment attend the man who, confiding in their promises and energy, ventures upon a difficult enterprise. "Never do to-day what you can put off until to-morrow," is the favourite proverb in Spain, and, unlike most proverbs, it is rigidly attended to.

CHAPTER IV

The commotion of Aranjuez had undeceived the French emperor; he perceived that he was engaged in a delicate enterprise, and that the people he had to deal with were any thing but tame and quiescent under insult. Determined, however, to persevere, he pursued his political intrigues, and, without relinquishing the hope of a successful termination to the affair by such means, he arranged a profound plan of military operations, and so distributed his forces, that, at the moment when Spain was pouring forth her swarthy bands, the masses of the French army were concentrated upon the most important points, and combined in such a manner, that, from their central position they had the power of overwhelming each separate province, no three of which could act in concert without first beating a French corps; and if any of the Spanish armies succeeded in routing a French force, the remaining corps of the latter could unite without difficulty, and retreat without danger. It was the skill of this disposition which enabled seventy thousand men, covering a great extent of country, to brave the simultaneous fury of a whole nation: an army less ably distributed would have been trampled under foot, and lost amidst the tumultuous uproar of eleven millions of people.

Historia de la Guerra contra Napoleon Buonaparte.

The inconvenience in a political point of view that would have arisen from suffering a regular army to take the field was evident. To have been able to characterise the opposition of the Spanish people as a partial insurrection of peasants, instigated by some evil-disposed persons to act against the wishes of the respectable part of the nation, would have given some colour to the absorbing darkness of the invasion: but to have permitted that which was at first an insurrection of peasants to take the form and consistence of regular armies and methodical warfare, would have been a military error, and dangerous in the extreme. Napoleon, who well knew that scientific war is only a wise application of force, laughed at the delusion of those who regarded the want of a regular army as a favourable circumstance, and who hailed the undisciplined peasant as the more certain defender of the country. He knew that a general insurrection can never last long, that it is a military anarchy, and incapable of real strength: he knew that it was the disciplined battalions of Valley Forge, not the volunteers of Lexington, that established American independence; that it was the veterans of Arcole and Marengo, not the republicans of Valmy, that fixed the fate of the French revolution; and consequently his efforts were directed to hinder the Spaniards from drawing together any great body of regular soldiers; an event that might easily happen, for the gross amount of the organized Spanish force was, in the month of May, about one hundred and twenty-seven thousand men of all arms. Fifteen thousand of these were in Holstein, under the marquis of Romana, but twenty thousand were already partially concentrated in Portugal. The remainder, in which were comprised eleven thousand Swiss and thirty thousand militia, were dispersed in various parts of the kingdom, principally in Andalusia. Besides this force, there was a sort of local reserve called the urban militia, much neglected, and indeed more a name than a reality. Nevertheless the advantage of such an institution was considerable; men were to be had in abundance: and as the greatest difficulty in a sudden crisis is to prepare the frame-work of order, it was no small resource to find a plan of service ready, the principle of which was understood by the people.

Napoleon's notes. Appendix, No. 3.
Thiebault.
Dupont's Journal. MSS.

The French army in the Peninsula about the same period, although amounting to eighty thousand men, exclusive of those under Junot in Portugal, had not more than seventy thousand capable of active operations; the remainder were sick or in depôts. The possession of the fortresses, the central position, and the combination of this comparatively small army, gave it great strength; but it had also many points of weakness; it was made up of the conscripts of different nations, French, Swiss, Italians, Poles, and even Portuguese, whom Junot had expatriated, partly to strengthen the French army, partly to weaken the nation which he held in subjection; and it is a curious fact, that some of them remained in Spain until the end of the war. A few of the imperial guards were also employed, and here and there an old regiment of the line was mixed with the young troops to give them consistence; but with these exceptions the French army must be considered as a raw levy fresh from the plough and unacquainted with discipline: so late even as the month of August many of the battalions had not completed the first elements of their drill, and if they had not been formed upon good skeletons, the difference between them and the insurgent peasantry would have been very trifling. This fact explains, in some measure, the otherwise incomprehensible checks and defeats which the French sustained at the commencement of the contest, and it likewise proves how little of vigour there was in Spanish resistance at the moment of the greatest enthusiasm.

Napoleon's notes, Appendix, No. 2.and b

In the distribution of these troops Napoleon attended principally to the security of Madrid. The capital city, and the centre of all interests, its importance was manifest, and the great line of communication between it and Bayonne was early and constantly covered with troops. But the imprudence with which the grand duke of Berg brought up the corps of Moncey and Dupont to the capital, the manner in which those corps were posted, cutting off the communication between the northern and southern provinces, and the haughty impolitic demeanour assumed by that prince, drew on the crisis of affairs before the time was ripe, and obliged the French monarch to hasten the advance of other troops, and to make a greater display of his force than was consistent with his policy; for Murat's movement, while it threatened the Spaniards and provoked their hostility, placed the French army in an isolated position, leaving the long line of communication with France unprovided with soldiers and requiring fresh battalions to fill up the void thus discovered; and this circumstance generated additional anger and suspicion at a very critical period of time. To supply the chasm left by Moncey's advance, the formation of a new corps was commenced in Navarre, y successive reinforcements so increased; that in June it amounted to twenty-three thousand men, who were placed under the command of marshal Bessieres, and took the title of the "army of the Western Pyrenees."

Bessieres, at the first appearance of the commotion, fixed his head quarters at Burgos and occupied Vittoria, Miranda de Ebro, and other towns, placing posts in his front towards Leon; this position, while it protected the line from Bayonne to the capital, enabled him to awe the Asturias and Biscay, and (by giving him the command of the valley of the Duero,) to keep the kingdom of Leon and the province of Segovia in check. The town and castle of Burgos, being put into a state of defence, contained his dépôts, and became the centre and pivot of his operations; while some intermediate posts and the fortresses connected him with Bayonne, where a reserve of twenty thousand men was formed under general Drouet, then commanding the eleventh military division of France.

St. Cyr.
Napoleon's notes, Appendix, No. 2.

By the convention of Fontainebleau, the emperor was entitled to send forty thousand men into the northern parts of Spain. The right thus acquired was grossly abused, but the exercise of it being expected, created at first but little alarm. It was different on the eastern frontier: Napoleon had never intimated a wish to pass forces by Catalonia; neither the treaty nor the convention authorized such a measure, nor could the pretence of supporting Junot in Portugal be advanced as a mask. Nevertheless, so early as the 9th of

February, eleven thousand infantry, sixteen hundred cavalry, and eighteen pieces of artillery, under the command of general Duhesme, crossed the frontier at La Jonquera, and marched upon Barcelona, leaving a detachment at the town of Figueras, the strong citadel of which commands the principal pass of the mountains. Arrived at Barcelona, Duhesme prolonged his residence there under the pretext of waiting for instructions from Madrid, relative to a pretended march upon Cadiz; but his secret orders were, to obtain exact information concerning the Catalonian fortresses, dépôts, and magazines, — to ascertain the state of public feeling, — to preserve a rigid discipline, — scrupulously to avoid giving any offence to the Spaniards, and to enter into close communication with marshal Moncey, at that time commanding the whole of the French army in the north of Spain.

The political affairs were even then beginning to indicate serious results, and as soon as Duhesme's report was received, and the troops in the north were in a condition to execute their orders, he was directed to seize upon the citadel of Barcelona, and the fort of Monjuick. The citadel was obtained by stratagem; the fort, one of the strongest in the world, was surrendered by the governor Alvarez. That brave and worthy officer, knowing the baseness of his court, was certain that he would receive no support from that quarter, and did not resist the demand of the French general, who having failed to surprise the vigilance of the garrison, impudently insisted upon a surrender of the place. Alvarez consented to relinquish his charge, although he felt the disgrace of his situation so acutely that, it is said, he had some thoughts of springing a mine beneath a French detachment during the conference; but his mind, unequal to the occasion, betrayed his spirit, and he sunk, oppressed by the force of unexpected circumstances.

What a picture of human weakness do these affairs present; the boldest men shrinking from the discharge of their trust like the meanest cowards, and the wisest following the march of events, confounded and without a rule of action! If such a firm man, as Alvarez afterwards proved himself to be, could think the disgrace of surrendering his charge at the demand of an insolent and perfidious guest a smaller misfortune than the anger of a miserable court, what must the state of public feeling have been, and how can those men who, like O'Farril and Azanza, served the intruder be with justice blamed, if, amidst the general stagnation, they could not perceive the elements of a salutary tempest? At the view of such scenes Napoleon might well enlarge his ambitious designs, his fault was not in the projection, but in the rough execution of his plan; another combination would have ensured success, and the resistance he encountered only shows, that nations as well as individuals are but the creatures of circumstances, at one moment weak, trembling, and submissive; at another proud, haughty, and daring; every novel combination of events has an effect upon public sentiment distinct from, and often at variance, with what is called national character.

The treacherous game played at Barcelona was renewed at Figueras, and with equal success; the citadel of that place fell into the hands of the detachment left there, and thus a free entrance, and a secure base of operations, was established in Catalonia, and the magazines of Barcelona being filled, Duhesme, whose corps took the name of the "army of the Eastern Pyrenees," concluded that his task was well accomplished.

The affair was indeed a momentous one, and Napoleon earnestly looked for its termination before the transactions at Madrid could give an unfavourable impression of his ulterior intentions; he saw the importance which, under certain circumstances, a war would confer upon Barcelona. With an immense population, great riches, a good harbour, and almost impregnable defences, that town might be called the key of the south of France or Spain, just as it happened to be in the possession of the one or the other nation. The proximity of Sicily, where a large British force was kept in a state of constant preparation, made it more than probable that if hostilities broke out between himself and the Spaniards, an English army would be quickly carried to Barcelona, and a formidable systematic war be established upon the threshold of France. Such an occurrence would have been fatal to his projects, he felt the full extent of the danger, and at the risk of rendering abortive the efforts to create a French party at Madrid, guarded against it by this open violation of Spanish independence; but the peril of exposing Barcelona to the English was too imminent to leave room for hesitation.

Thirty or forty thousand British troops occupying an entrenched camp in front of that town, supported by a powerful fleet, and having reserve magazines and dépôts in Sicily and the Spanish islands, might have been so wielded as to give ample occupation to a hundred and fifty thousand enemies. Under the protection of such an army, the Spanish levies might have been organised and instructed, and as the actual numbers assembled could have been at all times easily masked, increased, or diminished, and the fleet ready to co-operate, the south of France (from whence all the provisions of the enemy must have been drawn) would have been exposed to descents, and have sustained all the inconvenience of actual hostilities. The Spanish provinces of Valencia, Murcia, and even Andalusia, being thus covered, the war would have been drawn to a head, and concentrated about Catalonia, the most warlike, rugged, and sterile portion of Spain. But Duhesme's success having put an end to this danger, the affairs of Barcelona sunk into comparative insignificance. Nevertheless, the emperor kept a jealous watch upon that quarter, the corps employed there was increased to twenty-two thousand men, the general commanding it corresponded directly with Napoleon, and Barcelona was made the centre of a system complete in itself, and distinct from that which held the other corps, rolling round Madrid as their point of attraction.

The capital of Spain is situated in a sort of basin, formed by a semicircular range of mountains, which under the different denominations of the Sierra de Guadarama, the Carpentanos, and the Sierra de Guadalaxara, sweep in one unbroken chain from east to west, touching the Tagus at either end of an arch, of which that river is the chord.

All direct communications between Madrid and France, or between the former and the northern provinces of Spain, must necessarily pass over one or other of those Sierras, which are separated from the great range of the Pyrenees by the valley of the Ebro, and from the Biscayan and Asturian mountains by the valley of the Duero.

The four principal roads which lead from France directly upon Madrid are, first, the royal causeway, which passing the frontier at Irun runs under St. Sebastian, and then through a wild and mountainous country (full of dangerous defiles) to the Ebro, crosses that river by a stone bridge at Miranda, and leads upon Burgos, from which town it turns short to the left, is carried over the Duero at Aranda, and soon after encountering the Carpentanos and the Sierra de Guadalaxara, penetrates them by the strong pass of the Somosierra, and descends upon the capital. Vittoria stands in a plain about half way between St. Sebastian and Burgos.

The second, which is inferior to the first, commences at St. Jean Pied de Port, and unites at Pampelona: it runs through Taffalla, crosses the Ebro at Tudela, and enters the basin of Madrid by the eastern range of the Sierra de Guadalaxara, where the declination of the mountains presents a less rugged barrier than the snowy summits of the northern and western part of the chain.

The third threads the Pyrenees by the way of Jaca, passes the Ebro at Zaragoza, and uniting with the second, likewise crosses the Guadalaxara ridge.

The fourth is the great route from Perpignan by Figueras and Gerona to Barcelona; from this latter town it leads by Cervera and Lerida to Zaragoza.

Hence Zaragoza, the capital of Aragon, one of the great dépôts of Spain for arms and ammunition, and at that time containing fifty thousand inhabitants, was a strategetical point of importance. An army in position there could operate on either bank of the Ebro, intercept the communication between the armies of the Eastern and Western Pyrenees, and block three out of the four great roads leading upon Madrid; if the French had occupied it in force, their army in the capital would have been free and unconstrained in its operations, and might have acted with more security against Valencia; and the dangerous importance of the united armies of Gallicia and Leon would also have been diminished, when the road of Burgos ceased to be the only line of retreat from the capital. Nevertheless, Napoleon neglected Zaragoza at first, because that having no citadel, a small body of troops could not control the inhabitants, and a large force would have created suspicion too soon, and perhaps have prevented the success of the attempts against Pampelona and Barcelona (objects of still greater importance); neither was the heroic defence which that city afterwards made within a reasonable calculation.

The grand duke of Berg and the duke of Rovigo remained at Madrid, and from that central point appeared to direct the execution of the French emperor's projects; but he distrusted their judgment, and exacted the most detailed information of every movement and transaction.

In the course of June, Murat, who was suffering from illness, quitted Spain, leaving behind him a troubled people, and a name for cruelty which was foreign to his character. Savary remained the sole representative of the new monarch: his situation was delicate; he was in the midst of a great commotion; upon every side he beheld the violence of insurrection and the fury of an insulted nation; it behoved him, therefore, to calculate with coolness and to execute with vigour.

Each Spanish province had its own junta of government; but although equally enraged, they were not equally dangerous in their anger. The attention of the Catalonians was completely absorbed by Duhesme's operations; but the soldiers of the regiments which Cabanes' War in Catalonia, 1st Part.composed the Spanish garrisons of Barcelona, Monjuick, and Figueras, quitting their ranks after the seizure of those places, flocked to the patriotic standards in Murcia and Valencia. The greatest part belonged to the Spanish and Walloon guards, and they formed a good basis for an army which the riches of the two provinces and the arsenal of Carthagena afforded ample military resources to equip.

The French had, however, nothing to fear from any direct movement of this army against Madrid, as such an operation could only bring on a battle; but if by a march towards Zaragoza, the Valencians had united with the Aragonese and then operated against the line of communication with France, the insurrection of Catalonia would have been supported, and a point of union for three great provinces fixed. In the power of executing this project lay the sting of the Valencian insurrection. To besiege Zaragoza and prevent such a junction was the remedy.

The importance of Andalusia was greater; the division of regular troops which under the command of the unhappy Solano had been withdrawn from Portugal, was tolerably disciplined; a large veteran force was assembled at the camp of St. Roque under general Castaños; and the garrisons of Ceuta, Algeziras, Cadiz, Granada, and other places being united, the whole formed a considerable mass of troops; while a superb cannon foundry at Seville, and the arsenal of Cadiz, furnished the means of equipment and the materials for a train of artillery. An active intercourse was maintained between the patriots and the English: the juntas of Granada, Jaen, and Cordova Mr. Stuart's Letters, vide Parliamentary Papers, 1810.admitted the supremacy of the junta of Seville, and the army of Estremadura consented to obey their orders. The riches of the province, its distance from Madrid, the barrier of the Sierra Morena, which like a strong wall covered Andalusia, and favoured the insurrection, afforded the means of establishing a systematic war, and drawing together all the scattered elements of resistance in the southern and western provinces of Spain and Portugal; but this danger, although pregnant with future consequences, was not immediate: there was no line of offensive movement against the flank or rear of the French army open to the Andalusian patriots, and a march to the front against Madrid would have been tedious and dangerous; the true policy of the Andalusians was palpably defensive.

In Estremadura the activity and means of the junta were not at first sufficient to excite much attention; but in Leon, Old Castile, and Gallicia, a cloud was gathering that threatened a perilous storm. Don Gregorio Cuesta was captain-general of the two former kingdoms: inimical to popular movements, and of a haughty resolute disposition, he at first checked the insurrection with a rough hand; by this conduct he laid the foundation for quarrels and intrigues, which afterwards impeded the military operations, and split the northern provinces into factions; finally, however, he joined the side of the patriots. Behind him the kingdom of Gallicia, under the direction of Filanghieri, had prepared a large and efficient force. It was composed of the strong and disciplined body of troops Thiebault. Exped. Portugal.which, under the command of Tarranco, had taken possession of Oporto, and after that general's death had returned with general Belesta to Gallicia. The garrisons of Ferrol and Coruña and a number of soldiers, flying from the countries occupied by the French, swelled the regular army, the agents of Great Britain were actively employed in blowing the flame of insurrection; money, arms, and clothing, were poured into the province through their hands; Coruña afforded an easy and direct intercourse with England, and a strict connexion was maintained between the Gallician and Portuguese patriots.

The facility of establishing the base of a regular systematic war in Gallicia was therefore as great as in Andalusia, the resources perhaps greater on account of the proximity of Great Britain, and the advantage of position at this time was essentially in favour of Gallicia, because the sources of her strength were equally well covered from the direct line of the French operations, and the slightest offensive movement upon her part threatened the communications of the French army in Madrid, and endangered the safety of any corps marching from the capital against the southern provinces. To be prepared against the Gallician forces was, therefore, a matter of pressing importance; a defeat from that quarter would have been felt in all parts of the army; and no considerable or sustained operation could have been undertaken against the other insurgent forces until the strength of Gallicia had been first broken.

In Biscay and the Asturias the want of regular troops and fortified towns, and the contracted shape of those provinces, placed them completely within the power of the French, who had nothing to fear as long as they could maintain possession of the sea-ports.

From this sketch it results that Savary, in classing the dangers of his situation, should have rated Gallicia and Leon in the first, Zaragoza in the second, Andalusia in the third, and Valencia in the fourth rank, and by that scale he should have regulated his operations. It was thus Napoleon looked at the affair, but the duke of Rovigo, wavering in his opinions, neglected or misunderstood the spirit of his instructions, lost the control of the operations, and sunk amidst the confusion which he had himself created.

Nearly fifty thousand men and eighty guns were disposable for offensive operations in the beginning of June: collected into one mass such an army was more than sufficient to crush any or all of the insurgent armies combined; but it was necessary to divide it and to assail several points at the same time; in doing this the safety of each minor body depended upon the stability of the central point from whence it emanated; and again the security of that centre depended upon the strength of its communications with France; in other words, Bayonne was the base of operations against Madrid, and this town in turn became the base of operations against Valencia, Murcia, and Andalusia.

To combine all the movements of a vast plan which would embrace the operations against Catalonia, Aragon, Biscay, the Asturias, Gallicia, Leon, Castille, Andalusia, Murcia, and Valencia, in such a simple manner that the corps of the army working upon one principle might mutually support and strengthen each other, and at the same time preserve their communication with France, was the great problem to be solved. Napoleon felt that it required a master mind, and from Bayonne he put all the different armed masses in motion himself, and with the greatest caution; for it is a mistaken notion, although one very generally entertained, that he plunged headlong into this contest without precaution, as having to do with adversaries he despised.

In his instructions to the duke of Rovigo he says, "*In a war of this sort it is necessary to act with patience, coolness, and upon calculation.*" "*In civil wars it is the important points only which should be guarded, we must not go to all places;*" and he inculcates the doctrine that to spread the troops over the country without the power of uniting upon emergency would be a dangerous and useless display of activity. The principle upon which he proceeded may be illustrated by the comparison of a closed hand thrust forward and the fingers afterwards extended: as long as the solid part of the member was securely fixed and guarded, the return of the smaller portions of it and their flexible movement was feasible and without great peril; but a wound given to the hand or arm not only endangered that part but paralyzed the action of the whole limb. Hence all the care and attention with which his troops were arranged along the road to Burgos; hence all the measures of precaution already described, such as the seizure of the fortresses, and the formation of the reserves at Bayonne.

The insurrection having commenced, Bessieres was ordered to put Burgos into a state of defence, — to detach a division of four or five thousand men under general Lefebre Desnouettes against Zaragoza, — to keep down the insurgents of Biscay, Asturias, and Old Castille, — and to watch the army assembling in Gallicia; he was likewise enjoined to occupy and watch with jealous care the port of St. Ander and the coast towns. At the same time a reinforcement of nine thousand men was preparing for Duhesme, which, it was supposed, would enable him to tranquillize Catalonia, and co-operate with a division marching from Madrid against Valencia.

The reserve under general Drouet was nourished by drafts from the interior: it supplied Bessieres with reinforcements, and afforded a detachment of four thousand men to watch the openings of the valleys Napoleon's notes, Appendix, No. 2.of the Pyrenees, especially towards the castle of Jaca, which was in possession of the Spanish insurgents. A smaller reserve was established at Perpignan, and another detachment watched the openings of the eastern frontier. All the generals commanding corps, or even detachments, were directed to correspond daily with general Drouet.

The security of the rear being thus provided for, the main body at Madrid commenced offensive operations. Marshal Moncey was directed, with part of S. Journal of Moncey's Operations. MSS.his corps upon Cuenca, to intercept the march of the Valencian army upon Zaragoza, and general Dupont, with ten thousand men, marched towards Cadiz; the remainder of his and

Moncey's troops were kept in reserve and distributed in various parts of La Mancha and the neighbourhood of Madrid. Napoleon likewise directed, that Segovia should be occupied Napoleon's notes, Appendix, No. 1.and put in a state of defence, that a division (Gobert's) of Moncey's corps should co-operate with Bessieres on the side of Valladolid, and that moveable columns should scour the country in rear of the acting bodies, and unite again at stated times upon points of secondary interest. Thus linking his operations together, Napoleon hoped, by grasping as it were the ganglia of the insurrection, to paralyze its force, and reduce it to a few convulsive motions which would soon subside. The execution of his plan failed in the feebler hands of his lieutenants, but it was well conceived, and embraced every probable immediate chance of war, and even provided for the distant and uncertain contingency of an English army landing upon the flanks or rear of the corps at either extremity of the Pyrenean frontier.

Military men would do well to reflect upon the prudence which the French emperor displayed upon this occasion. Not all his experience, his power, his fortune, nor the contempt which he felt for the prowess of his adversaries, could induce him to relax in his precautions; every chance was considered, and every measure calculated with as much care and circumspection as if the most redoubtable enemy was opposed to him. The conqueror of Europe was as fearful of making false movements before an army of peasants, as if Frederick the Great had been in his front, and yet he failed! Such is the uncertainty of war!

CHAPTER V

All the insurrections of the Spanish provinces took place nearly at the same period; the operations of the French divisions were, of course, nearly simultaneous; I shall, therefore, narrate their proceedings separately, classing them by the effect each produced upon the stability of the intrusive government in Madrid, and commencing with the

FIRST OPERATIONS OF MARSHAL BESSIERES

Moniteur.
Victoires et Conquêtes des Français.

That officer had scarcely fixed his quarters at Burgos when a general movement of revolt took place. On his right, the bishop of St. Ander excited the inhabitants of the diocese to take arms. In his rear, a mechanic assembled some thousand armed peasants at the town of Logroño. In front, five thousand men took possession of the Spanish artillery dépôt at Segovia; an equal number assembling at Palencia armed themselves from the royal manufactory at that place, and advanced to the town of Torquemada; while general Cuesta, with some regular troops and a body of organized peasantry, posted themselves on the Pisuerga at Cabeçon.

Bessieres immediately divided his disposable force, which was not more than twelve thousand men, into several columns, and traversed the country in all directions, disarming the towns and interrupting the combinations of the insurgents; while a division of Dupont's corps, under general Frere, marched from the side of Madrid to aid his operations. General Verdier attacked Logroño on the 6th of June, dispersed the peasantry, and put the leaders to death after the action. General Lasalle, departing from Burgos with a brigade of light cavalry, passed the Pisuerga, fell upon the Spaniards at Torquemada on the 7th, broke them, and pursuing with a merciless sword, burnt that town, and entered Palencia on the 8th.

Meanwhile Frere defeated the Spanish force at Segovia taking thirty pieces of artillery; and general Merle marching through the country lying between the Pisuerga and the Douero with a division of infantry, joined Lasalle at Dueñas on the 12th. From thence they proceeded to Cabeçon, where Cuesta accepted battle, and was overthrown, with much slaughter, the loss of his artillery, and several thousand musquets. The flat country being thus subdued, Lasalle's cavalry remained to keep it under; but Merle, marching northward, commenced operations, in concert with general Ducos, against the province of St. Ander. On the 20th, the latter general drove the Spaniards from the pass of Soncillo; the 21st, he forced the pass of Venta de Escudo, and descending the valley of the river Pas, approached St. Ander; on the 22d, Merle, after some resistance, penetrated by Lantueño, and followed the course of the Besaya to Torre La Vega, then turning to his right entered St. Ander on the 23d; and Ducos arriving at the same time, the town submitted, and the bishop fled with the greatest part of the clergy. The authorities of Segovia, Valladolid, Palencia, and St. Ander, were compelled to send deputies to take the oath of allegiance to Joseph.

By these operations, the above-named provinces were completely disarmed, and so awed by the activity of Bessieres, that no further insurrections took place, and his cavalry raised contributions and collected provisions without the least difficulty. Frere's division then returned to Toledo, and from thence marched to San Clemente, on the borders of Murcia. The imprudence of Cuesta, and the general deficiency of talent and judgment manifested by the Spaniards throughout these proceedings, were very remarkable.

Cavallero.

While Bessieres thus broke the northern insurrections, the march of general Lefebre Desnouettes against the province of Aragon brought on the first siege of Zaragoza. Palafox being declared captain-general, recalled the retired officers into service; a number of volunteers repaired to him from distant parts, and the soldiers and officers who could escape from Pampelona and Madrid joined his standard, and among others the officers of engineers employed in the school of Alcala. With their assistance his forces were rapidly organized, and many battalions were formed and posted at different points on the roads leading towards Navarre. The baron de Versage, an officer of the Walloon guards, occupied Calatayud with a regiment composed of students who were volunteers; he raised more men in that quarter, kept up a communication with the juntas of Soria and Siguenza, and covered the powder-mills in Villa Felice. The arsenal of Zaragoza supplied the patriots with arms. At Tudela the people broke down the bridge over the Ebro, and Palafox detached five hundred fuzileers to assist them in defending the passage of that river.

S.
Journal of Lefebre's Operations. MSS.

Moniteur.

Victoire et Conquêtes des Français.

Cavallero.

In this situation of affairs Lefebre commenced his march from Pampelona the 7th of June, at the head of three or four thousand infantry, some field batteries, and a regiment of Polish cavalry. On the 9th he forced the passage of the Ebro, put the leaders of the insurrection to death after the action, and then continued his movement by the right bank to Mallen. Palafox, with ten thousand infantry, two hundred dragoons, and eight pieces of artillery, awaited him there in a position behind the Huecha. The 13th, Palafox was overthrown; the 14th, the French reached the Xalon; another combat and another victory carried Lefebre across that river; and the 15th, he was on the Huerba, in front of the heroic city.

FIRST SIEGE OF ZARAGOZA

Cavallero.

Siege of Zaragoza.

Zaragoza contained at that period fifty thousand inhabitants; situated on the right bank of the Ebro, it was connected with a suburb on the opposite side by a handsome stone bridge. The immediate vicinity is flat, and on the side of the suburb low and marshy. The small river Huerba, running through a deep cleft, cuts the plain on the right bank, and taking its course close to the walls, falls into the Ebro nearly opposite to the mouth of the Gallego, which, descending from the mountains on the opposite side, cuts the plain on the left bank. The convent of St. Joseph, built on the right of the Huerba, covered a bridge over that torrent; and, at the distance of cannon-shot, a step of land commenced, which, gradually rising, terminated at eighteen hundred yards from the convent, in a hill called the Monte Torrero. On this hill, which commanded all the plain and overlooked the town, several storehouses and workshops, built for the use of the canal, were entrenched, and occupied by twelve hundred men. The canal itself, a noble work, formed a water carriage without a single lock from Tudela to Zaragoza. The city, surrounded by a low brick wall, presented no regular defences, and possessed very few guns in a state fit for service, but the houses were strongly constructed, some of stone, others of brick; they were mostly of two stories high, each story being vaulted so as to be nearly proof against fire; and the massive walls of the convents, rising like castles all round the circuit as well as inside the place, were to be seen crowded with armed men.

S

Journal of Lefebre's Operations. MSS.

Cavallero.

Such was Zaragoza when Lefebre Desnouettes first appeared before it: his previous movements had cut the direct communication with Calatayud, and obliged the baron Versage to retire to Belchite with the volunteers and several thousand fresh levies. Palafox occupied the olive groves and houses on the step of land between the convent of St. Joseph and Monte Torrero; but his men, cowed by their previous defeats, were easily driven from thence on the 16th, and the town was closely invested on the right bank of the Ebro. Indeed so great was the terror and confusion of the Spaniards, that some of the French penetrated without difficulty into the street of St. Engracia, and the city was on the point of being taken that day, for Palafox, accompanied by his brother Francisco, an aide-de-camp, and one hundred dragoons, under pretence of seeking succour, endeavoured to go forth on the side of the suburb at the moment when the French were entering on the side of Engracia; but the plebeian leaders being suspicious of his intentions, would not suffer him to depart without a guard of infantry, and Tio Jorge[7] accompanied him to watch his conduct and to ensure his return. It was a strange proceeding, and ill-timed, that the chief should thus fly out at one gate while the enemy was pressing in at another, when the streets were filled with clamour, the dismayed garrison making little or no resistance, and all things in confusion. Zaragoza was that day on the very verge of destruction, when the French, either fearful of an ambuscade, or ignorant of their advantages, retired, and the people, as if inspired, changing from the extreme of terror to that of courage, suddenly fell to casting up defences, piercing loop-holes in the walls of the houses, constructing ramparts with sand-bags, and working with such vigour, that, under the direction of their engineers, in twenty-four hours they put the place in a condition to withstand an assault. Whereupon Lefebre confining his operations to the right bank of the Ebro, established posts close to the gates, and waited for reinforcements.

Cavallero.

Meanwhile Palafox crossing the Ebro at Pina, joined Versage at Belchite, and having collected seven or eight thousand men, and four pieces of artillery, gained the Xalon in rear of the French; from thence he proposed to advance through Epila and endeavour to relieve Zaragoza by a battle. His officers, struck with the imprudence of this measure, resisted his authority, and prepared to retire to Valencia. Palafox, ignorant of war, and probably awed by Tio Jorge, expressed his determination to fight, saying, with an imposing air, "that those who feared danger might retire." Touched with shame, all agreed to follow him to Epila; and he advanced: but two French regiments, detached by Lefebre, met him on the march, and a combat commencing at nine in the evening, the Spaniards were unable to form any order of battle, and, notwithstanding their superior numbers, were defeated with the loss of three thousand men. Palafox, who did not display that firmness in danger which his speech promised, must have fled early, as he reached Calatayud in the night, although many of his troops arrived there unbroken the next morning. After this disaster, Palafox, leaving Versage at Calatayud to make fresh levies, returned himself, with all the beaten troops that he could collect, to Belchite, and from thence regained Zaragoza on the 2d of July. Meanwhile Lefebre had taken the Monte Torrero by assault on the 27th of June.

S

Journal of Lefebre's Operations. MSS.

The 29th or 30th, general Verdier arrived on the Huerba with a division of infantry, and a large train of battering artillery; and the besiegers being now nearly twelve thousand strong, attacked the convents of St. Joseph and the Capuchins on the same day that Palafox returned; the first assault on St. Joseph's failed, the second succeeded; but the Capuchins, after some fighting, was set fire to by the Spaniards and abandoned. All this time the suburb was left open and free for the besieged. But Napoleon blamed this mode of attack, and sent orders to throw a bridge across the Ebro, — to press the siege on the left bank, — and to profit of the previous success by raising a breaching battery in the convent of St. Joseph. A bridge was accordingly constructed at St. Lambert, two hundred yards above the town, and two attacks were carried on at the same time.

Napoleon's Notes, Appendix, No. 2.

Hitherto the French troops employed in Aragon formed a part of marshal Bessieres' corps, but the emperor now directed Lefebre to repair with his brigade to reinforce that marshal, and constituting the ten thousand men who remained with Verdier a separate corps, gave this last general the command of it, and promised him reinforcements. Verdier continued to press the siege as closely as his numbers would permit, but, all around him, the insurgents were rapidly organising small armies, and threatened to enclose him in his camp. This obliged him to send detachments against them: and it is singular, that with so few men, while daily fighting with the besieged, he should have been able to scour the country, and put down the insurrection, as far as Lerida, Barbastro, Tudela, Jacca, and Calatayud; the garrison of Pampelona only assisting him from the side of Navarre. In one of these expeditions the powder-mills of Villa Felice, thirty miles distant, were destroyed, and the baron Versage being defeated, was forced to retire with his division towards Valencia.

Cavallero.

During the course of July, Verdier made several assaults on the gate of El Carmen, and others on the Portillo, but he was repulsed in all. The besieged having been reinforced by the regiment of Estremadura, composed of eight hundred old soldiers, in return made a sally with two thousand men to retake the Monte Torrero, but they were beaten, with the loss of their commander; regular approaches were then commenced by the French against the quarter of St. Engracia and the castle of Aljaferia. The 2d of August, the besieged were again reinforced by two hundred men of the Spanish guard and volunteers of Aragon, who brought some artillery with them; the French likewise were strengthened by two old regiments of the line, which increased their numbers to fifteen thousand men.

Ibid.

Cavallero.

On the 3d of August, the breaching batteries opened against St. Engracia and Aljaferia; the mortar batteries threw shells at the same time, and a Spanish magazine of powder blowing up in the Cosso (a public walk formed on the line of the ancient Moorish ramparts), destroyed several houses, and killed many of the defenders. The place was then summoned to surrender on terms, but Palafox having rejected all offers, on the 4th of August the town was stormed through a breach in the convent of St. Engracia; the French penetrated to the Cosso, and a confused and terrible scene ensued. Some defended the houses, some drew up in the streets, some fled by the suburb to the country, where the French cavalry fell upon them; cries of treason were every where heard, and became the signal for assassinations; all seemed lost, when a column of the assailants seeking the way to the bridge over the Ebro, got entangled in the Arco de Cineja, a long crooked street, and being attacked in that situation, were driven back to the Cosso; others began to plunder, and the Zaragozans recovering courage, fought with desperation, and set fire to the convent of Francisco. At the close of day the French were in possession of one side of the Cosso, and the Spaniards of the other. A hideous and revolting spectacle was exhibited during the action; the public hospital being taken and fired, the madmen confined there issued forth among the combatants, muttering, shouting, singing, and moping, according to the character of their disorder, while drivelling idiots mixed their unmeaning cries with the shouts of contending soldiers.

The Spaniards now perceived, that with courage the town might still be defended; and from that day the fighting was murderous and constant, one party endeavouring to take, the other to defend the houses. In this warfare, where skill was nearly useless, Verdier's force was too weak to make a rapid progress; and events disastrous to the French arms taking place in other parts of Spain, he received, about the 10th of August, orders from the king to raise the siege, and retire to Logroña. Of this operation I shall speak in due time.

OBSERVATIONS

1°. Mere professional skill and enterprise do not constitute a great general. Lefebre Desnouettes, by his activity and boldness, with a tithe of their numbers, defeated the insurgents of Aragon in several actions, and scoured the open country; but the same Lefebre, wanting the higher qualities of a general, failed miserably where that intuitive sagacity that reads passing events aright was required. There were thousands in the French army who could have done as well as him; probably not three who could have reduced Zaragoza, and yet it is manifest that Zaragoza owed her safety to accident, and that the desperate resistance of the inhabitants was more the result of chance than of any peculiar virtue.

2°. The feeble defence made at Mallen, at the Xalon; at the Monte Torrero, at Epila; the terror of the besieged on the 16th, when the French penetrated into the town; the flight of Palafox under the pretence of seeking succour, nay, the very assault which in such a wonderful manner called forth the energy of the Zaragozans, and failed only because the French troops plundered, and missing the road to the bridge, missed that to victory at the same time, proves, that the fate of the city was determined by accident in more than one of those nice conjunctures which men of genius know how to seize, but others leave to the decision of fortune.

3°. However, it must be acknowledged that Lefebre and Verdier, especially the latter, displayed both vigour and talent; for it was no mean exploit to quell the insurrections to a distance of fifty miles on every side, at the same time investing double their own numbers, and pushing the attack with such ardour as to reduce to extremity a city so defended.

4°. The current romantic tales of women rallying the troops, and leading them forward at the most dangerous periods of this siege, I have not touched upon, and may perhaps be allowed to doubt, although it is not unlikely that when suddenly environed with horrors, the delicate sensitiveness of women driving them to a kind of phrensy, might produce actions above the heroism of men; and in patient suffering their superior fortitude is manifest; wherefore I neither wholly believe, nor will deny, their exploits at Zaragoza; merely remarking that for a long time afterwards Spain swarmed with heroines, clothed in half uniforms, and loaded with weapons.

Cavallero.

5°. The two circumstances that principally contributed to the success of the defence were, first, the bad discipline of the French soldiers; and secondly, the system of terror which was established by the Spanish leaders, whoever those leaders were. Few soldiers can be restrained from plunder when a town is taken by assault; yet there is no period when the chances of war are so sudden and so decisive, none where the moral responsibility of a general is so great. Will military regulations alone secure the necessary discipline at such a moment? The French army are not deficient in a stern code, and the English army, taken altogether, is probably the best regulated of modern times; but here it is seen that Lefebre failed to take Zaragoza in default of discipline; and in the course of this work it will appear that no wild horde of Tartars ever fell with more licence upon their rich effeminate neighbours than did the English troops upon the Spanish towns taken by storm. The inference to be drawn is, that national institutions alone will produce that moral discipline necessary to make a soldier capable of fulfilling his whole duty; yet a British statesman[8] was not ashamed to declare in parliament that the worst men make the best soldiers; and this odious, narrow-minded, unworthy maxim, had its admirers. That a system of terror was at Zaragoza successfully employed to protract the defence is undoubted. The commandant of Monte Torrero, ostensibly for suffering himself to be defeated, but according to some, for the gratification of private malice, was tried and put to death; and a general of artillery was in a more summary manner killed without any trial; the chief engineer, a man of skill and undaunted courage, was arbitrarily imprisoned; and the slightest word or even gesture of discontent, was punished with instant death. A stern band of priests and plebeian leaders, in whose hands Palafox was a tool, ruled with such furious energy, that resistance to the enemy was less dangerous than disobedience to their orders. Suspicion was the warrant of death, and this system once begun, ceased not until the town was taken in the second siege.

CHAPTER VI

OPERATIONS IN CATALONIA

Cabanes, 1st Part.

When Barcelona fell into the power of the French, the Spanish garrison amounted to nearly four thousand men; but Duhesme daily fearing a riot in the city, connived at their escape in parties, and even sent the regiment of Estremadura (which was eight hundred strong) entire to Lerida, where, strange to relate, the gates were shut against it; and thus, discarded by both parties, it made its way into Zaragoza during the siege of that place. Many thousand citizens also fled from Barcelona, and joined the patriotic standards in the neighbouring provinces.

Napoleon's Notes, Appendix, No. 2.

Cabanes, 1st Part.

After the first ebullition at Manresa, the insurrection of Catalonia lingered awhile; but the junta of Gerona continued to excite the people to take arms, and it was manifest that a general commotion approached; and this was a serious affair, for there were in the beginning of June, including those who came out of Barcelona, five thousand veteran troops in the province, and in the Balearic islands above ten thousand. Sicily contained an English army, and English fleets covered the Mediterranean. Moreover, by the constitution of Catalonia, the whole of the male population fit for war are obliged to assemble at certain points of each district with arms and provisions, whenever the alarum bell, called the *somaten*, is heard to ring; hence the name of *somatenes*; and these warlike peasants, either from tradition or experience, are well acquainted with the military value of their mountain holds.

St. Cyr.
Victoire et Conquestes des Francois.
Foy.
Cabanes.

Hostilities soon commenced; Duhesme, following his instructions from Bayonne, detached general Chabran and five thousand two hundred men, with orders to secure Tarragona and Tortosa, to incorporate the Swiss regiment of Wimpfen with his own troops, and to aid marshal Moncey in an attack on Valencia. At the same time general Swartz having more than three thousand men, Swiss, Germans, and Italians, under his command, was detached by the way of Martorel and Montserrat to Manresa, with orders to raise contributions, to put down the insurrection, and to destroy the powder mills at the last town; then to get possession of Lerida, and to incorporate all the Swiss troops found there in his own brigade, placing five hundred men in the citadel; after which he was to penetrate into Aragon, and to co-operate with Lefebre against Zaragoza.

Ibid.

These two columns quitted Barcelona the 3d and the 4th of June. A heavy rain induced Swartz to stop all the 5th at Martorel: the 6th he resumed his march, but without any military precautions, although the object of his expedition was known, and the somaten ringing out among the hills, the peasants of eight districts were assembled in arms; these men took a resolution to defend the pass of Bruch, and the most active of the Manresa and Igualada districts, assisted by a few old soldiers, immediately repaired there, and posted themselves on the rocks. Swartz coming on in a careless manner, a heavy but distant fire opened from all parts on his column, and created a little confusion, but order was soon restored, and the Catalans being beaten from their strong holds, were pursued for four or five miles along the main road. At Casa Mansana, where a cross road leads to Manresa, one part broke away, the others continued their flight to Igualada. Swartz, a man evidently destitute of talent, halted at the very moment when his success was complete, and the road to Manresa open; the Catalans seeing his hesitation first rallied in the rear of Casa Mansana, then returned to the attack, and drove the advanced guard back upon the main body. The French general became alarmed, formed a square, and retired hastily towards Esparraguéra, followed and flanked by clouds of somatenes, whose courage and numbers increased every moment; at Esparraguéra, which was a long single street, the inhabitants had prepared an ambush; but Swartz, who arrived at twilight, getting intelligence of their design, passed to the right and left of the houses, and continuing his flight reached Martorel the 7th, having lost a gun and many men by this inglorious expedition, from which he returned in such disorder, and with his soldiers so discouraged, that Duhesme thought it necessary to recall Chabran from Tarragona.

The country westward of the Llobregat is rugged and difficult for an army, yet Chabran reached Tarragona on the 8th without encountering an enemy; but when he attempted to return, the line of his march was intercepted by the insurgents, who took post at Vendrill, Arbos, and

Villa Franca, and spread themselves along the banks of the Llobregat. As he approached Vendrill the somatenes fell back to Arbos, but a skirmish commencing at this latter place, the Catalans were defeated. Chabran set fire to the town, and proceeded to Villa Franca. Here the excesses so common at this time among the Spaniards were not spared; the governor, an old man, and several of his friends, were murdered, and the perpetrators of these crimes, as might be expected, made little or no defence against the enemy.

Meanwhile general Lechi moved out of Barcelona, and acting in concert with Swartz's brigade, which marched from Martorel, cleared the banks of the Llobregat, and formed a junction at San Felice with Chabran on the 11th. The latter, after a day's rest, having his division completed by the brigade of Swartz, marched against Manresa to repair the former disgrace; he arrived at Bruch the 14th, but the somatenes were also there, and assisted by some regular troops with artillery. Finding that in a partial skirmish he made no impression, Chabran, more timid even than Swartz, took the extraordinary resolution of retreating, or rather flying from those gallant peasants, who pursued him with scoffs and a galling fire back to the very walls of Barcelona.

This success spurred on the insurrection; Gerona, Rosas, Hostalrich, and Tarragona prepared for defence. The somatenes assembling in the Ampurdan obliged the French commandant to quit the town of Figueras, and shut himself up with three hundred men in the citadel, while others gathering between the Ter and the Besos, intercepted all communication between France and Barcelona.

In this predicament Duhesme resolved to make a sudden attempt on Gerona, and for this purpose drew out six thousand of his best troops, and eight pieces of artillery; but as the fortress of Hostalrich stood in the direct road, he followed the coast line, and employed a French privateer, then in the harbour, to attend his march. The somatenes got intelligence of his designs: one multitude took possession of the heights of Moncada, which are six miles from Barcelona, and overhang the road to Hostalrich; another multitude was posted on the ridge of Mongat, which, at the same distance from Barcelona, abuts on the sea; an intrenched castle, with a battery of fifteen guns, protected their left, and their right was slightly connected with the people at Moncada.

The 17th, Duhesme, after some false show to hide his real attack, fell upon the castle of Mongat, where the greater mass of the Catalans being posted, were defeated with slaughter; a detachment from Barcelona dispersing those of Moncada at the same time.

The 18th, the town of Mattaro being taken was plundered, although a few cannon-shot only had been fired in its defence. The somatenes were also defeated at the pass of San Pol. The 19th, the French halted at San Tione, but at nine o'clock on the morning of the 20th, they appeared before the walls of Gerona.

This town, built on the right bank of the Ter, is cut in two by the Oña. To the eastward it is confined by strong rocky hills, whose points filling the space between the right bank of the Oña and the Ter, overlook the town at different distances. Fort Mont Jouy, a regular fortification, crowned the nearest hill or table land, at five hundred yards distance, and three forts (that of the Constable, of queen Anne, and of the Capuchins), being connected by a ditch and rampart, formed one irregular outwork, a thousand yards in length, and commanding all the ridge to the south-east. The summit of this ridge is five, eight, and twelve hundred yards from Gerona, and sixteen hundred from Fort Mont Jouy, being separated from the latter by the narrow valley and stream of the Gallegan. South-west, between the left of the Oña and the Ter, the country, comparatively flat, is, however, full of hollows and clefts close to the town. The body of the place on that side was defended by a ditch and five regular bastions connected by a wall with towers. To the west the city was covered by the Ter, and on the east fortified by a long wall with towers having an irregular bastion at each extremity, and some small detached works placed at the opening of the valley of Gallegan. Three hundred of the regiment of Ultonia and some artillerymen composed the garrison of Gerona, but they were assisted by volunteers and by the citizens; and the somatenes also assembled on the left of the Ter to defend the passage of that river.

St. Cyr.

Duhesme, after provoking some cannon-shot from the forts, occupied the village of St. Eugenia in the plain, and making a feint as if to pass the Ter by the bridge of Salt, engaged the somatenes in a useless skirmish. Great part of the day was spent by him in preparing ladders for an attack; but at five o'clock in the evening the French artillery opened from the heights of Palau, and a column crossing the Oña passed between the outworks and the town, threw out a detachment to keep the garrison of the former in check, and assaulted the gate of El Carmen. This attempt failed completely and with great loss to the assailants. Two hours afterwards another column, advancing by the plain on the left of the Oña, made an assault on the bastion of Santa Clara, but with so little arrangement, or discipline, that the storming party moved forward without their ladders, and although the hollows favoured them so much that they arrived under the walls without being perceived, and that the Neapolitan colonel Ambrosio, with a few others, actually gained the ramparts by means of the single ladder brought up, the confusion was too great to be remedied. And a detachment of the regiment of Ultonia coming from the other side of the town, charged the assailants, bayoneted those who were upon the walls, and drove the rest back. Another feeble effort made after dark likewise failed.

Duhesme tried some useless negotiations on the following day; but dreading a longer absence from Barcelona, broke up on the 22d, and returned by forced marches. As he passed Mattaro he left Chabran with some troops in that town. Meanwhile the victorious somatenes of Bruch had descended the Llobregat, rallied those of the lower country, and getting artillery from Taragona and other fortresses, planted batteries at the different passages of the river, and entrenched a line from San Boy to Martorel. Regular officers now took the command of the peasants; colonel Milans assembled a body at Granollers; don Juan Claros put himself at the head of the peasants of the Ampurdan; and colonel Baget took the command of those at Bruch.

General Chabran, after a few days' rest at Mattaro, made a foraging excursion through the district of El Vallés. Milans, who held the valley of the Congosta, encountered him near Granollers; both sides claimed the victory, but Chabran retired to Barcelona, and Milans remained on the banks of the Besos. The 30th Duhesme caused the somatenes on the Llobregat to be attacked; general Lechi menaced those at the bridge of Molinos del Rey, while the brigades of Bessieres and Goullus, crossing at San Boy, surprised a battery at that point and turned the whole line. Lechi then crossed the river by the bridge of Molinos, ascended the left bank, took all the artillery, burnt several villages, killed a number of the somatenes, and put the rest to flight. They rallied again, however, at Bruch and Igualada, and returning the 6th of July, infested the immediate vicinity of Barcelona, taking possession of all the hills between San Boy and Moncada, and connecting their operations with colonel Milans. Other parties collected between the Besos and the Ter, and extended the line of insurrection to the Ampurdan; Juan Claros occupied the flat country about Rosas, and the French garrison of Figueras having burnt the town, were blocked up in the fort of San Fernando by two thousand somatenes of the Pyrenees. A nest of Spanish privateers was formed in Palamos Bay, and two English frigates, the Imperieuse and the Cambrian, watched the coast from Rosas to Barcelona.

A supreme junta being now established at Lerida, opened an intercourse with Aragon, Valencia, Seville, Gibraltar, and the Balearic islands, and decreed that forty tercios or regiments of one thousand men, to be selected from the somatenes, should be paid and organized as regular troops, and that forty others should be kept in reserve, but without pay.

Foy's History.

Lord Collingwood's despatch, Aug. 27.
Foy's History.

This state of affairs being made known to Napoleon through the medium of the moveable columns watching the valleys of the eastern Pyrenees, he ordered general Reille, commanding the reserve at Perpignan, to take the first soldiers at hand and march to the relief of Figueras, after which, his force being increased by drafts from the interior of France, to nine thousand men, he was to assault Rosas and to besiege Gerona. The emperor imagined, that the fall of the latter place would induce the surrender of Lerida, and would so tranquillize Catalonia, that five thousand men might again be detached towards Valencia. On receiving this order, Reille with two battalions of Tuscan recruits, conducted a convoy safely to Figueras and raised the blockade, but not without difficulty, for his troops were greatly terrified and could scarcely be kept to their colours. He relieved the place the 10th of July, and the same day Duhesme, who had been preparing for a second attack on Gerona, quitted Barcelona with six thousand infantry, some cavalry, a battering train of twenty-two pieces, and a great number of country carriages to transport his ammunition and stores, general Lechi remaining in the city with five thousand men. Meanwhile Reille having victualled Figueras and received a part of his reinforcements, proceeded to invest Rosas; but he had scarcely appeared before it when Juan Claros raised the country in his rear; and Captain Otway, of the Montague, landing with some marines, joined the migueletes: the French were forced to retire, and lost two hundred men in their retreat.

St. Cyr. Campaign in Catalonia.

Duhesme pursued his march by the coast, whereupon the somatenes of that part broke up the road in his front; Milans hung upon his left, and lord Cochrane, with the Imperieuse frigate and some Spanish vessels, cannonaded his right flank. In this dilemma he remained five days in front of Arenas de Mar; and then dividing his forces, sent one part across the mountains by Villagorguin, and another by St. Iscle; the first made an attempt on Hostalrich, but failed; the second beat away colonel Milans and dispersed the somatenes of the Tordera; finally, Duhesme united his people before Gerona on the 22d, but he had lost many carriages during the march. The 23d he passed the Ter and dispersed the migueletes that guarded the left bank. The 24th general Reille coming from Figueras with six thousand men, took post at Puente Mayor, and the town was invested with a line extending from that point by the heights of San Miguel to the Monte Livio; from Monte Livio by the plain to the bridge of Salt, and from thence along the left bank of the Ter to Sarria. The garrison consisting of five hundred migueletes and four hundred of the regiment of Ultonia, was reinforced on the 25th by thirteen hundred of the regiment of Barcelona, who entered the town with two guns. All the defences were in bad repair, but the people were resolute. The night of the 27th, a French column passing the valley of Galligan, gained the table land of Fort Mont Jouy, and made lodgements in three towers of masonry which the Spaniards had abandoned in the first moment of surprise. This advantage elated Duhesme so much, that he resolved, without consulting his engineers, to break ground on that side.

Cabanes' History.

Cabanes' History, 2d Part.

At this period a great change in the affairs of Catalonia took place; the insurrection had hitherto been confined to the exertions of the unorganised somatenes and was without system; but now a treaty between lord Collingwood, who commanded the British navy in the Mediterranean, and the marquis of Palacios, who was captain-general of the Balearic isles, having been concluded, the Spanish fleet and the troops in Minorca, Majorca, and Ivica, became disposable for the service of the patriots. Palacios immediately sent thirteen hundred to the port of San Felice di Quixols to reinforce the garrison of Gerona. These men entered that city, as we have seen, on the 25th, and Palacios himself disembarked four thousand others at Tarragona on the 22d, together with thirty-seven pieces of artillery; an event that excited universal joy, and produced a surprising eagerness to fight the French.

St Cyr.

Cabanes' History, 2d Part.

The supreme junta immediately repaired to Tarragona, declared Palacios their president, and created him commander-in-chief, subject, however, to the tutelar saint Narcissus, who was appointed generalissimo of the forces by sea and land, and the ensigns of authority, with due solemnity, placed on his coffin. The first object with Palacios was to re-establish the line of the Llobregat. To effect this, the count of Caldagues, with eighteen hundred men and four guns, marched from Tarragona in two columns, the one moving by the coast way to San Boy, and the other by the royal road, through Villafranca and Ordal. Caldagues, in passing by the bridge of Molino del Rey, established a post there, and then ascending the left bank, fixed his quarters at Martorel, where colonel Baget joined him with three thousand migueletes of the new levy.

Lord Collingwood's despatches.

St. Cyr.

The Llobregat runs within a few miles of Barcelona, but the right bank being much the steepest, the lateral communications easier, and the heights commanding a distinct view of every thing passing on the opposite side; the line taken by Caldagues was strong, and the country in his rear rough, full of defiles, and very fitting for a retreat after the loss of a battle. General Lechi, thus hemmed in on the west, was also hampered on the north, for the mountains filling all the space between the Llobregat and the Besos, approach in tongues as near as two and three miles from Barcelona; and the somatenes of the Manresa and Valls districts occupied them, and skirmished daily with the French outposts. Beyond the Besos, which bounds Barcelona on the eastward, a lofty continuous ridge extending to Hostalrich, runs parallel to, and at the distance of two or three miles from the sea coast, separating the main and the marine roads, and sending its shoots down to the water's edge. This ridge also swarmed with somatenes, who cut off all communication with Duhesme, and lay in leaguer round the castle of Mongat, in which were eighty or ninety French. The Cambrian and the Imperieuse frigates blockaded the harbour of Barcelona; and, on the 31st of July, lord Cochrane having brought his vessel alongside of Mongat, landed his marines, and, in concert with the somatenes, took it, blew up the works, and rolled the rocks and ruins down in such a manner as to destroy the road. Thus, at the very moment that Duhesme commenced the siege of Gerona, he was cut off from his own base of operations, and the communication between Figueras and general Reille's division, was equally insecure, for the latter's convoys were attacked the 28th of July, the 3d of August, and so fiercely on the 6th, that a Neapolitan battalion was surrounded, and lost one hundred and fifty men.

Palacios, whose forces increased daily, wished to make an effort in favour of Gerona, and with this view sent the count of Caldagues, at the head of three or four thousand men (part migueletes, part regulars), to interrupt the progress of the siege, intending to follow himself with greater forces. Caldagues left Martorel the evening of the 6th, marched by Tarrasa, Sabadell, Granollers, and San Celoni, and reached Hostalrich the morning of the 10th; there his force was increased to five thousand men and four guns. The 13th, he entered Llagostera; the 14th Castellar, a small place situated behind the ridges that overlook Gerona, and only five miles from the French camps. Don Juan Claros, with two thousand five hundred migueletes, mixed with some Walloon and Spanish guards from Rosas, met him at Castellar, as did also colonel Milans with eight hundred somatenes.

Caldagues having opened a communication with the junta of Gerona, found that Fort Mont Jouy was upon the point of surrendering, and that the French, who were ignorant of his approach, had, contrary to good discipline, heaped their forces in the plain between the left of the Oña and the Ter, but only kept a slender guard on the hills, while a single battalion protected the batteries raised against Mont Jouy. Being an enterprising man, Caldagues resolved to make an immediate effort for the relief of the place, and, after a careful observation on the 15th, divided his forces, and the 16th fell, with several columns, on the weakest part of the besiegers' line. The garrison sallied forth at the same time from Mont Jouy, and the French guards being taken between two fires, were quickly overpowered, and driven first to the Puente Mayor and finally over the Ter. The Spaniards re-formed on the hills, expecting to be attacked; but Duhesme and Reille remained quiet until dark, then breaking up the siege, they fled away, the one to Figueras, the other to Barcelona, leaving both artillery and stores behind.

Duhesme endeavoured to pass along the coast, but, on his arrival at Callella, he discovered that the road was cut by ditches, that an English frigate was prepared to rake his columns on the march, and that all the heights were occupied by the somatenes; whereupon, destroying his ammunition, throwing his remaining artillery over the rocks, and taking to by-ways in the mountains, he forced a passage through the midst of the somatenes to Mongat, where general Lechi met him the 20th, and covered his retreat into Barcelona. Thus ended Duhesme's second attempt against Gerona.

Observation 1.—Three great communications pierce the Pyrenean frontier of Catalonia, leading directly upon Barcelona.

The first, or Puycerda road, penetrates between the sources of the Segre and the Ter.

The second, or Campredon road, between the sources of the Ter and the Fluvia.

The third, or Figueras road, between the sources of the Muga and the sea-coast.

The first and second unite at Vicque; the second and third are connected by a transverse road running from Olot, by Castle Follit, to Gerona; the third also dividing near the latter town, leads with one branch through Hostalrich, and with the other follows the line of the coast. After the union of the first and second at Vicque, a single route pursues the stream of the Besos to Barcelona, thus turning the Muga, the Fluvia, the Ter, the Tordera, Besos, and an infinity of minor streams, that, descending from the mountains, in their rapid course to the Mediterranean, furrow all the country between the eastern Pyrenees and Barcelona. The third, which is the direct and best communication between Perpignan and the capital of Catalonia, crosses all the above-named rivers, whose deep channels and sudden floods offer serious obstacles to the march of an army.

All these roads, with the exception of that from Olot to Gerona, are separated by craggy ridges of mountains scarcely to be passed by troops; and the two first leading through wild and savage districts, are incommoded by defiles, and protected by a number of old castles and walled places, more or less capable of resistance. The third, passing through many rich and flourishing places, is however completely blocked to an invader by the strong fortresses of Figueras and Rosas on the Muga, of Gerona on the Ter, and Hostalrich on the Tordera. Palamos and several castles likewise impede the coast road, which is moreover skirted by rocky mountains, and exposed for many leagues to the fire of a fleet. Such is Catalonia, eastward and northward of Barcelona.

On the west, at five or six miles distance, the Llobregat cuts it off from a rough and lofty tract, through which the Cardena, the Noga, the Foix, Gaya, Anguera, and Francoli rivers, break in deep channels, descending in nearly parallel lines to the coast, and the spaces between being gorged with mountains, and studded with fortified places which command all the main roads. The plains and fertile valleys are so few and contracted, that Catalonia may, with the exception of the rich parts about Lerida and the Urgel, be described as a huge mass of rocks and torrents, incapable of supplying subsistence even for the inhabitants, whose prosperity depends entirely upon manufactures and commerce.

Barcelona, the richest and most populous city in Spain, is the heart of the province, and whoso masters it, if he can hold it, may suck the strength of Catalonia away. A French army, without a commanding fleet to assist, can scarcely take or keep Barcelona; the troops must be supplied by regular convoys from France; the fortresses on the line of communication must be taken and provisioned, and the active intelligent population of the country must be beaten from the rivers, pursued into their fortresses, and warred down by exertions which none but the best troops are capable of: for the Catalans are robust, numerous, and brave enough after their own manner.

Observation 2d. — It follows from this exposition, that Duhesme evinced a surprising want of forethought and military sagacity, in neglecting to secure Gerona, Hostalrich, and Tarragona, with garrisons, when his troops were received into those places. It was this negligence that rendered the timid operations of Swartz and Chabran capital errors; it was this that enabled some poor injured and indignant peasants to kindle a mighty war, and in a very few weeks obliged Napoleon to send thirty thousand men to the relief of Barcelona.

St Cyr.

Observation 3d.—Duhesme was experienced in battles, and his energy and resources of mind have been praised by a great authority; but undoubtedly an absence of prudent calculation and arrangement, a total neglect of military discipline, marked all his operations in Catalonia; witness his mode of attack on Gerona, the deficiency of ladders, and the confusion of the assaults. Witness also his raising of the second siege, and absolute flight from Caldagues, whose rash enterprise, although crowned with success, should have caused his own destruction.

Napoleon's Notes, Appendix, No. 2.

St. Cyr.Cabanes.

In those affairs it is certain Duhesme displayed neither talent nor vigour; but in the severities he exercised at the sacking of Mattaro, in the burning of villages, which he executed to the extreme verge of, if not beyond what the harshest laws of war will justify, an odious energy was apparent, and as the ardour of the somatenes was rather increased than repressed by these vigorous proceedings, his conduct may be deemed as impolitic as it was barbarous.

Observation 4th.—In Catalonia all the inherent cruelty of the Spaniards was as grossly displayed as in any other province of Spain. The Catalans were likewise vain and superstitious; but their courage was higher, their patriotism purer, and their efforts more sustained; the somatenes were bold and active in battle, the population of the towns firm, and the juntas apparently disinterested. The praise merited and bestowed upon the people of Zaragoza is great; but Gerona more justly claims the admiration of mankind; for the Aragonese troops were by Lefebre driven from the open country in crowds to their capital, and little was wanted to induce them to surrender at once; it was not until the last hour that, gathering courage from despair, the people of Zaragoza put forth all their energy: whereas those of Gerona, although attacked by a greater force, and possessing fewer means of defence, without any internal system of terror to counterbalance their fear of the enemy, manfully and successfully resisted from the first. The people of Zaragoza rallied at their hearthstone; those of Gerona stood firm at the porch. But quitting these matters, I must now, following the order I have marked out, proceed to relate the occurrences in Valencia.

OPERATIONS OF MARSHAL MONCEY

The execution of Calvo and his followers changed the horrid aspect of the Valencian insurrection; the spirit of murder was checked, and the patriotic energy assumed a nobler appearance. Murcia and Valencia were united as one province; and towards the end of June, nearly thirty thousand men, armed and provided with artillery, attested the resources of these rich provinces, and the activity of their chiefs. The Valencians then conceived the plan of marching to the assistance of the Aragonese; but Napoleon had already prescribed the measures which were to render such a movement abortive.

S. Journal of Moncey's Operations. MSS.

An order, dated the 30th of May, directed Moncey to move, with a column of ten thousand men, upon Cuenca; from that point he was to watch the country comprised between the lower Ebro and Carthagena, and he was empowered to act against the city of Valencia if he judged it fitting to do so. The position of Cuenca was advantageous; a short movement from thence to the left would place Moncey's troops upon the direct line between Valencia and Zaragoza, and enable him to intercept all communication between those towns; and a few marches to the right placed him upon the junction of the roads leading from Carthagena and Valencia to Madrid. If Moncey thought it essential to attack Valencia, the division of general Chabran was to co-operate from the side of Catalonia. By this combination the operations of Lefebre Desnouettes at Zaragoza, and those of Duhesme in Catalonia, were covered from the Valencians; and at the same time the flank of the French army at Madrid was protected on the side of Murcia.

Ibid.

The 6th of June Moncey marched from Aranjuez by Santa Cruz, Tarancon, Carascoso, and Villa del Orma, and reached Cuenca the 11th. There he received information of the rapid progress of the insurrection, of the state of the Valencian army, and of the projected movement to relieve Zaragoza; he immediately resolved to make an attempt against the city of Valencia, and wrote to general Chabran, whom he supposed to be at Tortosa, directing him to march upon Castellon de la Plana, a town situated at some distance eastward of the river Guadalaviar. Moncey himself proposed, by a march through Requeña, to clear the country westward of that river, and fixed upon the 25th of June as the latest period at which the two columns were to communicate in the immediate vicinity of Valencia.

Halting from the 11th to the 16th at Cuenca, he marched the 17th to Tortola, the 18th to Buenaches, the 19th to Matilla, the 20th to Minglanilla, and the 21st to Pesquiera. From Buenaches to Pesquiera no inhabitants were to be seen; the villages were deserted, and either from fear or hatred, every living person fled before his footsteps. At length, a Swiss regiment, some of the Spanish guards, and a body of armed peasantry, made a stand at the bridge of Pajaso, upon the river Cabriel; the manner in which the country had been forsaken, the gloomy and desolate marches, and the sudden appearance of an armed force ready to dispute this important pass, prognosticated a desperate conflict; but the event belied the omens; and scarcely any resistance was made; the French easily forced the passage of the bridge; the peasants fled, and the Swiss and Spanish guards came over to the side of the victors.

Ibid.

Moncey informed general Chabran of this success, and appointed the 27th and 28th for a junction under the walls of Valencia. The next day he took a position at Otiel; but hearing that the defeated patriots had rallied and being reinforced, were, to the number of ten or twelve thousand, intrenching themselves upon his left, he quitted the direct line of march to attack them in their post of Cabreras, which was somewhat in advance of the Siete Aguas. The Spanish position was of extraordinary strength, the flanks rested upon steep rocky mountains, and the only approach to the front was through a long narrow defile, formed by high scarped rocks, whose tops, inaccessible from the French side, were covered with the armed peasantry of the neighbourhood. A direct assault upon such a position could not succeed, and general Harispe was directed to turn it by the right, while the cavalry and artillery occupied the attention of the Spaniards in front; after overcoming many obstacles offered by the impracticable nature of the ground, Harispe reached the main body of the Spaniards, and then easily defeated them, taking all their cannon, ammunition, and baggage. This action, which took place upon the 24th, freed the left flank of Moncey's army, and he resumed his march upon the direct road to Valencia. The 25th he was at the Venta de Buñol, the 26th in advance of Chieva, and the 27th he arrived in front of Valencia.

A complete circuit of the ancient walls was in existence, and all the approaches were commanded by works which had been hastily repaired or newly raised by the inhabitants; the citadel was in a tolerable state of defence, and the population were preparing for a vigorous resistance. A city containing eighty thousand people, actuated by the most violent passions, cannot be easily overcome, and the Valencians derived additional strength from the situation of their town, built as it was upon low ground, and encircled with numerous canals and cuts, made for the purposes of irrigation; the deep ditches of the place were filled with water, so that no approach could be made by the small force under Moncey except against the gates. It is said that the marshal had corrupted a smuggler, who promised to betray the city during the heat of the assault, and it is probable that some secret understanding of that kind induced the French commander to make an attempt which would otherwise have been rash and unmilitary.

Don Joseph Caro, a brother of the marquis of Romana, was with four thousand men entrenched behind the canal of the Guadalaviar, which was five miles in advance of the city gates. The village of Quarte, and some thickly planted mulberry trees, helped to render this post very strong; and when Moncey attacked it upon the 27th, he met with a vigorous resistance. Caro was, however, beaten, and chased into the city, with the loss of some cannon, and on the 28th the French drove in the outposts, and occupied all the principal avenues of the town.

However enthusiastic the patriots were while their enemy was at a distance, his near approach filled them with terror, and it is possible that a vigorous assault might have succeeded at the first moment of consternation. But the favourable opportunity, if it really existed, quickly passed away; Padre Rico, a friar distinguished by his resolution, traversing the streets, with a cross in one hand and a sword in the other, aroused the sinking spirit and excited the fanaticism of the multitude; the fear of retaliation for the massacre of the French residents, and the certainty that Moncey's troops were few, powerfully seconded his efforts; and as it is usual for undisciplined masses of people to pass suddenly from one extreme to another, fear was soon succeeded by enthusiasm.

After disposing his field-pieces on the most favourable points, and while the impression of the first defeat was still fresh, Moncey summoned the governor to surrender. But the latter answered, "That he would defend the city." The French guns then opened upon the place; the heavy guns of the Spaniards, however, soon overpowered them, and a warm skirmish ensuing about the houses of the suburbs and the vicinity of the gates, the Valencians so obstinately resisted, that when the night fell, not only no serious impression had been made upon the defences, but the assailants were repulsed with loss at every point. The situation of the French marshal became delicate; the persons sent to seek Chabran could gain no intelligence of that general's movements; the secret connexions in the town, if any there were, had failed; the ammunition was nearly expended, and the army was encumbered with seven or eight hundred wounded men, and among them the general of engineers. Moncey, swayed by these embarrassments, relinquished his attack, and fell back to Quarte on the 29th, being harassed by Caro and the populace in his retreat.

When it is considered that in a great city only a small number of persons can estimate justly the immense advantages of their situation, and the comparative weakness of the enemy, it must be confessed that the spirit displayed by the Valencians upon this occasion was very great; unfortunately it ended there, nothing worthy of such an energetic commencement was afterwards performed, although very considerable armies were either raised or maintained in the province.

Journal of Moncey.

At Quarte Moncey, hearing that the captain-general, Serbelloni, was marching upon Almanza to intercept the communication with Chieva and Buñol, resolved to relinquish the line of Cuenca, and to attack Serbelloni before he could quit the kingdom of Murcia. This vigorous resolution he executed with great celerity; for, directing the head of his column towards Torrente, he continued his march until night, halting a short distance from that town. And a forced march the next day brought him near Alcira, only one league from the river Xucar; from his bivouac at that place he despatched advice to general Chabran of this change of affairs.

In the mean time the conde de Serbelloni, surprised in the midst of his movement, and disconcerted in his calculations by the decision and rapidity of Moncey, took up a position to defend the passage of the Xucar; the line of that river is strong, and offers many advantageous points of resistance; but the Spaniards imprudently occupied both banks, and in this exposed situation were attacked upon the morning of the 1st of July; the division on the French side was overthrown, and the passage forced without loss of time. Serbelloni then retired to the heights of San Felice, which covered the main road leading from Alcira to Almanza, hoping to secure the defiles in front of the latter town before the enemy could arrive there; but Moncey was again too quick for him; for leaving San Felice to his left, he continued his march on another route, and by a strenuous exertion seized upon the gorge of the defiles near Almanza late in the night of the 2d; the Spanish troops in the mean time approached his position, but were dispersed at daybreak on the 3d, and some of their guns captured; the road being now open, Moncey entered the town of Almanza the same day. The 4th he took post at Bonete. The 5th near Chinchilla, and the 6th at Albacete, where he got intelligence that general Frere, who should have been at St. Clemente with a division, was gone towards Mequeña.

To explain this movement it is necessary to observe that when Dupont marched towards Andalusia, and Moncey against Valencia, the remaining divisions of their corps were employed by Savary to scour the country in the neighbourhood of Madrid, and to protect the rear and connect the operations of those generals; thus general Gobert, who, following Napoleon's orders, should have been at Valladolid, was sent with the third division of Dupont towards Andalusia; and general Frere (commanding the second division of Moncey's), who should have been at San Clemente, a central point, from whence he could gain the road leading from Seville to La Mancha, and intercept the communication between Valencia and Cuenca, or seize upon the point of junction where the route from Carthagena and Murcia falls into the road of Valencia, was sent by Requeña to reinforce Moncey.

Meanwhile, the inhabitants of Cuenca rose in arms, and being joined by a force of seven or eight thousand peasants, overpowered and destroyed a French detachment left in that town. The duke of Rovigo, fearing that Moncey's column would be compromised by this insurrection, ordered general Caulaincourt, then at Taracon, to quell it with a force composed of cavalry and some provisional battalions. Caulaincourt arrived in front of Cuenca on the evening of the 3d of July; finding the insurgents in position, he attacked and dispersed them with great slaughter, and the town being deserted by the inhabitants, was given up to pillage.

Foy's History.

In the mean time, Frere, who had quitted San Clemente upon the 26th, made his way to Requeña; there he received intelligence of Caulaincourt's success, and that Moncey had passed the Xucar; whereupon, retracing his steps, he returned to San Clemente, his troops being wearied, sickly, and exhausted by these long and useless marches in the heats of summer. Moncey now re-organized his forces, and prepared artillery and other means for a second attempt against Valencia; but he was interrupted by Savary, who, alarmed at the advance of Cuesta and Blake, recalled Frere towards Madrid, and Moncey, justly offended that Savary, inflated with momentary power, should treat him with so little ceremony, broke up from San Clemente, and likewise returned by the way of Ocaña to the capital.

OBSERVATIONS

Appendix, No. 7.

1°. The result of marshal Moncey's campaign being published by the Spaniards as a great and decisive failure, produced extravagant hopes of final success; a happy illusion if the chiefs had not partaken of it, and pursued their wild course of mutual flattery and exaggeration, without reflecting that in truth there was nothing very satisfactory in the prospect of affairs. Moncey's operation was in the nature of a moveable column; the object of which was to prevent the junction of the Valencian army with the Aragonese. The attempt upon the town of Valencia was a simple experiment, which, if successful, would have produced great effects, but having failed, the evil resulting was but trifling in a military point of view.

Valencia was not the essential object of the expedition, and the fate of the general campaign depended upon the armies in Old Castile.

2°. It was consoling that a rich and flourishing town had not fallen into the power of the enemy; but at the same time a want of real nerve in the Spanish insurrection was visible. The kingdoms of Murcia and Valencia acted in concert, and contained two of the richest sea-port towns in the Peninsula; their united force amounted to thirty thousand organised troops, exclusive of the armed peasants in various districts; and the populace of Valencia were deeply committed by the massacre of the French residents. Here then, if in any place, a strenuous resistance was to be expected; nevertheless, marshal Moncey, whose whole force was at first only eight thousand French, and never exceeded ten thousand men, continued marching and fighting without cessation for a month, during which period he forced two of the strongest mountain passes in the world, crossed several large and difficult rivers, carried the war into the very streets of Valencia; and being disappointed of assistance from Catalonia, extricated his division from a difficult situation, after having defeated his opponents in five actions, killed and wounded a number of them, equal in amount to the whole of his own force, and made a circuit of above three hundred miles through a hostile and populous country, without having sustained any serious loss, without any desertion from the Spanish battalions incorporated with his own, and what was of more importance, having those battalions much increased by desertions from the enemy. In short, the great object of the expedition had been attained, the plan of relieving Zaragoza was entirely frustrated, and the organization of an efficient Spanish force retarded.

3°. Moncey could hardly have expected to succeed against the town of Valencia; for to use Napoleon's words, "*a city, with eighty thousand inhabitants, barricadoed streets, and artillery placed at the gates, cannot be* taken by the collar."

4°. General Frere's useless march to Requeña was very hurtful to the French; and the duke of Rovigo was rated by the emperor for his want of judgment upon the occasion; "it was a folly," the latter writes, "to dream of reinforcing Moncey; because if that marshal failed in taking the city by a sudden assault, it became an affair of artillery; and twenty thousand men, more or less, would not enable him to succeed." "Frere could do nothing at Valencia, but he could do a great deal at San Clemente; because from that post he could support either Madrid or general Dupont."

5°. Moncey was slightly blamed by the emperor for not halting within a day's march of Valencia, in order to break the spirit of the people, and make them feel the weight of the war; but this opinion was probably formed upon an imperfect knowledge of the local details. The marshal's line of operations from Cuenca was infested by insurgent bands, his ammunition was nearly exhausted, he could hear nothing of Chabran's division, and the whole force of Murcia was collecting upon his flank and rear. The country behind him was favourable for his adversaries, and his army was encumbered by a number of wounded men; it was surely prudent under such circumstances, to open his communication again with Madrid as quickly as possible.

By some authors, the repulse at Valencia has been classed with the inglorious defeat of Dupont at Baylen; but there was a wide difference between those events, the generals, and the results. Moncey, although an old man, was vigorous, active, and decided; and the check he received produced little effect. Dupont was irresolute, slow, and incapable, if not worse, as I shall hereafter show; but before describing his campaign, I must narrate the operations of the Gallician army.

CHAPTER VII

OPERATIONS OF BESSIERES AGAINST BLAKE AND CUESTA

While the moveable columns of Bessieres' corps ranged over the Asturian and Biscayan mountains, and dispersed the insurgent patriots of those provinces, Cuesta, undismayed by his defeat at Cabezon, collected another army at Benevente, and, in concert with the Gallician forces, prepared to advance again towards Burgos.

Filanghieri, the captain-general of Gallicia, had organised the troops in that kingdom without difficulty, because the abundant supplies poured in from England were beginning to be felt; and patriotism is never more efficacious than when supported by large sums of money. Taranco's soldiers joined to the garrisons of Ferrol and Coruña were increased, by new levies, to twenty-five thousand men, organised in four divisions, and being well equipped, and provided with a considerable train of artillery, were assembled at Manzanal, a strong post in the mountains, twelve miles behind Astorga.

The situation of that city offered great advantages to the Spaniards; the old Moorish walls which surrounded it were complete, and susceptible of being strengthened, so as to require a regular siege; but a siege could not be undertaken by a small force, while the army of Gallicia was entrenched at Manzanal, and while Cuesta remained at Benevente; neither could Bessieres, with any prudence, attack the Gallicians at Manzanal while Cuesta was at Benevente, and while Astorga contained a strong garrison. Filanghieri appears to have had some notion of its value, for he commenced forming an entrenched camp in the mountains; but being slain by his soldiers, don Joachim Blake succeeded to the command, and probably fearing a similar fate if the army remained stationary, left one division at Manzanal, and with the remainder marched towards Benevente to unite with Cuesta.

Journal of Bessieres' Operations. MSS.

Napoleon's Notes, Appendix, No. 2.

On the French side, marshal Bessieres collected his scattered columns at Palencia; his plan, founded upon instructions from Bayonne, was to make a S. rapid movement against Cuesta, in the hope of beating him, while Blake was still behind Leon; then wheeling to his right, to attack and drive the Gallicians back to the mountains, to overrun the flat country with his numerous cavalry, to open a communication with Portugal, and after receiving certain reinforcements then preparing for him, to subdue Gallicia, or assist Junot, as might seem most fitting at the time.

Ibid.

At this period the king was on his journey to Madrid, and the military system of Napoleon was brought to its first great crisis; for unless Bessieres was successful, there could be no sure footing for the French in the capital, and as Madrid was the base of Moncey's and Dupont's operations, the farther prosecution of their plans depended upon the result of the approaching struggle in the plains of Leon. Napoleon, foreseeing this crisis, had directed Savary to occupy Segovia, to send general Gobert's division to Valladolid, and to hold Vedel's and Frere's, the one in La Mancha, a few marches from the capital, and the other at San Clemente, a central point connecting Moncey, Dupont, and Madrid. But Savary, unable to estimate justly the relative importance of the different operations, sent Vedel and Gobert into Andalusia to reinforce Dupont, when he should rather have recalled the latter to the northern side of the Sierra Morena; he caused Frere, as we have seen, to quit San Clemente, and march by Requeña against Valencia, at the moment when Moncey was retiring from that city through Murcia to San Clemente, and thus dispersed and harassed his reserves by long marches to the south without any definite object when the essential interests were at stake in the north; and now, struck with fear at the approach of Cuesta and Blake, whose armies he had hitherto disregarded, he precipitately recalled Frere, Vedel, Gobert, and even Dupont to Madrid, too late to take part with Bessieres in the coming battle, but exactly timed to frustrate Moncey's projects, and, as we shall hereafter find, to ensure the ruin of Dupont. In this manner steering his vessel before every wind that blew, he could not fail of storms.

Greatly was Napoleon discontented with these errors; he relied, and with reason, on the ability of Bessieres for a remedy; but to Savary he sent the following instructions, dated the 13th of July:

"The French affairs in Spain would be in an excellent state if Gobert's division had marched upon Valladolid, and Frere's had occupied San Clemente, with a moveable column, three or four marches upon the route of general Dupont. Gobert having been directed upon Dupont, Frere being with Moncey, harassed and enfeebled by marches and countermarches, the position of the French army is become less advantageous.

"Marshal Bessieres is this day at Medina del Rio Seco with fifteen thousand men, infantry, cavalry, and artillery; the 15th or 16th he will attack Benevente, open

a communication with Portugal, drive the rebels into Gallicia, and seize upon Leon. If his operations succeed thus, and in a brilliant manner, the position of the French army will again be as good as it was.

"If general Cuesta retires from Benevente without fighting, he will move by Zamora and Salamanca to gain Avila and Segovia, certain that then Bessieres cannot pursue him, as, in that case, he would be menaced by the army of Gallicia, whose advanced guard is at Leon. The general who commands at Madrid must then be able to assemble six or seven thousand men and march upon Cuesta; the citadel of Segovia must be occupied by three or four hundred convalescents, with some guns and six weeks biscuit. It was a great fault not to have occupied this citadel when the major-general ordered it; of all the possible positions, Segovia is the most dangerous for the army; the capital of a province, situated between two routes, it deprives the army of all its communications, and the enemy once posted in the citadel, the French army cannot dislodge him. Three or four hundred convalescents, a good commandant, and a squad of artillery, will render the castle of Segovia impregnable for some time, and will insure to the army the important position of Segovia.

"If general Cuesta throws himself into Gallicia without fighting or suffering a defeat, the position of the army will become better; of course it will be still better if he does so after having suffered a defeat.

"If marshal Bessieres faces Cuesta at Benevente without attacking him, or if he is repulsed by him, his object will always be to cover Burgos, and to hold the enemy in check as long as possible; he could, perhaps, be reinforced with the three hundred troops of the line which accompany the king, but then there would be no room for hesitation. If Bessieres retires without a battle, he must be reinforced instantly with six thousand men. If he retreats after a battle wherein he has suffered great loss, it will be necessary to make great dispositions; to recall Frere, Gobert, Caulaincourt, and Vedel by forced marches to Madrid; to withdraw Dupont into the Sierra Morena, or even bring him nearer to Madrid (keeping him always, however, seven or eight marches off), then crush Cuesta and all the Gallician army, while Dupont will serve as an advanced guard to hold the army of Andalusia in check."

Before Bessieres could collect his troops, Blake effected a junction with Cuesta at Benevente. Three plans were open to those generals:

1°. To remove into the mountains, and take a position covering Gallicia.

2°. To maintain the head of the Gallician army in advance of Astorga, while Cuesta, with his Castilians, pushing by forced marches through Salamanca and Avila, reached Segovia.

3°. To advance farther into the plains, and try the fate of a battle.

This last plan was rash, seeing that Bessieres was well provided with horsemen, and that the Spaniards had scarcely any; but Cuesta, assuming the chief command, left a division at Benevente to protect his stores, and advanced, much against Blake's wishes, with twenty-five thousand infantry (regular troops), a few hundred cavalry, and from twenty to thirty pieces of artillery, in the direction of Palencia. His march, as we have seen, dismayed Savary. To use Napoleon's expressions, he who had been *"hitherto acting as if the army of Gallicia was not in existence,"* now acted *"as if Bessieres was already beaten;"* but that marshal, firm and experienced, rather than risk an action of such importance with insufficient means, withdrew even the garrison from the important post of St. Ander, and having quickly collected fifteen thousand men and thirty pieces of artillery at Palencia, moved forward on the 12th of July to the encounter. His line of battle consisted of two divisions of infantry, one of light cavalry, and twenty-four guns, his reserve was formed of four battalions and some horse grenadiers of the imperial guards, with six pieces of artillery.

S.
Journal of Bessieres' Operations.

The 13th he halted at Ampudia and Torre de Mormojon, from thence advancing on the 14th in two columns, he drove in an advanced guard of one hundred and fifty Spanish cavalry, and arrived about nine o'clock in front of Rio Seco, where Cuesta's army was drawn up like a heavy domestic animal awaiting the spring of some active wild beast.

BATTLE OF RIO SECO

The first line of the Spaniards was posted along the edge of a step of land, with an abrupt fall towards the French; the heaviest guns were distributed along the front. The second line, composed of the best troops, strengthened, or rather weakened, by seventeen or eighteen thousand peasants, was displayed at a great distance behind the first; the town of Rio Seco was in rear of the centre.

S
Journal of Bessieres' Operations.

Ibid.

Bessieres was at first startled at their numbers, and doubted if he should attack; but soon perceiving the vice of Cuesta's disposition, he ordered general Lasalle to make a feint against the front with the light cavalry, while he himself marching obliquely to the right, outstretched the left of the Spaniards, and suddenly thrust Merle's and Mouton's divisions and the imperial guards, horse and foot, between their lines, and threw the first into confusion; at that moment Lasalle charging furiously, the Spanish front went down at once, and fifteen hundred dead bodies strewed the field; but the victor's ranks were disordered, and Cuesta made a gallant effort to retrieve the day, for, supported by the fire of all his remaining artillery, he fell with his second line upon the French, and with his right wing broke in boldly and took six guns; but his left hanging back, the flank of the right was exposed. Bessieres, with great readiness, immediately charged on this naked flank with Merle's division and the horse grenadiers, while the fourteenth provisionary regiment made head against the front; a fierce short struggle ensued; and the Spaniards were overborne, were broken and dispersed; meanwhile the first line rallied in the town of Rio Seco, but were a second time defeated by Mouton's division, and fled over the plains, pursued by the light cavalry, and suffering severely in their flight.

Mr. Stuart's Papers.

From five to six thousand Spaniards were killed and wounded on the field, and twelve hundred prisoners, eighteen guns, and a great store of ammunition, remained in the hands of the French. The vanquished sought safety in all directions, but chiefly on the side of Benevente. Blake and Cuesta separated in wrath with each other, the former making for the mountains of Gallicia, the latter towards Leon, and the division left at Benevente dispersed.

The French, who had lost fifty killed and three hundred wounded, remained at Rio Seco all the 15th; the 16th they advanced to Benevente, where they found many thousand English muskets and vast quantities of ammunition, clothing, and provisions.

The communication with Portugal was now open, and Bessieres at first resolved to give his hand to Junot; but hearing that the fugitives were likely to rally on the side of Leon, he pursued them by the road of Villa-fere. On his march, learning that Cuesta was gone to Mayorga, he turned aside to that place, and on the 22d captured there another great collection of stores; for, the Spanish general, with the usual improvidence of his nation, had established all his magazines in the open towns of the flat country.

After this Bessieres entered the city of Leon and remained there until the 29th, during which time he received the submission of the municipality, and prepared to carry the war into Gallicia. The junta of Castile and Leon, whose power had hitherto been restrained by Cuesta, now retired to Puente-Ferrada and assumed supreme authority, and the quarrel between the generals becoming rancorous, they sided with Blake. This appearing to Bessieres a favourable occasion to tamper with the fidelity of those chiefs; he sent his prisoners back, and endeavoured, by offering the vice-royalty of Mexico to the one, and by reasoning on the hopeless state of the insurrection, and the promise of rank and honours to the other, to shake the loyalty of both; but neither would listen to him.

This failing, he marched to Puente Orvigo the 31st, intending to break into Gallicia, but he was suddenly recalled from thence to protect the retreat of the king from Madrid. Dupont had surrendered with a whole army in Andalusia, the court was in consternation, the victory of Rio Seco was rendered fruitless; and Bessieres retracing his steps to Mayorga, took a defensive position near that town.

OBSERVATIONS

1°. As Blake was overruled by Cuesta he is not responsible for the errors of this short campaign; but the faults were gross on both sides, and it seems difficult to decide whether Savary or Cuesta made the greatest number.

2°. If the former had sent Gobert's division to Valladolid, Bessieres would have had twenty-two thousand men and forty pieces of artillery in the field, a force not at all too great, when it is considered that the fate of three French armies depended upon the success of a battle to which Cuesta might have brought at least double that number. The latter having determined upon an offensive movement, disregarded the powerful cavalry of his enemy, chose a field of battle precisely in the country where that arm would have the greatest advantage, and when he should have brought every man to bear upon the quarter which he did attack, he displayed his ignorance of the art of war by fighting the battle of Rio Seco with twenty-five thousand men only, and leaving ten thousand disciplined troops guarding positions in his rear, which could not be approached until he himself was first beaten. Neither was the time well chosen for his advance; had he waited a few days the port of St. Ander would have been attacked by eight English frigates and a detachment of Spanish troops under the command of general da Ponte, an enterprise that would have distracted and weakened Bessieres, but which was relinquished in consequence of the battle of Rio Seco.

3°. Once united to Blake, Cuesta's real base of operations was Gallicia, and he should have kept all his stores within the mountains, and not have heaped them up in the open towns of the flat country, exposed to the marauding parties of the enemy, or covered, as in the case of Benevente, by strong detachments which weakened his troops in the field and confined him to a particular line of operations in the plain.

4°. The activity and good sense of marshal Bessieres overbalanced the errors of Savary; and the victory of Rio Seco was of infinite importance, because as we have seen a defeat in that quarter would have shaken the French military system to its centre and have obliged the king, then on his journey to Madrid, to halt at Vittoria, until the distant divisions of the army were recalled to the capital, and a powerful effort made to crush the victorious enemy. Napoleon's observations are full of strong expressions of discontent at the imprudence of his lieutenant. "*A check given to Dupont,*" he says, "*would have a slight effect, but a wound received by Bessieres would give a locked jaw to the whole army. Not an inhabitant of Madrid, not a peasant of the valleys that does not feel that the affairs of Spain are involved in the affair of Bessieres; how unfortunate, then, that in such a great event you have wilfully given the enemy twenty chances against yourself."* When he heard of the victory he exclaimed that it was the battle of Almanza, and that Bessieres had saved Spain.

Napoleon's Notes, Appendix, No. 3.

The prospect was indeed very promising; the king had arrived in Madrid, bringing with him the veteran brigade of general Rey and some of the guards, and all fears upon the side of Leon being allayed, the affairs of Andalusia alone were of doubtful issue; for Zaragoza, hard pushed by Verdier, was upon the point of destruction in despite of the noble courage of the besieged; nor did the subjugation of Andalusia appear in reason a hard task, seeing that Moncey was then at San Clemente, and from that point threatened Valencia without losing the power of succouring Dupont, and Frere's and Caulincourt's troops were disposable for any operation. The French army possessed the centre, and the Spaniards were dispersed upon a variety of points on the circumference without any connexion with each other, and in force only upon the side of Andalusia.

5°. The great combinations of the French emperor were upon the point of being crowned with success, when a sudden catastrophe overturned his able calculations and raised the sinking hopes of the Spaniards. It was the campaign in Andalusia which produced such important effects, and it offers one of the most interesting and curious examples recorded by history of the vicissitudes of war; for there disorder unaccompanied by superior valour triumphed over discipline; inexperienced officers were successful against practised generals; and a fortuitous combination of circumstances enabled the Spaniards, without any skill, to defeat in one day an immense plan wisely arranged, embracing a variety of interests, and until that moment happily conducted in all its parts. This blow, which felled Joseph from his throne, marked the French army with a dishonourable scar, the more conspicuous, because it was the only one of its numerous wounds that misbecame it.

CHAPTER VIII

OPERATIONS IN ANDALUSIA

Journal of Dupont's Operations. MS.

General Dupont received orders to march against Cadiz with a column, composed of two Swiss regiments (Preux and Reding), taken from the Spanish army, a French division of infantry under general Barbou, a division of cavalry commanded by general Fresia, a marine battalion of the imperial guards, and eighteen pieces of artillery. Three thousand infantry, five hundred cavalry, and ten guns, drawn from the army of Portugal, were to join him in Andalusia, and he was to incorporate among his troops three other Swiss regiments, quartered in that province.

The latter end of May he traversed La Mancha, entered the Sierra Morena, by the pass of Despeñas Perros, and proceeded by Carolina and Baylen to Andujar, where he arrived the 2d of June; there he was informed that a supreme junta of government was established at Seville, that minor juntas ruled in Granada, Jaen, and Cordoba, that war was formally declared against the French, that the whole of Andalusia was in arms, and the Swiss regiments ranged under the Spanish banners, and finally, that general Avril, commanding the detachment expected from Portugal, had halted in Tavora, and was preparing to return to Lisbon.

Alarmed by this intelligence, Dupont wrote to Murat and Savary to demand reinforcements, and in the mean time closed up the rear of his columns, and established an hospital in Andujar. The 6th he crossed the Guadalquivir, and continued his march towards Cordoba, following the left bank of the river. Two leagues from that ancient city the road recrossed the Guadalquivir by a long stone bridge, at the furthest end of which stood the village of Alcolea. The French general arrived there at day-break on the 7th, but his further progress was opposed by the Spanish general Echevaria, who, having fortified the head of the bridge, manned the works, placed twelve guns in battery on the right bank, and drawn together three thousand regular troops, and ten thousand new levies and smugglers, occupied the village, and was prepared to dispute the passage of the river. A small reserve remained in a camp close to Cordoba, and a cloud of armed peasants from the side of Jaen were also gathered on the hills behind the French army, ready to fall on its rear when the bridge should be attacked.

Dupont having observed this disposition, placed the cavalry, the Swiss regiments, and the marine battalion in reserve facing to the hills, and with the division of Barbou stormed the head of the bridge. The Spaniards, making a feeble resistance, were driven across the river, and their whole line immediately fled to the camp at Cordoba. The multitude on the hills descended during the battle, but were beaten back by the cavalry with loss, and the French general, leaving the marine battalion at Alcolea to secure the bridge, marched with the rest of his forces to complete the victory. At his approach the Spaniards abandoned their new position, took refuge in the town, and being summoned to surrender, opened a fire of musketry from the walls, whereupon the French bursting the gates with their field-pieces, broke into the town, and after a short and confused fight Echevaria's men fled in disorder along the Seville road, and were pursued by the cavalry. As the inhabitants took no part in the contest, and received the French without any signs of aversion, the town was protected from pillage, and Dupont fixing his quarters there, sent his patroles as far as Ecija without meeting with an enemy.

Nellerto.

In Seville the news of this disaster, and the arrival of fugitives, struck such a terror, that the junta were only prevented from retiring to Cadiz by their dread of the populace, and even entertained thoughts of abandoning Spain altogether, and flying to South America. Castaños, who a few days before had been declared captain-general of the armies, was at this time in march with seven thousand troops of the line from San Roque; being called to Seville, he arrived there on the 9th, and after a short conference with the junta proceeded to take the command of Echevaria's forces, the greater part of which were reassembled at Carmona, but in such confusion and so moody that he returned immediately, and having persuaded the president Saavedra to accompany him, fixed his head-quarters at Utrera, where he gathered two or three thousand regulars from the nearest garrisons, and directing the new levies to repair to him, hastened the march of his own men from St. Roche. He also pressed general Spencer to disembark, and take up a position with the British forces at Xeres; but Spencer, for reasons hereafter to be mentioned, sailed to Ayamonte, a circumstance that augmented a general distrust of the English prevailing at the time, and which was secretly fomented by Morla, and by several members of the junta.

Appendix, No. 13.

At this moment Andalusia was lost if Dupont had advanced; his inactivity saved it: instead of pushing his victory, he wrote to Savary for reinforcements, and to general Avril, desiring that he would without delay come to his assistance, but he himself remained in Cordoba, overwhelmed with imaginary dangers and difficulties; for although Castaños had in a few days collected at Carmona and Utrera seven or eight thousand regulars, and above fifty thousand new levies, and that Dupont's letters were intercepted and brought to him, such was the condition of affairs that, resigning all thoughts of making a stand, he had, under the pretence of completing the defences of Cadiz, embarked the heavy artillery and stores at Seville, and was prepared, if Dupont should advance, to burn the timbers and harness of his field artillery, and to retreat to Cadiz.

Sir H. Dalrymple's Papers.

Meanwhile continuing the organization of his forces, he filled up the old regiments with new levies, and formed fresh battalions, in which he was assisted by two foreigners, the marquis de Coupigny, a crafty French emigrant, of some experience in war, and Reding, a Swiss, a bold, enterprising, honest man, but without judgment, and of very moderate talents as an officer. Castaños wished to adopt a defensive plan, to make Cadiz his place of arms, and to form an entrenched camp, where he hoped to be joined by ten or twelve thousand British troops, and, in security, to organize and discipline a large army; but, in reality, he had merely the name and the troubles of a commander-in-chief, without the power; for Morla was his enemy, and the junta containing men determined to use their authority for their own emolument and the gratification of private enmity, were jealous lest Castaños should control their proceedings, and thwarted him; humouring the caprice and insolence of the populace, and meddling with affairs foreign to the matter in hand.

As the numbers at Utrera increased, the general confidence augmented, and a retreat was no longer contemplated: plans were laid to surround Dupont in Cordoba; one detachment of peasants, commanded by regular officers, was sent to occupy the passes of the Sierra Morena, leading into Estremadura; another marched from Grenada, accompanied by a regiment of the line, to seize Carolina, and cut off the communication with La Mancha; a third, under colonel Valdecanas, proposed to attack the French in Cordoba without any assistance, and this eagerness for action was increased by a knowledge of the situation of affairs in Portugal, and by rumours exaggerating the strength of Filanghieri and Cuesta. It was believed that the latter had advanced to Valladolid, and offered Murat the option of abiding an attack, or retiring immediately to France by stated marches, and that, alarmed at Cuesta's power, the grand duke was fortifying the Retiro.

These reports, so congenial to the wishes and vanity of the Andalusians, caused the plan proposed by Castaños to be rejected; and when Dupont's despatches magnifying his own danger, and pressing in the most urgent manner for reinforcements were again intercepted and brought to head-quarters, it was resolved to attack Cordoba immediately; but Dupont's fears outstripped their impatience.

Journal of Dupont's Operations.

After ten days of inactivity, by which he lost the immediate fruit of his victory at Alcolea, — the lead in an offensive campaign, and all the imposing moral force of the French reputation in arms, Dupont, finding that, instead of receiving direct reinforcements from Savary, he must wait until Moncey, having first subdued Valencia, could aid him by the circuitous route of Murcia, resolved to fall back to Andujar.

Napoleon's notes, Appendix, No. 1.

Whittingham. Journal of Dupont.

Foy's History.

Victoire et Conquêtes.

He commenced his retreat the 17th of June, being followed as far as Carpio by the advanced guard of the Andalusians, under general Coupigny. Along the line of march, and in the town of Andujar, where he arrived the evening of the 18th, he found terrible proofs of Spanish ferocity; his stragglers had been assassinated, and his hospital taken, the sick, the medical attendants, the couriers, the staff officers, in fine, all who had the misfortune to be weaker than the insurgents, were butchered, with circumstances of extraordinary barbarity; upwards of four hundred men had perished in this miserable manner since the fight of Alcolea. The fate of colonel Renè was horrible; he had been sent on a mission to Portugal previous to the breaking out of hostilities; and was on his return, travelling in the ordinary mode, without arms, attached to no army, engaged in no operations of war, but being recognised as a Frenchman he was seized, mutilated, and then placed between two planks and sawed alive.

Dupont now collected provisions, and prepared to maintain himself in Andujar until he should be reinforced; but wishing to punish the city of Jaen, from whence the bands had come that murdered his sick, he sent captain Baste, a naval officer, with a battalion of infantry and some cavalry, to accomplish that object. The French soldiers, inflamed by the barbarity of their enemies, inflicted a severe measure of retaliation, for it is the nature of cruelty to reproduce itself in war; and for this reason, although the virtue of clemency is to all persons becoming, it is peculiarly so to an officer, the want of it leading to so many and such great evils.

The Andalusian army having remained quiet, Dupont, who knew that Vedel's division, escorting a large convoy for the army, was marching through La Mancha, sent captain Baste with a second detachment to clear the pass of Despeñas Perros which was occupied by insurgents and smugglers from Grenada to the number of three thousand: the pass itself was of incredible strength, and the Spaniards had artillery, and were partially entrenched; but their commander, a colonel of the line, deserted to the enemy, and before Baste could arrive, Vedel forced the road without difficulty and reached Carolina. He posted a detachment there to keep open the communication with La Mancha, and then descended himself to Baylen, a small town sixteen miles from Andujar.

Dupont's Journal.

Foy's History.

Meanwhile other insurgents from Grenada having arrived at Jaen were preparing to move by the Linhares road to Carolina and Despeñas Perros. General Cassagne, with a brigade of Vedel's division, marched against them the 29th of June, and after fighting on the 2nd and 3d of July, he took possession of Jaen, and drove the Grenadans back with considerable slaughter, but lost two hundred men himself, and returned on the 25th to Baylen. Notwithstanding these successes, and that Vedel brought reinforcements for Barbou's division and the cavalry, Dupont's fears increased. His position at Andujar covered the main road from Seville to Carolina; but eight miles lower down the river it could be turned by the bridge of Marmolexo, and sixteen miles higher up by the roads leading from Jaen to the ferry of Mengibar and Baylen; and beyond that line by the roads from Jaen and Grenada to Uzeda, Linhares, and the passes of El Rey and the Despeñas Perros. The dryness of the season had also rendered the Guadalquivir fordable in many places. The regular force under Castaños was daily increasing in strength, the population around was actively hostile, and the young French soldiers were drooping under privations and the heat of the climate. Six hundred were in hospital, and the whole were discouraged. It is in such situations that the worth of a veteran is found: in battle the ardour of youth often appears to shame the cool indifference of the old soldier, but when the strife is between the malice of fortune and fortitude, between human endurance and accumulating hardships, the veteran becomes truly formidable, when the young soldier resigns himself to despair.

After the actions at Jaen, both sides remained quiet until the 14th of July, on which day general Gobert, who should have been at Rio Seco with Bessieres, arrived at Carolina with the greatest part of a division, the next day he joined Vedel at Baylen, and the latter general pushed on a brigade, under general Leger Bellair, to watch the ferry of Mengibar, and it was full time, for the Spanish army was already on the opposite bank of the river.

Whittingham's Correspondence.

Whittingham's Correspondence.

When Dupont's retreat from Cordoba had frustrated the plan of the Spaniards to surround him, Castaños returned to his old project of a rigorous defensive system. The junta at first acquiesced, but being unsettled in their policy, and getting intelligence of Vedel's march, they ordered Castaños to attack Dupont at Andujar before the reinforcements could arrive. The regular troops were about twenty-five thousand infantry, and two thousand cavalry. A very heavy train of artillery, and large bodies of armed peasantry, commanded by officers of the line, attended the army; the numbers, of course, varied from day to day, but the whole multitude that advanced towards the Guadalquivir could not have been less than fifty thousand men, hence the intelligence that Vedel had actually arrived did not much allay the general fierceness. Castaños, however, was less sanguine than the rest, and learning that Spencer had just returned to Cadiz with his division, he once more requested him to land and advance to Xeres, to afford a point of retreat in the event of a disaster; the English general consented to disembark, but refused to advance further than Port St. Mary.

Ibid.

The 1st of July the Spanish army occupied a position extending from Carpio to Porcuñas; the 11th a council of war being held, it was resolved that Reding's division should cross the Guadalquivir at the ferry of Mengibar, and gain Baylen; that Coupigny should cross at Villa Nueva, and support Reding; and that Castaños, with the other two divisions, advancing to the heights of Argonilla, should attack Andujar in front, while Reding and Coupigny should descend from Baylen and attack it in the rear. Some detachments of light troops under colonel Cruz were ordered to pass the Guadalquivir by Marmolexo, and to seize the passes leading through the Morena to Estremadura.

Ibid.

Dupont's Journal.

Foy.

The 13th, Reding, with the first division, and three or four thousand peasantry, marched towards Mengibar; and Coupigny, with the second division, took the road of Villa Nueva. The 15th, Castaños crowned the heights of Argonilla, in front of Andujar, with two divisions of infantry, and a multitude of irregular troops. Coupigny skirmished with the French picquets at Villa Nueva; and Reding crossing the river at Mengibar, attacked Leger Bellair; but Vedel came to the assistance of the latter, and Reding recrossed to the left bank. When Dupont saw the heights of Argonilla covered with Spanish troops, he sent to Vedel for a brigade of infantry, broke down the bridge of Marmolexo, occupied some works that he had thrown up to cover the bridge of Andujar, put a garrison in an old tower built over one of the arches, and drew the remainder of his troops up in position on the bank of the river; his cavalry being posted in the plain behind the town, with posts watching the fords above and below the position.

Dupont's Journal.

Ibid.

The 15th, Castaños merely cannonaded the bridge; the 16th, colonel Cruz crossed with four thousand men near Marmolexo, and fell upon Dupont's rear, while Castaños attacked him in front. Cruz was beaten, and chased into the mountains by a single battalion, and a few discharges checked Castaños. Meanwhile, Vedel, either thinking all safe at Baylen, or mistaking Dupont's meaning, instead of sending a brigade, marched during the night of the 15th with his whole division. The next day Reding again passed the Guadalquivir, and attacked Leger Bellair. General Gobert, who had just arrived at Baylen, marched to the latter's assistance; the combat became hot, Gobert fell mortally wounded, and the French retired to Baylen. General Darfour succeeded Gobert, and as Reding did not follow up his success, Darfour gave credit to a report that the Spanish general was moving by the Linhares road upon Carolina, and imprudently fell back to the latter town.

While this was passing, Dupont, already offended by Vedel's over-zeal, heard of Gobert's death, and obliged the former to return during the nights of the 16th and 17th, to Baylen, with orders to secure that important point; but Vedel also fell into the same error as Darfour, and marched the 18th to Carolina. Reding, who had never moved from Mengibar, being now joined by Coupigny, profited of this occasion to seize Baylen, and throwing out a detachment on the side of Carolina, drew up in position facing Andujar; his numbers, including the armed peasants, being about twenty thousand.

Dupont's Journal.

The armies were thus interlaced in a singular manner: Dupont being posted between Castaños and Reding; and Reding between Dupont and Vedel's division: the affair became one of time; Castaños rested tranquilly in his camp, apparently ignorant of Reding's situation; Dupont, more alive to what was passing, silently quitted Andujar on the evening of the 18th, marched all night, and at day-break came to Rio de las Tiedras, a torrent with rugged banks, two miles from the Spanish position, in front of Baylen. Reding's ground was strong, intersected with deep ravines, and planted with olive trees. Dupont hoping that Vedel would return upon the Spanish rear, and having no choice, passed the Tiedras, and leaving Barbou with a few battalions on that stream to keep Castaños in check, if he should arrive during the action, attacked Reding.

Whittingham.

Ibid.

For some time the French appeared to be gaining ground; but, fatigued with a long night march, and unable to force the principal points, they became discouraged; the Swiss brigade went over to the enemy; and at two o'clock, after losing about two thousand, killed and wounded, Dupont yielded to his destiny, and sent to desire a suspension of hostilities, with a view to a convention. Reding, who could hardly maintain his position, willingly acceded to the proposal. At this moment Barbou was attacked by general La Pena, who arrived on the Tiedras with a third Spanish division; for Castaños, when he had discovered Dupont's retreat eight hours after the latter had quitted his position, sent half the troops in pursuit, and remained with the rest at Andujar.

Victoires et Conquêtes.

Foy.

Dupont's Journal. MSS.

Vedel having heard the cannonade as early as three o'clock in the morning, quitted Carolina at five o'clock, and marched in the direction of Baylen. The continued sound of artillery became more distinct as he advanced, and left no doubt of the fact of Dupont's division being seriously engaged, notwithstanding which he halted at Guarroman, two Spanish leagues from Baylen, and remained inactive for seven hours. At three o'clock in the evening, when the firing had long ceased, he put himself in motion again, and coming upon the rear of Reding's troops, enveloped and made prisoners a battalion of the detached corps which was posted by that general to watch the road leading from Carolina. These troops relying upon the faith of the armistice just agreed upon with Dupont, made no resistance;

and Vedel being informed of what was passing, released them, and awaited the result of this singular crisis.

Whittingham's Correspondence.

Victoires et Conquêtes.

One Villontreys, an officer of the emperor's staff, opened the negotiation with Reding, by whom he was referred to Castaños then at Andujar; thither generals Chabert and Marescot repaired on the 20th. They demanded permission for the whole army to retire peaceably upon Madrid; and Castaños was at first inclined to grant this as the most certain and ready mode of freeing Andalusia from the French, and gaining time for further preparations; but Savary's letter to Dupont, written just before the battle of Rio Seco, to recall him to the defence of the capital, being intercepted, was brought at this moment to the Spanish head-quarters, and changed the aspect of affairs. A convention was no longer in question; Dupont's troops were required to lay down their arms and to become prisoners of war, on condition of being sent to France by sea. Vedel's troops were likewise required to surrender on condition of being sent to France with the others, but not to be considered as prisoners of war: and these terms were accepted.

Meanwhile Vedel, informed, in the night of the 20th, by Dupont, of this unexpected change, had retreated to Carolina. Castaños hearing of it, menaced Dupont with death if Vedel did not return; and the latter understanding that he was included in the capitulation, came back to Baylen and surrendered.

Foy's History.

Thus, above eighteen thousand French soldiers laid down their arms on the 22d, before a raw army incapable of resisting half that number if the latter had been led by an able man. Nor did this end the disgraceful affair; but, as if to show to what extent folly and fear combined will carry men, captain Villontrey's, with a Spanish escort, passed the Sierra Morena, and traversing La Mancha to within a short distance of Toledo, gathered up the escorts, the hospital attendants, and the detachments left by Dupont in that province, and constituting them prisoners under the capitulation, sent them to Andujar; and this unheard of proceeding was quietly submitted to by men who belonged to that army which for fifteen years had been the terror of Europe—a proof how much the firmness of soldiers depends upon the character of their immediate chief.

The capitulation, shameful in itself, was shamefully broken. The French troops, instead of being sent to France, were maltreated, and numbers of them murdered in cold blood, especially at Lebrixa, where above eighty officers were massacred in the most cowardly manner. Although armed only with their swords, they kept the assassins for some time at bay, and gathering in a company, upon an open space in the town, endeavoured to save their lives, but a fire from the neighbouring houses was kept up until the last of those unfortunate gentlemen fell.

Victoires et Conquêtes.

No distinction was made between Dupont's and Vedel's troops; all who survived the march to Cadiz, after being exposed to every species of indignity, were cast into some hulks, where the greatest number perished in lingering torments: a few hundreds, rendered desperate by their situation, contrived to escape, some years afterwards, by cutting the cables of their prison-ship, and drifting, under a heavy fire, and in the midst of a storm, upon a lee-shore, where two-thirds of them were picked up by their countrymen at that time blockading Cadiz. Dupont himself was permitted to return to France, and to take with him all the generals; and it is curious that general Privé, who had remonstrated strongly against the capitulation, and pressed Dupont on the field to force a passage through Reding's army, was the only one left behind.

Don Thomas Morla, after a vain attempt to involve lord Collingwood and sir Hew Dalrymple in the disgraceful transaction, formally defended the conduct of the junta in breaking the capitulation; his reasoning was worthy of the man who so soon afterwards betrayed his own country with the same indifference to honour that he displayed on this occasion.

OBSERVATIONS

Return of the French army. Appendix.

1°. The gross amount of Dupont's corps when it first entered Spain was about twenty-four thousand men, with three thousand five hundred horses; of these twenty-one thousand were fit for duty. It was afterwards strengthened by a provisionary regiment of cuirassiers, a marine battalion of the guard, and the two Swiss regiments of Preux and Reding. It could not therefore have been less than twenty-four thousand fighting men when Dupont arrived in Andalusia, and as the whole of Vedel's, and the greatest part of Gobert's division, had joined before the capitulation, and that eighteen thousand men laid down their arms at Baylen, Dupont must have lost by wounds, desertion, and deaths in hospital or the field, above four thousand men.

2°. The order which directed this corps upon Cadiz was despatched from Bayonne before the Spanish insurrection broke out; it was therefore strange that Dupont should have persevered in his march when he found affairs in such a different state from that contemplated by Napoleon at the time the instructions for this expedition were framed. If the emperor considered it necessary to reinforce the division which marched under Dupont's own command, with a detachment from the army in Portugal before the insurrection broke out, it was evident that he never could have intended that that general should blindly follow the letter of his orders, when a great and unexpected resistance was opposed to him, and that the detachment of Portugal was unable to effect a junction. The march to Cordoba was therefore an error, and it was a great error, because Dupont confesses in his memoir that he advanced under the conviction that his force was too weak to obtain success, and, consequently, having no object, his operations could only lead to a waste of lives.

3°. At Cordoba, Dupont remained in a state of torpor for ten days; this was the second error of a series which led to his ruin: he should either have followed up his victory and attacked Seville in the first moment of consternation, or he should have retired to Andujar while he might do so without the appearance of being compelled to it. If he had followed the first plan, the city would inevitably have fallen before him, and thus time would have been gained for the arrival of the 2d and 3d division of his corps.

Dupont's Journal of Operations.

4°. It may be objected that ten thousand men durst not penetrate so far into a hostile country; but at Alcolea, Dupont boasts of having defeated forty thousand men without any loss to himself; from such armies then he had nothing to fear, and the very fact of his having pushed his small force between the multitudes that he defeated upon the 7th, proves that he despised them. "He retired from Cordoba," he says in his memoir, "because to fight a battle when victory can be of no use is against all discretion;" but to make no use of a victory when it is gained comes to the same thing; and he should never have moved from Andujar unless with the determination of taking Seville.

5°. Those errors were, however, redeemable; the position behind the Guadalquivir, the checks given to the patriots at Jaen after the arrival of Vedel at Carolina upon the 27th, and above all the opportune junction of Gobert at the moment when Castaños and Reding appeared in front of the French line, proved that it was not fortune but common sense that deserted Dupont on this occasion, for the Spanish forces being divided and extended from Andujar to Mengibar were exposed to be beaten in detail; but their adversary was indulgent to them, and amidst the mass of errors committed upon both sides, this false disposition appeared like an act of wisdom, and being successful was stamped accordingly.

6°. At Mengibar a variety of roads branch off leading to Jaen, to Linhares, to Baylen and other places. From Andujar, a road nearly parallel to the Guadalquivir runs to the ferry of Mengibar and forms the base of a triangle, of which Baylen may be taken as the apex. From this latter town to the ferry is about six miles, from the ferry to Andujar is about eighteen, from the latter to Baylen the distance may be sixteen miles. Fifteen miles above Baylen the town of Carolina, situated in the gorge of the Sierra Morena, was the point of communication with La Mancha, and the line of retreat for the French in the event of a defeat, hence Baylen, not Andujar, was the pivot of operations.

Dupont's Journal. MS.

7°. The French force was inferior in number to that under Castaños, yet Dupont disseminated his divisions upon several points. The natural results followed. The Spaniards, although the most unwieldy body, took the lead and became the assailants; the French divisions were worn out by useless marches; the orders of their chief were mistaken or disobeyed; one position being forced, another was of necessity abandoned; confusion ensued, and finally Dupont says he surrendered with *eighteen thousand* men, because his fighting force was reduced to *two thousand*: such an avowal saves the honour of his soldiers, but destroys his own reputation as a general. The first question to ask is, what became of the remainder? Why had he so few when ten thousand of his army never fired a shot? It must be confessed that Dupont, unless a worse explanation can be given of his conduct, was incapable to the last degree.

8°. There were two plans, either of which promised a reasonable chance of success, under the circumstances in which the French army was placed on the 14th. 1st. To abandon Andujar, send all the incumbrances into La Mancha, secure the passes, unite the fighting men at Carolina, and fall in one mass upon the first corps of Spaniards that advanced; the result of such an attack could hardly have been doubtful; but if, contrary to all probability, the Spaniards had been successful, the retreat of the French was open and safe. 2dly. To secure Carolina by a detachment, and placing small bodies in observation at Andujar and the ferry of Mengibar, to unite the army on the 15th at Baylen, and in that central position await the enemy. If the two corps of the Spanish army had presented themselves simultaneously upon both roads, the position was strong for battle and the retreat open; if one approached before the other, each might have been encountered and crushed separately. Dupont had a force more than sufficient for this object, and fortune was not against him.

9°. The direction in which Reding marched was good, but it should have been followed by the whole army. The heights of Argonilla would have screened the march of Castaños, and a few troops with some heavy guns left in front of the bridge of Andujar, would have sufficed to occupy Dupont's attention. If the latter general had attacked Castaños upon the morning of the 16th, when Vedel's division arrived from Baylen, the fourteen thousand men thus united by accident would easily have overthrown the two Spanish divisions in front of Andujar; and Reding, if he had lost an hour in retreating to Jaen, might have been taken in flank by the victorious troops, and in front by Gobert, and so destroyed. Instead of availing himself of this opening, the French general sent Vedel back to Baylen, and followed himself the day after; being encountered by Reding, he vainly hoped that the divisions (which with so much pains he had dispersed) would reunite to relieve him from his desperate situation; it is difficult to say why those divisions did not arrive during the battle, and more difficult to assign to each person a just portion of censure where all were to blame.

Appendix, No. 6.

10°. In the action Dupont clung tenaciously to the miserable system of dividing his forces; his only chance of safety was to force Reding before Castaños could arrive upon the Tiedras; it was therefore a wretched misapplication of rules to have a reserve watching that torrent, and to fight a formal battle with a first and second line and half a dozen puny columns of attack. An energetic officer would have formed his troops in a dense mass and broken at once through the opposing force upon the weakest point; there are few armies so good, that such an assault would not open a passage through them; seven thousand infantry with cavalry and artillery is a powerful column of attack, and the Spanish line could not have withstood it for a moment. The battle should have been one of half an hour; Dupont, by his ridiculous evolutions, made it one of ten hours, and yet so badly did the patriots fight, that in all that time not a single prisoner or gun fell into their hands, and the fact of Reding's entering at all into a convention, proves his fears for the final result. It is truly astonishing that Dupont, who, from his rank, must have been well acquainted with Napoleon's Italian campaigns, should have caught so little of the spirit of his master. And then the inexplicable capitulation of Vedel after his retreat was actually effected! Vedel, who might have given battle and disputed the victory by himself without any great imprudence! Joseph called Dupont's capitulation a "*defection;*" perhaps he was right.

11°. Castaños, although active in preparation, discovered but little talent in the field, his movements were slow, uncertain, and generally false: the attempt to turn the French position at Andujar by detaching four thousand men across the river was ill conceived and badly supported; it was of that class of combinations to which the separate march of Reding's corps belonged. To the latter general the chief honour of the victory is due; yet, if Vedel had returned from Carolina upon the 19th, with the rapidity which the occasion required, Reding would have repented taking post at Baylen. It was undoubtedly a bold energetic step; but instead of remaining at that place, he should have descended instantly upon the rear of Dupont, leaving a corps of observation to delay the march of Vedel. Time not being taken into his calculation, Reding acted like a bold but rash and unskilful officer. Fortune, however, favoured his temerity, and with her assistance war is but a child's play.

Foy's History.

Intelligence of the capitulation of Baylen was secretly spread among the Spaniards in Madrid as early as the 23d or 24th of July, but the French, although alarmed by rumours of some great disaster, were unable to acquire any distinct information, until the king sent two divisions into La Mancha to open the communication; these troops arriving at Madrilejos, one hundred and twenty miles from Baylen, met captain Villontreys with his Spanish escort collecting prisoners, and apparently intending to proceed in his task to the very gates of Madrid. The extent of the disaster thus became known, and the divisions retraced their steps. Joseph called a council of war on the 29th, and Savary, enlightened by the instructions of Napoleon, proposed to unite all the French forces, to place a small garrison in the Retiro, and to fall upon the Spanish armies in succession as they advanced towards the capital; but a dislike to the war was prevalent amongst the higher ranks of the French army. The injustice of it was too glaring; and the reasons for a retreat, which might perchance induce Napoleon to desist, being listened to with more complacency than Savary's proposal, it was resolved to abandon Madrid and retire behind the Ebro.

The king commenced this operation on the 1st of August, marching by the Somosierra; while Bessieres posted at Mayorga, covered the movement until the court reached Burgos, and then fell back himself. In a short time the French invaders were all behind the Ebro, the siege of Zaragoza was raised, and the triumphant cry of the Spaniards was heard throughout Europe.

The retreat of the king was undoubtedly hasty and ill-considered; whether as a military or political measure it was unwise. Bessieres, with seventeen thousand victorious troops and forty pieces of artillery, paralized the northern provinces, the Spanish army of Andalusia was too distant from that of Valencia to concert a combined movement, and if they had formed a junction their united force could not have exceeded forty thousand fighting men, ill provided, and commanded by jealous independent chiefs. Now the king, without weakening Bessieres's corps too much, could have collected twenty thousand infantry, five thousand cavalry, and eighty pieces of artillery, and the battle of Rio Seco shows what such an army could have effected. Every motive of prudence and of honour called for some daring action to wipe off the ignominy of Baylen.

Let it be conceded that Joseph could not have maintained himself in Madrid; the line of the Duero was the true position for the French army. Taking Aranda as a centre, and occupying the Somosierra, Segovia, Valladolid, Palencia, Burgos, and Soria on the circumference; two ordinary marches would have carried the king to the succour of any part of his position, and the northern provinces would thus have been separated from the southern; for Blake durst not have made a flank march to the Guadarama, Castaños durst not have remained in the basin of Madrid, and the siege of Zaragoza might have been continued, because from Aranda to Zaragoza the distance is not greater than from Valencia or from Madrid, and from Soria it is only three marches; hence the king could have succoured Verdier in time if the Valencians attacked him, and it was impossible for Castaños to have arrived at Zaragoza under a month; now by taking up the line of the Ebro, Napoleon's plan of separating the provinces, and confining each to its own exertions, was frustrated, and Joseph virtually resigned the throne; for however doubtful the prudence of opposing the French might have been considered before the retreat, it became imperative upon all Spaniards to aid the energy of the multitude, when that energy was proved to be efficient.

In this manner Napoleon's first effort against Spain was frustrated; not that he had miscalculated either the difficulties of his task, or the means to overcome them; for although Bessieres was the only general who perfectly succeeded in his operations, the plan of the emperor was so well combined, that it required the destruction of a whole army to shake it at all, and even when the king, by committing the great faults of abandoning Madrid and raising the siege of Zaragoza, had given the utmost force to Dupont's catastrophe; the political position only of the French was weakened, their military hold of the country was scarcely loosened, and the Spaniards were unable to follow up their victory.

The moral effect of the battle of Baylen was surprising: it was one of those minor events which, insignificant in themselves, are the cause of great changes in the affairs of nations. The defeat of Rio Seco, the preparations of

Moncey for a second attack on Valencia, the miserable plight of Zaragoza, the desponding view taken of affairs by the ablest men of Spain, and, above all, the disgust and terror excited among the patriots by the excesses of the populace, weighed heavy against the Spanish cause. One victory more, and probably the moral as well as the physical force of Spain would have been crushed; but the battle of Baylen, opening as it were a new crater for the Spanish fire, all their pride, and vanity, and arrogance burst forth, the glory of past ages seemed to be renewed, every man conceived himself a second Cid, and perceived in the surrender of Dupont, not the deliverance of Spain, but the immediate conquest of France. "We are much obliged to our good friends the English," was a common phrase among them when conversing with the officers of Sir John Moore's army; "we thank them for their good-will, and we shall have the pleasure of escorting them through France to Calais: the journey will be pleasanter than a long voyage, and we shall not give them the trouble of fighting the French; we shall, however, be pleased at having them as spectators of our victories." This absurd confidence might have led to great things if it had been supported by wisdom, activity, or valour; but it was "a voice, and nothing more."

BOOK II

CHAPTER I

The uninterrupted success that for so many years attended the arms of Napoleon, gave him a moral influence doubling his actual force. Exciting at once terror, admiration, and hatred, he absorbed the whole attention of an astonished world, and openly or secretly all men acknowledged the power of his wonderful genius. The continent bowed before him, and even in England an increasing number of absurd and virulent libels on his person and character indicated the growth of secret fear. His proceedings against the Peninsula were, in truth, viewed at first with anxiety rather than with the hope of arresting their progress; yet when the full extent of the injustice became manifest, the public mind was vehemently excited, and a sentiment of some extraordinary change being about to take place in the affairs of the world prevailed among all classes of society; suddenly the Spanish people rose against the man that all feared; and the admiration which energy and courage exact, even from the base and timid, became enthusiastic in a nation conscious of the same virtues.

No factious feelings interfered to check this enthusiasm: the party in power, anxious to pursue a warlike system necessary to their own political existence, saw with joy that the stamp of justice and high feeling would, for the first time, be affixed to their policy. The party out of power having always derided the impotence of the ancient dynasties, and asserted that regular armies alone were insufficient means of defence, could not consistently refuse their approbation to a struggle originating with, and carried on entirely by the Spanish multitude. The people at large exulted that the manifest superiority of plebeian virtue and patriotism was acknowledged.

The arrival of the Asturian deputies was, therefore, universally hailed as an auspicious event. Their wishes were forestalled, their suggestions were attended to with eagerness; their demands were so readily complied with, and the riches of England were so profusely tendered to them by the ministers, that it can scarcely be doubted that the after arrogance and extravagance of the Spaniards arose from the manner in which their first applications were met; for there is a way of conferring a favour that appears like accepting one: and this secret being discovered by the English cabinet, the Spaniards soon demanded as a right what they had at first solicited as a boon. In politics it is a grievous fault to be too generous; gratitude, in state affairs, is unknown; and as the appearance of disinterested kindness never deceives, it should never be assumed.

The capture of the Spanish frigates had placed Great Britain and Spain in a state of hostility without a declaration of war. The invasion of Napoleon produced a friendly alliance between those countries without a declaration of peace, for the cessation of hostilities was not proclaimed until long after succours had been sent to the juntas.

The ministers seemed, by their precipitate measures, to be more afraid of losing the assistance of the Spaniards than prepared to take the lead in a contest which could only be supported by the power and riches of Great Britain. Instead of adopting a simple and decisive policy towards Spain, instead of sending a statesman of high rank and acknowledged capacity to sustain the insurrection, and to establish the influence of England by a judicious application of money and other supplies, the ministers employed a number of obscure men in various parts of the Peninsula who, without any experience of public affairs, were empowered to distribute succours of all kinds at their own discretion. Instead of sifting carefully the information obtained from such agents, and consulting distinguished military and naval officers in the arrangement of some comprehensive plan of operations which, being well understood by those who were to execute it, might be supported vigorously, the ministers formed crude projects, and parcelled out the forces in small expeditions, without any definite object in view, altering their plans with every idle report, and changing the commanders as lightly as the plans.

Mr. Stuart's Letters.
Lord W. Bentinck's ditto.

Entering into formal relations with every knot of Spanish politicians that assumed the title of a supreme junta, the government dealt with unsparing hands enormous supplies at the demand of those self-elected authorities, yet took no assurance that the succours should be justly applied, but, with affected earnestness, disclaimed all intention of interfering with the internal arrangements of the Spaniards, when the ablest men of Spain expected and wished for such an interference to repress the folly and violence of their countrymen, and when England was entitled, both in policy and justice, not only to interfere, but to direct the councils of the insurgents. The latter had solicited and obtained her assistance; the cause was become common to both nations, and their welfare demanded, that a prudent, just, and vigorous interference on the part of the most powerful and enlightened, should prevent that cause from being ruined by a few ignorant and conceited men, accidentally invested with authority.

Vide Instructions for sir Thos. Dyer, &c. &c.
Parliamentary Papers, 1809.

Appendix, No. 13, Section 5th.

The numbers and injudicious choice of military agents were also the source of infinite mischief; selected, as it would appear, principally because of their acquaintance with the Spanish language; few of those agents had any knowledge of war beyond the ordinary duties of a regiment; there was no concert among them, for there was no controlling power vested in any, but each did that which seemed good to him. Readily affecting to consult men whose inexperience rendered them amenable, and whose friendship could supply the means of advancing their own interests in a disorganised state of society, the Spanish generals received the agents with a flattering and confidential politeness, that diverted the attention of the latter from the true objects of their mission. Instead of ascertaining the real numbers and efficiency of the armies, they adopted the inflated language and extravagant opinions of the chiefs, with whom they lived; and their reports gave birth to most erroneous notions of the relative strength and situation of the contending forces in the Peninsula. Some exceptions there were; but the ministers seemed to be better pleased with the sanguine than with the cautious, and made their own wishes the measure of their judgments. Accordingly, enthusiasm, numbers, courage, and talent, were gratuitously found for every occasion; but money, arms, and clothing, were demanded incessantly, and supplied with profusion; the arms were, however, generally left in their cases to rot, or to fall into the hands of the enemy; the clothing seldom reached the soldier's back, and the money, in all instances misapplied, was in some, embezzled by the authorities, into whose hands it fell, and in others employed to create disunion, and to forward the private views of the juntas, at the expense of the public welfare. It is a curious fact, that from the beginning to the end of the war, an English musket was rarely to be seen in the hands of a Spanish soldier. But it is time to quit this subject, and to trace the progress of Junot's invasion of Portugal, that the whole circle of operations in the Peninsula being completed, the reader may take a general view of the situation of all parties, at the moment when sir Arthur Wellesley, disembarking at the Mondego, commenced those campaigns which form the proper subject of this history.

Thiebault.

Peremptory orders obliged Junot to commence operations at an unfavourable time of year, and before his preparations were completed. In his front the roads were nearly impracticable, and a part of his troops were still in the rear of Salamanca. Hence, his march from that town to Alcantara (where he effected his junction in the latter end of November, with the part of the Spanish force that was to act under his immediate orders) was very disastrous, and nearly disorganized his inexperienced army.

The succours he expected to receive at Alcantara were not furnished, and the repugnance of the Spanish authorities to aid him, was the cause of so much embarrassment, that his chief officers doubted the propriety of continuing operations under the accumulating difficulties of his situation; but Junot's firmness was unabated. He knew that no English force had landed at Lisbon, and the cowardice of the Portuguese court was notorious. Encouraged by these considerations, he undertook one of those hardy enterprises which astound the mind by their success, and leave the historian in doubt if he should praise the happy daring, or stigmatise the rashness of the deed.

Thiebault.

Without money, without transport, without ammunition sufficient for a general action, with an auxiliary force of Spaniards by no means well disposed to aid him, Junot, at the head of a raw army, penetrated the mountains of Portugal on the most dangerous and difficult line by which that country can be invaded. He was ignorant of what was passing in the interior; he knew not if he was to be opposed, nor what means were prepared to resist him; but trusting to the inertness of the Portuguese government, to the rapidity of his own movements, and to the renown of the French arms, he made his way through Lower Beira, and suddenly appeared in the town of Abrantes, a fearful and unexpected guest. There he obtained the first information of the true state of affairs. Lisbon was tranquil, and the Portuguese fleet was ready to sail, but the court still remained on shore. On hearing this, Junot, animated by the prospect of seizing the prince regent, pressed forward, and reached Lisbon in time to see the fleet, having the royal family on board, clearing the mouth of the Tagus. One vessel dragged astern within reach of a battery, the French general himself fired a gun at her; and on his return to Lisbon, meeting some Portuguese troops, he resolutely commanded them to form an escort for his person, and thus attended, passed through the streets of the capital. Nature alone had opposed his progress; yet such were the hardships his army had endured, that of a column which had numbered twenty-five thousand in its ranks, two thousand tired grenadiers only entered Lisbon with their general; fatigue, and want, and tempests, had scattered the remainder along two hundred miles of rugged mountains, inhabited by a warlike and ferocious peasantry, well acquainted with the strength of their fastnesses, and proud of many successful defences made by their fore-fathers against former invaders. Lisbon itself contained three hundred thousand inhabitants, and fourteen thousand regular troops were collected there. A powerful British fleet was at the mouth of the harbour; the commander, sir Sydney Smith, had urged the court to resist, and offered to land his seamen and marines to aid in the defence of the town; but his offers were declined; and the people, disgusted with the pusillanimous conduct of their rulers, and confounded by the strangeness of the scene, evinced no desire to impede the march of events. Thus three weak battalions sufficed to impose a foreign yoke upon this great capital, and illustrated the truth of Napoleon's maxim: — *that in war the moral is to the physical force as three parts to one.*

The prince regent, after having at the desire of the French government, expelled the British factory, ordered the British minister plenipotentiary away from his court, sequestered British property, and shut the ports of Portugal against British merchants; after having degraded himself and his nation by performing every submissive act which France could devise to insult his weakness, was still reluctant to forego the base tenure by which he hoped to hold his crown. Alternately swayed by fear and indolence, a miserable example of helpless folly, he lingered until the reception of a Moniteur, announcing that "*the house of Braganza had ceased to reign,*" awoke all the energy he was capable of. At that time lord Strangford, the British minister plenipotentiary, had resigned all hope of persuading the royal family to emigrate; but sir Sydney Smith, seizing the favourable moment, threatened to commence hostilities if the emigration should be longer delayed; and thus urged, the prince regent of Portugal, the old queen his mother, and the rest of the royal family, had embarked on the 27th; and quitting the Tagus on the 29th of November[9], sailed for the Brazils, a few hours only before Junot arrived with his slight escort of grenadiers.

This celebrated emigration was beneficial to the Brazils in the highest degree, and of vast importance to England in two ways, for it ensured great commercial advantages, and it threw Portugal completely into her power in the approaching conflict; but it was disgraceful to the prince, insulting to the brave people he abandoned, and impolitic, inasmuch as it obliged men to inquire how far subjects were bound to a monarch who deserted them in their need? how far the nation could belong to a man who did not belong to the nation?

It has been observed by political economists, that where a gold and paper currency circulate together, if the paper be depreciated it will drag down the gold with it, and deteriorate the whole mass; but that after a time, the metal revolts from this unnatural state, and asserts its own intrinsic superiority. So a privileged class, corrupted by power and luxury, drags down the national character; but there is a point when the people, like the gold, no longer suffering such a degradation, will separate themselves with violence from the vices of their effeminate rulers. Before that time arrives a nation may appear to be sunk in hopeless lethargy, when it is really capable of great and noble exertions. Thus it was with the Portuguese, who were at this time unjustly despised by enemies, and mistrusted by friends.

Thiebault.

Foy.

The invading army, in pursuance of the convention of Fontainebleau, was divided into three corps; the central one, composed of the French troops, and a Spanish division, under general Caraffa, had penetrated by the two roads, which from Alcantara lead, the one by Pedragoa, the other by Sobreira Formosa; but at Abrantes, Caraffa's division separated from the French, and took possession of Thomar. Meanwhile the right, under general Taranco, marching from Gallicia established themselves at Oporto, and the marquis of Solano, with the left, entered the Alemtejo, and fixed his quarters at Setuval. The Spanish troops did not suffer on their route; but such had been the distress of the French army, that three weeks afterwards it could only muster ten thousand men under arms, and the privations encountered on the march led to excesses which first produced that rancorous spirit of mutual hatred, so remarkable between the French and Portuguese. Young soldiers always attribute their sufferings to the ill-will of the inhabitants; it is difficult to make them understand that a poor peasantry have nothing to spare; old soldiers, on the contrary, blame nobody, but know how to extract subsistence in most cases without exciting enmity.

Junot passed the month of December in collecting his army, securing the great military points about Lisbon, and in preparations to supplant the power of a council of regency, to whom the prince at his departure had delegated the sovereign authority. As long as the French troops were scattered on the line of march, and that the fortresses were held by Portuguese garrisons, it would have been dangerous to provoke the enmity, or to excite the activity of this council, and the members were treated with studious respect; but they were of the same leaven as the court they emanated from, and the quick resolute proceedings of Junot soon deprived them of any importance conferred by the critical situation of affairs during the first three weeks.

Return of the French army. Appendix, No. 28.

The Spanish auxiliary forces were well received in the north and in the Alemtejo; but general Taranco dying soon after his arrival at Oporto, the French general Quesnel was sent to command that province. Junot had early taken possession of Elvas, and detached general Maurin to the Algarves, with sixteen hundred men; and, when Solano was ordered by his court to withdraw from Portugal, nine French battalions and the cavalry, under the command of Kellerman, took possession of the Alemtejo also, and occupied the fortress of Setuval. At the same time Junot replaced Caraffa's division at Thomar by a French force, and distributed the former in small bodies, at a considerable distance from each other, on both sides of the Tagus, immediately round Lisbon.

Foy.

The provisions of the treaty of Fontainebleau were unknown to the Portuguese, a circumstance that procured the Spanish troops a better reception than the French; but that treaty was now no longer regarded by Junot, whose conduct plainly discovered that he considered Portugal to be a possession entirely belonging to France.

Ibid.
Thiebault.

When all his stragglers were come up, his army recovered from its fatigues, and that he knew that a reinforcement of five thousand men had arrived at Salamanca on its march to Lisbon, Junot proceeded more openly to assume the chief authority; he commenced by exacting a forced loan of two hundred thousand pounds, and not only interfered with the different departments of state, but put Frenchmen into all the lucrative offices; and his promises and protestations of amity became loud and frequent in proportion to his encroachments and the increase of his power. At last being created by Napoleon duke of Abrantes, he threw off all disguise, suppressed the council of regency, seized the reins of government himself, and while he established many useful regulations, made the nation sensibly alive to the fact that he was a despotic conqueror.

The flag and the arms of Portugal were replaced by those of France; and of the Portuguese army, eight thousand men were selected and sent from the kingdom, under the command of the marquis d'Alorna and Gomez Frere, two noblemen of the greatest reputation for military talent among the native officers. Five thousand more were attached to the divisions of Junot's army, and the rest were disbanded.

Thiebault.

Foy.

An extraordinary contribution of four millions sterling, decreed by Napoleon, was then demanded, under the curious title of a ransom for the state; this sum was exorbitant, and Junot prevailed on the emperor to reduce it one half. He likewise on his own authority accepted the forced loan, the confiscated English merchandise, the church plate, and the royal property, in part payment; but the people were still unable to raise the whole amount, for the court had before taken the greatest part of the church plate and bullion of the kingdom, and had also drawn large sums from the people, under the pretext of defending the country, with which treasure they departed, leaving the public functionaries, the army, private creditors, and even domestic servants, unpaid.

But although great discontent and misery prevailed, the tranquillity of Lisbon, during the first month after the arrival of the French, was remarkable; no disturbance took place, the populace were completely controlled by the activity of a police, established under the prince regent's government by the count de Novion, a French emigrant, and continued by Junot on an extended scale.

No capital city in Europe suffers so much as Lisbon from the want of good police regulations, and the French general conferred an unmixed benefit on the inhabitants by giving more effect to Novion's plans; yet so deeply rooted is the prejudice in favour of ancient customs, that no act of the duke of Abrantes gave the Portuguese more offence than his having the streets cleansed, and the wild dogs (that infested them by thousands) killed. A French serjeant, distinguished by his zeal in destroying those disgusting and dangerous animals, was in revenge assassinated.

Thiebault.

In the course of March and April, Junot's military system was completed; the arsenal of Lisbon, one of the finest establishments of the kind in Europe, contained all kinds of naval and military stores in abundance, and ten thousand excellent workmen in every branch of business appertaining to war; hence the artillery, the carriages, the ammunition, and all the minor equipments of the army, were soon renewed and put in the best possible condition, and the hulks of two line-of-battle ships, three frigates, and seven lighter vessels of war, were refitted, armed, and moored across the river to defend the entrance, and to awe the town. The army itself, perfectly recovered from its fatigues, reinforced, and better disciplined, was grown confident in its chief from the success of the invasion, and being well fed and clothed, was become a fine body of robust men, capable of any exertion. In

March it was re-organized in three divisions of infantry and one of cavalry. General La Borde commanded the first, general Loison the second, general Travot the third, general Margaron the fourth, and general Taviel directed the artillery. General Kellerman commanded in the Alemtejo, general Quesnel at Oporto, general Maurin in the Algarves, and Junot himself in Lisbon.

The fortresses of Faro in Algarve, of Almeida, of Elvas, La Lippe, St. Lucie, Setuval, Palmela, and those between Lisbon and the mouth of the Tagus, of Ericia and Peniché, were furnished with French garrisons; and Estremos, Aldea-Gallegos, Santarem, and Abrantes were occupied, and put in such a state of defence as their decayed ramparts would permit.

Return of the French army. Appendix, No. 28.

The whole army, including the French workmen and marines attached to it, amounted to above fifty thousand men, of which above forty-four thousand were fit for duty; that is to say, fifteen thousand five hundred Spaniards, five thousand Portuguese, and twenty-four thousand four hundred French.

Of the latter 1000 were in Elvas and La Lippe,
1000 in Almeida,
1000 in Peniché,
1600 in the Algarves,
2892 in Setuval,
750 in Abrantes,
450 cavalry were kept in Valencia
d'Alcantara, in Spanish Estremadura,
and 350 distributed in the proportion of

fifteen men to a post, guarded the lines of communication which were established from Lisbon to Elvas, and from Almeida to Coimbra. Above fifteen thousand men remained disposable.

Thus Lisbon, the capital, containing all the civil, military, and naval, and the greatest part of the commercial establishments, the only fine harbour, two-eighths of the population, and two-thirds of the riches of the whole kingdom, was secured by the main body, which formed the centre, while on the circumference a number of strong posts gave support to the operations of the moveable column. By this disposition, the garrison of Peniché commanded the only harbour between the Tagus and the Mondego, in which a large disembarkation of English troops could take place; and the little port of Figueras, which was held by a small garrison, blocked the mouth of the latter river; while the division at Thomar secured all the great lines of communication to the north-east, and in conjunction with the garrison of Abrantes, commanded both sides of the Zezere.

From Abrantes to Estremos and Elvas, and from the former to Setuval, the lines of communication were short, and through an open country, suitable for the operations of the cavalry, which was all quartered on the south bank of the Tagus. Thus, without breaking up the mass of the army, the harbours were sealed against the English, and a great and rich tract was enclosed by posts, and rendered so pervious to the troops, that any insurrection could be reached by a few marches, and immediately crushed. The connexion between the right and left banks of the Tagus at Lisbon was secured, and the entrance to the port defended by the vessels of war which had been refitted and armed. A light squadron was also prepared to communicate with South America, and nine Russian line of battle ships, and a frigate under the command of admiral Siniavin, which had taken refuge some time before from the English fleet, were of necessity engaged in the defence of the harbour, and formed an unwilling, but not an unimportant auxiliary force.

These military arrangements were Junot's own, and suitable enough if his army had been unconnected with any other; but they clashed with the general views of Napoleon, who regarded the force in Portugal only as a division of troops, to be rendered subservient to the general scheme of subjecting the Peninsula; wherefore, in the month of May, he ordered that general Avril, with three thousand infantry, five hundred cavalry, and ten guns, should co-operate with Dupont in Andalusia, and that general Loison, with four thousand infantry, should proceed to Almeida, and from thence co-operate with Bessieres in the event of an insurrection taking place in Spain.

General Thiebault complains of this order as injurious to Junot, ill combined, and the result of a foolish vanity that prompted the emperor to direct all the armies himself; yet it would be difficult to show that the arrangement was faulty. Avril's division, if he had not halted at Tavora, for which there was no reason, would have ensured the capture of Seville, and if Dupont's defeat had not rendered the victory of Rio Seco useless, Loison's division would have been eminently useful in controlling the country behind Bessieres, in case the latter invaded Gallicia; and it was well placed to intercept the communication between the Castilian and the Estremaduran armies. Thus the emperor's combinations, if they had been fully executed, would have brought seventy thousand men to bear on the defence of Portugal.

Napoleon in Las Casas.

Foy.

Such was the military attitude of the French in May; their political situation was far from being so favourable. Junot's natural capacity was very considerable; but it was neither enlarged by study, nor strengthened by mental discipline. Of intemperate habits, indolent in business, yet prompt and brave in action, quick to give offence, ready to forget an injury; at one moment a great man, the next below mediocrity, Junot was at all times unsuited to the task of conciliating and governing a people like the Portuguese, who, with passions as sudden and vehement as his own, retain a sense of injury or insult with incredible tenacity; otherwise, although he had many difficulties to encounter, and his duty towards France was in some instances incompatible with good policy towards Portugal, he was not without resources for establishing a strong French interest. But he possessed neither the ability nor disposition to soothe a nation that, without having suffered a defeat, was suddenly bowed to a foreign yoke.

Foy.

The pride and the poverty of the Portuguese, and the influence of ancient usages, interfered with Junot's policy. The monks and friars, and most of the nobility, were inimical to his sway; and all the activity of the expelled British factory, and the secret warfare of spies and writers in the pay of England, were directed to undermine his plans, and to render him and his nation odious; but on the other hand, he was in possession of the government and of the capital, he had a fine army, and he could offer novelty so dear to the multitude, and he had the name and the fame of Napoleon to assist him. The promises of power are always believed by the many; and there were abundance of grievances to remedy, and wrongs to redress in Portugal. And such a strong feeling existed among the best educated men (and especially at the universities) of dislike to the Braganza family, and in favour of a reformed system, that steps were actually taken to have prince Eugene declared king of Portugal; and we shall find hereafter, that this spirit was not extinguished at a much later date.

With these materials, and the military vanity of the Portuguese to work upon, Junot might have established a powerful French interest; and under an active government, the people would not long have regretted the loss of an independence that had no wholesome breathing amidst the corrupt stagnation of the old system. But the arrogance of a conqueror, and the necessities of an army, which was to be subsisted and paid by an impoverished people, soon gave rise to all kinds of oppression; private abuses followed close upon the heels of public rapacity, and insolence left its sting to rankle in the wounds of the injured. The malignant humours broke out in quarrels and assassinations, and the severe punishments that ensued, many of them unjust and barbarous in the highest degree, created rage, not terror; for the nation had not tried its strength in battle, and would not believe that it was weak.

Thiebault.

The ports were rigorously blockaded by the English fleet, the troubles in Spain interrupted the commerce in grain, by which Portugal had been usually supplied from that country, and the unhappy people suffered under the triple pressure of famine, war-contributions, and a foreign yoke. With all external aliment thus cut off, and a hungry army gnawing at its vitals, the nation could not remain tranquil; and although the first five months of Junot's government was, with the exception of a slight tumult at Lisbon (when the arms of Portugal were taken down), undisturbed by commotion, the whole country was soon ripe for a general insurrection. The harvest, however, proved remarkably fine, and Junot hailed the prospect of returning plenty, as a relief from his principal difficulty; but as one danger disappeared, another presented itself. The Spanish insurrection excited the hopes of the Portuguese; agents from the neighbouring juntas communicated secretly with the Spanish generals in Portugal. The capture of the French fleet in Cadiz became known, assassinations multiplied; the pope's nuncio fled on board the English fleet, and all things tended to a general explosion. The English agents were of course actively engaged in promoting this spirit; and the appearance of two English fleets at different points of the coast, having troops on board, produced great alarm among the French, and augmented the impatient fierceness of the Portuguese.

Among the various ways in which the people discovered their hatred of the invaders, one was very characteristic: an egg was marked with certain letters by a chemical process, and then placed in a nest; being taken from thence, it was exhibited, and created a great sensation; the letters were interpreted to indicate the speedy coming of don Sebastian, king of Portugal, who, like Arthur of romantic memory, was supposed to be hidden in a secret island, waiting for the destined period when he was to re-appear and restore his country to her ancient glory. The trick was turned against the contrivers; other eggs prophesied in the most impatriotic manner, but the belief of the Sebastianists lost nothing of its zeal; many people, and those not of the most uneducated classes, were often observed upon the highest points of the hills, casting earnest looks towards the ocean, in the hopes of descrying the island in which their long lost hero was detained.

CHAPTER II

The first serious blow was struck at Oporto; the news of what had taken place all over Spain was known there in June. General Bellesta, the chief Spanish officer, immediately took an honourable and resolute part. He made the French general Quesnel, with his staff, prisoners; after which, calling together the Portuguese authorities, he declared that they were free to act as they judged most fitting for their own interests, and then marched to Gallicia with his army and captives.

The opinions of the leading men at Oporto were divided upon the great question of resistance; but, after some vicissitudes, the boldest side was successful, and the insurrection, although at one moment quelled by the French party, was finally established in Oporto, and soon extended along the banks of the Duero and the Minho, and to those parts of Beira which lie between the Mondego and the sea-coast.

Thiebault.

Junot being informed of this event, perceived that no time was to be lost in disarming the Spanish regiments quartered in the neighbourhood of Lisbon; but this was not an easy operation. Carraffa's division was above six thousand men, and without employing the garrisons of the citadel and forts of Lisbon, it was difficult to collect an equal force of French. The suspicions of the Spanish regiments had been already excited, they were reluctant to obey the French generals, and one quartered at Alcacer de Sal had actually resisted the orders of the general-in-chief himself. To avoid a tumult was the great object, because in Lisbon fifteen thousand Gallicians were ordinarily engaged as porters and water-carriers, and if a popular movement had been excited, these men would naturally have assisted their countrymen. Notwithstanding these difficulties, Junot, in the night of that day upon which he received the information of Bellesta's defection, arranged all his measures; and the next day the Spanish troops being, under various pretexts, assembled in such numbers, and in such places, that resistance became impossible, they yielded to necessity, and were disarmed, and placed on board the hulks in the Tagus: eight hundred of the regiment of Murcia and three hundred of that of Valencia only escaping. Thus Junot in the course of twenty-four hours, and with very little bloodshed, succeeded, by his promptness and dexterity, in averting a very serious danger.

The decision and success of this stroke against the Spanish division produced considerable effect, but not sufficient to prevent the insurrection from becoming general; all couriers, and officers carrying orders or commanding small posts of communications, were suddenly cut off, and Junot, reduced by a single blow from fifty to twenty-eight thousand men, found himself isolated, and dependent upon his individual resources, and the courage of his soldiers, for the maintenance of his conquest, and even for the preservation of his army.

The Russian squadron indeed contained six thousand seamen and marines, but, while they consumed a great quantity of provisions, it was evident, from certain symptoms, that they could not be depended upon as useful allies, except in the case of an English fleet attempting to force the entrance of the river. In this situation the duke of Abrantes at first thought of seizing Badajos, with a view to secure still more effectually the best line of retreat into Spain, but the Spanish army of Estremadura had assembled there, under the command of general Galuzzo, and frustrated that scheme.

Thiebault.

General Avril's column having failed to effect its junction with Dupont, returned to Estremos, and it is probable that Junot never intended that it should be otherwise; for no great efforts appear to have been made by Avril to attain the object of the march. Loison was in the north, but orders were sent to him, to repair with his column to Oporto and assume the command of that city. Upon the 5th of June, one day previous to Bellesta's defection, Loison had arrived at Almeida, and upon the 12th had made himself master of Fort Conception, a strong, but ill-placed Spanish fortification on the frontier. The commandant being partly persuaded, and partly frightened into a surrender of his charge, retired, with his garrison, to Ciudad Rodrigo.

Upon receipt of the despatch which directed him to march to Oporto, Loison quitted Almeida, and endeavoured to penetrate into the province of Entre Minho e Duero by the route of Amarante, but his division was too weak to force his way through such a strong country (where the population was in full insurrection), and to take a great city, and it was possible that general Bellesta might have returned and fallen upon his flank. Swayed by these reasons, Loison advanced cautiously, and without vigour. Being slightly opposed at the position of Mezam Frias, and hearing that his baggage had been attacked at the same time by insurgents in his rear, he fell back at once upon Villa Real, there he engaged in another trifling skirmish, and then quitting his first route, crossed the Douero at Lamego, and marched to Castro d'Airo, being harassed on the road by the armed peasantry of the mountains skirting his line of march. At Castro d'Airo he faced about, and dispersed the assailants with some slaughter, and then continued his movement to Celerico without further molestation; at Celerico a body of insurgents fled without firing a shot; and Loison dividing his troops, sent one half to Trancoso, and with the other marched to Guarda, intending to scour that part of the country, and to put down the insurrection; but at this time he received one of twenty-five despatches sent by Junot for the purpose of recalling him to Lisbon; all the rest had been intercepted. Loison, upon the receipt of this despatch, returned to Almeida the 1st of July. Leaving his sick, his wounded, and weak men there, and making up the garrison to the number of twelve hundred and fifty, he removed all the palisades, guns, and materials from Fort Conception, completely ruined the defences of that place, and then prosecuted his march to Lisbon by the route of Guarda.

While these events were passing in the north, another insurrection took place in the south: general Maurin commanded in the Algarves; and some Portuguese artillerymen and other native troops were attached to the French brigade under his orders. A rising of the people commenced in the neighbourhood of Faro, and soon extended to that town, and along the coast. Maurin was confined to his bed by illness, and fell into the hands of the insurgents; colonel Maransin supplied his place, but the country was too extensive to be controlled by sixteen hundred men. The Portuguese soldiers went over to their countrymen: the Spaniards from Andalusia threatened to move across the Guadiana, and general Spencer, with five thousand British soldiers, appeared off Ayamonte. Maransin immediately fell back in haste upon Mertola, leaving part of his baggage, his military chest, his accounts, and above a hundred prisoners, besides killed and wounded, in the hands of the patriots. At Mertola he was safe; and general Spencer merely landed a few officers, and ordered rations for five thousand men; while the Portuguese wisely remained within the range of the mountains which protect the northern frontier of Algarve.

The circle was now closing fast round Junot; emissaries from Oporto excited the people to rise as far as Coimbra. At that town a small French post was easily overpowered, and a junta formed; from thence new efforts spread the flame to Condexa, Pombal, and Leria; and a student of the Coimbra university, named Zagalo, with considerable address and boldness, got possession of the small, but important fort of Figueras, at the mouth of the Mondego; the commandant (a Portuguese officer), with a hundred men, capitulated; the terms were broken, but no violence seems to have been committed upon the prisoners.

On the other side, Abrantes was threatened by the insurgents of the valley of the Zezere; and the Spaniards, under Galuzzo, crossed the Guadiana at Juramenha, and occupied that place and Campo Mayor. Kellerman's head-quarters were at Elvas; a great, although confused body of men menaced his position, but, supported by the strength of the town and Fort La-Lyppe, he easily maintained himself. Avril remained unmolested at Estremos, and Evora, held by a small garrison, was tranquil; but the neighbourhood of Setuval was in commotion; the populace of Lisbon was unquiet; and at this critical moment general Spencer, whose force report magnified to ten thousand men, appeared at the mouth of the Tagus.

Thiebault.

Junot held a council of war. After hearing the opinions of the principal general officers, he decided on the following plan: 1°. To collect the sick in such hospitals as could be protected by the ships of war. 2°. To secure the Spanish prisoners by moving the hulks in which they were confined as far as possible from the city. 3°. To arm and provision the fortresses of Lisbon, and to remove the powder from the magazines to the ships. 4°. To abandon all the other fortresses in Portugal with the exception of Setuval, Almeida, Elvas, and Peniché, and, finally, to concentrate the army in Lisbon. In the event of bad fortune, the duke of Abrantes determined to defend the capital as long as he was able, and then to cross the Tagus, make way by the left bank upon Elvas, and from thence retreat to Madrid, Valladolid, or Segovia, as he might find expedient. This well-conceived plan was not executed, the first alarm soon died away, Spencer returned to Cadiz, and when the insurrection was grappled with, it proved to be more noisy than dangerous.

Kellerman recalled Maransin from Mertola and prepared himself to march to Lisbon, but the inhabitants of the town of Villa Viciosa having risen against a company of French troops quartered there, the latter took refuge in an old castle, and defended themselves until Kellerman sent general Avril from Estremos to succour them; this the latter effected without difficulty; the Portuguese fled the moment he appeared, and a very few were killed in the pursuit. But the town of Beja followed the example of Villa Viciosa, and colonel Maransin, who was preparing to retire from Mertola, being informed of it, marched in that direction with such rapidity, that he passed over forty miles in eighteen hours, and falling suddenly upon the patriots, defeated them with considerable slaughter, himself losing thirty killed and fifty wounded: the town was pillaged, and some houses were burned.

General Thiebault writes, that an obstinate combat took place in the streets, but the Portuguese never made head for a moment against a strong body, during the whole course of the insurrection. How, indeed, was it possible for a collection of miserable peasants, armed with scythes, pitchforks, a few old fowling pieces, and a little bad powder, under the command of some ignorant countryman or fanatic friar, to maintain a battle against an efficient and active corps of French soldiers? For there is this essential difference to be observed in judging between the Spanish and Portuguese insurrections; the Spaniards had many great and strong towns free from the presence of the French, and large provinces in which to collect and train forces at a distance from the invaders; but in Portugal the naked peasants were forced to go to battle the instant even of assembling. The loss which Maransin sustained must have arisen from the stragglers (who in a consecutive march of forty miles would have been numerous) having been cut off and killed by the peasantry. This blow, however, quieted the Alentejo for the moment, and Kellerman having cleared the neighbourhood of Elvas from the Spanish parties, placed a commandant in La-Lyppe, and concentrated the detachments under Maransin and Avril, proceeded towards Lisbon.

Thiebault.

Accursio de Neves.

The duke of Abrantes was in great perplexity; the intercepting of his couriers and isolated officers had been followed by the detection of all his spies, and he was exposed, without assistance, to every report which the fears of his army, or the ingenuity of the people, could give birth to. Now there are few nations that can pretend to vie with the Portuguese and Spaniards in the fabrication of plausible reports: among those current, the captivity of Loison was one; but nothing was certainly known except that the insurgents from the valley of the Mondego were marching towards Lisbon. General Margaron was therefore ordered to disperse them, and, if possible, to open a communication with general Loison: he advanced, with three thousand men and six pieces of artillery, to Leria, whither the patriots had retired in disorder when they heard of his approach. The greater part dispersed at once, but those who remained were attacked on the 5th of July, and a scene similar to that of Beja ensued; the French boasted of victory, the insurgents called it massacre and pillage.

In a combat with armed peasantry, it is difficult to know where the fighting ceases and the massacre begins: men dressed in peasants' clothes are observed firing, and moving about, without order, from place to place; when do they cease to be enemies? They are more dangerous when single than together; they can hide their muskets in an instant and appear peaceable; the soldier passes and is immediately shot from behind.

The example at Leria did not however deter the people of Thomar from declaring against the French; and the neighbourhood of Alcobaça rose at the same time. Thus Margaron was placed between two new insurrections at the moment he had quelled one. English fleets, with troops on board, were said to be hovering off the coast, and the most alarming reports relative to Loison were corroborated, his safety was despaired of, when suddenly authentic intelligence of his arrival at Abrantes revived the spirits of the general-in-chief and the army.

After arranging all things necessary for the security of Almeida, Loison had quitted that town the 2d of July, at the head of three thousand four hundred and fifty men, and arrived at Abrantes upon the 8th, having in seven days passed through Guarda, Atalaya, Sarsedas, Corteja, and Sardoval. During this rapid march he dispersed several bodies of insurgents that were assembled on the line of his route, especially at Guarda and Atalaya. It has been said that twelve hundred bodies were stretched upon the field of battle near the first town; this is absurd beyond all measure. Twelve hundred slain would give, at a low average, five thousand wounded: six thousand two hundred killed and wounded by a corps of three thousand four hundred and fifty men, in half an hour! and this without cavalry or artillery, and among fastnesses that vie in ruggedness with any in the world! The truth is, that the peasants, terrified by the reports that Loison himself spread to favour his march, fled on all sides, and if two hundred and fifty Portuguese were killed and wounded during the whole passage, it was the utmost. The distance from Almeida to Abrantes is more than a hundred and eighty miles, the greatest part is a mountain pathway rather than a road, and the French were obliged to gather their provisions from the country as they passed; now, to forage, to fight several actions, to pursue active peasants well acquainted with the country so closely as to destroy them by thousands, and to march a hundred and eighty miles over bad roads, and all in seven days, is impossible.

Thiebault.

Parliamentary Papers, 1809.

The whole French army was now concentrated; the insurrection at Alcobaça had been quelled by Kellerman, and that of Thomar was also quieted, but the insurgents from Oporto were gathering strength at Coimbra; the last of the native soldiers deserted the French colours; the Spanish troops at Badajos, strengthened by a body of Portuguese fugitives, and commanded by one Moretti, were preparing to enter the Alentejo, which was again in commotion: the English admiral had opened a communication with the insurgents on the side of Setuval, and the patriots were also assembled in considerable numbers at Alcacer do Sal.

In this dilemma Junot resolved to leave the northern people quiet for a while, and to bend his force against the Alentejo, because that was his line of retreat upon Spain; from thence only he could provision the capital, and there also his cavalry could act with the most effect. Accordingly, Loison, with seven thousand infantry, twelve hundred cavalry, and eight pieces of artillery, crossed the Tagus the 25th of July, and marched by Os Pegoens, Vendanovas, and Montemor. At the latter place he defeated an advanced guard, which fled to Evora, where the Portuguese general Leite had assembled the mass of the insurgents; and assisted by three or four thousand Spanish troops under Moretti, had taken a position to cover the town.

Thiebault.

Appendix, No. 12.

When Loison came up he directed Margaron and Solignac to turn the flanks of the patriots, and fell upon their centre himself. The Spanish auxiliaries performed no service, and the Portuguese soon took to flight, but there was a great and confused concourse; a strong cavalry was let loose upon them, and many being cut off from the main body, were driven into the town, which had been deserted by the principal inhabitants. There, urged by despair, they endeavoured to defend the walls and the streets for a few moments, but were soon overpowered, the greater part slain, and the houses pillaged. The French lost about two or three hundred men, but the number of the Portuguese and Spaniards that fell was very considerable; and disputes having arisen between the troops of those nations, the latter ravaged the country in their retreat with more violence than the French.

Loison, after resting two days at Evora, proceeded to Elvas, and drove away the numerous Spanish parties which had long infested the neighbourhood of that fortress, and were become extremely obnoxious to friends and enemies. His detachments scoured the country round, and were accumulating provisions to form great magazines at Elvas, when their labours were suddenly interrupted by a despatch from the duke of Abrantes, directing Loison to return to the right bank of the Tagus. The British army, so long expected, had descended upon the coast, and manly warfare reared its honest front amidst the desolating scenes of insurrection.

OBSERVATIONS

Thiebault.

1°. This expedition to the Alentejo was an operation of military police, rather than a campaign. Junot wished to repress the spirit of insurrection by sudden and severe examples. The actions of general Loison were therefore of necessity harsh, but they have been represented as a series of massacres and cruelties of the most revolting nature, because he himself disseminated such stories in order to increase the terror which it was the object of his expedition to create; and the credulity of the nation that produced the Sebastianists was not easily shocked. The Portuguese eagerly listened to tales so derogatory to their enemies and congenial to their own revengeful disposition. The anecdotes of French barbarity current for two years after the convention of Cintra, were notoriously false. The same story being related by persons remote from each other, is no argument of their truth. The reports that Loison was captured on his march from Almeida, reached Junot through fifty different channels; there were men to declare that they had beheld him bound with cords, others to tell how he had been entrapped, some named the places he had been carried through in triumph, and his habitual and characteristic expressions were quoted. The story was complete and the parts were consistent; yet the whole was not only false, but the rumour had not even the slightest foundation of truth.

2°. The Portuguese accounts of the events of this period are but angry amplifications of every real or pretended act of French barbarity and injustice, and the crimes of individuals are made matter of accusation against the whole army. The French accounts are more plausible, but scarcely more safe as authorities, seeing that they are written by men, who being for the most part actors in the scenes they describe, are naturally concerned to defend their own characters: their military vanity also has had its share in disguising the simple facts of the insurrection; for willing to enhance the merit of the troops, they have exaggerated the number of the insurgents, the obstinacy of the combats, and the loss of the patriots. English party writers, greedily fixing upon such relations, have changed the name of battle into massacre; and thus prejudice, conceit, and clamour, have combined, to violate the decorum of history, and to perpetuate error.

Napoleon in Las Casas.

3°. It would, however, be an egregious mistake to suppose, that because the French were not monsters, there existed no cause for the acrimony with which their conduct has been assailed. The duke of Abrantes, although not cruel, nor personally obnoxious to the Portuguese, was a sensual and violent person, and his habits were expensive; such a man is always rapacious, and as the character of the chief influences the manners of those under his command, it may be safely assumed that his vices were aped by many of his followers. Now the virtuous general Travot was esteemed, and his person respected, even in the midst of tumult, by the Portuguese, while Loison was scarcely safe from their vengeance when surrounded by his troops. The execrations poured forth at the mere mention of "the bloody Maneta," as, from the loss of his hand, he was called, proves that he must have committed many heinous acts; and Kellerman appears to have been as justly stigmatised for rapacity, as Loison was for violence.

4°. It has been made a charge against the French generals, that they repressed the hostility of the Portuguese and Spanish peasants by military executions; but in doing so they only followed the custom of war, and they are not justly liable to reproof, save where they may have carried their punishments to excess, and displayed a wanton spirit of cruelty. All armies have an undoubted right to protect themselves when engaged in hostilities. An insurrection of armed peasants is a military anarchy. Men in such circumstances cannot be restrained within the bounds of civilised warfare; they will murder stragglers, torture prisoners, destroy hospitals, poison wells, and break down all the usages that soften the enmities of modern nations. They wear no badge of an enemy, and their devices cannot, therefore, be guarded against in the ordinary mode. Their war is one of extermination, and it must be repressed by terrible examples, or the civilized customs of modern warfare must be discarded, and the devastating system of the ancients revived. Hence, the usage of refusing quarter to an armed peasantry, and burning their villages, however unjust and barbarous it may appear at first view, is founded upon a principle of necessity, and is in reality a vigorous infliction of a partial evil, to prevent universal calamity. But however justifiable it may be in theory, no wise man will hastily resort to it, and no good man will carry it to any extent.

CHAPTER III

Parliamentary Papers, 1809.

The subjugation of Portugal was neither a recent nor a secret project of Napoleon's. His intentions with respect to the house of Braganza were known in 1806 to Mr. Fox, who sent lord Roslyn, lord St. Vincent, and general Simcoe on a politico-military mission to Lisbon, instructing them not only to warn the court that a French force destined to invade Portugal was assembling at Bayonne, but to offer the assistance of an English army to repel the danger. The cabinet of Lisbon affected to disbelieve the information, Mr. Fox died during the negotiation, and the war with Prussia diverting Napoleon's attention to more important objects, he withdrew his troops from Bayonne. The tory administration, which soon after overturned the Grenville party, thought no further of the affair, or at least did not evince as much foresight and ready zeal as their predecessors. They kept, indeed, a naval force off Lisbon, under the command of sir Sydney Smith; but their views seem to have been confined to the emigration of the royal family, and they intrusted the conduct of the negotiations to lord Strangford, a young man of no solid influence or experience. Suddenly, the Russian squadron, under admiral Siniavin, took refuge in the Tagus, and this unexpected event produced in the British cabinet an activity which the danger of Portugal had not been able to excite.

Parliamentary Papers, 1809.

Sir John Moore's Journal, MS.

It was supposed, that as Russia and England were in a state of hostility, the presence of the Russian ships would intimidate the prince regent, and prevent him from passing to the Brazils, wherefore sir Charles Cotton, an admiral of higher rank than sir Sydney Smith, was sent out with instructions to force the entrance of the Tagus, and to attack admiral Siniavin. To ensure success, general Spencer, then upon the point of sailing with five thousand men upon a secret expedition, was ordered to touch at Lisbon, and sir John Moore, with ten thousand men, was withdrawn from Sicily, and directed to aid the enterprise; but before the instructions for the commanders were even written, the prince regent was on his voyage to the Brazils, and Junot ruled in Lisbon.

Sir John Moore, however, arrived at Gibraltar, but hearing nothing of sir Sydney Smith, nor of general Spencer, proceeded to England, and reached Spithead the 31st of December, from whence, after a detention of four months, he was despatched upon that well-known and eminently foolish expedition to Sweden, which ended in such an extraordinary manner, and which seems from the first to have had no other object than to keep an excellent general and a superb division of troops at a distance from the only country where their services were really required.

Meanwhile, general Spencer's armament, long baffled by contrary winds, and once forced back to port, was finally dispersed in a storm, and a part arrived at Gibraltar by single ships the latter end of January. Sir Hew Dalrymple, the governor of that fortress, being informed, on the 5th of February, that a French fleet had just passed the strait, and run up the Mediterranean, became alarmed for Sicily, then scantily furnished with troops, and caused the first comers to proceed to that island the 11th. General Spencer, whose instructions were to attack Ceuta, arrived on the 10th of March, and the deficiency in his armament being supplied by a draft from the garrison of Gibraltar, a council was held for the purpose of arranging the plan of attack: the operation was, however, thought to be impracticable, and consequently relinquished. General Spencer would then have carried the remainder of his troops to Sicily, but the insurrection in Spain broke out at the moment and altered his determination. In the relation of Dupont's campaign, I have already touched upon Spencer's proceedings at Cadiz; but in this place it is necessary to give a more detailed sketch of those occurrences, which, fortunately, brought him back to the coast of Portugal at the moment when sir Arthur Wellesley was commencing the campaign of Vimiero.

Sir Hew Dalrymple's Correspondence. MS.

When the French first entered Spain, general Castaños commanded the Spanish troops at St. Roque; in that situation he was an object of interest to Napoleon, who sent two French officers privately to sound his disposition. Castaños secretly resolving to oppose the designs of the emperor, thought those officers were coming to arrest him, and at first determined to kill them, and fly to Gibraltar; but soon discovering his mistake, he treated them civilly, and prosecuted his original plans. Through the medium of one Viale, a merchant of Gibraltar, he opened a communication with sir Hew Dalrymple, and the latter, who had been closely watching the progress of events, encouraged him in his views, and not only promised assistance, but recommended several important measures, such as the immediate seizure of the French squadron in Cadiz, the security of the Spanish fleet at Minorca, and a speedy communication with South America. But before

Castaños could mature his plans, the insurrection took place at Seville, and he acknowledged the authority of the junta.

Meanwhile Solano arrived at Cadiz, and general Spencer, in conjunction with admiral Purvis, pressed him to attack the French squadron, and offered to assist if he would admit the English troops into the town. Solano's mind was, however, not made up to resist the invaders, and expressing great displeasure at the proposal to occupy Cadiz, he refused to treat at all with the British. This was not unexpected by sir Hew; he knew that most of the Spaniards were mistrustful of the object of Spencer's expedition, and the offer was made without his concurrence; thus a double intercourse was carried on between the British and Spanish authorities; the one friendly and confidential between sir Hew and Castaños, the other of a character proper to increase the suspicions of the Spaniards; and when it is considered that Spain and England were nominally at war, that the English commanders were acting without the authority of their government, that the troops which it was proposed to introduce into Cadiz were in that part of the world for the express purpose of attacking Ceuta, and had already taken the island of Perexil, close to that fortress, little surprise can be excited by Solano's conduct.

Sir Hew Dalrymple's Correspondence. MS.

His death intervening, general Morla succeeded to the command, and Spencer and Purvis renewed their offers; but Morla likewise declined their assistance, and having himself forced the French squadron to surrender, by a succession of such ill-directed attacks, that some doubt was entertained of his wish to succeed, he commenced a series of low intrigues calculated to secure his own personal safety, while he held himself ready to betray his country if the French should prove the strongest. After the reduction of the enemy's ships, the people were inclined to admit the English troops, but the local junta, swayed by Morla's representations, were averse to it, and he, while confirming this disposition, secretly urged Spencer to persevere in his offer, saying that he looked entirely to the English troops for the future defence of Cadiz; and thus dealing, he passed with the people for an active patriot, yet made no preparations for resistance, and by his double falsehoods preserved a fair appearance both with the junta and the English general.

With these affairs sir Hew Dalrymple did not meddle, he early discovered that Morla was an enemy of Castaños, and having more confidence in the latter, carried on the intercourse at first established between them without reference to the transactions at Cadiz. He also supplied the Spanish general with arms and two thousand barrels of powder, and placing an English officer near him as a military correspondent, sent another in the capacity of a political agent to the supreme junta at Seville.

Castaños being appointed commander-in-chief of the Andalusian army, as I have before related, rallied Echevaria's troops, and asked for the co-operation of the British force; he had no objection to their entering Cadiz, but he preferred having them landed at Almeria to march to Xeres. General Spencer, however, confined his offers to the occupation of Cadiz; and when Morla pretended that to fit out the Spanish fleet was an object of immediate importance, colonel sir George Smith, an officer employed by general Spencer to conduct the negotiations, promised on his own authority, money to pay the Spanish seamen, who were then in a state of mutiny. Lord Collingwood and sir Hew Dalrymple refused to fulfil this promise, and the approach of Dupont causing Morla to wish Spencer's troops away, he persuaded that general to sail to Ayamonte, under the pretence of preventing Avril's division from crossing the Guadiana, although he knew well that the latter had no intention of doing so.

The effect produced upon colonel Maransin by the appearance of the British force off Ayamonte has been already noticed. General Thiebault says, that Spencer might have struck an important blow at that period against the French; but the British troops were unprovided with any equipment for a campaign, and to have thrown five thousand infantry, without cavalry and without a single place of arms, into the midst of an enemy who occupied all the fortresses, and who could bring twenty thousand men into the field, would have been imprudent to the greatest degree. General Spencer, who had by this time been rejoined by his detachment from Sicily, only made a demonstration of landing, and having thus materially aided the insurrection, returned to Cadiz, from whence he was almost immediately summoned to Lisbon, to execute a new project, which proved to be both ill-considered and fruitless.

Mr. Canning to lord Castlereagh, 28th Dec. 1807.

Sir Hew Dalrymple's Correspondence.

Parliamentary Papers, 1809.

Sir Hew Dalrymple's Correspondence.

Sir Charles Cotton, after superseding sir Sydney Smith, had blockaded the mouth of the Tagus with the utmost rigour, expecting to force the Russian squadron to capitulate for want of provisions. This scheme, which originated with lord Strangford, never had the least chance of success; but the privations and misery of the wretched inhabitants was so greatly aggravated thereby, that Junot had recourse to various expedients to abate the rigour of the blockade with regard to them, and among others, employed a Portuguese, named Sataro, to make proposals to the English admiral. This man at first pretended that he came without the privity of the French, and in the course of the communications that followed, sir Charles was led to believe that only four thousand French troops remained in Lisbon. Under this erroneous impression, he requested that general Spencer might be sent to him, for the purpose of attacking the enemy while they were so weak. Spencer, by the advice of sir Hew Dalrymple and lord Collingwood, obeyed the summons, but on his arrival was led to doubt the correctness of the admiral's information. Instead of four thousand, it appeared that there could not be much less than fifteen thousand French in or near Lisbon; and the attack was of course relinquished. When Spencer returned to Cadiz, Castaños again pressing him to co-operate with the Spanish forces, he so far consented, as to disembark them at the port St. Mary, and even agreed to send a detachment to Xeres; but being deceived by Morla, who still gave him hopes of finally occupying Cadiz, he resolved to keep the greater part close to that city.

At this period the insurrection of Andalusia attracted all the intriguing adventurers in the Mediterranean towards Gibraltar and Seville, and the confusion of Agramant's camp would have been rivalled, if the prudent firmness of sir Hew Dalrymple had not checked the first efforts of those political pests; but among the perplexing follies of the moment, one deserves particular notice, on account of some curious circumstances that attended it, the full explanation of which I must, however, leave to other historians, who may perhaps find in that and the like affairs, a key to that absurd policy, which in Sicily so long sacrificed the welfare of two nations to the whims and follies of a profligate court.

Sir Hew Dalrymple's Correspondence.

The introduction of the salique law had long been a favourite object with the Bourbons of Spain; but the nation at large would never agree to change the ancient rule of succession, which admitted females to the throne. The project was, however, secretly revived by some of the junta at this moment, and the party favouring the salique law wished to offer the regency to the prince of Sicily, who (Ferdinand and his brothers dying without sons) would, under that law, have succeeded, to the prejudice of the princess of the Brazils. The chevalier Robertoni, a Sicilian agent, appeared early at Gibraltar, and from thence (as if under the auspices of England), attempted to forward the views of his court; but sir Hew Dalrymple, being accidentally informed that the British cabinet disapproved of the object of his mission, sent him away. Meanwhile Castaños, deceived by some person engaged in the intrigue, was inclined to support the pretensions of the Sicilian prince to the regency, and proposed to make use of sir Hew Dalrymple's name to give weight to his opinions; a circumstance which must have created great jealousy in Spain, if sir Hew had not promptly refused his sanction.

Ibid.

After that, the affair seemed to droop for a moment; but in the middle of July an English man of war suddenly appeared at Gibraltar, having on board prince Leopold of Sicily, and a complete court establishment of chamberlains with their keys, and ushers with their white wands. The duke of Orleans, who attended his brother-in-law the prince, made no secret of his intention to negotiate for the regency of Spain, and openly demanded that he should be received into Gibraltar. Sir Hew, foreseeing all the mischief of this proceeding, promptly refused to permit the prince, or any of his attendants, to land; and the captain of the ship, whose orders were merely to carry him to Gibraltar, refused to take him back to Sicily. To relieve his royal highness from this awkward situation, sir Hew consented to receive him as a guest, provided that he divested himself of his public character, and that the duke of Orleans departed instantly from the fortress.

Appendix, No. 8.

Ibid.

Sir William Drummond, the British envoy at Palermo; Mr. Viale; and the duke of Orleans were the ostensible contrivers of this notable scheme, by which, if it had succeeded, a small party in a local junta would have appointed a regency for Spain, paved the way for altering the laws of succession in that country, established their own sway over the other juntas, and created interminable jealousy between England, Portugal, and Spain; but with whom the plan originated does not very clearly appear. Sir William Drummond's representations induced sir Alexander Ball to provide the ship of war, nominally for the conveyance of the duke of Orleans, but in reality for prince Leopold, with whose intended voyage sir Alexander does not appear to have been made acquainted. That the prince should have desired to be regent of Spain was natural, but that he should have been conveyed to Gibraltar in a British ship of the line, when the English government disapproved of his pretensions, was really curious. Sir William Drummond could scarcely have proceeded such lengths in an affair of so great consequence, without secret instructions from some member of his own government, yet lord Castlereagh expressed unqualified approbation of sir Hew's decisive conduct upon the occasion! Did the ministers act at this period without any confidential communication with each other? or was lord Castlereagh's policy secretly and designedly thwarted by one of his colleagues? But it is time to quit this digression and turn to

THE PROCEEDINGS IN PORTUGAL

The bishop of Oporto being placed at the head of the insurrectional junta of that town, claimed the assistance of England. "We hope," said he, "for an aid of three hundred thousand cruzado novas; of arms and accoutrements complete, and of cloth for forty thousand infantry and for eight thousand cavalry; three thousand barrels of cannon powder, some cargoes of salt fish, and other provisions, and an auxiliary body of six thousand men at least, including some cavalry." This extravagant demand would lead to the supposition than an immense force had been assembled by the prelate, yet he could never at any time have put five thousand organized men in motion against the French, and had probably not even thought of any feasible or rational mode of employing the succours he demanded; but the times were favourable for extravagant demands, and his were not rejected by the English ministers, who sent agents to Oporto and other parts, with power to grant supplies. The improvident system adopted for Spain being thus extended to Portugal, produced precisely the same effects, that is, cavils, intrigues, waste, insubordination, and inordinate vanity and ambition among the ignorant upstart men of the day.

Pary. Paps.

Ld. Castleh. to

S. A. Welly. 21st June, 1808.

More than half a year had now elapsed since Napoleon first poured his forces into the Peninsula; every moment of that time was marked by some extraordinary event, and one month had passed since a general and terrible explosion, shaking the unsteady structure of diplomacy to pieces, had left a clear space for the shock of arms; yet the British cabinet was still unacquainted with the real state of public feeling in the Peninsula and with the Spanish character; and although possessing a disposable army, of at least eighty thousand excellent troops, was totally unsettled in its plans, and unprepared for any vigorous effort. Agents were indeed despatched to every accessible province; the public treasure was scattered with heedless profusion, and the din of preparation was heard in every department; but the bustle of confusion is easily mistaken for the activity of business; time removing the veil of official mystery covering those transactions, has exposed all their dull and meagre features; and it is now clear that the treasure was squandered without judgment, and the troops dispersed without meaning. Ten thousand exiled to Sweden proved the truth of Oxenstern's address to his son; as many more idly kept in Sicily were degraded into the guards of a vicious court; Gibraltar was unnecessarily filled with fighting men; and general Spencer, with five thousand excellent soldiers, being doomed to wander between Ceuta, Lisbon, and Cadiz, was seeking, like the knight of La Mancha, for a foe to combat.

A considerable force remained in England; but it was not ready for service, when the minister resolved to send an expedition to the Peninsula, and nine thousand men collected at Cork by other hands and for other purposes, formed the only disposable army for immediate operations. The Grey and Grenville administration, so remarkable for unfortunate military enterprises, had assembled this handful of men with a view to permanent conquests in South America, upon what principle of policy it is not necessary to inquire, but such undoubtedly was the intention of that administration; perhaps in imitation of the Roman senate, who sent troops to Spain when Hannibal was at the gates of the city. The tory administration relinquished this scheme of conquest, and directed sir Arthur Wellesley to inform general Miranda, the military adventurer of the day, not only that he must cease to expect assistance, but that all attempts to separate the colonies of Spain from the parent state would be discouraged by the English government. Thus the troops assembled at Cork became available, and sir Arthur Wellesley being appointed to command them, sailed on the 12th of July, to commence that long and bloody contest in the Peninsula which he was destined to terminate in such a glorious manner.

Parliamentary Papers, 1808.

Ibid.

Ld. Castleh. to S. A. Welly. 30th June.

Ibid.

Ld. Castleh. to gl. Spencr. 28th and 30th June.

Do. to adl. Purvis, 28th June.

Two small divisions were soon after ordered to assemble for embarkation at Ramsgate and Harwich, under the command of generals Anstruther and Acland, but a considerable time elapsed before they were ready to sail; and a singular uncertainty in the views of the ministers at this period subjected all the military operations to perpetual and mischievous changes. General Spencer, supposed to be at Gibraltar, was directed to repair to Cadiz, and wait for sir Arthur's orders; and the latter was permitted to sail under the impression that Spencer was actually subject to his command; but other instructions empowered Spencer at his own discretion to commence operations in the south, without reference to sir Arthur Wellesley's proceedings; and admiral Purvis, who, after lord Collingwood's arrival, had no separate command, was also authorised to undertake any enterprise in that quarter, and even to control the operations of sir Arthur Wellesley by calling for the aid of his troops, that general being enjoined to "pay all due obedience to any such requisition!" Yet sir Arthur himself was informed, that "the accounts from Cadiz were bad;" that "no disposition to move either there or in the neighbourhood of Gibraltar was visible," and that "the cabinet were unwilling he should go far to the southward, whilst the spirit of exertion appeared to reside more to the northward." Again the admiral, sir Charles Cotton, was informed that sir Arthur Wellesley was to co-operate with him in a descent at the mouth of the Tagus; but sir Arthur himself had no definite object given for his own operations, although his instructions pointed to Portugal, and thus in fact no one officer, naval or military, knew exactly what his powers were, with the exception of admiral Purvis, who, being only second in command for his own service, was really authorised to control all the operations of the land forces, provided he directed them to that quarter which had been declared unfavourable for any operations at all.

Pary. Paps.
Ld. Castleh.to S. A. Welly. 30th June, 1808.

In recommending Portugal as the fittest field of action, the ministers were chiefly guided by the advice of the Asturian deputies; although having received sir Hew Dalrymple's despatches to a late date, their own information must have been more recent and more extensive than any that they could obtain from the deputies, who had left Spain at the commencement of the insurrection, and were ill informed of what was passing in their own province, utterly ignorant of the state of any other part of the Peninsula, and under any circumstances were incapable of judging rightly in such momentous affairs.

Pary. Paps.
Ld. Castleh. to S. A. Welly. 30th June, 1808.

The inconsistent orders of the ministers were well calculated to introduce all manner of confusion, and to prevent all vigour of action, but more egregious conduct followed. In sir Arthur Wellesley's instructions, although they were vague and undefined, as to immediate military operations, it was expressly stated that the intention of the government was to enable Portugal and Spain to throw off the French yoke, and ample directions were given to him as to his future political conduct in the Peninsula. He was informed how to demean himself in any disputes that might arise between the two insurrectional nations, how to act with relation to the settlement of the supreme authority during the interregnum; and directed to facilitate communications between the colonies and the mother country, and to offer his good offices to arrange any differences between them. The terms upon which Great Britain would acquiesce in any negotiation between Spain and France were stated, and finally he was empowered to recommend the establishment of a paper system in the Peninsula, as a good mode of raising money, and attaching the holders of it to the national cause. The Spaniards were not, however, sufficiently civilized to adopt this recommendation, and barbarously preferred gold to credit at a time when no man's life, or faith, or wealth, or power, was worth a week's purchase. Sir Hew Dalrymple was at this time also commanded to furnish sir Arthur with every information that might be of use to the latter in his operations.

Ibid.

Ld. Castleh. to S. H. Dalrymple, 28th June, 1808.

When the tenor of these instructions, and the great Indian reputation enjoyed by sir Arthur Wellesley are considered, it is not possible to doubt that he was first chosen as the fittest man to conduct the armies of England at this important conjuncture; yet scarcely had he sailed when he was superseded, not to make room for a man whose fame and experience might have justified such a change, but by an extraordinary arrangement, which can hardly be attributed to mere vacillation of purpose, he was reduced to the fourth rank in that army, for the future governance of which, he had fifteen days before received the most extended instructions.

Sir Hew Dalrymple was appointed to the chief command, and sir John Moore, who had suddenly and unexpectedly returned from the Baltic, (having by his firmness and address saved himself and his troops from the madness of the Swedish monarch), was, with marked disrespect, directed, to place himself under the orders of sir Harry Burrard and proceed to Portugal. Thus two men, comparatively unknown and unused to the command of armies, superseded the only generals in the British service whose talents and experience were indisputable. The secret springs of this proceeding are not so deep as to baffle investigation; but that task scarcely belongs to the general historian, who does enough when he exposes the effects of envy, treachery, and base cunning, without tracing those vices home to their possessors.

Ibid.

Ld. Castleh. to S. A. Welly. 15th July, 1808.

Notwithstanding these changes in the command, the uncertainty of the minister's plans continued. The same day that sir Hew Dalrymple was appointed to be commander-in-chief, a despatch, containing the following project of campaign, was sent to sir Arthur Wellesley: "The motives which have induced the sending so large a force to that quarter[10] are, 1st. to provide effectually for an attack upon the Tagus; and, 2dly, to have such an additional force disposable beyond what may be indispensably requisite for that operation, as may admit of a detachment being made to the southward, either with a view to secure Cadiz, if it should be threatened by the French force under general Dupont, or to co-operate with the Spanish troops in reducing that corps, if circumstances should favour such an operation, or any other that may be concerted. His Majesty is pleased to direct that the *attack upon the Tagus should be considered as the first object to be attended to.* As the whole force, of which a statement is enclosed, when assembled, will amount to not less than thirty thousand, *it is considered that both services may be provided for amply.* The precise distribution, as between Portugal and Andalusia, both as to time and proportion of force, must depend upon circumstances, to be judged of on the spot; and should it be deemed advisable to fulfil the assurance which lieutenant-general sir Hew Dalrymple appears to have given to the supreme junta of Seville[11], under the authority of my despatch of (no date), that it was the intention of his majesty to employ a corps of 10,000 men to co-operate with the Spaniards in that quarter. A corps of this magnitude may, I should hope, be detached without prejudice to the main operation against the Tagus, and may be reinforced, according to circumstances, after the Tagus has been secured. But if, previous to the arrival of the force under orders from England, Cadiz should be seriously threatened, it must rest with the senior officer of the Tagus, at his discretion to detach, upon receiving a requisition to that effect, such an amount of force as may place that important place out of the reach of immediate danger, *even though it should for the time suspend operations against the Tagus*[12]."

In England at this period, personal enmity to Napoleon, and violent party prejudices, had so disturbed the judgments of men relative to that monarch, that any information speaking of strength or success for him, was regarded with suspicion even by the ministers, who, as commonly happens in such cases, becoming the dupes of their own practices, listened with complacency to all those tales of mutiny among his troops, disaffection of his generals, and insurrections in France, which the cunning or folly of their agents transmitted to them. Hence sprung such projects as the one above, the false calculations of which may be exposed by a short comparative statement.

The whole English force was not much above thirty thousand men, distributed off Cadiz, off the coast of Portugal, on the eastern parts of England, and in the channel. The French force in Spain and Portugal was about a hundred and twenty thousand men: they possessed all the Portuguese, and most of the Spanish fortresses.

The English army had no reserve, no fixed plan, and it was to be divided, and to act upon a double line of operations. The French had a strong reserve at Bayonne, and the grand French army of four hundred thousand veterans was untouched, and ready to succour the troops in the Peninsula if they required it.

Happily, this visionary plan was in no particular followed by the generals entrusted with the conduct of it. A variety of causes combined to prevent the execution. The catastrophe of Baylen marred all the great combinations of the French emperor; fortune drew the scattered divisions of the English army together, and the decisive vigour of sir Arthur Wellesley sweeping away these cobweb projects, obtained all the success that the bad arrangements of the ministers would permit.

In the next chapter, resuming the thread of the history, I shall relate the proceedings of the first British campaign in the Peninsula; but I judged it necessary first to make an exposition of the previous preparations and plans of the cabinet, lest the reader's attention not being fully awakened to the difficulties cast in the way of the English generals by the incapacity of the government, should, with hasty censure, or niggard praise, do the former injustice; for, as a noble forest hides many noisome swamps and evil things, so the duke of Wellington's laurels have covered the innumerable errors of the ministers.

CHAPTER IV

Sir A. Wellesley's Narrative. Court of Inquiry.

A few days after sailing from Cork, sir Arthur Wellesley quitting the fleet, repaired in a frigate to Coruña, where he arrived the 20th of July, and immediately held a conference with the members of the Gallician junta, by whom he was informed of the battle of Rio Seco; but the account was glossed over in the Spanish manner, and the issue of that contest had caused no change in their policy, if policy that may be called, which was but a desire to obtain money and to avoid personal inconvenience; they rejected all succour in men, but earnestly pressed for arms and gold; and even while the conference went on, the last was supplied, for an English frigate entered the harbour with two hundred thousand pounds for their use. Whereupon, the junta recommended that the British troops should be employed in the north of Portugal, and promising to aid them by sending a Spanish division to Oporto, supported their recommendation by an incorrect statement of the number of men, Spanish and Portuguese, who, they asserted, were in arms near that city, and by a still more inaccurate estimate of the forces under Junot; and in this manner persuaded sir Arthur not to land in their province. Yet, at the moment they were rejecting the assistance of the British troops, the whole kingdom of Gallicia was lying at the mercy of marshal Bessieres, and there were neither men nor means to impede the progress of his victorious army.

Parliamentary Papers, 1809.

Sir A. Wellesley's Narrative. Court of Inquiry.

Mr. Charles Stuart, appointed to reside as British envoy near the junta, landed at Coruña, and sir Arthur Wellesley proceeded to Oporto, where he found colonel Browne, an active and intelligent officer, who had been sent there a short time before to collect intelligence, and to distribute supplies. From his information it appeared, that no Spanish troops were in the north of Portugal, and that all the Portuguese force was upon the Mondego, to the south of which river the insurrection had spread. A French division of eight thousand men was supposed to be in their front, and some great disaster was expected, for, to use colonel Browne's words, "with every good will in the people, their exertions were so short lived, and with so little combination, that there was no hope of their being able to resist the advance of the enemy;" in fact, only five thousand regulars and militia, half armed, and associated with ten or twelve thousand peasants without any arms, were in the field at all. A large army was, however, made out upon paper by the bishop of Oporto, who, having assembled his civil and military coadjutors in council, proposed various plans of operation for the allied forces, none of which sir Arthur was inclined to adopt; but after some discussion it was finally arranged that the prelate and the paper army should look to the defence of the Tras os Montes against Bessieres, and that the five thousand soldiers on the Mondego should co-operate with the British forces.

Sir A. Wellesley's Narrative. Court of Inquiry.

Sir H. Dalrymple's and lord Collingwood's Correspondence.

This being settled, sir Arthur Wellesley hastened to consult with sir Charles Cotton relative to the descent at the mouth of the Tagus, which had so long haunted the imaginations of the ministers. The strength of the French, the bar of the river, the disposition of the forts, and the difficulty of landing in the immediate neighbourhood, occasioned by the heavy surf playing upon all the undefended creeks and bays, convinced him that such an enterprise was unadvisable, if not impracticable. There remained the alternative of landing to the north of Lisbon at such a distance as to avoid the danger of a disputed disembarkation, or of proceeding to the southward to join general Spencer, and commence operations in that quarter against Dupont. Sir Arthur Wellesley decided against the latter, which promised no good result while Junot held Portugal, and Bessieres hung on the northern frontier. He foresaw that the jealousy of the Spaniards, evinced by their frequent refusal to admit English troops into Cadiz, would assuredly bring on a tedious negotiation, and waste the season of action before the army could obtain a place of arms, or that the campaign must be commenced without any secure base of operations. Nothing was then known of the Spanish troops, except that they were inexperienced; but without good aid from them it would have been idle with fourteen thousand men to take the field against twenty thousand strongly posted in the Sierra Morena and communicating freely with the main body of the French army. A momentary advance was useless; and if the campaign was protracted, the line of operations running nearly parallel to the frontier of Portugal, would have required a covering army on the Guadiana to watch the movements of Junot.

The double line of operations, proposed by lord Castlereagh, was contrary to all military principle, and as Spencer's despatches announced that his division was at St. Mary's, near Cadiz, and disengaged from any connexion with the Spaniards (a fortunate circumstance scarcely to have been expected), sir Arthur sent him orders to sail to the mouth of the Mondego, whither he himself also repaired, and joined the fleet having his own army on board. Off the Mondego he received the despatches announcing sir Hew Dalrymple's appointment and the sailing of sir John Moore's troops.

Sir A. Wellesley's Narrative. Court of Inquiry.

This mortifying intelligence did not relax his activity; he directed fast sailing vessels to look out for Anstruther's armament, and to conduct it to the Mondego, and having heard of Dupont's capitulation, resolved, without waiting for general Spencer's arrival, to disembark his own troops and commence the campaign—a determination that marked the cool decisive vigour of his character; for, although sure that (in consequence of Dupont's defeat) Bessieres would not enter Portugal, his information led him to estimate Junot's own force at sixteen to eighteen thousand men, a number, indeed, below the truth, yet sufficient to make the hardiest general pause before he disembarked with only nine thousand men, and without any certainty that his fleet could remain even for a day in that dangerous offing, at a moment also when another man was coming to profit from any success that might be obtained, and when a failure would have ruined his own reputation in the estimation of the English public, always ready to deride the skill of an Indian general.

It was difficult to find a good point of disembarkation, for the coast of Portugal from the Minho to the Tagus, presents, with few exceptions, a rugged and dangerous shore; all the harbours formed by the rivers have bars, that render most of them difficult of access even for boats, and with the slightest breeze from the sea-board a terrible surf breaks along the whole line of coast and forbids all approach, and when the south wind, which commonly prevails from August to the winter months, blows, a more dangerous shore is not to be found in any part of the world.

Sir A. Wellesley's Narrative. Court of Inquiry.

The small peninsula of Peniché, about seventy miles northward of the Lisbon Rock, alone offered a safe and accessible bay, perfectly adapted for a disembarkation, but the anchorage was completely within range of the fort, which contained a hundred guns and a garrison of a thousand men. The next best place was the Mondego river, and as the little fort of Figueras, taken, as I have before related, by the student Zagalo, and now occupied by English marines, secured a free entrance, sir Arthur commenced landing his troops there on the 1st of August. The weather was calm, but the operation was so difficult that it was not completed before the 5th. At that moment, by a singular good fortune, general Spencer arrived; he had not received sir

Arthur's orders, but with great promptitude had sailed for the Tagus the moment Dupont surrendered, and by sir Charles Cotton had been directed to the Mondego. The united forces, however, only amounted to twelve thousand three hundred men, because the fourth veteran battalion being destined for Gibraltar was left on board the ships.

The army being on shore, the British general repaired to Montemor Velho to confer with don Bernardim Freire de Andrada, the Portuguese commander-in-chief. The latter proposed that the troops of the two nations should relinquish all communication with the coast, and throwing themselves into the heart of Beira, commence an offensive campaign; he promised ample stores of provisions; but sir Arthur having already discovered the weakness of the insurrection, placed no reliance on those promises. He supplied Freire with five thousand stand of arms and ammunition, but refused to separate from his ships; and seeing clearly that the insurgents were unable to give any real assistance, he resolved to act with reference to the probability of their deserting him in danger. The Portuguese general, disappointed at this refusal, reluctantly consented to join the British army, but he pressed sir Arthur to hasten to Leria, lest a large magazine filled, as he affirmed, with provisions for the use of the British army, should fall into the enemy's hands. After this the two generals separated, and the necessary preparations for a march being completed, the advanced guard of the English army quitted the banks of the Mondego on the 9th, taking the road to Leria. The 10th sir Arthur Wellesley followed with the main body, and thus commenced the

FIRST CAMPAIGN IN PORTUGAL

His plan embraced three principal objects:

1°. To hold on by the sea coast, as well for the sake of his supplies as to avoid the drain upon his weak army, which the protection of magazines on shore would occasion, and also to cover the disembarkation of the reinforcements expected from England.

2°. To keep his troops in a mass, that he might strike an important blow.

3°. To strike that blow as near Lisbon as possible, that the affairs of Portugal might be quickly brought to a crisis.

Sir A. Wellesley's Narrative. Court of Inquiry.

He possessed very good military surveys of the ground in the immediate neighbourhood of Lisbon, and he was anxious to carry on his operations in a part of the country where he could avail himself of this resource; but the utter inexperience of his commissariat staff, and the want of cavalry, rendered his movements slow, and obliged him to be extremely circumspect, especially as the insurrection, although a generous, was but a feeble effort, and its prolongation rather the result of terror than of hope. The blow had been hastily struck in the moment of suffering, and the patriots, conscious of weakness, trembled when they reflected on their own temerity.

Proceedings of the Court of Inquiry.

From the English stores Bernardim Freire had received arms and equipments complete for five thousand soldiers, yet his army at Leria did not exceed six thousand men of all arms fit for action; and besides this force, there were in all the provinces north of the Tagus only three thousand infantry, under the command of the marquis of Valladeres, half of whom were Spaniards. Hence it appears, that nothing could be more insignificant than the insurrection, nothing more absurd than the lofty style adopted by the junta of Oporto in their communications with the British ministers.

Thiebault.

Upon the other side, Junot, who received information of the English descent in the Mondego as early as the 2d, was extremely embarrassed by the distance of his principal force, and the hostile disposition of the inhabitants of Lisbon. He also was acquainted with the disaster of Dupont, and exaggerated notions of the essential strength of the Portuguese insurgents were generated in his own mind and in the minds of his principal officers.

The patriots of the Alemtejo and Algarves, assisted by some Spaniards, and animated by the manifestos and promises assiduously promulgated from the English fleet, had once more assembled at Alcacer do Sal, from whence they threatened the garrisons of St. Ubes and the French posts on the south bank of the Tagus, immediately opposite to Lisbon. The capital itself was very unquiet; the anticipation of coming freedom was apparent in the wrathful looks and stubborn manners of the populace, and superstition was at work to increase the hatred and the hopes of the multitude. It was at this time that the prophetic eggs, denouncing death to the French, and deliverance to the Portuguese, appeared; but less equivocal indications of approaching danger were to be drawn from the hesitations of Junot, who, wavering between his fear of an insurrection in Lisbon, and his desire to check the immediate progress of the British army, gave certain proof of an intellect yielding to the pressure of events.

Thiebault.

At this period Loison, with between seven and eight thousand men, was in the neighbourhood of Estremos, two thousand five hundred men were in the fortresses of Elvas and Almeida, a few hundred were at Abrantes, a thousand were in Santarem, and the same number in Peniché. General Thomieres, with a brigade, was in the vicinity of Alcobaca, and the remainder were quartered in Lisbon and on a circuit round, including both sides of the river. The Tagus itself was guarded on the north bank by the forts of Cascaes, St. Antonio, St. Julians, Belem, and the citadel, between each of which smaller works kept up a continued line of offence against ships entering by the northern passage of the harbour. On the southern bank fort Bugio, built upon a low sandy point, crossed its fire with St. Julians in the defence of the entrance. Upon the heights of Almada or Palmela, stood the fort of Palmela. St. Ubes and Traffaria completed the posts occupied by the French on that side. The communication between the north and south banks was kept up by the refitted Portuguese ships of war, by the Russian squadron, and by the innumerable boats, most of them very fine and large, with which the Tagus is covered.

Such being the situation of the army on the 3d, Junot ordered Loison to march by Portalegre and Abrantes, and from thence effect a junction with general Laborde, who, with three thousand infantry, five or six hundred cavalry, and five pieces of artillery, quitted Lisbon upon the 6th, and proceeded by Villa Franca, Rio Mayor, and Candeiros, charged to observe the movements of the British, and to cover the march of Loison, with whom he expected to form a junction at Leria.

Thiebault.

Junot himself remained in Lisbon with a view of controlling the inhabitants by his presence. He embarked all the powder from the magazines, took additional precautions to guard his Spanish prisoners, and put the citadel and forts into a state of siege; but disquieted by the patriots assembled at Alcacer do Sal, he sent general Kellerman with a moveable column to disperse them, and to scour the country between that place and Setuval, ordering him to withdraw the garrison from the latter, to abandon all the French posts on the south of the Tagus except Palmela, and to collect the whole force in one mass on the heights of Almada, where an entrenched camp had been already commenced; but general Kellerman had scarcely departed when two English regiments, the one from Madeira, the other from Gibraltar, arriving off the bar of Lisbon, distracted anew the attention of the French, and increased the turbulence of the populace, and in this state of perplexity the duke of Abrantes lingered until the 15th, when the progress of sir Arthur Wellesley forced him to assume the command of the army in the field.

Loison entered Abrantes the 9th, and Laborde arrived at Candeiros the same day; from that point he could with facility carry his division upon Alcobaca and Leria, or form a junction with Loison upon the side of Santarem.

The armies on both sides were now in that state of attraction towards each other, which indicates an approaching shock. In the French camps the news of Bessieres' victory at Rio Seco became known, and produced a short-lived exultation; and at the same moment intelligence of Joseph's flight from Madrid reached the British army, and increased their confidence of victory. The 10th, Loison halted at Abrantes, and Laborde moved to Alcobaca, where he was joined by Thomieres and the garrison of Peniché.

Proceedings of the Court of Inquiry.

Sir Arthur's advanced guard also entered Leria, and was there joined by Bernardim Freire and the Portuguese army, who immediately seized the magazine without making any distribution to the British troops. The main body of the latter arrived the 11th, and the whole marched in advance upon the 12th.

Thiebault.

Laborde employed the 11th and 12th in looking for a position in the neighbourhood of Battalha; but the ground was too extensive for his numbers, and at the approach of the English, he fell back in the night of the 12th to Obidos, a small town, with an old Moorish castle situated on a gentle eminence in the middle of a valley. Having occupied Obidos with his picquets, and placed a small detachment at the windmill of Brilos, three miles in front, he retired the 14th to Roriça, a village four miles to the southward, situated at the intersection of the roads leading to Torres Vedras, to Montachique, and to Alcoentre, and overlooking the whole valley of Obidos.

This position enabled him to preserve his communication with Loison open, but as it uncovered Peniché, the fourth Swiss regiment, with the exception of the flank companies, was sent to regarrison that important point, and at the same time three hundred men were detached to the right by Bombarral, Cadaval, and Segura, to obtain intelligence of Loison.

That general, having made a demonstration on the side of Thomar the 11th, ascertained that Leria was in the hands of the British, and fell back the same day upon Torres Novas, then following the course of the Tagus he arrived at Santarem upon the 13th, but in such an exhausted state, that he was unable to renew his march until the 15th. Sir Arthur Wellesley's first movement had thus cut the line of communication between Loison and Laborde, caused a loss of several forced marches to the former, and obliged the latter to risk an action with more than twice his own numbers.

As the hostile troops approached each other, the Portuguese chiefs became alarmed, notwithstanding the confident language of their public manifestos and the bombastic style of their conversation, an internal conviction that a French army was invincible pervaded all ranks of the patriots. The leaders, aware of their own deficiency, and incredulous of the courage of the English soldiers, dreaded the being committed in a decisive contest, because a defeat (which they expected) would deprive them of all hope to make terms with the victors, whereas by keeping five or six thousand men together, they could at any time secure themselves by a capitulation. The junta of Oporto also, who were already aiming at supreme authority, foresaw that in the event of a successful battle, it would be more advantageous for their particular views, to be provided with an army untouched and entirely disconnected with a foreign general, and Freire being well instructed in the secret designs of his party, resolved not to advance a step beyond Leria; but, to cover his real motives, he required the British commander to supply him with provisions, choosing to forget the magazine which he had just appropriated to himself, and as readily forgetting the formal promises of the bishop of Oporto, who had undertaken to feed the English army.

This extraordinary demand, that an auxiliary force just disembarked should nourish the native soldiers, instead of being itself fed by the people, was met by sir Arthur Wellesley with a strong remonstrance. He easily penetrated the secret motive which caused it, but feeling that it was important to have a respectable Portuguese force acting in conjunction with his own, he first appealed to the honour and patriotism of Freire, and warmly admonished him, that he was going to forfeit all pretension to either, by permitting the British army to fight without his assistance; but this argument had no effect upon don Bernardim. He parried the imputations against his spirit and zeal by pretending that his intention was to operate independently on the line of the Tagus; and after some further discussion, sir Arthur, as a last effort, changed his tone of rebuke to one of conciliation, and recommended to him not to risk his troops by an isolated march, but to keep in the rear of the British, and wait for the result of the first battle. This advice was so agreeable to Freire, that at the solicitation of captain Trant, a military agent, he consented to leave fourteen hundred infantry, and two hundred and fifty cavalry, under the immediate command of the English general.

Thiebault.

The defection of the native force was a serious evil. It shed an injurious moral influence, and deprived sir Arthur of the aid of troops whose means of gaining intelligence, and whose local knowledge, might have compensated for his want of cavalry. Nevertheless, continuing his own march, his advanced guard entered Caldas the 15th, and that day also Junot reluctantly quitted Lisbon, with a reserve composed of two thousand infantry, six hundred cavalry, and ten pieces of artillery, carrying with him his grand parc of ammunition, and a military chest, containing forty thousand pounds. General Travot was left at Lisbon, with above seven thousand men, of which number two battalions were formed of stragglers and convalescents. He occupied both sides of the Tagus, distributing two thousand men in Palmela, the Bugio fort, and on the heights of Almada, in order to protect the shipping from the insurgents of the Alemtejo, who, under the orders of the Monteiro Mor, were again gathering at Setuval. A thousand French he kept on board the vessels of war, to guard the Spanish prisoners and the spare powder; with two thousand four hundred he garrisoned the citadel and supported the police. A thousand were distributed in the forts of Belem, St. Julians, Cascaes, and Ericeia (the last named place is situated to the northward of the rock of Lisbon, and commands a small harbour a few miles west of Mafra), and a thousand were at Santarem, protecting a large depôt of stores; thus, if the garrisons of Elvas, Peniché, and Almeida be included, nearly one half of the French army was, by Junot's combinations, rendered inactive, and those in the field were divided into three parts, without any certain point of junction in advance, yet each too weak singly to sustain an action. The duke of Abrantes seems to have reigned long enough in Portugal to forget that he was merely the chief of an advanced corps, whose safety depended upon activity and concentration.

The French reserve was transported to Villa Franca by water, from whence it was to march to Otta; but the rope ferry-boat of Saccavem being removed by the natives, it cost twenty-four hours to throw a bridge across the creek at that place. On the 17th the troops were on their march, when Junot hastily recalled them to Villa Franca. This retrograde movement was occasioned by a report that the English had landed near the capital. When the falsehood of this rumour became known, the reserve resumed the road to Otta, under the command of general Thiebault, Junot himself pushing forward to Alcoentre, where he found Loison, and assumed the personal direction of that general's division.

Sir A. Wellesley's Despatch.

During this time, sir Arthur Wellesley was pressing La Borde. The 15th he caused the post at Brilos to be attacked, and the piquets to be driven out of Obidos. Two companies of the 95th, and two of the 5th battalion, 60th, were employed in the former operation; they carried the windmill without loss, but pursued the retiring enemy with such inconsiderate eagerness, that at the distance of three miles from their support, they were outflanked by two superior bodies of French, and were only saved by the opportune advance of general Spencer. Two officers and twenty-seven men were killed and wounded in this slight affair, which gave a salutary check to the rashness, without lowering the confidence of the troops.

The 16th Laborde's position was examined. The road from Caldas to Obidos runs through a valley, formed by the ramifications of the Monte Junto. The high table land upon which Roriça is situated closed this valley to the southward, and Laborde's division being posted on a small plain immediately in front of that village, completely overlooked the country as far as Obidos. All the favourable points of defence in the valley, and on the nearest hills on each side, were occupied by small detachments. One mile in the rear, a steep ridge extending about three quarters of a mile from east to west, and parallel to the French position, offered a second line of great strength. The main road led by a deep defile over this ridge, which was called the height of Zambugeira, or Columbeira, and beyond it, very lofty mountains rose abruptly, stretching from the sea-coast to the Tagus like a wall, and filling all the space between that river and the ocean down to the rock of Lisbon.

The valley leading from Obidos to Roriça was bounded on the left by a succession of ridges that rose the one above the other like steps, until they were lost in the great mass of the Sierra de Baragueda, itself a shoot from the Monte-junto.

Laborde's situation was becoming truly embarrassing. Loison was at Alcoentre, and the reserve was at Villa Franca; that is one and two marches distant from Roriça. If he retired upon Torres Vedras, his communication with Loison would be lost. To fall back on Montachique was to expose the line of Torres Vedras and Mafra. To march upon Alcoentre, and unite with Loison, was to open the shortest road to Lisbon (that of Montachique) for the British army; and to remain at Roriça, it was necessary to fight three times his own force.

Animated, however, by the danger, encouraged by the local advantages of his position, and justly confident in his own talents, Laborde resolved to abide his enemy's assault, in the feeble hope that Loison might arrive during the action.

COMBAT OF RORIÇA

Sir Arthur Wellesley attacked upon the 17th.

Early in the morning of that day, a dense mass, consisting of thirteen thousand four hundred and eighty infantry, four hundred and seventy cavalry, and eighteen guns, issued from Obidos, and soon afterwards broke into three distinct columns of battle.

The left, commanded by lieutenant-general Ferguson, was composed of his own and major-general Bowe's brigades of infantry, reinforced by two hundred and fifty riflemen, forty cavalry, and six guns, forming a total of four thousand nine hundred combatants. They marched by the crests of the hills adjoining the Sierra de Baragueda, being destined to turn the right flank of Laborde's position, and to oppose the efforts of Loison, if that general (who was supposed to be at Rio Mayor) should appear during the action.

The column of the right, under captain Trant, composed of a thousand Portuguese infantry, and fifty horse of the same nation, moved by the village of St. Amias, with the intention of turning the left flank of the French.

The centre column, nine thousand in number, with twelve guns, was commanded by sir Arthur in person, and marched straight against the enemy by the village of Mahmed. It was composed of generals Hill's, Nightingale's, Catlin Craufurd's, and Fane's brigades of British infantry, four hundred cavalry, two hundred and fifty of which were Portuguese, and four hundred light troops of the same nation.

As this column advanced, general Fane's brigade, extending to its left, drove back the French skirmishers, and connected the march of Ferguson's division with the centre. When the latter approached the elevated plain upon which Laborde was posted, general Hill, who moved upon the right of the main road, being supported by the cavalry, and covered by the fire of his light troops, pushed forward rapidly to the attack. On his left general Nightingale displayed a line of infantry, preceded by the fire of nine guns. Craufurd's brigade, and the remaining pieces of artillery, formed a reserve.

At this moment, Fane's riflemen crowned the nearest hills on the right flank of the French; the Portuguese troops showed the head of a column beyond St. Amias upon the enemy's left, and general Ferguson was seen descending from the higher grounds in the rear of Fane. Laborde's position appeared desperate; but with the coolness and dexterity of a practised warrior, he evaded the danger, and covered by his excellent cavalry, fell back rapidly to the heights of Zambugeira. A fresh disposition of the English became indispensable to dislodge him from that formidable and well chosen post.

Colonel Trant continued his march, and turned the left of the new field of battle.

Ferguson and Fane being united, were directed to penetrate by the mountains, and outflank the French right.

Generals Hill and Nightingale advanced against the front, which was of singular strength, and only to be approached by narrow paths winding through deep ravines. A swarm of skirmishers starting forward, plunged into the passes, and spreading to the right and left, won their way with extreme difficulty among the rocks and tangled evergreens that overspread the steep ascent; with still greater difficulty the supporting columns followed, and their formation was soon disordered in the confined and rugged passes. The hollows echoed with a continued roll of musketry; the shouts of the advancing troops were loudly answered by the enemy, and the curling smoke that broke out from the sides of the mountain marking the progress of the assailants, showed how stoutly the defence was maintained. Laborde, watching anxiously for the arrival of Loison, gradually slackened his hold on the left, but clung tenaciously to the right, in the hope of yet effecting a junction with that general. The ardour of the 9th and 29th regiments, who led the attack, favoured this skilful conduct. They pressed forward with such vigour, as to force the two strongest passes and reach the plain above, long before the flank movements of Ferguson and Trant had shaken the credit of the position, the 29th first arrived in disorder at the top; ere they could form, a French battalion came forward at a rapid pace, poured in their fire, and breaking gallantly through the midst of the English regiment, slew the colonel and many others, and made the major and fifty or sixty men prisoners; but the 29th were not to be overthrown. They rallied, and being joined by the 9th, the colonel of which also fell in this bitter fight, maintained their dangerous footing. Laborde, who brought every arm into action at the proper time and place, made repeated efforts to destroy these regiments before they could be supported; failing in that, he yet gained time to withdraw his left wing and to rally it upon the centre and right; but the English troops were gathering thickly on the upper ground, and general Ferguson, who had at first taken an erroneous direction towards the centre, now regained the true line, and was rapidly passing the right flank of the position. The French general, seeing that the day was lost, commenced a retreat by alternate masses, protecting his movements by vigorous charges of cavalry. At the village of Zambugeira he made another desperate stand, but the English troops bore on him too heavily to be resisted, and thus disputing the ground, he fell back to the Quinta de Bugagliera, there he halted until his detachments on the side of Segura had rejoined him, and then taking to the narrow pass of Ruña he marched all night to gain the position of Montechique, leaving three guns on the field of battle, and the road to Torres Vedras open for the victors.

Thiebault.

Appendix, No. 19.

The loss of the French was six hundred killed and wounded; among the latter was Laborde himself. The British also suffered considerably; two lieutenant-colonels and nearly five hundred men being killed, taken, or wounded, and as not more than four thousand men were actually engaged, this hard fought action was very honourable to both sides.

Sir A. Wellesley's evidence. Court of Inquiry.

The firing ceased a little after four o'clock, and sir Arthur getting intelligence that Loison's division was at Bombaral, only five miles distant, took up a position for the night in an oblique line to that which he had just forced, his left resting upon a height near the field of battle, and his right covering the road to Lourinham. Believing that Loison and Laborde had effected their junction at the Quintade Bugagliera, and that both were retiring to Montechique, he resolved to march the next morning to Torres Vedras; but before night-fall he was informed that general Anstruther's and general Acland's[13] divisions, accompanied by a large fleet of store ships, were off the coast, the dangerous nature of which rendered it necessary to provide for their safety by a quick disembarkation. He therefore changed his plans, and resolved to seek for some convenient post, that, being in advance of his present position, would likewise enable him to cover the landing of these reinforcements. The vigour of Laborde's defence had also an influence upon this occasion; before an enemy so bold and skilful no precaution could be neglected with impunity.

The 18th sir Arthur marched to Lourinham, and Junot at the same time quitting Cereal with Loison's division, crossed the line of Laborde's retreat, and pushed for Torres Vedras, which he reached in the evening of the same day. The 19th being joined by Laborde, and the 20th by his reserve, he re-organized his army, and prepared for a decisive battle.

CHAPTER V

The day on which the combat of Roriça was fought the insurgents attacked Abrantes, and the feeble garrison being ill commanded, gave way, and was destroyed.

The 19th sir Arthur Wellesley took up a position at Vimiero, a village near the sea-coast, and from thence sent a detachment to cover the march of general Anstruther's brigade, which had, with great difficulty and some loss, been that morning landed on an open sandy beach called the bay of Maceira.

The French cavalry scoured the neighbouring country, carried off some of the women from the rear of the camp, and hemmed the army round so closely that no information of Junot's position could be obtained.

In the night of the 20th, general Acland's brigade was also disembarked, and this reinforcement increased the army to sixteen thousand fighting men, with eighteen pieces of artillery, exclusive of Trant's Portuguese and of two British regiments, under general Beresford, which were with the fleet at the mouth of the Tagus.

Appendix, No. 9.

Estimating Junot's whole force at eighteen thousand men, sir Arthur Wellesley judged, that after providing for the security of Lisbon, the French general could not bring more than fourteen thousand into the field; he designed, therefore, not only to strike the first blow, but to follow it up, so as to prevent the enemy from rallying and renewing the campaign upon the frontier. In this view he had, before quitting the Mondego, written to sir Harry Burrard, giving an exact statement of his own proceedings and intentions, and recommending that sir John Moore, with his division, should disembark at the Mondego, and march without delay to Santarem, by which he would protect the left of the army, block the line of the Tagus, and at the same time threaten the French communication between Lisbon and Elvas, and that without danger, because Junot would be forced to defend Lisbon against the coast army, or if, relinquishing the capital, he endeavoured to make way to Almeida by Santarem, the ground there was so strong that sir John Moore might easily maintain it against any efforts.

Moreover, the marquis of Valladeres commanded three thousand men at Guarda, and general Freire, with five thousand men, was at Leria, and might be persuaded to support the British at Santarem.

Sir A. Wellesley's evidence. Court of Inquiry.

The distance from Vimiero to Torres Vedras was about nine miles; but although the number and activity of the French cavalry completely shrouded Junot's position, it was known to be strong, and very difficult of approach, by reason of a long defile through which the army must penetrate in order to reach the crest of the mountain. There was, however, a road leading between the sea-coast and Torres Vedras, which, turning Junot's position, opened a way to Mafra. Sir Arthur possessed very exact military surveys of the country through which that road led, and he projected, by a forced march, on the 21st to turn the position of Torres Vedras, and to gain Mafra with a strong advanced guard, while the main body, seizing some advantageous heights a few miles short of that town, would be in a position to intercept the French line of march to Montachique. The army was reorganized during the 20th in eight brigades of infantry, and four weak squadrons of cavalry, and every preparation was made for the next day's enterprise; but at that critical period of the campaign the ministerial arrangements, which provided three commanders-in-chief, began to work.

Sir Harry Burrard arrived in a frigate off the bay of Maceira, and sir Arthur was checked in the midst of his operations on the eve of a decisive battle. Having repaired on board the frigate, he made his report of the situation of affairs, and renewed his former recommendation relative to the disposal of sir John Moore's troops; but Burrard, who had previously resolved to bring the latter down to Maceira, condemned this project, and forbid any offensive movement until the whole army should be concentrated; whereupon sir Arthur returned to his camp.

The ground occupied by the army, although very extensive, and not very clearly defined as a position, was by no means weak. The village of Vimiero, situated in a valley through which the little river of Maceira flows, contained the parc and commissariat stores. The cavalry and the Portuguese were on a small plain close behind the village, and immediately in its front a rugged isolated height, with a flat top, commanded all the ground to the southward and eastward for a considerable distance.

Upon this height Fane's and Anstruther's brigades of infantry with six guns were posted, the left of Anstruther's occupied a church and churchyard which blocked a road leading over the extremity of the height to the village, the right of Fane's rested on the edge of the other extremity of the hill, the base of which was washed by the Maceira.

A mountain that commenced at the coast swept in a half circle close behind the right of the hill upon which these brigades were posted, and commanded, at rather long artillery range, all its upper surface. Eight guns, and the first, second, third, fourth, and eighth brigades of infantry, occupied this mountain, which was terminated on the left by a deep ravine that divided it from another strong and narrow range of heights over which the road from Vimiero to Lourinham passed. The right of these last heights also overtopped the hill in front of the village, but the left, bending suddenly backward, after the form of a crook, returned to the coast, and ended in a lofty cliff. There was no water upon this range, and some piquets only were placed there.

The troops being thus posted, on the night of the 20th, about twelve o'clock, sir Arthur was aroused by a German officer of dragoons, who galloped into the camp, and with some consternation reported, that Junot, at the head of twenty thousand men, was coming on to the attack, and distant but one hour's march. The general, doubting the accuracy of this gentleman's information, merely sent out some patrolles, and warned the piquets and guards to be upon the alert. Before daybreak, according to the British custom, the troops were under arms; the sun rose, and no enemy was perceived; but at seven o'clock a cloud of dust was observed beyond the nearest hills, and at eight o'clock an advanced guard of horse was seen to crown the heights to the southward, and to send forward scouts on every side. Scarcely had this body been discovered, when a force of infantry, preceded by other cavalry, was descried moving along the road from Torres Vedras to Lourinham, and threatening the left of the British position; column after column followed in order of battle, and it soon became evident that the French were coming down to fight, but that the right wing of the English was not their object. The second, third, fourth, and eighth brigades were immediately directed to cross the valley behind the village, and to take post on the heights before-mentioned as being occupied by the piquets only. As those brigades reached the ground, the second and third were disposed in two lines facing to the left, and consequently forming a right angle with the prolongation of Fane and Anstruther's front. The fourth and eighth brigades were to have furnished a third line; but before the latter could reach the summit the battle commenced. From the flank of all these troops, a line of skirmishers was thrown out upon the face of the descent towards the enemy; the cavalry was drawn up in the plain a little to the right of the village of Vimiero; and the fifth brigade and the Portuguese were detached to the returning part of the crook to cover the extreme left, and to protect the rear of the army. The first brigade under general Hill remained on the mountain which the others had just quitted, and formed a support for the centre and a reserve for the whole.

The ground between the two armies was so wooded and broken, that after the French had passed the ridge where they had been first descried, no correct view of their movements could be obtained; and the British being so weak in cavalry were forced to wait patiently until the columns of attack were close upon them. Junot had quitted Torres Vedras the evening of the 20th, intending to fall on the English army at day-break; but the difficulty of the defile in his front retarded his march for many hours and fatigued his troops. When he first came in sight of the position of Vimiero, the British order of battle appeared to him as being on two sides of an irregular triangle, the apex of which formed by the hill in front of the village, was well furnished with men, while the left face appeared naked, for he could only see the piquets on that side, and the passage of the four brigades across the valley was hidden from him. Concluding, then, that the principal force was in the centre, he resolved to form two connected attacks, the one against the apex, the other against the left face; for he thought that the left of the position was an accessible ridge, whereas a deep ravine, trenched as it were along the base, rendered it utterly impervious to an attack, except at the extremity, over which the road from Torres Vedras to Lourinham passed. Junot had nearly fourteen thousand fighting men organized in four divisions, of which three were of infantry and one of cavalry, with twenty-three pieces of artillery, but of small calibre. Each division was composed of two brigades, and at ten o'clock, all being prepared, he commenced the

BATTLE OF VIMIERO

Thiebault.

Foy.

Laborde marched with one brigade against the centre; general Brennier led another against the left; Loison's division followed in the same order at a short distance. Kellerman, whose division (called the reserve) was composed of grenadiers, moved in one body behind Loison, and the cavalry under Margaron, about thirteen hundred in number, was divided, a part being on the right of Brennier, and the remainder in rear of the reserve. The artillery was distributed among the columns, and opened their fire whenever the ground was favourable for their practice.

Sir A. Wellesley's despatch.

Junot designed that Laborde's and Brennier's attacks should be simultaneous, but the latter coming unexpectedly upon the ravine before mentioned as protecting the left, got entangled among the rocks and water courses, and Laborde alone engaged Anstruther's brigade under a heavy and destructive fire of artillery that played on his front and flank, for the eighth brigade being then in the act of mounting the heights where the left was posted, observing the advance of the columns against the centre, halted, and opened a battery on their right flank. Junot, perceiving this failure in his combinations, ordered Loison to support Laborde's attack with one brigade of his division, and directed general Solignac, with the other, to turn the ravine in which Brennier was entangled, and to fall upon the extremity of the English line.

Loison and Laborde formed one grand and two secondary columns of attack; of the latter, the one advanced against Fane's brigade, while the other endeavoured to penetrate by a road which passed between the ravine and the church on the extreme left of Anstruther; but the principal column, headed by Laborde in person, and preceded by a multitude of light troops, mounted the face of the hill with great fury and loud cries; the English skirmishers were forced in upon the lines in a moment, and the French masses arrived at the summit; but, shattered by a terrible fire of the artillery, and breathless from their exertions, and in this state, first receiving a discharge of musketry from the fiftieth regiment at the distance of half pistol shot, they were vigorously charged in front and flank, and overthrown. At the same time Fane's brigade repulsed the attack on their side, and colonel Taylor, with the very few horsemen he commanded, passing out by the right, rode fiercely among the confused and retreating troops, and scattered them with great execution. Margaron's cavalry seeing this, came suddenly down upon Taylor, who was there slain, and the half of his feeble squadron cut to pieces, and Kellerman taking advantage of this check, threw one half of the reserve into a pine wood, that flanked the line of retreat followed by the beaten troops, and with the other endeavoured to renew the attack by the road leading to the church, where the forty-third regiment were engaged in a hot skirmish among some vineyards.

The grenadiers coming on at a brisk pace, beat back the advanced companies of the forty-third; but to avoid the artillery that swept their left, they dipped a little into the ravine, and were taken on the other flank by the guns of the eighth and fourth brigades, and at the same time the forty-third rallying in a mass, broke down upon the head of the column at a moment when the narrowness of the way and the discharges of the artillery had somewhat disordered its formation, a short yet desperate fight took place; the enemy were repulsed in disorder, but the regiment suffered very severely.

The French being now wholly discomfited in the centre, and the woods and hollows filled with their wounded and straggling men, retired up the edge of the ravine in a direction almost parallel to the British line, and left the road from Vimiero to Torres Vedras open to their opponents; but sir Arthur Wellesley strictly forbade any pursuit at that moment, partly because the grenadiers in the pine wood flanked the line of the French retreat, and partly because Margaron's horsemen, riding stiffly between the two armies, were not to be lightly meddled with. Meanwhile, (Brennier being still hampered in the ravine), general Solignac passed along the crest of the ridge above, and came upon general Ferguson's brigade, which was posted at the left of the English position. But where the French expected to find a weak flank, they encountered a front of battle on a depth of three lines protected by steep declivities on either side; a powerful artillery swept away their foremost ranks, and on their right the fifth brigade and the Portuguese were seen marching by a distant ridge towards the Lourinham road and threatening the rear. Ferguson instantly taking the lead, bore down upon the enemy, the ridge widened as the English advanced, and the regiments of the second line running up in succession, increased the front, and constantly filled the ground. The French falling fast under the fire drew back fighting, until they reached the declivity of the ridge, and their cavalry made several efforts to check the advancing troops, but the latter were too compact to be disturbed by these attempts. Solignac himself was carried from the field severely wounded, and his retiring column, continually outflanked on the left, was cut off from the line of retreat, and thrown into the low ground about the village of Perenza. There six guns were captured, and general Ferguson leaving the eighty-second and seventy-first regiments to guard them, was continuing to press the disordered columns, when Brennier having at last cleared the ravine, came suddenly in upon those two regiments, and re-took the artillery. His success was but momentary; the surprised troops rallied upon the higher ground, poured in a heavy fire of musquetry, and with a shout returning to the charge, overthrew him and recovered the guns. Brennier himself was wounded and made prisoner, and Ferguson having completely separated the French brigades from each other, would have forced the greatest part of Solignac's to surrender, if an unexpected order had not obliged him to halt, and then the discomfited troops re-forming under the protection of their cavalry with admirable quickness and steadiness, made an orderly retreat, and were soon united to the broken brigades which were falling back from the attack on the centre.

Brennier, who, the moment he was taken, was brought to sir Arthur Wellesley, eagerly demanded if the reserve under Kellerman had yet charged, and sir Arthur, ascertaining from other prisoners that it had, was then satisfied that all the enemy's attacks were exhausted, and that no considerable body of fresh troops could be hidden among the woods and hollows in his front. It was only twelve o'clock, the battle was already won;

thirteen guns were in his possession, for seven had been taken in the centre; the fourth and eighth brigades had suffered very little; the Portuguese, the fifth and the first brigades had not fired a shot, and the latter was two miles nearer to Torres Vedras than any part of the French army, which was moreover in great confusion. The relative numbers before the action were considerably in favour of the English; and the result of the action had increased that disparity. A portion of sir Arthur's army had defeated the enemy when entire; a portion then could effectually follow up his victory, and he resolved with the five brigades on the left to press Junot closely, and driving him over the Sierra da Baragueda, force him upon the Tagus, while Hill, Anstruther, and Fane, seizing the defile of Torres Vedras, should push on to Montachique and cut him off from Lisbon.

If this able and decisive operation had been executed, Junot would probably have lost all his artillery, and several thousand stragglers, and being buffeted and turned at every point, would have been glad to seek safety under the guns of Almeida or Elvas, and even that he could only have accomplished because sir John Moore's troops were not landed at the Mondego. But sir Harry Burrard, who was present during the action, although partly from delicacy, and partly from approving of sir Arthur's arrangements, he had not hitherto interfered, now assumed the chief command. From him, the order which arrested Ferguson in his victorious career had emanated, by him further offensive operations were forbidden, and he resolved to wait in the position of Vimiero until the arrival of sir John Moore. The adjutant-general Clinton and colonel Murray, the quarter-master-general, supported sir Harry Burrard's views, and sir Arthur's earnest representations could not alter his determination.

Proceedings of the Board of Inquiry.

Sir Harry's decision was certainly erroneous, but error is common in an art which at best is but a choice of difficulties. The circumstances of the moment were imposing enough to sway most generals; for although the French were beaten in the attacks, they rallied with surprising quickness under the protection of a strong and gallant cavalry; sir Harry knew that his own artillery carriages were so shaken as to be scarcely fit for service; that the draft horses were few and bad, and that the commissariat parc on the plain was in the greatest confusion. The hired Portuguese carmen were making off with their carriages in all directions; the English cavalry was totally destroyed, and finally, general Spencer had discovered a line of fresh troops on the ridge behind that occupied by the French army. Weighing all these things in his mind with the caution natural to age, Burrard was reluctant to hazard the fortune of the day upon what he deemed a perilous throw.

The duke of Abrantes, who had displayed all that reckless courage to which he originally owed his elevation, profited by this unexpected cessation of the battle, and re-formed his broken infantry. Twelve hundred fresh men joined him at the close of the contest, and, covered by his cavalry, he retreated with order and celerity until he regained the command of the pass of Torres Vedras, so that when the day closed, the relative position of the two armies was the same as on the evening before.

Thiebault.

One general, thirteen guns, and several hundred prisoners fell into the hands of the victors, and the total loss of the French was estimated at three thousand men, an exaggeration, no doubt, but it was certainly above two thousand, for their closed columns had been exposed for more than half an hour to sweeping discharges of grape and musquetry, and the dead lay thickly together. General Thiebault indeed reduces the number to eighteen hundred, and asserts that the whole amount of the French army did not much exceed twelve thousand men, from which number he deducts nearly three thousand for the sick, the stragglers, and all those other petty drains which form the torment of a general-in-chief. But when it is considered that this army was composed of men selected and organized into provisionary battalions expressly for the occasion; that one half had only been in the field for a fortnight, and that the whole had enjoyed three days rest at Torres Vedras, it is evident that the number of absentees bears too great a proportion to the combatants. A French order of battle found upon the field gave a total of fourteen thousand men present under arms, of which thirteen hundred were cavalry, and this amount agrees too closely with other estimates, and also with the observations made at the time, to leave any reasonable doubt of its authenticity or correctness.

Proceedings of the Board of Inquiry.

The arrangements made by sir Harry Burrard did not remain in force a long time. Early on the morning of the 22d, sir Hew Dalrymple disembarked and assumed the chief command. Thus, in the short space of twenty-four hours, during which a battle was fought, the army fell successively into the hands of three men, who, coming from different quarters, with different views, habits, and information, had not any previous opportunity of communing even by letter, so as to arrange a common plan of operations; and they were now brought together at a critical moment, when it was more than probable they must all disagree, and that the public service must suffer from that want of vigour which is inherent to divided councils; for when sir Hew Dalrymple was appointed to the command, sir Arthur Wellesley was privately recommended to him by the minister as a person who should be employed with more than usual confidence; and this unequivocal hint was backed up with too much force by the previous reputation and recent exploits of the latter, not to produce some want of cordiality; for sir Arthur could not do otherwise than take the lead in discussing affairs of which he had more than laid the foundation, and sir Hew would have forfeited all claims to independence in his command, if he had not exercised the right of judging for himself between the conflicting opinions of his predecessors.

Sir H. Dalrymple's Narrative.
Court of Inquiry.

Proceedings of the Board of Inquiry.d

After receiving information upon the most important points, and taking a hasty view of the situation of the army; although the wounded were still upon the ground, and that the wains of the commissariat were employed in removing them, sir Hew decided to advance upon the 23d, and gave orders to that effect; but, at the same time, he entirely agreed in opinion with sir Harry Burrard, that the operation was a perilous one, which required the concentration of all the troops, and the application of all his means, to bring to a good conclusion; and for this reason he did not rescind the order directing sir John Moore to fall down to Maceira. This last measure was disapproved of by sir Arthur, who observed that the provisions on shore would not supply more than eight or nine days consumption for the troops already at Vimiero; that the country would be unable to furnish any assistance, and that the fleet could not be calculated upon as a resource because the first of the gales common at that season of the year would certainly send it away from the coast, if it did not destroy a great portion of it. Sir Hew thought the evil of having the army separated, would be greater than the chance of distress from such events. His position was certainly difficult; the bishop of Oporto had failed in his promise of assisting the troops with raft cattle, as indeed he did in all his promises. Both the artillery and commissariat were badly supplied with mules and horses; the cavalry was a nullity; and the enemy was, with the exception of his immediate loss in killed and wounded, suffering nothing from his defeat, which, we have seen, did not deprive him of a single position necessary to his defence.

Thiebault.

Sir Hew, while weighing this state of affairs, was informed that general Kellerman, escorted by a strong body of cavalry, was at the outposts, and demanded an interview. It appears, that Junot having regained Torres Vedras and occupied Mafra with half his army, received news from Lisbon that gave him great uneasiness: the symptoms of an immediate explosion in that city threatened him with destruction, and he hastened to extricate himself while there was yet time. Sending forward a false account of a victory, he followed it up by a reinforcement for the garrison, and immediately afterwards called a council of war to advise with upon the measures fittest to pursue towards the English. It is an old and a sound remark, that "a council of war never fights," and Kellerman's mission was the result of the above consultation.

Proceedings of the Court of Inquiry.

That general being conducted to the quarters of the commander-in-chief, demanded a cessation of arms, and proposed the ground-work of a convention under which Junot offered to evacuate Portugal without further resistance. Nothing could be more opportune than this proposition, and sir Hew Dalrymple readily accepted of it as an advantage which would accrue, without any drawback to the general cause of the Peninsula. He knew, from a plan of operations sketched by the chief of the French engineers, colonel Bory de St Vincent, and taken by the Portuguese, that Junot possessed several very strong positions in front of Lisbon, and that a retreat either upon Almeida, or across the river upon Elvas, was not only within the contemplation of that general, but considered in this report as a matter of course, and perfectly easy of execution. Hence the proposed convention was an unexpected advantage offered in a moment of difficulty, and the only subject for consideration was the nature of the articles proposed by Kellerman as a basis for the treaty. Sir Hew was of necessity ignorant of many important details which bore upon the question, and he naturally had recourse to sir Arthur Wellesley for information. The latter, taking an enlarged view of the question in all its bearings, coincided with the opinion of the former as to the sound policy of agreeing to a convention by which a strong French army would be quietly got out of a country that it had complete military possession of, and by which not only a great moral effect in favour of the general cause would be produced, but likewise an actual gain made both of men and time, for the farther prosecution of the war in Spain. By the convention, he observed,

1°. That a kingdom would be liberated, with all its fortresses, arsenals, &c., and that the excited population of the Peninsula might then be pushed forward in the career of opposition to France, under the most favourable circumstances.

Ibid.

2°. That the Spanish army of Estremadura, which contained the most efficient body of cavalry in the Peninsula, (being first reinforced with the four or five thousand Spanish soldiers who were prisoners on board the vessels in the Tagus), would be enabled to unite with the other patriot armies at a critical period, when every addition of force must tend to increase the confidence, and forward the impulse, which the victory of

Baylen, and the flight of Joseph, had given to the Spaniards; and, finally, that the sacrifice of lives to be expected in carrying the French positions in Portugal, all the difficulties of reducing the fortresses, and the danger of losing a communication with the fleet, would be avoided by this measure; the result of which would be as complete as the most sanguine could expect from the long course of uncertain and unhealthy operations which must follow a rejection of the proposal. But, completely coinciding, as he did, with the commander-in-chief, as to the utility of the measure itself, he differed with him as to the mode of proceeding, and a long discussion (in which sir H. Burrard took a part) followed the opening of Kellerman's mission. Sir Arthur's first objection was, that, in point of form, Kellerman was merely entitled to negotiate a cessation of hostilities. But sir Hew Dalrymple judged, that as the good policy and the utility of the convention were recognised, it would be unwise to drive the French to the wall for the sake of a trivial ceremony. Wherefore the proposition was accepted, and the basis of a definitive treaty was arranged, subject, however, to the final approbation of sir Charles Cotton, without whose concurrence it was not to be binding.

Articles 1st and 2d declared the fact of the armistice, and provided for the mode of future proceedings.

Article 3d indicated the river Sizandre as the line of demarcation between the two armies. The position of Torres Vedras to be occupied by neither.

Article 4th. Sir Hew Dalrymple engaged to have the Portuguese included in the armistice, and their boundary line was to extend from Leria to Thomar.

Article 5th declared, that the French were not to be considered as prisoners of war, and that themselves and their property, public and private, were, without any detainder, to be transported to France. To this article sir Arthur objected, as affording a cover for the abstraction of Portuguese property. General Kellerman replied, that it was to be taken in its fair sense of property justly obtained; and upon this assurance it was admitted.

Article 6th provided for the protection of individuals. It guaranteed from political persecution all French residents, all subjects of powers in alliance with France, and all Portuguese who had served the invaders, or become obnoxious for their attachment to them.

Article 7th stipulated for the neutrality of the port of Lisbon as far as the Russian fleet was concerned. At first Kellerman proposed to have the Russian fleet guaranteed from capture, with leave to return to the Baltic; but this was peremptorily refused; and indeed the whole proceeding was designed to entangle the Russians in the French negotiation, that in case the armistice should be broken, the former might be forced into a co-operation with the latter.

Sir Arthur strenuously opposed this article: he argued, 1°, that the interests of the two nations were not blended, and that they stood in different relations towards the British army. 2°. That it was an important object to keep them separate, and that the French general, if pressed, would leave the Russians to their fate. 3°. That as the British operations had not been so rapid and decisive as to enable them to capture the fleet before the question of neutrality could be agitated, the right of the Russians to such protection was undoubted, and in the present circumstances it was desirable to grant it, because, independent of the chances of their final capture, they would be prevented from returning to the Baltic, which in fact constituted their only point of interest when disengaged from the French negotiation; but, that viewed as allies of the latter, they became of great weight. Lastly, that it was an affair which concerned the Portuguese, Russians, and British, but with which the French could have no right to interfere.

Sir Hew finding that the discussion of this question became lengthened, and considering that sir Charles Cotton alone could finally decide, admitted the article merely as a form, without acquiescing in the propriety of it.

Article 8th provided, that all guns of French calibre, and the horses of the cavalry, were to be likewise transported to France.

Article 9th stipulated, that forty-eight hours notice should be given of the rupture of the armistice.

To this article also sir Arthur objected; he considered it unnecessary for the interests of the British army, and favourable to the French, because if hostilities recommenced, the latter would have forty-eight hours to make arrangements for their defence, for the passage of the Tagus, and for the co-operation of the Russian fleet. Upon the other hand, sir Hew thought it was an absolute advantage to gain time for the preparations of the British army, and for the arrival of sir John Moore's reinforcements.

By an additional article it was provided, that all the fortresses held by the French, which had not capitulated before the 25th of August, should be given up to the British, and the basis of a convention being thus arranged, general Kellerman returned to his chief, and colonel George Murray was ordered to carry the proposed articles to the English admiral.

Previous to his landing, sir Hew had received none of the letters addressed to him by sir Arthur Wellesley, he had met with no person during his voyage from whom he could obtain authentic information of the state of affairs, and his time had been completely occupied since his arrival by the negotiations with Kellerman; he was consequently ignorant of many details of importance. The day after Kellerman's departure, don Bernardim Freire Andrada the Portuguese commander-in-chief, came to remonstrate against the armistice just concluded. Now, from the circumstances before-mentioned, it so happened that sir Hew was utterly ignorant of the existence of don Bernardim or his army at the time the armistice was discussed, and it was therefore difficult for him to manage this interview with propriety, because Andrada had some plausible, although no real ground of complaint. His remonstrances were, however, merely intended for the commencement of an intrigue, to which I shall hereafter revert.

Proceedings of the Court of Inquiry.

Colonel Murray soon reached the fleet, and presented the articles of convention to sir Charles Cotton, but the latter refused to concur therein, and declared that he would himself conduct a separate treaty for the Russian ships. With this answer colonel Murray returned on the 24th, having first, in reply to a question put by the French officer who accompanied him on board the Hibernia, declared that nothing had passed between him and sir Charles Cotton which ought to preclude further negotiation. Sir Hew Dalrymple was now urged by sir Arthur Wellesley to give notice, without further explanation, that hostilities would recommence, and to leave it to general Junot to renew propositions, if he chose to do so, separately from the Russians. But sir Hew felt himself in honour bound, by colonel Murray's observation to the French officer, not to take advantage of the occasion; and he likewise felt disinclined to relinquish a negotiation which, from certain circumstances, he deemed upon the point of being crowned with success. He therefore despatched colonel Murray to Lisbon, with directions, to inform Junot of the admiral's objection, and to give notice of the consequent rupture of the armistice, Murray himself being provided, however, with full powers to enter into and conclude a definitive treaty upon a fresh basis.

Ibid.

Procgs. Ct. of Inquiry.

The army was, at the same time, pushed forward to Ramalhal, and sir John Moore's troops commenced landing at Maceira Bay. When the order to repair to that place first reached them, a part had been already disembarked in the Mondego, and had to be re-shipped. This and contrary winds detained them for four days, and when they arrived at Maceira great difficulty was encountered, and some loss was sustained, in the getting of them ashore, an operation effected only by five days of incessant exertion on the part of the navy, for the boats were constantly swamped by the surf, and such was its fury that not more than thirty remained fit for service at the conclusion.

On the 27th, information was received from colonel Murray that a fresh treaty was in agitation upon an admissible basis. On the 28th, the army took a new position, a part occupying Torres Vedras, and the remainder being placed in the rear of that town.

Meanwhile in Lisbon the agitation of the public mind was excessively great, hope and fear were magnified by the obscurity of affairs, and the contradictory news which was spread by the French, and by those who held communication with the country, increased the anxious feelings of joy or grief almost to phrensy. Junot made every effort to engage admiral Siniavin in the negotiation, and the necessity by which the latter was forced to put his ships in a hostile and guarded attitude, contributed powerfully to control the populace, and to give strength to an opinion, industriously spread, that he would make common cause with the French. Siniavin had, however, no intention of this kind, and very early gave notice that he would treat separately.

The French, thus left to themselves, rested their hopes upon their own dexterity, and brought all the ordinary machinery of diplomatic subtlety into play. Among other schemes, Junot opened a separate communication with sir Hew Dalrymple at the moment when colonel Murray, invested with full powers, was engaged in daily conferences with general Kellerman, and the difficulty of coming to a conclusion was much increased by the natural sources of suspicion and jealousy incident to such a singular transaction, where two foreign nations were seen bargaining, and one of them honestly bargaining, for the goods and interests of a third, yet scarcely hinting even at the existence of the latter. The French were the weakest party, and having of course the most to dread, put forward claims which they knew could not be complied with, in order to preserve the vital questions untouched. On the other hand, the Portuguese leaders being relieved from all fear of a signal defeat, were loudly remonstrating against the terms of the convention, and taking advantage of the opportunity to attack some patroles of the French, passed the bounds of demarcation, and threatened the line of the Tagus by Santarem. This movement, and the breach of faith in attacking the patroles, were promptly and distinctly disavowed by sir Hew; but they kept suspicion awake, and the mutual misunderstandings arose at last to such a height, that Junot, seeming for a moment to recover all his natural energy, threatened to burn the public establishments, and to make his retreat good at the expense of the city; a menace which nothing could have prevented him from executing. Finally, however, a definitive treaty was concluded at Lisbon on the 30th, and soon afterwards ratified in form.

Vide Appendix, No. 10.

This celebrated convention, improperly called "of Cintra," consisted of twenty-two original, and three supplementary articles, upon the expediency of many of which, sir Arthur Wellesley and the commander-in-chief disagreed; but as their disagreement had reference to the details and not to the general principle, the historical importance is not sufficient to call for remark. An informality on the part of Junot caused some delay in the ratification of the instrument; but the British army marched notwithstanding to take up the position near Lisbon, assigned to it by the 11th article of the treaty.

On the march, sir Hew Dalrymple met two Russian officers, who were charged to open a separate negotiation for the Russian squadron. The British general refused to receive their credentials, and referred them to sir Charles Cotton. Baffled in this attempt to carry on a double treaty (for a naval one was already commenced), Siniavin, whose conduct appears to have been weak, was forced to come to a conclusion with the English admiral. At first he claimed the protection of a neutral port; but singly he possessed none of that weight which circumstances had given him before the convention with Junot, and his claim was answered by an intimation, that a British flag was flying on the forts at the mouth of the Tagus; and this was true, for the third and forty-second regiments, under the command of major-general Beresford, had landed and taken possession of them, in virtue of the convention, and the British colours were hoisted instead of the Portuguese. Foiled by this proceeding, the justice of which is somewhat doubtful, Siniavin finally agreed to surrender, upon the following terms:

1°. The Russian ships, with their sails, stores, &c. to be held by England, as a deposit, until six months after the conclusion of a peace between the two governments of the contracting parties.

2°. The admiral, officers, and seamen, without any restriction as to their future services, to be transported to Russia, at the expense of the British government.

Parliamentary Papers, 1809.

Two additional articles were, subsequently to the ratification of the original treaty, proposed by the Russians, and assented to by the English admiral. The first stipulated that the imperial flag should be displayed, even in the British harbours, as long as the Russian admiral remained on board. The second provided that the ships themselves and their stores should be delivered again at the appointed time, in the same state as when surrendered. The rights of the Portuguese were not referred to; but sir Charles Cotton individually was justified by his instructions in this breach of neutrality, for by them he was authorised to make prize of the Russian fleet, which thus suffered all the inconvenience of hostilities, and its commander the shame of striking his colours without having violated in any manner the relations of amity in which his nation stood with regard to the Portuguese. On the other hand, for the sake of a few old and decaying ships, the British government made an injudicious display of contempt for the independence of their ally, as, with singular inconsistency, they permitted the officers and crews, the real strength of the squadron, to return to the Baltic, although scarcely a year had elapsed since the national character was defiled to extinguish in that quarter the existence of a navy inimical to Great Britain.

Pary. Paps. 1809. Admiralty Instructions to sir C. Cotton, 16th April, 1808. Ibid. Mr. Welly. Pole to sir C. Cotton, 17th Sept. 1808.

This inconsistency belonged wholly to the ministers; for the two original articles of the treaty only were confirmed by them, and they were copied verbatim from the Admiralty instructions delivered to sir Charles Cotton four months previous to the transaction. Yet that officer, by the very men who had framed those instructions, was, with matchless inconsistency, rebuked, for having adopted a new principle of maritime surrender!

The 2d of September head-quarters were established at Oyeras. The right of the army occupied the forts at the mouth of the river, the left rested upon the heights of Bellas.

Thiebault.

Ibid.

The French army being concentrated in Lisbon, posted their piquets and guards as if in front of an enemy, and at night the sentries fired upon whoever approached their posts; the police disbanded of their own accord, and the city became a scene of turbulence, anarchy, and crime. Notwithstanding the presence of their enemies, the inhabitants of the capital testified their joy, and evinced their vengeful feelings in a remarkable manner; they refused to sell any provisions, or to deal in any manner with the French, they sung songs of triumph in their hearing, and in their sight fabricated thousands of small lamps for the avowed purpose of illuminating the streets at their departure. The doors of many of the houses occupied by the troops were marked in one night; men were observed bearing in their hats lists of Portuguese or Frenchmen designed for slaughter, and the quarters of Loison were threatened with a serious attack. Yet amidst all this disorder and violence, general Travot, and some others of the French army, fearlessly and safely traversed the streets, unguarded save by the reputation of their just and liberal conduct when in power; a fact extremely honourable to the

Portuguese, and conclusive of the misconduct of Loison. Junot himself was menaced by an assassin, but he treated the affair with magnanimity, and, in general, he was respected, although in a far less degree than Travot. The dread of an explosion, which would have compromised at once the safety of the French army and of the city, induced Junot to hasten the period when an English division was to occupy the citadel and take charge of the public tranquillity.

Emissaries from the junta of Oporto fomented the disposition of the populace to commit themselves by an attack upon the French; the convention was reprobated, and endeavours were fruitlessly made to turn the tide of indignation even against the English, as abettors of the invaders. The judge of the people, an energetic, but turbulent fellow, issued an inflammatory address calling for a suspension of the treaty, and designating the French as robbers and as insulters of religion. The Monteiro Mor, who commanded a rabble of peasantry which he dignified with the title of an army, had taken possession of the south bank of the Tagus, and from his quarters issued a protest against the convention, the execution of which he had the audacity to call upon sir Charles Cotton to interrupt. The latter sent his communications to sir Hew Dalrymple, who treated them with the contemptuous indignation they merited.

Sir John Hope being appointed the English commandant of Lisbon, took possession of the castle of Belem on the 10th, and of the citadel on the 12th, and, by his firm and vigorous conduct, soon reduced the effervescence of the public mind, and repressed the disorders which had arisen to a height that gave opportunity for the commission of any villany. The duke of Abrantes, with his staff, embarked the 13th. The first division of his army sailed the 15th, it was followed by the second and third divisions, and on the 30th all the French, except the garrisons of Elvas and Almeida, were out of Portugal.

Sir H. Dalrymple's Narrative. Court of Inquiry.

The execution of the convention had not been carried on thus far without much trouble and contestation. Lord Proby, the English commissioner appointed to carry the articles of the treaty into effect, was joined by major-general Beresford on the 5th, and their united labours were scarcely sufficient to meet the exigencies of a task in the prosecution of which disputes hourly arose. Anger, the cupidity of individuals, and opportunity, combined to push the French beyond the bounds of honour and decency, and several gross attempts were made to appropriate property which no interpretation of the stipulations could give a colour to; amongst the most odious were the abstraction of manuscripts and rare specimens of natural history from the national museum, and the invasion of the deposito publico, or funds of money awaiting legal decision for their final appropriation. Those dishonest attempts were met and checked with a strong hand, and at last a committee, consisting of an individual of each of the three nations, was appointed by the commissioners on both sides. Their office was to receive reclamations, to investigate them, and to do justice by seizing upon all contraband baggage embarked by the French. This measure was attended with excellent effect. It must, however, be observed, that the loud complaints and violence of the Portuguese, and the machinations of the bishop of Oporto, seem to have excited the suspicions of the British, and influenced their actions more than the real facts warranted; for the national character of the Portuguese was not then understood, nor the extent to which they supplied the place of true reports, by the fabrication of false ones, generally known. Writers have not been wanting to exaggerate the grounds of complaint. The English have imputed fraud, and evasions of the most dishonourable kind to the French, and the latter have retorted by accusations of gratuitous insult and breach of faith, asserting that their soldiers when on board the British ships were treated with cruelty in order to induce them to desert. It would be too much to affirm that all the error was on one side, but it does appear reasonable and consonant to justice to decide, that as the French were originally aggressors and acting for their own interest, and that the British were interfering for the protection of the Portuguese, any indecorous zeal upon the part of the latter, if not commendable, was certainly more excusable than in their opponents. Upon the ground of its being evidently impossible for him to know what was doing in his name, the British commissioners acquitted Junot of any personal impropriety of conduct, and his public orders, which denounced severe punishments for such malpractices, corroborated this testimony; yet Kellerman, in his communications with sir Hew Dalrymple, did not scruple to insinuate matter to the duke's disadvantage. But, amidst all these conflicting accusations, the British commander's personal good faith and scrupulous adherence to justice has never been called in question.

To define the exact extent to which each party should have pushed their claims is not an easy task; but an impartial investigator would begin by carefully separating the original rights of the French from those rights which they acquired by the convention. Much of the subsequent clamour in England against the authors of that treaty sprung from the error of confounding these essentially distinct grounds of argument. Conquest being the sole foundation of the first, defeat, if complete, extinguished them, if incomplete, nullified a part only. Now the issue of the appeal to arms not having been answerable to the justice of the cause, an agreement ensued, by which a part was sacrificed for the sake of the remainder, and upon the terms of that agreement the whole question of right hinges. If the French were not prisoners of war, it follows that they had not forfeited their claims founded on the right of conquest, but they were willing to exchange an insecure tenure of the whole for a secure tenure of a part. The difficulty consisted in defining exactly what was conceded, and what should be recovered from them. With respect to the latter, the restitution of plunder acquired anterior to the convention was clearly out of the question: if officially made, it was part of the rights bargained for, and if individually, to what tribunal could the innumerable claims which would follow such an article be referred? Abstract notions of right in such matters are misplaced. If an army surrenders at discretion, the victors may say with Brennus, "Woe to the vanquished;" but a convention implies some weakness, and must be weighed in the scales of prudence, not in those of justice.

CHAPTER VI

The interview that took place at Vimiero between don Bernardim Freire d'Andrada and sir Hew Dalrymple has been already noticed as the commencement of an intrigue of some consequence. The Portuguese general objected at the time to the armistice just concluded with Kellerman, ostensibly upon general grounds, but really, as it appeared, to sir Hew, because the bishop and junta of Oporto were not named in the instrument. At the desire of Freire, one Ayres Pinto de Souza was received at the English head-quarters as the protector of Portuguese interests during the subsequent negotiation. He was soon apprised that a treaty for a definitive convention was on foot, and both himself and his general were invited to state their views and wishes before any further steps were taken. Neither of them took any notice of this invitation, but when the treaty was concluded clamoured loudly against it.

The British army was, they said, an auxiliary force, and should only act as such; nevertheless it had assumed the right of treating with the French for Portuguese interests. A convention had been concluded which protected the enemy from the punishment due to his rapine and cruelty. It was more favourable than the strength of the relative parties warranted; no notice had been taken of the Portuguese government, or of the native army in the Alemtejo. Men who were obnoxious to their countrymen for having aided the invaders were protected from a just vengeance, and finally the fortresses were bargained for, as acquisitions appertaining to the British army; a circumstance which must inevitably excite great jealousy both in Portugal and Spain, and injure the general cause, by affording an opportunity for the French emissaries to create disunion among the allied nations. They dwelt upon the importance of the native forces, the strength of the insurrection, and insinuated that separate operations were likely to be carried on notwithstanding the treaty. Noble words often cover pitiful deeds: this remonstrance, apparently springing from the feelings of a patriot whose heart was ulcerated by the wrongs his country had sustained, was but a cloak for a miserable interested intrigue.

The bishop of Oporto, a meddling ambitious priest, had early conceived the project of placing himself at the head of the insurrectional authorities, and transferring the seat of government from Lisbon to Oporto. He was aware that he should encounter great opposition, and he hoped that by inveigling the English general to countenance these pretensions, he might, with the aid of Freire's force and his own influence, succeed in the object of his wishes. With this view he wrote a letter to sir Charles Cotton, dated the 4th of August, in which was enclosed (as the letter describes it) "The form of government with which they (the junta of Oporto) meant to govern Portugal when the city of Lisbon should be free from the French." This letter, together with its enclosure, being transmitted to sir Arthur Wellesley, he placed them among other public documents in the hands of sir Hew Dalrymple when the latter first landed at Maceira. In the document itself it was declared that "The body of government had taken the glorious resolution of restoring the Portuguese monarchy in all its extent, and of restoring the crown of Portugal to its lawful sovereign, don Juan VI., their prince, who was actually living in his estates of Brazil;" but this "glorious resolution" was burthened with many forms and restrictions; and although the junta professed the intention of restoring a regency, they provided, "that if this new regency should be interrupted by a new invasion of the French, (which God forbid!) or by *any other thing*, this government will immediately take the government on themselves, and exercise the authority and jurisdiction which it has done ever since its institution."

Thus prepared for some cabal, sir Hew Dalrymple was at no loss for an answer to Freire's remonstrance. He observed, that if the government of Portugal had not been mentioned in the treaty, neither had that of England nor that of France. The convention was purely military, and for the present concerned only the commanders in the field. With regard to the occupation of the fortresses, and the fact of the British army being an auxiliary force, the first was merely a measure of military precaution absolutely necessary, and the latter was in no way rendered doubtful by any act which had been committed; he sir Hew was instructed by his government to assist in restoring the prince regent of Portugal to his lawful rights, without any secret or interested motives; finally, the Portuguese general had been invited to assist in the negotiations, and if he had not done so, the blame rested with himself. And to this sir Hew might have justly added, that the conduct of Freire in withdrawing his troops at the most critical moment of the campaign, by no means entitled him to assume a high tone towards those whom he had so disgracefully deserted in the hour of danger.

The Portuguese general was silenced by this plain and decided answer; but the English general was quickly convinced that the bishop and his coadjutors, however incapable of conducting great affairs, were experienced plotters. In his first interview with Andrada, sir Hew Dalrymple had taken occasion to observe, that "no government lawfully representing the prince regent actually existed in Portugal." In fact, a junta, calling itself independent, was likewise established in Algarvé, and the members of the regency legally invested by the prince with supreme authority were dispersed, and part of them in the power of the French. This observation, so adverse to the prelate's views, was transmitted to him by Freire, together with a copy of the armistice. The junta were well aware that a definite convention, differing materially from the armistice, was upon the point of being concluded, and that the refusal of sir Charles Cotton to concur in the latter, had rendered it null and void; but preserving silence on that point, the bishop forwarded the copy of the armistice to the chevalier Da Souza, Portuguese minister in London, accompanied by a letter filled with invectives and misrepresentations of its provisions. The chevalier placed this letter with its inclosures, in the hands of Mr. Canning the English secretary of state for foreign affairs, and at the same time delivered to him an official note in which, adopting the style of the prelate and junta, he spoke of them as the representatives of his sovereign, and the possessors of the supreme power in Portugal.

But the efforts of the party were not confined to formal communications with the ministers; the daily press teemed with invectives against the English general's conduct, and ex-parte statements, founded on the provisions of an armistice that was never concluded, being thus palmed upon the public, (always hasty in judging of such matters), a prejudice against the convention was raised before either the terms of, or the events which led to it, were known. For, sir Hew, forgetting the ordinary forms of official intercourse, neglected to transmit information to his government until fifteen days after the commencement of the treaty, and the ministers, unable to contradict or explain any of Souza's assertions, were placed in a mortifying situation, by which their minds were irritated and disposed to take a prejudiced view of the real treaty. Meanwhile the bishop pretended to know nothing of the convention, hence the silence of Freire during the negotiations; but those once concluded, a clamour was, by the party, raised in Portugal, similar to that which they had already excited in England; and thus both nations appeared to be equally indignant at the conduct of the general, when, in fact, his proceedings were unknown to either.

Appendix, No. 11.

It would appear that the bishop had other than Portuguese coadjutors. The baron Von Decken, a Hanoverian officer, was appointed one of the military agents at Oporto: he was subject to sir Hew Dalrymple's orders, but as his mission was of a detached nature, he was also to communicate directly with the secretary of state in England. Von Decken arrived at Oporto upon the 17th August, and the same evening, in concert with the bishop, concocted a project admirably adapted to forward the views of the latter; they agreed that the prelate was the fittest person to be at the head of the government, and that as he could not, or pretended that he could not, quit Oporto, the seat of government ought to be transferred to that city. But two obstacles to this arrangement were foreseen; first, the prince regent at his departure had nominated a regency, and left full instructions for the filling up of vacancies arising from death or other causes; secondly, the people of Lisbon and of the southern provinces would certainly resist any plan for changing the seat of government. To obviate these difficulties, Von Decken wrote largely in commendation of the proposed arrangement, vilifying the conduct of the regency, and urging sir Hew not only to give his sanction to the ambitious project, but to employ the British troops in controlling the people of Lisbon should they attempt to frustrate the bishop's plans. To conciliate the members of the regency, it was proposed to admit a portion of them into the new government, and Francisco Noronha, Francisco da Cunha, the Monteiro Mor, and the principal Castro, were named as being the only men who were faithful to their sovereign. Now the last had accepted the office of ministre des cultes under the French, and was consequently unfaithful; but he was the brother of the bishop, Castro being legitimately born. Under the pretext of sparing the feelings of the people of Lisbon, it was further proposed to appoint a Portuguese commandant, subject to the British governor, but with a native force under his orders, to conduct all matters of police; and the bishop took the occasion to recommend a particular general for that office. Finally, civil dissension and all its attendant evils were foretold as the consequences of rejecting this plan.

Sir Hew Dalrymple's answer was peremptory and decisive. He reprimanded general Von Decken, and at once put an end to the bishop's hopes of support from the English army.

This second offence, for sir Hew's answer did not reach Oporto until after Freire's report had arrived there, completed the mortification of the bishop and the junta; they set no bounds to their violence. Efforts were made to stimulate the populace of Lisbon to attack not only the French but the English, in the hope that the terrible scene which must have ensued would effectually prevent the re-establishment of the old regency, and at the same time render the transfer of the seat of government to Oporto an easy task. Hence the outrageous conduct of the Monteiro Mor and of the judge of the people, and the former's insolent letter calling upon sir Charles Cotton to interrupt the execution of the convention.

The 3d of September, sir Hew Dalrymple received instructions from home relative to the formation of a new regency, which were completely at variance with the plan arranged between the bishop and general Von Decken, yet no difficulty attended the execution. Here, as in the case of prince Leopold, we are arrested by the singularity of the transaction. Is it likely that general Von Decken should plunge into such a delicate and important affair in one hour after his arrival at Oporto, if he had not been secretly authorised by some member of the English cabinet; and are we to seek for a clue to these mysteries in that shameful Machiavelian policy that soon afterwards forced lord Castlereagh to defend his public measures by a duel?

Appendix, No. 23.

The usual fate of plans laid by men more cunning than wise, attended the bishop of Oporto's projects; he was successful for a moment in rendering the convention of Cintra odious to the Portuguese, but the great mass of the people soon acknowledged with gratitude the services rendered them by the English, and rejoiced at the fulfilment of a treaty that freed their country at once from the invaders; and well might they rejoice when they beheld above twenty-five thousand bold and skilful soldiers reluctantly quitting the strong holds of the kingdom, and to the last maintaining the haughty air of an army unsubdued, and capable on the slightest provocation of resorting once more to the decision of battle.

Appendix, No. 12.

The Portuguese people were contented; but the Spanish general Galluzzo appears to have favoured the views of the Oporto faction. Detachments of his troops, and Portuguese refugees (principally from the northern provinces), commanded by a Spaniard, were acting in conjunction with the insurgents of the Alemtejo. Many disputes arose between the two nations, as I have already related, and the Spaniards treated Portugal as a conquered country, they denied the authority of the Portuguese general Leite, who was not of the bishop's party; they insulted him personally, seized his military chest at Campo Mayor, and in all things acted with the utmost violence and rapacity. Galluzzo himself was required by his own government to join the Spanish armies concentrating on the Ebro; but instead of obeying, he collected his forces near Elvas, and when he heard of the convention concluded at Lisbon, invested Fort Lalippe, and refused to permit the execution of the treaty relative to that impregnable fortress. Colonel Girod de Novillard commanded the French garrison, and profiting from its situation, had compelled the inhabitants of Elvas to shut their gates against the Spaniards, and to supply the fort daily with provisions. Galluzzo's proceedings were also manifestly absurd in a military point of view; his attacks were confined to a trifling bombardment of Lalippe from an immense distance, and the utmost damage sustained, or likely to be sustained by that fortress, was the knocking away the cornices and chimneys of the governor's house, every other part being protected by bomb proofs of the finest masonry.

Through lord Burghersh, who had been appointed to communicate with the Spanish troops in Portugal, Galluzzo was early in September officially informed of the articles of the convention, and also that the troops of his nation confined on board the hulks at Lisbon, were by that treaty released, and would be clothed and armed and sent to Catalonia. Upon the 5th of September, sir Hew Dalrymple wrote to the Spaniard, repeating the substance of the first communication, and requesting that his detachments might be withdrawn from the Alemtejo where they were living at the expense of the people. Galluzzo took no notice of either communication; he pretended that he had opened his fire against Lalippe before the date of the convention; that no third party had a right to interfere, and that he would grant no terms to the garrison, nor permit any but Portuguese to enter the fort. At this very moment the Spanish armies on the Ebro were languishing for cavalry, which he alone possessed; and his efforts were so despised by Girod that the latter made no secret of his intention, (if the fate of the French army at Lisbon should render such a step advisable), to blow up the works, and march openly through the midst of Galluzzo's troops.

Colonel Ross, with the 20th regiment, being appointed by sir Hew to receive the fort from colonel Girod, and to escort the garrison to Lisbon under the terms of the convention, sent a flag of truce to the French. Major Colborne, who carried it, was furnished with an autograph letter from Kellerman, and was received by Girod with civility; but the latter refused to surrender his post without more complete proof of the authenticity of the treaty; and with the view of acquiring that, he proposed that a French officer should proceed to Lisbon to verify the information; not that he affected to doubt the truth of Colborne's information, but that he would not surrender his charge while the slightest doubt, capable of being removed, was attached to the transaction; and so acting he did well, and like a good soldier.

Appendix, No. 12.

General Dearey, who commanded the investing force, was persuaded to grant a truce for six days, to give time for the journey of the officers appointed to go to Lisbon; but on their return it was not without great difficulty and delay that they were permitted to communicate with colonel Girod, and no argument could prevail upon the obstinate Galluzzo to relinquish the siege. After a warm intercourse of letters, sir Hew Dalrymple was forced to order sir John Hope to advance to Estremos with a considerable body of troops, for the purpose of giving weight to his remonstrances, or, if pushed to extremity, of forcing the Spaniard to desist from his unwarrantable pretensions. It must be observed that Galluzzo was not only putting aside the convention by which he profited himself, but also violating the independence of the Portuguese who desired his absence from their territory; and he was likewise setting at naught the authority of his own government, for the army of Estremadura pretended to act under the orders of the junta of Seville: and Laguna, an accredited agent of that junta, was at this moment receiving from sir Hew Dalrymple the Spanish prisoners liberated by the effect of the convention, together with money, arms, &c., to prepare them for immediate service in Catalonia, whither they were also to be transported in British vessels. One more effort was however made to persuade this intractable man to submit to reason, before recourse was had to violent measures which must have produced infinite evil. Colonel Graham repaired upon the 25th of September to Badajos, and his arguments being backed up by the near approach of the powerful division under Hope, were successful, and this troublesome affair ended in an amicable manner.

Appendix to col. De Bosset's Parga, p. 134.

Thiebault.

Colonel Girod evacuated the forts, and his garrison proceeded to Lisbon, attended by the 52d regiment as an escort. The rival troops agreed very well together, striving to out-do each other by the vigour and the military order of their marches; but the Swiss and French soldiers did not accord, and many of the latter wished to desert. At Lisbon the whole were immediately embarked; but the transports being detained for some time in the river, major de Bosset, an officer of the Chasseurs Britanniques, contrived to persuade near a thousand of the men to desert, who were afterwards received into the British service. Girod de Novillard complained of this as a breach of the convention, and it must be confessed that it was an equivocal act, yet one common to all armies, and if done simply by persuasion, very excusable.

The garrison of Almeida surrendered that fortress without any delay, and being marched to Oporto, were proceeding to embark, when the populace rose and would have slain them if great exertions had not been made by the British officers to prevent such a disgraceful breach of faith. The escort was weak, but resolute to sustain the honour of their nation, by firing upon the multitude if the circumstances became desperate. Nevertheless several of the French soldiers were assassinated, and in spite of every effort the baggage was landed, and the whole plundered; the excuse being that church plate was to be found amongst it, an accusation easily made, difficult to be disproved to the satisfaction of a violent mob, and likely enough to be true.

This tumult gives scope for reflection upon the facility with which men adapt themselves to circumstances, and regulate their most furious passions, by the scale of self-interest. In Oporto, the suffering, in consequence of the invasion, was trifling compared to the misery endured in Lisbon; yet the inhabitants of the former were much more outrageous in their anger. In Lisbon, the very persons who had inflicted the worst evils upon the people were daily exposed, more or less, to violence, yet suffered none; while in Oporto it was with extreme difficulty that men, until that moment unseen of the multitude, were rescued from their frantic revenge. In both cases fear regulated the degree of hatred shown, and we may conclude from hence, that national insurrections however spontaneous and vehement, if the result of hatred only, will never successfully resist an organized force, unless the mechanical courage of discipline be grafted upon the first enthusiasm.

While the vexatious correspondence with Galluzzo was going on, sir Hew Dalrymple renewed his intercourse with Castaños, and prepared to prosecute the war in Spain. The Spanish prisoners, about four thousand in number, were sent to Catalonia; and the British army was cantoned principally in the Alemtejo along the road to Badajos, but some officers were despatched to examine the roads through Beira with a view to a movement on that line; and general Anstruther was directed to repair to the fortress of Almeida, for the purpose of regulating every thing which might concern the passage of the army, if it should be found necessary to enter Spain by that route. Lord William Bentinck was also despatched to Madrid, having instructions to communicate with the Spanish generals and with the central junta, and to arrange with them the best line of march, the mode of providing magazines, and the plan of campaign. But in the midst of these affairs, and before the garrison of Elvas arrived at Lisbon, sir Hew Dalrymple was called home to answer for his conduct relative to the convention. The command then devolved upon sir Harry Burrard, but after holding it for a few days he also returned to England, there to abide the fury of the most outrageous and disgraceful public clamour that was ever excited by the falsehoods of base and venal political writers.

The editors of the daily press adopting all the misrepresentations of the Portuguese minister, and concluding that the silence of government was the consequence of its dissatisfaction at the convention, broke forth with such a torrent of rabid malevolence, that all feelings of right and justice were overborne, and the voice of truth stifled by their obstreperous cry. Many of the public papers were printed with mourning lines around the text which related to Portuguese affairs; all called for punishment, and some even talked of death to the guilty, before it was possible to know if any crime had been committed; the infamy of the convention was the universal subject of conversation, a general madness seemed to have seized all classes, and, like the Athenians after the sea fight of Arginusæ, the English people if their laws would have permitted the exploit, were ready to condemn their generals to death for having gained a victory!

A court of inquiry was assembled at Chelsea to inquire into the transactions relating to the armistice and the definite convention. Sir Arthur Wellesley, sir Harry Burrard, sir Hew Dalrymple, and the principal generals engaged at Vimiero, were called before it. A minute investigation of all the circumstances took place, and a detailed report was made by the board; at the end of which, it was stated that no further judicial measures seemed to be called for. This report was not satisfactory to the government, and the members of the court were required to state individually whether they approved or disapproved of the armistice and convention. It then appeared that four approved, and three disapproved, of the convention. Among the latter the earl of Moira distinguished himself by a laboured criticism, which, however, left the pith of the question entirely untouched. The proceedings of the board were dispassionate and impartial but the report was not luminous; a circumstance to be regretted, because the rank and reputation of the members were sufficiently great to secure them from the revenge of party, and no set of men were ever more favourably placed for giving a severe and just rebuke to popular injustice.

Thus ended the last act of the celebrated convention of Cintra, the very name of which will always be a signal record of the ignorant and ridiculous vehemence of the public feeling; for the armistice, the negotiations, the convention itself, and the execution of its provisions, were all commenced, conducted, and concluded, at the distance of thirty miles from Cintra, with which place they had not the slightest connexion, political, military, or local[14]!

OBSERVATIONS

RORIÇA.

1°. General Thiebault says, that the scattered state of the French army, in the beginning of August, rendered its situation desperate; but that the slowness of sir Arthur Wellesley saved it. Others again have accused the latter of rashness and temerity. Neither of these censures appear to be well founded. It is true that Junot's army was disseminated; but to beat an army in detail, a general must be perfectly acquainted with the country he is to act in, well informed of his adversary's movements, and rapid in his own.

Now rapidity in war depends as much upon the experience of the troops as upon the energy of the chief; and the English army was raw, the staff and commissariat mere novices, the artillery scantily and badly horsed, few baggage or draft animals were to be obtained in the country, and there were only a hundred and eighty cavalry mounted. Such impediments are not to be removed in a moment, and therein lies the difference betwixt theory and practice, between criticism and execution.

2°. To disembark the army without waiting for the reinforcements was a bold but not a rash measure. Sir Arthur Wellesley knew that the French troops were very much scattered, although he was not aware of the exact situation of each division, and from the bishop of Oporto's promises, he had reason to expect good assistance from the Portuguese, who would have been discouraged if he had not landed at once. Weighing these circumstances he was justified in disembarking his troops, and the event proved that he was right, for he had full time to prepare his army, his marches were methodical, and he was superior in numbers to his enemy in each battle. His plans were characterized by a due mixture of enterprise and caution well adapted to his own force, and yet capable of being enlarged without inconvenience when the reinforcement should arrive.

3°. In the action of Roriça there was a great deal to admire, and some grounds for animadversion. The movement against Laborde's first position was well conceived and executed; but the subsequent attack against the heights of Zambugeira was undoubtedly faulty. The march of Ferguson's and Trant's divisions would have dislodged Laborde from that strong ridge without any attack on the front. It is said that such was sir Arthur's project; but that some mistake in the orders caused general Ferguson to alter the direction of his march from the flank to the centre; this if true, does not excuse the error; because the commander-in-chief being present at the attack in front, might have restrained it until Ferguson had recovered the right direction. It is more probable that sir Arthur did not expect any very vigorous resistance, and wishing to press the French in their retreat pushed on the action too fast, and Laborde, who was unquestionably no ordinary general, made the most of both time and circumstances.

4°. Towards the close of the day when the French had decidedly taken to the mountains, the line of Loison's march was in the power of the English general. If he had sent two thousand men in pursuit of Laborde, left one thousand to protect the field of battle, and with the remaining ten thousand marched against Loison, whose advanced guard could not have been far off; it is probable that the latter would have been surprised and totally defeated, and at all events he could only have saved himself by a hasty retreat, which would have broken Junot's combinations and scattered his army in all directions.

5°. Sir Arthur Wellesley marched to Lourinham to cover the immediate disembarkation of his reinforcements and stores, and this was prudent, because a south-west wind would in one night have sent half the fleet on shore in a surf unequalled for fury; and such was the difficulty of a disembarkation, that a detachment from the garrison of Peniché would have sufficed to frustrate it. The existence of a French reserve estimated by report at four thousand men, was known; but its situation was unknown, and it might have been on the coast line; hence great danger to Anstruther if he attempted a landing without being covered, greater still if he remained at sea. The reasons then for the march to Lourinham were cogent, and perhaps outweighed the advantages of attacking Loison; but it seems to have been an error not to have occupied Torres Vedras on the 18th; as the disembarkation of Anstruther's force would have been equally secured, while the junction of the French army, and the consequent battle of Vimiero would have been prevented.

6°. It is an agreeable task to render a just tribute of applause to the conduct of a gallant although unsuccessful enemy; and there is no danger of incurring the imputation of ostentatious liberality in asserting that Laborde's operations were exquisite specimens of the art of war. The free and confident manner in which he felt for his enemy, the occupation of Brilos, Obidos, and Roriça in succession, by which he delayed the final moment of battle, and gained time for Loison; the judgment and nice calculation with which he maintained the position of Roriça, and the obstinacy with which he defended the heights of Zambugeira, were all proofs of a consummate knowledge of war and a facility of command rarely attained.

Sir A. Wellesley's evidence. Court of Inquiry.

7°. Sir Arthur Wellesley estimated Laborde's numbers at six thousand men, and his estimation was corroborated by the information gained from a wounded French officer during the action. It is possible that at Alcobaça they might have been so many, but I have thought it safer to rate them at five thousand, for the following reasons: first, it is at all times very difficult to judge of an enemy's force by the eye, and it is nearly impossible to do so correctly when he is skilfully posted, and as in the present case, desirous of appearing stronger than he really was; secondly, the six hundred men sent on the 14th to Peniché, and three companies employed on the 16th and 17th to keep open the communication with Loison by Bombaral, Cadaval, and Segura must be deducted; thirdly, Laborde himself after the convention, positively denied that he had so many as six thousand. General Thiebault indeed says, that only one thousand nine hundred were present under arms;

but this assertion is certainly inaccurate, and very injurious to the credit of general Laborde, because it casts ridicule upon a really glorious deed of arms. It is surprising that a well-informed and able writer should disfigure an excellent work by such trifling.

VIMIERO.

1°. The battle of Vimiero was merely a short combat, but it led to important results because Junot was unable to comprehend the advantages of his situation. Profitable lessons may however be drawn from every occurrence in war, and Vimiero is not deficient in good subjects for military speculation.

2°. To many officers the position of the British appeared weak from its extent, and dangerous from its proximity to the sea, into which the army must have been driven if defeated. The last objection is well founded, and suggests the reflection that it is unsafe to neglect the principles of the art even for a moment. The ground having been occupied merely as a temporary post, without any view to fighting a battle, the line of retreat by Lourinham was for the sake of a trifling convenience left uncovered a few hours. The accidental arrival of sir Harry Burrard arrested the advanced movement projected by sir Arthur Wellesley for the 21st, and in the mean time Junot took the lead, and had he been successful upon the left, there would have been no retreat for the British army.

3°. The extent of the position at Vimiero, although considerable to a small army, was no cause of weakness, because the line of communication from the right to the left was much shorter and much easier for the British defence than it was for the French attack, and the centre was very strong and perfectly covered the movement of the right wing. Sir Arthur, when he placed the bulk of the combatants in that quarter, did all that was possible to remedy the only real defect in his position, that of having no line of retreat.

4°. The project of seizing Torres Vedras and Mafra at the close of the battle, was one of those prompt daring conceptions that distinguish great generals, and it is absurd to blame sir Harry Burrard for not adopting it. Men are not gifted alike, and even if the latter had not been confirmed in his view of the matter by the advice of his staff, there was in the actual situation of affairs ample scope for doubt; the facility of executing sir Arthur's plan was not so apparent on the field of battle as it may be in the closet. The French cavalry was numerous, unharmed, and full of spirit. Upon the distant heights behind Junot's army, a fresh body of infantry had been discovered by general Spencer, and the nature of the country prevented any accurate judgment of its strength being formed. The gun carriages of the British army were very much shaken, and they were so badly and so scantily horsed, that doubts were entertained if they could keep up with the infantry in a long march. The commissariat was in great confusion, and the natives, as we have seen, were flying with the country transport. The Portuguese troops gave no promise of utility, and the English cavalry was destroyed. To overcome obstacles in the pursuit of a great object is the proof of a lofty genius; but the single fact that a man of sir George Murray's acknowledged abilities was opposed to the attempt, at once exonerates sir Harry Burrard's conduct from censure, and places the vigour of sir Arthur Wellesley's in the strongest light. It was doubtless ill-judged of the former (aware as he was of the ephemeral nature of his command) to interfere at all with the dispositions of a general who was in the full career of victory, and whose superior talents and experience were well known; but it excites indignation to find a brave and honourable veteran borne to the earth as a criminal, and assailed by the most puerile shallow writers, merely because his mind was not of the highest class. Sir Arthur Wellesley himself was the first to declare before the court of inquiry that sir Harry Burrard had decided upon fair military reasons.

GENERAL PLAN OF THE CAMPAIGN.

1°. Although double lines of operation are generally disadvantageous and opposed to sound principles, the expediency of landing sir John Moore's troops at the mouth of the Mondego, and pushing them forward to Santarem, was unquestionable, and unless the probable consequences of such a movement are taken into consideration, sir Arthur Wellesley's foresight cannot be justly appreciated.

Lisbon, situated near the end of the tongue of land lying between the sea-coast and the Tagus, is defended to the northward by vast mountains, that rising in successive and nearly parallel ranges, end abruptly in a line extending from Torres Vedras to Alhandra on the Tagus. As these ridges can only be passed at certain points by an army, the intersections of the different roads form so many strong positions.

The great mass of the Monte Junto appears to lead perpendicularly on to the centre of the first ridge; but stopping short at a few miles distance, sends a rugged shoot called the Sierra de Barragueda in a slanting direction towards Torres Vedras, from which it is only divided by a deep defile.

From this conformation it results, that an army marching from the Mondego to Lisbon, must either pass behind the Monte Junto, and follow the line of the Tagus, or keeping the western side of that mountain, come upon the position of Torres Vedras.

If sir Arthur Wellesley had adopted the first line of operations, his subsistence must have been drawn by convoys from the Mondego, the enemy's numerous cavalry would have cut his communications, and in that state he would have had to retreat, or to force the positions of Alhandra, Alverca, and finally the heights of Bellas, a strong position the right flank of which was covered by the creek of Saccavem, and the left flank by the impassable Sierra dos Infiernos. On the other line Torres Vedras was to be carried, and then Mafra or Montechique, following the direction of Junot's retreat. If Mafra was forced (and neither it nor Montechique could be turned), a line of march, by Cassim and Quelus, upon Lisbon would have been opened to the victors; but that route, besides being longer than the road through Montechique and Loures, would, while it led the English army equally away from the fleet, have entangled it among the fortresses of Ereceira, Sant Antonio, Cascaes, St. Julians, and Belem. Again, supposing the position of Montechique to be stormed, the heights of Bellas offered a third line of defence, and lastly, the citadel and forts of Lisbon itself would have sufficed to cover the passage of the river, and a retreat upon Elvas would have been secure.

Thus it is certain, that difficulties of the most serious nature awaited the English army while acting on a single line of operations; and the double line proposed by sir Arthur was strictly scientific. For if sir John Moore, disembarking at the Mondego, had marched first to Santarem and then to Saccavem, he would have turned the positions of Torres Vedras and Montechique, and then sir Arthur on the other side would have turned the heights of Bellas by the road of Quelus. Junot's central situation could not in this case have availed him, because the distance between the British corps would be more than a day's march, and their near approach to Lisbon would have caused an insurrection of the populace. The duke of Abrantes must either have abandoned that capital and fallen vigorously upon sir John Moore, with a view to overwhelm him and gain Almeida or Elvas, or he must have concentrated his forces, and been prepared to cross the Tagus if he lost a battle in front of Lisbon. In the first case, the strength of the country afforded Moore every facility for a successful resistance, and sir Arthur's corps would have quickly arrived upon the rear of the French. In the second case, Junot would have had to fight superior numbers, with an inveterate populace in his rear, and if, fearing the result of such an encounter he had crossed the Tagus, and pushed for Elvas, sir John Moore's division could likewise have crossed the river, and harassed the French in their retreat.

Captain Poulteney Malcolm's Evidence. Court of Inquiry.

2º. The above reasoning being correct, it follows, that to re-embark sir John Moore's army after it had landed at the Mondego, and to bring it down to Maceira bay, was an error which (no convention intervening) might have proved fatal to the success of the campaign. This error was rendered more important by the danger incurred from the passage; for, as the transports were not sea-worthy, the greatest part would have perished had a gale of wind come on from the south-west.

3°. Sir Arthur Wellesley's project of seizing Mafra by a rapid march on the morning of the 21st, was exceedingly bold; its successful execution would have obliged Junot to make a hurried retreat by Enxara dos Cavalleiros to Montechique, at the risk of being attacked in flank during his march; or if he had moved by the longer route of Ruña and Sobral, it is scarcely to be doubted that the British army would have reached Lisbon before the French. But was it possible so to deceive an enemy inured to warfare, as to gain ten miles in a march of sixteen? was it possible to evade the vigilance of an experienced general, who, being posted only nine miles off, possessed a formidable cavalry, the efforts of which could neither be checked nor interrupted by the small escort of horse in the British camp? was it in fine possible, to avoid a defeat during a flank march along a road crossed and interrupted by a river and several deep gullies, which formed the beds of mountain torrents? These are questions which naturally occur to every military man. The sticklers for a rigid adherence to system would probably decide in the negative. Sir Arthur Wellesley was however, not only prepared to try at the time, but he afterwards deliberately affirmed that, under certain circumstances of ground an operation of that kind would succeed; and to investigate such questions is the best study for an officer.

4°. A night march is the most obvious mode of effecting such an enterprise, but not always the best in circumstances where expedition is required; and great generals have usually preferred the day-time, trusting to their own skill in deceiving the enemy while their army made a forced march to gain the object in view. Thus, Turenne at Landsberg was successful against the archduke Leopold in broad daylight, and Cæsar in a more remarkable manner overreached Afranius and Petrieus near Lerida. Nor were the circumstances at Vimiero unfavourable to sir Arthur Wellesley. He might have pushed a select corps of light troops, his cavalry, the marines of the fleet, the Portuguese auxiliaries, and a few field pieces, to the entrance of the defile of Torres Vedras before daybreak, with orders to engage the French outposts briskly, and to make demonstrations as for a general attack. There is no doubt that such a movement if skilfully conducted, would have completely occupied the enemy's attention, while the main body of the army marching in great coats, and hiding the glitter of their arms, might have profited from the woods and hollows through which the by-road to Mafra led, and gained such a start as would have insured the success of the enterprise.

Let us, however, take a view of the other side; let us suppose that Junot, instructed by his spies and patroles, or divining the intention of the British general, held the masking division in check with a small force, and carrying the remainder of his army by the Puente de Roll, or some other cross road (and there were several) against the flank of the English, had fallen upon the latter while in march, hemmed in as they would be between the sea and the mountains, and entangled among hollows and torrents. What then would have been the result? History answers, by pointing to Condé and the battle of Senef. It must however be confessed, that it could be no ordinary general that conceived such a project, and, notwithstanding the small numbers of the opposing armies, success would have ranked sir Arthur high among the eminent commanders of the world, if he had never performed any other exploit. "The statue of Hercules, cast by Lysippus, although only a foot high, expressed," says Pliny, "the muscles and bones of the hero more grandly than the colossal figures of other artists."

5º. So many circumstances combine to sway the judgment of an officer in the field which do not afterwards appear of weight, that caution should always be the motto of those who censure the conduct of an unfortunate commander; nevertheless, the duke of Abrantes' faults, during this campaign, were too glaring to be mistaken. He lingered too long at Lisbon; he was undecided in his plans; he divided his army unnecessarily; and he discovered no skill on the field of battle. The English army having landed affairs were brought to a crisis, and Junot had only two points to consider. Could the French forces under his command defend Portugal without assistance? and if not, how were its operations to be made most available for furthering Napoleon's general plans against the Peninsula? The first point could not be ascertained until a battle with sir Arthur had been tried. The second evidently required that Junot should keep his army concentrated, preserve the power of retreating into Spain, and endeavour to engage the British troops in the sieges of Elvas and Almeida. If the two plans had been incompatible, the last was certainly preferable to the chance of battle in a country universally hostile. But the two plans were not incompatible.

6º. The pivot of Junot's movements was Lisbon; he had therefore to consider how he might best fall upon and overthrow the English army, without resigning the capital to the Portuguese insurgents during the operation. He could not hope to accomplish the first effectually without using the great mass of his forces, nor to avoid the last except by skilful management, and the utmost rapidity. Now the citadel and forts about Lisbon were sufficiently strong to enable a small part of the French army to control the populace, and to resist the insurgents of the Alemtejo for a few days. The Russian admiral, although not hostile to the Portuguese, or favourable to the French, was forced by his fear of the English, to preserve a guarded attitude, and in point of fact, did materially contribute to awe the multitude, who could not but look upon him as an enemy. The Portuguese ships of war which had been fitted out by Junot, were floating fortresses requiring scarcely any garrisons, and yet efficient instruments to control the city, without ceasing to be receptacles for the Spanish prisoners, and safe depôts for powder and arms which might otherwise have fallen into the power of the populace. Wherefore, instead of delaying so long in the capital, instead of troubling himself about the assemblage of Alcacer do Sal, instead of detaching Laborde with a weak division to cover the march of Loison; Junot should have taken the most vigorous resolutions in respect to Lisbon the moment he heard of the English descent. He should have abandoned the left bank of the Tagus, with the exception of Palmela and the Bugio, which were necessary to the safety of his shipping; he should have seized upon the principal families of the capital as hostages for the good behaviour of the rest; and he should have threatened and been prepared to bombard the city if refractory; then leaving nothing more than the mere garrisons of the citadel, forts, and ships behind him, have proceeded, not to Leria, which was too near the enemy to be a secure point of junction with Loison, but to Santarem, where both corps might have been united without danger and without fatigue. General Thomieres, in the mean time, putting a small garrison in Peniché, could have watched the movement of the British general, and thus from eighteen to twenty thousand men would have been assembled at Santarem by the 13th at farthest, and from thence one march would have brought the whole to Batalha, near which place the lot of battle might have been drawn without trembling.

7°. If it proved unfavourable to the French, the ulterior object of renewing the campaign on the frontier was in no manner compromised. The number of large boats that Lisbon can always furnish, would have sufficed to transport the beaten army over the Tagus from Santarem in a few hours, especially if the stores had been embarked before Junot moved towards Batalha, and the French army, once in the Alemtejo with a good garrison in Abrantes, could not have been followed until the forts at the mouth of the Tagus were reduced, and the fleet sheltered in the river. Thus, long before the British could have appeared in force in the Alemtejo, the fortress of Elvas would have been provisioned from the magazines collected by Loison after the battle of Evora, and the campaign could have been easily prolonged until the great French army, coming from Germany crushed all opposition.

The above is not a theory broached after the event. That Junot would attempt something of the kind, was the data upon which the English general formed his plans; the intercepted memoir of colonel Bory de St. Vincent, treated such an operation as a matter of course, and Junot's threats during the negotiation prove that he was not ignorant of his own resources; but his mind was depressed, and his desponding mood was palpable to those around him. It is a curious fact, that Sattaro, the Portuguese agent, who, for some purpose or other was in the British camp, told sir Arthur Wellesley before the battle of Vimiero, that Junot would willingly evacuate Portugal upon terms.

Thiebault.

8°. When the French, being fourteen thousand in number, occupied Torres Vedras, that position was nearly impregnable. Seventeen thousand British could scarcely have carried it by force; but they might have turned it in a single march by the coast road; yet Junot neither placed a detachment on that side nor kept a vigilant watch by his patroles. Now, if sir Arthur Wellesley's intended movement had not been arrested by orders from Burrard, it must have succeeded, because Junot was entangled in the defiles of Torres Vedras from six o'clock in the evening of the 20th, until late in the morning of the 21st. The two armies would thus have changed camps in the space of a few hours without firing a shot: Junot would have lost Lisbon, and have been placed in the most ridiculous situation.

9°. In the battle, the duke of Abrantes showed great courage, but no talent. His army was inferior in numbers, yet he formed two separate attacks, an evident error that enabled sir Arthur to beat him in detail without difficulty. And it was the less excusable, because the comparatively easy nature of the ground over which the road from Torres Vedras to Lourinham led, and the manner in which the English army was heaped to the right when the position first opened to the view of the French general, plainly indicated the true line of attack. Junot should, with all his forces concentrated for one effort, have fallen in upon the left of his opponent's position; if victorious, the sea would have swallowed those who escaped his sword. If repulsed, his retreat was open, and his loss could not have been so great in a well-conducted single effort, as it was in the ill-digested, unconnected attacks that took place.

10°. The rapidity with which the French soldiers rallied, and recovered their order after such a severe check, was admirable, but their habitual method of attacking in column cannot be praised. Against the Austrians, Russians, and Prussians, it may have been successful, but against the British it must always fail, because the English infantry is sufficiently firm, intelligent, and well disciplined, to wait calmly in lines for the adverse masses, and sufficiently bold to close upon them with the bayonet.

11°. The column is undoubtedly excellent for all movements short of the actual charge, but as the Macedonian phalanx was unable to resist the open formation of the Roman legion, so will the close column be unequal to sustain the fire and charge of a good line aided by artillery. The natural repugnance of men to trample on their own dead and wounded, the cries and groans of the latter, and the whistling of the cannon-shots as they tear open the ranks, produce the greatest disorder, especially in the centre of attacking columns, which, blinded by smoke, unstedfast of footing, and bewildered by words of command coming from a multitude of officers crowded together, can neither see what is taking place, nor make any effort to advance or retreat without increasing the confusion: no example of courage can be useful, no moral effect can be produced by the spirit of individuals, except upon the head, which is often firm, and even victorious at the moment when the rear is flying in terror. Nevertheless, well managed columns are the very soul of military operations; in them is the victory, and in them also is safety to be found after a defeat. The secret consists in knowing when and where to extend the front.

ARMISTICE. CONVENTION.

1°. It is surprising, that Junot having regained Torres Vedras, occupied Mafra, and obtained an armistice, did not profit by the terms of the latter to prepare for crossing the Tagus and establishing the war on the frontiers. Kellerman ascertained during his negotiation, that sir John Moore was not arrived; and it was clear, that until he did arrive the position of Montechique could neither be attacked nor turned. There was nothing in the armistice itself, nor the way in which it had been agreed to, which rendered it dishonourable to take such an advantage. The opening thus left for Junot to gain time, was sir Arthur Wellesley's principal objection to the preliminary treaty.

2°. With regard to the convention, although some of its provisions were objectionable in point of form, and others imprudently worded, yet taken as a whole, it was a transaction fraught with prudence and wisdom. Let it be examined upon fair military and political grounds; let it even be supposed for the sake of argument, that sir Arthur unimpeded by sir Harry Burrard, had pursued his own plan, and that Junot, cut off from Lisbon and the half of his forces had been driven upon the Tagus, he was still master of flying to Almeida or Elvas: the thousand men left in Santarem would have joined him in the Alemtejo, or fallen down to the capital; and what then would have been the advantages that could render the convention undesirable?

Proceedings of the Board of Inquiry.

Appendix, No. 22.

The British army, exclusive of sir John Moore's division, had only provisions, or transport for provisions, sufficient to last for ten or twelve days, and the fleet was the only resource when that supply should be exhausted. But a gale from any point between the southward and north-west, would have driven the ships away or have cast them on a lee-shore. Hence an indispensable preliminary measure would have been to open the mouth of the Tagus as a security for the fleet; but without occupying Cascaes, Bugio, and St. Julians, that was impossible. To take the last-named fort would have required ten days' open trenches at the least, and the heavy artillery must have been landed in some of the small creeks, and dragged by force of men over the mountains, because the artillery horses were scarcely able to draw the field guns, and the country was incapable of supplying assistance of that kind. In the mean time, the French troops in Lisbon, and those upon the heights of Almada and in the men-of-war, retiring tranquilly through the Alemtejo, would have united with Junot; or if he had fallen back upon Almeida, they could have retired upon Elvas and La-Lyppe. In this argument the Russians have not been considered, but whatever his secret wishes might have been, Siniavin must have joined the French or surrendered his squadron in a disgraceful manner. This would have increased Junot's force by six thousand men; and it may here be observed, that even after the arrival of sir John Moore, only twenty-five thousand British infantry were fit for duty.

Let it be supposed that the forts were taken, the English fleet in the river, the resources of Lisbon organized, and the battering guns and ammunition necessary for the siege of Elvas transported to Abrantes by water. Seventy miles of land remained to traverse, and then three months of arduous operations in the sickly season, and in the most pestilent of situations, would have been the certain consequences of any attempt to reduce that fortress. Did the difficulty end there? No! Almeida remained, and in the then state of the roads of Portugal, and taking into consideration only the certain and foreseen obstacles, it is not too much to say, that six months more would have been wasted before the country could be entirely freed from the invaders. But long before that period Napoleon's eagles would have soared over Lisbon again. The conclusion is inevitable; the convention was a great and solid advantage for the allies, a blunder on the part of the French.

With the momentary exception of Junot's threat to burn Lisbon if his terms were not complied with, we look in vain for any traces of that vigour which urged the march from Alcantara; we are astonished to perceive the man, who, in the teeth of an English fleet, in contempt of fourteen thousand Portuguese troops, and regardless of a population of three hundred thousand souls, dared, with a few hundred tired grenadiers, to seize upon Lisbon, so changed in half a year, so sunk in energy, that, with twenty-five thousand good soldiers, he declined a manly effort, and resorted to a convention to save an army which was really in very little danger. But such and so variable is the human mind, the momentary slave of every attraction, yet ultimately true to self-interest. When Junot entered Portugal, power, honours, fame, emolument, nay, even a throne, was within his reach, and toil and danger were overlooked in such gorgeous society; but when he proposed the convention he was only with the latter companions; fame flitted at a distance, and he easily persuaded himself that prudence and vigour could not be yoked together. A saying attributed to Napoleon perfectly describes the convention in a few words. "I was going to send Junot before a council of war, but, fortunately, the English tried their generals, and saved me the pain of punishing an old friend!"

BOOK III

CHAPTER I

The convention of Cintra being followed by the establishment of a regency at Lisbon, the plans of the bishop and junta of Oporto were disconcerted, and Portugal was restored to a state of comparative tranquillity; for the Portuguese people being of a simple character, when they found their country relieved from the presence of a French army, readily acknowledged the benefit derived from the convention, and refused to listen to the pernicious counsels of the factious prelate and his mischievous coadjutors.

Thus terminated what may be called the convulsive struggle of the Peninsular war. Up to that period a remarkable similarity of feeling and mode of acting betrayed the common origin of the Spanish and Portuguese people. A wild impatience of foreign aggression, extravagant pride, vain boasting, and a passionate reckless resentment, were common to both nations; but there the likeness ceased, and the finer marks of national character which had been impressed upon them by their different positions in the political world, became distinctly visible.

Spain, holding from time immemorial a high rank among the great powers, and more often an oppressor than oppressed, haughtily rejected all advice. Unconscious of her actual weakness and ignorance, and remembering only her former dignity, she ridiculously assumed an attitude which would scarcely have suited her in the days of Charles V.; while Portugal, always fearing the ambition of a powerful neighbour, and relying for safety as much upon her alliances as upon her own intrinsic strength, was from habit inclined to prudent calculation, and readily submitted to the direction of England. The turbulence of the first led to defeat and disaster; the docility and patience of the second were productive of the most beneficial results.

The difference between these nations was, however, not immediately perceptible, and at the period of the convention the Portuguese were despised, while a splendid triumph was anticipated for the Spaniards. It was affirmed and believed, that from every quarter enthusiastic multitudes of the latter were pressing forward to complete the destruction of a baffled and dispirited enemy; the vigour, the courage, the unmatched spring of Spanish patriotism, was in every man's mouth, and Napoleon's power and energy seemed weak in opposition. Few persons doubted the truth of such tales, and yet nothing could be more unsound, more eminently fallacious, than the generally-entertained opinion of French weakness and of Spanish strength. The resources of the former were unbounded, almost untouched; those of the latter were too slender even to support the weight of victory. In Spain the whole structure of society was shaken to pieces by the violence of an effort which merely awakened the slumbering strength of France: foresight, promptitude, arrangement, marked the proceedings of Napoleon; but with the Spaniards the counsels of prudence were punished as treason; and personal interests, every where springing up with incredible force, wrestled against the public good. At a distance, the insurrection appeared of towering proportions and mighty strength; but in truth it was a fantastic object, stained with blood, and tottering from weakness, and the helping hand of England alone was stretched forth for its support; all other assistance was denied, for the continental powers, although nourishing secret hopes of profit from the struggle, with calculating policy, turned coldly from the patriots' cause. The English cabinet was indeed sanguine, and resolute to act; but the ministers while anticipating success in a preposterous manner, displayed little industry and less judgment in their preparations for the struggle; nor does it appear that the real freedom of the Peninsula was much considered in their councils. They contemplated this astonishing insurrection, as a mere military opening through which Napoleon might be assailed, and they neglected, or rather feared, to look towards the great moral consequences of such a stupendous event, consequences which were in truth above their reach of policy. They were neither able nor willing to seize such a singularly propitious occasion for conferring a benefit upon mankind.

It is however certain, that this opportunity for restoring the civil strength of a long degraded people, by a direct recurrence to first principles, was such as had seldom been granted to a sinking nation. Enthusiasm was aroused without the withering curse of faction; and the multitude were ready to follow whoever chose to lead. The weight of ancient authority was, by a violent external shock, thrown off. The ruling power fell from the hands of the few, and was caught by the many, without the latter having thereby incurred the odium of rebellion, or excited the malice of mortified grandeur. There was nothing to deter the cautious, for there was nothing to pull down. The foundation of the social structure was laid bare, and all the materials were at hand for building a rare and noble monument of human genius and virtue. The architect alone was wanting. No anxiety to ameliorate the moral or physical condition of the people in the Peninsula was evinced by the ruling men of England, and if any existed amongst those of Spain, it evaporated in puerile abstract speculations. Napoleon indeed offered the blessing of regeneration in exchange for submission, but in that revolting form accompanied by the evils of war, it was rejected; and amidst the clamorous pursuit of national independence, the independence of man was trampled under foot. The mass of the Spanish nation, blinded by personal hatred, thought only of revenge. The leaders, arrogant and incapable, neither sought nor wished for any higher motive of action: without unity of design, devoid of arrangement, their policy was mean and personal, their military efforts were abortive, and a rude unscientific warfare disclosed at once the barbarous violence of Spanish character, and the utter decay of Spanish institutions.

After Joseph's retreat from Madrid, the insurrection of Spain may be said to have ceased; from that period it became a war between France and the Peninsula; the fate of the latter was intrusted to organised bodies of men, and as the first excitement subsided, and danger seemed to recede, all the meaner passions resumed their empire; but the transactions of that memorable period which intervened between the battles of Baylen and Coruña were exceedingly confused, and the history of them must necessarily partake somewhat of that confusion.

The establishment of a central supreme junta, the caprices of the Spanish generals, and their interminable disputes, the proceedings of the French army before the arrival of the emperor, the operations of the grand army after his arrival, and the campaign of the British auxiliary force, form so many distinct actions, connected it is true by one great catastrophe, yet each attended by a number of minor circumstances of no great historical importance taken separately, but when combined, showing the extent and complicated nature of the disease which destroyed the energy of Spain.

For the advantage of clearness therefore, it will be necessary to sacrifice chronological order; and as frequent reference must be made to the proceedings of a class of men whose interference had a decided, and in many cases a very disastrous influence upon the affairs of that period, I shall first give a brief account of the English agents, under which denomination both civil and military men were employed, but the distinction was rather nominal than real; for, generally speaking, each person assumed the right of acting in both capacities.

The envoy, Mr. Charles Stuart, was the chief of the civil agents; the persons subordinate to him were, Mr. Hunter, Mr. Duff, and others, consuls and vice-consuls.

Mr. Stuart sailed with sir A. Wellesley, and was left at Coruña when that officer touched there, previous to the operations in Portugal.

Mr. Hunter was stationed at Gihon in the Asturias.

Mr. Duff proceeded to Cadiz, and the others in like manner were employed at different ports. They were all empowered to distribute money, arms, and succours of clothing and ammunition: but the want of system and forethought in the cabinet was palpable from the injudicious zeal of the inferior agents, each of whom conceived himself competent to direct the whole of the political and military transactions. Mr. Stuart was even put to some trouble in establishing his right to control their proceedings.

The military agents were of two classes: those sent from England by the government, and those employed by the generals abroad.

Sir Thomas Dyer, assisted by major Roche and captain Patrick, proceeded to the Asturias. The last officer remained at Oviedo, near the junta of that province. Major Roche was sent to the head-quarters of Cuesta, and sir Thomas Dyer after collecting some information, returned to England.

Colonel Charles Doyle having organized the Spanish prisoners at Portsmouth, sailed with them to Coruña. He was accompanied by captain Carrol and captain Kennedy. During the passage a singular instance of turbulent impatience occurred: the prisoners, who had been released, armed, and clothed by England, and who had been as enthusiastic in their expressions of patriotism as the most sanguine could desire, mutinied, seized the transports, carried them into different ports in the Peninsula, disembarked, and proceeded each to his own home.

Colonel Browne was despatched to Oporto, and a major Green to Catalonia.

Those employed by the generals commanding armies were captain Whittingham, who was placed by sir Hew Dalrymple, near general Castaños, on the first appearance of the insurrection. He accompanied the head-quarters of the Andalusian army until the battle of Tudela put an end to his functions. Major Cox (appointed also by sir Hew Dalrymple) remained near the junta of Seville. The talents and prudent conduct of this officer were of great service. It would have been fortunate if all the persons employed as agents had acted with as much judgment and discretion. All the above named gentlemen were in full activity previous to the commencement of the campaign in Portugal.

When the convention of Cintra opened a way for operations in Spain, sir Hew Dalrymple sent lord William Bentinck to Madrid, that he might arrange a plan of co-operation with the Spanish generals, and transmit exact intelligence of the state of affairs. Such a mission was become indispensable. Up to the period of lord William's arrival in Madrid, the military intelligence received was very unsatisfactory. The letters from the armies contained abundance of commonplace expressions relative to the enthusiasm and patriotism visible in Spain. Vast plans were said to be under consideration, some in progress of execution, and complete success was confidently predicted; but, by some fatality, every project proved abortive or disastrous, without lowering the confidence of the prognosticators, or checking the mania for grand operations, which seemed to be the disease of the moment.

Sir H. Dalrymple's Papers. MS.

The English minister confirmed the appointment of lord William Bentinck, and at the same time re-organized the system of the military agents; by marking out certain districts and appointing a general officer to superintend each. Thus, major-general Broderick was sent to Gallicia. Major-general Leith, with a large staff, proceeded to the Asturias. Major-general Sontag went to Portugal. The scope of general Leith's mission was wide; Biscay, Castille, Leon, and even Catalonia were placed under his superintendence, and he appears to have had instructions to prepare the way for the disembarkation of an English army on the coast of Biscay. At the same time sir Robert Wilson was furnished with arms, ammunition, and clothing for organizing three or four thousand men levied by the bishop of Oporto. He took with him a large regimental staff, and a number of Portuguese refugees, and succeeded in forming a partizan corps, afterwards known by the title of the Lusitanian legion.

Brigadier-general Decken, a German, having been first destined for Spain, was countermanded at sea, and directed to Oporto, where he arrived on the 17th of August, and immediately commenced that curious intrigue which has been already mentioned in the campaign of Vimiero.

When sir John Moore assumed the command of the army, he sent colonel Graham to reside at the Spanish head-quarters on the Ebro, and directed lord William Bentinck to remain at Madrid to forward the arrangements for commencing the campaign. Lord William found in Mr. Stuart an able coadjutor, and in the letters of these two gentlemen, and the correspondence of major Coxe, then at Seville, is to be found the history of the evils which at this period afflicted unhappy Spain, and ruined her noble cause.

The power of distributing supplies, and the independent nature of their appointments, gave to those military agents immediately employed by the minister an extraordinary influence, and it was very injudiciously exercised. They forgot the real objects of their mission, and in many cases took a leading part in affairs with which it was not politic in them to have meddled at all.

Sir John Moore's Correspondence. MSS.

Whittingham's Letters. MS.

Colonel Doyle having left captain Kennedy at Coruña, and placed captain Carrol at the head-quarters of Blake's army, repaired in person to Madrid, where he was received with marked attention, and obtained the rank of a general officer in the Spanish service for himself, and that of lieutenant-colonel for captains Carrol and Kennedy. From colonel Doyle's letters it appears that he had a large share in conducting many important measures, such as the arrangement of a general plan of operations, and the formation of a central and supreme government. He seems to have attached himself principally to the duke of Infantado, a young man of moderate capacity, but with a strong predilection for those petty intrigues which constituted the policy of the Spanish court. Captain Whittingham gained the confidence of general Castaños to such a degree that he was employed by him to inspect the different Spanish corps on the Ebro early in September, and to report upon their state of efficiency previous to entering upon the execution of the plan laid down for the campaign. Notwithstanding the favourable position in which these officers stood, it does not appear that either of them obtained any clear idea of the relative strength of the contending forces, and their opinions, invariably and even extravagantly sanguine, were never borne out by the result.

Mr. Stuart's Letters. MS. Lord W. Bentinck's Letters. MS.

Appendix, No. 13. section 6.

The Spaniards were not slow to perceive the advantages of encouraging the vanity of inexperienced men who had the control of enormous supplies; but while all outward demonstrations of respect and confidence were by them lavished upon subordinate functionaries, and especially upon those who had accepted of rank in their service, the most strenuous exertions of lord William Bentinck and Mr. Stuart were insufficient to procure the adoption of a single beneficial measure, or even to establish the ordinary intercourse of official business.

Sir John Moore's Correspondence. MS.

The leading Spaniards wished to obtain a medium through which to create a false impression of the state of affairs, and thus to secure supplies and succours from England without being fettered in the application of them. The subordinate agents answered this purpose, and satisfied with their docility, the generals were far from encouraging the residence of more than one British agent at their head-quarters. Captain Birch, an intelligent engineer officer, writing from Blake's camp, says, "General Broderick is expected here; but I have understood that the appearance of a British general at these head-quarters to accompany the army might give jealousy. General Blake is not communicative, but captain Carrol appears to be on the best footing with him and his officers, and captain Carrol tells me that he informs him of more than he does any of his generals."

The object was perfectly accomplished; nothing could be more widely different than Spanish affairs, judged of by the tenor of the military agent's reports, and Spanish affairs when brought to the test of battle. The fault did not attach so much to the agents as to the ministers who selected them. It was difficult for inexperienced men to avoid the snare. Living with the chiefs of armies actually in the field, being in habits of daily intercourse with them, holding rank in the same service, and dependent upon their politeness for every convenience, the agent was in a manner forced to see as the general saw, and to report as he wished. A simple spy would have been far more efficacious!

Sir John Moore's Papers. MSS.

Sir John Moore, perceiving the evil tendency of such a system, recalled all those officers who were under his immediate control, and strongly recommended to ministers that only one channel of communication should exist between the Spanish authorities and the British army. He was convinced of the necessity of this measure, by observing, that each of the military agents considered the events passing under his own peculiar cognizance as the only occurrences of importance. Some of those officers even treated sir Hew Dalrymple and himself as persons commanding auxiliary bodies of men which might be moved, divided, and applied at the requisition of every inferior agent, and the forces of the British empire, a mere accessory aid, placed at their own disposal. Thus general Leith says: "Whatever may be the plan of operations, and whatever the result, I beg leave, in the strongest manner, to recommend to your consideration the great advantage of ordering all the disposable force of horse or car artillery, and light infantry, mounted on horses or mules of the country, without a moment's delay to move on Palencia, where the column or columns will receive such intelligence as may enable them to give the most effectual co-operation."

Captain Whittingham, at the same period, after mentioning the wish of general Castaños that some British cavalry should join him, says, "I cannot quit this subject without once more repeating, that the efforts of the cavalry will decide the fate of the campaign." And again: "Should it be possible for your excellency to send one thousand or fifteen hundred horse, the advantages that would result are incalculable." While one of these pressing recommendations came from Oviedo, the other from Tudela, colonel Doyle, writing from Madrid, thus expresses himself: "Certain it is, that if your army were here, the French would evacuate Spain before you got within a week's march of them; indeed, even the light cavalry and two thousand light troops sent on cars, to keep up with the cavalry, to show our friends the nature of outpost duty, would, I think, decide the question." — "A respectable corps of British troops, landed in Catalonia, would so impose, that I have no doubt of the good effects."

This last proposition relative to Catalonia was a favourite plan of all the leading men at Madrid; so certain were they of success on the Ebro, that finding no British force was likely to be granted for that purpose, they withdrew eight or nine thousand men from the army near Tudela, and directed them upon Lerida.

Thus much I have thought it necessary to relate about the agents, and now quitting that subject, I shall narrate

THE OPERATIONS OF THE SPANISH ARMIES IMMEDIATELY AFTER THE BATTLE OF BAYLEN

When that victory caused Joseph to abandon Madrid, the patriotic troops, guided by the caprice of the generals, moved in a variety of directions, without any fixed object in view, and without the slightest concert. Indeed all persons seemed to imagine that the war was at an end, and that rejoicing and triumph alone ought to occupy the minds of good Spaniards.

Cavallero.

The Murcian and Valencian army separated. General Llamas, with twelve thousand infantry, and a few cavalry, took the road to Madrid, and arrived there before any of the other generals. General St. Marc, a Fleming by birth, with greater propriety, carried the Valencians to the relief of Zaragoza. On the road he joined his forces with those of the baron de Versage, and the united troops, amounting to sixteen thousand, entered Zaragoza on the 15th, one day after Verdier and Lefebre had broken up the siege and retired to Tudela. The French left their heavy guns and many stores behind them. The Valencians and Arragonese pursued, and on the 19th their advanced guard overtook the retiring force, but were beaten by the French cavalry. On the 20th Lefebre abandoned Tudela and took a position at Milagro. On the 21st, St. Marc and Versage occupied Tudela. The peasantry of the valleys, encouraged by the approach of a regular army, and by the successful defence of Zaragoza, assembled on the left flank of the French, and threatened their communications. Meanwhile Palafox gave himself up to festivity and rejoicing, and did not even begin to repair the defences of Zaragoza until the end of the month. He assumed supreme authority, and in various ways discovered the most inordinate and foolish presumption; and among other acts he decreed that no Arragonese should henceforward be liable to the punishment of death for any crime.

Cox's Correspondence. MSS.

Whittingham's Correspondence. MSS.

The army of Andalusia was the most efficient body of men in arms throughout Spain: it contained thirty thousand regular troops, provided with a good train of artillery, and flushed with recent victory; but they were constrained to remain idle by the junta of Seville, who detained them to aid in asserting its own supremacy over the other juntas of Andalusia, and even brought back a part to Seville to assist in an ostentatious triumph. It was not until a full month after the capitulation of Dupont, that Castaños made his entry into the capital, at the head of a single division of seven thousand men, another of the same force being left at Toledo, and the rest of his army quartered at Puerto del Rey, St. Helena, and Carolina, in the Sierra Morena.

The infantry of the Estremaduran army was at first composed of new levies; but it was afterwards strengthened by the Walloon and royal guards, and sir Hew Dalrymple supplied general Galluzzo with every needful equipment. According to the stipulations of a treaty between the juntas of Seville and Badajos, the cavalry was to be placed under the command of Castaños; it was in number about four thousand, and with the exception of Cuesta, no other Spanish general possessed any efficient body of horsemen. Orders and entreaties, and even the intervention of sir Hew Dalrymple, were resorted to by the council of Castille, the generals and the military agents, to induce Galluzzo to send this body of cavalry forward to the capital; but he remained deaf to their representations, and occupied himself, as we have seen, in thwarting the execution of the convention of Cintra by a pretended siege of fort La Lippe.

Sir H. Dalrymple's papers. MS.

The Spanish captives, released by that treaty, were clothed, armed, and sent to Catalonia in British transports; and sir Hew Dalrymple, at the same time, forwarded ten thousand musquets, and ammunition in proportion, for the service of the Catalans.

Ibid.

Doyle's letters.

It has been before stated that one thousand five hundred Spaniards, commanded by the marquis of Valladeras, co-operated with the Portuguese during the campaign of Vimiero. But they never penetrated beyond Guarda, and being destitute of money, were reduced to great distress; they could not subsist where they were, nor yet march away. From this dilemma, sir Hew, by a timely advance of ten thousand dollars, relieved them, and Valladeras joined Blake. That general, after the defeat of Rio Seco, separated the Gallician army from the army commanded by Cuesta, and sheltered himself from the pursuit of Bessieres in the mountains behind Astorga. His reserve division had not been engaged in the battle, and the resources of the province, aided by the succours from England, were sufficient, to place him again at the head of thirty thousand infantry.

Mr. Stuart's Correspondence.

When Bessieres retreated after the defeat of Baylen, Blake occupied Leon, Astorga, and the pass of Mansanal: farther into the plains he durst not venture without cavalry. At this time Cuesta, with one thousand five hundred dragoons, was at Arevalo, and the junta of Castille and Leon, having taken refuge at Ponteferrada, commanded him to transfer his horsemen to Blake's army; but Cuesta, an arbitrary old man, exasperated by his defeat, and his mind rankling from his quarrel with Blake, instead of obeying retired to Salamanca, collected eight or ten thousand peasants, armed them, and then annulled the proceedings of the junta, and threatened the members with punishment for resisting his authority as captain-general. On the other hand Blake protected them, and while the generals disputed, three thousand French cavalry descending the Douero, scoured the plains, and raised contributions in the face of both their armies.

Capt. Carrol's letters.

Blake finding that the obstinacy of Cuesta was invincible, quitted his cantonments early in September, and skirting the plains on the north-east, carried his army by forced marches to the Montagna St. Ander, a small rugged district, dividing Biscay from the Asturias. The junta of the latter province had received enormous and very timely succours from England, but made no exertions answerable to the amount of the assistance granted, or to the strength and importance of the district. Eighteen thousand men were said to be in arms, but only ten thousand were promised to Blake, and but eight thousand joined his army.

In Catalonia the war was conducted by both sides without much connexion, or dependance on the movements of the main armies; and at this period it had little influence on the general plan of campaign.

Thus, it appears, that one month after the capitulation of Dupont, only nineteen thousand infantry without cavalry, and those under the command of more than one general, were collected at Madrid; that only sixteen thousand men were in line upon the Ebro, and that the remainder of the

Spanish armies, (exclusive of that in Catalonia computed at eleven thousand men,) were many days' march from the enemy, and from one another. The chiefs at discord with their respective juntas, and at variance among themselves, were inactive, or as in the case of Galluzzo, doing mischief.

The feeble and dilatory operations of the armies, were partly owing to the ineptitude of the generals; but the principal causes were the unbounded vanity, arrogance, and selfishness of the local governments, among whom the juntas of Gallicia and Seville were remarkable for their ambition. The time which should have been passed in concerting measures for pushing the victory of Baylen was spent by them in devising schemes to ensure the permanency of their own power, and the money and resources, both of England and Spain, were applied to further this pernicious object. In every part of the country a spirit of interested violence prevailed; the ardour of patriotism was chilled, and the exertions of sensible men were rendered nugatory, or served as a signal for their own destruction.

Appendix, No. 6.

Appendix, No. 4.

The argument to be drawn from this state of affairs is conclusive against the policy of Joseph's retreat. Without drafting a man from the garrisons of Pampeluna, Tortosa, and St. Sebastian; without interfering with the moveable columns employed on the communications of Biscay and Navarre; that monarch drew together about fifty thousand good troops, in twenty days after he had abandoned his capital. At the head of such a force, or even of two-thirds of it, he might have bid defiance to the inactive, half-organized, and scattered Spanish armies. It was so necessary to have maintained himself in Madrid, that scarcely any disproportion of numbers should have induced him to abandon it without an effort; but the disaster of Dupont had created in Joseph's mind a respect for Spanish prowess, while from his sagacious brother it drew the following observation: "*The whole of the Spanish forces are not capable of beating twenty-five thousand French in a reasonable position.*" The error of abandoning the capital would, if the Spaniards had been capable of pursuing any general plan of action, been fatal; but as if the stone of Cadmus had been cast among them, the juntas turned upon one another in hate, and forgot the common enemy.

Ferdinand was again proclaimed king of Spain, and the pomp and rejoicing attendant on this event put an end to all business, except that of intrigue. Castaños assumed the title of captain-general of Madrid. This step seems to have been taken by him, partly to forward his being appointed generalissimo, and partly with a view to emancipate himself from the injurious control of the Seville junta; for, although the authority of the captains-general had been superseded in most of the provinces by the juntas, it was not universally the case. Castaños expected, and with reason, to be appointed generalissimo of the Spanish armies; but he was of an indolent disposition, and it soon became manifest that until a central and supreme government was established, such a salutary measure would not be adopted. In the mean time the council of Castille, although not generally popular with the people, and hated by the juntas, was accepted as the provisional head of the state in the capital; but its authority was merely nominal, and the necessity of showing some front to the enemy seems to have been the only link of connexion between the Spanish armies.

The evil consequences flowing from this want of unity were soon felt. Scarcely had the French quitted Madrid, when the people of Biscay prepared to rise. Such an event, if prudently conducted and well supported, would have been of incalculable advantage; but the nicest arrangement, and the utmost prudence, were necessary to insure success, for the Biscayans had neither arms nor ammunition, the French were close to them, and the nearest Spanish force was the feeble Asturian levy. A previous junction of Blake's army with the latter was indispensable; that once effected, and due preparation made, the insurrection of Biscay, protected by forty thousand regular troops, and supplied from the sea-board with money and stores, would have forced the French to abandon the Ebro or to fight a battle, which Blake might have risked with little danger, provided that the Andalusian, Murcian, Valencian, and Arragonese troops assembling about Tudela, were prepared to move at the same time against the left flank of the enemy. But in every point of view it was an event pregnant with important consequences, and the impatience of the Biscayans should have been restrained rather than encouraged; yet the duke of Infantado, colonel Doyle, and others, at Madrid, made strenuous efforts to hasten the explosion. The crude manner in which they conducted this serious affair is exposed in the following extracts from colonel Doyle's despatches:

"I proposed to general Blake that he should send officers to Biscay to stir up the people there, and into the Asturias to beg that of their 15,000 men, 8,000 might be pushed into Biscay to Bilbao, to assist the people, who were all ready, and only waited for arms and ammunition, for both of which I wrote to Mr. Hunter at Gihon, and learned from him that he had sent a large supply of both, and some money to Bilbao, where already 14,000 men had enrolled themselves. The remainder of the Asturians I begged might instantly occupy the passes from Castille into the Asturias and Biscay, that is to say, from Reynosa in the direction of Bilbao." Some days after he says, — "My measures in Biscay and Asturias have perfectly succeeded; the reinforcements of arms, ammunition, and men (5,000 stand of arms, and ammunition in proportion) have reached Bilbao in safety, and the Asturians have taken possession of the passes I pointed out, so that we are all safe in that part of the world."

In this fancied state of security affairs remained until the 16th of August; general Blake was still in the mountains of Gallicia, the English succours arrived in the port of Bilbao, and the explosion took place. General Merlin, with three thousand grenadiers, immediately came down on the unfortunate Biscayans; Bilbao was taken, and to use the emphatic expression of king Joseph, "the fire of insurrection was quenched with the blood of twelve hundred men." Fortunately, the stores were not landed, and the vessels escaped from the river. Thus, at a blow, one of the principal resources which Blake had a right to calculate upon in his future operations was destroyed; and although the number admitted by the Spaniards to have fallen was less than the above quotation implies, the spirit of resistance was severely checked, and the evil was unmixed and deplorable.

Appendix, No. 6.

Whittingham's Letters. MSS.

This unfortunate event, however, created little or no sensation beyond the immediate scene of the catastrophe. Triumphs and rejoicings occupied the people of Madrid and Zaragoza, and it is difficult to say how long the war would have been neglected, if Palafox had not been roused by the re-appearance of a French corps, which re-took Tudela, and pushed on to the vicinity of Zaragoza itself. This movement took place immediately after the expedition against Bilbao, and was intended to suppress the insurrection of the valleys, and to clear the left flank of the French army. Palafox thus roughly aroused, wrote intemperately to the council of Castille, commanding that all the troops in the capital should be forwarded to the Ebro, and menacing the members personally for the delay which had already occurred. Being a young man without any weight of character, and his remonstrances being founded only upon his own danger, and not supported by any general plan or clear view of affairs, the presumptuous tone of his letters gave general offence; they were chiefly aimed at Castaños, who was not under his command; and moreover, the junta of Seville refused to pay or to subsist the Andalusian army if it moved beyond the capital before a central government should be established; at the same time resorting to every kind of intrigue, to retard, if not entirely to prevent, the execution of the latter measure.

Whittingham's Letters. MSS.

Mr. Stuart's Letters.

Parliamentary Papers.

It was, however, necessary to do something, and a council of all the generals commanding armies was held at Madrid on the 5th of September.

Castaños, Llamas, Cuesta, the duke of Infantado, and some others assembled; Blake gave his proxy to the duke, and Palafox was represented by a colonel of his own staff. Cuesta proposed that a commander-in-chief should be appointed: the others were too jealous to adopt this proposal, but they agreed to pursue the following plan of operations.

Llamas, with the Murcians, to occupy Tarascona, Agreda, and Borja. La-Peña, with the two divisions of Andalusia already in the capital, to march by Soria, and take possession of Logroña and Najera. The other divisions of that army to follow in due time. When La-Peña should be established in Logroña, Llamas was to advance to Cascante, Corella, and Calahorra.

> Sir H. Dalrymple's Correspce.
> Doyle's Letters.
> Cox's Do.

When this united force (to be called the army of the centre) was once securely fixed in its positions, Palafox, under whose command St. Marc's division acted, was to push forward to Sanguessa by the left bank of the Ebro, and to turn the enemy on the Aragon river. In the mean time it was hoped that Blake would arrive at Palencia, and form his junction with the Asturians. Cuesta promised to march upon Burgo del Osma, and to fill up the space between Blake and the army of the centre. The head of La-Peña's column was to be at Soria on the 17th of September, and the junta confidently expected that this vicious plan, in which every sound military principle was violated, and the enemy's troops, considered with regard to position, as a fixed immoveable mass, would cause the total destruction of the French army. The only fear entertained was, that a hasty flight into France would save it from Spanish vengeance! Thus captain Whittingham, echoing the sentiments of the Spanish generals with reference to this plan, writes, "As far as my poor judgment leads me, I am satisfied that if the French persist in maintaining their present position, we shall, in less than six weeks, have a second edition of the battle of Baylen!" But to enable La-Peña and Llamas to march, pecuniary aid was requisite. There was a difficulty in raising money at Madrid, and the maritime provinces intercepted all the English supplies. In this dilemma, colonel Doyle drew bills upon the English treasury, and upon the government at Seville, making the latter payable out of two millions of dollars, just transmitted to the junta through Mr. Duff.

It is probable that such an unprincipled body would not have hesitated to dishonour the bills, but major Coxe, before they were received, made energetic remonstrances upon the subject of the wants of the army; at first he received a haughty and evasive answer, but his representations were strongly seconded by a discovery made by the junta, that a plot against their lives, supposed to have been concocted at Madrid, was on the eve of execution. In fact, they had become hateful from their domineering insolence and selfishness, and the public feeling was strongly against them. Alarmed for the consequences, they sent off 200,000 dollars to Madrid, and published a manifesto, in which they inserted a letter, purporting to be from themselves to Castaños, dated on the 8th, and giving him full powers to act as he judged fitting for the public good. Their objects were to pacify the people, and to save their own dignity, by appearing to have acted voluntarily; but Castaños published the letter in Madrid with its true date of the 11th, and then it became manifest, that to major Coxe's remonstrance, and not to any sense of duty, this change of conduct was due.

Parliamentary Papers, 1810.

Doyle's bills having been negotiated, the troops were put in motion, and 40,000 fresh levies were enrolled, but the foresight and activity of Napoleon in disarming the country had been so effectual, that only 3,200 firelocks could be procured. A curious expedient then presented itself to the imagination of the duke of Infantado, and other leading persons in Madrid: colonel Doyle, at their desire, wrote to sir Hew Dalrymple in the name of the supreme council, to request that *the firelocks of Junot's army, and the arms of the Portuguese people,* might be forwarded to the frontier, and from thence carried by post to Madrid; a novel proposition, and made at a time when England had already transmitted to Spain 160,000 muskets; a supply considerably exceeding the whole number of men organized throughout the country; 50,000 of these arms had been sent to Seville, but the junta shut them up in the arsenals, and left the armies defenceless; for to neglect or misuse real resources, and to fasten with avidity upon the most extravagant projects, is peculiarly Spanish. No other people could have thought of asking for a neighbouring nation's arms at such a conjuncture; no other than Spanish rulers could have imagined the absurdity of supplying their levies (momentarily required to fight upon the Ebro) with the arms of a French army still unconquered in Portugal. But this project was only one among many proofs afforded at the time, that Cervantes was as profound an observer as he was a witty reprover of the extravagance of his countrymen.

CHAPTER II

INTERNAL POLITICAL TRANSACTIONS

Mr. Stuart's Letters. Parliamentary Papers.

Ibid.

Stuart's Letters. MS.

Ibid.

With the military affairs thus mismanaged, the civil and political transactions proceeded step by step, and in the same crooked path. Short as the period was between the first breaking forth of the insurrection, and the arrival of Mr. Stuart at Coruña, it was sufficient to create disunion of the worst kind. The juntas of Leon, of the Asturias, and of Gallicia, were at open discord, and those provinces were again split into parties, hating each other with as much virulence as if they had been of a hundred years growth. The money and other supplies sent by the English ministers were considered, by the authorities into whose hands they fell, as a peculiar donation to themselves, and appropriated accordingly. The junta of one province would not assist another with arms when there was a surplus, nor permit their troops to march against the enemy beyond the precincts of the particular province in which they were first organized. The ruling power was in the hands of the provincial nobility and gentry, men of narrow contracted views, unused to business, proud, arrogant — as extreme ignorance suddenly clothed with authority will always be — and generally disposed to employ their newly-acquired power in providing for their relations and dependants at the expense of the common cause, which with them was quite subordinate to the local interests of their own particular province. Hence a jealousy of their neighbours regulated the proceedings of all the juntas, and the means they resorted to for increasing their own, or depressing a rival government's influence, were equally characterised by absurdity and want of principle. The junta of Gallicia did their utmost to isolate that province, as if with a view to a final separation from Spain and a connexion with Portugal. They complained, Mr. as of an injury, that the army of Estremadura had obeyed the orders of the junta of Seville; they at once struck up an independent alliance with the junta and bishop of Oporto, and sent troops, as we have seen, under Valladeras, to aid the war in Portugal, but, at the same time, refused to unite in any common measure of defence with the provinces of Castille, until a formal treaty of alliance between them was negotiated, signed, and ratified. In the mean time their selfishness and incapacity created so much disgust in their own district, that plots were formed to overthrow their authority. The bishops of Orense and St. Jago became their decided enemies; and the last-named prelate, an intriguing man, secretly endeavoured to draw Blake, with the army, into his views, and even wrote to him, to desire that he would lead the forces against the government of Coruña; but the junta having intercepted the letters, arrested the bishop. Their own stability and personal safety were however still so insecure, that many persons applied to Mr. Stuart to aid in changing the form of government by force. The Asturians were even worse, they refused to assist Blake when his army was suffering, although the stores required by him, and supplied by England, were rotting in the harbours where they were first landed. Money also that was sent out in the Pluto frigate for the use of Leon was detained at Gihon, and Leon itself never raised a single soldier for the cause: and thus, only two months after the first burst of the insurrection, corruption, intrigue, and faction even to the verge of civil war, were raging in the northern parts of Spain.

Appendix, No. 13, section 5.

Ibid.

Sir Hew Dalrymple's Paprs.
Coxe's Correspondce.

Sir Hew Dalrymple's Paprs.
Coxe's Correspondce.

Appendix, No. 13, section 5.

Ibid.

The same passions were at work in the south, and the same consequences followed. The junta of Seville, still less scrupulous than that of Gallicia, made no secret of their ambitious views; they stifled all local publications, and even suppressed the public address of Florida Blanca, who, as president of the Murcian junta, had recommended the formation of a supreme central government. They wasted their time in vain and frivolous disputes, and neglecting every concern of real importance, sacrificed the general welfare to views of private advantage and interest. They made promotions in the army without regard to public opinion or merit; they overlaid all real patriotism; bestowed on their own creatures places of emolument, to the patronage of which they had not a legal right; and even usurped the royal prerogative of appointing canons in the church, for their cupidity equalled their ambition. They intercepted, as I have already related, the pecuniary supplies necessary to enable the army to act; they complained that La Mancha and Madrid, in whose defence they said "*their* troops were sacrificing themselves," did not subsist and supply the force under Castaños; under the pretence of forming a nucleus for disciplining thirty thousand levies as a reserve, they retained five battalions at Seville, and, having by this draft weakened the army in the field, they neglected the rest, and never raised a man. The canonries filled up by them had been vacant for several years, and the salaries attached to those offices were appropriated to the public service. The junta now applied the money to their own and their creatures' emolument; and at one period they appear to have contemplated an open partition of the funds received from England among themselves. Against this flagitious junta also the public indignation was rife; a plot was formed to assassinate the members; the municipal authorities remonstrated with them, the archbishop of Toledo protested against their conduct, and the junta of Grenada refused to acknowledge their supremacy; but so great was their arrogance, so unprincipled their ambition, that the decided and resolute opposition of Castaños alone prevented them from commencing a civil war, and marching the victorious army of Baylen against the refractory Granadans. Such was the real state of Spain, and such the patriotism of the juntas, who were at this time filling Europe with the sound of their own praise.

Stuart's Correspondence. Parliamentary Papers.

In the northern parts Mr. Stuart endeavoured to reduce this chaos of folly and wickedness to some degree of order, and to produce that unity of design and action without which it was impossible to resist the mighty adversary that threatened the independence of the Peninsula. He judged that to reduce the conflicting passions of the moment, a supreme authority, upon which the influence of Great Britain could be brought to bear with full force, was indispensable. To convoke the ancient cortez of the realm appeared to him the most certain and natural method of drawing the strength and energy of the nation into one compact mass; but there the foresight of Napoleon interfered; by an able distribution of the French forces, all direct communication between the northern and southern provinces was intercepted. Bessieres, Dupont and Moncey at that time occupied a circle round Madrid, and would have prevented the local governments of the north from uniting with those of the southern, if they had been inclined to do so. An union of the nearest provinces, to be called the northern cortez, then suggested itself to Mr. Stuart as a preliminary step, which would ensure the convocation of a general assembly when such a measure should become practicable. Accordingly he strenuously urged its adoption, but his efforts, at first, produced no good results. It was in vain that he represented the danger of remaining in a state of anarchy when so many violent passions were excited, and such an enemy was in the heart of the country. It was in vain that he pointed out the difficulties, that the want of a supreme authority fastened on the intercourse with the British cabinet, which could not enter into separate relations with every provincial junta. The Spaniards, finding that the supplies were not withheld, that their reputation for patriotism was not lowered in England by actions which little merited praise, finding, in short, that the English cabinet was weak enough to gorge their cupidity, flatter their vanity, and respect their folly, they assented to all Mr. Stuart's reasoning, but forwarded none of his propositions, and continued to nourish the disorders that, cancer-like, were destroying the common cause.

The jarring interests which agitated the northern provinces were not even subdued by the near approach of danger. The result of the battle of Rio Seco rather inflamed than allayed the violence of party feeling. If Bessieres had not been checked in his operations by the disaster of Dupont, he would have encountered few obstacles in establishing Joseph's authority in Gallicia and Old Castile. The enthusiasm of those provinces never rose to a great pitch; Bessieres was prepared to use address as well as force, and among the factions he must doubtless have found support. The reinforcements continually arriving from France would have enabled him to maintain his acquisition, and then the ability of the emperor's dispositions would have become apparent; for while Bessieres held Gallicia, and Dupont hung on the southern frontier of Portugal with twenty-five thousand men, Junot could have securely concentrated his army in the neighbourhood of Lisbon, and have rendered an English disembarkation on the coast nearly impracticable.

Azanza and O'Farril, Mem.

The whole of the French monarch's combinations were overturned by the disgraceful capitulation of Baylen, and when Joseph evacuated Madrid a fresh impulse was given to the spirit of the people; but, unfortunately for Spain, as a wider scope for ambition was obtained, the workings of self-interest increased, fresh parties sprung up, and new follies and greater absurdities stifled the virtue of the country, and produced irremediable confusion, ending in ruin. The fact of Dupont's capitulation was made known to the council of Castile before king Joseph was informed of it, and the council, foreseeing all the consequences of such an event, immediately refused, as I have already related, to promulgate officially his accession to the throne. Joseph permitted this act of obedience to pass without much notice. He was naturally averse to violence, and neither he, nor his brother Napoleon, did at any period of the contest for Spain constrain a Spaniard to accept or retain office under the intrusive government. Joseph went further; before he abandoned Madrid, he released his ministers from their voluntary oath of allegiance to himself, and left them free to choose their party once more. Don Pedro Cevallos and the marquis of Pinuelo changed with, what appeared to them, changing fortune; but five others remained steadfast, preferring an ameliorated government under a foreign prince to what they believed to be a hopeless struggle, but which, if successful, they knew must end in a degrading native despotism; perhaps, also, a little swayed by their dislike to England, and by the impossibility of obtaining that influence among their countrymen which, under other circumstances, their talents and character would have ensured.

Sir H. Dalrymple's Papers.
Coxe's Correspondence.

The boldness of the council of Castille was not publicly chastised by the intruding monarch, but secretly he punished the members by a dexterous stroke of policy. General Grouchy wrote to Castaños, saying, that circumstances had arisen which required the presence of the French troops in another quarter, and he invited the Spanish general to take immediate possession of Madrid for the preservation of public tranquillity. This communication gave rise to an opinion that the French were going to evacuate Spain; a report so congenial to the vanity and indolence of the Spaniards was greedily received, and contributed among other causes to the subsequent supineness of the nation in preparing for its defence; thus by appealing to Castaños, and affecting to treat the council of Castille as a body who had lost their influence with the nation, Joseph gave a handle to their enemies which the latter failed not to lay hold of. The juntas dreaded that the influence of such a body would destroy their own; that of Gallicia would not communicate with them, affirming that, individually, the members were attached to the French, and that, collectively, they had been the most active instrument of the usurper's government. The junta of Seville endeavoured not only to destroy the authority of the existing members, but to annul that of the council, as an acknowledged tribunal of the state. The council, however, was not wanting to itself, the individuals composing it did not hesitate to seize the reins of government the moment the French had departed; and the prudence with which they preserved tranquillity in the capital, and prevented all re-action, proves that they were not without merit; and forms a striking contrast to the conduct of the provincial juntas, under whose savage sway every kind of excess was committed, and even encouraged.

Aware of the hostility they had to encounter, the members of the council lost no time in forming a party to support themselves. Don Arias Mon y Velarde, dean or president for the time being, wrote a circular letter to the local juntas, pointing out the necessity of establishing a central and supreme power, and proposing that deputies from each province, or nation, as they were sometimes called, should repair to Madrid, and there concert with the council the best mode of carrying such a measure into effect. If this proposal had been adopted, all power would inevitably have fallen into the hands of the proposers. Confessedly the first public body in the state, and well acquainted with the forms of business; the council must necessarily have had a preponderating influence in the assembly of delegates, and it appeared so reasonable that it should take the lead, when an efficient authority was required to direct the violence of the people in a useful channel, before the moment of safety was passed; that all the juntas trembled at the prospect of losing their misused power. The minor ones submitted, and agreed to send deputies. The stronger and more ambitious felt that subtlety would avail more than open opposition to the project.

Mr. Stuart's Correspondence.

Cox's Corresponce.

Appendix, No. 13, section 5.

Mr. Stuart's Correspondence.

The council followed up this blow by the publication of a manifesto, containing an accurate detail of the events of the revolution, defending the part taken by its members, and claiming a renewal of the confidence formerly reposed in them by the nation. This important state paper was so ably written, that a large party, especially at Valladolid, was immediately formed in favour of its authors; and the junta of Seville were so sensible of the increasing influence of the council, that they intercepted a copy of this manifesto, addressed to sir Hew Dalrymple, and strictly suppressed all writings favourable to the formation of a supreme central authority. Nothing they dreaded more; but it was no longer possible to resist the current, which had set strongly in favour of such a measure. The juntas, however they might oppose its progress, could not openly deny the propriety of it, and in every province, individuals of talent and consideration called for a change in the Hydra polity, which oppressed the country, and was inefficient against the enemy. Every British functionary, civil or military, in communication with the Spaniards, also urged the necessity of concentrating the executive power.

Ibid.

The provincial juntas were become universally odious. Some of the generals alone, who had suddenly risen to command under their rule, were favourable to them; but Palafox was independent, as a captain-general, whose power was confirmed by success; Castaños openly declared that he would no longer serve under their control, and Cuesta was prepared to put them down by force, and to re-establish the royal audienzas and the authority of the captains-general according to the old practice. In this state of affairs, the retreat of Bessieres' army freed the communication with the southern parts, and removed all excuse for procrastination. The juntas of Gallicia, Castille, Leon, and the Asturias, gave way to the unceasing remonstrances of Mr. Stuart, and at his instance agreed to meet in cortez, at Lugo; Gallicia, however, first insisted upon a formal ratification of the treaty with Castille already mentioned.

When the moment of assembling arrived, the Asturians, without assigning any reason, refused to fulfil the engagement they had entered into, and the three remaining juntas held the session without them. The bishop of Orense, and the junta of Gallicia, were prepared to assert the supremacy of that province over the others, but the Baily Valdez of Castille, an able and disinterested man, being chosen president of the convocation, proposed, on the first day of assembly, that deputies should be appointed to represent the three provinces in a supreme junta, to be assembled in some central place, for the purpose of convoking the ancient cortez of the whole kingdom according to the old forms, and of settling the administration of the interior, and the future succession to the throne. This proposition was immediately carried by the superior number of the Castillians and Leonese; but the bishop of Orense protested against it, and the Gallician members strongly opposed an arrangement, by which their province was placed on the same footing as others, a glaring injustice (in their opinion) when the numbers of the Gallician army were taken into consideration; for the local feeling of ambition was uppermost, and the general cause disregarded. The other party answered, with great force, that the Gallician army was paid, armed, and clothed, by England, and fed by Castille and Leon.

Mr. Stuart's Correspondence.

Meanwhile the influence of the council of Castille greatly increased, and the junta of Seville, quickened by fear, took the lead in directing what they could not prevent. The convocation of the cortez they knew would be fatal to their own existence; wherefore, in a public letter, addressed to the junta of Gallicia, dated one day previous to the circular of don Arias Mon, but evidently written after the receipt of the latter, they opposed the assembling of the cortez on the ground that it was "the prerogative of the king to convoke that body, and if it was called together by any other authority, the provinces would not obey." "There would be no unanimity." The futility of this argument is apparent. The question was not one of form, but of expediency. If the nation was in favour of such a step, (and after facts proved that the people were not opposed to it) the same necessity which constituted the right of the junta to declare war against the French, (another prerogative of the monarch) would have sufficed to legalize the convocation of the national assembly. But their sole object was to preserve their own power. They maintained that the juntas, being chosen by the nation, were the only legitimate depositaries of authority, and that to members of their own bodies only could any of that authority be delegated; and adopting thereupon the suggestion contained in the letter of Arias Mon, they proposed that two deputies from each supreme junta should repair, not to Madrid, but to Ciudad Real, or Almagro, and at the moment of meeting should be in fact constituted governors-general of the kingdom, and as such obeyed. Nevertheless, the local governments were, with due subordination to the central junta, to retain and exercise in their own provinces all the authority with which they had already invested themselves. Thus they had only to choose subservient deputies, and their power would be more firmly fixed than before.

This arrangement would, doubtless, have been readily adopted by the junta of Gallicia; but the rapidity with which Valdez carried his proposition, prevented that cause of discord from being added to the numerous disputes which already distracted the northern provinces. Mr. Stuart, impelled by the political tide, proceeded onward to Madrid, observing, wherever he passed, the same violence of local party feeling, and the general disgust occasioned by the conduct of the oligarchical provincial governments. Pride, vanity, corruption, and improvidence, were every where obtrusively visible.

Stuart's Correspondence.

The dispute between Blake and Cuesta, which was raging at the period of the battle of Rio Seco, a period when division was most hurtful to the military operations, was now allayed between the generals; but their political partizans waged war with more bitterness than ever, as if with the intent to do the greatest possible mischief, by continuing the feud among the civil branches of the government, when union was most desirable in that quarter. The seeds of division had taken deep root. The Baily Valdez chosen, as I have said, a deputy to the supreme junta, was obnoxious to general Cuesta, a man not to be offended with impunity when he had power to punish.

Don Gregorio Cuesta was haughty and incredibly obstinate. He had been president of the council of Castille, and he was captain-general of Castille and Leon when the insurrection first broke out. Disliking all revolutionary movements, although as inimical to a foreign domination as any of his countrymen, he endeavoured to repress the public effervescence, and to maintain the tranquillity of the country at the risk of losing his life as a traitor. He was an honest man, insomuch as the Spanish and French interests being put in competition, he would aid the former, but, between his country's cause and his own passions, he was not honest. He disliked, and with reason, the sway of the local juntas, and with consistency of opinion, he wished to preserve the authority of the captains-general and the royal audienzas, both of which had been overturned by the establishment of those petty governments; but, sullen and ferocious in his temper, he supported his opinion with an authority and severity which had no guide but his own will, and he was prepared, if an opportunity offered, to exercise military influence over the supreme, as well as over the subordinate juntas. He had himself appointed one for Leon and Castille as a sort of council, subordinate to the authority of captain-general; but, after the battle of Rio Seco, the members fled to Ponteferrada, assumed the supreme authority, and putting themselves under the protection of his enemy Blake, disregarded Cuesta's orders, and presumed to command him, their superior, to deliver up his cavalry to the former general; wherefore he annulled all their proceedings at Ponteferrada, and now asserting that the election of Valdez and his colleagues was void, as being contrary to the existing laws, he directed new juntas to be assembled in a manner more conformable to existing usages, and a fresh election to be made.

His mandates were disregarded; Valdez and the other deputies proceeded in defiance of them towards the place appointed for the assembly of the central and supreme government, and Cuesta, in return, without hesitation, abandoned the operations of the campaign, which, in the council of war held at Madrid, he had promised to aid, and falling back to Segovia with twelve thousand men, seized the deputies, and shut up Valdez a close prisoner in the tower of that place, declaring his intention to try him by a military tribunal for disobedience; and such was the disorder of the times, that Cuesta was not without plausible arguments to justify this act of stubborn violence; for the original election of members to form the junta of Castille and Leon had been any thing but legal; several districts had been omitted altogether in the representation of those kingdoms, many deputies had been chosen by the city of Leon alone, and Valdez was named president, although neither a native nor a proprietor, and for those reasons ineligible to be a deputy at all. The kingdom of Leon also had appointed representatives for those districts in Castille which were under the domination of the French, and when the enemy retired, the Castillians in vain demanded a more equitable arrangement.

However, amidst all this confusion and violence, the plan of uniting to form a central government gained ground all over the kingdom. Seville, Catalonia, Arragon, Murcia, Valencia, and Asturias, appointed their deputies. Fresh disputes relative to the place of assembly now arose, but after some time it was agreed to meet at Aranjuez. This royal residence was chosen contrary to the wishes of many, and notably against the opinion of Jovellanos, an eloquent person, and of great reputation for integrity, but of a pertinacious temper, unsuitable to the times. He urged that the capital was the meetest spot; but he was answered, that the turbulent disposition of the inhabitants of Madrid would impede the formation of a government, and that the same objection would exist against the choice of any other large town. It is extraordinary that such an argument should be held in Spain at a moment when the people were, in all the official and public papers, represented as perfectly enthusiastic, and united in one common sacred pursuit, and in the British parliament were denominated the "universal Spanish nation!"

Cox's Correspondence.

To seek thus for protection in a corner, instead of manfully and confidently identifying themselves with the people, and courting publicity, augured ill for the intentions of the deputies, nor was the augury belied by the event. The junta of Seville, who had so bitterly reviled the council of Castille, for having partially submitted to the usurper, had, notwithstanding, chosen for their own deputies, don Vincente Hore, a known creature of the prince of peace, and the count de Tilly Gusman, who was under the stigma of a judicial sentence for robbery. Hore declined the appointment; but Tilly, braving the public disgust, repaired to Aranjuez, and his place as resident with the head-quarters of the Andalusian army was filled up by Miñiano, another member of the junta, who received an enormous salary for performing the mischievous duties of that office. The instructions given by the different provinces to the deputies were to confine their deliberations and votes to such subjects as they should, from time to time, receive directions from their constituents to treat of. Seville again took the lead in this fraudulent policy, and when public indignation and the remonstrances of some right-minded persons, obliged the juntas of that town and of Valencia to rescind these instructions, both substituted secret orders of the same tenor; in short the greater part of the deputies were the mere tools of the juntas; agents, watching over the interests of their employers, and (conscious of demerit) anxious to hide themselves from the just indignation of the public until they had consolidated their power; hence the dislike to large towns and the intrigues for fixing the government at Aranjuez.

Count Florida Blanca, a man in the last stage of decrepitude, was chosen first president in rotation for three months, and all idea of choosing an independent executive was abandoned; Jovellanos proposed to establish a regency selected from their own body; but his plan was rejected on the ground that the members were not authorised to delegate their powers even to one another. It was palpable that the juntas had merely appeared to comply with the public wish for a central government, but were determined not to part with one iota of their own real power.

Mr. Stuart's Correspondence.
Col. Graham's ditto.

The first act of authority executed by the assembly was, however, a necessary assertion of its own dignity, which had been violated in the case of Valdez. Cuesta, who was personally unpopular, and feared by the central, as well as by the provincial juntas, was summoned to release his captive, and to repair to Aranjuez, that cognizance might be taken of his proceedings; he was at the same time denounced by the juntas of Castille and Leon as a traitor, and exposed to great danger of popular commotion. At first Cuesta haughtily repelled the interference of Castaños and Florida Blanca, but finally he was forced to bend, and after a sharp correspondence with Mr. Stuart, whose influence was usefully employed to strengthen the central government, he released his prisoner, and quitting the command of the army, appeared at Aranjuez. No formal proceedings were had upon the case; but after much mutual recrimination, Valdez was admitted to the exercise of his functions, and the old general was detained at the seat of government, a kind of state prisoner at large, until, for the misfortune of his country, he was, by subsequent events, once more placed at the head of an army.

About this time lord William Bentinck joined Mr. Stuart at Madrid. Perfectly coinciding in opinions, they laboured earnestly to give a favourable turn to affairs, by directing the attention of the central junta, to the necessity of military preparations, and active exertion for defence; but the picture of discord, folly, and improvidence exhibited in the provinces, was here displayed in more glaring colours. The lesser tribunals being called upon to acknowledge the authority of the assembled deputies, readily obeyed; but the council of Castille, reluctant to submit, and too weak to resist, endeavoured to make terms; they were forced, however, to an unconditional submission.

Mr. Stuart's Correspondence.

A good management of the revenue, a single chief for the army, and, above all, the total suppression of the provincial juntas, were the three objects of public anxiety. With respect to the army, no doubt was at first entertained that Castaños would be appointed commander-in-chief; his services entitled him to the office, and his general moderation and conciliating manners fitted him for it at a time when so much jealousy was to be soothed and so many interests to be reconciled. The past expenditure of the money received from England was also a subject of great importance, and it was loudly required that an account of its disbursement should be demanded of the local juntas, and a surrender of the residue instantly Ibid. enforced. These just expectations lasted but a short time; scarcely were the deputies assembled, when every prospect of a vigorous administration was blasted. Dividing themselves into sections, answering in number to the departments of state under the old king, they appointed a secretary not chosen from their own body, to each, and declared all and every one of these sections, supreme and independent, having equal authority.

Parliamentary Papers.

Florida Blanca informed Mr. Stuart and lord William Bentinck that Castaños would be named generalissimo, and the latter was even appointed to confer with him upon the plan of campaign for the British troops, then marching from Portugal to the assistance of the Spaniards. The necessity of having a single chief at the head of the armies was imperious, and acknowledged by every individual, military or civil; yet such was the force of jealousy, and so stubborn were the tools of the different juntas, that all the exertions of Mr. Stuart and lord William Bentinck, and all the influence of the British cabinet, failed to get one appointed. The generals were all confirmed in their separate and independent commands, the old and miserable system of the Dutch deputies in Marlborough's time, and of the commissaries of the convention, during the French revolution, was partially revived, and the expressed wishes of the English government were totally disregarded at a time when it had supplied Spain with two hundred thousand musquets, clothing, ammunition of all kinds in proportion, and ten millions of dollars. Such ample succours, if rightly managed, ought to have secured to the English cabinet unlimited influence; but as the benefits came through one set of persons, and the demands through another, the first were taken as of right, the last unheeded, and the resources of Great Britain were wasted without materially improving the condition of Spain; the armies were destitute, the central government was without credit, and notwithstanding the ample subsidies, contracted a large debt.

Stuart's Correspce.
Lord W. Bentinck's Ditto.

Lord W. Bentinck's Correspce.

Appendix, No. 13, section 6.

The provincial juntas were still permitted to retain their power within their own districts, and the greatest timidity marked all the proceedings of the central government in relation to those obnoxious bodies. Attentive, however, to their own interests, the members of the supreme junta decreed, 1st. that their persons should be inviolable; 2d. that the president should have the title of highness, with a salary of 25,000 crowns a year; 3d. that each of the deputies, taking the title of excellency, should have a yearly salary of

5,000 crowns; and lastly, that the collective body should be addressed by the title of majesty. Thinking that they were now sufficiently confirmed in power to venture upon a public entry into Madrid, the junta made preparations to ensure a favourable reception from the populace. They resolved to declare a general amnesty, to lower the duties on tobacco, and to fling large sums among the people during the procession; but, in the midst of all this pomp and vanity, the presence of the enemy on the soil was scarcely remembered, and the details of business were totally neglected, a prominent evil that extended to the lowest branches of administration. Self-interest, indeed, produced abundance of activity, but every department, almost every man, seemed struck with torpor when the public welfare was at stake; and withal, an astonishing presumption was common to the highest and the lowest.

Lord W. Bentinck's Correspce.

To supply the place of a generalissimo, a council or board of general officers was projected, on whose reports the junta proposed to regulate the military operations. Castaños was destined to be president; but some difficulty arising relative to the appointment of the other members, the execution of the plan was deferred, with the characteristic remark "that when the enemy was driven across the frontier, Castaños would have leisure to take his seat." The idea of a defeat, the possibility of failure, never entered their minds; the government evincing neither apprehension, nor activity, nor foresight, were contented if the people believed the daily falsehoods they promulgated relative to the enemy; and the people, equally presumptuous, were content to be so deceived; in fine, all the symptoms of a ruined cause were already visible to discerning eyes. The armies neglected even to nakedness, and the soldier's constancy under privations cruelly abused; disunion, cupidity, incapacity, in the higher orders; the patriotic ardour visibly abating among the lower classes; the rulers grasping, improvident, and boasting; the enemy powerful; the people insubordinate, and the fighting men without arms or bread; as a whole, and in all its parts, the government unfitted for its task; cumbrous and ostentatious, its system, to use the comprehensive words of Mr. Stuart, "was neither calculated to inspire courage nor to increase enthusiasm."

The truth of this picture will be recognized by men who are yet living, and whose exertions were as incessant as unavailing to remedy those evils at the time. It will be recognized by the friends of a great man, who fell a victim to the folly and base intrigues of the day; and finally, it will be recognized by that general and army, who, afterwards winning their own unaided way through Spain, found that to trust Spaniards in war was to lean against a broken reed. To others it may appear exaggerated; for without having seen it is difficult to believe the extent of a disorder that paralized the enthusiasm of a whole people.

EXTERNAL POLITICAL RELATIONS OF SPAIN

At first these were of necessity confined to a few foreign courts; England, Sicily, and Portugal; the rest of the Old World was either subject to Buonaparte or directly under his influence; but in the New World it was different: the Brazils, after the emigration of the royal family of Braganza, became important under every point of view, and relations were established between the junta and that court, that afterwards under the cortez created considerable interest, and threatened serious embarrassments to the operations of the duke of Wellington.

Mr. Stuart's Correspce. MS.
Sir Hew Dalrymple.

The ultra-marine possessions of Spain were, of course, a matter of great anxiety to both sides; Napoleon's activity balanced the natural preponderance of the mother country. The slowness of the local juntas, or rather their want of capacity to conduct such an affair, gave the enemy a great advantage. It was only owing to the exertions of Mr. Stuart in the north, and of sir Hew Dalrymple and lord Collingwood in the south, that, after the insurrection broke out, vessels were despatched to South America to confirm the colonists in their adherence to Spain, and to arrange the mode of securing the resources of those great possessions for the parent state. The hold which Spain retained over her colonies was, however, very slight; her harsh restrictive system had long before weakened the attachment of the South Americans; the expedition of Miranda, although unsuccessful, had kindled a fire which could not be extinguished; and it was apparent to all able statesmen, that Spain must relinquish her arbitrary mode of governing, or relinquish the colonies altogether; the insurrection at home only rendered this more certain; every argument, every public manifesto put forth in Europe, to animate the Spaniards against foreign aggression, told against them in America. Yet for a time the latter transmitted the produce of the mines, and many of the natives served in the Spanish armies.

Napoleon, notwithstanding his activity, and the offers which he made of the vice-royalty of Mexico to Cuesta, Castaños, Blake, and probably to others residing in that country, failed to create a French party of any consequence. The Americans were unwilling to plunge into civil strife for a less object than their own independence: the arrogance and injustice of Old Spain, however, increased, rather than diminished, under the sway of the insurrectional government, and at last, as it is well known, a general rebellion of the South American states established the independence of the fairest portion of the globe, and proved, how little the abstract love of freedom influenced the resistance of the old country to Napoleon.

The intercourse with the English court, which had been hitherto carried on through the medium of the deputies, who first arrived in London to claim assistance, was now placed upon a regular footing. The deputies, at the desire of Mr. Canning, were recalled, and admiral Apodaca was appointed envoy extraordinary and minister plenipotentiary at St. James's, and Mr. John Hookham Frere was accredited, with the same diplomatic rank, near the central junta.

Mr. Stuart, whose knowledge of the state of the country, whose acquaintance with the character of the leading persons, and whose able and energetic exertions had so much contributed to the formation of a central government, was superseded by this injudicious appointment, and thus a great political machine, with every wheel in violent action, was, at the critical moment, left without any controlling power or guiding influence; for Mr. Stuart, who, on his own responsibility, had quitted Coruña, and repaired to Madrid, and had remitted the most exact and important information of what was passing, remained for three months without receiving a single line from Mr. Canning, approving or disapproving of his proceedings, or giving him instructions how to act at this important crisis: a strange remissness, indicating the bewildered state of the ministers, who slowly and with difficulty followed, when they should have been prepared to lead. Their tardy abortive measures demonstrated, how wide the space between a sophist and a statesman, and how dangerous to a nation is that public feeling which, insatiable of words, disregards the actions of men, esteeming more the interested eloquence and wit of an orator like Demades, than the simple integrity, sound judgment, and great exploits, of a general like Phocion.

Such were the preparations made by Spain in September and October, to meet the exigencies of a period replete with danger and difficulty. It would be instructive to contrast the exertions of the "enthusiastic Spaniards" during these three months of their insurrection, with the efforts of "discontented France," in the hundred days of Napoleon's second reign. The junta were, however, not devoid of ambition, for even before the battle of Baylen, that of Seville was occupied with a project of annexing the Algarves to Spain, and the treaty of Fontainebleau was far from being considered as a dead letter.

CHAPTER III

Letter to Murat.
Las Casas.

The French emperor, although surprised and chagrined at the disgrace which, for the first time, his armies had sustained, was nothing dismayed by a resistance which he had early contemplated as not improbable. With a piercing glance he had observed the efforts of Spain, and calculated the power of foreign influence in keeping alive the spirit of resistance. Assigning a just value to the succours which England could afford, he foresaw the danger which might accrue, if he suffered an insurrection of peasants, that had already dishonoured the glory of his arms, to attain the consistency of regular government, to league with powerful nations, and to become disciplined troops.

To defeat the raw levies which the Spaniards had hitherto opposed to his soldiers, was an easy matter, but it was necessary to crush them to atoms, that a dread of his invincible power might still pervade the world, and the secret influence of his genius remain unabated. The constitution of Bayonne would, he was aware, weigh heavy in the scale against those chaotic governments, neither monarchical, nor popular, nor aristocratic, nor federal, which the Spanish revolution was throwing up; but before the benefit of that could be felt by the many, before he could draw any advantages from his moral resources, it was necessary to develop all his military strength. The moment was critical and dangerous. He was surrounded by enemies whose pride he had wounded, but whose means of offence he had not destroyed. If he bent his forces against the Peninsula, England might again excite the continent to arms, and Russia and Austria once more banding together, might raise Prussia and renew the eternal coalitions. The designs of Austria, although covered by the usual artifices of that cunning rapacious court, were not so hidden but that, earlier or later, a war from that quarter was to be expected as a certain event.

Baron Fain's Campaign. 1813.

The inhabitants of Prussia, subdued and oppressed, could not be supposed tranquil: the secret societies, that, under the name of Tugenbunde, Gymnasiasts, and other denominations, have since been persecuted by those who were then glad to avail themselves of such assistance, were just beginning to disclose their force and plans. A baron de Nostiz, Stein, the Prussian counsellor of state, generals Sharnhost and Gneizenau, and colonel Schill, appear to have been the principal contrivers and patrons of these societies, so characteristic of Germans, who, regular and plodding, even to a proverb in their actions, possess the most extravagant imaginations of any people on the face of the earth. Whatever the ulterior views of these associations may have been, at this period they were universally inimical to the French, their intent was to drive the latter over the Rhine, and they were a source of peril to the emperor, the more to be feared, as the extent of their influence could not be immediately ascertained.

Russia also, little injured by her losses, was more powerful perhaps from her defeats, because more enlightened as to the cause of them: Napoleon felt, that the hostility of such a great empire would require all his means to repel, and that, consequently, his Spanish operations must be confined in a manner unsuitable to the fame of his arms. Of a long-sighted policy he had, however, prepared the means of obviating this danger, by drawing the emperor of Russia into a conference at Erfurth, whither the French monarch repaired, confident in the resources of his genius for securing the friendship of the czar.

At this period, it may be truly said, that Napoleon supported the weight of the world; every movement of his produced a political convulsion; yet so sure, so confident was he, of his intellectual superiority, that he sought but to gain one step, and doubted not to overcome all resistance, and preserve his ascendancy. Time was to him victory; if he gained the one, the other followed. Sudden and prompt in execution, he prepared for one of those gigantic efforts which have stamped this age with the greatness of antiquity.

His armies were scattered over Europe. In Italy, in Dalmatia, on the Rhine, the Danube, the Elbe; in Prussia, Denmark, Poland, his legions were to be found. Over that vast extent, above five hundred thousand disciplined men maintained the supremacy of France. From those bands he drew the imperial guards, the select soldiers of the warlike nation he governed, and the terror of the other continental troops. The veterans of Jena, of Austerlitz, of Friedland, reduced in number, but of confirmed hardihood, were collected into one corps, and marched towards Spain. A host of cavalry, unequalled for enterprise and knowledge of war, were also directed against that devoted land, and a long train of gallant soldiers followed, until two hundred thousand men, accustomed to battle, had penetrated the gloomy fastnesses of the western Pyrenees. Forty thousand men of inferior reputation, drawn from the interior of France, from Naples, from Tuscany, and from Piedmont, were assembled at Perpignan.

The march of this multitude was incessant, and as they passed the capital, Napoleon, neglectful of nothing which could excite their courage and swell their military pride, addressed to them one of those nervous orations that shoot like fire to the heart of a real soldier. In the tranquillity of peace it may seem inflated, but on the eve of battle it is thus a general should speak.

"Soldiers! after triumphing on the banks of the Vistula and the Danube, with rapid steps you have passed through Germany. This day, without a moment of repose, I command you to traverse France. Soldiers! I have need of you! The hideous presence of the leopard contaminates the peninsula of Spain and Portugal. In terror he must fly before you. Let us bear our triumphal eagles to the pillars of Hercules, there also we have injuries to avenge! Soldiers! you have surpassed the renown of modern armies, but have you yet equalled the glory of those Romans who, in one and the same campaign, were victorious upon the Rhine and the Euphrates, in Illyria and upon the Tagus! A long peace, a lasting prosperity, shall be the reward of your labours. A real Frenchman could not, ought not, to rest until the seas are free and open to all. Soldiers! all that you have done, all that you will do, for the happiness of the French people and for my glory, shall be eternal in my heart!"

Thus saying, he caused his troops to proceed towards the frontiers of Spain, and himself hastened to meet the emperor Alexander at Erfurth. Their conference, conducted upon the footing of intimate friendship, produced a treaty of alliance offensive and defensive, and the fate of Spain was, by the one, with calm indifference, abandoned to the injustice of the other.

The accession of strength which this treaty, and the manifest personal partiality of Alexander, gave to the French emperor, inspired him perhaps with the idea, that the English cabinet would, if a fair occasion offered, gladly enter into negotiations for a general peace. The two emperors wrote a joint letter to the king of England. "The circumstances of Europe had," they said, "brought them together; their first thought was to yield to the wish and the wants of every people, and to seek, in a speedy pacification, the most efficacious remedy for the miseries which oppressed all nations. The long and bloody war which had torn the continent was at an end, without the possibility of being renewed. Many changes had taken place in Europe, many states had been overthrown; the cause was to be found in the state of agitation and misery in which the stagnation of maritime commerce had placed the greatest nations: still greater changes might yet take place, and all of them contrary to the policy of the English nation. Peace, then, was, at once, the interest of the people of the continent, as it was the interest of the people of Great Britain. We entreat your majesty," they concluded, "we unite to entreat your majesty to listen to the voice of humanity, to silence that of the passions; to seek, with the intention of arriving at that object, to conciliate all interests, and thus preserve all powers which exist, ensure the happiness of Europe and of this generation, at the head of which Providence has placed us."

To this joint letter Mr. Canning replied by two letters to the French and Russian ministers, accompanied by an official note. In that addressed to the Russian, he observed, that "however desirous the king might be to reply personally to the emperor, he was prevented, by the unusual mode of communication adopted, which had deprived it of a private and personal character. It was impossible to pay that mark of respect to the emperor, without at the same time acknowledging titles which he had never acknowledged. The proposition for peace would be communicated to Sweden, and to the existing government of Spain. It was necessary that his majesty should receive an immediate assurance, that France acknowledged the government of Spain as a party to the negotiation. That such was the intention of the emperor could not be doubted, when the lively interest manifested by his imperial majesty for the welfare and dignity of the Spanish monarchy was recollected. No other assurance was wanted, that the emperor could not have been induced to sanction by his concurrence or approbation, usurpations, the principles of which were not less unjust than their example was dangerous to all legitimate sovereigns."

The letter addressed to Mons. de Champagny, duke of Cadore, merely reiterated the claim for Sweden and Spain being admitted as parties to the negotiation. The official note commenced by stating the king's desire for peace, on terms consistent with his honour, his fidelity to his engagements, and the permanent repose of Europe. The miserable condition of the continent, the convulsions it had experienced, and those with which it was threatened, were not imputable to his majesty. If the cause of so much misery was to be found in the stagnation of commercial intercourse, although his majesty could *not be expected to hear with unqualified regret,* that the system devised for the destruction of the commerce of his subjects had recoiled upon its authors or its instruments; yet, as it was neither the disposition of his majesty, nor in the character of the people over whom he reigned to rejoice in the privations and unhappiness even of the nations which were combined against him, he anxiously desired the termination of the sufferings of the continent. The note, after stating that the progress of the war had imposed new obligations upon Great Britain, claimed for Sicily, for Portugal, for Sweden, and for Spain, a participation in the negotiations.

Treaties, it stated, existed with the three first, which bound them and England in peace and war. With Spain indeed no formal instrument had yet been executed, but the ties of honour were, to the king of England, as strong as the most solemn treaties; wherefore it was assumed, that the central junta, or government of Spain, was understood to be a party to any negotiation, in which his majesty was invited to engage.

The reply of Russia was peremptory. The claims of the sovereigns, allies of Great Britain, she would readily admit. But the insurgents of Spain, Russia would not acknowledge as an independent power. The Russians (and England, it was said, could recollect one particular instance) had always been true to this principle; moreover, the emperor had acknowledged Joseph Buonaparte as king of Spain, and was united to the French emperor for peace and for war; he was resolved not to separate his interests from those of Napoleon. After some further arguments touching the question, the reply concluded by offering to treat upon the basis of the "uti possidetis," and the respective power of the belligerent parties, or upon *any basis*; for the conclusion of an honourable, just, and equal peace.

The insulting tone of Mr. Canning's communication produced an insulting reply from monsieur de Champagny, which also finished by proposing the "uti possidetis" as a basis for a treaty, and expressing a hope, that without losing sight of the inevitable results of the force of states, it would be remembered, that between great powers there could be no solid peace but that which was equal and honourable for both parties. Upon the receipt of these replies, the English minister broke off the negotiations, and all chance of peace vanished; but previous to the conclusion of this remarkable correspondence, Napoleon had returned to Paris.

O'Meara. Voice from St. Helena. Vol. 2.

What his real views in proposing to treat were, it is difficult to determine; he could not have expected that Great Britain would relinquish the cause of Spain, he must therefore have been prepared to make some arrangement upon that head, unless the whole proceeding was an artifice to sow distrust among his enemies. The English ministers asserted that it was so; but what enemies were they among whom he could create this uneasy feeling? Sweden, Sicily, Portugal! the notion as applied to them was absurd; it is more probable that he was sincere. He said so at Saint Helena, and the peculiar circumstances of the period at which the conferences of Erfurth took place, warrant a belief in that assertion. The menacing aspect of Austria, the recent loss of Portugal, the hitherto successful insurrection of Spain, the secret societies of Germany, the desire of consolidating the Polish dominions, and placing, while he might, a barrier to the power of Russia on that side, the breach which the events of the Peninsula made in his continental system of excluding British goods, and the commercial distresses of Europe, were cogent reasons for a peace, they might well cause him to be suspicious of the future, and render him anxious for an excuse to abandon an unjust contest, in which he could not fail to suffer much, and to risk more than he could gain. In securing the alliance of Russia, he only disentangled a part of the Gordian knot of politics; to cut the remainder with his sword was at this conjuncture a task which even he might have been doubtful of. The fact that his armies were marching upon Spain, proves nothing to the contrary of this supposition. Time was to him of the utmost consequence. His negotiations proving abortive, it would have been too late to have reinforced his troops on the Ebro; and the event evinced the prudence of his measures in that respect. The refusal to admit the Spaniards as a party to the conferences for peace is scarcely more conclusive; to have done that would have been to resign the weapon in his hands before he entered the lists. That England could not abandon the Spaniards is unquestionable; but that was not a necessary consequence of continuing the negotiations. There was a bar put to the admission of a Spanish diplomatist, but no bar was thereby put to the discussion of Spanish interests; the correspondence of the English minister would not of necessity have compromised Spanish independence, it need not have relaxed in the slightest degree the measures of hostility, nor retarded the succours preparing for the patriots; and when we consider the great power of Napoleon's arms, the subtlety and force of his genius, the good fortune which had hitherto attended his progress in war, and the vast additional strength which the alliance of Russia conferred at the moment, and when, to oppose all this, we contrast the scanty means of Spain, and the confusion into which she was plunged, it does appear as if her welfare would have been better consulted by an appeal to negotiation rather than to battle. It is true that Austria was arming; but Austria had been so often conquered, was so sure to abandon the cause of the patriots, and every other cause when pressed, so certain to sacrifice every consideration of honour or faith to the suggestions of self-interest, that the independence of Spain through the medium of war could only be regarded as the object of uncertain hope, a prize to be gained, if gained at all, by wading through torrents of blood, and sustaining every misery that famine, and the fury of devastating armies could inflict. To avoid, if possible, such dreadful evils by negotiating was surely worth trial, and the force of justice, when urged by the minister of a great nation, would have been difficult to withstand; no power, no ambition can resist it and be safe. But such an enlarged mode of proceeding was not in accord with the shifts and subterfuges that characterized the policy of the day[15], when it was thought wise to degrade the dignity of such a correspondence by a ridiculous denial of Napoleon's titles; and praiseworthy to render a state paper, in which such serious interests were discussed, offensive and mean by miserable sarcasms, evincing the pride of an author more than the gravity of a statesman. Mr. Whitbread declared in the House of Commons that he saw no reason for refusing to treat with France at that period; and although public clamour afterwards induced him to explain away this expression, he had no reason to be ashamed of it; for if the opinion of Cicero, that an unfair peace is preferable to the justest war, was ever worthy of attention, it was so at this period, when the success of Spain was doubtful, her misery certain, her salvation only to be obtained through the baptism of blood!

Imperial Decree, 11th Sept. 1808.

Upon the 18th of October Napoleon returned to Paris, secure of the present friendship and alliance of Russia, but uncertain of the moment when the stimulus of English subsidies would quicken the hostility of Austria into life; but if his peril was great, his preparations to meet it were likewise enormous. First he called out two conscriptions, of which the one taken from the classes of 1806, 7, 8, and 9, afforded eighty thousand men arrived at maturity; these were destined to replace the veterans directed against Spain.

The second conscription, taken from the class of 1810, also produced eighty thousand, which were disposed of as reserves in the dépôts of France.

The force in Germany was concentrated on the side of Austria. Denmark was evacuated, and one hundred thousand soldiers were withdrawn from the Prussian states.

The army of Italy was powerfully reinforced, and placed under the command of prince Eugene, who was assisted by marshal Massena. Murat also, who had succeeded Joseph in the kingdom of Naples, was directed to assemble a Neapolitan army on the shores of Calabria, and to threaten Sicily. In short, no measures that prudence could suggest were neglected by this wonderful man, to whom the time required by Austria for the mere preparation of a campaign seemed sufficient for the subjection of the whole Peninsula.

Exposé de l'Empire, 1808.

The session of the legislative body was opened on the 24th of October; the emperor, in his speech from the throne, after giving a concise sketch of the political situation of Europe, touched upon Spain. "In a few days I go," said he, "to put myself at the head of my armies, and, with the aid of God, to crown the king of Spain in Madrid, and to plant my eagles on the towers of Lisbon," and then departing from Paris he repaired to Bayonne; but the labours of his ministers continued; their speeches and reports, more elaborately explicit than usual, exposed the vast resources of France, and were well calculated to impress upon the minds of men the danger of provoking the enmity of such a powerful nation. From those documents it appeared that the expenses of the year, (including the interest of the national debt), being between twenty-nine and thirty millions sterling, were completely covered by the existing taxes, drawn from a metallic currency, and that no fresh burthens would be laid upon the nation. Numerous public works were in progress, internal trade, and that commerce which was carried on by land, were flourishing, and nearly one million of men were in arms!

The readiness with which Mr. Canning broke off the negotiation of Erfurth, and defied this stupendous power, would lead to the supposition that on the side of Spain at least he was prepared to encounter it with some chance of success; but no trace of a matured plan is to be found in the instructions to the generals commanding in Portugal previous to the 25th of September, nor was the project then adopted one which discovered any adequate knowledge of the force of the enemy, or of the state of affairs. Indeed the conduct of the cabinet relative to the Peninsula was scarcely superior to that of the central junta itself. Several vague projects, or rather speculations, were communicated to the generals in Portugal, but in none of them was the strength of the enemy alluded to, in none was there a settled plan of operations visible. It was evident that the prodigious activity of the emperor was not taken into consideration, and that a strange delusion relative to his power, or to his intentions existed among the English ministers.

Ld. Castles. Despatch.
Pary. Paps.

It was the 6th of October before a despatch, containing the first determinate plan of campaign, arrived at Lisbon. Thirty thousand infantry and five thousand cavalry were to be employed in the north of Spain; of these numbers ten thousand were to be embarked at the English ports, and the remainder were to be composed of regiments, drafted from the army then in Portugal. Lieutenant-general sir John Moore was appointed to command the whole, and he was authorised (at his own discretion) to effect a junction by a voyage round the coast, or by a march through the interior. He chose the latter, 1°. because a voyage at that season of the year would have been tedious and precarious; 2°. because the intention of sir Hew Dalrymple had been to enter Spain by Almeida, and the few arrangements which that general had power to make were made with a view to such a march; and 3°. because he was informed that the province of Gallicia was scarcely able to equip the force coming from England, under the command of lieutenant-general sir David Baird. Sir John Moore was directed to take the field with the troops under his own immediate command without delay; and he was to fix upon some place either in Gallicia or on the borders of Leon for concentrating the whole army. The specific plan of operations was to be concerted afterwards with the Spanish generals.

This was a light and idle proceeding, promising no good result, for the Ebro was to be the theatre of war. The head of the great French host coming from Germany was already in the passes of the Pyrenees, and the local difficulties impeding the English general's progress were abundant, and of a nature to render that which was ill begun, end worse, and that which was well arranged, fail. To be first in the field is a great and decided advantage; but here the plan of operations was not even arranged, when the enemy's first blows were descending.

Sir John Moore's Papers.

Appendix, No. 13, sections 1st and 3d.

Appendix, No. 13, section 1st.

Sir John Moore had, indeed, much to execute, and with little help. First, he was to organize an army of raw soldiers; then, in a poor and unsettled country, just relieved from the pressure of a harsh and griping enemy, he was to procure the transport necessary for his stores, ammunition, and even for the conveyance of the officers' baggage. Assisted by an experienced staff, such obstacles do not very much impede a good general; but here, few, if any, of the officers, except the commander-in-chief, had served a campaign; and every branch of the administration, civil and military, was composed of new men, very zealous and willing, but ignorant of a service, where no energy can prevent the effects of inexperience from being severely felt. The roads through Portugal were very bad; the rainy season, so baleful to an army, was upon the point of setting in; time pressed sorely, it was essential to be quick, but gold, that turns the wheels of war, was wanting; and this, at all times a great evil, was the more grievously felt at the moment, inasmuch as the Portuguese, accustomed to fraud on the part of their own government, and to forced contributions by the French, could not readily be persuaded that an army of foreigners, paying with promises alone, might be trusted; nor was this natural suspicion allayed by observing, that while the general and his troops were thus kept without money, all the subordinate agents dispersed throughout the country were amply supplied. Sir David Baird, who, with his portion of troops, was to land at Coruña, and to equip in a country already exhausted by Blake's army, was likewise encompassed with difficulties. From Coruña to the nearest point where he could effect a junction with the forces marching from Lisbon was two hundred miles, and he also was without money.

Appendix, No. 13, section 4th.

No general-in-chief was appointed to command the Spanish armies; nor was sir John Moore referred by the English ministers to any person with whom he could communicate at all, much less concert a plan of operations for the allied forces. He was unacquainted with the views of the Spanish government, he was uninformed of the numbers, composition, or situation of the troops with which he was to act, as well as those with whom he was to contend, and 25,000*l.* in his military chest, and his own genius, constituted his resources for a campaign, which would probably lead the army far from the coast, and from all its means of supply. He was first to unite the scattered portions of his forces by a winter march of three hundred miles; another three hundred were to be passed before he reached the Ebro; then he was to concert a plan of operations with generals acting each independent of the other; their corps reaching from the northern sea-coast to Zaragoza; themselves jealous and quarrelsome, their men insubordinate, differing in customs, discipline, language, and religion from the English, and despising all foreigners; and this was to be accomplished in time to defeat an enemy who was already in the field, accustomed to great movements, and conducted by the most rapid and decided of men. It must be acknowledged that the ministers' views were equally vast and inconsiderate, and their miscalculations are the more remarkable, as there was not wanting a man in the highest military situation to condemn their plan at the time, and to propose a better.

Appendix, No. 24.

The duke of York, in a formal minute drawn up for the information of the government, observed, that the Spanish armies being unconnected, and occupying a great extent of ground, were weak. That the French being concentrated, and certain of reinforcements, were strong. That there could be no question of the relative value of Spanish and French troops, and that, consequently, the allies might be beaten before the British could arrive at the scene of action; the latter would then unaided have to meet the French army; hence it was essential to provide a sufficient number of troops to meet such an emergency; that number he judged should not be less than sixty thousand men, and by a detailed statement, he proved that such a number could have been furnished without detriment to any other service.

Mr. Stuart's letters. MS.

Appendix, No. 13, section 6th.

At this period, also, the effects of that incredible folly and weakness which marked all the proceedings of the central junta, were felt throughout Spain. In any other country the conduct of the government would have been attributed to insanity. So apathetic with respect to the enemy as to be contemptible; so active in pursuit of self-interest as to become hateful. The junta was occupied in devising how to render itself at once despotic and popular; how to excite enthusiasm and check freedom of expression; how to enjoy the luxury of power without its labour; how to acquire great reputation without trouble; how to be indolent and victorious at the same moment. Fear prevented it from removing to Madrid after every preparation had been made for a public entrance into that capital. The members passed decrees, repressing the liberty of the press on the ground of the deceptions practised upon the public; but themselves never hesitated to deceive the British agents, the generals, the government, and their own countrymen, by the most flagitious falsehoods upon every subject, whether of greater or less importance. They hedged their own dignity round, with ridiculous and misplaced forms opposed to the vital principle of an insurrectional government; they devoted their attention to abstract speculations, recalled the exiled Jesuits, and inundated the country with long and laboured state papers, but left the pressing business of the moment to shift for itself. Every application on the part of lord William Bentinck and Mr. Stuart, even for an order to expedite a common courier, was met by difficulties and delays, and it was necessary to have recourse to the most painful solicitations to obtain the slightest attention; nor did that mode always succeed.

Appendix, No. 13, section 3.

Sir John Moore strenuously grappled with the difficulties besetting him: well knowing the value of time in military transactions, he urged forward the preparations with all possible activity. He was very desirous, that troops who had a journey of six hundred miles to make previous to meeting the enemy, should not, at the commencement, be overwhelmed by the torrents of rain which in Portugal descend at this period with such violence as to destroy the shoes, ammunition, and accoutrements of a soldier, and render him almost unfit for service. The Spanish generals recommended that the line of march should be conducted by Almeida, Ciudad Rodrigo, Salamanca, Valladolid, and Burgos, and that the magazines for the campaign should be formed at one of the latter towns; and as this coincided with the previous preparations, the army was organized in three columns, two of which were directed upon Almeida, by the routes of Coimbra and Guarda, and the third, comprising the artillery, the cavalry, and the regiments quartered in the Alemtejo, was destined to move by Alcantara, upon Ciudad Rodrigo. Almeida itself was chosen for a place of arms, and all the reserve-stores and provisions were forwarded there, as time and circumstances would permit; but the want of money, the unsettled state of the country, and the inexperience of the commissariat, rendered it difficult to procure the means of transport even for the light baggage of the regiments, although the quantity of the latter was reduced so much as to create discontent. One Sattaro (the same person who has been already mentioned as an agent of Junot's in the negotiation with sir Charles Cotton) engaged to supply the army, but dishonestly failing in his contract, so embarrassed the operations, that the general resigned all hope of being able to move with more than the light baggage, the ammunition necessary for immediate use, and a scanty supply of medicines. The formation of the magazines at Almeida was also retarded, and the future subsistence of the troops was thus thrown upon a raw commissariat, unprovided with money. The general, however, relying upon its increasing experience, and upon the activity of lord William Bentinck and Mr. Stuart, did not delay his march, but sent agents to Madrid and other places to make contracts, and to endeavour to raise money, for such was the policy of the ministers, that they supplied the Spaniards with gold, and left the English army to get it back in loans.

Many of the regiments were actually in movement when an unexpected difficulty forced the commander-in-chief to make a fresh disposition of the troops. The state of the Portuguese roads north of the Tagus was unknown; the native officers and the people declared that they were impracticable for artillery. The opinion of colonel Lopez, a military commissary, sent by the Spanish government to facilitate the march of the British, coincided with this information, and the reports of one of the most intelligent and enterprising of the officers of the quarter-master-general's department, who were employed to examine the lines of route, corroborated the general opinion[16]. Junot, indeed, with infinite pains, had carried his guns along these roads, but his carriages had been broken, and the batteries rendered unserviceable by the operation. In this dilemma, sir John Moore reluctantly determined to send his artillery and cavalry by the south bank of the Tagus, to Talavera de la Reyna, from whence they might gain Naval Carneiro, the Escurial, the pass of the Guadarama mountains, Espiñar, Arevalo, and Salamanca. He would have marched the whole army by the same route, if this disagreeable intelligence respecting the northern roads had been obtained earlier; but when the arrangements were all made for the supplies to go to Almeida, and when most of the regiments were actually in movement towards that town, it was too late to alter their destination.

This separation of the artillery violated a great military principle, which prescribes that the point of concentration for an army should be beyond the reach of the enemy. But it was a matter of apparent necessity, and, moreover, no danger was apprehended from the offensive operations of an adversary represented to be incapable of maintaining his own line of defence. Valladolid and Burgos were considered by the Spaniards as safe places for the English magazines, and sir John Moore shared so much of the universal confidence in the Spanish enthusiasm and courage, as to suppose that Salamanca would not be an insecure point of concentration for his columns, under the protection of such numerous patriotic armies as were said to be on the Ebro. One brigade of six-pounders he retained with the head-quarters, the remainder of his artillery, twenty-four pieces; the cavalry, amounting to a thousand troopers; the great parc of the army, containing many hundred carriages, and escorted by three thousand infantry, he sent by the road of Talavera, under the command of sir John Hope, an officer qualified by his talents, firmness, and zeal, to conduct the most important enterprises.

The rest of the army marched in three columns, the first by Alcantara, the second by Abrantes, the third by Coimbra, in the direction of Almeida and Ciudad Rodrigo; and with such energy did the general overcome all obstacles, that the whole of the troops were in movement, and head-quarters quitted Lisbon by the 26th of October, just twenty days after the receipt of the despatch which appointed him to the chief command; a surprising diligence, but rendered necessary by the pressure of circumstances. "The army," to use his own words, "run the risk of finding itself in front of the enemy with no more ammunition than the men carried in their pouches:" "but had I waited," he adds, "until every thing was forwarded, the troops would not have been in Spain until the spring, and I trust that the enemy will not find out our wants as soon as they will feel the effects of what we have."

The Spaniards, however, who expected "every body to fly except themselves," thought him slow, and were impatient, and from every quarter indeed letters arrived, pressing him to advance. Lord William Bentinck and Mr. Stuart, witnesses of the sluggish incapacity of the Spanish government, judged that such a support was absolutely necessary to sustain the reeling strength of Spain. The supreme government were even awakened for a moment. Hitherto, as a mask for its ignorance, it had treated the French power with contempt, and the Spanish generals and the people echoed the sentiments of the government: but now, a letter addressed by the governor of Bayonne to general Jourdan, stating, that sixty thousand infantry, and seven thousand cavalry, would reinforce the French armies between the 16th of October and the 16th of November, was intercepted, and made the junta feel that a crisis for which it was unprepared was approaching. With the folly usually attendant on improvidence, these men, who had been so slow themselves, required that others should be supernaturally quick when danger pressed.

In the mean time sir David Baird's forces arrived at Coruña. Lord William Bentinck had given intimation of their approach, and the central junta had repeatedly assured him, that every necessary order was given, and that every facility would be afforded, for the disembarkation and supply of the troops. This was untrue; no measures of any kind had been taken, no instructions issued, and no preparations were made. The junta of Coruña disliked the personal trouble of a disembarkation in that port, and in the hope that Baird would be driven to another, refused him permission to land, until a communication was had with Aranjuez; but fifteen days elapsed before an answer could be obtained from a government, who were daily pestering sir John Moore with complaints of the tardiness of his march.

Appendix, No. 13, section 1.
Sir J. Moore to lord Castlereagh, 27th Oct.

Appendix, No. 13, section 5 and 6.

Sir David Baird came without money, sir John could only give him 8000*l.*, a sum which might have been mistaken for a private loan, if the fact of its being public property were not expressly mentioned. But at this time Mr. Frere, the plenipotentiary, arrived at Coruña, with two millions of dollars, intended for the use of the Spaniards; and while such large sums, contrary to the earnest recommendations of Mr. Stuart and major Cox, were lavished in that quarter, the penury of the English general obliged him to borrow from the funds in Mr. Frere's hands. Thus assisted, the troops were put in motion; but, wanting all the equipments essential to an army, they were forced to march by half battalions, conveying their scanty stores on country cars, hired from day to day, nor was that meagre assistance obtained but at great expense, and by compliance with a vulgar mercenary spirit predominant among the authorities of Gallicia. The junta frequently promised to procure the carriages, but did not; the commissaries pushed to the wall by the delay, offered an exorbitant remuneration: the cars were then forthcoming, and the procrastination of the government proved to be a concerted plan, to defraud the military chest. In fine, the local rulers were unfriendly, crafty, fraudulent, the peasantry suspicious, fearful, rude, disinclined towards strangers, and indifferent to public affairs. A few shots only were required to render theirs a hostile instead of a friendly greeting.

Sir H. Dalrymple's Correspondence.

With Mr. Frere came a fleet, conveying a Spanish force, under the marquis of Romana. When the insurrection first broke forth, that nobleman commanded fourteen or fifteen thousand troops, who were serving with the French armies. How to recover this disciplined body of men from the enemy was a subject of early anxiety with the junta of Seville; and Castaños, in his first intercourse with sir Hew Dalrymple, signified his wish that the British government should adopt some mode of apprising Romana, that Spain was in arms, and should endeavour to extricate him and his army from the toils of the enemy. A gentleman named M'Kenzie was employed by the English ministers to conduct the enterprise; the Spanish troops were quartered in Holstein, Sleswig, Jutland, and the islands of Funen, Zealand, and Langeland; Mr. M'Kenzie, through the medium of one Robertson, a catholic priest, opened a communication with Romana. Neither the general, nor the soldiers he commanded, hesitated, and a judicious plan being concerted, sir Richard Keats, with a squadron detached from the Baltic fleet, suddenly appeared off Nyborg, in the island of Funen. A majority of the Spanish regiments quartered in Sleswig immediately seized all the Danish craft in the different harbours of that coast, and pushed across the channel to Funen, where Romana, with the assistance of Keats, had already seized the port and castle of Nyborg without opposition, save from a small ship of war that was moored across the mouth of the harbour. From Nyborg Romana passed to Langeland, and there awaited the arrival of sir James Saumarez with the English fleet, on board of which he embarked with about nine thousand five hundred men. Of the remainder, some were disarmed, or overawed by the Danish troops in Zealand, and some did not escape from Sleswig. This enterprise was conducted with prudent activity, and the unhesitating patriotism of the Spanish soldiers was very honourable, but the danger was trifling; Mr. Robertson incurred the most. Romana, after touching at England, repaired to Coruña; his troops did not, however, land at that port, but after a while coasted to St. Andero, and being there disembarked, and equipped from the English stores, proceeded by divisions to join Blake's army in Biscay.

Among the various subjects calling for sir John Moore's attention, there was none of greater interest than the appointment of a generalissimo to the Spanish armies. Impressed with the imminent danger of procrastination, or uncertainty in such a matter, he desired lord William Bentinck and Mr. Stuart to urge the central government with all their force upon that head; to lord Castlereagh he represented the injury that must accrue to the cause, if the measure was delayed, and he proposed to go himself to Madrid, with a view of adding weight to his representations. Subsequent events, which left him no time for the journey, frustrated this intention, and there seems no reason to imagine, that his personal remonstrances would have weighed with a government, described by Mr. Stuart, after a thorough experience of their qualities, as, "never having made a single exertion for the public good, neither rewarding merit nor punishing guilt," and being for all useful purposes "absolutely null." The junta's dislike to a single military chief was not an error of the head, and reason is of little avail against the suggestions of self-interest.

The march of the British troops was as rapid as the previous preparations had been. Head-quarters reached Almeida on the 8th of November. The infantry were already assembled at that town. The condition of the men was superb, and their discipline exemplary; on that side all was well, but from the obstacles encountered by sir David Baird, and the change of direction in the artillery, it was evident, that no considerable force could be brought into action before the end of the month. Meanwhile, the Spaniards were hastening events. Despatches from lord William Bentinck announced that the enemy remained stationary on the Ebro, although reinforced by ten thousand men; that Castaños was about to cross that river at Tudela; and that the army of Aragon was moving by Sor upon Roncevalles, with a view to gain the rear of the French, while Castaños assailed their left flank. The general, judging that such movements would bring on a battle, the success of which must be very doubtful, became uneasy for his own artillery: his concern was increased by observing, that the guns might have kept with the other columns; "and if any thing adverse happens, I have not," he wrote to general Hope, "necessity to plead; the road we are now travelling, that by Villa Velha and Guarda, is practicable for artillery. The brigade under Wilmot has already reached Guarda, and as far as I have already seen, the road presents few obstacles, and those easily surmounted; this knowledge was, however, only acquired by our own officers; when the brigade was at Castello Branco, it was not certain if it could proceed." Wherefore, he desired Hope no longer to trust any reports, but seek a shorter line, by Placentia, across the mountains to Salamanca.

Up to this period, all reports from the agents, all information from the government at home, all communications public and private, coincided upon one subject. *The Spaniards were an enthusiastic, a heroic people, a nation of unparalleled energy! their armies were brave; they were numerous; they were confident! one hundred and eighty thousand men were actually in line of battle, extending from the sea-coast of Biscay to Zaragoza; the French, reduced to a fourth of this number, cooped up in a corner, shrunk from an encounter; they were deserted by the emperor; they were trembling; they were spiritless!* Nevertheless, the general was somewhat distrustful; he perceived the elements of disaster in the divided commands, and the lengthened lines of the Spaniards; and early in October he had predicted the mischief that such a system would produce. "As long as the French remain upon the defensive," he observed, "it will not be so much felt; but the moment an attack is made, some great calamity must ensue." However, he was not without faith in the multitude and energy of the patriots, when he considered the greatness of their cause.

Appendix, No. 13, section 7.

Castaños was at this time pointed out by the central junta as the person with whom to concert a plan of campaign, and sir John Moore, concluding that it was a preliminary step towards making that officer generalissimo, wrote to him in a conciliatory style, well calculated to ensure a cordial co-operation. This was an encouraging event; the English general believed it to be the commencement of a better system, and looked forward with more hope to the opening of the war; but this favourable state soon changed. Far from being created chief of all, Castaños was superseded in the command he already held, the whole folly of the Spanish character broke forth, and confusion and distress followed. But even at that moment clouds were arising in a quarter, which had hitherto been all sunshine. The military agents, as the crisis approached, lowered their tone of confidence, they no longer dwelt upon the enthusiasm of the armies; they admitted, that the confidence of the troops was sinking, and that even in numbers they were inferior to the French. In truth, it was full time to change their note, for the real state of affairs could no longer be concealed, and a great catastrophe was at hand; but what of wildness in their projects, or of skill in the enemy's; what of ignorance, vanity, and presumption in their generals; what of fear among their soldiers; and what of fortune in the events; combined to hasten the ruin of the Spaniards, and how that ruin was effected, I, quitting the English army for a time, will now relate.

CHAPTER IV

In the preceding chapters I have exposed the weakness, the folly, the improvidence of Spain, and shown how the bad passions and sordid views of her leaders were encouraged by the unwise prodigality of England. I have dissected the full boast and meagre preparations of the governments in both countries; laying bare the bones and sinews of the insurrection; and by comparing their loose and feeble structure with the strongly knitted frame and large proportions of the enemy, prepared the reader for the inevitable issue of a conflict between such ill-matched champions. In the present book, I shall recount the sudden and terrible manner in which the Spanish armies were overthrown, and the tempestuous progress of the French emperor.

But previous to relating these disasters I must revert to the period immediately following the retreat of king Joseph, and trace those early operations of the French and Spanish forces which, like a jesting prologue to a deep tragedy, unworthily ushered in the great catastrophe.

CAMPAIGN OF THE FRENCH AND SPANISH ARMIES BEFORE THE ARRIVAL OF THE EMPEROR

After general Cuesta was removed from the command, and that the junta of Seville was, by major Cox, forced to disgorge so much of the English subsidy as sufficed for the immediate relief of the troops in Madrid, all the Spanish armies closed upon the Ebro.

General Broderick's Correspondence.

General Blake, reinforced by eight thousand Asturians, established his base of operations at Reynosa, opened a communication with the English vessels off the port of St. Andero, and directed his views towards Biscay.

The Castillian army, conducted by general Pignatelli, resumed its march upon Burgo del Osma and Logroña.

Capt. Whittingham's.

The two divisions of the Andalusian troops under Lapeña, and the Murcian division of general Llamas, advanced to Taranzona and Tudela.

Colonel Doyle's.

Palafox, with the Aragonese and Valencian divisions of St. Marc, operated from the side of Zaragoza.

Castaños's Vindication.

Fourteen or fifteen thousand of the Estremaduran troops were drafted, and placed under the conduct of the conde de Belvedere, a weak youth, not twenty years of age. They were at first directed upon Logroña, as forming part of Castaños's command, but finally, as we shall find, received another destination.

Whittingham's Correspondence.

Between these armies there was neither concert nor connexion; their movements were regulated by some partial view of affairs, or by the silly caprices of the generals, who were ignorant of each other's plans, and little solicitous to combine operations. The weak characters of many of the chiefs, the inexperience of all, and the total want of system, opened a field for intriguing men, and invited unqualified persons to interfere in the direction of affairs. Thus we find colonel Doyle making a journey to Zaragoza, and priding himself upon having prevailed with Palafox to detach seven thousand men to Sanguessa; and captain Whittingham, without any knowledge of Doyle's interference, earnestly dissuading the Spaniards from such an enterprise. The first affirmed, that the movement would "turn the enemy's left flank, threaten his rear, and have the appearance of cutting off his retreat." The second argued, that Sanguessa, being seventy miles from Zaragoza, and only a few leagues from Pampeluna, the detachment would itself be cut off. Doyle judged that it would draw the French from Caparosa and Milagro, and expose those points to Llamas and La-Peña; that it would force the enemy to recall the reinforcements said to be marching against Blake, and enable that general to form a junction with the Asturians, when he might, with forty thousand men, possess himself of the Pyrenees; and if the French army, estimated at thirty-five thousand men, did not fly, cut it off from France, or by moving on Miranda, sweep clear Biscay and Castille. Palafox, pleased with this plan, sent Whittingham to inform Llamas and La-Peña, that O'Neil would, with six thousand men, march on the 15th of September to Sanguessa. Those generals disapproved of the movement as dangerous, premature, and at variance with the plan arranged in the council of war held at Madrid. Palafox, regardless of their opinion, persisted. O'Neil occupied Sanguessa, drew the attention of the enemy, and was immediately driven across the Alagon river.

Ld. W. Bentinck's Correspondce. MS.
Doyle's Correspondence. MS.

In this manner all their projects, characterized by a profound ignorance of war, were lightly adopted and as lightly abandoned, or ended in disasters; yet victory was more confidently anticipated, than if consummate skill had presided over the arrangements; and this vain-glorious feeling, extending to the military agents, was by them propagated in England, where the fore-boasting was nearly as loud, and as absurd, as in the Peninsula. The delusion was universal; even lord William Bentinck and Mr. Stuart, deceived by the curious consistency of the Spanish falsehoods, doubted if the French army was able to maintain its position, and believed that the Spaniards had obtained a moral ascendancy in the field. Drunk with vanity and folly, the leading Spaniards in the capital, feeling certain that the "remnants," as they were called, of the French army on the Ebro, estimated at from thirty-five to forty thousand men, would be immediately destroyed, proposed that the British army should be directed upon Catalonia, and when they found that this proposal was not acceded to, they withdrew ten thousand men from the Murcian division, and sent them to the neighbourhood of Lerida.

Appendix, No. 6.

The natural pride and arrogance of the Spaniards were greatly aided by the timid and false operations of king Joseph. Twenty days after the evacuation of Madrid, that monarch was at the head of above fifty thousand fighting men, exclusive of eight thousand employed to maintain the communications, and to furnish the garrisons of Pampeluna, Tolosa, Irun, St. Sebastian, and Bilbao.

The French army of Catalonia, seventeen thousand in number, was, as we have seen, distinct from the king's command; but a strong reserve, assembled at Bayonne, under general Drouet, supplied him with reinforcements, and was itself supported by drafts from the depôts in the interior of France.

Six thousand men, divided into several moveable columns, watched the openings of the Pyrenees, from St. Jean Pied de Port to Rousillon, and guarded the frontier from Spanish incursions; and a second reserve, composed of Neapolitans, Tuscans, and Piedmontese, was commenced at Belgarde, with a view of supporting Duhesme in Catalonia.

How the king quelled the nascent insurrection at Bilbao, and how he dispersed the insurgents of the valleys in Aragon, I have already related. After those operations the French army was re-organized and divided into three grand divisions and a reserve. Marshal Bessieres retained the command of the right wing; marshal Moncey assumed that of the left; and marshal Ney arriving at this period from Paris, took charge of the centre; while the reserve, chiefly composed of detachments from the imperial guard, remained near the person of the king. The old republican general, Jourdan, a man whose day of glory belonged to another era, re-appeared upon the military stage, and filled the office of major-general to the army.

Napoleon's notes. Appendix, Nos. 4 and 5.

S

Journal of the king's operations. MS.

With such a force, and so assisted, there was nothing in Spain, turn which way he would, capable of opposing king Joseph's march; but the incongruity of a camp with a court is always productive of indecision and of error; the truncheon does not fit every hand, and the French army soon felt the inconvenience of having at its head a monarch who was not a warrior. Joseph remained on the defensive; but he did not understand the force of the maxim, "*that offensive movements are the foundation of a good defence.*" He held Bilbao, but he abandoned Tudela contrary to the advice of the generals who had conducted the operations on that side, and in its place Milagro, a small town, situated upon the rivers Arga and Aragon, just above their confluence with the Ebro, was by him chosen as the position of battle for the left wing. As long as Bessieres held Burgos in force, his cavalry commanded the valley of the Douero, menaced Palencia and Valladolid, and scouring the plains, kept Blake and Cuesta in check. Instead of reinforcing a post so advantageous, the king relinquished Burgos as a point beyond his line of defence, and Bessieres' troops were posted in successive divisions behind it, as far as Puente Lara on the Ebro. Ney's force lined that river down to Logroña; the reserve was quartered behind Miranda; and Trevino, a small obscure place, was chosen as the point of battle, for the right and centre. In this disadvantageous situation the army, with some trifling changes, remained from the middle of August until late in September. During that time the artillery and carriages of transport were repaired, magazines were collected, the cavalry remounted, and the preparations made for an active campaign when the reinforcements should arrive from Germany.

The line of resistance thus offered to the Spaniards, evinced a degree of timidity which the relative strength of the armies by no means justified; the left of the French evidently leaned towards the great communication with France, and seemed to refuse the support of Pampeluna. Tudela was abandoned, and Burgos resigned to the enterprise of the Spaniards. All this indicated fear, a disposition to retreat if the enemy advanced. The king complained with what extreme difficulty he obtained intelligence; yet he neglected by forward movements to feel for his adversaries. Wandering as it were in the dark, he gave a loose to his imagination, and conjuring up a phantom of Spanish strength, which had no real existence, anxiously waited for the development of their power, while they were exposing their weakness by a succession of the most egregious blunders.

Joseph's errors did not escape the animadversion of his brother, whose sagacity enabled him, although at a distance, to detect, through the glare of the insurrection, all the inefficiency of the Spaniards; but, despising them as soldiers, he dreaded the moral effect produced by their momentary success, and he was preparing to crush the rising hopes of his enemies. Joseph's retreat, and subsequent position, therefore, displeased him; and he desired his brother to check the exultation of the patriots, by acting upon a bold and well-considered plan, of which he sent him the outline.

Appendix, No. 5.

His notes, dictated upon the occasion, are replete with genius, and evince his absolute mastery of the art of war. "It was too late," he said, "to discuss the question, whether Madrid should have been retained or abandoned? Idle to consider, if a position, covering the siege of Zaragoza, might not have been formed; useless to examine, if the line of the Douro was not better than that of the Ebro for the French army. The line of the Ebro was actually taken, and it must be kept; to advance from that river without a fixed object would create indecision; this would bring the troops back again, and produce an injurious moral effect; but why abandon Tudela? Why relinquish Burgos? Those towns were of note, and of reputation; the possession of them gave a moral influence, and moral force constituted two-thirds of the strength of armies. Tudela and Burgos had also a relative importance; the first possessing a stone bridge, was on the communication of Pampeluna and Madrid. It commanded the canal of Zaragoza. It was the capital of a province. When the army resumed offensive operations, their first enterprise would be the siege of Zaragoza; from that town to Tudela, the land carriage was three days, but the water carriage was only fourteen hours; wherefore to have the besieging artillery and stores at Tudela was the same as to have them at Zaragoza. If the Spaniards got possession of the former, all Navarre would be in a state of insurrection, and Pampeluna exposed. Tudela then was of vast importance; but Milagro was of none. It was an obscure place, without a bridge, and commanding no communication; in short, it was without interest, defended nothing! led to nothing! A river," said this great commander, "though it should be as large as the Vistula, and as rapid as the Danube at its mouth, is nothing, unless there are good points of passage, and a head quick to take the offensive. The Ebro as a defence was less than nothing, a mere line of demarcation! and Milagro was useless. The enemy might neglect it, be at Estella, and from thence gain Tolosa, before any preparation could be made to receive him; he might come from Soria, from Logroña, or from Zaragoza. Again, Burgos was the capital of a province, the centre of many communications, a town of great fame, and of relative value to the French army. To occupy it in force, and offensively, would threaten Palencia, Valladolid, Aranda, and even Madrid. It is necessary," observed the emperor, "to have made war a long time to conceive this. It is necessary to have made a number of offensive enterprises to know how much the smallest event, or even indication, encourages or discourages, and decides the adoption of one enterprise instead of another." "In short, if the enemy occupies Burgos, Logroña, and Tudela, the French army will be in a pitiful position. It is not known if he has left Madrid; you are ignorant of what has become of the Gallician army, and we have reason to suspect that it may have been directed upon Portugal; in such a state to take up, instead of a bold, menacing, and honourable position like Burgos, a confined shameful one like Trevino, is to say to the enemy, you have nothing to fear, go elsewhere, we have made our dispositions to go farther, or we have chosen our ground to fight; come there, without fear of being disturbed. But what will the French general do if the enemy marches the next day upon Burgos? Will he let the citadel of that town be taken by six thousand insurgents? or if the French have left a garrison in the castle, how can four or five hundred men retire in such a vast plain? and, from that time, all is gone; the enemy master of the citadel, it cannot be retaken; if, on the contrary, we should guard the citadel, we must give battle to the enemy, because it cannot hold out more than three days, and if we wish to fight a battle, why should Bessieres abandon the ground where we wish to fight? These dispositions appear badly considered, and when the enemy shall march, our troops will meet with such an insult as will demoralize them if there are only insurgents or light troops advancing against them. If fifteen thousand insurgents enter into Burgos, retrench themselves in the town, and occupy the castle, it will be necessary to calculate a march of several days to enable us to post ourselves there, and to retake the town, which cannot be done without some inconvenience. If, during the time, the real attack is upon Logroña or Pampeluna, we shall have made countermarches without use, which will have fatigued the army. If we hold it with cavalry only, is it not to say we do not intend stopping, and to invite the enemy to come there? It was the first time," he said, "that an army had quitted all its offensive positions to take up a bad defensive line, and to affect to choose its field of battle, when the thousand and one combinations which might take place, and the distance of the enemy, did not leave a probability of being able to foresee if the battle would take place at Tudela, between Tudela and Pampeluna, between Soria and the Ebro, or between Burgos and Miranda;" and then followed an observation which may be studied with advantage by those authors who, unacquainted with the simplest rudiments of military science, censure the conduct of a general, and are pleased, from some obscure nook, to point out his errors to the world; authors who, profoundly ignorant of the numbers, situation, and resources of the opposing armies, pretend, nevertheless, to detail with great accuracy the right method of executing the most difficult and delicate operations of war. As the rebuke of Turenne, who frankly acknowledged to Louvois that he could pass the Rhine at a particular spot if the latter's finger were a bridge, has been lost upon such men, perhaps the more recent opinion of Napoleon may be disregarded. "But it is not permitted," says that consummate general, "*it is not permitted, at the distance of three hundred leagues, and without even a state of the situation of the army, to direct what should be done!*"

After having thus protected himself from the charge of presumption, the emperor proceeded to recommend certain dispositions for the defence of the Ebro. The Spaniards, he said, were not to be feared in the field; twenty-five thousand French in a good position would suffice to beat all their armies united, and this opinion he deduced from the events of Dupont's campaign, of which he gave a short analysis. Let Tudela, he said, be retrenched if possible, at all events it should be occupied in force, and offensively towards Zaragoza. Let the general commanding there collect provisions on all sides; secure the boats, with a view to future operations when the reinforcements should arrive, and maintain his communication with Logroña by the right bank if he can, but certainly by the left. Let his corps be considered as one of observation; if a body of insurgents only approach, he may fight them, or keep them constantly on the defensive by his movements against their line or against Zaragoza. If regular troops attack him, and he is forced across the Ebro, let him then manœuvre about Pampeluna until the general-in-chief has made his dispositions for the main body. In this manner no prompt movement upon Estella and Tolosa can take place, and the corps of observation will have amply fulfilled its task. Let marshal Bessieres, with all his corps united, and reinforced by the light cavalry of the army, encamp in the wood near Burgos; let the citadel be well occupied, the hospital, the dépôts, and all encumbrances sent over the Ebro; let him keep in a condition to manœuvre, be under arms every day at three o'clock in the morning, and remain until the return of his patroles. He should send parties to a great extent, as far as two days' march. Let the corps of the centre be placed at Miranda and Briviesca, and all the encumbrances be likewise sent across the Ebro behind Vittoria. This corps should be under arms every morning, and send patroles by the road of Soria, and wherever the enemy may be expected. It must not be lost sight of, that these two corps, being to be united, they should be connected as little as possible with Logroña, and consider the left wing as a corps detached, having a line of operations upon Pampeluna, and a separate part to act. Tudela is preserved as a post contiguous to the line. Be well on the defensive, he continues, in short, make war, that is to say, get information from the alcaldes, the curates, the posts, the chiefs of convents, and the principal proprietors, you will then be perfectly informed; the patroles should always be directed upon the side of Soria, and of Burgos, upon Palencia, and upon the side of Aranda. They could thus form three posts of interception, and send three reports of men arrested; these men should be treated well, and dismissed, after they had given the information desired of them. Let the enemy then come, and we can unite all our forces; hide our marches from him, and fall upon his flank at the moment he is meditating an offensive movement.

With regard to the minor details, the emperor thus expressed himself: "Soria is not, I believe, more than two short marches from the actual position of the army; that town has constantly acted against us; an expedition sent there to disarm it, to take thirty of the principal people as hostages, and to obtain provisions, would have a good effect. It would be useful to occupy St. Ander. It will be of advantage to move by the direct road of Bilbao to St. Ander. It will be necessary to occupy and disarm Biscay and Navarre. Every Spaniard taken in arms there should be shot[17]. The manufactories of arms at Palencia should be watched, to hinder them from working for the rebels. The port of Pancorbo should be armed and fortified with great activity; ovens, and magazines of provisions and ammunition, should be placed there. Situated nearly half way between Madrid and Bayonne, it is an intermediate post for the army, and a point of support for troops operating towards Gallicia. The interest of the enemy," he resumes, "is to mask his forces. By hiding the true point of attack, he operates in such a manner, that the blow he means to strike is never indicated in a positive way, and the opposing general can only guess it by a well-matured knowledge of his own position, and of the mode in which he makes his offensive system act, to protect his defensive system. We have no accounts of what the enemy is about; it is said that no news can be obtained, as if this case was extraordinary in an army, as if spies were common: they must do in Spain, as they do in other places. Send parties out. Let them carry off, sometimes the priest, sometimes the alcalde, the chief of a convent, the master of the post or his deputy, and, above all, the letters. Put them under arrest until they speak. Question them twice each day, or keep them as hostages. Charge them to send foot messengers, and to get news. When we know how to take measures of vigour and force, it is easy to get news. All the posts, all the letters, must be intercepted. The single motive of procuring intelligence will be sufficient to authorise a detachment of four or five thousand men, who will go into a great town, will take the letters from the post, will seize the richest citizens, their letters, papers, gazettes, &c. It is beyond doubt, that even in the French lines, the inhabitants are all informed of what passes; of course, out of that line, they know more; what, then, should prevent you from seizing the principal men? Let them be sent back again without being ill treated. It is a fact, that when we are not in a desert, but in a peopled country, if the general is not well instructed, it is because he is ignorant of his trade. The services which the inhabitants render to an enemy's general, are never given from affection, nor even to get money. The truest method to obtain them is by safeguards and protections to preserve their lives, their goods, their towns, or their monasteries!"

Appendix, No. 6.

Joseph, although by no means a dull man, seems to have had no portion of his brother's martial genius, and the operations recommended by the latter did not appear to the king to be applicable to the state of affairs. He did not adopt them, but proposed others; in discussing which, he thus defended the policy of his retreat from Madrid.

"When the *defection* of twenty-two thousand men (Dupont's) caused the king to quit the capital, the disposable troops remaining were divided in three corps: that immediately about his person; that of marshal Bessieres; and that of general Verdier, then besieging Zaragoza: but these bodies were spread over a hundred leagues of ground, and with the last the king had little or no connexion. His first movement was to unite the two former at Burgos, and afterwards to enter into communication with the third. The line of defence on the Ebro was adopted." This operation Joseph affirmed to have been dictated by sound reason. — Because "when the events of Andalusia foreboded a regular and serious war, prudence did not permit three corps, the strongest of which was only eighteen thousand men, to separate to a greater distance than six days' march, in the midst of eleven millions of people in a state of hostility. But fifty thousand French could defend with success a line of sixty leagues, guarding the two grand communications of Burgos and Tudela, against enemies who had not, up to that period, been able to carry to either point above twenty-five thousand men; because fifteen thousand French could be united upon either."

Joseph was dissatisfied with Napoleon's plans, and preferred his own. The disposable troops at his command, exclusive of those in Bilbao, were fifty thousand; these he distributed as follows. The right wing occupied Burgos, Pancorbo, and Puente Lara. The centre was posted between Haro and Logroña; the left extended from Logroña to Tudela; the latter town was not occupied. He contended that this arrangement, at once offensive and defensive, might be advantageously continued, if the great army directed upon Spain arrived in September, since it tended to refit the army already there, and menaced the enemy; but that it could not be prolonged until

November, because in three months the Spaniards must make a great progress, and would very soon be in a state to take the offensive with grand organized corps, obedient to a central administration, which would have time to form in Madrid. Every thing announced, he said, that the month of October was one of those decisive epochs which gave to the party who knew how to profit from it, the priority of movements and success, the progress of which it was difficult to calculate.

In this view of affairs, the merits of six projects were discussed by the king.

First. To remain in the actual position. This was declared to be unsustainable, because the enemy could attack the left with forty thousand, the centre with forty thousand, the right with as many. Tudela and Navarre, as far as Logroña, required twenty-five thousand men to defend them. Burgos could not be defended but by an army in a state to resist the united forces of Blake and Cuesta, which would amount to eighty thousand men, and it was doubtful if the twenty thousand bayonets which could be opposed, could completely beat them; if they did not, the French would be harassed by the insurgents of the three provinces (Biscay, Navarre, and Guipuscoa), who would interpose between the left wing and France.

Second project. To carry the centre and reserve by Tudela, towards Zaragoza or Almazan; united with the left, they would amount to thirty thousand men, who might seek for, and, doubtless, would defeat the enemy, if he was met with on that side. In the meantime, the right wing, leaving garrisons in the citadel of Burgos and the fort of Pancorbo, could occupy the enemy, and watch any movements in the Montagna St. Ander, or disembarkations that might take place at the ports; but this task was considered difficult, because Pancorbo was not the only defile accessible to artillery. Three leagues from thence, another road led upon Miranda, and there was a third passage over the point of the chain which stretched between Haro and Miranda.

Third project. To leave the defence of Navarre to the left wing. To carry the centre, the reserve, and the right wing, to Burgos, and to beat the enemy before he could unite; an easy task, as the French would be thirty thousand strong. Meanwhile, Moncey could keep the Spaniards in check on the side of Tudela, or if unable to do that, he was to march up the Ebro, by Logroña and Briviesca, and join the main body. The communication with France would be thus lost, but the army might maintain itself until the arrival of the emperor. A modification of this project proposed that Moncey, retiring to the entrenched camp of Pampeluna, should there await either the arrival of the emperor, or the result of the operations towards Burgos.

Fourth project. To pass the Ebro in retreat, and to endeavour to tempt the enemy to fight in the plain between that river and Vittoria.

Fifth project. To retire, supporting the left upon Pampeluna, the right upon Montdragon.

Sixth project. To leave garrisons, with the means of a six weeks' defence, in Pampeluna, St. Sebastian, Pancorbo, and Burgos. To unite the rest of the army march against the enemy, attack him wherever he was found, and then wait either near Madrid or in that country, into which the pursuit of the Spaniards, or the facility of living, should draw the army. This plan relinquished the communications with France entirely, but it was said that the grand army could easily open them again, and the troops already in Spain would be sufficiently strong to defy all the efforts of the enemy, to disconcert all his projects, and to wait in a noble attitude the general impulse which would be given by the arrival of the emperor.

Of all these projects the last was the favourite with the king, who strongly recommended it, and asserted, that if it was followed, affairs would be more prosperous when the emperor arrived than could be expected from any other plan. Marshal Ney and general Jourdan approved of it; but it would appear that Napoleon had other views, and too little confidence in his brother's military judgment, to intrust so great a matter to his guidance.

OBSERVATIONS

1°. It is undoubted, that there must always be some sympathy of genius in the man who is to execute another's conception in military affairs. Without that species of harmony between their minds, the thousand accidental occurrences and minor combinations which must happen contrary to expectation, will inevitably embarrass the executor to such a degree, that he will be unable to see the most obvious advantages, and in striving to unite the plan he has received with his own views, he will adopt neither, but steer an unsteady reeling course between both, and fail of success. The reason of this appears to be, that a strong, and, if the term may be used, inveterate attention must be fixed upon certain great principles of action in war, to enable a general to disregard the minor events and inconveniences which cross his purpose; minor they are to the great object, but in themselves sufficient to break down the firmness and self-possession of any but extraordinary men.

2°. The original memoir from which Joseph's projects have been extracted is so blotted and interlined, that it would be unfair to consider it as a matured production. The great error which pervades it, is the conjectural data upon which he founds his plans, and the little real information which he appears to have had relative to the Spanish forces, views, or interior policy.

Thus he was prepared to act upon the idea, that the central junta would be able and provident; the parties united, and the armies strong and well administered; none of which things really took place. Again, he estimated Cuesta and Blake's armies at eighty thousand, and considered them as one body; but they were never united at all, and if they had, they would scarcely have amounted to sixty thousand. The bold idea of throwing himself into the interior came too late; he should have thought of that before he quitted Madrid, or at least before the central government was established at that capital. His operations might have been successful against the miserable armies opposed to him; against good and moveable troops they would not, as the emperor's admirable notes prove.

The first project, wanting those offensive combinations discussed by Napoleon, was open to all his objections, as being timid and incomplete. The second was crude and ill-considered, for, according to the king's estimate of the Spanish force, thirty thousand men on each wing might oppose the heads of his columns, sixty thousand could still have been united at Logroña, pass the Ebro, excite an insurrection in Navarre, Guipuscoa, and Biscay, seize Tolosa and Miranda, and fall upon the rear of the French army, which thus cut in two, and its communications intercepted, would have been extremely embarrassed. The third was not better judged. Burgos as an offensive post, protecting the line of defence, was very valuable, and to unite a large force there was so far prudent; but if the Spaniards retired, and refused battle with their left, while the centre and right operated by Logroña and Sanguessa, what would have been the result? the French right must without any definite object either have continued to advance, or remained stationary without communication, or returned to fight a battle for those very positions which they had just quitted. The fourth depended entirely upon accident, and is not worth argument. The fifth was an undisguised retreat. The sixth was not applicable to the actual situation of affairs. The king's force was no longer an independent body, it was become the advanced guard of the great army, marching under Napoleon. It was absurd, therefore, to contemplate a decisive movement, without having first matured a plan suitable to the whole mass that was to be engaged in the execution. In short, to permit an advanced guard to determine the operations of the main body, was to reverse the order of military affairs, and to trust to accident instead of design. It is curious, that while Joseph was proposing this irruption into Spain, the Spaniards and the military agents of Great Britain were trembling lest he should escape their power by a precipitate flight. *"War is not a conjectural art!"*

CHAPTER V

Journal of the king's operations, MS.

Appendix, No. 28.

The emperor overruled the offensive projects of the king, and the latter was forced to distribute the centre and right wing in a manner more consonant to the spirit of Napoleon's instructions; but he still neglected to occupy Tudela, and covered his left wing by the Aragon river.

The 18th of September the French army was posted in the following manner:

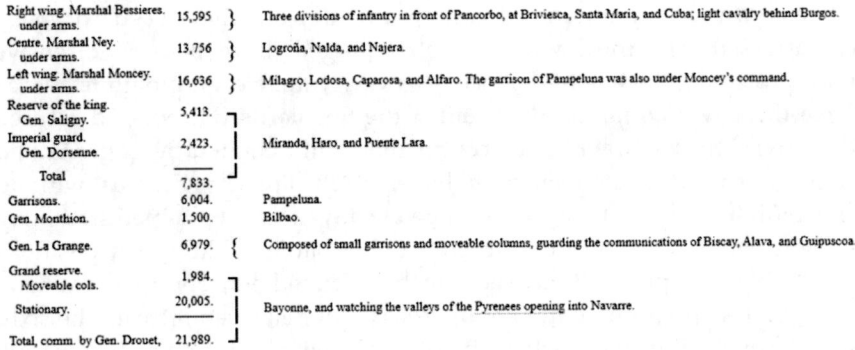

Right wing. Marshal Bessieres. under arms.	15,595	}	Three divisions of infantry in front of Pancorbo, at Briviesca, Santa Maria, and Cuba; light cavalry behind Burgos.
Centre. Marshal Ney. under arms.	13,756	}	Logroña, Nalda, and Najera.
Left wing. Marshal Moncey. under arms.	16,636	}	Milagro, Lodosa, Caparosa, and Alfaro. The garrison of Pampeluna was also under Moncey's command.
Reserve of the king. Gen. Saligny.	5,413.	⌐	
Imperial guard. Gen. Dorsenne.	2,423.	|	Miranda, Haro, and Puente Lara.
Total	7,833.	⌐	
Garrisons.	6,004.		Pampeluna.
Gen. Monthion.	1,500.		Bilbao.
Gen. La Grange.	6,979.	{	Composed of small garrisons and moveable columns, guarding the communications of Biscay, Alava, and Guipuscoa.
Grand reserve. Moveable cols.	1,984.	⌐	
Stationary.	20,005.	|	Bayonne, and watching the valleys of the Pyrenees opening into Navarre.
Total, comm. by Gen. Drouet,	21,989.	⌐	

Total 90,289 present under arms, exclusive of the troops in Catalonia. Hence the communication being secured, the fortresses garrisoned, and the fort of Pancorbo armed, there remained above fifty thousand sabres and bayonets disposable on a line of battle extending from Bilbao to Alfaro.

To oppose this formidable force the Spanish troops were divided into three principal masses, denominated the armies of the right, centre, and left.

	Infantry.	Cavalry.	Guns.		1st Line.	
					Men.	Guns.
The first, composed of the divisions of St. Marc and O'Neil, numbered about	17,500	500	24	⎤		
The second, composed of the divisions of La Pena, Llamas, and Caro	26,000	1,300	36	⎟	75,400	86
The third, consisting entirely of Gallicians, about	30,000	100	26	⎦		

		2d Line.	
In the second line the Castillians were at Segovia	12,000	⎤	
The Estremadurans at Talavera	13,000	⎟	
Two Andalusian divisions were in La Mancha	14,000	⎟	57,000
And the Asturians (posted at Llanes) were called	18,000	⎦	

This estimate, founded upon a number of contemporary returns and other documents, proves the monstrous exaggerations put forth at this time to deceive the Spanish people and the English government. The Spaniards pretended that above one hundred and forty thousand men in arms were threatening the French positions on the Ebro, whereas less than seventy-six thousand were in line of battle, and those exceedingly ill-armed and provided. The right, under Palafox, held the country between Zaragoza and

Sanguessa, on the Aragon river; the centre, under Castaños, occupied Borja, Taranzona, and Agreda; the left, under Blake, was posted at Reynosa, near the sources of the Ebro.

The relative position of the French and Spanish armies was very disadvantageous for the latter. From the right to the left of their line, that is, from Reynosa to Zaragoza, was twice the distance between Bayonne and Vittoria, and the roads more difficult; the reserve under Drouet was consequently in closer military communication with king Joseph's army, than the Spanish wings were with another. The patriots were acting without concert upon double external lines of operation, and against an enemy far superior in quickness, knowledge, and organization, and even in numbers. The French were superior in cavalry, and the base of their operations rested on three great fortresses, Bayonne, St. Sebastian, and Pampeluna; and they could in three days carry the centre and the reserve to either flank, and unite thirty thousand combatants without drawing a man from their garrisons. The Spaniards held but one fortress (Zaragoza), and being disseminated in corps under different generals of equal authority, they could execute no combined movement with rapidity or precision, nor under any circumstances could they unite more than 40,000 men at any given point.

Correspce. of Captain Carrol.

Ibid. General Broderick.

In this situation of affairs, general Blake, his army organized in six divisions (each five thousand strong), of which four were numbered, and the other two called the advanced guard, and the reserve, broke up from Reynosa on the 17th of September. One division advanced on the side of Burgos, to cover the march of the main body, which, threading the valley of Villarcayo, turned the right of marshal Bessieres, and reached the Ebro. Two divisions occupied Traspaderna and Frias, and established a post at Oña, on the right bank of that river; a third division took a position at Medina, and a fourth held the town of Erran and the Sierra of that name. A fifth halted in the town of Villarcayo, to preserve the communication with Reynosa, and at the same time, 8,000 Asturians under general Acevedo, quitted the camp at Llanes, and advanced to St. Ander. General Broderick now arrived in the Spanish camp; Blake importuned him for money, and obtained it, but treated him otherwise with great coldness, and withheld all information relative to the movements of the army.

Correspce. of general Leith.

Journal of the king's operations, MS.

English vessels hovering on the coast were prepared to supply the Biscayans with arms and ammunition, and general Blake thought himself in a situation to revive the insurrection in that province, and to extend it to Guipuscoa. With this view he detached his 4th division, and five guns, under the command of the marquis of Portazgo, to attack general Monthion at Bilbao. The king getting knowledge of the march of this division, ordered a brigade from his right wing to fall on its flank by the valley of Orduña, and caused general Merlin to reinforce Monthion by the valley of Durango. Bessieres aided these dispositions by a demonstration on the side of Frias, but the combination was made too late. Portazgo was already master of Bilbao. Monthion retired on the 20th to Durango, and Bessieres fell back with his corps to Miranda, Haro, and Puente Lara, having first injured the defences of Burgos.

Correspondence of gen. Leith.

The king took post with the reserve at Vittoria. Marshal Ney immediately abandoned his position on the Ebro, and carried his whole force by a rapid march to Bilbao, where he arrived on the evening of the 26th. At the same time, general Merle's division executed a combined movement from Miranda upon Osma and Barbaceña. Portazgo being overmatched, occupied the heights above Bilbao, until nightfall, and then retreated to Valmaceda, where he found the third division, for Blake had changed his position, and now occupied Frias with his right, Quincoes with his centre, and Valmaceda with his left. In this situation, holding the passes of the mountain, he awaited the arrival of the Asturians, who were marching by the valley of Villarcayo. All the Spanish artillery remained in the town of that name, being guarded by a division of infantry. Thus the second effort to raise Biscay failed of success.

Journal of the king's operations. MS.

Ibid.

In the mean time, O'Neil, following colonel Doyle's plan before mentioned, entered Sanguessa, and was beaten out of it again, with the loss of two guns. However, the Castillian army approached the Ebro by the road of Soria. General La-Peña occupied Logroña, Nalda, and Najera. Llamas and Caro occupied Corella, Cascante, and Calahorra, and O'Neil took post in the mountains, on the left bank of the Aragon facing Sanguessa. The peasantry of the valleys assembled in considerable numbers, and the country between Zaragoza and the Aragon river appeared to be filled with troops. Marshal Moncey withdrew from the Ebro, and took a position, with his left flank at the pass of Sanguessa, his centre at Falces, and his right at Estella. Ney, leaving Merlin with three thousand men at Bilbao, returned to the Ebro; but finding that Logroña was occupied in force by the Spaniards, halted at Guardia on the 5th of October, and remained in observation.

Journal of the king's operations. MS.

On the 4th the king and Bessieres, at the head of Mouton's and Merle's divisions, quitted Miranda, and advanced along the road of Osma, with the intention of feeling for Blake on the side of Frias and Medina, but the Spaniards were in force at Valmaceda. Joseph, deceived by false information, imagined that they were again in march towards Bilbao, and pushed on to Lodio, with the intention of attacking Blake during his movement. At Lodio the king ascertained the truth and halted. He was uneasy about Moncey, and therefore returned to Murquia on the 7th. In that town he left Merle to protect the rear of the troops at Bilbao, and proceeded to Miranda with the division of Mouton. On the 12th, Blake, still intent upon the insurrection of Biscay, placed a division at Orduña, and attacked Bilbao with fifteen thousand men. Merlin retired fighting up the valley of Durango as far as Zornosa, but being joined there by general Verdier, at the head of six battalions, he turned and checked the pursuit. At this time the leading columns of the great French army were passing the Spanish frontier, and Laval's division advanced to Durango. Sebastiani, with six thousand men, relieved Merle at Murquia; the latter repaired to Miranda, and Verdier returned to Vittoria. Marshal Lefebre, duke of Dantzic, assumed the command of the three divisions posted at Durango.

Parliamentary Papers.

Vindication of Castaños.

On the Spanish side, the marquis of Romana's division disembarked on the 9th at St. Ander, and being completely equipped and provided from the English stores, the infantry, eight thousand in number, proceeded by slow marches to join Blake. The Asturians halted at Villarcayo; but the Estremaduran army, under the conde de Belvedere, was put in motion, and the Castillian forces arrived upon the Ebro. The first and third divisions of the Andalusian army were on the march from La Mancha, and Castaños, quitting Madrid, proceeded towards Tudela. All things announced the approach of a great crisis. Yet such was the apathy of the supreme junta, that the best friends of Spain hoped for a defeat, as the only mode of exciting sufficient energy in the government to save the state, and by some it was thought, that even that sharp remedy would be insufficient. A momentary excitement was, however, caused by the intercepted letter to Jourdan before spoken of. The troops in the second line were ordered to proceed to the Ebro by forced marches, letters were written pressing for the advance of the British army, and Castaños was enjoined to drive the enemy, without delay, beyond the frontier; but this sudden fury of action ended with those orders. Sir David Baird's corps was detained in the transports at Coruña, waiting for permission to land; no assistance was afforded to sir John Moore, and although the subsidies already paid by England amounted to ten millions of dollars, and that Madrid was rich, and willing to contribute to the exigencies of the moment, the central junta, although complaining of the want of money, would not be at the trouble of collecting patriotic gifts, and left the armies "to all the horrors of famine, nakedness, and misery." The natural consequence of such folly and wickedness ensued; the people ceased to be enthusiastic, and the soldiers deserted in crowds.

General Broderick's Letter.
Pary. Paps.

Birch's Letters to Leith. MS.

The conduct of the generals was scarcely less extraordinary. Blake had voluntarily commenced the campaign without magazines, and without any plan, except that of raising the provinces of Biscay and Guipuscoa. With the usual blind confidence of a Spaniard, he pressed forward, ignorant of the force or situation of his adversaries, never dreaming of a defeat, and so little experienced in the detail of command, that he calculated upon the ordinary quantity of provision contained in an English frigate, which cruised off the coast, as a resource for his army, if the country should fail to supply him with subsistence. His artillery had only seventy rounds for each gun, his men were without great coats, many without shoes, and the snow was beginning to fall in the mountains. That he was able to make any impression is a proof that king Joseph possessed little military talent: the French marshals, from the habitude of war, were able to baffle Blake without difficulty, but the stratagetical importance of the valley of Orduña they did not appreciate, or he would have been destroyed. The lesson given by Napoleon, when he defeated Wurmser in the valley of the Brenta, might have been repeated, under more favourable circumstances, at Orduña and Durango; but if genius was asleep with the French, it was dead with the Spaniards.

As long as Blake remained between Frias and Valmaceda his position was tolerably secure from an attack, because the Montagna St. Ander is exceedingly rugged, and the line of retreat by Villacayo was open; but he was cooped up in a corner, and ill-placed for offensive movements, which were the only operations he thought of. Instead of occupying Burgos, and repairing the citadel, he descended on Bilbao with the bulk of his army, thereby discovering his total ignorance of war; for several great valleys, the upper parts of which were possessed by the French, met near that town, and it was untenable. The flank of his army was exposed to an attack from the side of Orduña, and his line of retreat was always in the power of Bessieres. To protect his flank and rear, Blake detached largely, but that weakened the main body without obviating the danger, nor did he make amends for his bad dispositions by diligence, for his movements were slow, his attacks without vigour, and his whole conduct displayed temerity without decision, and rashness without enterprise.

Appendix, No. 27.

The armies of the centre and right were not better conducted. Castaños, having quitted Madrid on the 8th of October, arrived at Tudela on the 17th, and on the 20th held a conference with Palafox at Zaragoza. The aggregate of their forces did not much exceed forty-five thousand men, of which from two to three thousand were cavalry. Sixty pieces of artillery followed the divisions, and the whole was posted in the following manner:

ARMY OF THE CENTRE,
27,000

General Pignatelli, with ten thousand Castillian infantry, one thousand five hundred cavalry, and fourteen guns, at Logroña.

General Grimarest, with the second division of Andalusia, five thousand men, at Lodosa.

General La-Peña, with the fourth division, five thousand infantry, at Calahorra.

The parc of artillery, and a division of infantry, four thousand, at Centruenigo.

The remainder at Tudela and the neighbouring villages.

ARMY OF ARAGON,
18,000

O'Neil, with seven thousand five hundred men, held Sos, Lumbar, and Sanguessa.

Thirty miles in the rear, St. Marc occupied Exca, with five thousand five hundred men.

Palafox, with five thousand men, remained in Zaragoza.

The Ebro rolled between these two corps. Taken as one army, their front lines occupied two sides of an irregular triangle, of which Tudela was the apex, and Sanguessa and Logroña the extremities of the base. Those points being taken as the chord, the rivers Ebro and Aragon meeting at Milagro, describe, in their double course, an arc, the convex of which was opposed to the Spaniards. The streams of the Ega, the Arga, and the Zidasco rivers, descending from the Pyrenees in parallel courses, cut the chord of this arc at nearly equal distances, and fall, the two first into the Ebro, and the last into the Aragon. All the roads leading from Pampeluna to the Ebro follow the course of those torrents.

Marshal Moncey's right was at Estella on the Ega, his centre held Falces and Tafalla on the Arga and the Zidasco, his left was in front of Sanguessa on the Aragon. The bridges of Olite and Peralta were secured by advanced parties, and Caparosa, where there was another bridge, he occupied in force. In this situation he could operate freely between the torrents, which intersected his line; he commanded all the roads leading to the Ebro, and he could, from Caparosa, at any moment, issue forth against the centre of the Spanish armies. Now from Tudela to Sanguessa is fifty miles, from Tudela to Logroña is sixty miles, but from Tudela to Caparosa is only twelve miles of good road; wherefore, the extremities of the Spanish line were above one hundred miles, or six days' march from each other, while a single day would have sufficed to unite the French within two hours' march of the centre.

Sir John Moore's Papers.
Colonel Graham's Correspondence.

Ibid.
Col. Doyle's Correspondence.

The weakness of the Spaniards' position is apparent. If Palafox, crossing the Aragon at Sanguessa, advanced towards Pampeluna, Moncey would be on his left flank and rear; if he turned against Moncey, the garrison of Pampeluna would fall upon his right. If Castaños, to favour the attack of Palafox, crossed the Ebro at Logroña, Ney, being posted at Guardia, was ready to take him in flank; if the two wings endeavoured to unite, their line of march was liable to be intercepted at Tudela by Moncey, and the rear of Castaños attacked by Ney, who could pass the Ebro at Logroña or Lodosa. If they remained stationary, they might easily be beaten in detail. Any other than Spanish generals would have been filled with apprehension on such an occasion. But Palafox and Castaños, heedless of their own danger, tranquilly proceeded to arrange a plan of offensive operations singularly absurd. They agreed that the army of the centre, leaving a division at Lodosa and another at Calahorra, should make a flank march to the right, and take a position along the Aragon, the left to be at Tudela, the right at Sanguessa; that is, with less than twenty thousand men to occupy fifty miles of country close to a powerful enemy. In the meantime, Palafox, with the Aragonese, crossing the river at Sanguessa, was to extend in an oblique line to Roncesvalles, covering the valleys of Talay, Escay, and Roncal, with his centre, and reinforcing his army by the armed inhabitants, who were ready to flock to his standard. Blake was invited to operate, in combination with them, by Guipuscoa, and to pass in the rear of the whole French army, so as to unite with Palafox, and thus cut off the enemy's retreat into France, and intercept his reinforcements at the same time.

S

Journal of the king's operations, MS.

Castaños returned to Tudela on the 23d, and proceeded to Logroña on the 25th; the grand movement being to commence on the 27th. But on the 21st, Grimarest had pushed forward strong detachments across the Ebro to Mendavia, Andosilla, Sesma, and Carcur, and one over the Ega to Lerim. The Castillian outposts also occupied Viana on the left bank of the Ebro. The Aragonese divisions were already closing upon Sanguessa, and a multitude of peasants crowded to the same place in the hope of obtaining arms and ammunition. Moncey, deceived by this concourse of persons, estimated the force in Sanguessa at twenty thousand, when, in fact, it was only eight thousand regular troops. His report, and the simultaneous movements of the Spaniards on both extremities, made the king to apprehend a triple attack from Logroña, Lodosa, and Sanguessa. He immediately reinforced Ney with a division (Merlin's) of Bessieres' corps, and directed him to clear the left bank of the Ebro, while a second division (Bonnet's) of Bessieres descended the right bank from Haro to Briones. A division of Moncey's corps, stationed at Estella, received orders to follow the course of the Ega, and second Ney's operations; and a part of the garrison of Pampeluna, posted at Montreal and Salinas, was commanded to advance upon Nardues, and make a demonstration against Sanguessa.

Whittingham's Correspondence. MS.

Colonel Graham's Correspondence. MS.

When Castaños arrived at Logroña these operations were in full activity. Ney had advanced on the 24th, driven back the Castillian outposts, crowned the height opposite that town on the 25th, and was cannonading the Spaniards' position. On the 26th, he renewed his fire briskly until twelve o'clock, at which time Castaños, after giving Pignatelli strict orders to defend his post unless he was turned by a force descending the right bank of the Ebro, proceeded himself to Lodosa and Calahorra. As the road winded by the river, the Spanish general was exposed to the fire of light troops posted in a wood on the opposite side, but escaped without injury. Meanwhile the French from Estella falling down the Ega, drove the Spanish parties out of Mendavia, Andosilla, Carcur, and Sesma; and Grimarest retired from Lodosa to La Torre with such precipitation, that he left colonel Cruz, a valuable officer, with a light battalion, and some volunteers, at Lerim. A squadron of cavalry escaped, but Cruz, with the infantry, being surrounded in a convent, was, after a creditable resistance, taken. Pignatelli, regardless of Castaños' orders, retired from Logroña, and abandoned all his guns at the foot of the Sierra Ibid.de Nalda, only a few miles from the enemy, then crossing the mountains gained Centruenigo in such disorder, that his men continued to arrive for twenty-four hours consecutively. On the right, O'Neil skirmished with the garrison of Pampeluna, and lost six men killed, and eight wounded; but, in the Spanish fashion, announced, that, after a hard action of many hours, the enemy was completely overthrown. On the 27th, Merlin's division rejoined Bessieres at Miranda, and Bonnet, retiring from Briones, took post in front of Pancorbo. Castaños, incensed at the ill conduct of the Castillians, dismissed Pignatelli, and incorporated his troops with the Andalusian divisions. Fifteen hundred men of the latter, commanded by the Conde de Cartoajal, being sent back to Nalda, recovered the lost guns, and brought them safe to Centruenigo.

Castaños' Vindication.

Colonel Graham's Correspondence. MS.

Whittingham's Correspondence. MS.

Internal dissensions succeeded to external troubles. Palafox arrogantly censured Castaños, and a cabal, of which general Coupigny appears to have been the principal mover, was formed against the latter. The junta, exasperated that Castaños had not already driven the enemy beyond the frontier, encouraged his traducers, and circulated slanderous accusations themselves, as if his inaction alone enabled the French to remain in Spain. Don Francisco Palafox, brother of the captain-general, and a member of the supreme junta, was sent to head-quarters avowedly to facilitate, but really to interfere with, and control the military operations. He arrived at Alfaro on the 29th, accompanied by Coupigny and the conde de Montijo, a turbulent, factious man, shallow and vain, but designing and unprincipled. Castaños waited upon the representative of the government, and laid before him the denuded state of the army, and the captain-general, Palafox, coming up from Zaragoza, a council of war was held at Tudela on the 5th of November. The rough manner in which the troops were driven from the left bank of the Ebro was not sufficient to divert the attention of the Spanish generals from the grand project of gaining the rear of the French army. The council agreed to persevere, although certain advice was received that the enemy were strengthened by thirty thousand fresh men. Deeming it, however, fitting, that Blake should act the first, it was resolved to await his time, but, as an intermediate operation, it was agreed that the army of the centre, leaving six thousand men at Calahorra, and a garrison at Tudela, should cross the Ebro and attack Caparosa. French parties were, however, pushed as far as Voltierra, and in the skirmishes which ensued, the conduct of the Castillian battalions was discreditable.

Ibid.

Joseph Palafox returned to Zaragoza, and the deputy separated himself from Castaños. The loss sustained by desertion and the previous combats was considerable, but some Murcian levies, and a part of the first and third Andalusian divisions joined the army of the centre, which now mustered twenty-six thousand infantry, and nearly three thousand cavalry under arms, with fifty or sixty pieces of artillery. The positions of the army extended from Calahorra, by Haro, to Tudela. La-Peña held the first town with five thousand men; Grimarest and Caro commanded eight thousand at the second; and head-quarters, with thirteen thousand five hundred men, were fixed in the last. Cartoajal remained with eleven hundred in the Sierra de Nalda, and eight hundred were posted at Ansejo.

Graham's Correspondence. MS.

Castaños' Vindication

In pursuance of the plan arranged, the troops were in movement to cross the Ebro, when despatches from Blake announced that he had met with some disaster on the 31st, the extent of which he did not communicate. This news arrested the attack; and the preposterous transactions that ensued, resembled the freaks of Caligula rather than the operations of real war. First, it was arranged that the army should abandon Tudela, and take a position in two lines, the extremities of the one to rest on Calahorra and Amedo, the second to extend from Alfaro to Fitero. The deputy ordered O'Neil, with the army of Aragon, to occupy the latter of these lines forthwith, but O'Neil refused to stir without instructions from the captain-general. This was on the 9th, on the 10th the plan was changed. Castaños fixed his head-quarters at Centruenigo, and the deputy proposed that O'Neil should descend the right bank of the Aragon river, and attack Caparosa in the rear; that the troops in Tudela should attack it in front; and that a division should make a demonstration of passing the Ebro in boats, opposite to Milagro, in order to favour this attack. Castaños assented. On the 12th a division assembled opposite Milagro, and La-Peña with two divisions marched against Caparosa. Suddenly, the whimsical deputy sent them orders to repair to Lodosa, forty miles higher up the Ebro, and attack the bridge at that place, while Grimarest crossing in the boats at Calahorra, should ascend the left bank of the Ebro, and take it in rear. La-Peña and Villarcayo, confounded by this change, wrote to Castaños for an explanation. This was the first intimation that the latter, who was lying sick at Centruenigo, received of the altered dispositions. He directed his lieutenants to obey; but being provoked beyond endurance, wrote sharply to the junta, demanding to know who was to command the army; and after all this insolence and vapouring on the part of Francisco Palafox, no operation took place at all. He declared, that his intention was merely to make a demonstration, ordered the troops to their quarters, and then, without assigning any reason, deprived La-Peña of his command, and appointed Cartoajal in his place.

Vindication of Castaños.

It was at this time that sir John Moore's letter arrived; but Castaños, no longer master of his own operations, could ill concert a plan of campaign with the general of another army. He could not even tell what troops were to be at his nominal disposal; for the Estremaduran force, originally destined for his command, was now directed by the junta upon Burgos, and the remainder of his own first and third division was detained in Madrid.

His enemies, especially Montijo, were active in spreading reports to his disadvantage; the deserters scattered over the country declared that all the generals were traitors, and the people of the towns and villages, deceived by the central junta, and excited by false rumours, respected neither justice nor government, and committed the most scandalous excesses.

Blake's situation was not more prosperous.

The road from Bayonne to Vittoria was encumbered with the advancing columns of the great French army. An imperial decree, issued early in September, commanded that the troops already in Spain should be incorporated with the grand army then marching from Germany. The united forces were to compose eight divisions, called "Corps d'Armée," an institution analogous to the Roman legion, because each "Corps d'Armée," although adapted to act with facility as a component part of a large army, was also provided with light cavalry, a parc, and train of artillery, engineers, sappers, and miners, and a complete civil administration, to enable it to take the field as an independent force. The imperial guards and the heavy cavalry of the army were not included in this arrangement; the first had a constitution of their own, and at this time all the heavy cavalry, and all the artillery, not attached to the "Corps d'Armée," were formed into a large reserve. As the columns arrived in Spain, they were united to the troops already there, and the whole was disposed conformably to the new organization.

Marshal Victor, duke of Belluno, commanded the	first corps.
Marshal Bessieres, duke of Istria	second corps.
Marshal Moncey, duke of Cornegliano	third corps.
Marshal Lefebre, duke of Dantzic	fourth corps.
Marshal Mortier, duke of Treviso	fifth corps.
Marshal Ney, duke of Elchingen	sixth corps.
General St. Cyr	seventh corps.
General Junot, duke of Abrantes	eighth corps.

S
Journal of the king's operations, MS.

The seventh corps was appropriated to Catalonia; the remainder were in the latter end of October assembled or assembling in Navarre and Biscay. General Merlin, with a division, held Zornosa, and observed Blake, who remained tranquilly at Bilbao. Two divisions of the fourth corps occupied

Durango and the neighbouring villages. One division and the light cavalry of the first corps was at Vittoria, a second division of the same corps guarded the bridge of Murguia on the river Bayas, and commanded the entrance to the valley of Orduña. Haro, Puente Lara, Miranda, and Pancorbo were maintained by the infantry of the king's body guard and the second corps, and the light cavalry of the latter covered the plains close up to Briviesca.

The reinforcements were daily crowding up to Vittoria, and the king, restrained by the emperor's orders to a rigorous system of defence, occupied himself with the arrangements attendant on such an immense accumulation of force, and left Blake in quiet possession of Bilbao. The latter mistook this apparent inactivity for timidity; he was aware that reinforcements, in number equal to his whole army, had joined the enemy; but, with wonderful rashness, he resolved to press forward, and readily agreed to attempt a junction with Palafox, in the rear of the French position. At this time Romana's infantry were approaching Bilbao, and the Estremadurans were in march for Burgos; but the country was nearly exhausted of provisions; both armies felt the scarcity, and desertion prevailed among the Spaniards. The Biscayans, twice abandoned, were fearful of a third insurrection. Prudence dictated a retreat towards Burgos. Blake resolved to advance.

Carrol's Correspondence.

Brodrick's Correspondence.

Having posted general Acevedo with the Asturians and the second division at Orduña, he left a battalion at Miravelles, to preserve the communication with Bilbao, and the 24th of October marched himself at the head of seventeen thousand fighting men, divided in three columns, to attack Zornosa. The right ascended the valley of Durango by Galdacano, the centre by Larabezua, the left by Rigoytia; at the same time general Acevedo penetrated through the mountains of Gorbea by Ozoco and Villaro, with a view to seize Manares and St. Antonia d'Urquitiola. It was intended by this operation to cut the communication between Miranda on the Ebro, and the town of Durango, and thus to intercept the retreat of marshal Ney, and oblige him to surrender with sixteen thousand men; for Blake was utterly ignorant of his adversary's position, and imagined that he had only two corps to deal with. He believed that the king, with one, was in his front at Durango and Mont Dragon, and that Ney, with the other, was at Miranda, when in fact, the latter was at that moment attacking Pignatelli at Logroña. As the Spanish army approached Zornosa, Merlin abandoned the town, and drew up on some heights in the rear. Bad weather, and the want of provisions, checked further operations until the 25th. On the evening of that day, the Spanish division at Rigoytia attempted to turn the right flank of the French. At the same time Blake marched against the centre and left, and Merlin fell back to Durango.

S.

Journal of the king's operations, MS.

The duke of Dantzic, alarmed by these movements, concentrated his whole force, consisting of two divisions of infantry (Sebastiani's and Laval's), and a Dutch brigade at Durango; his third division (Valence's) being yet in France. The king reinforced him with a division of the first corps (Villatte's), and ordered Merlin's troops, which were composed of detachments, to join their respective regiments. From the 25th to the 30th the armies remained quiet; but at day-break on the 31st, the Spaniards were formed in order of battle, five miles beyond Zornosa, and close to the enemy's position. The vanguard drew up across the road to Durango; the reserve at some distance in the rear. The third and fourth divisions occupied the intermediate space, so disposed as to outflank the others, in a chequer shape. The first division occupied a height on the left of the road, and behind the reserve.

Ibid.

Carrol's Correspondence.

The duke of Dantzic, apprised by the previous movements, that he was going to be attacked, became impatient; the state of the atmosphere prevented him from discovering the order of march, or the real force of the Spaniards; he knew that Blake had the power of uniting nearly fifty thousand men, and concluding that such a force was in his front, he resolved to anticipate his adversaries by a sudden and vigorous assault. In fact, the Spanish generals were so little guided by the rules of war, that before their incapacity was understood, their very errors being too gross for belief contributed to their safety. Blake had commenced a great offensive movement, intending to beat the troops in his front, and to cut off and capture Ney's corps of sixteen thousand men. In six days, although unopposed, he advanced less than fifteen miles, and so disposed his forces, that out of thirty-six thousand men, he concentrated only seventeen thousand infantry, without artillery, upon the field of battle!

S

Journal of Operations, MS.

Leith's Correspondence. MS.

The duke of Dantzic, at the head of twenty-five thousand men, formed in three columns of attack, descended the heights of Durango. A thick fog covering the mountain sides, filled all the valleys; and a few random shots alone indicated the presence of the hostile armies. Suddenly Villatte's division appeared close to the Spanish vanguard; and with a brisk onset forced it back upon the third division. Sebastiani's and Leval's followed in succession; a fire of artillery, to which Blake could make no reply, opened along the road: the day cleared, and the Spanish army, heaped in confused masses, was, notwithstanding the example of personal courage given by Blake, and the natural strength of the country, driven from one position to another. At mid-day it was beyond Zornosa, and at three o'clock in full flight for Bilbao, which place it gained in a state of great confusion during the night. The next day Blake crossed the Salcedon, and took a position at Nava. The duke of Dantzic pursued as far as Guenes, and then leaving general Villatte, with seven thousand men, to observe the enemy, returned to Bilboa. Twelve vessels, laden with English stores, were in the river, but contrived to escape.

S

Journal of Operations, MS.

The king was displeased with the precipitancy of marshal Lefebre, but endeavoured to profit from the result. The division of the first corps, stationed at Murguia, was ordered to descend the valley of Orduña, as far as Amurio, to aid the operations of the fourth corps. At the same time, Mouton's division was detached from the second corps towards Barbareña, from whence it was, according to circumstances, either to join the troops in the valley of Orduña, or to watch Medina and Quincoes, and press Blake in his retreat, if he retired by Villarcayo. The French were ignorant of the situation of general Acevedo. On the day of the action at Zornosa, that general was at Villaro, from whence he endeavoured to rejoin Blake, by marching to Valmaceda. He reached Miravalles, in the valley of Orduña, on the 3d, at the moment when the head of the French troops coming from Murguia appeared in sight. After a slight skirmish, the latter thinking they had to deal with the whole of Blake's army, retired to Orduña, and Acevedo immediately pushed for the Salcedon river. Villatte first got notice of his march, and dividing his own troops, posted one half at Orantia, on the road leading from Miravalles to Nava, the other on the road to Valmaceda, thus intercepting the line of retreat.

Captain Carrol.

Blake, who was informed of Acevedo's danger, in the night of the 4th, with great decision and promptitude, instantly passed the bridge of Nava, and at daybreak crowned the heights of Orantia with three divisions, meaning to fall suddenly upon the French; but they were aware of his intention, and sending a detachment to occupy Gordujuela, a pass in the mountains, leading to Bilbao, rejoined Villatte on the Valmaceda road. Five Spanish divisions and some of Romania's troops were now assembled at Orantia: Blake left two in reserve, detached one against Gordujuela, and marched with the other two against the French position. Villatte was overpowered and driven across the Salcedon; but rallied on the left bank and renewed the action. At this moment Acevedo appeared in sight; he sent two battalions by a circuit to gain the rear of the French, and with the remainder joined in the combat. Villatte retired fighting, and encountering the two battalions in his retreat, broke through them, and reached Guenes, but not without considerable loss of men, and he also left one gun and part of his baggage in the hands of the Spaniards. Thus ended a series of operations and combats, which had lasted for eleven days.

OBSERVATIONS

1°. The duke of Dantzic's attack at Zornosa was founded upon false data; it was inconsistent with the general plan of the campaign, hasty, ill-combined, and feebly followed up. It was an unpardonable fault to leave Villatte without support, close to an army that had met with no signal defeat, and that was five times his strength. The march of Victor's division was too easily checked at Miravalles. For five days, general Acevedo, with at least eight thousand men, was wandering unmolested in the midst of the French columns, and finally escaped without any extraordinary effort.

2°. General Blake's dispositions, with the exception of his night-march from Nava to Orantia, will, if studied, afford useful lessons in an inverse sense. From the 24th of October to the 4th of November, he omitted no error that the circumstances rendered it possible to commit; and then, as if ashamed of the single judicious movement that occurred, he would not profit by it. Romana's infantry being partly arrived, and the remainder in the vicinity of Nava, the whole Spanish army was, contrary to all reasonable expectation, concentrated; Blake had then above thirty thousand fighting men united in one mass, harassed, but not much discouraged, and the conde de Belvedere, with twelve thousand infantry, twelve hundred cavalry, and thirty pieces of artillery, was close to Burgos.

If Blake had been at all acquainted with the principles of his art, he would have taken advantage of Villatte's retreat, to march by Espinosa, and Villarcayo, to the upper Ebro; from thence have gained Burgos; brought up the artillery from Reynosa; united Belvedere's troops to his own; opened a communication with the English army; and in that position, with a plentiful country behind him, his retreat open, and his army provided with cavalry, he might have commenced a regular system of operations; but with incredible obstinacy and want of judgment, he determined to attack Bilbao again, and to renew the ridiculous attempt to surround the French army and unite with Palafox at the foot of the Pyrenees.

Lord W. Bentinck's Correspondence.

Such were the commanders, the armies, the rulers, upon whose exertions the British cabinet relied for the security of sir John Moore's troops, during their double march from Lisbon and Coruña. It was in such a state of affairs that the English ministers, anticipating the speedy and complete destruction of the French forces in Spain, were sounding the trumpet for an immediate invasion of France! Of France, defended by a million of veteran soldiers, and governed by the mightiest genius of two thousand years! As if the vast military power of that warlike nation had suddenly become extinct; as if Baylen were a second Zama, and Hannibal flying to Adrumetum instead of passing the Iberus! But Napoleon, with an execution more rapid than other men's thoughts, was already at Vittoria, and his hovering eagles cast a gloomy shadow over Spain.

BOOK IV

CHAPTER I

S.
Journal of the king's operations, MS.

After the opening of the legislative sessions, the emperor quitted Paris, and repaired to Bayonne. He arrived there on the 3d of November. It was his intention that the presumption of the Spanish generals should be encouraged by a strict defensive system until the moment, when the blow he was prepared to strike, could fall with the greatest effect. The precipitate attack at Zornosa displeased him, and he was also dissatisfied with the subsequent measures of the king. He thought that the safety of Mouton's division would be compromised between the armies of Blake and the conde de Belvedere. To prevent any accident, he judged it necessary that Bessieres should advance with the whole of the second corps to Burgos; that marshal Victor should march by Amurio to Valmaceda; and that marshal Le-Febre should immediately renew his attack on that position, from the side of Bilbao. These dispositions were executed, and thus at the very moment when Blake was leading his harassed and starving troops back to Bilbao, two corps, amounting to fifty thousand men, were in full march to meet him, and a third had already turned his right flank, and was on his rear.

Captain Carrol's Correspce.

General Leith's Correspce.

The Spanish general advanced from Valmaceda on the 7th, and thinking that only fifteen hundred men were in Guenes, prepared to surround them. Two divisions making a circuit to the left, passed through Abellana and Sopoerte, with a view to gain the bridge of Sodupe, in the rear of Guenes, while two other divisions attacked that position in front; the remainder of the army followed at some distance. The advanced guard of the 4th corps was in Guenes, and after an action of two hours, the Spaniards were thrown into confusion; but the night saved them from a total rout. The same day, one of their flanking divisions was encountered and beaten near Sopoerte, and the retreat of the other being intercepted on the side of Abellana, it was forced to make for Portagalete on the sea-coast, and from thence to St. Andero. Blake's eyes being now opened a little to the peril of his situation, he resolved to retreat to Espinosa de los Monteros, a strong mountain position, two days' march in the rear; intending to rest his troops there, and to draw supplies from the magazines at Reynosa. Retreating during the night to Valmaceda, he gained Nava on the 8th, and finally reached Espinosa on the 9th. The remainder of Romana's infantry came up during this retreat, and the whole army was, with the exception of the division cut off at Abellana, concentrated in a strong position, which covered the intersection of the roads from St. Andero, Villarcayo, and Reynosa.

Napoleon, accompanied by the dukes of Dalmatia and Montebello, quitted Bayonne the morning of the 8th, and reached Vittoria in the evening. He was met by the civil and military chiefs at the gates of the town; but refusing to go to the house prepared for his reception, he jumped off his horse, entered the first small inn that he observed, and calling for his maps, and a report of the situation of the armies on both sides, proceeded to study the plan of his campaign.

The first and fourth corps, after uniting at Valmaceda, had separated again at Nava on the 9th, Victor pursuing the track of Blake, and Lefebre marching upon Villarcayo by Medina. The second corps was concentrating at Briviesca, the third corps occupied Tafalla, Peraltes, Caparosa, and Estrella. The sixth corps, the guards, and the reserve, were distributed from Vittoria to Miranda, and a division, under the command of general La Grange, was at Guardia, connecting the positions of the third and sixth corps. The fifth corps was still behind the frontier, and the eighth composed of the troops, removed from Portugal by the convention of Cintra, was marching from the French sea-ports, where it had disembarked.

On the Spanish side, the conde de Belvedere was at Burgos, Castaños and Palafox, unknowing of their danger, were planning to cut off the French army, and Blake was flying to Espinosa. The English army were scattered from Coruña to Talavera de la Reyna.

S.

Marshal Soult's Operations, MSS.

In two hours the emperor had arranged his plans. Moncey was directed to leave a division in front of Pampeluna, to observe the Spaniards on the Aragon, to concentrate the remainder of the third corps at Lodosa, and to remain on the defensive until further orders. Lagrange was reinforced by Colbert's brigade of light cavalry from the sixth corps, and directed upon Logroña. The first and fourth corps were to press Blake without intermission.

The sixth to march towards Aranda de Douero. The duke of Dalmatia was appointed to command the 2d corps, and ordered to fall headlong upon the conde de Belvedere. The emperor, with the imperial guards and the reserve, followed the movement of the second corps.

These instructions being issued, the enormous mass of the French army was put in motion with a celerity that marked the vigour of Napoleon's command. Marshal Soult having departed on the instant for Briviesca, arrived there at day-break on the 9th, received the second corps from the hands of Bessieres, and in a few hours, the divisions composing it were in full march for the terrace of Monasterio, which overlooks the plains of Burgos. Head-quarters were established there, and, during the night, general Franceschi's brigade of light cavalry took the road of Zaldueño to Arlanzon, having orders to cross the river of that name, and descending the left bank, to cut the communication of the Spaniards with Madrid, and to prevent them from rallying at the convent of the Chartreuse, if defeated near Burgos.

S.
Journal of Operations, MS.

At four o'clock on the morning of the 10th, the French were in march from Monasterio, and at six o'clock general Lassalle's cavalry reached Villa Fria. The conde de Belvedere, being informed of their approach, posted the Spanish army at Gamonal, and taking four thousand infantry, eight guns, and the whole of his cavalry, fell upon Lassalle. The latter skirmished for a while, and then following his orders, retired slowly to Rio Bena. At eight o'clock, the French infantry, which had advanced by two roads, was reunited at this town, and immediately pushed forward on Villa Fria. Belvedere was soon driven back upon Gamonal, and the Spanish army was discovered in line of battle. The right occupied a wood, leaving a clear space of some extent between it and the river Arlazon. The left was posted in the walled park of Vellimer. Thirty pieces of artillery covered the front, and seven or eight thousand armed peasants were arrayed on the heights, immediately behind the regular troops. These latter amounted to eleven thousand one hundred and fifty infantry, and eleven hundred and fifty cavalry, following a field state of their numbers, found after the action. This was the best army at that time in Spain; it was composed of the Walloon and Spanish guards, the regiments of Mayorca, Zafra, and Valencia de Alcantara; the hussars of Valencia, the royal carbineers, and some volunteers of good families. It was completely equipped, and armed principally from the English stores; but its resistance was even more feeble than that made by the half-famished peasants of Blake's force.

Appendix, No. 15.

General Lassalle, with the light cavalry, led down upon the Spanish right, and filled the plain between the river and the wood. At the same moment the Spanish artillery opened along the whole of their line, and the French infantry formed in columns of regiments arrived. Mouton's division, composed of old soldiers, broke at once into the wood at a charging pace. General Bonnet followed closely, but so rapid and effectual was the assault of Mouton's veterans, that Bonnet's troops never fired a shot. The Spaniards fled in disorder, the left wing, although not attacked, followed the example of the right, and the whole mass, victors and vanquished, rushed into the town of Burgos with extraordinary violence and uproar. At the same moment, Bessieres, who retained the command of all the heavy cavalry, passed at full gallop toward the Madrid road, where it crosses the Arlazon, sabring the fugitives, and taking all the guns which had escaped Mouton's vehement attack; and on the other side of the river, Franceschi was seen to cut in pieces some Catalonian light troops stationed there, and to bar all hopes of flight. Never was a defeat more instantaneous, or more complete. Two thousand five hundred Spaniards were killed; twenty guns, thirty ammunition waggons, six pair of colours, and nine hundred men, were taken on the field. Four thousand musquets were found unbroken, and the fugitives were dispersed far and wide. Belvedere himself escaped to Lerma, where he arrived in the evening of the day on which the battle was fought. Meeting some battalions, principally composed of volunteers, on their march to join his army, he retired with them to Aranda de Douero during the night; but first, with true Spanish exaggeration, wrote a despatch, in which he asserted, that the French were repulsed in two desperate attacks; but that after thirteen hours hard fighting, they succeeded in a third.

All the ammunition and stores of the Spanish army were captured in Burgos; and the indefatigable marshal Soult, who was still upon the post-horse, which he mounted at Briviesca; not content with travelling from Bayonne to Burgos, taking the latter town, and gaining a decisive victory within the space of fifty hours; now rallied his corps, and detaching one column in pursuit on the side of Lerma, and another towards Valencia and Valladolid, marched himself with a third, on the very day of the battle, towards Reynosa, where he hoped to intercept Blake's line of retreat to the plains of Leon.

Carrol's Correspce.

Ibid.

This last-mentioned general reached Espinosa, as we have seen, on the evening of the 9th, with six divisions, including Romana's infantry, who also dragged with them six guns of a small calibre. The separation of the fourth division at Abellana, the deserters, and the losses sustained in battle, had reduced the army below twenty-five thousand fighting men. The parc of ammunition and the artillery, guarded by two thousand infantry, were behind Reynosa, at Aquilar del Campo, on the road to Leon. Blake's position was strong, and he hoped to remain in it for some days unmolested. His left wing, composed of the Asturians, and the first division, occupied some heights which covered the road of St. Andero. The centre, consisting of the third division and the reserve, formed a line across the road of Reynosa, which led through Espinosa directly to the rear. The second division was established on a commanding height, a little on the right hand of the town; Romana's infantry were posted in a wood, two miles in advance of the right; and the vanguard, with six guns, formed a reserve behind the centre of the position.

BATTLE OF ESPINOSA

At two o'clock in the afternoon of the 10th, the head of marshal Victor's columns drove back Romana's infantry[18], and seized the wood; but the Spaniards, reinforced by the third division, renewed the combat. A second French column, however, opened its fire upon the Spanish centre, thus weakened by the advance of the third division; and at the same time some light troops ascending the heights on the left, menaced that wing of Blake's army. The contest on the right was maintained with vigour, and the Spaniards, supported by the fire of the six guns in their centre, appeared to be gaining ground, when the night closed and put an end to the action, leaving the French in possession of the wood, and of a ridge of hills, which, at the distance of a cannon-shot, run parallel to the centre of the position. Generals St. Roman and Riquielmé were mortally wounded this day on the Spanish side.

At daylight the next morning, Victor, who had relieved his left with fresh troops during the night, renewed the attack. General Maison throwing out a cloud of skirmishers along the front of the Spanish centre and left wing, under cover of their fire, passed rapidly to his own right, and fell upon the Asturians and the first division. Blake, observing this movement, detached a column of grenadiers to reinforce the latter, and advanced in person with three regiments from the centre to take Maison in flank during his march. It was too late. Three Asturian generals fell at the first fire, and the troops of that kingdom fled without waiting for the enemy. They were soon followed by the first division, and Maison, continuing his course without a check, intercepted the line of retreat by St. Andero, and also that by the town of Espinosa. In the mean time, the French troops posted on the parallel ridge before spoken of, attacked the centre, and the division in the wood advancing against the right of the Spaniards, their whole army gave way in terrible confusion and distress, and crowded towards the river Trueba, which encircled the rear of the position. Some tried the fords, some rushed to the town, others fled to the right and left; but the weather was bad, the roads deep, the country rugged and difficult, and the overthrow was fatal. Those who escaped went to their own provinces, carrying dismay into the remotest parts of Gallicia, Asturias, Leon, and Castille. The guns, the baggage, and ammunition, fell into the hands of the French. Blake himself reached Reynosa on the 12th, and there rallied about seven thousand fugitives, but without arms, without spirit, and without hope.

S.
Journal of Operations, MS.

The line of retreat by Aguilar del Campo, where his artillery remained, was still open to him; and he proposed to remain at Reynosa as long as the enemy would permit him; to restore order, and then to retire through Leon upon sir David Baird's division, the head of which was now near Astorga. But his total ignorance of the French operations and strength again misled him. He looked only to the side of Espinosa, and already Soult's cavalry was upon his line of retreat, and the duke of Dantzic was hastening by the valley of Villarcayo towards Reynosa. Upon the 13th, he was attacked by the advanced guard of the second corps, and being now utterly confounded, he fled with four or five thousand men through the valley of Cabuerniga, and took refuge at Arnedo, in the heart of the Asturian mountains. There the marquis of Romana joined him, and assumed the command of all that remained of the unfortunate army of the left.

S
Journal of Operations, MS.

Blake being thus disposed of, the fourth French corps, after a halt of a few days to refresh the troops, took the road of Carrion and Valladolid; but Soult recalling his detachments, concentrated the second corps at Reynosa, seized St. Ander, and captured a quantity of English stores; leaving a division there under general Bonnet, he then spread his columns over the whole of the Montagna, pursuing, attacking, and dispersing every body of Spaniards that yet held together, capturing their baggage, and filling all places with alarm. After some partial actions with unconnected parties, every thing military belonging to the patriots was driven over the snowy barrier of the Asturian hills; and Soult having left a detachment at St. Vincent de Barqueira, scoured the banks of the Deba, took the town of Potes, and overrun Leon with his cavalry as far as Sahagun and Saldaña. Meanwhile the duke of Belluno quitting Espinosa, joined the emperor, whose head-quarters were fixed at Burgos, after the defeat of Belvedere.

The battles of Espinosa and Gamonal, and the subsequent operations of marshal Soult, laid the north of Spain prostrate, and secured the whole coast from St. Sebastian to the frontier of the Asturias. By a judicious arrangement of small garrisons, and moveable columns, the provinces of Guipuscoa, Navarre, Biscay, and the Baston de Laredo were fettered; the communication of the army with France could no longer be endangered by insurrections in the rear; and the wide and fertile plains of Old Castille and Leon were thrown open to the French, and forbidden to the separated divisions of the British army. These great advantages, the result of Napoleon's admirable combinations, the fruits of ten days of active exertion, obtained so easily, and yet so decisive of the fate of the campaign, prove the weakness of the system upon which the Spanish and British governments were at this time acting; if that can be called a system where no one general knew what another had done — was doing — or intended to do.

Sir John Moore's Papers.

Burgos, instead of Vittoria, was now become the pivot of operations, and the right of his army being secured, the emperor prepared to change his front, and bear down against the armies of Castaños and Palafox, with a similar impetuosity; but it was first necessary to ascertain the exact situation of the British force. Napoleon believed that it was concentrated at Valladolid, and he detached three divisions of cavalry and twenty-four pieces of artillery, by Lerma and Palencia, with orders to cross the Douero, to turn the flank of the English, threaten their communications with Portugal, and thus force them to retire. It was soon discovered that the heads of their columns had not penetrated beyond Salamanca and Astorga, and that many days must elapse before they could be concentrated, and in a condition to act offensively. Certain of this fact, the emperor let loose his three divisions of cavalry, and eight thousand horsemen sweeping over the plains, vexed all Leon and Castille. The authorities showed no firmness; the captain-general, Pignatelli, fled in consternation; the people submissive and fearful, displayed no enthusiasm, and disconcerted by the rapid movements of the French, spread a thousand confused and contradictory reports. The incursions of the cavalry extended to the neighbourhood of Astorga, to Benevente, Zamora, Toro, Tordesillas, and even to the vicinity of Salamanca. Such was the fear, or the apathy of the inhabitants, that thirty dragoons were sufficient to raise contributions at the gates of the largest towns; and after the overthrow of Espinosa was known, ten troopers could safely traverse the country in any direction.

The front of the French army being now changed, the second corps, hitherto the leading column of attack, became a corps of observation, covering the right flank, and protecting the important point of Burgos, where large magazines were establishing, and upon which the reinforcements continually arriving from France were directed. The exact situation of the other corps was as follows: The first corps, the guards, and a part of the reserve, were at Burgos; and Ney, with the sixth, occupied Aranda de Douero; the march of his force from the Ebro had been made with a view to intercept the army of Estremadura on the side of Madrid; but the sudden destruction of that body of troops having rendered this precaution useless, Ney was equally well placed to cut the communication of Castaños with the capital. General Lagrange occupied Logroña, and Moncey, with three divisions of infantry and his light cavalry, was at Lodosa. The Spanish army of the centre was consequently turned and cut off from Madrid even before Castaños was aware that the campaign had commenced.

Baron Larrey's Surgical Campaigns.

In passing the mountains near Tolosa, marshal Lasnes, duke of Montebello, fell from his horse, and was left at Vittoria; his hurts were dangerous, but a rapid and interesting cure being effected by wrapping him in the skin of a sheep newly slain, the emperor directed him to assume the command of Lagrange's division and Colbert's light cavalry, to unite them with the third corps at Lodosa, and to fall upon Castaños in front. At the same time he ordered Ney to ascend the course of the Douero with the light cavalry and two divisions of the sixth corps, to connect his left with the right of Lasnes, and to gain Agreda by the road of Osma and Soria, from whence he could intercept the retreat of Castaños, and place himself on the rear of the Spanish army. To support this operation, the first corps, and Latour Maubourg's division of heavy cavalry being drawn from the reserve, proceeded by Lerma and Aranda, and from thence slowly followed the direction of Ney's march. The emperor, with the guards, and the remainder of the reserve, continued at Burgos, the citadel was repaired and armed, magazines were formed, and arrangements made to render it the great dépôt of the army. All the reinforcements coming from France were directed upon this town, and proclamations were issued assuring the country people of protection if they would be tranquil and remain in their houses.

Mr. Stuart. Lord W. Bentinck. MSS.

Ibid.

Ten days had now elapsed since Napoleon, breaking forth from Vittoria, had deluged the country with his troops, and each day was marked by some advantage gained over the Spaniards; but these misfortunes were still unknown at Tudela and disregarded at the capital. The remnants of Belvedere's army having rallied in the pass of the Somosierra and on the side of Segovia, the troops belonging to the army of the centre, which had been detained in Madrid, were forwarded to the former place, and those left behind from Cuesta's levies were ordered to the latter. General St. Juan, an officer of high reputation, took the command at the Somosierra, general Heredia repaired to Segovia, and an intermediate camp of detachments being formed at Sepulveda, the men thus collected were, by the junta, magnified into a great army sufficient to protect Madrid.

Ibid.

That the left wing of the French army was still upon the Ebro, the central junta attributed, not to the enemy's strength, but to the dilatory proceedings of Castaños, and depriving him of the command, they gave it to Romana, precisely at the moment when it was impossible for the latter to reach the army he was to lead. The junta wanted a battle, and, uncorrected by Blake's destruction, doubted not of victory.

Castaños' Vindication.

Ibid.

Colonel Graham's Correspce. MSS.

The proceedings at Tudela were also worthy of the times; there the madness of the generals, and the folly of the deputy, increased rather than abated. The freaks of Francisco Palafox, and their ridiculous termination on the 12th of November, I have already related. A few days sufficed to give birth to new plans equally absurd, but more dangerous, as the crisis approached nearer. This time Castaños took the lead. He knew upon the 10th that the Estremaduran army was at Burgos, and that the French were marching on that town; from that moment, despairing of the junction of the British army, and likewise of his own first and third divisions, which were in Madrid, he sent orders to Belvedere to unite himself with Blake; but his letters never reached that officer, who was defeated before they were written, and Castaños, feeling that he himself was in a dangerous position, and that some decided measure was required, conceived so extraordinary a plan, that it would be difficult to credit it upon any authority but his own. He proposed to carry the army of the centre, reduced in numbers and ill-disciplined as it was, by the Concha de Haro and Soria, towards Burgos, and to fall upon the emperor's rear guard; and, as a preliminary step, he determined to beat the army in his front; but Palafox had also a plan, of attacking Moncey on the side of Sanguessa, and the first measure necessary was to combine these double operations. It was agreed that Caparosa should be garrisoned by four thousand infantry, that the bridge head at that place should be fortified, and that O'Neil should be reinforced at Sanguessa by detachments from the centre until his force amounted to nineteen thousand infantry and twelve hundred cavalry. He was then to break down the bridge, place guards at all the passages on the Aragon, and by a flank march gain Caparosa, cross the river, and threaten Peraltes and Olite on the 17th; but on the 18th turning suddenly to the left to get in rear of Lodosa, while general La-Peña and Coupigny, marching from Centruenigo, should attack Moncey in front.

Ibid.

This great movement was openly talked of at the head-quarters of the Spanish generals for several days before its execution, and these extraordinary commanders, who were ignorant of Blake's disasters, announced their intention of afterwards marching towards Vittoria to lighten the pressure on that officer if he should be in difficulty, or if (as his despatches of the 5th had assured them) he was successful, then to join in a general pursuit. Castaños, however, concealed his real project, which was to move by the Concha de Haro towards Burgos.

Ibid.

Castaños' Vindication.

It was found impossible to procure a sufficient number of boats to lay a bridge over the Ebro at Alfaro: thus the reinforcements intended for O'Neil were forced to make a circuit by Tudela, and lost three or four days. On the 14th O'Neil arrived at Caparosa, after breaking the bridge of Sanguessa; the 15th the reinforcements joined him. On the 17th, the day appointed for the execution of the plan, Castaños received notice of his own dismissal from the command, but he persevered in his project; La-Peña and Coupigny were put in motion to pass the bridges of Logroña and Lodosa, and the fords between them; but general O'Neil, instead of executing his part, first refused to stir without an order from Joseph Palafox who was at Zaragoza, and then changing his ground, complained that he was without bread. Castaños besought him to move upon the 18th, urging the necessity of the measure, and the danger of delay. But the deputy, Palafox, who had hitherto approved of the project, suddenly quitted the head-quarters, and went to Caparosa, from whence, in concert with O'Neil, he wrote to demand a farther reinforcement from the centre, of six thousand infantry and some more cavalry, without which, they affirmed, that it would be dangerous to pass the Aragon river. Castaños preserved his temper, invited the deputy to return to the right bank of the Ebro, and opposed the demand for more troops on the ground of the delay it would cause; but now the captain-general Palafox, agreeing with neither side, proposed a new plan. It is difficult to say how long these strange disputes would have continued if an umpire had not interposed, whose award was too strongly enforced to be disregarded.

Castaños' Vindication.

Castaños' Account of the Battle of Tudela.

Castaños was with the divisions of Coupigny and La-Peña at Calahorra on the 19th, when he received information that a French corps was advancing upon Logroña. It was Lasnes', with Lagrange's and Colbert's troops, but the Spaniard concluded it to be Ney, for he was ignorant of the changes which had taken place since the 8th of the month. It was likewise reported, that Moncey, whose force he estimated at twelve thousand, when it really was above twenty thousand, had concentrated at Lodosa, and, at the same time, the bishop of Osma announced that twelve thousand men, under Dessolles, were marching from the side of Aranda de Douero. On the 21st, the intelligence that Dessolles had passed Almazan, and that Moncey was in motion, was confirmed. Then Castaños, relinquishing his offensive projects, prepared to retire, and it was full time. For marshal Ney, who left Aranda on the 19th, had passed Almazan on the 20th, dispersed several small bands of insurgents, and entered Soria on the 21st, so that when Castaños determined to fall back on the 21st, his flank was already turned, and his retreat upon Madrid in the enemy's power. His artillery was at Centruenigo, and a large detachment of his army was with O'Neil at Caparosa.

Castaños' Official Account of the Battle of Tudela.

During the night of the 21st and 22d he retired to the heights which extend from Tudela by Cascante, Novellas, Taranzona, and Monteguda. The advanced guard of Lasnes was in sight of the Spanish rear-guard at Calahorra on the morning of the 22d. At this moment the only supply of money which the central junta had yet transmitted for the use of the army arrived at Tudela, and, to complete the picture of distracted councils, O'Neil refused to fall back from Caparosa without the orders of the captain-general. The latter, however, fortunately arrived at Tudela in person, and a conference taking place between him and Castaños the same day, they agreed that the Aragonese army should cross the Ebro, and occupy the heights over Tudela, while the rest of the troops should stretch away in line as far as Taranzona; but in defiance of all orders, entreaties, or reasoning, the obstinate O'Neil remained in an olive wood on the right bank of the river during the night of the 22d, leaving the key of the position open to the enemy.

Ibid, and his Vindication.

A council of war was held, but the discussion was turbulent, and the opinions were discordant. Palafox insisted on the defence of Aragon, as the principal, or rather the only object to be attended to, and he wished the whole army to pass to the left bank of the Ebro, and confine its operations to the protection of Zaragoza on that side, a proposal which alone was sufficient to demonstrate his total incapacity for military affairs. Castaños reasoned justly against this absurdity, but the important moments passed in useless disputation, and the generals came to no conclusion.

In the meantime, marshal Lasnes, bringing with him a division of the sixth corps (Maurice Mathieu's), which had just arrived from France, concentrated above thirty thousand infantry, four or five thousand cavalry, and sixty pieces of artillery, at Lodosa on the 22d, and marching by Alfaro, appeared, at eight o'clock in the morning of the 23d, in front of the Spanish outposts, close to Tudela, just at the moment when the Aragonese were passing the bridge and ascending their position. From forty to fifty guns were distributed along the front of the Spanish army, which, numbering about forty-five thousand fighting men, was extended on a range of easy hills from Tudela to Taranzona, a distance of more than ten miles. Two divisions of the army of the centre connected the Aragonese with the fourth division, which occupied Cascante. Three divisions were in Taranzona, and there were no intermediate posts between these scattered bodies. The weakness attendant on such an arrangement being visible to the enemy at the first glance, Lasnes hastened to make his dispositions, and at nine o'clock commenced

THE BATTLE OF TUDELA

General Morlot, with one division, attacked the heights above the town. Maurice Mathieu, supported by the cavalry, of Lefebre Desnouettes, assailed the centre, and general Lagrange advanced against Cascante. The whole of the artillery followed the columns of attack. The Aragonese resisted Morlot with vigour, and even pressed him in the plain at the foot of the hills, but Maurice Mathieu having gained possession of an olive wood, and a small ridge which was connected with the centre of the Spanish position, after some sharp fighting pierced the line, and Lefebre, breaking through the opening with his cavalry, wheeled up to his left, and threw the right wing into hopeless confusion. The defeated soldiers fled towards the bridge of Tudela, pursued by the victorious horsemen. In the meantime La-Peña, descending from Cascante with the fourth division, drove in Lagrange's advanced guard of cavalry, and pressed forward briskly; but being met at a charging pace by the infantry, was beaten, and fell back to Taranzona, where three divisions remained during the whole of the action, which, strictly speaking, was confined to the heights above Tudela. Palafox, with the right wing and the centre, fled to Zaragoza with such speed that some of the fugitives are said to have arrived there the same evening.

When La-Peña was driven back upon Taranzona, the four divisions of the left wing commenced an orderly retreat towards Borja, but some cavalry, detached by Ney from the side of Soria, coming in sight, the Spaniards got into confusion; a magazine blew up, and in the midst of the disorder cries of treason were heard, the columns dissolved in a few moments, the road to Borja was covered with a disorganised multitude; and so ended the celebrated battle of Tudela, in which forty thousand men were beaten and dispersed by an effort that, being in itself neither very vigorous nor well sustained, was nevertheless sufficient for its purpose, and demonstrative of the incapacity of Spanish generals, and the want of steadiness in Spanish soldiers.

Eleventh Bulletin. Victoires et Conquêtes.

Several thousand prisoners, thirty pieces of artillery, and all the ammunition and baggage, fell into the hands of the French, who rated the killed and wounded very high. The total loss may be estimated at eight or nine thousand men. Fifteen thousand escaped to Zaragoza; a detachment of two thousand, under the Conde de Cartoajal and general Lille, left in the mountains of Nalda, were cut off by the result of the action, and two divisions, whose numbers were increased by fugitives from the others, were rallied at Calatayud on the 25th, but they were half starved and mutinous.

Castaños' Account of the Battle of Tudela, and Vindication.

At Calatayud, Castaños received two despatches from the central junta, virtually restoring him to the command. For the first empowered him to unite the Aragonese army with his own; and the second, informing him that St. Juan was at the Somosierra, required his co-operation with that general to protect the capital. The battle of Tudela disposed of the first despatch, the second induced Castaños to march by Siguenza upon Madrid.

S

Journal of Operations, MS.

Eleventh Bulletin.

In the meantime, Napoleon, recalling the greatest part of his cavalry from the open country of Castille, left seven or eight thousand men in Burgos, and fixed his head-quarters at Aranda de Douero on the 23d. From the difficulty of transmitting despatches through a country in a state of insurrection, intelligence of the victory at Tudela only reached him on the 26th. He was exceedingly discontented that Castaños should have escaped the hands of Ney. That marshal had been instructed to reach Soria by the

21st, to remain there until Lasnes should be in front of the Spaniards, and then to pass by Agreda, and intercept the retreat of the latter.

On the evening of the 21st, general Jomini and colonel D'Esmenard, staff officers of the sixth corps, arrived at Soria with an escort of eighty cavalry. That town is situated upon a rocky height, with a suburb below, and the conde de Cartoajal, who was retiring from the mountain of Nalda, happening to be in the upper part, the magistrates endeavoured to entrap the French officers. The latter were met at dusk by the municipality, and invited to enter the town with great appearance of cordiality; but their suspicions were excited, and the plan failed. Cartoajal marched during the night, and the next day the sixth corps occupied the place.

S   .

Journal of Operations, MS.

General Jomini, whose profound knowledge of the theory of war enabled him to judge accurately of the events which were likely to occur, urged Ney to continue his march upon Calatayud, without any rest; but the marshal, either offended with the heat of Jomini's manner, or from some other cause, resolved to follow the letter of his instructions, and remained at Soria the 23d and 24th, merely sending out some light cavalry on the side of Medina Celi and Agreda. On the 25th he marched to the latter town; the 26th he crossed the field of battle, passing through Cascante. The 27th, he arrived, with one division, at Mallen, a town situated between Tudela and Zaragoza, his advanced guard being at Arlazon on the Zilo.

To the erroneous direction and dilatory nature of these movements, Castaños owed the safety of the troops, which were reassembled at Calatayud. Ney must have been acquainted with the result of the battle on the 25th, and it is remarkable that he should have continued on the road towards Agreda, when a single march by Medina Celi would have brought him upon the line of retreat from Calatayud to Siguenza. By some writers these errors have been attributed to Ney's jealousy of marshal Lasnes; by others it has been asserted that the plunder of Soria detained him. The falsehood of the latter charge is evident from the fact, that, with the exception of a requisition for some shoes and great coats, no contribution was exacted from Soria, and no pillage took place at all; and with respect to the former accusation, a better explanation may be found in the peculiar disposition of this extraordinary man, who was notoriously indolent, and unlearned in the abstract science of war. It was necessary for him to see, in order to act; his character seemed to be asleep until some eminent danger aroused all the marvellous energy and fortitude with which nature had endowed him.

S

Journal of Operations, MS.

The success at Tudela fell short of what Napoleon had a right to expect from his previous dispositions, but it sufficed to break the Spanish strength on that side, and to lay the kingdoms of Aragon and Navarre, and the province of New Castille, as bare as the northern part of Spain was laid by the victory of Espinosa. From the frontiers of France to those of Portugal, from the sea-coast to the Tagus, the country was now overwhelmed. Madrid, Zaragoza, and the British army, indeed, lifted their heads a little way above the rising waters, but the eye looked in vain for an efficient barrier against the flood, which still poured on with unabated fury. The divided, weak state of the English troops led the emperor to conclude that sir John Moore would instantly retire into Portugal. Lasnes he commanded to pursue Palafox, to seize the important position of Monte Toreño, to summon Zaragoza, and to offer a complete amnesty to all persons in the town, without reservation, thus bearing testimony to the gallantry of the first defence. His own attention was fixed on Madrid. That capital was the rallying point of all the broken Spanish, and of all his own pursuing divisions, and it was the centre of all interests, a commanding height from whence a beneficial stream of political benefits might descend to allay, or a driving storm of war pour down to extinguish, the fire of insurrection.

CHAPTER II

The French patroles sent towards the Somosierra ascertained, on the 21st, that above six thousand men were entrenching themselves in the gorge of the mountains; that a small camp at Sepulveda blocked the roads leading upon Segovia; and that general Heredia was preparing to secure the passes of the Guadarama. Napoleon, however, having resolved to force the Somosierra, and reach the capital before Castaños could arrive there, ordered Ney to pursue the army of the centre without intermission, and directed the fourth corps to continue its march from Carion by Palencia, Valladolid, Olmedo, and Segovia.

The movement of this corps is worthy of the attention of military men. We shall find it confusing the spies and country people; overawing the flat country of Leon and Castile; protecting the right flank of the army; menacing Gallicia and Salamanca; keeping the heads of Moore's and Baird's columns from advancing, and rendering it dangerous for them to attempt a junction; threatening the line of Hope's march from the Tagus to the Guadarama; dispersing Heredia's corps, and finally turning the pass of Somosierra, without ever ceasing to belong to the concentric movement of the great army upon Madrid.

S.
Journal of Operations, MS.

The time lost in transmitting the intelligence of the victory at Tudela was productive of serious consequences. The officer despatched with these fresh instructions, found Ney and Moncey (Lasnes remained sick at Tudela), each advanced two days' march in the wrong direction.

The first, as we have seen, was at Mallen, preparing to attack Zaragoza; the second was at Almunio, near Calatayud, pursuing Castaños. They were consequently obliged to countermarch, and during the time thus lost, the people of Zaragoza recovering from the consternation into which they were at first thrown by the appearance of the flying troops, made arrangements for a vigorous defence. Castaños also escaped to Siguenza, without any further loss than what was inflicted in a slight action at Burvieca, where general Maurice Mathieu's division came up with his rear-guard.

The emperor quitted Aranda on the 28th with the guards, the first corps, and the reserve, and marched towards Somosierra. Head-quarters were at Boucequillas on the 29th. A detachment sent to attack the camp at Sepulveda failed, with a loss of fifty or sixty men; but the Spaniards, struck with a panic after the action, quitted their post, which was very strong, and fled in disorder towards Segovia. The 30th, the French advanced guard reached the foot of the Somosierra. General St. Juan, whose force now amounted to ten or twelve thousand men, was judiciously posted; sixteen pieces of artillery, planted in the neck of the pass, swept the road along the whole ascent, which was exceedingly steep and favourable for the defence. The infantry were advantageously placed on the right and left, in lines, one above another, and some entrenchments made in the more open parts strengthened the whole position.

PASSAGE OF THE SOMOSIERRA

At day-break, three French battalions attacked St. Juan's right, three more assailed his left, and as many marched along the causeway in the centre, six guns supported the last column. The French wings soon spread over the mountain side, and commenced a warm skirmishing fire. At this moment Napoleon arrived. He rode into the mouth of the pass, and attentively examined the scene before him. The infantry were making no progress; a thick fog mixed with smoke hung upon the ascent; suddenly, as if by inspiration, he ordered the Polish lancers of his guard to charge up the causeway, and seize the Spanish battery. The first squadron was thrown into confusion, by a fire which levelled the foremost ranks. General Krazinski rallied them in a moment, and under cover of the smoke, and the thick vapours of the morning, the regiment, with a fresh impetus, proceeded briskly up the mountain, sword in hand. As those gallant horsemen passed, all the Spanish infantry fired, and fled from the entrenchments on each side, towards the summit of the causeway; so that, when the Poles fell in among the gunners, and took the battery, the whole Spanish army was in flight, abandoning arms, ammunition, baggage, and a number of prisoners.

This surprising exploit, in the glory it conferred upon one party, and the disgrace it heaped upon the other, can hardly be paralleled in the annals of war. It is indeed almost incredible, even to those who are acquainted with Spanish armies, that a position, in itself nearly impregnable, and defended by twelve thousand men, should, without any panic, but merely from a deliberate sense of danger, be abandoned, at the wild charge of a few squadrons, which two companies of good infantry would have effectually stopped. Yet some of the Spanish regiments so shamefully beaten here, had been victorious at Baylen a few months before; and general St. Juan's dispositions at Somosierra were far better than Reding's at the former battle; but thus absolutely does Fortune govern in war!

The charge of the Poles, viewed as a simple military operation, was extravagantly foolish, but taken as the result of Napoleon's sagacious estimate of the real value of Spanish troops, and his promptitude in seizing the advantage, offered by the smoke and fog that clung to the side of the mountain, it was a felicitous example of intuitive genius.

Col. Graham's Correspondce.

The routed troops were pursued towards Buitrago by the French cavalry. St. Juan himself broke through the French on the side of Sepulveda, and gained the camp of Heredia at Segovia; but the cavalry of the fourth corps approached, and the two generals crossing the Guadarama, united some of the fugitives from Somosierra, on the Madrid side of the mountains, and endeavoured to enter that capital. The appearance of a French patrole terrified the vile cowards that followed them; the multitude once more fled to Talavera de la Reyna, and there consummated their intolerable villany by murdering their unfortunate general, and fixing his mangled body to a tree; after which, dispersing, they carried dishonour and fear into their respective provinces.

The Somosierra being forced, the imperial army came down from the mountains; the sixth corps hastened up from the side of Alcala and Guadalaxara; the central junta fled from Aranjuez; and the remnant of the forces under Castaños, being intercepted on the side of Madrid, and pressed by Ney in the rear, turned towards the Tagus. The junta, while flying with indecent haste, spread a thousand false reports, and with more than ordinary pertinacity, endeavoured to deceive the people and the English general; a task, in which they were strongly aided by the weak credulity of Mr. Frere, the British plenipotentiary, who accompanied them in their flight to Badajos. Mr. Stuart, with greater discretion and firmness, remained at Madrid until the enemy had actually commenced the investment of that town.

Castaños' Vindication.

The army of the centre, after the combat of Burvieca, had continued its retreat unmolested by Ney. The time lost, in the false movement upon Mallen, was never recovered. The Spaniards escaped the sword, but their numbers daily diminished; their sufferings increased, and their insubordination kept pace with their privations. At Alcazar del Rey, Castaños resigned the command to general La-Peña, and proceeded to Truxillo himself, with an escort of thirty infantry and fifteen dragoons, a number scarcely sufficient to protect his life from the ferocity of the peasants, who were stirred up and prepared, by the falsehoods of the central junta, and the villany of the deserters, to murder him.

Madrid was in a state of anarchy seldom equalled. A local and military junta were formed, to conduct the defence; the inhabitants took arms, a multitude of peasants from the neighbourhood entered the place, and the regular forces, commanded by the marquis of Castellar, amounted to six thousand men, with a train of sixteen guns. The pavement was taken up, the streets were barricadoed, the houses were pierced, and the Retiro, a weak irregular work, which commanded the city, was occupied in strength. Don Thomas Morla, and the prince of Castelfranco, were the chief men in authority. The people demanded ammunition, and when they received it, discovered, or said, that it was mixed with sand. Some person accused the marquis of Perales, a respectable old general, of the deed; a mob rushed to his house, murdered him, and dragged his body about the streets. Many others of inferior note fell victims to this fury, for no man was safe, none durst assume authority to control, none durst give honest advice; the houses were thrown open, the bells of the convents and churches rung incessantly, and a band of ferocious armed men traversed the streets in all the madness of popular insurrection.

Eight days had now elapsed since the first preparations for defence were made; each day the public effervescence increased, the dominion of the mob became more decisive, their violence more uncontrollable, and the uproar was extreme, when, on the morning of the 2d of December, three heavy divisions of French cavalry suddenly appeared on the high ground to the north-west, and like a dark cloud overhung the troubled city.

Fourteenth Bulletin.

At twelve o'clock the emperor himself arrived, and the duke of Istria, by his command, summoned the town. The officer employed was upon the point of being massacred by the irregulars, when the Spanish soldiers, ashamed of such conduct, rescued him. This determination to resist was, notwithstanding the fierceness displayed at the gates, very unpalatable to many of the householders, numbers of whom escaped from different quarters; deserters also came over to the French, and Napoleon, while waiting for his infantry, examined all the weak points of the city.

Madrid was for many reasons incapable of defence. First, there were no bulwarks; secondly, the houses, although strong and well built, were not like many Spanish towns, fire proof; thirdly, there were no outworks, and the heights on which the French cavalry were posted, the palace, and the Retiro, completely commanded the city; fourthly, the perfectly open country around would have enabled the French cavalry to discover and cut off all convoys, and no precaution had been taken to provide subsistence for the hundred and fifty thousand people contained within the circuit of the place.

Appendix, No. 3.

The desire of the central junta, that this metropolis should risk the horrors of a storm, was equally silly and barbarous. Their own criminal apathy had deprived Madrid of the power of procrastinating its defence until relieved from without, and there was no sort of analogy between the situation of Zaragoza and this capital. Napoleon knew this well; he was not a man to plunge headlong into the streets of a great city, among an armed and excited population; he knew that address in negotiation, a little patience, and a judicious employment of artillery, would soon reduce the most outrageous to submission, and he had no wish to destroy the capital of his brother's kingdom.

Fourteenth Bulletin.

In the evening the infantry and artillery arrived; they were posted at the most favourable points; the night was clear and bright, the French camp was silent and watchful; but the noise of tumult was heard from every quarter of the city, as if some mighty beast was struggling and howling in the toils.

At midnight a second summons was sent through the medium of a prisoner. The captain-general Castellar attempted to gain time by an equivocal reply, but he failed in his object. The French light troops then stormed some houses, and one battery of thirty guns opened against the Retiro, while another threw shells from the opposite quarter, to distract the attention of the inhabitants.

The Retiro, situated on a rising ground, was connected with a range of buildings erected on the same side of the Prado, a public walk which nearly encircled the town. Some of the principal streets opened into the Prado nearly opposite to those buildings. In the morning a practicable breach being made in the Retiro wall, the difference between military courage and ferocity became apparent, for Villatte's division breaking in easily, routed the garrison, and pursuing its success, seized the public buildings above spoken of, crossed the Prado, gained the barriers erected at the entrance of the streets, and took possession of the immense palace of the duke of Medina Celi, which was in itself the key to the city on that side. This vigorous commencement created great terror, and the town was summoned for the third time.

In the afternoon, Morla and another officer came out to demand a suspension of arms, necessary, they said, to persuade the people to surrender. Being admitted to the emperor's presence, he addressed Morla in terms of great severity; he reproached him for his scandalous conduct towards Dupont's army. "Injustice and bad faith," he exclaimed, "always recoil upon those who are guilty of either." This saying was well applied to that Spaniard, and Napoleon himself confirmed its philosophic truth in after times. "The Spanish ulcer destroyed me," was an expression of deep anguish which escaped from him in his own hour of misfortune.

Morla returned to the town: his story was soon told: before six o'clock the next morning Madrid must surrender or perish. A division of opinion arose; the violent excitement of the populace was considerably abated, but the armed peasantry from the country, and the poorest inhabitants, still demanded to be led against the enemy. A constant fire was kept up from the houses in the neighbourhood of the Prado; the French general Maison was wounded, and general Bruyeres was killed; but the disposition to fight became each moment weaker, and Morla and Castelfranco prepared a capitulation. The captain-general Castellar refused to sign it, and as the town was only invested on one side, he effected his escape with the regular troops during the night, carrying with him sixteen guns. The people now sunk into a quiescent state, and at eight o'clock in the morning of the 4th, Madrid surrendered.

That Morla was a traitor there is no doubt, and his personal cowardice was excessive; but Castelfranco appears to have been rather weak and ignorant than treacherous, and certainly the surrender of Madrid was no proof of his guilt; that event was inevitable. The boasting uproar of the multitude when they are permitted to domineer for a few days is not enthusiasm. The retreat of Castellar with the troops of the line during the progress of the negotiation was the wisest course to pursue, and proves that he acquiesced in the propriety of surrendering. That the people neither could nor would defend the city is quite evident, for it is incredible that Morla and Castelfranco should have been able to carry through a capitulation in so short a period, if the generals, the regular troops, the armed peasantry, and the inhabitants, had been all, or even a part of them, determined to resist.

The emperor, cautious of giving offence to a population so lately and so violently excited, carefully provided against any sudden reaction, and preserved the strictest discipline. A soldier of the imperial guard was shot in one of the squares for having a plundered watch in his possession. The infantry were placed in barracks and convents, and the cavalry were kept ready to scour the streets at the first alarm. The Spaniards were disarmed, and Napoleon fixed his own quarters at Chamartin, a country house four miles from Madrid. In a few days every thing presented the most tranquil appearance; the shops were opened, the public amusements recommenced, and the theatres were frequented. The inhabitants of capital cities are easily moved, and easily calmed; self-interest and the pursuit of pleasure unfit them for noble and sustained efforts; they can be violent, ferocious, cruel, but are seldom constant and firm.

It was during this operation that La-Peña, after escaping from the sixth corps, arrived at Guadalaxara with about five thousand men. On the 2d, the dukes of Infantado and Albuquerque having left Madrid, joined him, and on the 4th, Venegas came up with two thousand men. While the generals were hesitating what course to pursue, Napoleon being apprized of their vicinity, directed Bessieres with sixteen squadrons upon Guadalaxara, supporting him by Ruffin's division of the first corps. At the approach of the cavalry, the main body retired through the hills by Sanctorcaz towards Aranjuez, and the artillery crossed the Tagus at Sacedon. Ruffin's division immediately changed its direction, and cut the Spaniards off from La Mancha by the line of Ocaña. A mutiny among the Spanish troops having forced La-Peña to resign his command, the duke of Infantado was chosen in his place, the army crossed the Tagus at several points, and after some slight actions with the advanced cavalry of the French, this miserable body of men finally saved themselves at Cuenca. Many deserters and fugitives, and the brigades of Cartoajal and Lilli, which had escaped the different French columns, also arrived there, and the duke proceeded to organize another army.

Sir John Moore's Papers.

In the mean time the fourth French corps reached Segovia, passed the Guadarama, dispersed some armed peasants assembled at the Escurial, and then marched toward Almaraz, to attack general Galluzzo, who, having assembled five or six thousand men to defend the left bank of the Tagus, was, with the usual skill of a Spanish general, occupying a line of forty miles. The first corps entered La Mancha; Toledo immediately shut its gates, and the junta of that town publicly proclaimed their resolution to bury themselves under the ruins of the city; but at the approach of a French division, betrayed the most contemptible cowardice.

Thus, six weeks had sufficed to dissipate the Spanish armies; the glittering bubble bursted, and a terrible reality remained. From St. Sebastian to the Asturias, from the Asturias to Talavera de la Reina, from Talavera to the gates of the noble city of Zaragoza, all was submission, and beyond that boundary all was apathy or dread. Ten thousand French soldiers could safely (as far as regarded the Spaniards) have marched from one extremity of the Peninsula to the other.

After the fall of Madrid, king Joseph remained at Burgos, issuing proclamations, and carrying on a sort of underplot, through the medium of his native ministers. The views of the latter being naturally turned towards the Spanish interests as distinct from the French, a source of infinite mischief to Joseph's cause was opened; for that monarch, anxious to please and conciliate his subjects, ceased to be a Frenchman without becoming a Spaniard. At this time Napoleon assumed and exercised all the rights of conquest; and it is evident, from the tenor of his speeches, proclamations, and decrees, that some ulterior project, in which the king's personal interests were not concerned, was contemplated by him. It appeared as if he wished the Spaniards to offer the crown to himself a second time, that he might obtain a plausible excuse for adopting a new line of policy by which to attract the people, or at least to soften their pride, which was now the main obstacle to his success.

Moniteur.

An assemblage of the nobles, the clergy, the corporations, and the tribunals of Madrid, waited upon him at Chamartin, and presented an address, in which they expressed their desire to have Joseph among them again. The emperor's reply was an exposition of the principles upon which Spain was to be governed, and offers a fine field for reflection upon the violence of those passions which induce men to resist positive good, and eagerly seek for danger, misery, and death, rather than resign their prejudices.

"I accept," said he, "the sentiments of the town of Madrid. I regret the misfortunes that have befallen it, and I hold it as a particular good fortune that I am enabled, under the circumstances of the moment, to spare that city, and to save it from yet greater misfortunes.

"I have hastened to take measures fit to tranquillize all classes of citizens, knowing well that to all people, and to all men, uncertainty is intolerable.

"I have preserved the religious orders; but I have restrained the number of monks. No sane person can doubt that they are too numerous. Those who are truly called to this vocation by the grace of God will remain in their convents; those who have lightly adopted their vocation, or from worldly motives, will have their existence secured among the secular ecclesiastics, from the surplus of the convents. I have provided for the wants of the most interesting and useful of the clergy, the parish priests.

"I have abolished that tribunal against which Europe and the age alike exclaimed. Priests ought to guide consciences; but they should not exercise any exterior and corporal jurisdiction over men.

"I have taken the satisfaction which was due to myself and to my nation, and the part of vengeance is completed. Ten[19] of the principal criminals bend their heads before her; but for all others there is absolute and entire pardon.

"I have suppressed the rights usurped by the nobles during civil wars, when the kings have been too often obliged to abandon their own rights to purchase tranquillity and the repose of their people.

"I have suppressed the feudal rights; and every person can now establish inns, mills, ovens, weirs, and fisheries, and give free play to their industry; only observing the laws and customs of the place. The self-love, the riches, and the prosperity of a small number of men, was more hurtful to your agriculture than the heats of the dog days.

"As there is but one God, there should be in one estate but one justice; wherefore all the particular jurisdictions having been usurped, and being contrary to the national rights, I have destroyed them. I have also made known to all persons that which each can have to fear, and that which they may hope for.

"The English armies I will drive from the Peninsula. Zaragoza, Valencia, Seville, shall be reduced either by persuasion or by the force of arms.

"There is no obstacle capable of retarding for any length of time the execution of my will. But that which is above my power, is to constitute the Spaniards a nation, under the orders of the king, if they continue to be imbued with the principle of division, and of hatred towards France, such as the English partizans and the enemies of the continent have instilled into them. I cannot establish a nation, a king, and the Spanish independence, if that king is not sure of the affection and fidelity of his subjects.

"The Bourbons can never again reign in Europe. The divisions in the royal family were concerted by the English. It was not either king Charles or his favorite, but the duke of Infantado, the instrument of England, that was upon the point of overturning the throne. The papers recently found in his house prove this; it was the preponderance of England that they wished to establish in Spain. Insensate project! which would have produced a land war without end, and caused torrents of blood to be shed.

"No power influenced by England can exist upon the continent. If any desire it, their desire is folly, and sooner or later will ruin them. I shall be obliged to govern Spain, and it will be easy for me to do it by establishing a viceroy in each province. However, I will not refuse to concede my rights of conquest to the king, and to establish him in Madrid, when the thirty thousand citizens assemble in the churches, and on the holy sacrament take an oath, not with the mouth alone, but with the heart, and without any jesuitical restriction, 'to be true to the king, to love and to support him.' Let the priests from the pulpit and in the confessional, the tradesmen in their correspondence and their discourses, inculcate these sentiments in the people; then I will relinquish my rights of conquest, then I will place the king upon the throne, and I will take a pleasure in showing myself the faithful friend of the Spaniards.

"The present generation may differ in opinions; too many passions have been excited; but your descendants will bless me as the regenerator of the nation: they will mark my sojourn among you as memorable days, and from those days they will date the prosperity of Spain. These are my sentiments: go, consult your fellow citizens, choose your part, but do it frankly, and exhibit only true colours."

The dispositions now made by Napoleon indicated a vast plan of operations. It would appear that he intended to invade Gallicia, Andalusia, and Valencia, by his lieutenants, and to carry his arms to Lisbon in person. Upon the 20th December the sixth corps, the guards, and the reserve, were assembled under his own immediate control. The first corps was stationed at Toledo, but the light cavalry attached to it scoured the roads leading to Andalusia, up to the foot of the Sierra Morena. The fourth corps was at Talavera, on the march towards the frontier of Portugal. The second corps was on the Carrion river, preparing to advance against Gallicia. The eighth corps was broken up; the divisions composing it ordered to join the second, and Junot, who commanded it, repaired to the third corps, to supply the place of marshal Moncey, who was called to Madrid for a particular service; doubtless an expedition against Valencia. The fifth corps, which had arrived at Vittoria, was directed to reinforce the third, then employed against Zaragoza. The seventh was always in Catalonia.

Appendix, No. 28.

Vast as this plan of campaign appears, it was not beyond the emperor's means; for without taking into consideration his own genius, activity, and vigour, he counted on his muster-rolls, above three hundred and thirty thousand men, and above sixty thousand horses; above two hundred pieces of field artillery followed the corps to battle, and as many more remained in reserve. Of this monstrous army, two hundred and fifty-five thousand men, and fifty thousand horses, were actually under arms, with their different regiments; thirty-two thousand were detached or in garrisons, preserving tranquillity in the rear, and guarding the communications of the active force. The remainder were in hospital, and so slight had been the resistance of the Spanish armies, that only nineteen hundred prisoners were to be deducted from this multitude. Of the whole host, two hundred and thirteen thousand were native Frenchmen, the residue were Poles, Germans, and Italians.

Of the disposable troops, thirty-five thousand men and five thousand horses were appropriated to Catalonia, and about the same number to the siege of Zaragoza. Above one hundred and eighty thousand men, and forty thousand horses, were therefore available for any enterprise, without taking a single man from the service of the lines of communication.

What was there to oppose this fearful array? What consistency or vigour in the councils? What numbers? What discipline and spirit in the armies of Spain? What enthusiasm among the people? What was the disposition, the means? What the activity of the allies of that country? The answers to these questions demonstrate, that the fate of the Peninsula hung at this moment upon a thread, and that the deliverance of that country was due to other causes than the courage, the patriotism, or the constancy of the Spaniards.

Infantado's Letters.
Narrative of Moore's Campaign.

First, with regard to their armies. The duke of Infantado resided among, rather than commanded, a few thousand wretched fugitives at Cuenca, destitute, mutinous, and cowed in spirit. At Valencia there was no army, for that which belonged to the province was shut up in Zaragoza, and dissensions had arisen between Palafox and the local junta in consequence.

Stuart's and Frere's Letters.

Sir J. Moore's Papers.

Appendix, No. 13, Section 5.

The passes of the Sierra Morena were occupied by five thousand raw levies, hastily made by the junta of Seville, after the defeat of St. Juan. Galluzzo, who had undertaken to defend the Tagus, with six thousand timid and ill-armed soldiers, was at this time in flight, having been suddenly attacked and defeated at Almaraz by a detachment of the fourth corps. Romana was near Leon, at the head of eighteen or twenty thousand runaways, collected by him after the dispersion at Reynosa; but of this number only five thousand were armed, and none were subordinate or capable of being disciplined; for when checked for misconduct, the marquis complained that they deserted. In Gallicia there was no army; in the Asturias, the local government were so corrupt, so faithless, and so oppressive, that the spirit of the people was crushed, and patriotism reduced to a name.

Stuart.

The central junta, having first repaired to Badajos, were terrified, and fled from thence to Seville, and their inactivity was more conspicuous in this season of adversity than before, and contrasted strangely with the pompous and inflated language of their public papers. Their promises were fallacious, their incapacity glaring, their exertions ridiculous and abortive; and the junta of Seville, still actuated by their own ambitious views, had now openly reassumed all their former authority.

In short, the strength and spirit of Spain was broken, the enthusiasm was null, except in a few places, and the emperor was, with respect to the Spaniards, perfectly master of his operations. He was in the centre of the country; he held the capital; the fortresses; the command of the great lines of communication between the provinces; and on the wide military horizon, no dark cloud intercepted his view, save the heroic city of Zaragoza on the one side, and a feeble British army on the other. Sooner or later, he observed, and with truth, that the former must fall; it was an affair of artillery calculation. The latter, he naturally supposed to be in full retreat for Portugal; but the fourth corps were nearer to Lisbon than the British general; a hurried retreat alone could bring the latter in time to that capital, and consequently no preparations for defence could be made sufficient to arrest the sixty thousand Frenchmen which the emperor could carry there at the same moment. The subjugation of Spain appeared inevitable, when the genius and vigour of one man frustrated Napoleon's plans at the very moment of execution; and the Austrian war breaking out at the instant, drew the master-spirit from the scene of contention. England then put forth all her vast resources; fortunately those resources were wielded by a general equal to the task of delivering the Peninsula, and it was delivered. But through what changes of fortune; by what unexpected helps; by what unlooked-for and extraordinary events; under what difficulties; and by whose perseverance, and in despite of whose errors, let posterity judge; for in that judgment only will impartiality and justice be found.

CHAPTER III

The 20th of December, Napoleon became aware that sir John Moore (having relinquished his communication with Lisbon, and adopted a new one upon Coruña) was menacing the French line of operations on the side of Burgos. This intelligence obliged him to suspend all his designs against the south of Spain and Portugal, and to fix his whole attention upon

THE OPERATIONS OF THE BRITISH ARMY

The reasons which induced the English general to divide his army, and to send general Hope with one column by the Tagus, while the other marched under his own personal command, by Almeida and Ciudad Rodrigo, have been already related; as likewise the arrangements which brought sir David Baird to Coruña, without having permission to land his troops, and without money to equip them, when they were at last suffered to disembark.

The 8th of November, sir John Moore being at Almeida, on the frontier of Portugal, his artillery was at Truxillo, in Spanish Estremadura, and sir David Baird's division was at Coruña.

General Blake, pursued by fifty thousand enemies, was that day flying from Nava to Espinosa, and Castaños and Palafox were quarrelling at Tudela.

The conde de Belvedere was at Burgos, with thirteen thousand bad troops.

Napoleon was at Vittoria with a hundred and seventy thousand good troops.

At this time the letters of lord William Bentinck and colonel Graham, exposing all the imprudence of the Spanish generals, being received, created uneasiness in the mind of sir John Moore; he already foresaw that his junction with the other divisions of his army might be impeded by the result of an action, which the Spaniards appeared to be courting, contrary to all sound policy; but as no misfortune had yet befallen them, he continued his march, hoping, "that all the bad which might happen, would not happen."

Sir John Moore's Journal, MSS.

The 11th he crossed the frontier of Spain, and marched to Ciudad Rodrigo; on that day Blake was completely discomfited at Espinosa, and the Estremaduran army beaten the day before at Gamonal, was utterly ruined and dispersed.

The 13th, the head of the British columns entered Salamanca, at the moment when Blake's fugitive force was finally disorganized at Reynosa, leaving the first, second, and fourth French corps, amounting to near seventy thousand men, free to act against any quarter.

Appendix, No. 14.

Sir John Moore participated at first in the universal belief, that the nation was enthusiastic, and fixed in a determination to dispute every step with the invaders; even after he had detected the exaggerations of the military agents, and perceived the want of capacity in the Spanish generals and rulers, he trusted that the spirit of the people would compensate for their deficiency of skill, and his mind was bent upon succouring them with all his power; what then was his surprise to find, that the defeat of the conde de Belvedere, an event which laid Castille open to the incursions of the enemy, which uncovered the march of the British, and compromised their safety, had created no sensation among the people; that the authorities had spread no alarm, taken no precautions, delivered out no arms, although many thousands were stored in the principal towns, and neither encouraged the inhabitants by proclamations, nor enrolled any of them for defence? He himself was informed of this important occurrence a full week after it had happened, and then through a single official channel. Valladolid was but three marches from Salamanca, and only four thousand British troops had arrived in the latter town; if the enemy had advanced in force, a retreat upon Ciudad Rodrigo would have become inevitable. The general, therefore, assembled the local authorities, explained to them the danger of his position, and endeavoured to excite their ardour; his exhortations produced no effect, either upon the junta or the people; the latter loudly declared their detestation of the invaders, but remained tranquil; the former were timid and stupid. The first feeling of indignation against the French was exhausted, and there was nothing to supply its place; the fugitives from the armies passed daily, without shame, and without reproach from their countrymen. Notwithstanding this unfavourable appearance, sir John Moore resolved not to retire until forced to do so; but hastening the arrival of his own rear divisions, he sent orders to sir David Baird and to sir John Hope to concentrate their troops, yet to be prepared for a retreat if the enemy advanced.

Mr. Frere's Letter to the Junta.

In this state he remained until the 18th, his army was closing up, and the French cavalry withdrew from Valladolid to Placentia. But the news of Blake's defeat now reached Salamanca, not by rumour, or by any direct communication from the Montagna St. Ander, but through Mr. Stuart, eight days subsequent to the date of the action; the central junta did not even inform the minister plenipotentiary until thirty hours after having received official intelligence of it themselves.

The want of transport and supplies obliged the British to march in small and successive divisions. It was, therefore, the 23d of November before the centre, consisting of twelve thousand infantry, and a battery of six guns, were concentrated at Salamanca. On that day Castaños and Palafox were defeated at Tudela, their armies scattered without a chance of rallying again in the field, and the third and sixth French corps became disposable.

Sir John Moore's Papers.

The emperor, victorious on both flanks, and with a fresh base of operations fixed at Burgos, was free to move, with the guards and the reserve, either against Madrid or in the direction of Salamanca; and detachments of his army were already in possession of Valladolid; the very town which, a few days before, the Spanish government had indicated for the base of sir John Moore's operations, and the formation of his magazines.

The 26th the head of sir David Baird's column was in Astorga, but the rear extended beyond Lugo. The head of general Hope's division was at the Escurial, the rear at Talavera. The second French corps was on the Deba, threatening Leon and the Asturias; the cavalry covered the plains; the fourth corps was descending by Carrion and Valladolid, to seize the pass of the Guadarama; and the emperor himself was preparing to force the Somosierra.

From this summary of contemporary events, it is evident, that notwithstanding sir John Moore had organised, equipped, supplied, and carried his troops four hundred miles in the space of six weeks, he was too late in the field. The campaign was decided against the Spaniards before the British had, strictly speaking, entered Spain as an army; it is also certain, that if, instead of being at Salamanca, Escurial, and Astorga, on the 23d, the troops had been united at Burgos on the 8th, such was the weakness of the Spanish forces, the strength of the enemy, and such the skill with which Napoleon directed his movements, that a difficult and precarious retreat was the utmost favour that could be expected from Fortune by the English general.

Appendix, No. 13, sect. 1 and 4.

The situation in which he was placed on his arrival at Salamanca, gave rise to serious reflections in the mind of sir John Moore. He had been sent forward without a plan of operations, or any data upon which to found one. By his instructions he was merely directed to open communication with the Spanish authorities, for the purpose of "framing the plan of campaign;" but general Castaños, with whom he was desired to correspond, was superseded immediately afterwards, and the marquis of Romana, his successor, was engaged in rallying the remains of Blake's force in the Asturias, at a distance of two hundred miles from the only army with which any plan of co-operation could be formed, and of whose proceedings he was as ignorant as sir John Moore. No channel of intelligence had been pointed out to the latter, and as yet a stranger in the country, and without money, he could not establish any certain one for himself. It was the will of the people of England, and the orders of the government, that he should push forward to the assistance of the Spaniards; and he had done so, without magazines, and without money to form them; trusting to the official assurance of the minister, that above a hundred thousand Spanish soldiers covered his march, and that the people were enthusiastic and prepared for any exertion to secure their deliverance; but he found them supine and unprepared; the French cavalry, in parties as weak as twelve men, traversed the country, and raised contributions, without difficulty or opposition. This was the state of Castille.

Appendix, No. 13, sect. 5 and 6.

The letters of Mr. Stuart and lord William Bentinck amply exposed the incapacity, selfishness, and apathy of the supreme government at Aranjuez.

Ibid.

The correspondence of colonel Graham painted in the strongest colours the confusion of affairs on the Ebro, the jealousy, the discord of the generals, the worse than childish folly of the deputy, Palafox, and his creatures.

Ibid.

Sir David Baird's experience proved, that in Gallicia the people were as inert as in Castille and Leon, and the authorities more absurd and more interested. General Hope expressed a like opinion as to the ineptitude of the central junta; and even the military agents, hitherto so sanguine, had lowered their tone of exultation in a remarkable manner.

The real force of the enemy was unknown to sir John Moore, but he knew that it could not be less than eighty thousand fighting men, and that thirty thousand more were momentarily expected, and might have arrived; he knew that Blake and the conde de Belvedere were totally defeated, and that Castaños must inevitably be so if he hesitated to retreat.

The only conclusion to be drawn from these facts was, that the Spaniards were unable, or unwilling, to resist the enemy, and that the British would have to support the contest alone, unless they could form a junction with Castaños, before the latter was entirely discomfited and destroyed; but there was no time for such an operation, and the first object was, to unite the parcelled divisions of the English army. From Astorga to Salamanca was four marches, from Salamanca to the Escurial was six marches; but it would have required five days to close up the rear upon Salamanca, six days to enable Hope to concentrate at the Escurial, and sixteen to enable Baird to assemble at Astorga. Under twenty days it would have been impossible for the English army to unite and act in a body; and to have advanced in their divided state would have been equally contrary to military principle and to common sense.

Appendix, No. 14.

A retreat, although it was prescribed by the rules of scientific war, and in unison with the instructions of the government, which forbad the general to commit his troops in any serious affair, before the whole were united, would have been (while the Spanish army of the centre still held the field) ungenerous, and the idea was repugnant to the bold and daring spirit of Moore. Rather than resort to such a remedy for the false position his government had placed him in, he contemplated a hardy and dangerous enterprise, such as none but great minds are capable of. He proposed, if he could draw the extended wings of his army together in good time, to abandon all communication with Portugal, and throwing himself into the heart of Spain, to rally Castaños' army (if it yet existed) upon his own, to defend the southern provinces, and trust to the effect which such an appeal to the patriotism and courage of the Spaniards would produce. But he considered that the question was not purely military; the Spanish cause was not one which could be decided by the marches of a few auxiliary troops; its fate rested on the vigour of the rulers, the concert of the generals, the unity of the exertions, and the fixed resolution of the people to suffer all privations, and die rather than submit. To sir John Moore it appeared doubtful that such a spirit, or the means of creating it, existed, and more doubtful that there was capacity in the government to excite or to direct it when aroused. No men of talent had yet appeared, and good-will was in itself nothing if improperly treated.

With the English plenipotentiary, who had just superseded Mr. Stuart near the central junta, the general had been directed by the ministers to communicate upon all important points, and to receive with deference his opinion and advice. The present was an occasion to which those instructions were peculiarly applicable. Mr. Frere had come fresh from the English government, he was acquainted with its views, and he was in the most suitable position to ascertain what degree of elasticity the Spanish cause really possessed. The decision of the question belonged as much to him as to the general; it involved the whole policy of the English cabinet with respect to Spain. As a simple operation of war the proposed movement was rash; all the military and many political reasons called for a retreat upon Portugal, which would take the army back upon its own resources, ensure its concentration, increase its strength, protect British interests, and leave it free either to return to Spain if a favourable opportunity should occur, or to pass by sea to Andalusia, and commence the campaign in the south.

Such were the reflections that induced sir John Moore to solicit Mr. Frere's opinion upon the general policy of the proposed operation, but in so doing he never had the least intention of consulting him upon the mode of executing the military part, of which he conceived himself to be the best judge.

While awaiting the reply, he directed sir David Baird, if the enemy showed no disposition to molest him, to push the troops on to Salamanca as fast as they should arrive at Astorga. Sir David was proceeding to do so, when Blake advised him that a considerable French force was collecting at Rio Seco and Ampudia with a view of interrupting the march. This arrested the movement, and Baird, after destroying some of his stores at Astorga, fell back to Villa Franca. As sir John Moore's information led him to believe that Blake's report was false, he recalled Baird; but valuable time was thus lost. It was the march of the fourth corps, then traversing the line from Carrion to the Guadarama, that gave rise to the contradictory intelligence.

At this time, the various changes in the French positions, and the continual circulation of their light cavalry through the plains, bewildered the spies and the peasants. The force of the enemy on different points also confused the higher agents, who, believing the greatest amount of the invading army to be from a hundred to a hundred and twenty thousand men, could never reconcile the reports with this standard, and therefore concluded that Napoleon exaggerated his real numbers to create terror.

Appendix, No. 14.

Sir John Moore wrote to Mr. Frere on the 27th of November, and the arrangements for the execution of his project were all prepared. Baird was to march by Benevente on the 1st, Hope was to move on Tordesillas, and the force at Salamanca was to advance to Zamora and Toro; but in the night of the 28th, a despatch from Mr. Stuart made known the disaster at Tudela. This changed the aspect of affairs; the question proposed to Mr. Frere was no longer doubtful; the projected movement had been founded upon *the chance of rallying the Spanish armies behind the Tagus;* a hazardous and daring experiment when first conceived; but now that Castaños had no longer an army, now that the strength of Spain was utterly broken, to have persisted in it would have been insanity. The French could be over the Tagus before the British, and there were no Spanish armies to rally. The defeat at Tudela took place the 23d of November; Baird's brigades could not be united at Astorga before the 5th of December, and to concentrate the whole of the army at Salamanca required a flank march of several days over an open plain; an operation not to be thought of, within a few marches of a skilful enemy who possessed such an overwhelming force of artillery and cavalry. As long as Castaños and Palafox kept the field there was reason to believe that the French stationed at Burgos would not make any serious attempt on the side of Astorga, but that check being now removed, an unmilitary flank march would naturally draw their attention, and bring them down upon the parcelled divisions of the English troops. The object of succouring the Spaniards called for great but not for useless sacrifices. The English general was prepared to confront any danger and to execute any enterprise which held out a chance of utility, but he also remembered that the best blood of England was committed to his charge, that not an English army, but the very heart, the pith of the military power of his country was in his keeping, it was entrusted to his prudence, and his patriotism spurned the idea of seeking personal renown by betraying that sacred trust.

The political reasons in favour of marching towards Madrid, scarcely balanced the military objections before the battle of Tudela; but after that event, the latter acquiring double force, left no room for hesitation in the mind of any man capable of reasoning at all; and sir John Moore resolved to fall back into Portugal. He ordered sir David Baird to regain Coruña or Vigo, and to carry his troops by sea to Lisbon; but wishing, if possible, to unite with Hope before the retrograde movement commenced, he directed Baird to show a bold front for a few days in order to attract the enemy's attention.

Appendix, No. 13, section 5.

The negligence, the false intelligence, the frauds, the opposition approaching to hostility, experienced by sir David Baird during his march from Coruña, had so reduced that general's hopes, that he prepared to retreat without reluctance. He was in direct communication with Romana, but the intercourse between them had rather confirmed than weakened the impression on sir David's mind, that it was impossible to depend upon the promises, the information, or the judgment of any Spanish general.

Sir John Moore's Papers.

Hope's Letters.

In the meantime, Napoleon forced the Somosierra, and summoned Madrid. The supreme junta fled to Badajos. St. Juan was murdered at Talavera. The remnant of Castaños's army was driven towards the Tagus; and as the fourth corps approached Segovia, sir John Hope's situation became very critical. His column, consisting of three thousand infantry, nine hundred cavalry, the artillery, and the great parc of ammunition had been obliged, from the want of money and supplies, to move in six divisions, each being a day's march behind the other. At Almaraz, Hope endeavoured to discover a way across the mountains to Ciudad Rodrigo; a road did exist, but the peasants and muleteers declared it to be impracticable for carriages, and consequently unfit for the convoy. The truth of their assertions was much doubted; but sir John was daily losing horses from the glanders, and, with a number but just sufficient to drag his guns and convoy along a good road, he feared to explore a difficult passage over the Sierras.

Lord W. Bentinck's Letters.

Appendix, No. 13, section 6.

When his leading division had reached Talavera, don Thomas Morla, then secretary at war, anxious to have the troops more minutely divided, proposed that the regiments should march through Madrid in ten divisions on as many successive days, the first to reach the capital on the 22d of November, which would exactly have brought the convoy into the jaws of the French army. Hope immediately repaired in person to Madrid, held a conference with Morla, and quickly satisfied himself that every thing was in confusion, and that the Spanish government had neither arranged a general plan, nor was capable of conducting one. Convinced of this unfortunate truth, he paid no attention to Morla's proposition, but carried his troops at once to the Escurial by the road of Naval Carnero. At the Escurial he halted to close up the rear, and to obtain bullocks to assist in dragging the parc over the Guadarama. The 28th he crossed the mountain, and entered the open flat country. The 28th and 29th the infantry and guns were at Villa Castin and St. Antonia, the parc being at Espinar, and the cavalry advanced on the road to Arevalo. General Heredia was still at Segovia. The duke of Dantzic was at Valladolid and Placentia, and his patroles were heard of at Coca, only a few miles from Arevalo.

General Hope's Reports. MS.

In the course of the day a despatch from Mr. Stuart announced the catastrophe at Tudela, and the flight from the camp of Sepulveda. At the same time the outposts of cavalry in the front reported that four hundred French horse were at Olmedo, only twelve miles from Arevalo, and that four thousand others were in the neighbourhood. The scouts at St. Garcia, on the right, also tracked the French again at Añaya, near Segovia. The general's situation was now truly embarrassing. If he fell back to the Guadarama, the army at Salamanca would be without ammunition or artillery. If he advanced, it must be by a flank march of three days, with a heavy convoy, over a flat country, and within a few hours march of a very superior cavalry. If he delayed where he was even for a few hours, the French on the side of Segovia might get between him and the pass of Guadarama, and then, attacked in front, flank, and rear, he would be reduced to the shameful necessity of abandoning his convoy and guns to save his men in the mountains of Avila. A man of less intrepidity and calmness would have been ruined; but Hope, as enterprising as he was prudent, without any hesitation ordered the cavalry to throw out parties cautiously towards the French, and to maintain a confident front if the latter approached; then moving the infantry and guns from Villacastin, and the convoy from Espinosa by cross roads to Avila, he continued his march day and night until they reached Peneranda: the cavalry covering this movement closed gradually to the left, and finally occupied Fontiveros on the 2d of December.

The infantry and the draft animals were greatly fatigued, but the danger was not over; the patroles reported, that the enemy, to the number of ten thousand infantry, two thousand cavalry, and forty guns, were still in Olmedo. This was the eternal fourth corps, which thus traversing the country, continually crossed the heads of the English columns, and seemed to multiply the forces of the French at all points. Hope now drew his infantry and cavalry up in position, but obliged the artillery and the convoy to proceed without rest to Alba de Tormes, where a detachment from Salamanca met them, and covered their march to that town. This vigorous and skilful operation concluded, the division remained at Peneranda, collected its stragglers, and pushed outposts to Medina del Campo, Madrigal, and Torecilla, while the fourth corps unwittingly pursued its march to the Guadarama.

Mr. Stuart's Correspondence.

Narrative of Moore's Campaign.

Sir John Moore's resolution to retreat upon Portugal created a great sensation at Madrid and at Aranjuez. The junta feared, and with reason, that such a palpable proof of the state to which their negligence and incapacity had reduced the country would endanger their authority, and perhaps their lives; and although they were on the point of flying to Badajos themselves, they were anxious that others should rush headlong into danger. Morla, and those who, like him, were prepared to abandon the cause of their country, felt mortified at losing an opportunity of commemorating their defection by a signal act of perfidy. The English plenipotentiary was surprised and indignant that a general of experience and reputation should think for himself, and decide upon a military operation without a reference to his opinion. Mr. Frere, although a person of some scholastic attainments, greatly overrated his own talent for public affairs. He was ill qualified for the duties of his situation, which at this moment required temper, sagacity, and judgment. He had come out to Spain impressed with false notions of what was passing in that country, and clinging tenaciously to the pictures of his imagination, he resented the intrusion of reason, and petulantly spurned at facts. The defeat of the conde de Belvedere at Gamonal, a defeat that broke the centre of the Spanish line, uncovered the flank and rear of Castaños's army, opened a way to Madrid, and rendered the concentration of the British divisions unsafe, if not impossible; he curiously called the "unlucky affair of the 10th at Burgos." After the battle of Tudela he estimated the whole French army on the side of Burgos and Valladolid at eleven thousand men, when they were above one hundred thousand; and yet, with information so absurdly defective, he was prompt to interfere with, and eager to control, the military combinations of the general, although they were founded upon the true and acknowledged principles of the art of war.

Moore's Papers.

Mr. Stuart's Correspondence.

Moore's Papers.

Frere's Correspondence.

While sir John Moore was anxiously watching the dangerous progress of sir John Hope, he was suddenly assailed by the representations and remonstrances of all these offended, mortified, and disappointed persons. The question of retiring was, by the defeat of Tudela, rendered so purely military, and the necessity of it was so palpable, that the general, although anticipating some expressions of discontent from the Spanish government, was totally unprepared for the torrent of puerile impertinencies with which he was overwhelmed. Morla, a subtle man, endeavoured first to deceive Mr. Stuart; by treating the defeat of Castaños lightly, and stating officially that he had saved the greatest part of his army at Siguenza, and was on the march to join St. Juan at the Somosierra; to this he added, that there were only small bodies of French cavalry in the flat country of Castille and Leon, and no force on that side capable of preventing the junction of sir John Moore's division. This was on the evening of the 30th. The emperor had forced the pass of the Somosierra on that morning, and the duke of Dantzic was at Valladolid. The same day Mr. Frere, writing from Aranjuez, (in answer to the general's former communication, and before he was acquainted with his intention to fall back), deprecated a retreat upon Portugal, and asserted, that the enthusiasm of the Spaniards was unbounded, except in Castille and Leon, where he admitted they were more passive than they should be. He even stated, that twenty thousand men were actually assembled in the vicinity of the capital, and that Castaños was falling back upon them; that reinforcements were arriving daily from the southern provinces, and that the addition of the British army would form a force greatly superior to any the French could bring against that quarter, in sufficient time. It was certain, he said, that the latter were very weak, and would be afraid to advance, while the whole country, from the Pyrenees to the capital, was in arms upon their left flank. Rumours also were rife that the conscription had been resisted, and this was the more probable, because every great effort made by France was accompanied by weakness and internal disturbance; and a pastoral letter of the bishop of Carcassonne seemed to imply that it was so at that time. "Good policy, therefore, required, that the French should be attacked before their reinforcements joined them, as any success obtained at that moment would render a conscription for a third attempt infinitely difficult, if not impracticable; but if, on the other hand," said this inconsiderate person, "the French are allowed, with their present forces, to retain their present advantages, and to wait the completion of their conscription, they would pour into Spain, with a number of troops which would give them immediate possession of the capital and the central provinces." Two days after the date of this letter, the emperor was actually at the capital; and Mr. Frere, notwithstanding the superior Spanish force which his imagination had conjured up, was, with the junta, flying in all haste from those very central provinces: France remaining, meanwhile, strong, and free from internal dissension. This rambling letter was not despatched when the general's intention to fall back upon Portugal was made known to Mr. Frere; but the latter thought it so admirably calculated to prevent a retreat, that he forwarded it, accompanied by a short explanatory note, which was offensive in style, and indicative of a petulant disposition.

Moore's Papers.

At this time, don Augustin Bueno and don Ventura Escalente arrived at head-quarters. These two generals were deputed by the junta to remonstrate against sir John Moore's intended retreat; and they justified the choice of their employers, being in folly and presumptuous ignorance the very types of the government they represented. They began by asserting, that St. Juan, with twenty thousand men under his command, had so fortified the pass of the Somosierra, that it could not be forced by any number of enemies, and then affirming that reinforcements were daily joining him, they were proceeding to create immense Spanish armies, when the general stopped their garrulity by introducing colonel Graham, who had been a witness of the dispersion of Castaños's army, and had just left the unfortunate St. Juan at Talavera, surrounded by the villanous runagates, who murdered him the next day. It may be easily supposed, that such representations and from such men could have no weight with the commander of an army; in fact, the necessity of retreating was rendered more imperious by these glaring proofs that the junta and the English plenipotentiary were totally ignorant of what was passing around them. But Napoleon was now in full career; he had raised a hurricane of war, and directing its fury as he pleased, his adversaries were obliged to conform their movements to his, and as the circumstances varied from hour to hour, the determination of one moment was rendered useless in the next.

The appearance of the French cavalry in the plains of Madrid sent the junta and Mr. Frere headlong to Badajos; but the people of Madrid, as we have seen, shut their gates, and displayed the outward signs of a resolution to imitate Zaragoza. The neighbouring peasants flocked in to aid the citizens, and a military junta (composed of the duke of Infantado, the prince of Castel Franco, the marquis of Castellar, and don Thomas Morla) was appointed to manage the defence. Morla now resolved to make a final effort to involve the British army in the destruction of his own country, and as the duke of Infantado was easily persuaded to quit Madrid on a mission to the army of the centre, the traitor was left sole master of the town, because the duke and himself only had any influence with that armed mob, which had murdered the marquis of Perales, and filled the city with tumult.

When the French emperor summoned the junta to surrender, Morla, in concert with the prince of Castel Franco, addressed a paper to sir John Moore, in which it was stated that twenty-five thousand men under Castaños, and ten thousand from the Somosierra, were marching in all haste to the capital, where forty thousand others were in arms; but that, apprehending an increase of force on the enemy's side, the junta hoped that the English army would either march to the assistance of the capital, or take a direction to fall upon the rear of the French, and not doubting that the English general had already formed a junction with Blake's army, they hoped he would be quick in his operations. This paper was sent by a government messenger to Salamanca; but ere he could reach that place, Morla, who had commenced negotiations, before the despatch was written, capitulated, and Napoleon was in Madrid. This communication alone would not have been sufficient to arrest sir John Moore's retrograde movement. He was become too well acquainted with what facility Spanish armies were created on paper, to rely on any statement of their numbers; but Mr. Stuart also expressed a belief that Madrid would make a vigorous resistance, and the tide of false information having set in with a strong current, every moment brought fresh assurances that a great spirit had arisen.

On the day that Morla's communication arrived, there also appeared at head-quarters one Charmilly, a French adventurer. This man, who has been since denounced in the British parliament as an organizer of assassination in St. Domingo, and a fraudulent bankrupt in London, came as the confidential agent of Mr. Frere. He had been in Madrid during the night of the 1st, and left it (immediately after having held a conference with Morla), on the morning of the 2d. Taking the road to Talavera, he met with the plenipotentiary, to whom he spoke with enthusiasm of the spirit and preparations of the inhabitants in the capital. Mr. Frere readily confided in him, and imparting his own views, not only intrusted this stranger with letters to the British general, but charged him with a mission to obstruct the retreat into Portugal. Thus instructed, Charmilly hastened to Salamanca, and presented Mr. Frere's first missive, in which that gentleman, after alluding to former representations, and to the information of which colonel Charmilly was the bearer, viz. the enthusiasm in the capital, made a formal remonstrance, to the effect that propriety and policy demanded an immediate advance of the British to support this generous effort. Charmilly also demanded a personal interview, which was granted; but sir John Moore having some suspicion of the man, whom he had seen before, listened to his tale of the enthusiasm and vigorous character displayed at Madrid, with an appearance of coldness that baffled the penetration of the adventurer, who retired under the impression that a retreat was certain.

Appendix, No. 13, section 7.

For many years so much ridicule had been attached to the name of an English expedition, that weak-headed men claimed a sort of prescriptive right to censure without regard to subordination, the conduct of their general. It had been so in Egypt, where a cabal was formed to deprive lord Hutchinson of the command; it had been so at Buenos Ayres, at Ferrol, and in Portugal. It was so at this time in sir John Moore's army; and it will be found in the course of this work, that the superlative talents, vigour, and success of the duke of Wellington, could not even at a late period of the war secure him from such vexatious folly. The three generals who commanded the separate divisions of the army, and who were in consequence acquainted with all the circumstances of the moment, were perfectly agreed as to the propriety of a retreat; but in other quarters indecent murmurs were so prevalent among officers of rank as to call for rebuke. Charmilly, ignorant of the decided character of the general-in-chief, concluded that this temper was favourable to the object of his mission, and presented a second letter, which Mr. Frere had charged him to deliver, should the first fail of effect. The purport of it was to desire that if sir John Moore still persisted in his intention of retreating, "*the bearer might be previously examined before a council of war,*" in other words, that Mr. Frere, convinced of sir John Moore's incapacity and want of zeal, was determined to control his proceedings even by force. And this to a British general of long experience and confirmed reputation, and by the hands of a foreign adventurer!! The indignation of a high spirit at such a foolish, wanton insult, may be easily imagined. He tore the letter in pieces, and ordered Charmilly to quit the cantonments of the British army without delay. His anger, however, soon subsided. Quarrels among the servants of the public could only prove detrimental to his country, and he put his personal feelings on one side. The information brought by Charmilly, separated from the indecorum of his mission, was in itself important. It confirmed the essential fact, that Madrid was actually resisting, and that the spirit and energy of the country was awaking. Hitherto his own observation had led sir John Moore to doubt, if the people took sufficient interest in the cause to make any effectual effort; all around himself was apathetic and incapable, and his correspondents, with the exception of Mr. Frere, nay, even the intercepted letters of French officers, had agreed in describing the general feeling of the country as subsiding into indifference. To use his own words, "*Spain was without armies, generals, or a government.*" But now the fire essential to the salvation of the nation appeared to be kindling, and Moore feeling conscious of ability to lead a British army, hailed the appearance of an enthusiasm which promised success to a just cause, and a brilliant career of glory to himself.

Appendix, No. 14.

That the metropolis should thus abide the fury of the conqueror was surprising. It was a great event and full of promise. The situation of the army was likewise improved; general Hope's junction was accomplished, and as the attention of the French was turned toward Madrid, there was no reason to doubt that Baird's junction could likewise be effected. On the other hand, there was no certainty, that the capital would remain firm when danger pressed, none that it would be able to resist, none that the example would spread; yet without it did so, nothing was gained, because it was only by an union of heart and hand throughout the whole country, that the great power of the French could be successfully resisted.

In a matter so balanced, sir John Moore, as might be expected from an enterprising general, adopted the boldest and most generous side. He ordered sir David Baird to concentrate his troops at Astorga, and he himself prepared for an advance; but as he remained without any further information of the fate of Madrid, he sent colonel Graham to obtain intelligence of what was passing, and to carry his answer to Morla. This resolution being taken, he wrote to Mr. Frere, calmly explaining the reasons for his past conduct, and those which actuated him in forming a fresh plan of operation. "I wish anxiously," said this noble-minded man in conclusion, "I wish anxiously, as the king's minister, to continue upon the most confidential footing with you, and I hope as we have but one interest, the public welfare, though we occasionally see it in different aspects, that this will not disturb the harmony which should subsist between us. Fully impressed as I am with these sentiments, I shall abstain from any remarks upon the two letters from you delivered to me last night and this morning by colonel Charmilly, or on the message which accompanied them. I certainly at first did feel and expressed much indignation at a person like him being made the channel of a communication of that sort from you to me. Those feelings are at an end, and I dare say they never will be created towards you again."

The plan of operations now occupied his mind. The Somosierra and the Guadarama were both in possession of the enemy, no direct movement could therefore be made towards Madrid; besides, the rear of Baird's troops was still several marches behind Astorga, and a general movement on the side of the capital could not commence before the 12th of the month. Zaragoza, the general knew, was determined to stand a second siege, and he had the guarantee of the first that it would be an obstinate stand. He had received from the junta of Toledo a formal assurance of their resolution to bury themselves under the ruins of the town sooner than submit; and he was informed from several quarters that the southern provinces were forwarding crowds of fresh levies. Romana at this time also was in correspondence with him, and with the usual exaggeration of a Spaniard, declared his ability to aid him with an army of twenty thousand men. Upon this data sir John Moore formed a plan, bearing the stamp of genuine talent and enterprise, whether it be examined as a political or a military measure.

Appendix, No. 14.

He supposed the French emperor to be more anxious to strike a heavy blow against the English, and to shut them out of Spain, than to overrun any particular province, or get possession of any town in the Peninsula. He resolved, therefore, to throw himself upon the communications of the French army, hoping, if fortune was favourable, to inflict a severe loss upon the troops which guarded them before aid could arrive. If Napoleon, suspending his operations against the south, should detach largely, Madrid would thereby be succoured; if he did not detach largely, the British could hold their ground. Sir John Moore knew well that a great commander would in such a case be more likely to unite his whole army, and fall upon the troops which thus ventured to place themselves on his line of operations. But, to relieve the Spaniards at a critical moment, and to give time for the southern provinces to organise their defence and recover courage, he was willing thus to draw the whole of the enemy upon himself. He felt that in doing so, he compromised the safety of his own army, that he must glide along the edge of a precipice, that he must cross a gulf on a rotten plank; but he also knew the martial qualities of his soldiers, he had confidence in his own genius; and the occasion being worthy of a great deed, he dared essay it even against Napoleon.

Colonel Graham returned on the 9th, bringing the first intimation of the capitulation of the capital. He had been able to proceed no further than Talavera, where he encountered two members of the supreme junta. By them he was told that the French, being from twenty to thirty thousand strong, possessed the Retiro, but that the people retained their arms, and that La-Peña, with thirty thousand men of the army of the centre, was at Guadalaxara; that fourteen thousand of St. Juan's and Heredia's forces were assembled at Almaraz, and that Romana, with whom they anxiously desired that sir John Moore would unite, had likewise an army of thirty thousand fighting men. Finally, they assured colonel Graham that the most energetic measures were in activity wherever the enemy's presence did not control the patriots.

Mortifying as it was to find that Madrid, after so much boasting, should have held out but one day, the event itself did not destroy the ground of sir John Moore's resolution to advance. Undoubtedly it was so much lost; it diminished the hope of arousing the nation, and it increased the danger of the British army by letting loose a greater number of the enemy's troops; but as a diversion for the south it might still succeed; and as long as there was any hope, the resolution of the English general was fixed, to prove that he would not abandon the cause even when the Spaniards were abandoning it themselves.

CHAPTER IV

The forward movement of the British army commenced on the 11th of December. Sir John Moore's first intention was to march with his own and Hope's division to Valladolid, with a view to cover the advance of his stores and to protect the junction of sir David Baird's troops, the rear of which was still several marches behind Astorga. The preparations for a retreat upon Portugal were, however, continued, and sir David was ordered to form magazines at Benevente, Astorga, Villa Franca, and Lugo. This arrangement secured two lines of operation, and permitted a greater freedom of action.

The 13th, head-quarters were at Alaejos. Two brigades, and the cavalry under lord Paget at Toro. General Hope was at Torrecilla. The cavalry under brigadier-general Charles Stewart, was at Rueda; having the night before surprised a French post of fifty infantry and thirty dragoons, killing or taking almost the whole number. The prisoners declared that in the French army it was believed that the English were retreating to Portugal.

Appendix, No. 13, section 4.

At Alaejos an intercepted despatch of the prince of Neufchatel was brought to head-quarters; the contents were important enough to change the direction of the march. It was addressed to the duke of Dalmatia. Madrid was said to be perfectly tranquil, the shops opened, and the public amusements going forward as in a time of profound peace. The fourth corps of the army was at Talavera, on its way towards Badajos; this movement, it was observed, would force the English to retire to Portugal, if, contrary to the emperor's belief, they had not already done so. The fifth corps were on the march to Zaragoza, and the eighth to Burgos. The duke was directed to drive the Spaniards into Gallicia, to occupy Leon, Benevente, and Zamora, and to keep the flat country in subjection, for which purpose his two divisions of infantry, and the cavalry brigades of Franceschi and Debelle, were considered sufficient. It is remarkable that the first correct information of the capitulation of Madrid should have been acquired by the perusal of this document, ten days after the event had taken place; nor is it less curious, that while Mr. Frere's letters were filled with vivid descriptions of Spanish enthusiasm, Napoleon should have been so convinced of their passiveness as to send this important despatch by an officer, who rode post, without an escort and in safety, until his abusive language to the postmaster at Valdestillos created a tumult, by which he lost his life. Captain Waters, an English officer sent to obtain intelligence, happening to arrive in that place, heard of the murder, and immediately purchased the despatch for twenty dollars. The accidental information thus obtained was the more valuable, that neither money nor patriotism had induced the Spaniards to bring any intelligence of the enemy's situation, and each step the army had hitherto made was in the dark.

It was now certain that Burgos was or would be strongly protected, and that Baird's line of march was unsafe if Soult, following these instructions, advanced. On the other hand, as the French appeared to be ignorant of the British movements, there was some chance of surprising and beating the second corps before Napoleon could come to its succour. Hope immediately passed the Douero at Tordesillas, and directed his march upon Villepando; head-quarters were removed to Toro, and Valderas was given as the point of junction to Baird's division, the head of which was now at Benevente.

Sir John Moore's Papers. MSS.

The 16th, Mr. Stuart arrived at Toro, accompanied by don F^e. X^r. Caro, a member of the Spanish government, who brought two letters, the one from the junta, the other from Mr. Frere. That from the junta complained, that when Romana proposed to unite fourteen thousand picked men to the British army, with a view to make a forward movement, his offer had been disregarded, and a retreat determined upon, in despite of his earnest remonstrances; this retreat they declared to be uncalled for, and highly impolitic, "as the enemy was never so near his ruin as in that moment." If the Spanish and British armies should unite, they said, it would give "liberty to the Peninsula," that "Romana, with his fourteen thousand select men," was still ready to join sir John Moore, and that "thirty thousand fresh levies would in a month be added to the ranks of the allied force."

Ibid.

This tissue of falsehoods, for Romana had approved of the intention to retreat, and never had above six thousand men armed, was addressed to Mr. Frere, and by him transmitted to the general, together with one from himself, which, in allusion to the retreat upon Portugal, contained the following extraordinary passages: "I mean the immense responsibility with which you charge yourself by adopting, upon a supposed military necessity, a measure which must be followed by immediate, if not final, ruin to our ally, and by indelible disgrace to the country with whose resources you are entrusted." "I am unwilling to enlarge upon a subject in which my feelings must be stifled, or expressed at the risk of offence, which, with such an interest at stake, I should feel unwilling to excite, but this much I must say, that if the British army had been sent abroad for the express purpose of doing the utmost possible mischief to the Spanish cause, with the single exception of not firing a shot against their troops, they would, according to the measures now announced as about to be pursued, have completely fulfilled their purpose."

Appendix, No. 13, section 7.

These letters were dated at Truxillo; for the junta, not thinking themselves safe at Badajos, had proceeded so far on their way to Seville. On that side the French had continued to advance, the remnants of the Spanish armies to fly, and every thing bore the most gloomy appearance. Mr. Frere knew this. In a subsequent letter he acknowledged that the enthusiasm was extinguished, and a general panic commencing, at the moment when he was penning these offensive passages. He was utterly ignorant of the numbers, the situation, and the resources of the enemy, but he formed hypotheses, and upon the strength of them insulted sir John Moore, and compromised the interests of his country; and in this manner the British general, while struggling with unavoidable difficulties, had his mind harassed by a repetition of remonstrances and representations in which common sense, truth, and decency were alike disregarded. On this occasion he furnished a remarkable instance of the control he exercised over his personal feelings, when the public welfare was at stake. As Mr. Frere had acknowledged the receipt of a letter of the 10th, it was probable that he had also received the general's answer (written before the 10th) to the communication made through Charmilly; but as he did not say so, Sir John Moore took advantage of the omission, and with singular propriety and dignity thus replied to him: "With respect to your letter delivered to me at Toro by Mr. Stuart, I shall not remark upon it. It is in the style of the two which were brought to me by colonel Charmilly, and consequently was answered by my letter of the 6th, of which I send you a duplicate; that subject is I hope at rest!"

Sir John Moore's Papers.

Col Symes' Correspce.

Gen. Leith.

Appendix, No. 13, section 5.

Appendix, No. 13, Section 7.

At Toro sir John Moore ascertained that Romana, although aware of the advance of the British, and engaged to support them, was retiring into Gallicia. That nobleman, nominally commander-in-chief of the Spanish armies, was at the head of a few thousand miserable soldiers; for the Spaniards, with great ingenuity, contrived to have no general when they had an army, and no army when they had a general. After the dispersion of Blake's people at Reynosa, Romana rallied about five thousand men at Renedo, in the valley of Cabernigo, and endeavoured to make a stand on the borders of the Asturias, but without any success, for the vile conduct of the Asturian junta, joined to the terror created by the French victories, had completely subdued the spirit of the peasantry, and ruined the resources of that province. Romana complained that, when checked for misconduct, his soldiers quitted their standards; indeed that any should have been found to join their colours is to be admired; for among the sores of Spain there were none more cankered, more disgusting, than the venality, the injustice, the profligate corruption of the Asturian authorities, who, without a blush, openly divided the English subsidies, and defrauded, not only the soldiers of their pay and equipments, but the miserable peasants of their hire, doubling the wretchedness of poverty, and deriding the misery they occasioned by pompous declarations of their own virtue. From the Asturias the marquis led the remnants of Blake's force to Leon about the period of sir John Moore's arrival at Salamanca; like others, he had been deceived as to the real state of the country, and at this time repented that he had returned to Spain.

Romana was a person of talent, quickness, and information, but disqualified by nature for military command; a lively principle of error pervaded all his notions of war; no man ever bore the title of a general who was less capable of directing an army, neither was he exempt from the prevailing weakness of his countrymen. At this moment, when he had not the strength to stand upright, his letters were teeming with gigantic offensive projects, and although he had before approved of the intention to retreat, he was now as ready to urge a forward movement, promising to co-operate with twenty thousand soldiers when he could scarcely muster a third of that number of men, who, half armed, were hardly capable of distinguishing their own standards; and at the very time he made the promise, he was retiring into Gallicia; not that he meant to deceive, for he was as ready to advance as to retreat, but this species of boasting is inherent in his nation, and Romana was a true Spaniard.

It has been asserted that Caro offered the chief command of the Spanish armies to sir John Moore, and that the latter refused it; this is not true: Caro had no power to do so, and if he had, there were no armies to command; but that gentleman in his interview either was, or affected to be, satisfied of the soundness of the English general's views, and ashamed of the folly of the junta.

The 18th, head-quarters were at Castro Nuevo; from that place sir John Moore wrote to Romana, informing him of his intention to fall upon Soult, desiring his co-operation, and requesting that the Marquis would, according to his own plan given to the British minister in London, reserve the Asturias for his line of communication, and leave the Gallicias open to the British.

The army was now in full march, Baird was at Benevente, Hope at Villapando; the cavalry scoured the country on the side of Valladolid, and in several successful skirmishes took a number of prisoners. The French could be no longer ignorant of the march, and the English general brought forward his columns rapidly. On the 20th the whole of the forces were united; the cavalry at Melgar Abaxo, and the infantry at Mayorga, and as much concentrated as the necessity of obtaining cover in a country devoid of fuel, and deep with snow, would permit. The weather was exceedingly severe, and the marches long, but a more robust set of men never took the field: their discipline was admirable, and there were very few stragglers; the experience of one or two campaigns alone was wanting to make a perfect army.

Appendix, No. 25.

The number was however small; nominally it was nearly thirty-five thousand, but four regiments were still in Portugal, and three more were left by sir David Baird at Lugo and Astorga. One thousand six hundred and eighty-seven men were detached, and four thousand and five were in hospital. The actual number present under arms on the 19th of December was only nineteen thousand and fifty-three infantry, two thousand two hundred and seventy-eight cavalry, and one thousand three hundred and fifty-eight gunners, forming a total of twenty-three thousand five hundred and eighty-three men, with sixty pieces of artillery: the whole being organized in three divisions, a reserve, and two light brigades of infantry, and one division of cavalry. Of the artillery four batteries were attached to the infantry, and two to the cavalry; one was kept in reserve.

Romana, who had been able to bring forward very few men, promised to march in two columns by Almanzer and Guarda, and sent some information of the enemy's position; but sir John Moore depended little upon his intelligence, when he found him, even so late as the 19th of December (upon the faith of information from the junta), representing Madrid as still holding out; and when the advanced posts were already engaged at Sahagun, proposing an interview at Benevente to arrange the plan of operations.

S
Journal of Operations. MS.

Ibid.

S

Journal of Operations. MS.

On the French side, Soult's corps was concentrating on the Carrion. After the rapid and brilliant success of this marshal at the opening of the campaign, his corps was ordered to remain on the defensive until the movements against Tudela and Madrid were completed; the despatches commanding him to recommence his offensive operations were, as we have seen, intercepted on the 12th, but on the 16th he became acquainted with the advance of the English army. At that period general Bonnet's division occupied Barquera de San Vincente and Potes, on the Deba; and watched some thousand Asturians that Ballasteros had collected near Llanes. Merle's and Mermet's divisions were on the Carrion; Franceschi's dragoons at Valladolid; and general Debelle's at Sahagun. The whole formed a total of sixteen or seventeen thousand infantry, and twelve hundred cavalry, present under arms, of which only eleven thousand infantry and twelve hundred cavalry could, without uncovering the important post of St. Andero, be opposed to the advance of the British. Soult, alarmed at this disparity of force, required general Mathieu Dumas, commandant at Burgos, to direct all the divisions and detachments passing through that town, (whatever might be their original destination) upon the Carrion; and this decisive conduct was approved of by the emperor. The 21st, Bonnet's division remaining on the Deba, Mermet's occupied the town of Carrion; Merle's was at Saldaña; and Franceschi's cavalry retired from Valladolid to Riberos de la Cuesca. Debelle's continued at Sahagun, and thirteen hundred dragoons, under general Lorge, arrived at Palencia from Burgos.

Meanwhile, the fifteenth and tenth British hussars quitting Melgar Abaxo during the night, arrived close to Sahagun before daylight on the 21st; the tenth marched straight to the town, the fifteenth turned it by the right, and endeavoured to cut off the enemy, but meeting with a patrole, the alarm was given, and when lord Paget, with four hundred of the fifteenth, arrived at the rear of the village, he was opposed by a line of six hundred French dragoons. The tenth not being in sight, the fifteenth, after a few movements, charged, broke the enemy's line, and pursued them for some distance. Fifteen to twenty killed, two lieutenant-colonels, and eleven other officers, with a hundred and fifty-four men prisoners, were the result of this affair, which lasted about twenty minutes. Debelle then retired to Santerbas.

The English infantry occupied Sahagun, and head-quarters were established there. Romana remained at Mancilla, and it was evident that no assistance could be expected from him; the truth was, that ashamed of exposing the weakness and misery of his troops, he kept away, for, after all his promises, he could not produce six thousand fighting men; his letters, however, were, as usual, extremely encouraging. *The French force in Spain was exceedingly weak, Palafox had not been defeated at Tudela, Soult, including Sonnet's division, had scarcely nine thousand men of all arms. It was an object to surround and destroy him before he could be succoured* — and other follies of this nature.

S

Journal of Operations. MS.

The English troops having outmarched their supplies, halted the 22d and 23d. Soult, whose intention was to act on the defensive, hastened the march of the reinforcements from the side of Burgos, and being fearful for his communication with Placentia, abandoned Saldaña on the 23d, and concentrated his infantry at Carrion. Debelle's cavalry again advanced to Villatilla and Villacuenda, Franceschi remained at Riberos, the dragoons of general Lorge occupied Paredes, and general Dumas pushed on the divisions of the eighth corps, of which, Laborde's was already arrived at Palencia, and Loison's and Heudelet's followed at the distance of two days' march; but these last were very weak.

Sir John Moore's plan was to move during the night of the 23d, so as to arrive at Carrion by daylight on the 24th, to force the bridge, and afterwards ascending the river, fall upon the main body of the enemy, which his information led him to believe was still at Saldaña. This attack was however but a secondary object, his attention was constantly directed towards Madrid. He might beat the corps in his front, but the victory could be of little use beyond the honour of the day, for the eighth and third corps were too near to admit of farther success. The whole operation, was one of time, a political bait to tempt the emperor, whose march from Madrid must be the signal for a retreat that sooner or later was inevitable. To draw Napoleon from the south was the great object, but it behoved the man to be alert that interposed between the lion and his prey.

The 23d, Romana gave notice that the French were in motion on the side of Madrid. The night of the 23d the troops were in march towards Carrion, when Romana's intelligence was confirmed by the general's spies; all their reports agreed that the whole French army was in movement to crush the English. The fourth corps had been halted at Talavera, the third at Vittoria, the eighth was closing up to reinforce the second, and the emperor in person was marching towards the Guadarama; the principal objects of sir John Moore's advance were thus attained. The siege of Zaragoza was delayed, the southern provinces were allowed to breathe, and it now remained for him to prove, by a timely retreat, that this offensive operation, although hazardous, was not the result of improvident rashness, nor weakness of mind, but the hardy enterprise of a great commander acting under peculiar circumstances: as a military measure, his judgment condemned it; as a political one, he thought it of doubtful advantage, because Spain was really passive, but he was willing to give the Spaniards an opportunity of making one more struggle for independence. That was done. If they could not, or would not profit of the occasion, if their hearts were faint or their hands feeble, the shame and the loss were their own; the British general had done enough, enough for honour, enough for utility, more than enough for prudence; but the madness of the times required it. His army was already on the verge of destruction, the enemy's force was hourly increasing in his front; the first symptoms of a retreat would bring it headlong on; and in the meantime the emperor threatened the line of communications with Gallicia, and by the rapidity of his march left no time for consideration.

After the first burst, by which he swept the northern provinces, and planted his standards on the banks of the Tagus, that monarch had put all the resources of his subtle genius into activity, endeavouring to soften the public mind, and by engrafting benefits on the terror his victories had created, to gain over the people; but, at the same time, he was gathering in his extended wings, and preparing for a new flight, which would have carried him over the southern kingdoms of the Peninsula, and given him the rocks of Lisbon as a resting-place for his eagles.

Madrid was tranquil; Toledo, notwithstanding her heroic promises, never shut her gates; one division of the first corps occupied that town, another was in Ocaña, and the light cavalry scoured the whole of La Mancha, even to the borders of Andalusia. The fourth corps, and Milhaud's and Lasalle's horsemen, were at Talavera preparing to march to Badajos, and sixty thousand men, with one hundred and fifty guns and fifteen days' provisions in carts, were reviewed at the gates of Madrid upon the 19th. Three days afterwards they were in full march to intercept the line of sir John Moore's retreat.

The emperor was informed of that general's advance on the 21st; in an instant the Spaniards, their juntas, and their armies were dismissed from his thoughts; the different corps were arrested in their movements, ten thousand men were left to control the capital, and on the evening of the 22d, fifty thousand men were at the foot of the Guadarama. A deep snow choked the passes of the Sierra, and, after twelve hours of ineffectual toil, the advanced guards were still on the wrong side; the general commanding reported that the road was impracticable, but Napoleon, rebuking him fiercely, urged the columns to another attempt, and the passage of the mountain was effected amidst storms of hail and drifting sleet. The cold and fatigue being so intense that many soldiers and draft animals died during the two days that the operation lasted.

S   .
Journal of Operations. MS.

Personally urging on the troops with unceasing vehemence the emperor arrived at Villacastin, fifty miles from Madrid, on the 24th, and the 26th he was at Tordesillas with the guards and the divisions of La-Pisse and Dessolles. The dragoons of La Houssaye were at Valladolid on the same day, and marshal Ney, with the sixth corps, was at Rio Seco. From Tordesillas Napoleon communicated with Soult, informed him of these movements, and concluded his despatch thus: "*Our cavalry scouts are already at Benevente. If the English pass to-day in their position, they are lost; if on the contrary, they attack you with all their force, retire one day's march: the farther they proceed the better for us. If they retreat, pursue them closely;*" and then, full of hope, he hastened to Valderas, but had the mortification to learn that, notwithstanding his rapid march, having scarcely rested night or day, he was twelve hours too late. The British were across the Esla!

S   .
Journal of Operations. MS.

In fact Soult was in full pursuit when this letter was written, for sir John Moore, who was well aware of his real situation, had given orders to retreat the moment the intelligence of Napoleon's march from Madrid reached him. The heavy baggage and stores had been immediately moved to the rear; but the reserve, the light brigades, and the cavalry remained at Sahagun, the latter pushing their patroles up to the enemy's lines and skirmishing, with a view to hide the retrograde march. The 24th, general Hope, with two divisions, fell back by the road of Mayorga, and general Baird, with another, by that of Valencia de San Juan, where there was a ferry-boat to cross the Esla river. The marquis of Romana undertook to guard the bridge of Mansilla. The enemy's dragoons, under Lorge, arrived the same day at Frechilla, and the division of Laborde at Paredes. The 25th the general-in-chief, with the reserve and light brigades, followed the route of Hope's column to Valderas; the 26th Baird passed the Esla at Valencia, and took post on the other side, but with some difficulty, for the boat was small, the fords deep, and the river rising. The troops, under the commander-in-chief, approached the bridge of Castro Gonzalo early in the morning of the 26th. The stores and baggage were a long time passing, a dense fog intercepted the view, and so nicely timed was the march that the scouts of the imperial horsemen were already infesting the flank of the column, and even carried off some of the baggage. The left bank of the river being high, and completely commanding the bridge, the second light brigade, under general Robert Crawfurd, and two guns, were posted on that side to protect the passage, for the cavalry were still on the march from Sahagun, and Soult, aware of the retreat, was pressing forward vigorously. When lord Paget had passed Mayorga he discovered a strong body of horse, appertaining to Ney's corps, embattled on a swelling mound close to the road. The soil was deep, and soaked with snow and rain. Two squadrons of the tenth riding stiffly against the enemy, mounted the hill, and, notwithstanding the superiority of numbers and position, overthrew him, killed twenty men, and took a hundred prisoners. This was a bold and hardy action; but the English cavalry had been engaged more or less for twelve successive days, and with such fortune and bravery that above five hundred prisoners had already fallen into their hands, and their leaders being excellent, their confidence was unbounded. From Mayorga lord Paget proceeded to Benevente, but the duke of Dalmatia, with great judgment, directed his march towards Astorga by the road of Mancilla; and Romana, leaving three thousand men and two guns to defend the bridge at that place, fell back to Leon.

Thus by a critical march, sir John Moore had recovered his communications with Astorga and so far baffled the emperor; but his position was by no means safe, or even tenable. The town of Benevente, a rich open place, remarkable for a small but curious Moorish palace or castle containing a fine collection of ancient armour, is situated in a plain that, extending from the Gallician mountains to the neighbourhood of Burgos, appeared to be boundless. On the left it was skirted by the hills near the town of Leon, which was enclosed with walls, and capable of resisting a sudden assault. The river Esla winded through the plain about four miles in front of Benevente, and the bridge of Castro Gonzalos was the key to the town, but the right bank of the Esla, as I have before observed, was completely commanded from the further side, and there were many fords. Eighteen miles higher up, at Valencia de San Juan, a shorter road from Mayorga to Astorga, crossed the river by the ferry-boat, and at Mancilla, the passage being only defended by Spaniards, was, in a manner, open to Soult, for Romana had not destroyed the arches of the bridge. In this exposed situation sir John Moore resolved to remain no longer than was necessary to clear out his magazines at Benevente, and to cover the march of his stores; but the road to Astorga by Leon being much shorter than that through Benevente, he wrote to Romana to request that he would maintain himself at Leon as long as he could; hearing also that the marquis intended to retreat into Gallicia, sir John repeated his desire to have that road left open for the English army. Romana, who assented to both these requests, had a great rabble with him, and as Leon was a walled place, and that a number of citizens and volunteers were willing, and even eager, to fight, the town might have made a formidable resistance. Sir John Moore hoped that it would do so, and gave orders to break down the bridge at Castro Gonzalo in his own front, the moment the stragglers and baggage should have passed.

At this time the bad example of murmuring given by officers of high rank had descended lower; many regimental officers neglected their duty, and what with the dislike to a retreat, the severity of the weather, and the inexperience of the army, the previous fine discipline of the troops was broken down. Very disgraceful excesses had been committed at Valderas, and the general issued severe orders, justly reproaching the soldiers for their evil deeds, and appealing to the spirit of the men and of the officers, to amend them.

On the night of the 26th, the chasseurs of the imperial guard rode close up to the bridge of Castro Gonzalo, and captured some women and baggage[20]. The 27th, the cavalry and the stragglers being all over the river, general Crawfurd commenced the destruction of the bridge; torrents of rain and snow were descending; and half the troops worked while the other half kept the enemy at bay from the heights on the left bank, for the cavalry scouts of the imperial guard were spread over the plain. At ten o'clock at night a large party following some waggons endeavoured to pass the piquets and gallop down to the bridge; that failing, a few dismounted, and extending to the right and left, commenced a skirmishing fire, while others remained ready to charge, if the position of the troops, which they expected to ascertain by this scheme, should offer an opportunity; but the event did not answer their expectations. This anxiety to interrupt the work induced general Crawfurd to destroy two arches of the bridge, and to blow up the connecting buttress; but the masonry was so solid and difficult to pierce, that it was not until twelve o'clock in the night of the 28th that all the preparations were completed. The troops then descended the heights on the left bank, and passing with the greatest silence by single files over planks laid across the broken arches, gained the other side without loss; an instance of singular good fortune, for the night was dark and tempestuous; the river rising rapidly with a roaring noise, was threatening to burst over the planks, and the enemy was close at hand. To have resisted an attack in such an awkward situation would have been impossible, but happily the retreat of the troops was undiscovered, and the mine being sprung with good effect, Crawfurd marched to Benevente, where the cavalry and the reserve still remained[21].

The army gained two days rest at Benevente, but as very little could be done to remove the stores, the greater part of them were destroyed. The troops were, and had been from the first, without sufficient transport, the general was without money to procure it, and the ill-will of the Spaniards, and the shuffling conduct of the juntas, added infinitely to these difficulties. The 28th, Hope's and Fraser's divisions marched to Labaneza; and the 29th, to Astorga, where Baird's division joined them from Valencia San Juan. On the same day the reserve and Crawfurd's brigade quitted Benevente, but the cavalry remained in the town, leaving parties to watch the fords of the Esla. Soon after daybreak, general Lefebre Desnouettes, seeing only a few cavalry posts on the great plain, rather hastily concluded that there was nothing to support them, and crossing the river at a ford a little way above the bridge with six hundred horsemen of the imperial guards, he advanced into the plain. The piquets at first retired fighting, but being joined by a part of the third German hussars, they charged the leading French squadrons with some effect. General C. Stewart then took the command, and the ground was obstinately disputed. At this moment the plain was covered with stragglers, and baggage-mules, and followers of the army; the town was filled with tumult; the distant piquets and vedettes were seen galloping in from the right and left; the French were pressing forward boldly, and every appearance indicated that the enemy's whole army was come up and passing the river. Lord Paget ordered the tenth hussars to mount and form under the cover of some houses at the edge of the town; he desired to draw the enemy, whose real situation he had detected at once, well into the plain before he attacked. In half an hour, every thing being ready, he gave the signal: the tenth hussars galloped forward, the piquets, that were already engaged, closed together, and the whole charged. In an instant the scene changed: the enemy were seen flying at full speed towards the river, and the British close at their heels; the French squadrons, without breaking their ranks, plunged into the stream, and gained the opposite heights, where, like experienced soldiers, they wheeled instantly, and seemed inclined to come forward a second time; but a battery of two guns being opened upon them, after a few rounds they retired. During the pursuit in the plain, an officer was observed separating from the main body, and making towards another part of the river; being followed, and refusing to stop when overtaken, he was cut across the head and brought in a prisoner. He proved to be general Lefebre.

Surgical Campaigns.

Although the imperial guards were outnumbered in the end, they were very superior at the commencement of this fight, which was handsomely contested on both sides. The British lost fifty men killed and wounded; the French left fifty-five killed and wounded on the field, and seventy prisoners, besides the general and other officers. According to baron Larrey, seventy other wounded men escaped, making a total loss of above two hundred excellent soldiers. Lord Paget maintained his posts on the Esla under an occasional cannonade until the evening, and then withdrew to La Baneza.

Bulletin.

S

Journal of Operations. MS.

While these things were passing, Napoleon arrived at Valderas, Ney at Villaton, and Lapisse at Toro; the French troops were worn down with fatigue, yet the emperor still urged them forward. The duke of Dalmatia, he said, would intercept the retreat of the English at Astorga, and their labours would be finally rewarded; but the destruction of the bridge of Castro Gonzalo was so well accomplished, that twenty-four hours were required to repair it, and the fords were now impassable. It was the 30th before Bessieres could cross the Esla; but on that day he passed through Benevente with nine thousand cavalry, and bent his course towards La Baneza. The same day, Franceschi forced the bridge of Mansilla de las Mulas by a single charge of his light horsemen, and captured the artillery and one half of the division left by Romana to protect it. The latter immediately abandoned Leon and many stores. The 31st the duke of Dalmatia entered that town without firing a shot, and the duke of Istria, with his cavalry, took possession of La Baneza; the advanced posts were pushed forward to the Puente d'Orvigo on one side, and the Puente de Valembre on the other.

The rear of the English army was still in Astorga, the head-quarters having arrived there on the day before. In the preceding month large stores had been gradually brought up to that town by sir David Baird, and as there were no means of transport to remove them, orders were given, after supplying the immediate wants of the army, to destroy them; but Romana, who would neither defend Leon nor Mansilla, had, contrary to his promises, pre-occupied Astorga with his fugitive army; and when the English divisions marched in, such a tumult and confusion arose, that no orders could be executed with regularity, no distribution made, nor the destruction of the stores be effected. The disorder thus unexpectedly produced was very detrimental to the discipline of the troops, which the unwearied efforts of the general had partly restored. The resources which he had depended on for the support of his soldiers became mischievous, and contributed to disorganise instead of nourishing them, and he had the farther vexation to hear Romana the principal cause of this misfortune, proposing, (with an army unable to resist a thousand light infantry), to commence offensive operations and plans, in comparison of which the visions of don Quixote were wisdom.

The 31st, the light brigades separated from the army at Bonillas, and bent their course by cross roads towards Orense and Vigo. This detachment was made to lessen the pressure on the commissariat, and to cover the flanks of the army. Fraser's and Hope's divisions entered Villa Franca, Baird's division was at Bembibre. The reserve, with the head-quarters, halted at Cambarros, a village six miles from Astorga, but the cavalry fell back in the night to the same place, and then the reserve marched to Bembibre.

The marquis of Romana, after doing so much mischief by crossing the line of march, left his infantry to wander as they pleased, and retired with his cavalry and guns to the valley of the Mincio.

Upon the 1st of January the emperor took possession of Astorga. On that day seventy thousand French infantry, ten thousand cavalry, and two hundred pieces of artillery, after many days of incessant marching, were there united. The congregation of this mighty force, while it evinced the power and energy of the French monarch, attested also the genius of the English general, who, with a handful of men, had found the means to arrest the course of the conqueror, and to draw him, with the flower of his army, to this remote and unimportant part of the Peninsula, at the moment when Portugal, and the fairest provinces of Spain, were prostrate beneath the strength of his hand. That Spain, being in her extremity, sir John Moore succoured her, and in the hour of weakness intercepted the blow which was descending to crush her, no man of candour and honesty can deny. For what troops, what preparations, what courage, what capacity, was there in the south to have resisted, even for an instant, the progress of a man, who, in ten days, and in the depth of winter, crossing the snowy ridge of the Carpentinos, had traversed two hundred miles of hostile country, and transported fifty thousand men from Madrid to Astorga in a shorter time than a Spanish diligence would have taken to travel the same distance?

S

Journal of Operations. MS.

This stupendous march was rendered fruitless by the quickness of his adversary; but Napoleon, though he had failed to destroy the English army, resolved, nevertheless, to cast it forth of the Peninsula, and being himself recalled to France by tidings that the Austrian storm was ready to burst, he fixed upon the duke of Dalmatia to continue the pursuit, adding for this purpose three divisions of cavalry, and three of infantry to his former command; but of these last, the two commanded by generals Loison and Heudelet, were several marches in the rear, and general Bonnet's remained always in the Montagna de St. Ander; hence the whole number bearing arms, which the duke led immediately to the pursuit, was about twenty-five thousand men, of which four thousand two hundred were cavalry[22]. The guns were fifty-four. Loison's and Heudelet's divisions, however, followed him by forced marches, and he was supported by marshal Ney with the sixth corps, wanting its third division; but mustering above sixteen thousand men under arms, (the flower of the French army), together with thirty-seven pieces of artillery. Thus including Laborde, Heudelet, and Loison's division, nearly sixty thousand men and ninety-one guns were put on the track of the English army.

The emperor returned to Valladolid, where he received the addresses of the notables and deputies from Madrid and the great towns, and strove, by promises and other means, to win the good opinion of the public. Appointing Joseph to be his lieutenant-general, he allotted separate provinces for each "*corps d'armée*," and directing the imperial guard to return to France; after three days he departed himself with scarcely any escort, but with a speed that frustrated the designs that (as some say) the Spaniards had formed against his person.

CHAPTER V

The duke of Dalmatia, a general, who, if the emperor be excepted, was no wise inferior to any of his nation, commenced his pursuit of the English army with a vigour that marked his eager desire to finish the campaign in a manner suitable to the brilliant opening at Gamonal.

S

Journal of Operations. MS.

The main body of his troops followed the route of Foncevadon and Ponteferrada, a second column took the road of Cambarros and Bembibre, and general Franceschi, with the light cavalry, entering the valley of the Syl, ascended the course of that river, and turned the position of Villa Franca del Bierzo. Thus sir John Moore, after having twice baffled the emperor's combinations, was still pressed in his retreat with a fury that seemed to increase every moment. The separation of his light brigades, a measure which he adopted, after the advice of his quarter-master-general, weakened the army by three thousand men; but he still possessed nineteen thousand of all arms, good soldiers to fight, and strong to march, yet by the disorders at Valderas and Astorga, much shaken in their discipline; for the general's exertions to restore order and regularity were by many officers slightly seconded, and by some with scandalous levity disregarded.

There was no choice but to retreat. The astonishing rapidity with which the emperor had brought up his overbearing numbers, and thrust the English army into Gallicia, had rendered the natural strength of the country unavailing. The resources were few, even for an army in winter quarters, and for a campaign in that season, there were none at all. All the draft cattle that could be procured would scarcely have supplied the means to transport ammunition for two battles, but the French, sweeping the rich plains of Castille with their powerful cavalry, might have formed magazines at Astorga and Leon, and from thence have been supplied in abundance, while the English were starving.

Appendix, No. 13, sections 2 and 8.

Sir John Moore's Papers. MSS.

Before he advanced from Salamanca, sir John Moore, foreseeing that his movement must sooner or later end in a retreat, had sent officers to examine the roads of Gallicia and the harbours which offered the greatest advantages for embarkation. By the reports of those officers, which arrived from day to day, and by the state of the magazines he had directed to be formed, his measures were constantly regulated. The magazines of Astorga, Benevente, and Labaneza, we have seen, were, by untoward circumstances, and the deficiency of transport, rendered of no avail beyond the momentary supply they afforded; and part of their contents falling into the enemy's hands, gave him some cause of triumph; but those at Villa Franca and Lugo contained about fourteen days' consumption; and there were other small magazines formed on the line of Orenze and Vigo; more than this could not have been accomplished.

Appendix, No. 28.

It was now only the fifteenth day since sir John Moore had left Salamanca, and already the torrent of war, diverted from the south, was foaming among the rocks of Gallicia. Nineteen thousand British troops, posted in strong ground, might have offered battle to very superior numbers; but where was the use of merely fighting an enemy who had three hundred thousand men in Spain? Nothing could be gained by such a display of courage; but the English general, by a quick retreat, might reach his ships unmolested, embark, and carrying his army from the narrow corner in which it was cooped, to the southern provinces, establish there a good base of operations, and renew the war under favourable circumstances. It was by this combination of a fleet and army, that the greatest assistance could be given to Spain, and the strength of England become most formidable. A few days' sailing would carry the troops to Cadiz; but six weeks' constant marching would not bring the French army from Gallicia to that neighbourhood. The northern provinces were broken, subdued in spirit, and possessed few resources. The southern provinces had scarcely seen an enemy, were rich and fertile, and there also was the seat of government. Sir John Moore reasoned thus, and resolved to fall down to the coast and embark, with as little loss or delay as might be. Vigo, Coruña, and Ferrol were the principal harbours; and their relative advantages could not be determined except by the reports of the engineers, none of which were yet received, so rapidly had the crisis of affairs come on; but as those reports could only be obtained from day to day, the line of retreat became of necessity subject to daily change.

Appendix, No. 13, section 2d,
see colonel Carmichael Smith's report.

When the duke of Dalmatia took the command of the pursuing army, Hope's and Fraser's divisions were, as I have said, at Villa Franca, sir David Baird's at Bembibre, the reserve and cavalry at Cambarros, six miles from Astorga. Behind Cambarros the mountains of Gallicia rose abruptly, but there was no position, because, after the first rise at the village of Rodrigatos, the ground continually descended to Calcabellos, a small town, only four miles from Villa Franca, and the old road of Foncevadon and Ponteferrada, which turned the whole line, was choked with the advancing columns of the enemy. The reserve and the cavalry marched during the night to Bembibre: on their arrival Baird's division proceeded to Villa Franca, but the immense wine-vaults of Bembibre had such temptations, that many hundred of his men remained behind inebriated; the followers of the army crowded the houses, and a number of Romana's disbanded men were mixed with this heterogeneous mass of marauders, drunkards, muleteers, women, and children; the weather was dreadful, and, notwithstanding the utmost exertions of the general-in-chief, when the reserve marched the next morning, the number of those unfortunate wretches was not diminished. Leaving a small guard to protect them, sir John Moore proceeded to Calcabellos; but scarcely had the reserve marched out of the village, when some French cavalry appeared. In a moment the road was filled with the miserable stragglers, who came crowding after the troops, some with loud shrieks of distress and wild gestures, others with brutal exclamations; many, overcome with fear, threw away their arms. Those who preserved theirs were too stupidly intoxicated to fire; and kept reeling to and fro, alike insensible to their danger and to their disgrace. The enemy's horsemen perceiving this confusion, bore down at a gallop, broke through the disorderly mob, cutting to the right and left as they passed, and riding so close to the columns, that the infantry were forced to halt in order to check their audacity.

At Calcabellos the reserve took up a position, and the general-in-chief went on to Villa Franca. In that town great excesses had been committed by the preceding divisions; the magazines were plundered, the bakers driven away from the ovens, the wine stores forced, and the commissaries prevented from making the regular distributions; the doors of the houses were broken, and the scandalous insubordination of the soldiers proved that a discreditable relaxation of discipline on the part of the officers had taken place. The general immediately arrested this disorder, caused one man taken in the act of plundering a magazine to be shot in the market-place, and issued severe orders to prevent a recurrence of such inexcusable conduct, after which he returned to the reserve at Calcavellos.

The Guia, a small, but at this season of the year a deep stream, run through that town, and was crossed by a stone bridge. On the Villa Franca side, a lofty ridge, rough with vineyards and stone walls, was occupied by two thousand five hundred infantry, with a battery of six guns. Four hundred[23] riflemen and about the same number of cavalry were posted on a hill two miles beyond the river, to watch the two roads of Bembibre and Foncevadon. The 3d of January, a little after noon, the French general Colbert approached this hill with six or eight squadrons; but observing the ground behind Calcabellos strongly occupied, he demanded reinforcements. Marshal Soult, believing that the English did not mean to make a stand, sent orders to Colbert to charge without delay; and the latter, stung by the message, obeyed with precipitate fury. From one of those errors so frequent in war, the British cavalry, thinking a greater force was riding against them, retired at speed to Calcabellos. The riflemen, who, following their orders, had withdrawn when the French first came in sight, were just passing the bridge, when a crowd of staff officers, the cavalry, and the enemy, came in upon them in one mass; in the confusion thirty or forty men were taken, and Colbert crossing the river, charged on the spur up the road. The remainder of the riflemen threw themselves into the vineyards, and permitting the enemy to approach within a few yards, suddenly opened such a deadly fire, that the greatest number of the French horsemen were killed on the spot, and among the rest Colbert himself. His fine martial figure, his voice, his gestures, and, above all, his daring valour had excited the admiration of the British, and a general feeling of sorrow was predominant when the gallant soldier fell. The French voltigeurs now crossed the river; a few of the 52d regiment descended from the upper part of the ridge to the assistance of the riflemen, and a sharp skirmish commenced, in which two or three hundred men of both sides were killed or wounded: towards evening Merle's division of infantry appeared on the hills in front of the town, and made a demonstration of crossing the river opposite to the left of the English position; but the battery of the latter checked this movement, and night coming on the combat ceased.

From Villa Franca to Lugo the road led through a rugged country; the cavalry were therefore sent on to the latter town at once. During the night the French patroles broke in upon the rifle piquets, and wounded some men, but were beaten back without being able to discover that the English troops had abandoned the position.

The reserve reached Herrerias, a distance of eighteen miles, on the morning of the 5th. Baird's division was at Nogales, Hope's and Fraser's near Lugo. At Herrerias, sir John Moore, who constantly directed the movements of the rear-guard himself, received the first reports of the engineers relative to the harbours. It appeared that Vigo, besides its greater distance, offered no position to cover the embarkation, but Coruña and Betanzos did. This induced him to relinquish his first intention of going to Vigo, and made him regret the absence of his light brigades. The transports were now ordered round from Vigo to Coruña; and in the mean time the general sent orders to the leading division to halt at Lugo, his intention being to rally the army there, to restore discipline, and to offer battle to the enemy if he was inclined to accept it.

These orders were carried to sir David Baird by one of the aides-de-camp of the commander-in-chief; but sir David forwarded them by a private dragoon, who got drunk and lost the despatch. This blameable irregularity was ruinous to general Fraser's troops: in lieu of resting two days at Lugo, that general unwittingly pursued his toilsome journey towards St. Jago de Compostella, and then returned without food or rest, losing by this pilgrimage above four hundred stragglers. The 4th, the reserve reached Nogales, having by a forced march of thirty-six miles gained twelve hours' start of the enemy. At the entrance of this village they met a large convoy, consisting of English clothing, shoes, and ammunition; intended for Romana's army but moving towards the enemy; a circumstance perfectly characteristic of the Spanish mode of conducting public affairs. There was a bridge at Nogales which the engineers failed to destroy; but this was a matter of little consequence, as the river was fordable above and below; indeed the general was unwilling, unless for some palpable advantage, which seldom presented itself, to injure the communications of a country that he was unable to serve. The bridges were commonly very solidly constructed, and the arches having very little span, could be rendered passable again in a shorter time than they could be destroyed.

At this period of the retreat the road was crowded with stragglers and baggage; the peasantry, although armed, did not molest the French; but fearing both sides alike, drove their cattle and carried off their effects into the mountains on each side of the line of march; even there the villanous marauders contrived to find them, and in some cases were by the Spaniards killed; a just punishment for quitting their colours. Under the most favourable circumstances, the tail of a retreating force exhibits terrible scenes of distress; and on the road near Nogales, the followers of the army were dying fast from cold and hunger. The soldiers, barefooted, harassed, and weakened, by their excesses at Bembibre and Villa Franca, were dropping to the rear by hundreds. Broken carts, dead animals, and the piteous appearance of women with children, struggling or falling exhausted in the snow, completed a picture of war, which, like Janus, has a double face.

Towards evening the French recovered their lost ground, and passed Nogales, galling the rear-guard with a continual skirmish; and here it was that dollars to the amount of twenty-five thousand pounds were abandoned. This small sum was kept near head-quarters to answer sudden emergencies, and the bullocks that drew it being tired, the general, who could not save the money without risking an ill-timed action, had it rolled down the side of the mountain; part of it was gathered by the enemy, part by the Gallician peasants[24].

S

Journal of Operations, MS.

This day also, general Franceschi, who after turning Villa Franca and scouring the valley of the Syl, had ascended the banks of the Minho with his cavalry, fell into the line of march at Becerea, and rejoined the French army. Towards evening the reserve approached Constantino; the French were close upon the rear, and a hill within pistol shot of the bridge offered them such an advantage, that there was little hope to effect the passage without great loss. The general caused the riflemen and artillery to take possession of the hill, under cover of which the remainder of the reserve hastily passed across the river without being perceived by the enemy, who were unusually cautious, and not aware of the vicinity of the bridge; the guns then descended at a trot, the riflemen followed, and when the French, now undeceived, came up at a brisk pace, the passage was effected, and a good line of battle formed at the other side; a fight commenced, but notwithstanding that the assailants were continually reinforced as their columns of march arrived, general Paget maintained the post with two regiments until nightfall, and then retired to Lugo, in front of which the whole army was assembled. A few of the French cavalry showed themselves on the 6th, but the infantry did not appear.

The 7th, sir John Moore, in a general order, gave a severe but just rebuke to the officers and soldiers for their previous want of discipline, and at the same time announced his intention to offer battle. It has been well said, that a British army may be gleaned in a retreat, but cannot be reaped. Whatever may be their misery, the soldiers will always be found clean at review, and ready at a fight. Scarcely was this order issued, when the line of battle, so attenuated before, was filled with vigorous men, full of confidence and valour. Fifteen hundred had fallen in action, or dropped to the rear; but as three fresh battalions left by sir David Baird in his advance to Astorga had joined the army between Villa Franca and Lugo, nineteen thousand combatants were still under arms when the French columns appeared in sight. The right of the English position was in comparatively flat ground, and partially protected by a bend of the Minho. The centre was amongst vineyards, with low stone walls. The left, which was somewhat withdrawn, rested on the mountains, being supported and covered by the cavalry. It was the intention of the general to engage deeply with his right and centre before he closed with his left wing, in which he had posted the flower of his troops, hoping thus to bring on a decisive battle, and trusting to the valour of the men to handle the enemy in such sort as that he should be glad to let the army continue its retreat unmolested. Other hope than this, to re-embark the troops without loss, there was none, except by stratagem; for Soult, an experienced general, commanding soldiers habituated to war, might be tempted, but could never be forced to engage in a decisive battle among those rugged mountains, where whole days would pass in skirmishing, without any progress being made towards crippling an adversary.

It was mid-day before the French marshal arrived in person at the head of ten or twelve thousand men; the remainder of his power followed in some disarray; for the marches had not been so easy but that many even of the oldest soldiers had dropped behind. As the French columns came up, they formed in order of battle along a strong mountainous ridge fronting the English. The latter were not distinctly seen, from the inequalities of the ground, and Soult feeling doubtful if they were all before him, took four guns, and some squadrons commanded by colonel Lallemande, advanced towards the centre, and opened a fire, which was soon silenced by a reply from fifteen pieces. The marshal being then satisfied that something more than a rear guard was in his front, retired. About an hour after he made a feint on the right, and at the same time sent a column of infantry and five guns against the left. On that side the three regiments which had lately joined were drawn up. The French pushed the outposts hard, and were gaining the advantage; when the English general-in-chief arriving, rallied the light troops, and with a vigorous charge broke the adverse column, and treated it very roughly in the pursuit. The estimated loss of the French was between three and four hundred men.

S
Journal of Operations, MS.

As it was now evident that the British meant to give battle, the duke of Dalmatia hastened the march of Laborde's division, which was still in the rear, and requested marshal Ney, who was then at Villa Franca, to detach a division of the sixth corps by the Val des Orres to Orense. Ney, however, merely sent some troops into the valley of the Syl, and pushed his advanced posts in front as far as Nogales, Poyo, and Dancos.

Ibid.

At daybreak on the 8th the two armies were still embattled. On the French side, seventeen thousand infantry, four thousand cavalry, and fifty pieces of artillery were in line, but Soult deferred the attack until the 9th. On the English part, sixteen thousand infantry, eighteen hundred cavalry, and forty pieces of artillery, impatiently awaited the assault, and blamed their adversary for delaying a contest which they ardently desired; but darkness fell without a shot having being fired, and with it fell the English general's hope to engage his enemy on equal terms.

What was to be done? assail the French position? remain another day in expectation of a battle? or, in secrecy, gain a march, get on board without being molested, or at least obtain time to establish the army in a good situation to cover the embarkation? The first operation was warranted neither by present nor by future advantages, for how could an inferior army expect to cripple a superior one, posted as the French were, on a strong mountain, with an overbearing cavalry to protect their infantry should the latter be beaten; and when twenty thousand fresh troops were at the distance of two short marches in the rear. The British army was not provided to fight above one battle. There were no draught cattle, no means of transporting reserve ammunition, no magazines, no hospitals, no second line, no provisions. A defeat would have been ruin, a victory useless. A battle is always a serious affair; but two battles under such circumstances, though both should be victories, would have been destruction.

But why fight at all, after the army had been rallied, and the disasters of the march from Astorga had been remedied? What, if beating first Soult and then Ney, the British had arrived once more above Astorga, with perhaps ten thousand infantry, and half as many hundred cavalry? From the mountains of Gallicia their general might have cast his eyes as far as the Sierra Morena, without being cheered by the sight of a single Spanish army; none were in existence to aid him, none to whom he might give aid. Even Mr. Frere acknowledged that at this period six thousand ill-armed men collected at Despeñas Peros formed the only barrier between the French and Seville, and sir John Moore was sent out not to waste English blood in fruitless battles, but to assist the universal Spanish nation!

Sir John Moore's Papers.

The second proposition was decided by the state of the magazines; there was not bread for another day's consumption remaining in the stores at Lugo. It was true that the army was in heart for fighting, but distressed by fatigue and bad weather, and each moment of delay increased privations that would soon have rendered it inefficient for a campaign in the south, which was the only point where its services could now be effectual. For two whole days sir John Moore had offered battle; this was sufficient to rally the troops, to restore order, and to preserve the reputation of the army. Lugo was strong ground in itself, but it did not cover Coruña. The road leading from Orense to St. Jago de Compostella turned it; the French ought to have been on that line, and there was no reason to suppose that they were not. Soult, we have seen, pressed Ney to follow it. It was then impossible to remain at Lugo, and useless if it had been possible.

The general adopted the third plan, and prepared to decamp in the night; he ordered the fires to be kept bright, and exhorted the troops to make a great exertion, which he trusted would be the last required of them.

The country immediately in the rear of the position was intersected by stone walls and a number of intricate lanes; precautions were taken to mark the right tracks, by placing bundles of straw at certain distances, and officers were appointed to guide the columns. At ten o'clock the troops silently quitted their ground, and retired in excellent order; but a moody fortune pursued sir John Moore throughout this campaign, baffling his prudence, and thwarting his views, as if resolved to prove the unyielding firmness of his mind. A terrible storm of wind and rain, mixed with sleet, commenced as the army broke up from the position; the marks were destroyed, and the guides lost the true direction; only one of the divisions happily gained the main road, the other two were bewildered, and when daylight broke, the rear columns were still near to Lugo. The fatigue, the depression of mind, occasioned by this misfortune, and the want of shoes, broke the order of the march, and the stragglers were, becoming numerous, when unfortunately, one of the generals commanding a leading division, thinking to relieve the men during a halt which took place in the night, desired them to take refuge from the weather in some houses a little way off the road. Complete disorganization followed this imprudent act: from that moment it became impossible to make the soldiers of the division keep their ranks; plunder succeeded, the example was infectious, and what with real suffering, and evil propensity encouraged by this error of inexperience, the main body of the army, which had *bivouaced* for six hours in the rain, arrived at Betanzos on the evening of the 9th, in a state very discreditable to its discipline.

Mr. James Moore's Narrative.

The commander-in-chief, with the reserve and the cavalry, as usual, covered the march; in the course of it he ordered several bridges to be destroyed, but the engineers failed of success in every attempt. Fortunately, the enemy did not come up with the rear before the evening, and then only with their cavalry, otherwise many prisoners must have fallen into their hands. The number of stragglers uncovered by the passage of the reserve was so numerous, that being pressed by the enemy's horse, they united in considerable bodies and repulsed them, a signal proof that the disorder was occasioned as much by insubordination in the regiments as by the fatigue of the march.

The reserve, commanded by general Edward Paget, an officer distinguished during the retreat by his firmness, ability, and ardent zeal, remained in position, during the night, a few miles from Betanzos. The rest of the army was quartered in that town, and as the enemy could not gather in strength on the 10th; the commander-in-chief halted that day, and the cavalry passed from the rear-guard to the head of the column.

The 11th, the French interrupted those employed to destroy the bridge of Betanzos; the twenty-eighth regiment repulsed the skirmishers, but the bridge, though constructed of wood, was only partially destroyed.

Appendix, No. 26.

In the meantime sir John Moore assembled the army in one solid mass. The loss of men in the march from Lugo to Betanzos had been greater than that in all the former part of the retreat, added to all the waste of the movement in advance and the loss sustained in the different actions: nevertheless fourteen thousand infantry were still in column, and by an orderly march to Coruña under the personal direction of the commander-in-chief, demonstrated, that inattention and the want of experience in the officers was the true cause of those disorders which had afflicted the army far more than the sword of the enemy or the rigour of the elements.

As the troops approached Coruña the general's looks were directed towards the harbour; an open expanse of water painfully convinced him, that to Fortune at least he was no way beholden; contrary winds detained the fleet at Vigo, and the last consuming exertion made by the army was thus rendered fruitless! The men were now put into quarters, and their leader awaited the progress of events. Three divisions occupied the town and suburbs, the reserve was posted with its left at the village of El Burgo, and its right on the road of St. Jago de Compostella. For twelve days these hardy soldiers had covered the retreat, during which time they had traversed eighty miles of road in two marches, passed several nights under arms in the snow of the mountains, were seven times engaged with the enemy, and they now assembled at the outposts, having fewer men missing from the ranks (including those who had fallen in battle) than any other division in the army. An admirable instance of the value of good discipline, and a manifest proof of the malignant injustice with which sir John Moore has been accused of precipitating his retreat beyond the measure of human strength.

The bridge of El Burgo was immediately destroyed, and an engineer was sent to blow up that of Cambria, situated a few miles up the Mero river; this officer was mortified at the former failures, and so anxious to perform his duty in an effectual manner, that he remained too near the mine, and was killed by the explosion; but there was also a bridge at Celas, two leagues higher up, and at that place Franceschi's cavalry crossed on the 12th, intercepted some stores coming from St. Jago, and made a few prisoners.

The town of Coruña, although sufficiently strong to oblige an enemy to break ground before it, was weakly fortified, and to the southward commanded by some heights close to the walls. Sir John Moore caused the land front to be repaired and strengthened, and also disarmed the sea face of the works, and occupied the citadel. The inhabitants cheerfully and honourably joined in the labour, although they were fully aware that the English intended to embark, and that they compromised their own safety by aiding the operation. Such flashes of light from the dark cloud which at this moment covered Spain may startle the mind of the reader, and make him doubt if the Spaniards could have been so insufficient to their own defence as they have been represented in the course of this history. I can only answer, that the facts were as I have told them, and that it was such paradoxical indications of character that deceived the world at this time, and induced men to believe that the reckless daring defiance of the power of France so loudly proclaimed by the patriots, would be strenuously supported. Of proverbially vivid imagination and quick resentments, the Spaniards feel and act individually rather than nationally; and during this war, that which appeared to be in them constancy of purpose, was in reality a repetition of momentary fury, a succession of electric sparks generated by a constant collision with the French army, and daily becoming fainter as custom reconciled them to those injuries and insults which are commonly the attendants of war.

Procrastination and improvidence are the besetting sins of the nation: at this moment a large magazine of arms and ammunition was in Coruña; these stores had been sent in the early part of the preceding year from England, and they were still unappropriated and unregarded by a nation infested with three hundred thousand enemies, and possessing a hundred thousand soldiers unclothed and without weapons.

Three miles from the town, four thousand barrels of powder were piled in a magazine built upon a hill; a smaller quantity, collected in another storehouse, was at some distance from the first: to prevent these magazines from falling a prey to the enemy, they were both exploded on the 13th. The inferior one blew up with a terrible noise and shook the houses in the town; but when the train reached the great store, there ensued a crash like the bursting forth of a volcano, the earth trembled for miles, the rocks were torn from their bases, and the agitated waters rolled the vessels as in a storm;

a vast column of smoke and dust, shooting out fiery sparks from its sides, arose perpendicularly and slowly to a great height, and then a shower of stones, and fragments of all kinds, bursting out of it with a roaring sound, killed several persons who remained too near the spot. A stillness, only interrupted by the lashing of the waves on the shore, succeeded, and the business of the war went on.

The ground in front of Coruña is impracticable for cavalry, and as the horses still left alive were generally foundered, and that it was impossible to embark them all in the face of an enemy, a great number were reluctantly ordered to be shot. These poor animals, already worn down and feet broken, would otherwise have been distributed among the French cavalry, or used as draft cattle, until by procrastinated sufferings of the nature they had already endured, they should be killed.

The enemy were now collecting in force on the Mero, and it became necessary to choose a position of battle. A chain of rocky elevations commencing on the sea-coast, north-west of the place, and ending on the Mero just behind the village of El Burgo, offered an advantageous line of defence; covered by a branch of the Mero, which, washing a part of the base, would have obliged the enemy to advance by the road of Compostella; but this ridge was too extensive for the English army, and if not wholly occupied, the French might have turned it by the right, and moved along a succession of eminences to the very gates of Coruña. There was no alternative but to take post on an inferior range, enclosed as it were within the other, and completely commanded by it within cannon-shot.

The French army had been so exhausted by continual toil, that it was not completely assembled on the Mero before the 12th. The infantry took post opposite El Burgo; the cavalry of La Houssaye lined the river as far as the ocean, and Franceschi, as we have seen, crossed at the bridge of Celas, seven miles higher up. The 14th, the bridges of El Burgo being rendered practicable for artillery, two divisions of infantry, and one of cavalry, passed the river. To cover this march some guns opened on the English posts at El Burgo, but were soon silenced by a superior fire. The same evening, the transports from Vigo hove in sight, and soon after entered the harbour of Coruña, and the dismounted cavalry, the sick, all the best horses, and fifty-two pieces of artillery, were embarked during the night; eight British, and four Spanish guns, were, however, retained on shore ready for action.

Noble's Expedition de Galice.

The 15th, La Borde's division arrived, and the French occupied the great ridge enclosing the British position, placing their right on the intersection of the roads leading from St. Jago and Betanzos, and their left upon a rocky eminence which overlooked both lines. Towards evening, their cavalry, supported by some light troops, extended towards the left, and a slight skirmish took place in the valley below. At the same time the English piquets opposite the right of the French, got engaged, and being galled by the fire of two guns, colonel M'Kenzie of the fifth, at the head of some companies, endeavoured to seize the battery; but a line of infantry, hitherto concealed by some stone walls, arose, and poured in such a fire of musketry, that the colonel was killed, and his men forced back with loss.

Noble's Expedition de Galice.

In the course of the night, marshal Soult with great difficulty established a battery of eleven guns, (eight and twelve-pounders,) on the rocks which formed the left of his line of battle. Laborde's division was posted on the right; half of it occupied the high ground, the other half was placed on the descent towards the river. Merle's division was in the centre. Mermet's division formed the left. The position was covered in front of the right by the villages of Palavia Abaxo, and Portosa, and in front of the centre by a wood; the left was strongly posted on the rugged heights where the great battery was established. The distance from that battery to the right of the English line was about twelve hundred yards, and, midway, the little village of Elvina was held by the piquets of the latter nation.

Sir John Moore's Letter to Ld. Castleh.

The late arrival of the transports, the increasing force of the enemy, and the disadvantageous nature of the ground, augmented the difficulty and danger of the embarkation so much, that several general officers proposed to the commander-in-chief, that he should negotiate for leave to retire to his ships upon terms. There was little chance of such a proposal being agreed to by the enemy, and there was no reason to try. The army had suffered, but not from defeat; its situation was dangerous, but far from desperate; and the general would not consent to remove the stamp of energy and prudence which marked his retreat, by a negotiation that would have given an appearance of timidity and indecision to his previous operations, as opposite to their real character as light is to darkness. His high spirit and clear judgment revolted at the idea, and he rejected the degrading advice without hesitation.

All the encumbrances of the army were shipped in the night of the 15th and on the morning of the 16th, and every thing was prepared to withdraw the fighting men as soon as the darkness would permit them to move without being perceived. The precautions taken would, without doubt, have insured the success of this difficult operation, but a more glorious event was destined to give a melancholy but graceful termination to the campaign.

About two o'clock in the afternoon a general movement along the French line gave notice of the approaching

BATTLE OF CORUÑA

Vide Plan of the Battle.

The British infantry, fourteen thousand five hundred strong, occupied the inferior range of hills already spoken of. The right was formed by Baird's division, and, from the oblique direction of the ridge, approached the enemy, while the centre and left were of necessity withheld in such a manner that the French battery on the rocks raked the whole of the line. General Hope's division, crossing the main road, prolonged the line of the right's wing, and occupied strong ground abutting on the muddy bank of the Mero. A brigade from Baird's division remained in column behind the extremities of his line, and a brigade of Hope's was posted on different commanding points behind the left wing. The reserve was drawn up near Airis, a small village situated in the rear of the centre. This last point commanded the valley which separated the right of Baird's division from the hills occupied by the French cavalry; the latter were kept in check by a regiment detached from the reserve, and a chain of skirmishers extending across the valley connected this regiment with the right of Baird's line. General Fraser's division remaining on the heights immediately before the gates of Coruña, was prepared to advance to any point, and also watched the coast road. These dispositions were as able as the unfavourable nature of the ground would admit of, but the advantage was all on the enemy's side. His light cavalry, under Franceschi, reaching nearly to the village of St. Christopher, a mile in the rear of Baird's division, obliged sir John Moore to weaken his front by keeping back Fraser's division until Soult's plan of attack should be completely developed. There was, however, one circumstance to compensate for these disadvantages. In the Spanish stores were found many thousand English muskets; the troops exchanged their old rusty and battered arms for these new ones; their ammunition also was fresh, and their fire was therefore very superior to their adversary's in proportion to the numbers engaged.

General Laborde's division being come up, the French force could not be less than twenty thousand men; and the duke of Dalmatia having made his arrangements, did not lose any time in idle evolutions, but distributing his lighter guns along the front of his position, opened a heavy fire from the battery on his left, and instantly descended with three solid masses to the assault. A cloud of skirmishers led the way, and the British piquets being driven back in disorder, the village of Elvina was carried by the first column, which afterwards dividing, one half pushed on against Baird's front, the other turned his right by the valley. The second column made for the centre. The third engaged the left by the village of Palavia Abaxo. The weight of the French guns overmatched the English six-pounders, and their shot swept the position to the centre.

Sir John Moore observing, that, according to his expectations, the enemy did not show any body of infantry beyond that which, moving up the valley, outflanked Baird's right, ordered general Paget to carry the reserve to where the detached regiment was posted, and, as he had before arranged with him, to turn the left of the French attack and menace the great battery. Then directing Fraser's division to support Paget, he threw back the fourth regiment, which formed the right of Baird's division, opened a heavy fire upon the flank of the troops penetrating up the valley, and with the fiftieth and forty-second regiments met those breaking through Elvina.

Moore's Narrative.

The ground about that village was intersected by stone walls and hollow roads; a severe, scrambling fight ensued, but in half an hour the French were borne back with great loss. The fiftieth regiment entered the village with them, and after a second struggle drove them for some distance beyond it. Meanwhile the general bringing up a battalion of the brigade of guards to fill the space in the line left vacant by those two regiments, the forty-second mistook his intention, and retired, and at that moment the enemy, being reinforced, renewed the fight beyond the village, the officer commanding the fiftieth[25] was wounded and taken prisoner, and Elvina became the scene of a second struggle; this being observed by the commander-in-chief, who directed in person the operations of Baird's division, he addressed a few animating words to the forty-second, and caused it to return to the attack. General Paget, with the reserve, now descended into the valley, and the line of skirmishers being thus supported, vigorously checked the advance of the enemy's troops in that quarter, while the fourth regiment galled their flank. At the same time the centre and left of the army also became engaged; sir David Baird was severely wounded, and a furious action ensued along the line, in the valley, and on the hills.

Mr. James Moore's Narrative.

Hardinge's Letter.

Sir John Moore, while earnestly watching the result of the fight about the village of Elvina, was struck on the left breast by a cannon shot; the shock threw him from his horse with violence; he rose again in a sitting posture; his countenance unchanged, and his stedfast eye still fixed upon the regiments engaged in his front; no sigh betrayed a sensation of pain; but in a few moments, when he was satisfied that the troops were gaining ground, his countenance brightened, and he suffered himself to be taken to the rear. Then was seen the dreadful nature of his hurt; the shoulder was shattered to pieces, the arm was hanging by a piece of skin, the ribs over the heart broken, and bared of flesh, and the muscles of the breast torn into long strips, which were interlaced by their recoil from the dragging of the shot. As the soldiers placed him in a blanket his sword got entangled, and the hilt entered the wound. Captain Hardinge, a staff officer, who was near, attempted to take it off, but the dying man stopped him, saying, "*It is as well as it is. I had rather it should go out of the field with me.*" And in that manner, so becoming to a soldier, Moore was borne from the fight.

During this time the army was rapidly gaining ground. The reserve, overthrowing every thing in the valley, and obliging La Houssaye's dragoons (who had dismounted) to retire, turned the enemy's left, and even approached the eminence upon which the great battery was posted. On the left, colonel Nicholls, at the head of some companies of the fourteenth, carried Palavio Abaxo (which general Foy defended but feebly), and in the centre, the obstinate dispute for Elvina terminated in favour of the British; so that when the night set in their line was considerably advanced beyond the original position of the morning, and the French were falling back in confusion.

If at this time general Fraser's division had been brought into action along with the reserve, the enemy could hardly have escaped a signal overthrow; for the little ammunition Soult had been able to bring up was nearly exhausted, the river Mero, with a full tide, was behind him, and the difficult communication by the bridge of El Burgo was alone open for a retreat. On the other hand, to continue the action in the dark was to tempt fortune, for the French were still the most numerous, and their ground was strong. The disorder they were in offered such a favourable opportunity to get on board the ships, that sir John Hope, upon whom the command of the army had devolved, satisfied with having repulsed the attack, judged it more prudent to pursue the original plan of embarking during the night, and this operation was effected without delay; the arrangements being so complete that neither confusion nor difficulty occurred.

The piquets kindling a number of fires, covered the retreat of the columns, and were themselves withdrawn at daybreak, and embarked, under the protection of general Hill's brigade, which was posted near the ramparts of the town. When the morning dawned, the French, observing that the British had abandoned their position, pushed forward some battalions to the heights of St. Lucie, and about mid-day succeeded in establishing a battery, which playing upon the shipping in the harbour, caused a great deal of disorder among the transports. Several masters cut their cables, and four vessels went ashore; but the troops being immediately removed by the men of war's boats, the stranded vessels were burnt, and the whole fleet at last got out of harbour. General Hill's brigade then embarked from the citadel; but general Beresford, with a rear guard, still kept possession of that work until the 18th, when the wounded being all put on board, his troops likewise embarked[26]. The inhabitants faithfully maintained the town against the French, and the fleet sailed for England.

Thus ended the retreat to Coruña; a transaction which, up to this day, has called forth as much of falsehood and malignity as servile and interested writers could offer to the unprincipled leaders of a base faction, but which posterity will regard as a genuine example of ability and patriotism.

Captain's Hardinge's Letter.

Mr. James Moore's Narrative.

From the spot where he fell, the general who had conducted it was carried to the town by a party of soldiers. The blood flowed fast, and the torture of his wound increased; but such was the unshaken firmness of his mind, that those about him judging from the resolution of his countenance that his hurt was not mortal, expressed a hope of his recovery. Hearing this, he looked stedfastly at the injury for a moment, and then said, "*No, I feel that* to be impossible." Several times he caused his attendants to stop and turn him round, that he might behold the field of battle, and when the firing indicated the advance of the British he discovered his satisfaction, and permitted the bearers to proceed. Being brought to his lodgings the surgeons examined his wound, but there was no hope; the pain increased, and he spoke with great difficulty. At intervals he asked if the French were beaten, and addressing his old friend colonel Anderson, he said, "*You know that I always wished to die this way.*" Again he asked if the enemy were defeated, and being told they were, observed, "*It is a great satisfaction to me to know we have beaten the French.*" His countenance continued firm, and his thoughts clear; once only, when he spoke of his mother, he became agitated. He inquired after the safety of his friends, and the officers of his staff, and he did not even in this moment forget to recommend those whose merit had given them claims to promotion. His strength was failing fast, and life was just extinct, when, with an unsubdued spirit, as if anticipating the baseness of his posthumous calumniators, he exclaimed, "*I hope the people of England will be satisfied! I hope my country will do me justice!*" The battle was scarcely ended, when his corpse, wrapped in a military cloak, was interred by the officers of his staff in the citadel of Coruña. The guns of the enemy paid his funeral honours, and Soult, with a noble feeling of respect for his valour, raised a monument to his memory.

Thus ended the career of sir John Moore, a man whose uncommon capacity was sustained by the purest virtue, and governed by a disinterested patriotism more in keeping with the primitive than the luxurious age of a great nation. His tall graceful person, his dark searching eyes, strongly defined forehead, and singularly expressive mouth, indicated a noble disposition and a refined understanding. The lofty sentiments of honour habitual to his mind, adorned by a subtle playful wit, gave him in conversation an ascendancy that he could well preserve by the decisive vigour of his actions. He maintained the right with a vehemence bordering upon fierceness, and every important transaction in which he was engaged increased his reputation for talent, and confirmed his character as a stern enemy to vice, a stedfast friend to merit, a just and faithful servant of his country. The honest loved him, the dishonest feared him; for while he lived, he did not shun but scorned and spurned the base, and, with characteristic propriety, they spurned at him when he was dead.

A soldier from his earliest youth, he thirsted for the honours of his profession, and feeling that he was worthy to lead a British army, hailed the fortune that placed him at the head of the troops destined for Spain. The stream of time passed rapidly, and the inspiring hopes of triumph disappeared, but the austerer glory of suffering remained; with a firm heart he accepted that gift of a severe fate, and confiding in the strength of his genius, disregarded the clamours of presumptuous ignorance; opposing sound military views to the foolish projects so insolently thrust upon him by the ambassador, he conducted a long and arduous retreat with sagacity, intelligence, and fortitude. No insult could disturb, no falsehood deceive him, no remonstrance shake his determination; fortune frowned without subduing his constancy; death struck, and the spirit of the man remained unbroken when his shattered body scarcely afforded it a habitation. Having done all that was just towards others, he remembered what was due to himself. Neither the shock of the mortal blow, nor the lingering hours of acute pain which preceded his dissolution, could quell the pride of his gallant heart, or lower the dignified feeling with which (conscious of merit) he asserted his right to the gratitude of the country he had served so truly.

If glory be a distinction, for such a man death is not a leveller!

CHAPTER VI

OBSERVATIONS

GENERAL VIEW OF THE CAMPAIGN.

Mr. Canning, in an official communication to the Spanish deputies in London, observed, that "the conduct of the campaign in Portugal was unsatisfactory, and inadequate to the brilliant successes with which it opened." In the relation of that campaign it has been shown how little the activity and foresight of the cabinet contributed to those successes, and the following short analysis will prove that, with respect to the campaign in Spain, the proceedings of the ministers were marked by tardiness and incapacity.

Joseph abandoned Madrid the 3rd of August, and on the 11th of the same month the French troops from the most distant parts of Europe were in motion to remedy the disasters in the Peninsula.

The 1st of September a double conscription, furnishing one hundred and sixty thousand men, was called out to replace the troops withdrawn from Poland and Germany.

The 4th of September the emperor announced to the senate, that "he was resolved to push the affairs of the Peninsula with the greatest activity, and to destroy the armies which the English had disembarked in that country."

The 11th, the advanced guard of the army coming from Germany reached Paris, and was there publicly harangued by the emperor.

The 8th of November he burst into Spain at the head of three hundred thousand men, and the 5th of December not a vestige of the Spanish armies remaining, he took possession of Madrid.

Now the Asturian deputies arrived in London the 6th of June.

The 20th of August (the battle of Vimiero being then unfought, and, consequently, the fate of the campaign in Portugal uncertain,) the English minister invited sir Hew Dalrymple to discuss three plans of operations in Spain, each founded upon data utterly false, and all objectionable in the detail. He also desired that sir Arthur Wellesley should go to the Asturias to ascertain what facilities that country offered for the disembarkation of an English army; and the whole number of troops disposable for the campaign (exclusive of those already in Portugal) he stated to be twenty thousand, of which one half was in England and the other in Sicily. He acknowledged that no information yet received had enabled the cabinet to decide as to the application of the forces at home, or the ulterior use to be made of those in Portugal, yet, with singular rashness, the whole of the southern provinces, containing the richest cities, finest harbours, and most numerous armies, were discarded from consideration, and sir Hew Dalrymple, who was well acquainted with that part of Spain, and in close and friendly correspondence with the chiefs, was directed to confine his attention to the northern provinces, of which he knew nothing.

The reduction of Junot's army in Portugal, and the discomfiture of Joseph's on the Ebro, were regarded as certain events. The observations of the minister were principally directed, not to the best mode of attacking, but to the choice of a line of march that would ensure the utter destruction or captivity of the whole French army; nay, elated with extravagant hopes and strangely despising Napoleon's power, he instructed lord William Bentinck to urge the central junta to an invasion of France, as soon as the army on the Ebro should be annihilated.

Thus it appears that the English ministers were either profoundly ignorant of the real state of affairs, or that with a force scattered in England, Portugal, and Sicily, and not exceeding forty-five thousand men, they expected in one campaign, first to subdue twenty-six thousand French under Junot, and then destroying eighty thousand under Joseph, to turn the tide of war, and to invade France.

The battle of Vimiero took place, and sir Arthur Wellesley naturally declined a mission more suitable to a staff captain than a victorious commander; but before sir Hew's answer, exposing the false calculations of the minister's plans, could be received in England, a despatch, dated the 2d of September, announced the resolution of the government to employ an army in the northern provinces of Spain, and directed twenty thousand men to be held in readiness to unite with other forces to be sent from England; nevertheless, this project also was so immature, that no intimation was given how the junction was to be effected, whether by sea or land; nor had the ministers even ascertained that the Spaniards would permit English troops to enter Spain at all; for three weeks later, lord William Bentinck, writing from Madrid, says, "I had an interview with Florida Blanca: he expressed his surprise that there should be a doubt of the Spaniards wishing for the assistance of the English army." Such also was the confusion at home, that lord Castlereagh repeatedly expressed his fears lest the embarkation of Junot's troops should have "absorbed all the means of transport" in the Tagus, when a simple reference to the transport office in London would have satisfied him, that although the English army should also be embarked, there would still remain a surplus of twelve thousand tons.

When the popular cry arose against the convention of Cintra, the generals in chief were recalled in succession, as rapidly as they had been appointed; the despatches addressed to one generally fell into the hands of his successor; but the plans of the ministers becoming at last mature, on the 6th of October sir John Moore was finally appointed to lead the forces into Spain. At this period the head of the grand French army was already in the passes of the Pyrenees, and the hostile troops on the Ebro coming to blows. The Spaniards were weak and divided, and the English were forty marches from the scene of action; yet, said the minister to sir John Moore, "there will be full time to concert your plan of operations with the Spanish generals before the equipment of your army can be completed." Was this the way to oppose Napoleon! Could such proceedings lead to ought but disaster! It has been said, that sir Hew Dalrymple's negligence was the cause of this delay; that he should have had the troops in readiness: but that general could not prudently incur the expense of equipping for a march, an army that was likely to be embarked; he could not, in short, divine the plans of the ministers before they were formed; and it is evident that the error attaches entirely to the government.

The incapacity of the Spanish generals has been already sufficiently exposed by occasional observations in the narrative; their faults, glaring and fatal, call for no further remark; but the exact combinations, the energy and rapidity of the French emperor, merit the most careful examination; his operations were not, as they have been generally considered, a pompous display of power, to create an appearance of conquest that was unreal, not a mere violent irruption with a multitude of men, but a series of skilful and scientific movements, worthy of so great a general and politician. It is true that his force was immense, and that the Spaniards were but contemptible soldiers; but he never neglected the lessons of experience, nor deviated from the strictest rules of art. With astonishing activity, and when we consider the state of his political relations on the continent, we may add, with astonishing boldness, he first collected ample means to attain his object, then deceiving his enemies with regard to his numbers, position, and intentions, and choosing his time with admirable judgment, he broke through the weak part of their line, and seized Burgos, a central point, which enabled him to envelop and destroy the left wing of the Spaniards before their right could hear of his attack, the latter being itself turned by the same movement, and exposed to a like fate. This position also enabled him to menace the capital, to keep the English army in check, and to cover the formation of those magazines and stores which were necessary to render Burgos the base and pivot of further operations.

Napoleon's forces were numerous enough to have attacked Castaños and Palafox, while Blake was being pursued by the first and fourth corps; but trusting nothing to chance, he waited for twelve days, until the position of the English army was ascertained, the strength of the northern provinces quite broken, and a secure place of arms established. Then leaving the second corps to cover his communications, and sending the fourth corps into the flat country, to coast, as it were, the heads of the English columns on his right, and to turn the passes of the Carpentino mountains, he caused the Spanish right wing to be destroyed, and himself approached the capital, at a moment when not a vestige of a national army was left, when he had good reason to think that the English were in full retreat, when the whole of his own corps were close at hand, and consequently when the greatest moral effect could be produced, and the greatest physical power concentrated at the same time to take advantage of it. Napoleon's dispositions were indeed surprisingly skilful; for although marshal Lefebre's precipitation at Zornoza, by prolonging Blake's agony, lost six days of promise, it is certain that reverses in battle could neither have checked the emperor, nor helped the Spaniards.

For if Soult had been beaten at Gamonal, Napoleon was close at hand to support the second corps, and the sixth corps would have fallen upon the flank and rear of the Spaniards.

If the first corps had been defeated at Espinosa, the second and fourth corps, and the emperor's troops, would have taken Blake in flank and rear.

If Lasnes had been defeated at Tudela, he could have fallen back on Pampeluna; the fifth and eighth corps were marching to support him, and the sixth corps would have taken the Spaniards in flank.

If the emperor had been repulsed at the Somosierra, the sixth corps would have turned that position by Guadalaxara, and the fourth corps by Guadarama.

If sir John Moore had retreated on Portugal, the fourth corps was nearer to Lisbon than he was.

If he had overthrown Soult, the fifth and eighth corps were ready to sustain that marshal, and Napoleon, with fifty thousand men, as we have seen, was prepared to cut the British line of retreat into Gallicia. In short, no possible event could have divided the emperor's forces, and he constantly preserved a central position that enabled him to unite his masses in sufficient time to repair any momentary disaster. By a judicious mixture of force and policy also, he obliged Madrid to surrender in two days, and thus prevented the enthusiasm which would doubtless have arisen if the capital had been defended for any time, and the heart burnings if it had been stormed. The second sweep that he was preparing to make when sir John Moore's march called off his attention from the south would undoubtedly have put him in possession of the remaining great cities of the Peninsula. Then the civil benefits promised in his decrees and speeches would have produced their full effect, and the result may be judged of by the fact that in 1811 and 12, Andalusia and Valencia were under the able administration of marshals Soult and Suchet, as tranquil and submissive as any department of France, and the former even raised numerous Spanish battalions, and employed them not only to preserve the public peace, but to chase and put down the guerillas of the neighbouring provinces.

Sir John Moore's talents saved the Peninsula from this great danger, and here perhaps a military error of Napoleon's may be detected. Forgetting that war is not a conjectural art, he took for granted that the English army was falling back to Portugal, and without ascertaining that it was so, acted upon the supposition. This apparent negligence, so unlike his usual circumspection, leads to the notion, that through Morla he might have become acquainted with the peculiar opinions and rash temper of Mr. Frere, and trusted that the treacherous arts of the Spaniard, in conjunction with the presumptuous disposition of the plenipotentiary, would so mislead the English general, as to induce him to carry his army to Madrid, and thus deliver it up entire and bound. It was an error; but Napoleon could be deceived or negligent only for a moment. With what vigour he recovered himself, and hastened to remedy his error! How instantaneously he relinquished his intentions against the south, turned his face away from the glittering prize, and bent his whole force against the only man among his adversaries that had discovered talent and decision! Let those who have seen the preparations necessary to enable a small army to act, even on a pre-conceived plan, say what uncontrollable energy that man possessed, who, suddenly interrupted in such great designs, could, in the course of a few hours, put fifty thousand men in movement on a totally new line of operations, and in the midst of winter execute a march of two hundred miles with a rapidity hardly to be equalled under the most favourable circumstances.

The indefatigable activity of the duke of Dalmatia greatly contributed to the success of the whole campaign, and it is a remarkable circumstance, that Soult and Napoleon, advancing from different bases, should have so combined their movements, that (after marching, the one above a hundred, and the other two hundred miles, through a hostile country) they effected their junction at a given point, and at a given hour, without failure; and it is no less remarkable that such a decided and well-conducted operation should have been baffled by a general at the head of an inexperienced army.

OBSERVATIONS ON SIR JOHN MOORE'S RETREAT

When Sylla, after all his victories, styled himself a happy, rather than a great general, he discovered his profound knowledge of the military art. Experience had taught him that the urgent speed of one legion, the inactivity of another, the obstinacy, the ignorance, or the treachery of a subordinate officer, was sufficient to mar the best concerted plan, nay, that the intervention of a shower of rain, an unexpected ditch, or any apparently trivial accident, might determine the fate of a whole army. It taught him that the vicissitudes of war are so many, that disappointment will attend the wisest combinations; that a ruinous defeat, the work of chance, often closes the career of the boldest and most sagacious of generals; and that to judge of a commander's conduct by the event alone, is equally unjust and unphilosophical, a refuge for vanity and ignorance.

These reflections seem to be peculiarly applicable to sir John Moore's campaign, which has by sundry writers been so unfairly discussed. Many of the subsequent disasters of the French can now be distinctly traced to the operations of the British army. It can be demonstrated that the reputation of that excellent man was basely sacrificed at the period of his death, and that the virulent censures passed upon his conduct have been as inconsiderate as they were unmerited and cruel.

Sir John Moore's Journal, MSS.

The nature of the commands held by sir John Moore in the years 1807-8-9, forced him into a series of embarrassments from which few men could have extricated themselves. After refusing the charge of the absurd expedition to Egypt in 1806, which ended, as he judged it must do, unfavourably, he succeeded to the command of the troops in Sicily, a situation which immediately involved him in unpleasant discussions with the queen of Naples and the British envoy: discussions to which the subsequent well-known enmity of the cabinet of that day may be traced. By his frank conduct, clear judgment, and firm spirit, he obtained an influence over the wretched court of Palermo that promised the happiest results. The queen's repugnance to a reform was overcome, the ministers were awed, and the miserable intrigues of the day were for the time put down. The Sicilian army was reorganized, and a good military system was commenced under the advice of the British general. This promising state of affairs lasted but a short time; the Russian fleet put into the Tagus, the French threatened

Portugal, and Sicily was no longer considered! Sir John Moore was ordered to quit that island, and to assemble a large force at Gibraltar for a specific service; but the troops to be gathered were dispersed in the Mediterranean from Egypt to the straits, and their junction could not be effected at all unless the English ambassador at Constantinople should succeed in bringing a negotiation then pending between the Turks and Russians to a happy issue. The special service in question had two objects, 1°. to aid sir Sydney Smith in carrying off the royal family of Portugal to the Brazils; and 2°. to take possession of Madeira; but neither were made known to the general before his arrival at Gibraltar, which was not until after Junot had taken possession of Lisbon. Sir John Moore then (following his instructions) proceeded home, and thus our interests in Sicily were again abandoned to the vices and intrigues of the court of Palermo. On the passage he crossed general Spencer going with a force against Ceuta, and soon after he had reached England, he was despatched to Sweden, without any specific object, and with such vague instructions, that an immediate collision with the unfortunate Gustavus was the consequence. Having with much dexterity and judgment withdrawn himself and his army from the capricious violence of that monarch, sir John was superseded and sent to Portugal, with the third rank in an army which at that time no man had such good claims to command as himself[27].

The good fortune of England was never more conspicuous than at this period, when her armies and fleets were thus bandied about, and a blind chance governed the councils at home. For first a force collected from all parts of the Mediterranean was transported to the Baltic sea, at a time when an expedition composed of troops which had but a short time before come back from the Baltic were sailing from England to the Mediterranean. An army intended to conquer South America was happily assembled in Ireland at the moment when an unexpected event called for their services in Portugal, and a division destined to attack the Spaniards at Ceuta arrived at Gibraltar at the instant when the insurrection of Andalusia fortunately prevented them from making an attempt that would have materially aided Napoleon's schemes against the Peninsula. Again, three days after sir John Moore had withdrawn his army from Sweden, orders arrived to employ it in carrying off the Spanish troops under Romana, an operation for which it was not required, and which would have retarded, if not entirely frustrated, the campaign in Portugal; nor was it the least part of that fortune, that in such long continued voyages in bad seasons, no disaster befell those huge fleets thus employed in bearing the strength of England from one extremity of Europe to the other.

After the convention of Cintra, sir John Moore was again placed at the head of an army; an appointment unexpected by him, for the frank and bold manner in which he expressed himself to the ministers on his return from Gottingen left him little to hope; but the personal good-will of the king, and other circumstances, procured him this command. Thus, in a few months after he had quitted Sweden, Moore, with an army not exceeding twenty-four thousand men, was in the heart of Spain, opposed to Napoleon, who having passed the Pyrenees at the head of three hundred and thirty thousand men, could readily bring two hundred thousand to bear on the British; a vast disproportion of numbers, and a sufficient answer to all the idle censures passed upon the retreat to Coruña.

The most plausible grounds of accusation against sir John Moore's conduct rest on three alleged errors:

1st. That he divided his forces.

2dly. That he advanced against Soult.

3dly. That he made a precipitate and unnecessary retreat.

When a general, aware of the strength of his adversary, and of the resources to be placed at his own disposal, arranges a plan of campaign, he may be strictly judged by the rules of art; but if, as in the case of sir John Moore, he is suddenly appointed to conduct important operations without a plan being arranged, or the means given to arrange one, then it is evident that his capacity or incapacity must be judged of, by the energy he displays, the comprehensive view he takes of affairs, and the rapidity with which he accommodates his measures to events, that the original vice of his appointment will not permit him to control.

The first separation of the English army was the work of the ministers, who sent sir David Baird to Coruña. The after separation of the artillery was sir John Moore's act; the reasons for which have been already stated; but it is worth while to examine what the effect of that measure was, and what it might have been; and here it may be observed, that, although a brigade of light six-pounders did accompany the troops to Almeida, the road was *not practicable*; for the guns were in some places let down the rocks by ropes, and in others, carried over the difficult places; a practicable affair with one brigade; but how could the great train of guns and ammunition waggons that accompanied sir John Hope have passed such places without a loss of time that would have proved more injurious to the operations than the separation of the artillery?

The advance of the army was guided by three contingent cases, any one of which arising would have immediately influenced the operations; 1°. Blake on the left, or Castaños and Palafox upon the right, might have beaten the French, and advanced to the Pyrenees. 2°. They might have maintained their position on the Ebro. 3°. The arrival of reinforcements from France might have forced the Spaniards to fall back upon the upper Douero, on one side, and to the mountains of Guadalaxara on the other. In the first case, there was no risk in marching by divisions towards Burgos, which was the point of concentration given by the British and Spanish ministers. In the second case, the army could safely unite at Valladolid; and in the third case, if the division of sir David Baird had reached Toro early in November (and this it was reasonable to expect, as that general arrived at Coruña the 13th of October), the retrograde movement of the Spanish armies would probably have drawn the English to the Guadarama, as a safe and central point between the retiring Spanish wings. Now the artillery marching from the Alemtejo by the roads of Talavera and Naval Carnero, to Burgos, would pass over one hundred and two Spanish leagues. To Aranda de Douero, eighty-nine leagues. To Valladolid, ninety-two leagues. While the columns that marched by Almeida and Salamanca would pass over one hundred and sixteen leagues to Burgos, and ninety-eight to Valladolid. Wherefore supposing the Spaniards successful, or even holding their own, the separation of the artillery was an advantage, and if the Spaniards were driven back, their natural line of retreat would have brought them towards Madrid, Blake by Aranda to the Somosierra, and Castaños and Palafox by Siguenza and Tarancon, to cover the capital, and to maintain an interior communication between the Somosierra and the Henares river. The British artillery would then have halted at Espinar, after a march of only eighty leagues, and Baird and Moore's corps uniting at Salamanca early in November, might, by a flank march to Arevalo, have insured the concentration of the whole army.

Thus, in the three anticipated cases, the separation of the artillery was prudent, and promised to be advantageous. There was indeed a fourth case, that which really happened. All the Spanish armies were dispersed in an instant!—utterly effaced! but sir John Moore could not have divined such a catastrophe, while his ears were ringing with the universal clamour about the numbers and enthusiasm of the patriots; and if he had foreseen even a part of such disasters, he would never have advanced from Portugal. With the plans of the Spanish government he was unacquainted; but he was officially informed that above one hundred and forty thousand Spanish soldiers were between him and a feeble dispirited enemy; and as the intercepted letter from the governor of Bayonne stated that reinforcements would only arrive between the 18th of October and the 18th of November, it was reasonable to suppose that the French would not commence offensive operations before the latter period, and that ample time would be afforded to concentrate the English troops under the protection of the Spanish armies. If sir John Moore could have suspected the delusion under which the British government acted, the incredible folly of the central junta and the Spanish generals, or the inaccuracy of the military agents, if he could have supposed that the Spanish armies were weak in numbers, weaker in spirit, and destitute of food and clothing; or that, while the Spanish authorities were pressing him to advance, they would wantonly detain sir David Baird's troops seventeen days on board the transports; if he could have imagined all this, undoubtedly his arrangements ought and would have been different; his army would have been kept together, and the road through Coria, however difficult, would have been preferred to a divided march.

The dangerous and absurd position of the Spanish armies, and the remote situation of the British troops in October, may be explained by the annexed diagram. Lisbon being taken as a centre, and the distance a between Lisbon and Coruña being the radius, let a circle passing through Madrid be described. Let the tangential line c be drawn perpendicular to the radius a, meeting the secant b at Sanguessa.

The extreme right of the Spaniards was posted at Sanguessa. Castaños was at Calahorra, and Blake was near Durango, but the main body of the French was at Vittoria; and not only divided the Spaniards, but was actually twenty-five miles nearer to Burgos and Valladolid, (the points of concentration for Moore's and Baird's corps) than either Castaños or Blake, and seventy-five miles nearer than Palafox.

The 10th, the emperor struck the first blow, by beating Belvedere and seizing Burgos. Sir David Baird did not march from Coruña until the 12th, and did not bring up the whole of his troops to Astorga before the 4th of December; hence it is clear, that whatever road the artillery had taken, the British army could not have averted the ruin of the Spaniards. Let us suppose the troops assembled at Salamanca on the 13th of November. They must have advanced either to Valladolid or to Madrid. If to Valladolid, the emperor was at Burgos with the imperial guards, ten or twelve thousand cavalry, and a hundred pieces of artillery. The first corps was within a day's march, the second and fourth corps within three marches, and the sixth corps within two marches. Above a hundred thousand French soldiers could, therefore, have been concentrated in three days; and it is to be observed that sir John Moore never had twenty-five thousand in the field.

It is said, he might have gone to Madrid: in that case the separation of the artillery was a decided advantage, and the separation of Baird's corps (which was not the general's arrangement) was the error. The army could not have marched from Salamanca to Madrid in less than seven days; on the 21st of November then, twenty-four thousand British soldiers could have been collected in the capital; but the fourth French corps, which reached

Segovia the 1st of December, would have cut off their communication with Portugal, and the emperor with forty thousand men was at Aranda de Douero. Castaños was defeated on the 23d; the remnants of his army were only at Guadalaxara about the 1st of December, and the sixth corps was in full pursuit of them. The English general must then have done one of three things; advanced to the relief of Castaños's retreating army, joined St. Juan at the Somosierra, or retreated across the Tagus. In the first case, the emperor would have forced the Somosierra, and uniting with the fourth corps, have placed sixty thousand men upon sir John Moore's rear; in the second case, the sixth and fourth corps, turning both his flanks, would have effected a junction behind the Somosierra, and cut him off from Madrid, while Napoleon, with forty thousand men, assailed him in front. To retreat over the Tagus was to adopt the southern provinces for a new base of operations, and might have been useful if the Spaniards would have rallied round him with enthusiasm and courage; but would they have done so when the emperor was advancing with his enormous force? After-experience proves that they would not. The duke of Dalmatia, in 1810, with an army very inferior to that under Napoleon, reached the gates of Cadiz without a serious blow being struck to oppose him, and at this time the people of the south were reckless of the opportunity procured for them by sir John Moore's march on Sahagun; but, it has been said, that twenty-four thousand British troops acting vigorously, could have checked the emperor, and raised the courage of the Spaniards. To such an observation I will oppose a fact. In 1815, Napoleon crossed the Sambre with one hundred and fifteen thousand men, and the two hundred and ten thousand regular troops in his front, among which were more than thirty thousand English, could with difficulty stop his progress after four days' fighting, in three of which he was successful.

If sir John Moore, at a subsequent period, was willing to risk the danger of a movement on the capital, it was because he was misinformed of the French strength, and the Spaniards were represented to be numerous and confident; he was also unacquainted with the defeat at Tudela. His object was, by assisting Castaños, to arouse the spirit of the patriots: and nothing more strongly evinces his hardihood and prompt judgment, for, in his letter to Mr. Frere, he distinctly stated the danger to be incurred, and carefully separating the military from the political reasons, only proposed to venture the army if the envoy was satisfied that the Spanish government and people would answer to such an appeal, and that the British cabinet would be willing to incur the risk for such an object. If he did not follow up his own proposal, it was because he had discovered that the army of Castaños was, not simply defeated, but destroyed; because the Somosierra had been forced by a charge of cavalry, and because the passes of the Guadarama, on his line of march to Madrid, were seized by the enemy before his own army could be concentrated.

Why then did he not retreat into Portugal? Because Napoleon, having directed the mass of his forces against the capital, the British army was enabled to concentrate; because Madrid shut her gates; because Mr. Frere and the Spanish authorities deceived him by false information; because the solemn declaration of the junta of Toledo, that they would bury themselves under the ruins of that town rather than surrender, joined to the fact that Zaragoza was fighting heroically, seemed to guarantee the constancy and vigour of that patriotic spirit which was apparently once more excited; because the question was again become political, and it was necessary to satisfy the English people, that nothing was left undone to aid a cause which they had so much at heart; and, finally, because the peculiar position of the French army at the moment, afforded the means of creating a powerful diversion in favour of the southern provinces. These are the unanswerable reasons for the advance towards Sahagun. In the details of execution, that movement may be liable to some trifling objections; perhaps it would have been better to have carried the army on the 21st at once to Carrion and neglected Sahagun and Saldanha; but in its stratagetical and political character it was well conceived and well timed, hardy and successful.

The irritating interference that sir John Moore was called upon to repel, and the treachery and the folly, equal in its effects to treachery, that he was obliged to guard against, have been sufficiently dwelt upon already; but before discussing the retreat from Astorga, it may be of some military interest to show that the line of Portugal, although the natural one for the British army to retire upon, was not at this period necessarily either safe or useful, and that greater evils than those incurred by a retreat through Gallicia would probably have attended a retrograde march upon Lisbon.

The rugged frontier of Portugal lying between the Douero and the Tagus, is vulnerable in many points to an invading army of superior force. It may be penetrated between the Douero and Pinhel, and between Pinhel and Guarda, by roads leading into the valleys of the Zezere and the Mondego. Between the Sierra de Estrella and the Sierra de Gata, by the road from Alfayates to Sabugal and Penamacor, or that by Guarda and Coria. Again, it may be pierced between the Sierra de Gata and the Tagus by Idanha Velha, Castello Branco, and Sobreira Formosa; and from the Tagus to the Guadiana, a distance of about twenty leagues, the Alentejo presents an open country without any strong fortress, save Lalippe, which may be disregarded and passed without danger.

Sir John Moore commenced his forward movement from Salamanca on the 12th of December, and at that period, the fourth corps being at Talavera de la Reyna, was much nearer to Lisbon than the British army was, and the emperor was preparing to march on that capital with the sixth corps, the guards, and the reserve. He could, as the duke of Berwick did, penetrate by both sides of the Tagus, and what was to prevent him from reaching Lisbon before the British force, if the latter had retreated from Salamanca? he marched on a shorter line and a better road; he could supply his troops by requisitions, a system that, however fatal it may be in the end, is always advantageous at first. Sir John Moore must, from a scanty military chest, have purchased his supplies from a suspicious peasantry, rendered more distrustful by the retreat. In Lisbon, sir John Craddock commanded six thousand infantry and two hundred and fifty-eight cavalry; but the provisional government, who had only organized a few ill-composed battalions, were so inactive, that it was not until the 8th of December that a proclamation, calling on the people to arm, was issued. In the arsenal there were scarcely musquets and equipments for eight thousand men, and the new levies were only required to assemble when Portugal should be actually invaded. Sir Robert Wilson, indeed, having with great activity organized about two thousand of the Lusitanian legion, marched in the middle of December from Oporto; but this was all that could be opposed to an army more numerous, more favourably situated for invasion, and incomparably better commanded than that with which Massena invaded the country in 1810. Thus it may be affirmed, that if a retreat from Lisbon was advisable, before Napoleon took Madrid, it was not a safe operation after that event, and it is clear that sir John Moore neither lightly nor injudiciously adopted the line of Gallicia.

The arguments of those who deny the necessity of falling back, even behind the Esla, are scarcely worth notice; a simple reference to the numbers under the emperor, and the direction of his march, is sufficient to expose their futility; but the necessity of the continued, and as it has been unjustly called, the precipitate retreat to Coruña, may not be quite so obvious. The advance to Sahagun was intended to create a diversion, and give the Spaniards an opportunity of making head in the south; but although it succeeded in drawing away the enemy, the Spaniards did not make any head. The central junta displayed no energy or wisdom; a few slight demonstrations by the marquis of Palacios, on the side of the Sierra Morena, and by the duke of Infantado on the side of Cuenca, scarcely disturbed the first corps which remained in La Mancha; ten thousand men were sufficient to maintain Madrid in perfect tranquillity, and a part of the fourth corps even marched from Talavera by Placentia on Salamanca. By the letters of Mr. Stuart, and the reports of his own spies, sir John Moore was informed of all these disheartening circumstances; but the intelligence arrived slowly and at intervals, and he, hoping that the Spaniards would finally make an effort, announced his intention to hold the Gallicias; but Mr. Stuart's correspondence deprived him of that hope; and the presence of the emperor, the great amount of his force, and the vehemence with which he pressed forward, confirmed the unhappy truth that nothing could be expected from the south.

Appendix, No. 13, sect. 2.

Sir John Moore could not with twenty-three thousand men maintain himself against the whole French army, and until he reached Astorga his flanks were always exposed. From thence, however, he retreated in comparative security; but the natural strength of the country between that town and Coruña misled persons of shallow judgment, who have since inconsiderately advanced many vague accusations, such as that passes where a hundred men could stop an army were lightly abandoned; that the retreat was a flight, and the general's judgment clouded by the danger of his situation. There might be some foundation for such observations if military commanders were like prize-fighters, bound to strike always at the front; but as long as armies are dependent for their subsistence and ammunition upon lines of communication, the safety of their flanks and rear must be considered as of consequence. Sir John Moore was perfectly aware that he could fight any number of men in some of the mountainous positions on the road to Coruña; but unless he could make a permanent defence, such battles would have been worse than useless, and a permanent defence was impossible, inasmuch as there were none but temporary magazines nearer than Coruña, and there were neither carriages of transport, nor money to procure them; a severe winter had just set in, and the province being poor, and the peasantry disinclined to aid the troops, few resources could be drawn from the country itself, neither was there a single position between Astorga and Coruña which could be maintained for more than a few days against a superior force, for that of Rodrigatos could be turned by the old road leading to Villa Franca, Villa Franca itself by the valley of the Syl, and from thence the whole line to Coruña might be turned by the road of Orense, which also led directly to Vigo, and until he reached Nogales, sir J. Moore's intention was to retire to Vigo. The French could have marched through the richest part of Gallicia to St. Jago and Coruña on the left, or from the

Asturias, by the way of Mondonedo, on the right. If it be asked why they did not do so? the answer is prompt. The emperor having quitted the army, the jealousies and misunderstandings usual between generals of equal rank impeded the operations. A coolness subsisted between marshal Ney and the duke of Dalmatia, and without entering into the grounds of their difference it is plain that, in a military point of view, the judgment of the latter was the soundest. The former committed a great error by remaining at Villa Franca instead of pushing his corps, or a part of it, (as recommended by Soult) along the valley of Orense to St. Jago de Compostella. The British army would have been lost if the sixth corps had reached Coruña before it; and what would have been the chances in the battle if three additional French divisions had been engaged?

Granting, therefore, that the troops could have been nourished during the winter, Villa Franca, Nogales, Constantino, and Lugo, were not permanently defensible by an army whose base of operations was at Coruña. Hence it was that sir John Moore resolved to regain his ships with the view to renew the war in the south, and Hannibal himself could have done no more. Nor was the mode of executing the retreat at all unbecoming the character of an able officer.

Lord Bacon observes, that "honourable retreats are no ways inferior to brave charges, as having less of fortune, more of discipline, and as much of valour." That is an honourable retreat in which the retiring general loses no trophies in fight, sustains every charge without being broken, and finally, after a severe action, re-embarks his army in the face of a superior enemy without being seriously molested. It would be honourable to effect this before a foe only formidable from numbers, but it is infinitely more creditable, when the commander, while struggling with bad weather and worse fortune, has to oppose veterans with inexperienced troops, and to contend against an antagonist of eminent ability, who scarcely suffers a single advantage to escape him during his long and vigorous pursuit. All this sir John Moore did, and finished his work by a death as firm and glorious as any that antiquity can boast of.

Put to lord Bacon's test, in what shall the retreat to Coruña be found deficient? something in discipline perhaps, but that fault does not attach to the general. Those commanders who have been celebrated for making fine retreats were in most instances well acquainted with their armies; and Hannibal, speaking of the elder Scipio, derided him, although a brave and skilful man, for that, being unknown to his own soldiers, he should presume to oppose himself to a general who could call to each man under his command by name: thus inculcating, that, unless troops be trained in the peculiar method of a commander, the latter can scarcely achieve any thing great. Now sir John Moore had a young army suddenly placed under his guidance, and it was scarcely united, when the superior numbers of the enemy forced it to a retrograde movement under very harassing circumstances; he had not time, therefore, to establish a system of discipline, and it is in the leading events, not the minor details, that the just criterion of his merits is to be sought for.

Was the retreat uncalled for? Was it unnecessarily precipitate? Was any opportunity of crippling the enemy lost? Was any weakness to be discovered in the personal character of the general? These are the questions that sensible men will ask; the first has been already examined, the second is a matter of simple calculation. The rear guard quitted Astorga on the 1st of January; on the 3rd, it repulsed the enemy in a sharp skirmish at Calcabelos; the 6th it rejoined the main body at Lugo, having three times checked the pursuers during the march. It was unbroken, and lost no gun, suffered no misfortune; the whole army offered battle at Lugo for two successive days, it was not accepted, and the retreat recommencing, the troops reached Betanzos on the morning of the 10th, and Coruña on the 11th; thus in eleven days, three of which were days of rest, a small army passed over a hundred and fifty miles of good road. Now Napoleon, with fifty thousand men, left Madrid on the 22d of December, the 28th he was at Villapando, having performed a march, on bad roads, of a hundred and sixty-four miles in seven days. The retreat to Coruña was consequently not precipitate, unless it can be shown, that it was unnecessary to retreat at all beyond Villa Franca, neither can it be asserted, that any opportunity of crippling the enemy was lost. To fight a battle was the game of the French marshal, and if any censure will apply to his able campaign, it is that he delayed to attack at Lugo; victorious or beaten, the embarrassments of his adversary must have been increased; sir John Moore must have continued his retreat encumbered with the wounded, or the latter must have been abandoned without succour in the midst of winter.

Appendix, No. 26.
Ibid.

At Coruña the absence of the fleet necessarily brought on a battle; that it was honourable to the British troops is clear from the fact that they embarked without loss after the action; and that it was absolutely necessary to embark notwithstanding the success, is as certain a proof how little advantage could have been derived from any battle fought farther inland, and how prudently sir John Moore acted in declining an action the moment he had rallied his army at Lugo, and restored that discipline which the previous movements had shaken; but, notwithstanding the clamour with which this campaign has been assailed, as if no army had ever yet suffered such misfortunes, it is certain that the nominal loss was small, the real loss smaller, and that it sinks into nothing when compared with the advantages gained. An army which, after marching in advance or retreat above five hundred miles before an enemy of immensely superior force, has only lost, including those killed in battle, four thousand men, or a sixth part of its numbers, cannot be said to have suffered severely, nor would the loss have been so great but for the intervention of the accidental occurrences mentioned in the narrative. Night marches are seldom happy; that from Lugo to Betanzos cost the army in stragglers more than double the number of men lost in all the preceding operations; nevertheless the reserve in that, as in all the other movements, suffered little; and it is a fact, that the light brigades detached by the Vigo road, which were not pursued, made no forced marches, slept under cover, and were well supplied, left, in proportion to their strength, as many men behind as any other part of the army; thus accumulating proof upon proof that inexperience was the primary and principal cause of the disorders which attended the retreat. Those disorders were sufficiently great, but many circumstances contributed to produce an appearance of suffering and disorganization which was not real. The intention of sir John Moore was, to have proceeded to Vigo, in order to restore order before he sailed for England: instead of which the fleet steered home directly from Coruña; a terrible storm scattered it; many ships were wrecked, and the remainder, driving up the channel, were glad to put into any port. The soldiers, thus thrown on shore, were spread from the Land's End to Dover. Their haggard appearance, ragged clothing, and dirty accoutrements, things common enough in war, struck a people only used to the daintiness of parade, with surprise; the usual exaggerations of men just escaped from perils and distresses were increased by the uncertainty in which all were as to the fate of their comrades; a deadly fever, the result of anxiety, and of the sudden change from fatigue to the confinement of a ship, filled the hospitals at every port with officers and soldiers, and thus the miserable state of sir John Moore's army became the topic of every letter, and a theme for every country newspaper along the coast. The nation, at that time unused to great operations, forgot that war is not a harmless game, and judging of the loss positively, instead of comparatively, was thus disposed to believe the calumnies of interested men, who were eager to cast a shade over one of the brightest characters that ever adorned the country. Those calumnies triumphed for a moment; but Moore's last appeal to his country for justice will be successful. Posterity, revering and cherishing his name, will visit such of his odious calumniators as are not too contemptible to be remembered with a just and severe retribution; for thus it is that time freshens the beauty of virtue and withers the efforts of baseness; and if authority be sought for in a case where reason speaks so plainly, future historians will not fail to remark, that the man whose talents exacted the praises of Soult, of Wellington, and of Napoleon, could be no ordinary soldier.

Appendix, No. 16.

"Sir John Moore," says the first, "took every advantage that the country afforded to oppose an active and vigorous resistance, and he finished, by dying in a combat that must do credit to his memory."

Vivian's Conversations at Elba.

Voice from St. Helena

Napoleon more than once affirmed, that if he committed a few trifling errors they were to be attributed to his peculiar situation, for that his talents and firmness alone had saved the English army from destruction.

"In sir John Moore's campaign," said the duke of Wellington, "I can see but one error; when he advanced to Sahagun he should have considered it as a movement of retreat, and sent officers to the rear to mark and prepare the halting-places for every brigade; but this opinion I have formed after long experience of war, and especially of the peculiarities of a Spanish war, which must have been seen to be understood; finally, it is an opinion formed after the event."

APPENDIX

The following five Notes, dictated by the emperor Napoleon, and signed by general Bertrand, were found in king Joseph's portfolio, at the battle of Vittoria.

No. I

OBSERVATIONS ADDRESSÉES AU GÉNÉRAL SAVARY SUR LES AFFAIRES D'ESPAGNE.

Le 13 Juillet, 1808.

1ere *Observation.*—Les affaires des Français en Espagne seroient dans une excellente position si la division Gobert avait marché sur Valladolid, et si la division Frère eut occupé San Clemente, ayant une colonne mobile à trois ou quatre journées sur la route du général Dupont.

Le g^{al} Gobert ayant été dirigé sur le général Dupont, le g^{al} Frère étant avec le maréchal Moncey, harassé et affaibli par des marches et des contremarches, la position de l'armée Française est devenue moins belle.

2e *Observation.*—Le maréchal Bessières est aujourd'hui à Medina del Rio Secco avec 15 mille hommes, infanterie, cavalerie, artillerie. Le 15 ou le 16, il attaquera Bénavente, se mettra en communication avec le Portugal, jettera les rebelles en Galice, et s'emparera de Léon. Si toutes les opérations réussissent ainsi, et d'une manière brillante, la position de l'armée Française redeviendra ce qu'elle était.

Si le général Cuesta se retire de Bénavente sans combattre, il se retirait sur Zamora, Salamanque, pour venir gagner Avila et Segovia, certain qu'alors le maréchal Bessières ne pourrait point le poursuivre, puisque, dans cette supposition, il serait menacé par l'armée de Galice, dont l'avant-garde est réunie à Léon.

Alors il faut que le général qui commande à Madrid puisse promptement réunir 6 à 7000 hommes pour marcher sur le général Cuesta. Il faut que la citadelle de Ségovie soit occupée par quelques pièces de canon, trois à 400 convalescens, avec six semaines de biscuit.

C'est une grande faute de n'avoir pas occupé cette citadelle, quand le major-général l'a mandé. De toutes les positions possibles, Ségovie est la plus dangereuse pour l'armée: capitale d'une province, assise entre les deux routes, elle ôterait a l'armée toutes ses communications, et l'ennemi une fois posté dans cette citadelle, l'armée Française ne pourrait plus l'en déloger. Trois ou 400 convalescens et un bon chef de bataillon, une escouade d'artillerie, rendront le château de Ségovie imprégnable pendant bien de tems, et assureront à l'armée l'importante position de Ségovie.

Si le général Cuesta se jette en Galice, sans combattre, sans éprouver de défaite, la position de l'armée devient toujours meilleure; à plus forte raison, s'il est jetté en Galice après avoir éprouvé une forte défaite.

3e *Observation.*—Si le maréchal Bessières, arrivé devant Bénavente, reste en présence sans attaquer le g^{al} Cuesta, ou s'il est repoussé, son but sera toujours de couvrir Burgos, en tenant le plus possible l'ennemi en échec; il peut être renforcé de 3000 hommes de troupes de ligne, qui accompagnent le roi, mais alors il n'y a point à hésiter. Si le maréchal Bessières a fait une marche rétrograde sans bataille, il faut sur le champ lui envoyer 6000 hommes de renforts. S'il a fait son mouvement après une bataille, où il ait éprouvé de grandes pertes, il faudra faire de grandes dispositions: rappeler à marche forcée sur Madrid le g^{al} Frère, le g^{al} Caulaincourt, le g^{al} Gobert, le g^{al} Vedel, et laisser le g^{al} Dupont sur les montagnes de la Sierra Morena, ou le rapprocher même de Madrid, en le tenant toujours, cependant, à sept ou huit marches, afin de pouvoir écraser le g^{al} Cuesta et toute l'armée de Galice, pendant que le g^{al} Dupont servira d'avant-garde pour tenir l'armée d'Andalousie en échec.

4e *Observation.*—Si le général Dupont éprouvait un échec, cela serait de peu de conséquence. Il n'aurait d'autre résultat que de lui faire repasser les montagnes; mais le coup qui serait porté au maréchal Bessières serait un coup porté au cœur de l'armée, qui donnerait le tetanos, et qui se ferait sentir à toutes les points extrêmes de l'armée. Voilà pourquoi il est très malheureux que toutes les dispositions ordonnées n'aient pas été suivis. L'armée du maréchal Bessières devrait se trouver avoir au moins huite mille hommes de plus, afin qu'il n'y eut aucune espèce de chance contre l'armée du maréchal Bessières.

La vraie manière de renforcer le général Dupont, ce n'est pas de lui envoyer des troupes, mais c'est d'envoyer des troupes au maréchal Bessières. Le général Dupont et le général Vedel sont suffisans pour se maintenir dans les positions qu'ils ont retranchés; et si le maréchal Bessières avait été renforcé, et l'armée de Galice écrasée, le général Dupont immédiatement après se trouverait dans la meilleure position, non seulement par des forces qu'on pourrait alors lui envoyer, mais encore par la situation morale des affaires. Il n'y a pas un habitant de Madrid, pas un paysan des vallées qui ne sente que toutes les affaires d'Espagne aujourd'hui sont dans l'affaire du maréchal Bessières. Combien n'est-il pas malheureux que dans cette grande affaire on se soit donné volontairement 20 chances contre soi.

5e *Observation*.—L'affaire de Valence n'a jamais été d'aucun considération. Le maréchal Moncey seul était suffisant. C'était une folie que de songer à le secourir. Si le m^{al} Moncey ne pouvait pas prendre Valence, 20 mille hommes de plus ne le lui auraient pas fait prendre, parcequ'alors c'était un affaire d'artillerie, et non une affaire d'hommes: car on ne prend pas d'un coup de collier une ville de 80 ou 100 mille âmes, qui a barricadé ses rues, mis de l'artillerie à toutes les portes et dans toutes les maisons. Or, dans cette hypothèse, le m^{al} Moncey était suffisant pour former une colonne mobile, faire face à l'armée de Valence, et faire sentir dans toute leur force les horreurs de la guerre.

Le g^{al} Frère ne pouvait donc rien pour faire prendre Valence, et le g^{al} Frère pouvait beaucoup posté à San Clemente, soit qu'il dût revenir à Madrid, soit qu'il dût prendre une position intermédiaire pour secourir le g^{al} Dupont.

C'était une autre erreur que de songer à faire aller le m^{al} Moncey à Valence pour ensuite le faire marcher en Murcie et sur Grenade. C'était vouloir fondre ce corps d'armée en détail et sans fruit. Comme le dit fort bien le général Dupont, il valait mieux lui envoyer directement un régiment que de lui envoyer trois dans cette direction là.

Dans les guerres civiles ce sont les points importans qu'il faut garder: il ne faut pas aller partout. Si cependant on a dirigé le mal Moncey sur Valence, c'était à une époque où la situation des affaires n'était pas la même; c'était lorsque l'armée de Valence pouvait envoyer en Catalogne ou à Saragosse comme elle en menaçait.

6e *Observation*.—Le but de tous les efforts de l'armée doit être de conserver Madrid. C'est là qu'est tout. Madrid ne peut être menacé que par l'armée de Galice. Elle peut l'être aussi par l'armée de l'Andalousie, mais d'une manière beaucoup moins dangereux, parcequ'elle est simple et directe, et que par toutes les marches que fait le g^{al} Dupont sur ses derrières, il se renforce. Les généraux Dupont et Vedel étaient suffisans, ayant plus de 20,000 hommes; le m^{al} Bessières ne l'est pas proportionnellement, vû que sa position est plus dangereuse. Un échec que recevrait le g^{al} Dupont serait peu de chose; un échec que recevrait le m^{al} Bessières serait plus considérable et se ferait sentir à l'extremité de la ligne.

Résumé.—Faire reposer et rapprocher de Madrid le g^{al} Frère, le g^{al} Caulaincourt, le g^{al} Gobert, afin qu'ils puissent arriver à Madrid avant le g^{al} Cuesta, si celui-ci battait le m^{al} Bessières. Immédiatement après l'événement qui aura lieu le 15 ou le 16, prendre un part selon les événemens qui auront eu lieu, et dans le but d'écraser l'armée ennemie en Galice.

Si le maréchal Bessières a eu grand succès, sans éprouver de grandes pertes, tout sera bien dans la direction actuelle. S'il a un succès après avoir éprouvé beaucoup de pertes, il faut se mettre en mesure de le renforcer. S'il se tient en observation sans attaquer, il faut le renforcer. S'il a été défait et bien battu, il faut se concentrer et rassembler toutes ses troupes dans le cercle de sept ou huit journées de Madrid, et étudier les dispositions dans les différentes directions pour savoir où placer les avant-gardes, afin de profiter de l'avantage qu'on a d'être au milieu, pour écraser successivement avec toutes ses forces les divers corps de l'ennemi. Si on n'ordonne pas sur le champ au g^{al} Dupont de repasser les montagnes, c'est qu'on espère que malgré la faute faite, le m^{al} Bessières a la confiance (qu'on partage) qu'à la rigueur il est suffisant pour écraser l'ennemi. Le m^{al} Bessières a eu le bon esprit de tellement réunir toutes ses forces, qu'il n'a pas même laissé un seul homme à St. Ander. Quelqu' avantage qu'il y eut à laisser là un millier d'hommes, il a senti qu'un millier d'hommes pouvait décider sa victoire.

Quant à la division du g^{al} Verdier devant Saragosse, elle a rempli aux trois quarts son but. Elle a désorganisé tous les Arragoniens, a porté le découragement parmi eux, les a reduits à défendre les maisons de leur capitale, a soumis tous les environs, a bloqué la ville, et réuni tous les moyens pour s'en emparer sans que cela devienne trop conteux.

Voilà l'esprit de la guerre d'Espagne.

Dictated by the emperor Napoleon. Taken at the battle of Vittoria.

No. II

NOTE POUR LE ROI D'ESPAGNE.

Bayonne, le Juillet, 1808.

L'armée d'Espagne a son quartier général à Madrid; voici sa composition actuelle:

1°. *Corps des Pyrénées Occidentales.*

Le maréchal Bessières commande le corps des Pyrénées Occidentales, qui est fort de 23 mille hommes, infanterie, cavalerie, artillerie, occupe la place de St. Sebastian, les trois Biscays, les montagnes de St. Ander, la place de Burgos, et est chargée de combattre l'armée ennemie des Asturies et de Galice.

Toutes les troupes sont en mouvement pour composer l'armée de la manière suivante.

Division du g[al] Mouton.	⌐ 1ere brigade, │ le g[al] Reynaud.	⌐ le 4e reg[t] d'infanterie legère │ 15e d'infanterie de ligne └ 1er bat[on] de Paris en marche	⌐
	│ total 3000 hom. présens sous les armes, et 6 pièces de canon, ci 3000 h[es] ┤ (Cette brigade marche sur Bénévent.)		├ 5100[hes]
	│ 2e brigade, { 2e regt d'infanterie legère │ le g[al] Rey. { 12e idem		│
	│ total 2100 hommes et 6 pièces de canon, ci 2100 └ (Cette brigade est à Burgos avec le roi, et doit joindre sa division.)		

— —

À reporter 5100 [hes]

De l'autre part 5100[hes]

Division du g[al] Merle.	⌐ Brigade d'Armagnac	1800	⌐
	│ Brigade Gaulois	1800	│
	│ Brigade Sabathier	2800	│ 8400 h[es]
	└ Brigade Ducos	2000	┘

— —

Total 8400 h[es]
et 16 pièces de canon.

Garde. ⌐
        └ Infanterie   1900 h[es]
        et 6 pièces de canon.
(Toutes ces troupes marchent sur Bénévent.)

Cavalerie.	⌐ 10e de chasseurs	450	⌐
	│ 22e id.	450	│
	│ Garde	300	│
	│ *(Ces troupes marchent sur Bénévent.)*		│
	│ Escadrons de dragons	200	│
	┤ *(Ces escadrons sont en marche et ont dépassé la frontière.*		├ 1950 hes
	│ 26e de chasseurs	450	│
	│ *(Arrivant à Bayonne sous peu de jours.)*		│
	│	— —	│
	│ Total de la cavalerie	1950 h[es]	│
	└	====	┘

Les forces actives du maréchal Bessières sont donc de 17,000 h[es]. Il n'en a guère que 15,000 pour l'affaire de Bénévent.

S'il obtenait à Bénévent et à Léon un grand succès contre l'armée de Galice, peut-être serait-il convenable pour profiter de la victoire et de la terreur des premiers moments de se jetter dans la Galice. Toutefois, il devrait d'abord prendre position à Léon, en s'emparant de la plaine, jettant l'ennemi dans les montagnes, et interceptant au moins à Astorga la communication de la grande route.

Garnison de Burgos. — *Il y a dans le château de Burgos une garnison de dépôt[28]*   600 h^{es}

         — — —

         À reporter   17,950 hes

         — — —

         De l'autre part   17,950 hes

Colonne du général Bonnet. — Il y a encore à Burgos le g^{al} de division Bonnet, faisant partie du corps du m^{al} Bessières: ce g^{al} va avoir sous ses ordres une colonne mobile de 1200 hommes, pour maintenir la tranquillité dans la ville et ses environs. Cette colonne est composée comme il suit:

4e bataillon du 118e, formant   450 h^{es}

(*Actuellement existant à Burgos.*)

3e bataillon du dépôt gal actuellement à Vittoria   450   1500 hes

2 comp^{ies} du 4e d'infanterie legère, formant un petit bataillon   400

     — —

     1300 h^{es}

(*En marche, ayant passé la frontière.*)

Escadron de dragons (en marche)   200

2 pièces de canon en marche

     — —

     1500 h^{es}

     ====

Colonne d'Aranda. — Cette colonne, formée du 1er bataillon de marche, fort de 1000 h^{es} et de 4 pièces de canon, peut se réunir au bésoin avec la colonne du g^{al} Bonnet: elles doivent assurer la communication jusqu'aux montagnes en avant d'Aranda, ci   1000 h^{es}

Colonne de Vittoria. — Le général de brigade Monthion, et le colonel Barerre, occupent Vittoria avec une colonne composée comme il suit:

2 compagnies du 15e de ligne, formant un petit bataillon de   300 h^{es}

Le 2e baton du 12e d'infanterie legère   600

Le 2e baton du 2e id.   600

     — —

(Ce qui fait en infanterie)   1500 hes

1 escadron de dragons (en marche)   200

2 pièces de canon.

     — —

(Tous ces corps sont en marche)   1700 ci   1700

         — — —

         À reporter   22,150 h^{es}

         — — —

De l'autre part	22,150 h^{es}

Garnison de St. Sebastian. — Le général Thouvenot commande à St. Sebastian avec mille hommes de garnison, ci — 1000

— — —

Recapitulation. — Le corps du mal Bessières est de — 23,150
Et 36 pièces de canon.
======

Les détachemens et troisièmes bataillons des corps qui sont aux divisions actives du mal Bessières pourront sous 15 jours le réjoindre, vû qu'ils seront remplacés à Vittoria et à Burgos par d'autres corps.

2°. Arragon.

Jusqu'à cette heure les troupes qui sont en Arragon, faisaient partie du corps des Pyrénées Occidentales. Mais le corps des Pyrénées Occidentales se portant sur la Galice, il devient indispensable d'en faire une division à part.

Aujourd'hui, ce commandement comprend Pampelune, la Navarre, et les troupes qui forment le siège de Saragosse, sous les ordres du général Verdier.

Ces troupes sont divisées en quatre brigades, et sont composées ainsi qu'il suit:

3 regimens d'infanterie de ligne de la Vistule, ayant sous les armes	3600 h^{es}
Les 4e, 6e et 7e bataillons de marche	1500
Le 3e bataillon du 14e provisoire	1300
Le 1er regiment supplémentaire	900
Les 47e, 15e et 70^e	1600
Un bataillon des gardes nationales d'élite	600

— —

Total.		9500 h^{es}
La cavalerie consiste dans un regiment de lanciers Polonais	700 }	1100
Plus un escadron de marche	400 }	

À *Pampelune* le g^{al} Dagout commande. Indépendamment d'une dépôt de 800 hommes, formant 800 la garnison de la citadelle; il a une colonne mobile composée du 1er bataillon de marche du Portugal, du troisième bataillon du 118e, fort de 650 hommes, et d'un escadron de dragons, ce qui forme un total de 1400 hommes disponibles pour se porter sur tous les points de la Navarre, et sur — (ci 800

— — —

À reporter	11,400

De l'autre part	11,400
Et les communications de Saragosse, pour y mettre l'ordre: ci	1,400
Artillerie	200

— — —

Il y a donc en cernement en Arragon et en Navarre	13,000

======

Aussitôt que Saragosse sera pris, et que le corps de l'Arragon sera constitué, il sera nécessaire de fairer entrer au corps du mar^l Bessières le bataillon du 47e, celui du 15e, et les trois bataillons du 14e provisoire; ce qui augmentera le m^al Bessières de deux mille hommes, afin de tenir les corps réunis. Il est possible qu'on fasse partir de Bayonne le 19,300 hommes de bonnes troupes de ligne, pour se diriger sur Saragosse et enlever la prise de cette place, si toutefois elle n'est pas encore prise.

Si Saragosse était pris, le corps du m^al Bessières pourrait être renforcé de ces trois mille hommes d'élite et de 2000 hommes du corps de Saragosse, ce qui lui ferait un corps nombreux pour la campagne de Galice.

Indépendamment de Saragosse, les rebelles occupent la ville de Jaca et plusieurs points dans les vallées. À tous les débouchés des vallées en France il y a un général de brigade avec une colonne mobile. On attendra la prise de Saragosse pour entrer dans ces vallées et y marcher dans les deux sens. En général l'esprit des vallées est bon; mais des troupes de contrebandiers que les chefs des rebelles ont enrégimentés les vexent.

3°. Catalogne.

Le général Duhesme occupe Barcelone, qui est une place qui a deux très belles forteresses, qui la dominent. C'est la plus grande ville de la monarchie.

Le général Duhesme a deux divisions, la division Chabran et la division Lechi, formant 11,000 h^es d'infanterie, 1600 h^es de cavalerie et 18 pièces de canon.

Le général Duhesme a eu plusieurs événemens; il a brulé un grand nombre de villages, et maintenu en respect le pays à 15 lieues à la ronde.

La ville de Géronne, n'ayant pas été occupée, les insurgés de la Catalogne ont établis là leur Junte, d'où ils donnent le mouvement au reste de la province. 2000 insurgés assiégeaint le fort de Figuéras. On y avait heureusement laissé 300 Français: ils ont été obligés de tirer beaucoup de coups de canon et de bruler le village.

Le g^al de division Reille, avec deux bataillons Toscans; a marché sur Figuéras, l'a débloqué, le 6 du mois, et y a fait entrer une grande quantité de vivres, dont on manquait. Le 10, il réunissait sa division, qui arrivait de divers points de la France; il avait déjà 6000 hommes, et il doit avoir aujourd'hui 9000 h^es; il doit s'assurer de Roses et marcher sur Géronne, établir ses communications avec le général Duhesme et ensemble pacifier la Catalogne.

Les forces réunies des généraux Duhesme et Reille s'élevent donc à	22,000 h^es
Ainsi le corps des Pyrénées Occidentales est fort de	23,000
Celui d'Arragon, de	13,000
Celui de Catalogne, de	22,000
	— — —
Total	68,000 h^es.
	======

Nous venons de faire connaître la situation de l'armée dans les provinces de la Biscaye, de St. Ander, de la Castille, de la Navarre, de l'Arragon et de la Catalogne; c'est à dire, sur toute la frontière de France.

Voici actuellement la situation dans les autres points:

Les deux corps qui se sont rendus à Madrid sous les ordres du général Dupont et du m^{al} Moncey portaient, et portent encore; le premier, le nom de corps d'observation de la Gironde, commandé par le g^{al} Dupont; le second, le nom de corps d'observation des Côtés de l'Océan, commandé par le m^{al} Moncey.

Le corps d'observation de la Gironde est composé de trois divisions: deux sont en Andalousie avec le général Dupont; la 3eme, celle du général Frere, doit être à present à San Clemente.

Le corps d'observation des Côtés de l'Océan est composé également de trois divisions. La première est avec le maréchal Moncey, sous Valence: les deux autres sont à Madrid, et disséminés en differentes colonnes, pour maintenir la communication avec le général Dupont. Les états de situation vous feront connaître la force de ces divisions: mais on peut en général les considérer les unes dans les autres comme fortes de 6000 hommes présens sous les armes.

Il y a *à Madrid* deux bataillons de la garde, formant 1000 hommes, et à-peu-près 900 hommes de cavalerie de la garde.

Ainsi il y a *à Madrid*, et du côté *de Valence* et *de l'Andalousie*, la valeur de 40,000 hommes d'infanterie, huit mille hommes de cavalerie et 80 pièces de canon attelées.

Le général Junot a en Portugal trois divisions, formant présens sous les armes, compris son artillerie, sa cavalerie, 23 mille hommes[29].

Telle est la situation de l'armée en Espagne et en Portugal.

1ere *Observation.* — Les événemens qui se passent aujourd'hui et demain amélioreront beaucoup la situation de toutes les affaires, en jettant dans la Galice le général Cuesta, en lui ôtant ses communications avec l'Estramadure, Madrid et l'Andalousie, en assurant nôtre communication avec le Portugal, et en assurant la soumission des provinces de Salamanque, Zamora, Toro, &^{a}.

La manière dont ces événemens auront lieu décideront à entrer sur le champ en Galice, à soumettre les Asturies, ou à différer encore quelques jours.

2e *Observation.* — La Navarre et la Biscaye se sont maintenues tranquilles.

En Arragon le plat pays a été soumis, les rebelles ont été battus plusieurs fois; avec deux seuls bataillons, 8 à 10 mille insurgés ont été détruits ou dispersés; le découragement est à dernier point parmi eux. Ils se sont défendus dans leurs maisons à Saragosse; on les a bombardé; on leur a fait beaucoup de mal; on achève aujourd'hui de bloquer la ville en jettant un pont sur l'Ebre. Une fois cette ville soumise, il n'y a pas de doute que tout l'Arragon ne devienne tranquille. Une partie des troupes sera cependant nécessaire pour maintenir la province; une petite partie pourra aider à la soumission de la Catalogne. La partie qui est nécessaire pour le bien du service du maréchal Bessières ira le rejoindre. Ainsi cet événement équivaudra à un secours considérable.

3eme *Observation.* — La première opération du général Reille a débloqué Figuères: il soumet à présent tous les environs. Il ne tardera pas sans doute à s'emparer de Géronne et à établir sa communication par terre avec le général Duhesme. La reduction de Géronne éntamera probablement celle de Lerida; on pourra avoir alors une colonne de deux trois ou mille hommes, qu'on dirigera par Tortose sur Valence.

4eme Observation. — On n'a point de nouvelles de l'expédition de Valence, et le maréchal Moncey a huit mille hommes. Avec ces forces il n'a rien à craindre. Il peut ne pas prendre la ville, qui est très grande, si les paysans s'y sont renfermés et ne craignent point de la ruiner: mais le mal Moncey se maintiendra dans le plat pays, occupera les revoltés, qu'il empêchera de se porter ailleurs, et fera porter au pays tout le poids de la guerre.

5e *Observation.* — On compte que le général Dupont a aujourd'hui près de 20,000 hommes. Si les opérations du maréchal Bessières réussissent bien, il n'y aura pas d'inconvénient à appuyer encore le général Dupont et à lui permettre de reprendre l'offensive. Ainsi les deux points importans, et où on fera une véritable guerre reglée, sont la Galice et l'Andalousie, parceque les troupes du camp de St. Roche, de Cadiz, des Algarves, sont près de 25 mille hommes, qu'elles ont pris parti pour la sedition de Seville en Andalousie, et que tout ce qui était à Porto a pris parti pour les rebelles de Galice.

Le point le plus important de tous est celui du m^{al} Bessières, comme on l'a déjà vu dans la note qu'on a envoyé. On doit tout faire pour que ce corps n'éprouve aucun mouvement rétrograde, aucun échec; celui du général Dupont vient après.

Les affaires de Saragosse sont au 3e ordre; celles de Valence ne sont qu'en 4me.

Voilà la véritable situation des affaires militaires du royaume.

Il parait convenable de former dans l'Arragon une division de 10 à 12 mille hommes que pourra commander le g^{al} Verdier. Il devra corréspondre directément avec l'état major du roi, avec le m^al Bessières (pour s'éntendre), avec le g^al Duhesme pour se concerter, et avec le général de la 11e division militaire, qui se tiendra à Bayonne, afin de connaître toujours la situation de cette frontière. Son commandement doit embrasser la Navarre et tout l'Arragon.

Alors l'armée sera composée du corps des Pyrénées Occidentales, de la division de l'Arragon (il est inutile d'en faire un corps), du corps de la Catalogne composé de trois divisions, y compris celle du général Reille, et des six divisions que forment les corps d'observation de la Gironde et des Côtés de l'Océan.

Cela fera à-peu-près 12 divisions réunies et en outre un certain nombre de petites colonnes mobiles et de garnisons.

Dictated by the emperor Napoleon. Taken at Vittoria.

No. III

NOTE SUR LA POSITION ACTUELLE DE L'ARMÉE EN ESPAGNE.

Bayonne, le 21 Juillet, 1808.

1ere *Observation.* — La bataille de Medina del Rio Secco a mis les affaires de l'armée dans la meilleure situation. Le maréchal Bessières ne donne plus aucune inquiétude, et toutes les sollicitudes doivent se tourner du côté du général Dupont.

2de *Observation.* — Dans la position actuelle des affaires, l'armée Française occupe le centre; l'ennemi, un grand nombre de points de la circonférence.

3me *Observation.* — Dans une guerre de cette nature, il faut du sang froid, de la patience, et du calcul; et il ne faut pas épuiser les troupes en fausses marches et contremarches; il ne faut pas croire, quand on a fait une fausse marche de trois à quatre jours, qu'on l'aie réparé par une contremarche: c'est ordinairement deux fautes au lieu d'une.

4me *Observation.* — Toutes les opérations de l'armée ont réussies jusqu'à cette heure, autant qu'elles devaient réussir. Le général Dupont s'est maintenu au-delà des montagnes, et dans le bassin de l'Andalousie; trois fois il a défait les insurgés. Le maréchal Moncey a défait les insurgés à Valence; il n'a pas pu prendre la ville, ce qui est une chose qui n'est pas extraordinaire. Peut-être eût-on pu désirer qu'il eût pu se camper à une journée de la ville, comme a fait le général Dupont; mais, enfin, qu'il soit à une journée ou à cinq, comme à Saint Clément, la différence n'est pas très grande. En Arragon, on a battu sur tous les points, et dans toutes les circonstances, l'ennemi, et porté le découragement partout. Saragosse n'a pas été pris; il est aujourd'hui cerné; et une ville de 40 à 50 mille âmes, défendue par une mouvement populaire, ne se prend qu'avec du tems et de la patience. Les histoires des guerres sont pleins des catastrophes des plus considérables pour avoir brusqué et s'être enfourré dans les rues étroites des villes. L'exemple de Buenos Ayres, et des 12 milles Anglais d'élite qui y ont péri, en est une preuve.

5me Observation. — Ainsi la position de l'armée est bonne, le maréchal Moncey étant à Saint Clément, ou environs, et les généraux Gobert et Vedel réunis au général Dupont en Andalousie; ce serait une faute, à moins d'incidents et d'un emploie immédiat, à donner à ces troupes dans un autre point, que de concentrer toutes les troupes trop près de Madrid. L'incertitude des événemens du maréchal Bessières, et les 25 chances qu'il avoit contre lui sur cent, pouvaient déterminer à faire arrêter la marche de toutes les troupes qui s'éloignaient de la capitale, afin que les colonnes pussent être rappellés à Madrid si le maréchal Bessières était battu, et pussent arriver dans cette ville avant l'ennemi; mais ce serait une faute si on eut fait retrograder ces colonnes, et si on eut agi comme si le maréchal Bessières avait été battu, lorsque quelques jours avant on agissait comme si l'armée de Galice n'existait pas. 500 chevaux et 1800 hommes d'infanterie dirigés sur Valladolid étaient tous ce qu'il fallait. Si cette colonne était partie trois jours plutôt, elle y serait arrivé le 15. Le maréchal Bessières a été vainqueur, et avait pour être vainqueur 75 chances contre 25; mais la fatigue qu'on a donné à l'armée, et les mouvemens rétrogrades qu'on a ordonné inutilement, puisque même le maréchal Bessières battu, on avait 8 à 10 jours pour réunir l'armée, ont fait un mal moral et physique. Il faut espérer que la nouvelle de la victoire arrivée à tems aura mis l'état major à même d'arrêter toute mouvement sur Madrid, et que chaque colonne se trouvera plus près du point où elle doit se trouver.

6me *Observation.* — Dans la situation actuelle des affaires, le plus important de tous est le général Dupont. On doit lui envoyer le reste de la division Gobert, et employer d'autres troupes pour maintenir la communication; il faut tenir la tête de la division du maréchal Moncey, sur Saint Clement, et menacer toujours la province de Valence. Si le maréchal Bessières a battu sans effort, et avec peu de perte, l'armée de Galice, et a eu moins de huit milles hommes engagés, il n'y a pas de doute qu'avec 20 milles le général Dupont ne culbute tout ce qu'il a devant lui.

7me *Observation.* — La brigade du général Rey rend à l'armée plus qu'elle n'a perdu par le détachement qui a été fait sur Valladolid. Toutes les probabilitées humaines sont que le maréchal Bessières n'a plus besoin d'aucun renfort, du moins pour être maître de toute la Castille et du royaume de Léon. Ce n'est que lorsqu'on aura reçu la nouvelle de ce qu'il aura fait à Bénévent et à Léon qu'on pourra décider s'il doit attaquer la Galice.

8me Observation. — Le général Verdier, en Arragon, a cerné Saragosse: le 14eme et le 44eme de ligne partent demain pour s'y rendre. Les partis Français vont jusqu'à moitié chemin de Lerida, de Barbastro, et de Jaca. Dans dix jours toute l'artillerie sera arrivée. Cette belle et bonne brigade de troupes de ligne porte à près de quinze mille hommes l'armée du général Verdier. Il est probable que Saragosse tombera bientôt, et que les deux tiers de ces 15 milles hommes deviendrons disposibles.

9eme *Observation.* — Ainsi le corps du maréchal Bessières a pris l'offensive, il est depuis sa victoire renforcé de la brigade Lefebre et de la brigade Gaulois; il est donc dans le cas de conserver l'offensive. Le corps du général Verdier en Arragon a battu partout les insurgés, a cerné la ville avec des forces beaucoup moindres; il vient d'être considérablement renforcé; ainsi il peut donner une nouvelle activité aux opérations du siège, et conserver son activité offensive sur les deux rives de l'Ebre. Le corps de Catalogne a joliment agi, ayant pour point d'appui Barcelonne, l'ajonction sera faite aujourd'hui ou demain devant Géronne, avec le gén[l] Reille.

10eme *Observation.* — Voilà pour les trois corps d'armée situés du côté de la France. La communication de Madrid avec la France est important sous tous les points de vue. Il faut donc que les colonnes qui viennent d'être organisées à Burgos et à Vittoria et qui seront journellement renforcées et augmentées, soient laissées dans ces stations.

Ci joint la note de la formation de ces colonnes. Elles sont presque toutes composées de 3eme bataillons et de conscrits, mais avec de bons cadres; 15 à 20 jours de stations à Burgos et à Vittoria les mettront à-peu-près à l'école de bataillon. Ce serait une très grande faute que de rappeller trop tôt ces troupes pour en renforcer les cadres principaux; il faut attendre jusqu'à ce qu'on ait pu les remplacer à Vittoria et à Burgos par de nouvelles troupes.

11eme *Observation.* — Il n'y a donc rien à craindre du côté du maréchal Bessières, ni dans le nord de la Castille, ni dans le royaume de Léon.

Il n'y a rien à craindre en Arragon; Saragosse tombera un jour plus tôt ou un jour plus tard.

Il n'y a rien à craindre en Catalogne.

Il n'y a rien à craindre pour les communications de Burgos à Bayonne, moyennant les deux colonnes organisées dans ces deux villes, et qui seront renforcées. S'il y avait des événemens en Biscaye, la force qui se réunit à Bayonne, formant une réserve, seroit suffisante pour mettre tout en ordre.

S'il arrive à Burgos quelque événement trop considérable pour que la colonne mobile qui est à Burgos puisse y mettre ordre, le maréchal Bessières ne sera pas assez loin pour ne pouvoir faire un détachement.

Le général Monthion a la surveillance de toutes les Biscayes. Le général Bonnet à Burgos est chargé de maintenir la communication de Vittoria avec le maréchal Bessières et avec Madrid. Il est nécessaire que ces deux généraux correspondent tous les jours entr'eux et avec le général Drouet, qui est laissé en réserve à Bayonne, de même que le gén¹ Verdier de Saragosse et le gén¹ Dagoult de Pampelune doivent correspondre tous les jours avec le général Drouet à Bayonne, et avec Madrid, par le canal de Bayonne et de Vittoria: jusqu'à ce que les communications directes soient rétablies, un courier partant de Madrid peut se rendre par Vittoria, Tolosa, Pampelune, devant Saragosse. Le seul point important donc aujourd'hui est le général Dupont. Si l'ennemi parvenait jamais à s'emparer des défiles de la Sierra Morena, il serait difficile de l'en chasser; il faut donc renforcer le gén¹ Dupont, de manière qu'il ait 25 mille hommes, compris ce qu'il faudra pour gardes les passages des montagnes et une partie du chemin de La Manche. Il pourra disposer les troupes de manière que le jour où il voudra attaquer, la brigade de deux à trois mille hommes, destinée à garder les montagnes, arrive au camp du gén¹ Dupont à marches forcées, et soit successivement remplacée par les colonnes qui seraient en arrière, de sorte que le gén¹ Dupont ait pour le jour de la bataille plus de 23 mille hommes à mettre en ligne.

Une fois qu'on aura bien battu l'ennemi, une partie des troupes se dissipera, et selon que la victoire sera plus ou moins décidée, on pourra faire continuer le mouvement à d'autres troupes sur le général Dupont.

12eme *Observation.*—Saragosse pris, on aura des troupes disponibles, soit pour renforcer l'armée de Catalogne, soit pour marcher sur Valence de concert avec le maréchal Moncey, soit pour renforcer le maréchal Bessières et marcher en Galice, si après la victoire qu'il a déjà remporté, et celle qu'il remportera à Léon, il ne croit pas assez fort pour s'y porter d'abord.

13eme Observation.—Il serait important de choisir deux points intermédiaires entre Andujar et Madrid, pour pouvoir y laisser garnison permanente, un commandant, un dépôt de cartouches, munitions, canons, magazins de biscuit, des fours, du farine, et un hôpital, de sorte que 3 à 400 hommes défendent le magazin et l'hôpital contre toute une insurrection. Il est difficile de croire qu'il n'y ait point quelque château ou donjon, pouvant être retranché promptement et propre à cela. C'est par ce seul moyen qu'on peut raccourcir la ligne d'opération, et être sur d'avoir toutes les trois ou quatre grandes marches, une manutention et un point de repos.

14eme *Observation.*—En résumé, le partage de l'armée parait devoir être celui-ci:

Corps de Catalogne, tel qu'il existe à-peu-près		20,000 h^es.
Corps d'Arragon, tel qu'il existe à-peu-près 15 mille hommes, jusqu'à ce que Saragosse soit pris		15,000
Corps du maréchal Bessières, ce qu'il a à-peu-près	17,000	
Colonne de Burgos	2,000	
Colonne de Vittoria	2,000	
Garnison de St. Sebastian	1,500	
Corps d'Aranda	1,000	
	— — —	
Total du corps du mar^l Bessières.		24,000 h^es.

Après la prise de Saragosse, lorsque les affaires de Catalogne seront un peu appaisées, on pourra, selon les circonstances, ou renforcer le maréchal Bessières, ou renforcer le général Dupont, ou entreprendre l'opération de Valence.

Aujourd'hui, le seul point qui menace, où il faut promptement avoir un succès, c'est du côté du général Dupont, avec 25 mille hommes infanterie, cavalerie, et artillerie comprise: il a beaucoup plus qu'il ne faut pour avoir de grands résultats; à la rigueur, avec 21 mille hommes présent sur le champ de bataille, il peut hardiment prendre l'offensive, il ne sera pas battu, et il aura pour lui plus de 80 chances.

Dictated by Napoleon. Taken at Vittoria.

No. IV

NOTE SUR LES AFFAIRES D'ESPAGNE.

St. Cloud, le 30 août, 1808.

1ere Observation.—Dans la position de l'armée d'Espagne on a à craindre d'être attaqué sur le droite par l'armée de Galice, sur le centre par l'armée venant de Madrid, sur le gauche par l'armée venant de Saragosse et Valence. Ce serait une grande faute que de laisser l'armée de Saragosse et de Valence prendre position à Tudela.

Tudela doit être occupé, parceque c'est une position honorable, et Milagro une position obscure.

Tudela est sur les communications de Pampelune, a un beau pont en pierre, est l'aboutissant d'un canal sur Saragosse. C'est une position offensive sur Saragosse telle que l'ennemi ne peut pas la négliger; cette position seule couvre la Navarre. En gardant Tudela, on garde une grande quantité de bateaux, qui nous seront bientôt nécessaires pour le siège de Saragosse.

Si l'ennemi était maître de Tudela, toute la Navarre s'insurgerait, l'ennemi pourrait arriver à Estella, en négligeant la position de Milagro et en coupant la communication avec Pampelune.

D'Estella il serait sur Tolosa; il y serait sans donner le tems de faire les dispositions convenables; il n'est pas à craindre, au contraire, que l'ennemi fasse aucune opération sur Pampelune; tant que nous aurons Tudela, il serait lui-même coupé sur Saragosse.

Le général qui commande à Tudela peut couvrir les hauteurs de redoutes; si c'est une armée d'insurgés, s'en approcher et la battre, la tenir constamment sur le defensive par les reconnoissances et ses mouvemens sur Saragosse.

Et si, au lieu de cela, une partie de l'armée de ligne Espagnole marchait sur Tudela, le général Français repassera l'Ebre, s'il y est forcé, disputera le terrein sur Pampelune, et donnera le tems au général en chef de l'armée Française de prendre ses mésures. Ce corps d'observation remplira alors son but, et aucune opération prompte sur Tolosa ni Estella n'est à craindre.

Au lieu qu'en occupant la position de Milagro, l'ennemi sera à Estella, le même jour qu'on l'apprendra au quartier général. Si on occupe Tudela, il faut s'y aider de redoutes, et s'y établir, n'y conserver aucune espèce d'embarras, et les tenir tous dans Pampelune. Si l'ennemi l'occupe, il faut l'en chasser, et s'y établir; car dans l'ordre défensif, ce serait une grande faute, qui entrainerait de fâcheuses consequences.

2e *Observation.* — La position de Burgos était également importante à tenir, comme ville de haute réputation, comme centre de communication et de rapports.

Delà des partis non seulement de cavalerie, mais encore de deux ou de trois mille hommes d'infanterie, et même quatre ou cinq mille hommes en échelons peuvent poster les premières patrouilles d'housards dans toutes les directions jusqu'à deux marches, et parfaitement informés de tout ce qui ce fait, en instruire le quartier général, de manière que si l'ennemi se présente en force sur Burgos, les différentes divisions puissent à temps s'y porter pour le soutenir et livrer la bataille, ou si cela n'est pas jugé convenable, éclairer les mouvemens de l'ennemi, lui laisser croire qu'on veut se porter sur Burgos, et pouvoir ensuite faire sa retraite pour se porter ailleurs.

Un corps de 12 à 15 mille hommes ne prend-il pas 20 positions dans la journée au seul commandement d'un adjudant major? et nos troupes seraient-elles devenues des levées en masse, qu'il faudroit placer 15 jours d'avance dans les positions où on voudroit qu'elles se battent?

Si cela eut été jugé ainsi, le corps du maréchal Bessières eut pris la position de Miranda ou de Briviesca; mais lorsque l'ennemi est encore à Madrid, lorsqu'on ignore où est l'armée de Galice, et qu'on a le soupçon que les rebelles pourront employer une partie de leurs efforts contre le Portugal, prendre, au lieu d'une position menaçante, offensive, honorable comme Burgos, une position honteuse, borgne comme Trevino, c'est dire à l'ennemi, "Vous n'avez rien à craindre; portez vous ailleurs; nous avons fait nos dispositions pour aller plus loin, ou bien nous avons choisi un champ de bataille pour nous battre; venez ici, vous ne craignez pas d'être inquiétés." Mais que fera le général Français, si l'on marche demain sur Burgos? laissera-t-il prendre par 6,000 insurgés la citadelle de cette ville, ou si les Français ont laissés garnison dans le château (car on ignore la position et la situation de l'armée), comment une garnison de 4, 6, ou 800 hommes se retira-t-elle dans une si vaste plaine? Et des lors·c'est comme s'il n'y avoit rien: l'ennemi maître de cette citadelle, on ne la reprendra plus.

Si, au contraire, on veut garder la citadelle, on veut donc livrer bataille à l'ennemi; car cette citadelle ne peut pas tenir plus de trois jours; et si on veut livrer bataille à l'ennemi, pourquoi le mal. Bessières abandonne-t-il le terrein où on veut livrer bataille?

Ces dispositions paraissent mal raisonneés, et quand l'ennemi marchera on fera essuyer à l'armée un affront qui demoralisera les troupes, n'y eut-il que des corps légers ou des insurgés qui marchassent.

En résumé, la position de Burgos devait être gardée; tous les jours à trois heures du matin on devait être sous les armes, et à une heure du matin il devait partir des reconnaissances dans toutes les directions. On devait ainsi recueillir des nouvelles à huit ou dix lieux à la ronde, pour qu'on peut prendre ensuite le parti que les circonstances indiqueraient.

C'est la première fois qu'il arrive à une armée de quitter toutes les positions offensives, pour se mettre dans de mauvaises positions défensives, d'avoir l'air de choisir des champs de bataille, lorsque l'éloignement de l'ennemi, les mille et une combinaisons différentes qui peuvent avoir lieu, ne laissent point la probabilité de prévoir si la bataille aura lieu à Tudela, entre Tudela et Pampelune, entre Soria et l'Ebre, ou entre Burgos et Miranda.

La position de Burgos, tenue en force et d'une manière offensive, menace Palencia, Valladolid, Aranda. Madrid même. Il faut avoir longtems fait la guerre pour la concevoir; il faut avoir entrepris un grand nombre d'opérations offensives pour savoir comme le moindre événement ou indice encourage ou décourage, décide une opération ou une autre.

En deux mots, si 15 mille insurgés entrent dans Burgos, se retranchent dans la ville, et occupent le château, il faut calculer une marche de plusieurs jours pour pouvoir s'y poster et reprendre la ville; ce qui ne sera pas sans quelque inconvenient; si pendant ce tems-là la véritable attaque est sur Logroño ou Pampelune, on aura fait des contremarches inutiles, qui auront fatigué l'armée; et enfin, si l'ennemi occupe Logroño, Tudela, et Burgos, l'armée Française serait dans une triste et mauvaise position.

Quand on tiens à Burgos de la cavalerie sans infanterie, n'est-ce pas dire à l'ennemi qu'on ne veut pas y tenir; n'est-ce pas l'engager à y venir? Burgos a une grande influence dans le monde par son nom, dans la Castille parceque c'en est la capitale, dans les opérations parcequ'elle donne une communication directe avec St. Ander. Il n'est pas permis à 300 lieues, et n'ayant pas même un état de situation de l'armée, de prescrire ce qu'on doit faire; mais on doit dire que si aucune force majeure ne l'empêche, il faut occuper Burgos et Tudela.

Le corps détaché de Tudela a son mouvement assuré sur Pampelune, a la rôle de garder la Navarre, a ses ennemis à tenir en échec, Saragosse et tous les insurgés. Il était plus que suffisant pour surveiller Tudela, l'Ebre, et Pampelune, pour dissiper les rassemblemens s'il n'y avait que des insurgés, contenir l'ennemi, donner des renseignemens, et retarder la marche sur Pampelune. Si au lieu des insurgés, c'est l'armée ennemie qui marche de ce côté, il suffit encore pour donner le tems à l'armée de Burgos, à celle de Miranda, de marcher réunie avec 36 mille hommes, soit pour prendre l'offensive, soit pour prendre en flanc l'ennemi qui marche sur Pampelune, soit pour se replier et rentrer dans la Navarre, si toute l'armée ennemie avait pris cette direction.

Si ces observations paraissent bonnes et qu'on les adopte, que l'ennemi n'ait encore montré aucun plan, il faut que le général qui commande le corps de Sarragosse fasse construire quelque redoutes autour de Tudela, pour favoriser ses champs de bataille, réunisse des vivres de tous les côtés, et soit là dans une position offensive sur Sarragosse en maintenant sa communication avec Logroño par sa droite, mais au moins par la rive gauche de l'Ebre. Il faut que le maréchal Bessières, avec tout son corps, renforcé de la cavalerie légère, soit campé dans le bois près Burgos, la citadelle bien occupée; que tous les hôpitaux, les dépôts, les embarras soient au delà de l'Ebre; qu'il soit là en position de manœuvrer, tous les jours, à trois heures du matin, sous les armes, jusqu'au retour de toutes les reconnaissances, et éclairant le pays dans la plus grande étendue; que le corps du ma^l Moncey soit à Miranda et à Briviesca, tous ses embarras et hôpitaux derrière Vittoria, toujours en bataille avant le jour, et envoyant des reconnaissances sur Soria et les autres directions de l'ennemi.

Il ne faut pas perdre de vue que les corps des maréchaux Bessières et Moncey, devant être réunis, il faut se lier le moins possible avec Logroño, et cependant considérer le corps du général Lefebre comme un corps détaché, qui a une ligne d'opération particulière sur Pampelune et un rôle séparé; vouloir conserver Tudela comme une partie contigue de la ligne, c'est se desseminer beaucoup. Enfin, faire la guerre, c'est à dire, avoir des nouvelles par les curés, les alcaldes, les chefs de couvent, les principaux proprietaires, les postes: on sera alors parfaitement informé.

Les reconnaissances qui tous les jours se dirigeront du côté de Soria, de Burgos, sur Palencia, et du côté d'Aranda, peuvent former tous les jours trois postes d'interception, trois rapports d'hommes arrêtés, qu'on traitera bien, et qu'on rélachera quand ils auront donné les renseignemens qu'on desire. On verra alors venir l'ennemi, on pourra réunir toutes ses forces, lui dérober des marches, et tomber sur ses flancs au moment ou il meditera un projet offensif.

3me Observation.—L'armée Espagnole d'Andalousie étoit peu nombreuse. Toutes les Gazettes Anglaises, et les rapports de l'officier Anglais qui était au camp, nous le prouvent. L'inconcevable ineptie du général Dupont, sa profonde ignorance des calculs d'un général en chef, son tâtonnement, l'ont perdu. 18 mille hommes ont posé les armes, six mille seulement se sont battus, et encore ces 6000 hommes que le genl Dupont a fait battre à la pointe du jour, après les avoir fait marcher toute la nuit, étaient un contre trois. Malgré tout cela, l'ennemi c'est si mal battu, qu'il n'a pas fait un prisonnier, pris une pièce de canon, gagné un pouce de terrein, et l'armée de Dupont est restée intacte dans sa position; ce qui sans doute a été un malheur; car il eût mieux valu que cette division eût été mise en déroute, éparpillée, et détruite, puisque les divisions Vedel et Dufour, au lieu de se rendre par la capitulation, auraient fait leur retraite. Comment ces deux divisions ont-elles été comprises dans la capitulation? c'est par la lâcheté insultante et l'imbécilité des hommes qui ont négocié, et qui porteront sur l'échaffaud la peine de ce grand crime national.

Ce que l'ont vient de dire prouve que les Espagnols ne sont pas à craindre; toutes les forces Espagnols ne sont pas capables de culbuter 25 mille Français, dans une position raisonnable.

Depuis le 12 jusqu'au 19, le général Dupont n'a fait que des bêtises, et malgré tout cela, s'il n'avait pas fait la faute de se séparer de Vedel, et qu'il eût marché avec lui, les Espagnols auraient été battus et culbutés. A la guerre les hommes ne sont rien, c'est un homme qui est tout. Jusqu'à cette heure nous n'avons trouvé ces exemples que dans l'histoire de nos ennemis: aujourd'hui, il est fâcheux que nous puissions les trouver dans la nôtre.

Une rivière, fût-elle aussi large que la Vistule, aussi rapide que le Danube à son emboucheur, n'est rien si on n'a des débouchés sur l'autre rive, et une tête prompte à reprendre l'offensive. Quand à l'Ebre, c'est moins que rien; on ne la regarde que comme une trace.

Dans toutes ces observations, on a parlé dans la position où se trouvait l'armée du 20 au 26, lorsqu'elle n'avait nulle part nouvelle de l'ennemi.

Si on continue à ne prendre aucune mésure pour avoir des nouvelles, on n'apprendra que l'armée de ligne Espagnol est arrivée sur Tudela et Pampelune, qu'elle est sur les communications, sur Tolosa, que lorsqu'elle y sera déjà rendue. On a fait connaître dans la note précédente comment on faisait à la guerre pour avoir des nouvelles. Si la position de Tudela est occupée par l'ennemi, on ne voit pas que l'Ebre soit tenable. Comment a-t-on évacué Tudela, lorsqu'on avait mandé dans des notes précédentes qu'il fallait garder ce point, et que l'opinion même des généraux qui venaient de Sarragosse étaient d'occuper cette importante position.

Dictated by Napoleon. Taken at Vittoria.

No. V

NOTE SUR LES AFFAIRES D'ESPAGNE.

St. Cloud, Août, 1808.

1ere *Observation*. — Tudela est importante sous plusieurs points de vue: il a un pont sur l'Ebre, et protège parfaitement la Navarre: c'est le point d'intersection du canal qui va à Sarragosse.

Les convois d'artillerie et de vivres mettent pour se rendre de Pampelune à Tudela trois jours, de Tudela à Sarragosse trois jours. Mais en se servant du canal, on va de Tudela à Sarragosse en 14 heures. Lorsque donc les vivres, les hôpitaux, sont à Tudela, c'est comme s'ils étaient à Sarragosse.

La première opération qui doit faire l'armée lorsqu'elle reprendra son système d'offensive, et qu'elle sera forte de tous ses moyens, ce doit être d'investir et de prendre Sarragosse; et si cette ville résiste comme elle l'a fait la première fois, en donner un exemple qui retentisse dans toute l'Espagne.

Une vingtaine de pièces de 12 de campagne, une vingtaine d'obsusiers de six pièces de campagne, une douzaine de mortières, et une douzaine de pièces de 16 et de 24, parfaitement approvisionée, seront nécessaires, ainsi que des mineurs pour remplir ce but.

Il n'est aucun de ces bouches de feu qui doive consommer son approvisionement de campagne.

Un approvisionement extraordinaire de 80 mille coups de canon, bombes ou obus, parait nécessaire pour prendre cette ville.

Il faudrait donc, pour ne pas retarder la marche de la grande armée, 15 jours avant qu'elle ne puisse arriver, commencer le transport de Pampeluna à Tudela, et que dans les 48 heures après l'investissement de Sarragosse, l'artillerie y arrivât sur des bâteux, de manière que quatre jours après on put commencer trois attaques à la fois, et avoir cette ville en peu de jours, ce qui serait une partie des succès, en y employant 25 à 30 mille hommes, ou plus s'il était nécessaire.

On suppose que, si l'ennemi a pris position entre Madrid et Burgos, il aura été battu.

Il faut donc occuper Tudela. Ce point est tellement important qu'il serait à desirer qu'on put employer un mois à le fortifier et à s'y retrancher de manière qu'un millier d'hommes avec 8 à 10 pièces de canon s'y trouvassent en sûreté et à l'abri de toutes les insurrections possibles. Il ne faut pas surtout souffrir que les revoltés s'y retranchât; ce serait deux sièges au lieu d'une; et il serait impossible de prendre Sarragosse avant d'avoir Tudela, à cause du canal.

On trouvera ci-joint des observations du colonel Lacoste sur Tudela; puisque les localités empêchent de penser à le fortifier, il eût été utile de l'occuper au lieu de Milagro, qui n'aboutit à rien.

2de. Soria n'est je crois qu'à deux petits marches des positions actuelles de l'armée. Cette ville s'est constamment mal comportée. Une expedition qui se porterait sur Soria, la désarmerait, en prendrait une trentaine d'hommes des plus considerables, qu'on enverrait en France pour ôtages, et qui enfin lui ferait fournir des vivres pour l'armée, serait d'un bon effet.

3me. Une troisième opération qui serait utile serait l'occupation de St. Ander. Il serait bien avantageux qu'elle put ce faire par la route directe de Bilbao à St. Ander.

4me. Il faut s'occuper de désarmer la Biscaye et la Navarre; c'est un point important; tout Espagnol pris les armes à la main doit être fusillé.

Il faut veiller sur la fabrique d'armes de Palencia, ne point laisser travailler les ouvriers pour les rebelles.

Le fort de Pancorvo doit être armé et fortifie avec la plus grande activité. Il doit y avoir dans ce fort des fours, des magazins de bouches et de guerre. Situé presqu'à mi-chemin de Bayonne à Madrid, c'est une poste intermédiare pour l'armée, et un point d'appui pour les opérations de la Galicie.

Il y a dans l'armée plus de généraux qu'il n'en faut; deux seraient nécessaires au corps qui était sous Sarragosse. Les généraux de division La Grange, Belliard, et Grandjean sont sans emploi, et tous trois bons généraux.

Il faut renvoyer, le plus promptement possible, le regiment et le général Portugais pour joindre leurs corps à Grenobles, où il doit se former.

5ᵐᵉ. On ne discutera pas ici si la ligne de l'Ebre est bonne, si elle a la configuration requise pour être défendu avec avantage.

On discutera encore moins si on eût pu ne pas evacuer Madrid, conserver la ligne du Duero, ou prendre une position qui eût couvert le siège de Sarragosse et eût permis d'attendre que cette ville fut prise; toutes ces questions sont oiseuses.

Nous nous contenterons de dire, puisqu'on a pris la ligne de l'Ebre, que les troupes s'y desout et s'y reposent, qu'elle a au moins l'avantage que le pays est plus sain, étant plus élevé, et qu'on peut y attendre que les chaleurs soient passées.

Il faut surtout ne point quitter cette ligne sans avoir un projet déterminé, qui ne laisse aucune incertitude dans les opérations à suivre. Ce serait un grand malheur de quitter cette ligne pour être ensuite obligé de la reprendre.

A la guerre les trois quarts sont des affaires morales; la balance des forces réelles n'est que pour un autre quart.

6ᵐᵉ. En gardant la ligne de l'Ebre il faut que le général ait bien prévu tout ce que l'ennemi peut faire dans tous les hypothèses.

L'ennemi peut se présenter devant Burgos, partir de Soria, et marcher sur Logroño, ou, en partant de Sarragosse, se porter sur Estella, et menacer ainsi Tolosa. Il faut, dans tous ces hypothèses, qu'il n'y ait point un longtems perdu en déliberations, qu'on puisse se ployer de sa droite à sa gauche, et de sa gauche à sa droite, sans faire aucun sacrifice. Car dans des manœuvres combinées, les tâtonnements, l'irrésolution qui naissent des nouvelles contradictoires qui se succedent rapidement, conduisent à des malheurs.

Cette diversion de Sarragosse sur Tolosa est une des raisons qui a longtems fait penser que la position de Tudela devait être gardée, soit sur la rive droite, soit avec la faculté de repasser sur la rive gauche. Elle est offensive sur Sarragosse, elle previent à tem de tous les mouvemens qui pourraient se faire de ce côté.

7me. Une observation qu'il n'est pas hors de propos de faire ici c'est, que l'ennemi, qui a intérêt de masquer ses forces, en cachant le véritable point de son attaque, opère de manière que le coup qu'il veut porter n'est jamais indiqué d'une manière positive, et le général ne peut deviner que par la connaissance bien approfondie de sa position, et la manière dont il fait entrer son système offensive, pour proteger et garantir son système défensive.

8me. On n'a point de renseignemens sur ce que fait l'ennemi. On dit toujours qu'on ne peut pas avoir des nouvelles, comme si cette position était extraordinaire dans une armée, comme si on trouvait ordinairement des éspions. Il faut en Espagne, comme partout ailleurs, envoyer des parties qui enlevent tantôt le curé ou l'alcalde, tantôt un chef de couvent ou le maître de poste, et surtout toutes les lettres, quelquefois le maître de la poste, aux douanes, ou celui qui en fait les fonctions, ou les met aux arrêts jusqu'à ce qu'ils parlent, en les faisant interroger deux fois par jour; on les garde en ôtage, et on les charge d'envoyer des piétons, et de donner des nouvelles.

Quand on saura prendre des mésures de force et de vigueur, on aura des nouvelles; il faut intercepter toutes les postes, toutes les lettres.

Le seul motif d'avoir des nouvelles peut determiner à faire un gros détachement de quatre à cinq milles hommes, qui se portent dans une grande ville, prennent les lettres à la poste, se saississent des citoyens les plus aisés de leurs lettres, papiers, gazettes, etc.

Il est hors de doute que même dans la ligne des Français les habitans sont tous informés de ce qui se passe: à plus forte raison hors de la ligne. Qui empêche donc, qu'on prenne les hommes marquants, et qu'on les renvoyé ensuite sans les maltraiter?

Il est donc de fait, lorsqu'on n'est point dans un désert, et qu'on est dans un pays peuple, que si le general n'est pas instruit, c'est qu'il n'a pas su prendre les mésures convenables pour l'être.

Les services que les habitans rendent à un général ennemi, ils ne le font jamais par affection, ni même pour avoir de l'argent; les plus réels qu'on obtient c'est pour avoir de sauve-gardes, et de protections; c'est pour conserver ses biens, ses jours, sa ville, son monastère.

The original of the following memoir is a rough draft, written by king Joseph. It has many erasures and interlineations, and was evidently composed to excuse his retreat from Madrid. The number of the French troops was undoubtedly greater than is here set down, unless the infantry alone be meant.

No. VI

Lorsqu'on a quitté Madrid a la nouvelle de la defection d'un corps de vingt-deux mille hommes, il y avoit dans Madrid dix-sept mille hommes, au corps du maréchal Bessières quinze mille cinq cent, au corps de Sarragosse onze mille sept cent: l'armée se composait done de quarante-cinq mille hommes; mais ces trois corps étaient distans entre eux de près de cent lieus. La première idée fut de réunir le corps de Madrid à celui de Léon, à Burgos, et par suite d'entrer en communication avec celui de Sarragosse, avec lequel l'état major de Madrid n'avoit jamais eu aucune relation directe, et dont il ignorait absolument la situation et la composition.

Vingt jours après sa sortie de Madrid le roi s'est trouvé à la tête d'une armée de cinquante mille hommes. Le feu de la sedition n'a pas pu se communiquer sur les points parcourus par les trois corps d'armée alors réunis; les communications avec la France out été gardées; l'insurrection de Bilbao a été eteinte dans le sang de 1200 insurgés. Peu de jours après, 20,000 d'entre eux réunis a 60 lieus delà, à Tudela, à l'autre extrémité de la ligne, out été dispersés et poursuivis rigoureusement. Les provinces de la Biscaye, de Burgos, et le royaume de Navarre ont été contenus. Une organization intérieure a prepare les moyens de nourrir l'armée, d'approvisionner les places de Pampelune, St. Sebastien, les forts de Pancorvo et de Burgos, en rendant le moins insupportable possible à ces provinces cette charge évidemment disproportionnée à leurs moyens.

Le matériel de l'artillerie a été réparé et mis en état d'agir, l'armée réorganisée, les hommes et les chevaux sont aujourd'hui en bon état.

C'est ainsi que s'est passé le mois d'Août et partie de Septembre. Les renforts arrivés de France ont à peine indemnisé l'armée des pertes qu'elle a éprouvés par les maladies et le siège de Sarragosse.

Voici sa force, et son organisation actuelle:

Le corps de droite, commandé par m[r] le mar[al] Bessières, est forte de 18,000 hommes.

Celui de gauche, commandé par m^r le mar^{al} Moncey, est de 18,000 hommes.

Celui du centre, aux ordres de m^r le mar^{al} Ney, est de onze mille hommes.

La reserve du roi est de quatre mille hommes[30].

Le corps de droite occupe le pays depuis Burgos jusqu'à Pancorvo, et Ponte de Lara.

Le corps de gauche depuis Tudela jusqu'à Logroño.

Le corps du centre depuis Logroño jusqu'à Haro.

La reserve Miranda.

La nouvelle position prise par l'armée depuis que les événemens de l'Andalousie avaient fait présager une guerre réelle en Espagne, était évidemment commandée par les simples notions de la saine raison, qui ne pouvait permettre sa séparation à plus de dix jours de marche, de trois corps d'armée, dont le plus fort n'arrivait pas à 18,000 hommes, au milieu d'une nation de onze millions d'habitans, qui se déclarait ennemi, et se mettait universellement en état de guerre.

Cinquante mille Français ont pu se tenir avec succès sur une ligne de plus de 60 lieus, gardant les deux grandes communications de Burgos et de Tudela contre des ennemis qui n'ont pu jusqu'ici porter sur l'un ou l'autre de ces points plus de 25,000 hommes; puisque 15,000 Français pouvaient être réunis sur l'une ou l'autre de ces deux communications principales en 24 heures.

Si les corps d'armée dirigés sur l'Espagne devaient arriver dans le mois de Septembre, ce système défensif et offensif à la fois se continuerait avec avantage, puisqu'il tend à refaire l'armée, à attendre celle qui doit arriver, et continue à menacer l'ennemi; mais il ne saurait se prolonger jusqu'au mois de Novembre. L'ennemi n'a pu rester trois mois sans faire de grands progrès; bientôt il sera en état de prendre l'offensif avec de grands corps organisés, obéissans à une administration centrale, qui aura eu le tems de se former à Madrid. Tout nous annonce que le mois d'Octobre est une de ces époques décisives qui donne à celui qui sait s'en emparer la priorité des mouvemens et des succès dont la progression est incalculable.

Quel est le parti à prendre dans la position où se trouve l'armée, et avec l'assurance qu'elle a? de voir entrer en Espagne dans le mois de Novembre deux cent mille Français.

Six manières de voir se présentent à l'esprit.

1ere. D'essayer de rester encore dans l'état où l'on est.

Ce système est évidemment insoutenable. De Tudela à Burgos et à Bilbao il y a plus de 60 lieus. L'ennemi pourra attaquer la gauche de cette ligne avec quarante mille hommes, la droite avec quarante mille hommes, le centre avec des forces égales. Tudela et la Navarre jusqu'à Logroño demandent 25,000 hommes pour être défendues. Burgos ne peut être défendue que par une armée en état de résister aux forces réunis de MM. Blake, Cuesta, qui peuvent présenter 80,000 hommes. Il est douteux que les 20,000 bayonettes qu'il serait possible de leur presente puissent les battre complètement. Si le succès est douteux, ces 20,000 hommes seront harcelés par les insurgés, qui pourront alors soulever les trois provinces, les séparer totalement d'avec le corps de gauche et de la France.

2de. Porter le corps du centre et la reserve par Tudela au devant de l'ennemi sur la route de Sarragosse, ou sur celle d'Albazan; on réunirait ainsi 30,000 hommes, on chercherait l'ennemi, et nul doute on le battrait si on le rencontrait de ce côté.

Le maréchal Bessières serait chargé d'observer la grande communication de Burgos à Miranda, laisserait garnison dans le château de Burgos, dans le fort de Pancorvo, occuperait l'ennemi, surveillerait les mouvemens des montagnes de Reynosa, les débarquemens possibles de Santander. Sa tâche serait difficile si l'on considère que le défilé de Pancorvo n'est pas le seul accessible à l'artillerie, qu'à trois lieus delà on arrive sur Miranda par une route practicable à l'artillerie, que quelques lieus plus loin l'Ebre offre un troisième passage sur le point de la chaîne qu'il traverse entre Haro et Miranda.

3eme. Laisser le maréchal Moncey à la défence de la Navarre, et se porter avec le corps du centre et la reserve sur Burgos. Réuni au maréchal Bessières on pourroit chercher l'ennemi, et attaquer avec avantage, on marcherait à lui avec trente mille hommes, et on n'attendrait pas qu'il fut réuni avec toutes ses forces. Il serait peut-être possible de donner pour instruction au maréchal Moncey, dans le cas ou il serait débordé sur sa gauche, et qu'il ne verrait pas probabilité de battre l'ennemi, de faire un mouvement par sa droite, et se porter par Logroño sur Briviesca, où il se réunirait au reste de l'armée. Dans ce cas, la Navarre s'insurgerait, les communications avec la France seraient coupées, mais l'armée réunie dans la plaine serait assez forte pour attendre les corps qui arrivent de France, et qui seront assez forts pour pénétrer partout. Il serait aussi possible que, dans tous les cas, le maréchal Moncey se maintienne dans le camp retranché de Pampelune; manœuvrant autour de cette place, il y attendrait le résultat des opérations des deux corps d'armée qui auraient été au devant de l'ennemi dans la plaine de Burgos, et l'arrivée des corps de la grande armée.

4ᵉᵐᵉ. Passer l'Ebre, et chercher à amener l'ennemi à une bataille dans la plaine que est entre Vittoria et l'Ebre.

5ᵉᵐᵉ. Se retirer appuyant sa gauche sur Pampelune, et sa droite dans les montagnes de Mondragone.

6eme. Laisser une garnison en état de se défendre pendant six semaines à Pampelune, St. Sebastien, Pancorvo, et Burgos, réunir le reste de l'armée, marcher à la rencontre de l'ennemi sur l'une ou l'autre des grandes communications, le battre partout où on le trouverait, attendre, ou près de Madrid, ou dans le pays où les mouvemens de l'ennemi et la possibilité de vivre aurait porté l'armée, les troupes de France; on abandonnerait ses derrières, ses communications; mais la grande armée serait assez forte pour en ouvrir pour elle-même. Et quant à l'armée qui est en Espagne, réunie ainsi elle serait en état de braver tous les efforts, de déconcerter tous les projets de l'ennemi, et d'attendre dans une noble attitude le mouvement général qui sera imprimé par vôtre majesté lors de l'arrivée de toutes les troupes dans ce pays.

De tous les projets le dernier parait preférable; il est plus noble et aussi sur que le 5ᵉᵐᵉ.

Ces deux projets sont seuls entiers absolument offensif ou absolument défensif. On peut les regarder, l'un et l'autre, comme propres à assurer la conservation de l'armée jusqu'à l'arrivée des renforts. Le dernier a sur l'autre l'avantage d'arrêter le progrès de l'ordre nouveau qui s'établit en Espagne; il est plus digne des troupes Françaises, et du frère de vôtre majesté. Il est aussi sur que celui de la sévère et honteuse défensive proposée par l'article cinq. Je l'ai communiqué au marᵃˡ Jourdan et au marᵃˡ Ney, qui l'un et l'autre sont de cet avis. Je ne doute point que les autres maréchaux ne partagent leur opinion.

Au premier Octobre je puis avoir la réponse de V. M., et même avant, puisque je lui ai manifesté cette opinion par ma lettre du 14 Septembre.

Si V. M. approuve ce plan, il sera possible qu'elle n'ait pas de mes nouvelles jusqu'à l'arrivée des troupes; mais je suis convaincu qu'elle trouvera les affaires dans une bien meilleure situation qu'en suivant aucun des autres cinq projets.

Miranda, le 16 Sept. 1808.

No. VII

S.

EXTRAIT DE LA LETTER DU MAJOR GÉNÉRAL AU GÉNÉRAL SAVARY, À MADRID.

Bayonne, 12e Juillet, 1808.

Section 1.—J'ai rendu compte à l'empereur, général, de vôtre lettre du 8me. S. M. trouve que vous vous étes dégarni de trop de monde à Madrid, que vous avez fait marcher trop de troupes au secours du gal Dupont, qu'on ne doit pas agir offensivement jusqu'à ce que les affaires de la Galice soient éclairées. De tous les points de l'armée, général, le plus important est la Galice, parceque c'est la seule province qui ait réellement conclu un traité avec l'Angleterre. La division de ligne des troupes Espagnoles qui était à Oporto s'est joint à celle qui était en Galice, et enfin par la position de cette province extrêmement près de l'Angleterre. Indépendamment de ces considérations, la position la rend encore plus interessante; car les communications de l'armée se trouveraient compromises si le maréchal Bessières n'avait pas un entier succès, et il faudrait bien alors reployer toutes vos troupes, et marcher isolément au secours du maréchal Bessières. Encore une fois, général, vous vous étes trop dégarni de Madrid, et si un bon régiment de cuirassiers, quelque pièces d'artillerie, et 1000 à 1200 hommes d'infanterie avaient pu arriver à l'appui du maréchal Bessières, le 14, cela lui aurait été d'un éminent secours. Q'importe que Valence soit soumis? Q'importe que Sarragosse soit soumis? Mais, général, le moindre succès de l'ennemi du côté de la Galice aurait des inconvéniens immenses. Instruit comme vous l'étiez des forces du général Cuesta, de la désertion de troupes d'Oporto, &a.... S. M. trouve que pour bién manœuvrer il aurait fallu vcus arranger de manière à avoir du 12e au 15e 8000 hommes pour renforcer le maréchal Bessières. Une fois nos derrières debarassées, et cette armée de Galice détruite, tout le reste tombe et se soumit de soi-même, &c. &c.

S.

EXTRAIT DE LA LETTRE, &c.

Bayonne, 13 Juillet, 1808.

Section 2.—Nous recevons vos lettres du 9e et du 10e, général. L'empereur me charge de vous faire connaître que si le général Gobert était à Valladolid, le général Frère à San Clemente ayant une colonne dans la Manche, si 300 à 400 convalescens, un bon commandant, 4 pièces de canon, un escouade d'artillerie, et vingt mille rations de biscuit étaient dans le château de Ségovie, la position de l'armée serait superbe et à l'abri de toute sollicitude. La conduite du général Frère ne parait pas claire. Let nouvelles qu'il a eues de maréchal Moncey paraissent apocryphes. Il est possible que ses 8000 hommes et son artillerie n'aient pas été suffisans pour enlever la ville de Valence. Cela étant, le maréchal Moncey ne l'enleverait pas d'avantage avec 20,000 hommes, parcequ'alors c'est une affaire de canons et de mortiers, &a. &a.... Valence est comme la Catalogne et l'Arragon; ces trois points sont secondaires. Les deux vrais points importans sont le général Dupont et particulièrement le maréchal Bessières, parceque le premier a devant lui le corps du camp de St. Roch et le corps de Cadiz, et le maréchal Bessières parcequ'il a devant lui les troupes de la Galice et celles qui etaient à Oporto. Le général Dupont a près de 20,000 hommes; il ne peut pas avoir contre lui un pareil nombre de troupes; il a déjà obtenu des succès très marquans, et au pis aller il ne peut être contraint qu'à repasser les montagnes, ce qui n'est qu'un événement de guerre. Le maréchal Bessières est beaucoup moins fort que le général Dupont, et les troupes Espagnoles d'Oporto et de la Galice sont plus nombreuses que celles de l'Andalousie, et les troupes de la Galice n'ont pas encore été entamées. Enfin le moindre insuccés du maréchal Bessières intercepte tous les communications de l'armée et compromettrait même sa sûreté. Le général Dupont se bat pour Andujar, et le maréchal Bessières se bat pour les communications de l'armée et pour les opérations les plus importans aux affaires d'Espagne, &c. &c.

S.

EXTRAIT DE LA LETTRE, &c. &c.

Bayonne, 18 Juillet, 1808, à dix heures du soir.

Section 3.—Je reçois, général, vos lettres du 14. L'aide-de-camp du maréchal Moncey a donné à sa majesté tous les détails sur ce qui s'est passé. La conduite du maréchal a été belle. Il a bien battu les rebelles en campagne. Il est tout simple qu'il n'ait pu entrer à Valence; c'étoit une affaire de mortiers et de pièces de siège. Sa position à San Clement est bonne, de là il est à même de remarcher sur Valence. De reste, général, l'affaire de Valence est une affaire du second ordre, même celle de Sarragosse, qui cependant est plus importante. L'affaire du maréchal Bessières était d'un intérêt majeur pour les affaires d'Espagne, et la première après cette affaire c'est celle du général Dupont, et c'est le moment de laisser le général Gobert suivre la route. Le maréchal Moncey se repose; le général Reille marche sur Gironne: ainsi trois colonnes pourront marcher ensemble sur Valence; le corps du général Reille, celui de Sarragosse, et celui du maréchal Moncey, ce qui formera les 20,000 hommes que ce maréchal croit nécessaire. Mais l'empereur, général, trouve que vous avez tort de dire qu'il n'y a rien été fait depuis six semaines. On a battu les rassemblemens de la Galice, de St. Ander, ceux d'Arragon et de Catalogne, qui dans leur aveuglement croyaient qu'ils n'avaient qu'à marcher pour détruire les Français: le maréchal Moncey, les généraux Duhesme, Dupont, Verdier, ont fait de bonne besogne, et tous les hommes sensés en Espagne ont changé dans le fonds de leur opinion, et voient avec la plus grande peine l'insurrection. Au reste, général, les affaires d'Espagne sont dans la situation la plus prospère depuis la bataille de Medina del Rio Seco, &c. &c. Le 14e et le 44e arrivent demain; après demain ils partent pour le camp de Sarragosse; non pas que ces troupes puissent avancer la reddition, qui est une affaire de canon, mais elles serviraient contre les insurgés de Valence, s'ils voulaient renforcer ceux de Sarragosse. Enfin, si le général Gobert et les détachemens qui sont à moitié chemin pour rejoindre le général Dupont font juger à ce général qu'il a des forces suffisantes pour battre le général Castaños, il faut qu'elles continuent leur direction, et qu'il attaque l'ennemi, s'il croit devoir le faire, &a. &a.

(Cette lettre a été ecrite le jour de la bataille de Baylen.)

EXTRAIT DE LA LETTRE, &a.

Bourdeaux, 3 Août, 1818.

Section 4.—Les événemens du général Dupont sont une chose sans exemple, et la rédaction de sa capitulation est de niveau avec la conduite tenue jusqu'à cette catastrophe. L'empereur pense qu'on n'a pas tenue compte du vague de la rédaction de l'acte, en permettant que les corps en échellons sur la communication entre vous et le général Dupont aient marché pour se rendre aux Anglais: car on ne doit pas presumer qu'ils aient la loyauté de laisser passer les troupes qui s'embarquent. Comme vous ne parlez pas de cela, on pense que vous avez retiré ces échellons sur Madrid. Après avoir lu attentivement la rélation du général Dupont, on voit qu'il n'a capitulé que le lendemain de la bataille, et que les corps des généraux Vedel et Dufour, qui se trouvent compris pour quelque chose dans la capitulation (on ne sait pourquoi), ne se sont pas battus. Par la relation même du général Dupont, tout laisse penser que l'armée du général Castaños n'était pas à beaucoup près aussi forte qu'on le dit, et qu'il avait réuni à Baylen tout ce qu'il avait de forces. S. M. ne lui calcule pas plus de 25,000 hommes de troupes de ligne et plus de 15,000 paysans. Par la lettre du général Belliard il parait que l'ordre est donné de lever le siège de Sarragosse, ce qui serait prématuré; car vous comprendrez qu'il n'est pas possible qu'on ne laisse un corps d'armée, qui couvre Pampelune, et contienne la Navarre, sans quoi l'ennemi peut cerner Pampelune, insurger la Navarre, et alors la communication de France par Tolosa serait coupée, et l'ennemi sur les derrières de l'armée. Supposant l'ennemi réuni à Pampelune, la ville bloquée, il peut se trouver en cinq à six marches sur les derrières de Burgos. L'armée qui assiège Sarragosse est donc à-peu-près nécessaire pour contenir la Navarre, les insurgés de l'Arragon et de Valence, et pour empêcher de percer sur nôtre flanc gauche; car si, comme le dit le général Belliard, le général Verdier se porte avec ses troupes à Logroño, en jetant 2000 hommes dans Pampelune, la communication de Bayonne, qu'eut sur le champ être interceptée le général Verdier, serait mieux à Tudela qu'à Logroño. Si le général Castaños s'avance, et que vous puissiez lui livrer la bataille, on ne peut en prévoir que les plus heureux résultats: mais de la manière dont il a marché vis-à-vis du général Dupont, tout donne à croire qu'il mettra la plus grande circonspection dans ses mouvemens. Si par le canal des parlementaires l'on peut établir une suspension d'armes sans que le roi y soit pour rien en apparence, cette espèce d'armistice pourrait se rompre en se prévenant de part et d'autre huit jours d'avance, donnant aux Français la ligne du Duero passant par Almazan pour joindre l'Ebre. Cette suspension d'armes, que les insurgés pourraient regarder comme avantageuse, afin de s'organiser à Madrid ne nous serait pas défavorable, parcequ'on verrait pendant ce temps l'organisation que prendraient les parties insurgés de l'Espagne, et ce que veut la nation, &c. &c.

LE MAJOR GÉNÉRAL AU ROI D'ESPAGNE.

Nantes, 11 Août, 1808.

Section 5.—Sire, le général Savary ni vos ministres Azanza et Urquijo ne sont arrivés: il parait qu'il y a des rassemblemens à Bilbao d'après les nouvelles que nous recevons. S. M. pense qu'il est important d'y faire marcher le plutôt possible une colonne pour y rétablir l'ordre. V. M. sait que la moitié de Sarragosse était en nôtre pouvoir, et que sous peu on esperait avoir le reste de la ville. Lorsque le général Belliard a donné l'ordre de lever le siège, il eût été à désirer que cet ordre fut conditionnel, comme cela paraissait être l'intention de V. M., ainsi qu'on le voit dans sa correspondance; c'est à dire, que le siège ne fut levé que dans le cas où l'on n'aurait pas cru être maître de la ville avant cinq ou six jours. Cela aurait présenté des circonstances meilleurs; car si le général Verdier évacu en entier la Navarre et l'Arragon, il est à craindre que la Navarre ne s'insurge, et Pampelune ne tarderait pas à être cernée. J'ai mandé à V. M. que déjà des corps entiers de la grande armée sont en mouvement pour se rendre en poste en Espagne. Les dispositions les plus vigoureuses sont prises de tous côtés, et dans six semaines ou deux mois l'Espagne sera soumise. L'empereur, qui continue à jouir d'une bonne santé, quoiqu'il soit très occupé, part dans une heure pour continuer sa route sur Angers, Tours, et Paris. V. M. doit être persuadée que toutes nos pensées sont sur elle et sur l'armée qu'elle commande.

No. VIII

LETTER FROM MR. DRUMMOND TO SIR ALEXANDER BALL.

Palermo, July 4th, 1808.

MY DEAR SIR,

His highness the duke of Orleans has applied to me to write to you on a subject about which he appears to be extremely interested. I take it for granted that you are acquainted with all the events which have lately happened in Spain. The duke thinks that the appearance of a member of the house of Bourbon in that country might be acceptable to the Spaniards, and of great service to the common cause. In this I perfectly concur with his highness, and if you be of the same opinion you will probably have no objection to send a ship here to carry his highness to Gibraltar. He himself is exceedingly sanguine. We have letters from London down to the 5th of June. Portugal has followed the example of Spain, and Lisbon is probably now in other hands: an invitation has been sent to sir Charles Cotton.

(Signed) William Drummond.

P.S. "* * *"

MR. DRUMMOND TO SIR HEW DALRYMPLE.

Palermo, July 24th, 1808.

DEAR SIR,

This letter will be delivered to you by his royal highness prince Leopold, second son of the king of the Two Sicilies. This prince goes immediately to Gibraltar to communicate immediately with the loyal Spaniards, and to notify to them that his father will accept the regency, if they desire it, until his nephew Ferdinand the Seventh be delivered from captivity. Don Leopold and his cousin the duke of Orleans will offer themselves as soldiers to the Spaniards, and will accept such situations as may be given to them suitable to their illustrious rank. If their visit should not be acceptable to the Spaniards, don Leopold will return to Sicily, and his serene highness the duke of Orleans will proceed to England. Being of opinion that the appearance of an infant of Spain may be of the greatest utility at the present crisis, and in all events can hardly be productive of harm, I have urged his Sicilian majesty to determine upon this measure, which I conceive to be required at his hands, in consequence of the manifesto of Palafox, which you have probably seen. At the distance of 1000 miles, however, we cannot be supposed to be accurately informed here of many circumstances with which you probably may be intimately acquainted; prince Leopold therefore will be directed to consult with you, and to follow your advice, which I have no doubt you will readily and cheerfully give him. I take the liberty at the same time of recommending him to your care and protection.

(Signed) Wm. Drummond.

EXTRACT OF A LETTER FROM SIR HEW DALRYMPLE TO LORD CASTLEREAGH.

Gibraltar, August 10th, 1808.

MY LORD,

Last night the Thunderer arrived here, having on board the duke of Orleans, the second prince of the Two Sicilies, and a considerable number of noblemen and others, the suite of the latter. As the ship came to anchor at a late hour, I had not the honour of seeing the duke of Orleans until near ten at night, when he came accompanied by captain Talbot. The duke first put into my hands a letter from Mr. Drummond, as captain Talbot did a despatch from sir Alexander Ball, copies of which I have the honour to enclose. As the latter seemed bulky, I did not immediately open it, and therefore did not immediately remark that sir Alexander Ball did not seem aware that the prince of the Two Sicilies was coming down, much less that he meditated establishing his residence at Gibraltar for the avowed purpose of negotiating for the regency of Spain. Of this object the duke of Orleans made no mystery, and proceeded to arrange the time and manner of the prince's reception in the morning, and the accommodation that should be prepared for him, suited to his rank, and capable of containing his attendants. I took early occasion first to remark the ill effect this measure might produce in Spain at the moment when the establishment of a central government had become obviously necessary, and would naturally lead to much intrigue and disunion, until the sentiments of the people and the armies (which would naturally assemble for the purpose of expelling the enemy from their territory) should be pronounced....

EXTRACT OF A LETTER FROM LORD CASTLEREAGH TO SIR HEW DALRYMPLE.

Downing Street, Nov. 4th, 1808.

"I have great pleasure, however, in assuring you that the measures pursued by you on that delicate and important subject" (the unexpected arrival of prince Leopold and the duke of Orleans at Gibraltar) "received his majesty's entire approbation."

* * *

(Signed) Castlereagh.

No. IX

SIR A. WELLESLEY TO SIR HARRY BURRARD.

Head-quarters, at Lavos, August 8th, 1808.

SIR,

Having received instructions from the secretary of state that you were likely to arrive on the coast of Portugal with a corps of 10,000 men, lately employed in the north of Europe under the orders of sir John Moore, I now submit to you such information as I have received regarding the general state of the war in Portugal and Spain, and the plan of operations which I am about to carry into execution.

The enemy's force at present in Portugal consists, as far as I am able to form an opinion, of from 16,000 to 18,000 men, of which number there are about 500 in the fort of Almeida, about the same number in Elvas, about 6 or 800 in Peniché, and 16 or 1800 in the province of Alemtejo, at Setuval, &c.; and the remainder are disposable for the defence of Lisbon, and are in the forts of St. Julian and Cascaes, in the batteries along the coast as far as the Rock of Lisbon, and the old citadel of Lisbon, to which the enemy have lately added some works.

Of the force disposable for the defence of Lisbon, the enemy have lately detached a corps of about 2000, under general Thomieres, principally I believe to watch my movements, which corps is now at Alcobaça; and another corps of 4000 men, under gen[l]. Loison, was sent across the Tagus into Alemtejo on the 26th of last month, the object of which detachment was to disperse the Portuguese insurgents in that quarter, to force the Spanish corps, consisting of about 2000 men, which had advanced into Portugal as far as Evora from Estremadura, to retire, and then to be enabled to add to the force destined for the defence of Lisbon the corps of French troops which had been stationed at Setuval and in the province of Alemtejo; at all events Loison's corps will return to Lisbon, and the French corps disposable for the defence of that place will probably be about 14,000 men, of which at least 3000 must be left in the garrisons and forts on the coast and in the river.

The French army under Dupont, in Andalusia, surrendered on the 20th of last month to the Spanish army under Castaños; so that there are now no French troops in the south of Spain. The Spanish army of Gallicia and Castille, to the northward, received a check at Rio Seco, in the province of Valladolid, on the 14th of July, from a French corps supposed to be under the command of general Bessieres, which had advanced from Burgos.

The Spanish troops retired on the 15th to Benevente, and I understand there has since been an affair between the advanced posts in that neighbourhood, but I am not certain of it; nor am I acquainted with the position of the Spanish army, or of that of the French, since the 14th July. When you will have been a short time in this country, and will have observed the degree to which the deficiency of real information is supplied by the circulation of unfounded reports, you will not be surprised at my want of accurate knowledge on these subjects.

It is however certain that nothing of importance has occurred in that quarter since the 14th July; and from this circumstance I conclude that the corps called Bessieres attacked the Spanish army at Rio Seco solely with a view to cover the march of king Joseph Buonaparte to Madrid, where he arrived on the 21st July. Besides their defeat in Andalusia, the enemy, as you may probably have heard, have been beat off in an attack upon Sarragossa, in Arragon, in another upon the city of Valencia (in both of which it is said that they have lost many men); and it is reported that in Catalonia two of their detachments have been cut off, and that they have lost the fort of Figueras in the Pyrenees, and that Barcelona is blockaded. Of these last-mentioned actions and operations I have seen no official accounts, but the report of them is generally circulated and believed; and at all events, whether these reports are founded or otherwise, it is obvious that the insurrection against the French is general throughout Spain; that large bodies of Spaniards are in arms; amongst others, in particular, an army of 20,000 men, including 4000 cavalry, at Almaraz on the Tagus in Estremadura, and that the French cannot carry on their operations by means of small corps. I should imagine from their inactivity, and from the misfortunes they have suffered, that they have not the means of collecting a force sufficiently large to oppose the progress of the insurrection and the efforts of the insurgents, and to afford supplies to their different detached corps, or that they find that they cannot carry on their operations with armies so numerous as they must find it necessary to employ without magazines.

In respect to Portugal, the whole kingdom, with the exception of the neighbourhood of Lisbon, is in a state of insurrection against the French; their means of resistance are, however, less powerful than those of the Spaniards, their troops had been completely dispersed, their officers had gone off to the Brazils, and their arsenals pillaged, or in the power of the enemy, and their revolt under the circumstances in which it has taken place is still more extraordinary than that of the Spanish nation.

The Portuguese may have in the northern part of the kingdom about 10,000 men in arms, of which number 5000 are to march with me towards Lisbon. The remainder, with a Spanish detachment of about 1500 men which came from Gallicia, are employed in a distant blockade of Almeida, and in the protection of Oporto, which is now the seat of government.

The insurrection is general throughout Alemtejo and Algarve to the southward, and Entre Minho et Douero and Trasasmontes and Beira to the northward; but for want of arms the people can do nothing against the enemy.

Having consulted sir C. Cotton, it appeared to him and to me that the attack proposed upon Cascaes bay was impracticable, because the bay is well defended by the fort of Cascaes and the other works constructed for its defence, and the ships of war could not approach sufficiently near to silence them. The landing in the Passa d'Arcos in the Tagus could not be effected without silencing fort St. Julian, which appeared to be impracticable to those who were to carry that operation into execution.

There are small bays within which might admit of landing troops, and others to the northward of the rock of Lisbon, but they are all defended by works which must have been silenced; they are of small extent, and but few men could have landed at the same time. There is always a surf on them which affects the facility of landing at different times so materially, as to render it very doubtful whether the troops first landed could be supported in sufficient time by others, and whether the horses for the artillery and cavalry, and the necessary stores and provisions could be landed at all. These inconveniences attending a landing in any of the bays near the rock of Lisbon would have been aggravated by the neighbourhood of the enemy to the landing-place, and by the exhausted state of the country in which the troops would have been landed. It was obviously the best plan, therefore, to land in the northern parts of Portugal, and I fixed upon Mondego bay as the nearest place which afforded any facility for landing, excepting Peniché, the landing-place of which peninsula is defended by a fort occupied by the enemy, which it would be necessary to attack regularly in order to place the ships in safety.

A landing to the northward was farther recommended, as it would ensure the co-operation of the Portuguese troops in the expedition to Lisbon. The whole of the corps placed under my command, including those under the command of general Spencer, having landed, I propose to march on Wednesday, and I shall take the road by Alcobaça and Obidos, with a view to keep up my communication by the sea-coast, and to examine the situation of Peniché, and I shall proceed towards Lisbon by the route of Mafra, and by the hills to the northward of that city.

As I understand from the secretary of state that a body of troops under the command of brigadier-general Ackland may be expected on the coast of Portugal before you arrive, I have written to desire he will proceed from hence along the coast of Portugal to the southward; and I propose to communicate with him by the means of captain Bligh of the Alfred, who will attend the movements of the army with a few transports, having on board provisions and military stores. I intend to order brigadier-general Ackland to attack Peniché, if I should find it necessary to obtain possession of that place, and if not, I propose to order him to join the fleet stationed off the Tagus, with a view to disembark in one of the bays near the rock of

Lisbon as soon as I shall approach sufficiently near to enable him to perform that operation. If I imagined that general Ackland's corps was equipped in such a manner as to be enabled to move from the coast, I should have directed him to land at Mondego, and to march upon Santarem, from which station he would have been at hand either to assist my operations, or to cut off the retreat of the enemy, if he should endeavour to make it either by the north of the Tagus and Almeida, or by the south of the Tagus and Elvas; but as I am convinced that general Ackland's corps is intended to form a part of some other corps which is provided with a commissariat, that he will have none with him, and consequently that his corps must depend upon the country; and as no reliance can be placed upon the resources of this country, I have considered it best to direct the general's attention to the sea-coast; if, however, the command of the army remained in my hands, I should certainly land the corps which has lately been under the command of sir John Moore at Mondego, and should move it upon Santarem. I have the honour to enclose a return of the troops, &c. &c.

(Signed) Arthur Wellesley.

SIR ARTHUR WELLESLEY TO SIR HARRY BURRARD.

Camp at Lugar, 8 miles north of Lerya, August 10, 1808.

SIR,

Since I wrote to you on the 8th inst. I have received letters from Mr. Stuart and colonel Doyle at Corunna, of which I enclose copies. From them you will learn the state of the war in that part of Spain, and you will observe that Mr. Stuart and colonel Doyle are of opinion that marshal Bessieres will take advantage of the inefficiency of the Gallician army under general Blake to detach a corps to Portugal to the assistance of general Junot; we have not heard yet of that detachment, and I am convinced it will not be made till king Joseph Buonaparte will either be reinforced to such a degree as to be in safety in Madrid, or till he shall have effected his retreat into France, with which view it is reported that he left Madrid on the 29th of last month.

I conceive, therefore, that I have time for the operations which I propose to carry on before a reinforcement can arrive from Leon, even supposing that no obstacles would be opposed to its march in Spain or Portugal; but it is not probable that it can arrive before the different reinforcements will arrive from England; and as marshal Bessieres had not more than 20,000 men in the action at Rio Seco on the 14th July, I conceive that the British troops, which will be in Portugal, will be equal to contend with any part of that corps which he may detach.

The possibility that, in the present state of affairs, the French corps at present in Portugal may be reinforced, affords an additional reason for taking the position of Santarem, which I apprised you in my letter of the 8th I should occupy, if the command of the army remained in my hands after the reinforcements should arrive. If you should occupy it, you will not only be in the best situation to support my operations, and to cut off the retreat of the enemy, but if any reinforcements of French troops should enter Portugal, you will be in the best situation to collect your whole force to oppose him, &c. &c.

(Signed) Arthur Wellesley.

No. X

ARTICLES OF THE DEFINITIVE CONVENTION FOR THE EVACUATION OF PORTUGAL BY THE FRENCH ARMY.

The generals commanding in chief, &c. &c. being determined to negotiate, &c. &c.

Article 1. All the places and forts in the kingdom of Portugal occupied by the French troops shall be given up to the British army in the state in which they are at the period of the signature of the present convention.

Art. 2. The French troops shall evacuate Portugal with their arms and baggage, they shall not be considered as prisoners of war, and on their arrival in France they shall be at liberty to serve.

Art. 3. The English government shall furnish the means of conveyance for the French army, which shall be disembarked in any of the ports of France between Rochefort and L'Orient inclusively.

Art. 4. The French army shall carry with it all its artillery of French calibre, with the horses belonging thereunto, and the tumbrils supplied with 60 rounds per gun: all other artillery, arms, and ammunition, as also the military and naval arsenals, shall be given up to the British army and navy, in the state in which they may be at the period of the ratification of the convention.

Art. 5. The French army shall carry with it all its equipments, and all that is comprehended under the name of property of the army; that is to say, its military chest, and carriages attached to the field commissariat and field hospital; or shall be allowed to dispose of such part of the same on its account, as the commander-in-chief may judge it unnecessary to embark. In like manner, all individuals of the army shall be at liberty to dispose of their private property of every description, with full security hereafter for the purchasers.

Art. 6. The cavalry are to embark their horses, as also the generals and other officers of all ranks. It is however fully understood that the means of conveyance for horses, at the disposal of the British commanders, are very limited; some additional conveyance may be procured in the port of Lisbon. The number of horses to be embarked by the troops shall not exceed 600, and the number embarked by the staff shall not exceed 200. At all events every facility will be given to the French army to dispose of the horses belonging to it which cannot be embarked.

Art. 7. In order to facilitate the embarkation, it shall take place in three divisions, the last of which will be principally composed of the garrisons of the places, of the cavalry, the artillery, the sick, and the equipment of the army. The first division shall embark within seven days of the date of the ratification, or sooner if possible.

Art. 8. The garrison of Elvas and its forts, and of Peniché and Palmela, will be embarked at Lisbon. That of Almeida at Oporto, or the nearest harbour. They will be accompanied on their march by British commissaries, charged with providing for their subsistence and accommodation.

Art. 9. All the sick and wounded who cannot be embarked with the troops are intrusted to the British army. They are to be taken care of whilst they remain in this country at the expense of the British government, under the condition of the same being reimbursed by France when the final evacuation is effected. The English government will provide for their return to France, which will take place by detachments of about one hundred and fifty or two hundred men at a time. A sufficient number of French medical officers shall be left behind to attend them.

Art. 10. As soon as the vessels employed to carry the army to France shall have disembarked in the harbours specified, or in any other of the ports of France to which stress of weather may force them, every facility shall be given them to return to England without delay, and security against capture until their arrival in a friendly port.

Art. 11. The French army shall be concentrated in Lisbon, and within a distance of about two leagues from it. The English army will approach within three leagues of the capital, and will be so placed as to leave about one league between the two armies.

Art. 12. The forts of St. Julien, the Bugio, and Cascaes, shall be occupied by the British troops on the ratification of the convention. Lisbon and its citadel, together with the forts and batteries as far as the lazaretto or Trafaria on one side, and fort St. Joseph on the other, inclusively, shall be given up on the embarkation of the 2d division; as shall also the harbour and all armed vessels in it of every description, with their rigging, sails, stores, and ammunition. The fortresses of Elvas, Almeida, Peniché, and Palmela, shall be given up as soon as the British troops can arrive to occupy them. In the meantime the general-in-chief of the British army will give notice of the present convention to the garrisons of those places, as also to the troops before them, in order to put a stop to all further hostilities.

Art. 13. Commissioners shall be named on both sides to regulate and accelerate the execution of the arrangements agreed upon.

Art. 14. Should there arise doubts as to the meaning of any article, it will be explained favourably to the French army.

Art. 15. From the date of the ratification of the present convention, all arrears of contributions, requisitions, or claims whatever, of the French government against subjects of Portugal, or any other individuals residing in this country, founded on the occupation of Portugal by the French troops, in the month of December, 1807, which may not have been paid up, are cancelled; and all sequestration laid upon their property, moveable or immoveable, are removed, and the free disposal of the same is restored to the proper owners.

Art. 16. All subjects of France, or of powers in friendship or alliance, domiciliated in Portugal, or accidentally in this country, shall be protected; their property of every kind, moveable and immoveable, shall be respected; and they shall be at liberty either to accompany the French army or to remain in Portugal. In either case their property is guaranteed to them, with the liberty of retaining or of disposing of it, and passing the produce of the sale thereof into France, or any other country where they may fix their residence; the space of one year being allowed them for that purpose. It is fully understood that shipping is excepted from this arrangement, only however in as far as regards leaving the port, and that none of the stipulations above mentioned can be made the pretext of any commercial speculations.

Art. 17. No native of Portugal shall be rendered accountable for his political conduct during the period of the occupation of this country by the French army; and all those who have continued in the exercise of their employments, or who have accepted situations under the French government, are placed under the protection of the British commanders; they shall sustain no injury in their persons or property; it not having been at their option to be obedient or not to the French government, they are also at liberty to avail themselves of the stipulations of the 16th article.

Art. 18. The Spanish troops detained on board ship, in the port of Lisbon, shall be given up to the commander-in-chief of the British army, who engages to obtain of the Spaniards to restore such French subjects, either military or civil, as may have been detained in Spain without having been taken in battle, or in consequence of military operations, but on occasion of the occurrences of the 29th of last May, and the days immediately following.

Art. 19. There shall be an immediate exchange established for all ranks of prisoners made in Portugal since the commencement of the present hostilities.

Art. 20. Hostages of the rank of field officers shall be mutually furnished, on the part of the British army and navy, and on that of the French army, for the reciprocal guarantee of the present convention. The officer of the British army shall be restored on the completion of the articles which concern the army; and the officer of the navy on the disembarkation of the French troops in their own country. The like is to take place on the part of the French army.

Art. 21. It shall be allowed to the general-in-chief of the French army to send an officer to France with intelligence of the present convention. A vessel will be furnished by the British admiral to convey him to Bourdeaux or Rochefort.

Art. 22. The British admiral will be invited to accommodate his excellency the commander-in-chief and the other principal officers of the French army on board ships of war.

Done and concluded at Lisbon this 30th day of August, 1808.

(Signed) George Murray, quarter-master-general.
Kellerman, le général de division.

ADDITIONAL ARTICLES.

Art. 1. The individuals in the civil employment of the army, made prisoners either by the British troops or by the Portuguese, in any part of Portugal, will be restored, as is customary, without exchange.

Art. 2. The French army shall be subsisted from its own magazines up to the day of embarkation. The garrisons up to the day of the evacuation of the fortresses. The remainder of the magazines shall be delivered over in the usual forms to the British government, which charges itself with the subsistence of the men and horses of the army from the above mentioned periods till their arrival in France, under the condition of being reimbursed by the French government for the excess of the expense beyond the estimation to be made by both parties, of the value of the magazines delivered up to the British army. The provisions on board the ships of war in the possession of the French army will be taken on account by the British government, in like manner with the magazines of the fortresses.

Art. 3. The general commanding the British troops will take the necessary measures for re-establishing the free circulation of the means of subsistence between the country and the capital.

Done and concluded at Lisbon this 30th day of August, 1808.

(Signed) George Murray, quarter-master-general.
Kellerman, le général de division.

Ratified, &c. &c.

No. XI

1st. LETTER FROM BARON VON DECKEN TO THE GENERAL COMMANDING THE ARMY IN PORTUGAL.

Oporto, August 18th, 1808.

SIR,

The bishop of Oporto having expressed to me his wish to see me in private, in order to make me an important communication, which he desired to be kept secret, I went to his palace last night at a late hour. The bishop told me that he had taken the government of Portugal in his hands to satisfy the wish of the people, but with the intention to re-establish the government of his lawful sovereign; and he hoped that his majesty the king of Great Britain had no other point in view in sending troops to this country. After having given him all possible assurance on that head, the bishop continued, that as the prince regent, in leaving Portugal, had established a regency for the government of this country during his absence, he considered it his duty to resign the government into the hands of that regency as soon as possible. My answer was, that I had no instruction from my government on that head, but that I begged him to consider whether the cause of his sovereign would not be hurt in resigning the government into the hands of a regency which, from its having acted under the influence of the French, had lost the confidence of the nation, and whether it would not be more advisable for him to keep the government until the pleasure of the prince regent was known. The bishop allowed that the regency appointed by the prince regent did not possess the confidence of the people, that several members of it had acted in such a manner as to show themselves as friends and partisans of the French, and that, at all events, all the members of the late regency could not be re-established in their former power; but he was afraid that the provinces of Estramadura, Alemtejo, and Algarvé, would not acknowledge his authority if the British government did not interfere. After a very long conversation, it was agreed that I should inform our ministers with what the bishop had communicated to me, and in order to lose no time in waiting for an answer, the bishop desired me to communicate the same to you, expressing a wish that you would be pleased to write to him an official letter, in order to express your desire that he might continue the government until the pleasure of his sovereign was known, for the sake of the operations of the British and Portuguese troops under your command.

The secretary of the bishop, who acted as interpreter, told me afterwards in private, that the utmost confusion would arise from the bishop resigning the government at this moment, or associating with people who were neither liked nor esteemed by the nation.

I beg leave to add, that although the bishop expressed the contrary, yet it appeared to me that he was not averse to his keeping the government in his hands, if it could be done by the interference of our government. I have the honour to be, &c. &c.

(Signed) Frederick Von Decken, brig. gen.

2d. DITTO TO DITTO.

Oporto, August 22, 1808.

SIR,

Your excellency will have received the secret letter which I had the honour to send you by brigadier-general Stuart, on the 18th, respecting the communication of his excellency the bishop of Oporto relative to his resignation of the government into the hands of the regency established by the prince regent.—In addition to what I have had the honour to state upon that subject, I beg leave to add, that his excellency the bishop has this day desired me to make your excellency aware, in case it might be wished that he should keep the government in his hands until the pleasure of the prince regent may be known, that he could not leave Oporto; and the seat of government must in that case necessarily remain in this town. His excellency the bishop thinks it his duty to inform you of this circumstance as soon as possible, as he foresees that the city of Lisbon will be preferred for the seat of government, as soon as the British army have got possession of it. If the seat of the temporary government should remain at Oporto, the best method to adopt with respect to the other provinces of Portugal appears to be, to cause them to send deputies to that place for the purpose of transacting business relative to their own provinces; in the same manner as the provinces of Entre Douro y Minho and Tras los Montes now send their representatives. One of the principal reasons why his excellency the bishop can only accede to continue at the head of the government under the condition of remaining at Oporto is, because he is persuaded that the inhabitants of this town will not permit him to leave it, unless by order of the prince regent. It might also be advisable to keep the seat of government at Oporto, as it may be supposed that Lisbon will be in a state of great confusion for the first two months after the French have left it. I have the honour to be, sir, &c. &c.

(Signed) Frederick Von Decken, brig. gen.

3d.

Oporto, August 28.

SIR,

Your excellency will have received my secret letters of the 18th and 22d instant relative to the temporary government of this kingdom. His excellency the bishop of Oporto has received lately deputies from the province of Alemtejo and the kingdom of Algarve. Part of Estremadura, viz. the town of Leria has also submitted to his authority, and it may be therefore said that the whole kingdom of Portugal has acknowledged the authority of the temporary government, of which the bishop of Oporto is at the head, with the exception of Lisbon and the town of Setubal (St. Ubes). Although the reasons why these towns have not yet acknowledged the authority of the temporary government may be explained by their being in possession of the French, yet the bishop is convinced that the inhabitants of Lisbon will refuse to submit to the temporary government of Oporto, in which they will be strongly supported by the members of the former regency established by the prince regent, who of course will be very anxious to resume their former power. The bishop in assuming the temporary government complied only with the wishes of the people: he was sure that it was the only means of saving the country; but having had no interest of his own in view, he is willing to resign the authority which he has accepted with reluctance, as soon as he is convinced that it can be done without hurting the cause of his sovereign, and throwing the country into confusion. There is every reason to apprehend that the inhabitants of the three northern provinces of Portugal will never permit the bishop to resign the government, and submit to the former regency. They feel extremely proud of having first taken to arms, and consider themselves as the deliverers and saviours of their country; and as the inhabitants of Lisbon will be as much disinclined to submit to the temporary government of Oporto; a division of the provinces, which will excite internal commotion, will naturally follow, if not supported by your excellency. It has appeared to me that the best way to reconcile these opposite parties would be in endeavouring to unite the present government at Oporto with such of the members of the former regency who have not forfeited by their conduct the confidence of the people; and having opened my idea to the bishop, his answer was, that he would not object to it if proposed by you. I therefore take the liberty of suggesting, that the difficulty above mentioned would be in a great measure removed if your excellency would be pleased to make it known after Lisbon has surrendered, that until the pleasure of the prince regent was known, you would consider the temporary government established at Oporto as the lawful government, with the addition of the four members of the late regency, who have been pointed out to me by the bishop as such who have behaved faithfully to their sovereign and country; viz. don Francisco Noronha, Francisco da Cunha, the Monteiro Mor, and the principal Castro. These members to be placed at the head of the different departments, and to consider the bishop as the president, whose directions they are to follow, a plan which will meet with the less difficulty, as the president of the former regency, named by the prince regent, has quitted Portugal, and is now in France. The circumstance that Lisbon is now in a state of the greatest confusion will furnish a fair pretext for fixing the seat of the temporary government in the first instance at Oporto, to which place the gentlemen above named would be ordered to repair without loss of time, and to report themselves to the bishop. Independent of the reasons which I had the honour of stating to your excellency in my letter of the 22d instant, why it is impossible for the bishop to leave Oporto, I must beg leave to add, that, from what I understand, the greater part of the inhabitants of Lisbon are in the French interest, and that it will require a garrison of British troops to keep that city in order. The bishop of Oporto, although convinced of the necessity of considering Lisbon at present as a military station, and of placing a British commandant and a British garrison there, yet from a desire that the feelings of the inhabitants might be wounded as little as possible, wishes that you would be pleased to put also some Portuguese troops in garrison at Lisbon, together with a Portuguese commandant, who, though entirely under the orders of the British governor, might direct the police in that town, or at least be charged with putting into execution such orders as he may receive from the British governor under that head. If your excellency should be pleased to approve of this proposal, the bishop thinks brigadier Antonio Pinto Bacelar to be the properest officer of those who are now with the Portuguese army to be stationed at Lisbon, and who might also be directed to organise the military force of the province of Estremadura. The bishop is fully convinced that the temporary government of the country cannot exist without the support of British troops: he hopes that our government will leave a corps of 6000 men in Portugal after the French have been subdued, until the Portuguese troops may be sufficiently organised and disciplined to be able to protect their own government. I have the honour to be, sir, your most obedient and humble servant,

Frederick Von Decken, brig. gen.

No. XII

(Translation.)

LETTER FROM GENERAL LEITE TO SIR HEW DALRYMPLE.

MOST ILLUSTRIOUS AND MOST EXCELLENT SIR,

Strength is the result of union, and those who have reason to be grateful should be most urgent in their endeavours to promote it. I therefore feel it to be my duty to have recourse to your excellency to know how I should act without disturbing the union so advantageous to my country. The supreme junta of the Portuguese government established at Oporto, which I have hitherto obeyed as the representatives of my sovereign, have sent me orders by an officer, dated the 1st instant, to take possession of the fortress of Elvas as soon as it shall be evacuated. After having seen those same Spaniards who got possession of our strong places as friends, take so much upon themselves as even to prevent the march of the garrison which I had ordered to replace the losses sustained in the battle of Evora, which deprived me of the little obedience that was shown by the city of Beja, always favoured by the Spanish authorities; after having seen the Portuguese artillery which was saved after the said battle taken possession of by those same Spaniards, who had lost their own, without being willing even to lend me two three-pounders to enable me to join his excellency the Monteiro Mor; after having the arms which were saved from the destructive grasp of the common enemy made use of by those same Spaniards, who promised much and did nothing; after having seen a Spanish brigadier dispute my authority at Campo Mayor, where I was president of the junta, and from whence his predecessor had taken away 60,000 crowns without rendering any account; in a word, after having seen the march of these Spaniards marked by the devastation of our fields, and the country deserted to avoid the plunder of their light troops, I cannot for a moment mistake the cause of the orders given by the supreme junta of Oporto. A corps of English troops having yesterday passed Estremos, on their road to Elvas, knowing that in a combined army no officer should undertake any operation which may be intended for others, thereby counteracting each other, I consulted lieutenant-general Herre (Hope), who has referred me to your excellency, to whom in consequence I send lieut.-colonel the marquis of Terney, my quarter-master-general, that he may deliver you this letter, and explain verbally every thing you may wish to know which relates to my sovereign and the good of my country, already so much indebted to the English nation.

God preserve your excellency many years.

(Signed) Francisco de Paulo Leite, lieut.-general.

(Dated) *Estremos, 16th September, 1808.*

To the most illustrious and most excellent sir Hew Dalrymple.

EXTRACT OF A LETTER FROM SIR HEW DALRYMPLE TO LIEUTENANT-GENERAL SIR JOHN HOPE.

Head-quarters, Benefico, 25th Sept. 1808.

SIR,

Impediments having arisen to the fulfilment of that article of the convention which relates to the cession of Elvas by the French to the British army, in consequence of the unexpected and unaccountable conduct of the commander in chief of the army of Estremadura, in bombarding that place, and endeavouring to impose upon the French garrison terms of capitulation different from those which were agreed upon by the British and French generals in chief; and as the British corps sent to take possession of the above fortress, and to hold it in the name of the prince regent until reinforced by a body of Portuguese troops, is not of sufficient strength to preclude the possibility of insult, should the general above mentioned persevere in the contemptuous and hostile disposition he has hitherto shown; I have therefore thought it advisable to order the remainder of your division, and general Paget's advanced guard, to cross the Tagus, and to occupy cantonments as near as possible to the place above mentioned. In the mean time colonel Graham is gone to Badajos to expostulate with general Galluzzo on the singular and very inexplicable line of conduct he has seen cause to adopt....

No. XIII

JUSTIFICATORY EXTRACTS FROM SIR JOHN MOORE'S AND OTHER CORRESPONDENCE.

SECTION I. – RELATING TO WANT OF MONEY.

Sir John Moore to lord William Bentinck, October 22, 1808.

"Sir David Baird has unfortunately been sent out without money. He has applied to me, and I have none to give him." ... "I undertake my march in the hope that some will arrive; if it does not, it will add to the number of a great many distresses."

Sir John Moore to general Hope, October 22, 1808.

"Baird has sent his aide-de-camp Gordon to me: he is without money, and his troops only paid to September. He can get none at Coruña."

Sir John Moore to sir David Baird, October 22, 1808.

"We are in such want of money at this place that it is with difficulty I have been able to spare 800*l*., which went to you in the Champion this day."

Sir John Moore to lord Castlereagh, October 27.

"It is upon the general assurance of the Spanish government that I am leading the army into Spain without any established magazines. In this situation nothing is more essentially requisite than money, and unfortunately we have been able to procure very little here."

Sir John Moore to Mr. Frere, November 10, 1808.

"I understand from sir David Baird that you were kind enough to lend him 40,000*l*. from the money you brought with you from England. We are in the greatest distress for money. I doubt if there is wherewithal after the 24th of this month to pay the troops their subsistence."

Sir John Moore to lord Castlereagh, Nov. 24, 1808.

"I am without a shilling of money to pay, and I am in daily apprehension that from the want of it our supplies will be stopped. It is impossible to describe the embarrassments we are thrown into from the want of that essential article."

SECTION II. — RELATING TO ROADS.

Sir John Moore to general Anstruther, at Almeida, dated Lisbon, October 12, 1808.

"A division under Beresford is marching upon Coimbra, and a part of it will proceed on to Oporto or not, as information is received from you, that the road from thence to Almeida is or is not practicable. Some officers of the Spanish engineers, employed in the quarter-master-general's department, with commissaries, are sent from Madrid to obtain information on the subjects you will want with respect to roads, subsistence, &c. &c. from Almeida to Burgos."

Sir John Moore to lord William Bentinck, October 22, 1808.

"Colonel Lopez has no personal knowledge of this part of Spain; but what he has told me accords with other information I had before received, that the great Madrid road was the only one by which artillery could travel; the French brought theirs from Ciudad Rodrigo to Alcantara, but by this *it was destroyed*." ... "The difficulty of obtaining correct information of roads, and the difficulties attending the subsistence of troops through Portugal, are greater than you can believe."

Sir John Hope to sir John Moore, Madrid, Nov. 20.

"I sent Wills of the engineers by Placentia to Salamanca, and before this time I suppose he may have made his report to you of the roads from the Tagus at Almaraz and Puente de Cardinal to Salamanca." ... "Delancy is upon this road, and I have directed him to communicate with you at Salamanca, as soon as possible."

Sir John Moore to lord Castlereagh, Oct. 27, 1808.

"I am under the necessity of sending lieutenant-general Hope, with the artillery, &c. by the great road leading from Badajos to Madrid, as *every information* agreed that no other was fit for the artillery."

Substance of a report from captain Carmichael Smyth of the engineers, 26th December, 1808.

"The country round about Astorga is perfectly open, and affords no advantage whatsoever to a small corps to enable it to oppose a large force with any prospect of success. In retreating, however, towards Villa Franca, at the distance of about two leagues from Astorga, the hills approaching each other form some strong ground; and the high ground in particular in the rear of the village of Rodrigatos appears at first sight to offer a most advantageous position. One very serious objection presents itself nevertheless to our making a stand near Rodrigatos, or indeed at any position before we come to the village of Las Torres (about one league from Bembibre), as the talus, or slope of the ground, from Manzanal (close to Rodrigatos) until Las Torres, would be in favour of an enemy should we be forced at Rodrigatos, and we should be consequently obliged to retreat down hill for nearly two leagues, the enemy having every advantage that such a circumstance would naturally give them.

"From Las Torres to Bembibre the ground becomes more open, but with the disadvantage, however, of the slope being still against us. From Bembibre to Villa Franca there is great variety of ground, but no position that cannot easily be turned, excepting the ground in the rear of Calcavellos, and about one league in front of Villafranca. This is by far the strongest position between Astorga and Villafranca. It is also necessary to add, that the position at Rodrigatos can easily be turned by the Foncevadon road (which, before the establishment of the Camina real, was the high road towards Coruña). This is not the case with the position in front of Villafranca, as the Foncevadon road joins the Camina real at Calcavallos in front of the proposed position."

SECTION III.—RELATING TO EQUIPMENT AND SUPPLIES.

Sir John Moore to lord Castlereagh, October 9, 1808.

"At this instant the army is without equipment of any kind, either for the carriage of the light baggage of regiments, artillery stores, commissariat stores, or other appendages of an army, and not a magazine is formed on any of the routes by which we are to march."

Sir John Moore to lord Castlereagh, Oct. 18, 1808.

"In none of the departments is there any want of zeal, but in some of the important ones there is much want of experience." ... "I have no hope of getting forward at present with more than the light baggage of the troops, the ammunition immediately necessary for the service of the artillery, and a very scanty supply of medicines."

Sir John Moore's Journal.

"My anxiety is to get out of the rugged roads of Portugal before the rains."

Sir John Moore to lord William Bentinck, Oct. 22, 1808.

"The season of the year admitting of no delay, there was a necessity for beginning the march, and trusting for information and supplies as we get on unfortunately our commissariat is inexperienced, and a **** of a contractor, Mr. Sattaro, has deceived us."

Sir David Baird to sir John Moore, October 29, 1808.

"The want of provisions for the men and forage for the horses has been one of the most serious obstacles we have had to contend with. Nor do I at present feel at all easy upon that subject." — "The horses are suffering very severely, both for want of proper accommodations and food." ... "From lord Castlereagh's letter, I was led to expect that every preparation for our equipment had been made previous to our leaving England; I need hardly say how different the case was, and how much I have been disappointed."

Mr. Stuart to sir John Moore, November 17, 1808.

"The continued slowness of the junta is the only explanation I can offer for the want of proper arrangements on the routes for the reception of the English troops."

SECTION IV.—RELATING TO THE WANT OF INFORMATION.

Sir John Moore's Journal, November 28, 1808.

"I am not in communication with any of the (Spanish) generals, and neither know their plans nor those of the government. No channel of information has been opened to me, and I have no knowledge of the force or situation of the enemy, but what, as a stranger, I pick up."

Ditto, Salamanca.

"It is singular that the French have penetrated so far (Valladolid), and yet no sensation has been made upon the people. They seem to remain quiet, and the information was not known through any other channel but that of a letter from the captain-general of the province to me."

Sir David Baird to sir John Moore, Astorga, Nov. 19, 1808.

"The local authorities have not only failed in affording us the least benefit in that respect (supplies), but have neglected to give us any kind of information as to the proceedings of the armies or the motions of the enemy."

Ditto, Astorga, 23d November.

"It is clearly apparent how very much exaggerated the accounts generally circulated of the strength of the Spanish armies have been." ... "It is very remarkable that I have not procured the least intelligence, or received any sort of communication from any of the official authorities at Madrid, or either of the Spanish generals."

Sir David Baird to sir John Moore, Villafranca, Dec. 12, 1808.

"I also enclose a letter from the marquis of Romana; you will be fully able to appreciate the degree of reliance that may be placed on the *verbal* communication made to him by the extraordinary courier from Madrid. It was from the same kind of authority that he desired the information he conveyed to me of a supposed brilliant affair at Somosierra, which turned out to be an inconsiderable skirmish altogether undeserving of notice."

Colonel Graham to sir John Moore, Madrid, Oct. 4, 1808.

"The deputies sent over knew nothing but just concerning their own provinces and *pour se faire valoir*, they exaggerated every thing; for example, those of the Asturias talked louder than any body, and Asturias as yet has never produced a man to the army; thus government, with all their wish to get information (which cannot be doubted), failed in the proper means."

Lord Wm. Bentinck to sir John Moore, Madrid, Nov. 20, 1808.

"I must at the same time take the liberty of stating my belief, that reliance cannot be placed upon the correctness of information, even if such information should not be kept back, which does not come through the channel of a British officer. It is the choice of officers, rather than the system, that seems to have failed."

Mr. Stuart to sir John Moore, Madrid, Nov. 19, 1808.

"In your direct communications with Spanish generals, you must, however, be contented with their version of the state of affairs, which I do not think can always be relied on, because they only put matters in the view in which they wish you to see them."

Ditto, Nov. 29.

"The calculation of force which the junta hope may be united in the army under your command will be as follows, if no impediment prevents the different corps reaching the points selected for their junction."

		Remarks by the author.
British	35,000	They were only 23,500.
La Romana	20,000	... only 5000 armed.
San Juan	15,000	Totally dispersed.
Levies from the south, say	10,000	None ever arrived.
	— — —	
	80,000	Real total, 28,500.
	— — —	

Lieut. Boothby, royal engineers, to sir John Moore, La Puebla, Jan. 1, 1809.

"I shall consider of any means that may more completely ensure the earliest information of the enemy's movements towards this quarter; but the Spaniards are the most difficult people in the world to employ in this way, they are so slow, so talkative, and so credulous."

SECTION V.—RELATING TO THE CONDUCT OF THE LOCAL JUNTAS.

Sir David Baird to sir John Moore, Coruña, Oct. 24, 1808.

"The answer of the supreme government to our application as read by Mr. Frere last night in the presence of the junta of this province, is certainly very different from what I expected. Instead of expressing an anxiety to promote our views and dissatisfaction at the impediments thrown in the way of our measures by the Gallician government, it merely permits us to land here in the event of its being found impracticable to send us by sea to St. Andero, and directs that if our disembarkation takes place, it should be made in detachments of 2000 or 3000 men each! to be successively pushed on into Castille, without waiting for the necessary equipment of mules and horses."

Sir David Baird to sir John Moore, Coruña, Nov. 7.

"We have received no sort of assistance from the government."

Ditto, Astorga, Nov. 19.

"Had the Spanish government afforded us any active assistance, the state of our equipments would have been much more advanced."

Colonel Graham to sir John Moore, Madrid, Oct. 4, 1808.

"All this instead of at once appointing the fittest men in the country to be ministers, looks much like private interest and patronage being the objects more than the public good."

Colonel Graham to sir John Moore, Tudela, Nov. 9, 1808.

"*It is hoped* that the Arragonese army will come over to fill it" (the line) "up, but being an independent command, no order has yet been sent. An express went after Palafox, who will return here this morning, and *then, it is hoped*, that he will send an order to general O'Neil at Sanguessa to march instantly; and *further, it is hoped*, that general O'Neil will obey this order without waiting for one from his immediate chief, Palafox, the captain-general of Arragon, who is at Zaragoza; at all events, there is a loss of above 24 hours by the happy system of independent commands, which may make the difference of our having 18,000 men more or less in the battle that may be fought whenever the French are ready." ... "Making me compliments of there being no secrets with their allies, they" (the members of the council of war) "obliged me to sit down, which I did for a quarter of an hour, enough to be quite satisfied of the miserable system established by this junta" ... "In short, I pitied poor Castaños and poor Spain, and came away disgusted to the greatest degree."

Col. Graham to Lord W. Bentinck, Centruenigo, Nov. 13, 1808.

"If any thing can make the junta sensible of the absurdity of their conduct this will. It would indeed have been more felt if a great part of the division had been lost, as might well have happened. But the difficulty of passing so many men with artillery, and in small boats, and the time that would have been required so great, that I can hardly persuade myself these people can be so foolish as ever seriously to have entertained the idea. But with whatever intentions, whether merely as a pretence for assuming the command for the purpose of irritating Castaños; whether from the silly vanity of exercising power, and doing something which, if by great good luck it had succeeded, might have proved what might be done with a more active commander; or whether from a real conviction of the excellence of the scheme, it must be equally evident to every military man, indeed to every man of common sense, that it is impossible things can succeed in this way; and then the junta itself interferes, and to worse purpose."

Castaños's Vindication.

"The nation is deceived in a thousand ways; as an example, it believed that our armies were greatly superior to those of the enemy, reckoning

80,000 men that of the centre, when your excellencies" (the junta) "knew that it only amounted to 26,000 men." ... "Madrid possessed money and riches; the nobles and loyal inhabitants of that capital wished to give both the one and the other; but whilst the armies were suffering the horrors of famine, naked, and miserable, the possessions and jewels of the good Spaniards remained quiet in Madrid, that they might be soon seized by the tyrant, as they were in the end."

Stuart's Despatch, August 7, 1808.

"No province shares the succours granted by Great Britain, although they may not be actually useful to themselves. No gun-boats have been sent from Ferrol to protect St. Ander or the coast of Biscay; and the Asturians have in vain asked for artillery from the dépôts of Gallicia. The stores landed at Gihon, and not used by the Asturians, have remained in that port and in Oviedo, although they would have afforded a seasonable relief to the army of general Blake. The money brought by the Pluto for Leon, which has not raised a man, remains in the port where it was landed."

Major Cox to sir Hew Dalrymple, Seville, August 3, 1808.

"I freely confess that I cannot help feeling some degree of apprehension that this great and glorious cause may be ruined by the baneful effects of jealousy and division."

Major Cox to sir Hew Dalrymple, Seville, August 27.

"The fact is, their" (the junta of Seville) "attention has been for some time past so much occupied by vain and frivolous disputes, and by views of private interest and advantage, that they seem to have neglected entirely every concern of real importance, and almost to have lost sight of the general interests of the country." ... "A million of dollars have, I understand, been sent out." ... "It certainly would not be prudent to intrust so large a sum to the management of the temporary government of a particular province, without having a sufficient security for its proper application. My own opinion is, that the less money which is given to them the better, until the general government is formed. This junta have shown too evident signs of a wish to aggrandize themselves, and a disinclination to afford those aids to other provinces, which they had it in their power to grant, not to afford just grounds of suspicion, that their boasted loyalty and patriotism have at times been mixed with unworthy considerations of self-interest and personal advantage."

Ditto, Sept. 5.

"By Mr. Duff's present instructions, he would have had no option" (distributing the money), "even though the *iniquitous project of partition*, which your excellency knows was once contemplated, were still in existence."

Ditto, Sept. 7.

"A dispute between the two juntas" (Seville and Grenada), "which had nearly been productive of the most serious consequences, and would probably have ended in open hostility, had it not been prevented by the moderate, but decided conduct, of general Castaños."

Ditto, Sept. 10.

"The supreme junta of Seville have latterly manifested very different views, and, I am sorry to say, they seem almost to have lost sight of the common cause, and to be wholly addicted to their particular interests: instead of directing their efforts to the restoration of their legitimate sovereign and the established form of national government, they are seeking the means of fixing the permanency of their own, and endeavouring to separate its interests from those of the other parts of Spain. To what other purpose can be attributed the order given to general Castaños, not to march on any account beyond Madrid? To what the instructions given to their deputy, don Andrea Miñiano, to uphold the authority, and preserve the integrity of the junta of Seville; to distinguish the army to which he is attached by the name of the army of Andalusia; to preserve constantly the appellation, and not to receive any orders but what came directly from this government? And above all, what other motive could induce the strong and decided measure of enforcing obedience to those orders, by withholding from general Castaños the means of maintaining his troops, in case of his refusing to comply with them?" — "What has been the late occupation of the junta of Seville? Setting aside the plans which were formed for augmenting the Spanish army in these provinces, and neglecting the consideration of those which have been proposed in their stead, their attention has been taken up in the appointment of secretaries to the different departments, in disposing of places of emolument, in making promotions in the army, appointing canons in the church, and instituting orders of knighthood. Such steps as these make their designs too evident."

Captain Carrol to sir David Baird, Llanes, Dec. 17, 1808.

"This province" (Asturias), "the first to declare war with France, has, during seven months, taken no steps that I can discover to make arrangements against the event of the enemy's entering the province." ... "What has been done with the vast sums of money that came from England, you will naturally ask? Plundered and misapplied: every person who had or has any thing to do with money concerns endeavouring to keep in hand all he can, and be ready, let affairs turn out as they may, to help himself."

Lord William Bentinck to sir Hew Dalrymple, Seville, Sept. 19, 1808.

"Notwithstanding the professions of the Junta, their conduct has evidently fallen short of them, and I think it would be very desirable that more money should not fall into their hands."

Major Cox to sir H. Dalrymple, Seville, 10 July and 27th do.

"The proclamation of Florida Blanca was received here some time ago, but was carefully suppressed by the government."

Other publications containing maxims similar to those inculcated by the proclamation of Florida Blanca have appeared, but are suppressed here with equal care.

SECTION VI. — CENTRAL JUNTA.

Lord Wm. Bentinck to sir John Moore, Madrid, Oct. 4, 1808.

"I am sorry to say that the new government do not seem to proceed with the despatch and energy which the critical situation of the country demands."

Ditto to sir H. Burrard, Madrid, Oct. 8.

"In my last letter I adverted to the inactivity and apparent supineness which prevailed in the central council in regard to the military, as well as to the other business of the government."

Ditto to sir John Moore, Nov. 8.

"But it is upon the spot where the exact state of the armies, and the extraordinary inefficiency of the government, whose past conduct promises so little for the future, are known, that the danger must be the more justly appreciated." ... "The most simple order, however urgent the case, cannot be obtained from the government without a difficulty, solicitation, and delay, that is quite incredible."

Sir John Hope to sir John Moore, Madrid, Nov. 20, 1808.

"It is perfectly evident that they" (the junta) "are altogether without a plan as to their future military operations, either in the case of success or misfortune. Every branch is affected by the disjointed and inefficient construction of their government."

Mr. Stuart to sir John Moore, Madrid, Oct. 18, 1808.

"Lord William Bentinck, as well as myself, have made repeated representations, and I have given in paper after paper to obtain something like promptitude and vigour; but though loaded with fair promises in the commencement, we scarcely quit the members of the junta before their attention is absorbed in petty pursuits and the wrangling which impedes even the simplest arrangements necessary for the interior government of a country." ... "In short, we are doing what we can, not what we wish; and I assure you we have infamous tools to work with."

Mr. Stuart to sir John Moore, Seville, Jan. 2, 1809.

"Morla's treason is abused, but passed over; and the arrival of money from Mexico, which is really the arrival of spoil for the French, seems to have extinguished every sentiment the bad views and the desperate state of things ought to have created."

Mr. Stuart to sir John Moore, Jan. 10, 1809.

"Castaños, Heredia, Castelar, and Galluzzo, are all here. These unfortunate officers are either prisoners or culprits, waiting the decision of government on their conduct in the late transactions. If the state of affairs should allow the government to continue in existence they will probably wait many months, for no determination is to be expected from people who have in no one instance punished guilt or rewarded merit since they ruled the country. The junta indeed, to say the truth, is at present absolutely null, and although they represent the sovereign authority I have never witnessed the exercise of their power for the public good."

Mr. Frere to sir John Moore. Las Santos, Dec. 16, 1808.

"The subject of the ships in Cadiz had not escaped me, but I thought it so *very dangerous* to suggest to the junta any idea except that of living and dying on Spanish ground, that I avoided the mention of any subject that could seem to imply that I entertain any other prospects."

SECTION VII.—RELATING TO THE PASSIVE STATE OF THE PEOPLE.

Sir John Moore's Journal, Dec. 9, 1808.

"In this part the people are passive. We find the greatest difficulty to get people to bring in information."

Sir John Moore to Mr. Frere. Sahagun, Dec. 23, 1808.

"If the Spaniards are enthusiastic or much interested in this cause, their conduct is the most extraordinary that was ever exhibited."

Sir John Moore to lord Castlereagh, Dec. 31, 1808, Astorga.

"I arrived here yesterday, where, contrary to his promise, and to my expectation, I found the marquis la Romana, with a great part of his troops. Nobody can describe his troops to be worse than he does, and he complains as much as we do of the indifference of the inhabitants, his disappointment at their want of enthusiasm; and said to me in direct terms, that had he known how things were, he neither would have accepted the command nor have returned to Spain. With all this, however, he talks of attacks and movements which are quite absurd, and then returns to the helpless state of his army and of the country."

Mr. Stuart to sir John Moore, Nov. 17, 1808.

"The tranquillity of Madrid is truly wonderful."

Sir David Baird to sir John Moore, Dec. 6.

"Destitute as we are of magazines, and without receiving even a show of assistance either from the government or inhabitants of the country, who, on the contrary, in many instances, even thwarted our plans and measures; we could not have advanced without exposing ourselves to almost certain destruction."

Sir David Baird to lord Castlereagh, Nov. 22, 1808, Astorga.

"Major Stuart of the 95th regiment, who was despatched in front of this place to obtain information, reports that the inhabitants appear perfectly depressed by their losses, and seem to abandon all hope of making a successful resistance."

Captain Carrol to sir John Moore, Dec. 17, 1808.

"On my arrival at Oviedo all was confusion and dismay; the confidence between the people, the army, and the junta destroyed." ... "Is it to be expected that the peasantry can be as hearty in the cause of patriotism as if they were treated with justice."

Lieut. Boothby to sir J. Moore. La Puebla, Jan. 1. 1809.

"The Spanish soldiers now here (about 700) are merely on their way to the marquis de la Romana; and as to any neighbouring passes, there are no people whom I can call upon to occupy them, or should expect to defend them, however naturally strong they may be, for I see no people who are thinking of the enemy's advance with any sentiments beyond passive dislike, and hopes of protection from God and the English army."

The prince of Neufchatel to the duke of Dalmatia, Dec. 10, 1808.

"The city of Madrid is quite tranquil, the shops are all open, the public amusements are resumed."

General Thouvenot to the prince of Neufchatel. St. Sebastian, 29th Nov. 1808.

"The successes obtained by the armies of the emperor, and those which are also foreseen, begin to make a sensible impression upon the authorities of the country, who become from day to day more affable towards the French, and more disposed to consider the king as their legitimate sovereign."

The commandant Meslin to the prince of Neufchatel. Vittoria, 29th Nov. 1808.

"The public feeling is still bad, still incredulous of our successes." ... "As to the tranquillity of the country, it appears certain."

Mr. Frere to sir John Moore. Merida, Dec. 14, 1808.

"A thousand barriers would be interposed against that deluge of panic which sometimes overwhelms a whole nation, and of which at one time I was afraid I saw the beginning in this country." ... "*The extinction of the popular enthusiasm in this country*, and the means which exist for reviving it, would lead to a very long discussion."

SECTION VIII.—MISCELLANEOUS.

Lord Collingwood to sir H. Dalrymple. Ocean, Cadiz, June 23, 1808.

"At Minorca and Majorca they describe themselves to be strong, and having nothing to apprehend. However, they made the proposal for entering into a convention with us for their defence, and in the course of it demanded money, arms, and the protection of the fleet. When, in return for them, it was required that their fleet should be given up to us, to be held for their king Ferdinand, or that a part of them should join our squadron against the enemy, they rejected all those proposals: so that whatever we did for them was to be solely for the honour of having their friendship."

Captain Whittingham to sir Hew Dalrymple, June 12, 1808.

"12th June. I returned to Xerez at three o'clock, a.m. The general sent for me and requested I would go without delay to Gibraltar, and inform lieut.-general sir Hew Dalrymple that he at present occupied Carmona with 3000 men (regulars), having his head-quarters at Utrera, where his regular force would amount to 12,000 men; that it was not his intention to attempt to defend Seville; that the heavy train of artillery, consisting of 80 pieces, was already embarked for Cadiz, under the pretext that they were wanting for the defence of its works; and that every thing was prepared for burning the harness, timbers, &c. &c. of the field pieces; that he intended to fall gradually back upon Cadiz, if forced to retreat; and that he did not at present desire that any English troops should be landed till their numbers should amount to 8 or 10,000 men, lest the ardour of the people should oblige him to commence an offensive system of warfare before the concentration of a considerable Spanish and English force should afford reasonable hopes of success."

Capt. Whittingham to sir H. Dalrymple. Utrera, June 29, 1808.

"The president approved of the idea, condemned the policy which had led Spain to attempt to establish manufactories by force, and showed clearly that the result had been the loss of a considerable branch of the revenue, the increase of smuggling, and consequently an enormous expense, in the payment of nearly *one hundred thousand* custom or rather excise officers, distributed about the country, and the ruin of numberless families seduced by the prospect of immediate profit to engage in illicit traffic."

Lord William Bentinck to sir H. Dalrymple. Madrid, Oct. 2, 1808.

"A passage of lord Castlereagh's letter, of which I received from you a copy, instructed you, if possible, to ascertain the intentions of the Spanish government after the expulsion of the French. Though not positively directed by you to ask this information, yet the occasion appeared to make the question so natural, and seemingly of course, and even necessary, that I availed myself of it, and gave to general Castaños, to be laid before count Florida Blanca, a memorandum, of which I enclose a copy, marked A."

Extract from the copy marked A.

"It seems probable in such case that no diversion could be more effectual or more formidable to Buonaparte than the march of a large combined British and Spanish army over the Pyrenees, into that part of France where there are no fortified places to resist their passage into the very heart of the country, and into that part where great disaffection is still believed to exist."

Major Fletcher, royal engineers, to sir John Moore. Betanzos, Jan. 5, 1809.

"I have the honour to report to your excellency that, in obedience to your orders, I have examined the neck of land between the harbour of Ferrol and the bridge of Puente de Humo. This ground does not appear to possess any position that has not several defects." ... "I did not find any ground so decidedly advantageous, and containing a small space, as to render it tenable for the vanguard of an army to cover the embarkation of the main body." ... "I should have sent this report much sooner, but found it impossible to procure post horses until my arrival at Lugo, and since that time I have had very bad ones."

Ditto to Ditto. Coruña, Jan. 6, 1809.

"I am therefore led to suggest, that as Coruña is fortified, reveted, and tolerably flanked (though the ground about it is certainly not favourable), as it could not be carried by a coup-demain if properly defended, as it contains a great quantity of cover for men; and as, even against artillery, it might make resistance for some days, it may be worth consideration whether, under present circumstances, it may not be desirable to occupy it in preference to the peninsula of Betanzos, should the army not turn off for Vigo."

No. XIV

JUSTIFICATORY EXTRACTS FROM SIR JOHN MOORE'S CORRESPONDENCE.

Sir J. Moore to Mr. Frere. Salamanca, Nov. 27, 1808.

"The movements of the French give us little time for discussion. As soon as the British army has formed a junction I must, upon the supposition that Castaños is either beaten or retreated, march upon Madrid, and throw myself into the heart of Spain, and thus run all risks and share the fortunes of the Spanish nation, or I must fall back upon Portugal." ... "The movement into Spain is one of greater hazard, as my retreat to Cadiz or Gibraltar must be very uncertain. I shall be entirely in the power of the Spaniards, but perhaps this is worthy of risk, if the government and people of Spain are thought to have still sufficient energy, and the means to recover from their defeats; and by collecting in the south be able, with the aid of the British army, to resist, and finally repel, the formidable attack which is prepared against them."

Sir John Moore's Journal. Salamanca, Nov. 30, 1808.

"In the night of the 28th I received an express from Mr. Stuart, at Madrid, containing a letter from lieut.-colonel Doyle, announcing the defeat of Castaños's army near Tudela. They seem to have made but little resistance, and are, like Blake's, flying; this renders my junction with Baird so hazardous that I dare not attempt it; but even were it made, what chance has this army, now that all those of Spain are beaten, to stand against the force which must be brought against it. The French have 80,000 in Spain, and 30,000 were to arrive in 20 days from the 15th of this month. As long as Castaños's army remained there was a hope, but I now see none. I am therefore determined to withdraw the army."

Ditto, Dec. 9.

"After Castaños's defeat, the French marched for Madrid, the inhabitants flew to arms, barricaded their streets, and swore to die rather than submit. This has arrested the progress of the French, and Madrid still holds out; this is the first instance of enthusiasm shown; there is a chance that the example may be followed, and the people be roused; in which case there is still a chance that this country may be saved. Upon this chance I have stopt Baird's retreat, and am taking measures to form our junction whilst the French are wholly occupied with Madrid. We are bound not to abandon the cause as long as there is hope; but the courage of the populace of Madrid may fail, or at any rate they may not be able to resist; in short, in a moment things may be as bad as ever, unless the whole country is animated and flock to the aid of the capital, and in this part the people are passive."

Sir John Moore to lord Castlereagh. Salamanca, Dec. 10, 1808.

"I certainly think the cause desperate, because I see no determined spirit any where, unless it be at Zaragoza. There is however a chance, and whilst there is that I think myself bound to run all risks to support it I am now differently situated from what I was when Castaños was defeated: I have been joined by general Hope, the artillery, and all the cavalry (lord Paget, with three regiments, is at Toro); and my junction with sir David Baird is secure, though I have not heard from him since I ordered him to return to Astorga."

Ditto to Ditto, Dec. 12.

"I shall threaten the French communications and create a diversion, if the Spaniards can avail themselves of it; but the French have in the north of Spain from 80 to 90,000 men, and more are expected. Your lordship may therefore judge what will be our situation if the Spaniards do not display a determination very different from any they have shown hitherto."

Sir John Moore's journal. Sahagan, Dec. 24, 1808.

"I gave up the march on Carrion, which had never been undertaken but with the view of attracting the enemy's attention from the armies assembling in the south, and in the hope of being able to strike a blow at a weak corps, whilst it was still thought the British army was retreating into Portugal; for this I was aware I risked infinitely too much, but something I thought was to be risked for the honour of the service, and to make it apparent that we stuck to the Spaniards long after they themselves had given up their cause as lost."

Sir J. Moore to lord Castlereagh. Coruña, Jan. 13, 1808.

"Your lordship knows that had I followed my own opinion, as a military man, I should have retired with the army from Salamanca. The Spanish armies were then beaten; there was no Spanish force to which we could unite; and from the character of the government, and the disposition of the inhabitants, I was satisfied that no efforts would be made to aid us, or favour the cause in which they were engaged. I was sensible, however, that the apathy and indifference of the Spaniards would never have been believed; that had the British been withdrawn, the loss of the cause would have been imputed to their retreat; and it was necessary to risk this army to convince the people of England, as well as the rest of Europe, that the Spaniards had neither the power nor the inclination to make any efforts for themselves. It was for this reason that I marched to Sahagun. As a diversion it has succeeded. I brought the whole disposable force of the French against this army, and it has been allowed to follow it, without a single movement being made by any of what the Spaniards call armies to favour its retreat."

No. XV

This despatch from the count of Belvedere to the count of Florida Blanca, relative to the battle of Gamonal, is an example of the habitual exaggerations of the Spanish generals.

(Translation.)

Since my arrival at Burgos I have been attacked by the enemy: in two affairs I repulsed him; but to-day, after having sustained his fire for thirteen hours, he charged me with double my force, besides cavalry, as I believe he had three thousand of the latter, and six thousand infantry at least, and I have suffered so much that I have retired on Lerma, and mean to assemble my army at Aranda de Douero. I have sustained a great loss in men, equipage, and artillery; some guns have been saved, but very few. Don Juan Henestrosa, who commanded in the action, distinguished himself, and made a most glorious retreat; but as soon as the cavalry attacked, all was confusion and disorder. I shall send your excellency the particulars by an officer when they can be procured. The volunteers of Zafra, of Sezena, of Valentia, and the first battalion of infantry of Truxillo, and the provincials of Badajoz, had not arrived at Burgos, and consequently I shall be able to sustain myself at Aranda, but they are without cartridges and ammunition. I lament that the ammunition in Burgos could not be brought off. The enemy followed me in small numbers: I am now retiring (10 P.M.), fearing they may follow me in the morning. I yesterday heard from general Blake, that he feared the enemy would attack him to-day, but his dispositions frustrated the enemy's designs, beginning the action at eleven at night.

(Signed) Conde de Belvedere.

No. XVI

EXTRACT OF A LETTER FROM THE DUKE OF DALMATIA TO THE AUTHOR.

"Dans la même lettre que vous m'avez fait l'honneur de m'écrire vous me priez aussi, monsieur, de vous donner quelques lumières sur la poursuite de Mr. le général sir John Moore, quand il fit sa retraite sur la Corogne en 1809. Je ne pense pas que vous désiriez des détails sur cette operation, car ils doivent vous être parfaitement connus, mais je saisirai avec empressement l'occasion que vous me procurez pour rendre à la mémoire de sir John Moore le témoignage que ses dispositions furent toujours les plus convenables aux circonstances, et qu'en profittant habilement des avantages que les localités pouvaient lui offrir pour seconder sa valeur, il m'opposa partout la resistance la plus énergique et la mieux calculée; c'est ainsi qu'il trouva une mort glorieuse devant la Corogne, au milieu d'un combat qui doit honorer son souvenir."

"*Paris, ce 15 Novembre, 1824.*"

No. XVII

LETTER FROM MR. CANNING TO MR. FRERE.

London, Dec. 10, 1808.

"SIR,

"The messenger, Mills, arrived here yesterday with your despatches, No. 19 to No. 26 inclusive; and at the same time advices were received from lieutenant-general sir David Baird, dated on the 29th ultimo at Astorga, which state that general to have received intelligence from sir John Moore of the complete defeat of general Castaños's army, and of the determination taken by sir John Moore, in consequence, to fall back upon Portugal, while sir David Baird is directed by sir John Moore to re-embark his troops, and to proceed to the Tagus. Thus at the same moment at which I receive from you the caution entertained in your No. 20, that a retreat into Portugal would be considered by the central junta as indicating an intention to abandon the cause of Spain, his majesty's government receive the information that this measure has actually been adopted, but under circumstances, which, it is to be supposed, could not have been in the contemplation of the central junta. To obviate, however, the possibility of such an impression, as you apprehend, being produced upon the Spanish government by the retreat of the British armies, I lose no time in conveying to you his majesty's commands, that you should forthwith give the most positive assurance, that the object of this retreat is no other than that of effecting in Portugal the junction which the events of the war have unfortunately rendered impracticable in Spain, with the purpose of preparing the whole army to move forward again into Spain whenever, and in whatever direction their services may be best employed in support of the common cause. In proof of this intention, you will inform the Spanish government, that an additional reinforcement of cavalry is at this moment sailing for Lisbon, and that the British army in Portugal will be still further augmented, if necessary, so as to make up a substantive and effective force adequate to any operation, for which an opportunity may be offered in the centre or south of Spain, according to the course which the war may take. But while you make this communication to the Spanish government, it is extremely necessary that you should accompany it with a distinct and pressing demand for the communication to you and to the British general of whatever be the plan of operations of the Spanish armies. Sir John Moore complains that he had not received the slightest intimation of any such plan at the date of his last despatch of the 20th ultimo; and I am afraid the appointment which you mention in your No. 20 of general Morla to discuss with the British commanders the mode of co-operation between the British and Spanish armies will not have taken place till after the defeat of the Spanish armies will have entirely disposed of that question for the present. The language of sir David Baird, with respect to defect of information, is precisely the same as that of sir John Moore. Sir D. Baird has indeed had the advantage of some intercourse with the marquis de la Romana; but the marquis de la Romana himself does not appear to have been in possession of any part of the views of his government, nor to have received any distinct account of the numbers, state, or destination even, of either of the armies which he was himself appointed to command. The British government has most cautiously and scrupulously abstained from interfering in any of the counsels of the junta, or presuming to suggest to them, by what plan they should defend their country. But when the question is as to the co-operation of a British force, they have a right, and it is their duty to require, that some plan should have been formed, and being formed, should be communicated to the British commander, in order that he may judge of, and (if he shall approve), may be prepared to execute the share intended to be assigned to him. You will recollect, that the army which has been appropriated by his majesty to the defence of Spain and Portugal is not merely a considerable part of the disposeable force of this country: it is, in fact, the British army. The country has no other force disposeable. It may by a great effort reinforce the army for an adequate purpose; but another army it has not to send. The proposals, therefore, which are made somewhat too lightly for appending parts of this force, sometimes to one of the Spanish armies, sometimes to another, and the facility with which its services are called for, wherever the exigency of the moment happens to press, are by no means suited to the nature of the force itself, or consonant to the views, with which his majesty has consented to employ it in Spain. You are already apprised by my former despatch (enclosing a copy of general Moore's instructions), that the British army must be kept together under its own commander, must act as one body for some distinct object, and on some settled plan.

"It will decline no difficulty, it will shrink from no danger, when, through that difficulty and danger, the commander is enabled to see his way to some definite purpose. But, in order to this, it will be necessary that such purpose should have been previously arranged, and that the British army should not again be left as that of sir John Moore and sir David Baird have recently been, in the heart of Spain, without one word of information, except such as they could pick up from common rumour, of the events passing around them. Previously, therefore, to general sir John Moore's again entering Spain, it will be expected that some clear exposition should be made to him of the system upon which the Spaniards intend to conduct the war; the points which they mean to contest with the advancing enemy, and those which, if pressed by a series of reverse, they ultimately propose to defend.

"The part assigned to the British army in the combined operation must be settled with sir John Moore, and he will be found not unambitious of that in which he may be opposed most directly to the enemy. The courage and constancy displayed by the junta, under the first reverses, are in the highest degree worthy of admiration.[31] And if they shall persevere in the same spirit, and can rouse the country to adequate exertions, there is no reason to despair of the ultimate safety of Spain. But it is most earnestly to be hoped, that the same confidence which they appear to have placed in the ability of their armies, under Blake and Castaños, to resist the attacks of the enemy, will not be again adopted as their guide, again to deceive them in the ulterior operations of the war. It is to be hoped that they will weigh well their really existing means of defence against the means of attack on the part of the enemy, and that if they find them unequal to maintain a line of defence as extended, as they have hitherto attempted to maintain, they will at once fall back to that point, wherever it may be, at which they can be sure that their stand will be permanent, and their resistance effectual. It is obvious, that unless they can resist effectually in the passes of the Guadarama, or in the Sierra Morena, the ultimate point of retreat, after a series of defeats more or less numerous and exhausting, according as they shall the sooner or the later make up their minds to retreat, is Cadiz. Supported by Cadiz on one side, and by the fortress of Gibraltar on the other, the remaining armies of Spain might unquestionably make such a stand, as no force which France could bring against them could overpower; and the assistance of the British army would be in this situation incalculably augmented by the communication with Gibraltar and the sea. I am aware of the jealousy with which the mention of a British force of any sort coupled with the name of Cadiz will be received. But the time seems to be arrived at which we must communicate with each other (the Spanish government and England) without jealousy or reserve. His majesty has abjured, in the face of the world, any motive of interested policy,—you are authorised to repeat in the most solemn manner, if necessary, that abjuration. But if in the midst of such sacrifices and such exertions as Great Britain is making for Spain; if after having foregone all objects of partial benefit, many of which the state of Spain (if we had been so ungenerous as to take that advantage of it) would have brought within our reach, the fair opinion of the British government cannot be received without suspicion; there is little hope of real cordiality continuing to subsist under reverses and misfortunes, such as Spain must but too surely expect, and such as are at all times the tests of sincerity and confidence. It is the opinion of the British government that the last stand (if all else fails) must be made at Cadiz. It is the opinion of the British government, that this stand will be made in vain only if the necessity of resorting to it is too late acknowledged, and the means of making it effectually not providently prepared. It is the opinion of the British government, that on no account should the naval means of Spain be suffered to fall into the hands of France, or those of France to be recovered by her. It is their opinion that this may be prevented, but to prevent it, the object must be fairly looked at beforehand; and it is hoped that a spirit of distrust unworthy both of those who entertain it, and of those with respect to whom it is entertained, will not be suffered to interfere between an object of so great importance and the means of ensuring its accomplishment. It is absolutely necessary to lose no time in bringing this subject fairly before the Spanish government, and if in doing so, you should see either in M. Cevallos or in count Florida Blanca marks of that distrust and suspicion which must fatally affect any measure of co-operation between the British and Spanish forces, it will be right that you should at once anticipate the subject, and you are at liberty to communicate this despatch in extenso, as the surest mode of proving the openness with which the British government is desirous of acting, and the disdain which it would feel of any imputation upon its disinterestedness and sincerity. But while this object is thus to be stated to the central government, it is not to this object alone that the services of the British army are to be appropriated. The commander-in-chief will have both the authority and the inclination to listen to any proposal for any other practicable undertaking. And it is only in the event of no such object or undertaking being presented to him in Spain, that he is directed to confine himself to the defence of Portugal. I am, &c. &c. &c.

(Signed) "George Canning."

EXTRACTS FROM A LETTER FROM MR. CANNING TO MR. FRERE, OF THE SAME DATE AS THE ABOVE.

December 10, 1808.

"The timely preparation of the fleets of France and Spain, now in the harbour of Cadiz, is also a point to be pressed by you with earnestness, but at the same time with all the delicacy which belongs to it. In the event of *an emigration to America* it is obvious that this preparation should be made beforehand. And in the case of this project not being adopted, and of a resolution being taken to defend Cadiz to the utmost, it would still be desirable that the fleets should be prepared for removal to Minorca, in order to be out of the reach of any use which the disaffected in Cadiz (of whom general Morla is represented to have expressed considerable apprehensions), might be disposed to make of them for compromise with the enemy."

EXTRACT FROM A LETTER FROM MR. CANNING TO MR. FRERE.

December 11, 1808.

"SIR,

"Complaints have been justly made of the manner in which the British troops, particularly those under sir David Baird, have been received in Spain.

"The long detention of sir David Baird's corps on board the transports at Coruña may but too probably have contributed to render the difficulties of a junction between the two parts of the British army insurmountable, by giving the enemy time to advance between them. In addition to this it is stated, that there was a total want of preparation for supply of any sort, and the unwillingness with which those supplies appear to have been administered, have undoubtedly occasioned as much disappointment as inconvenience to the British commanders. Unless some change is effected in these particulars when the army again moves into Spain, the advance of the British troops through that country will be attended with more difficulty than a march through a hostile country."

No. XVIII

RETURN OF BRITISH TROOPS EMBARKED FOR PORTUGAL AND SPAIN, IN 1808.

Extracted from the adjutant-general's returns.

Artil.	Caval.	Infantry.	Total.	
357	349	8688	9394	Commanded by sir A. Wellesley; embarked at Cork the 15th, 16th, and 17th June, 1808; sailed 12th July; landed at Mondego, August 1st.
379	...	4323	4702	Commanded by generals Ackland and Anstruther; embarked at Harwich, July 18th and 19th; landed at Maceira, August 20th, 1808.
66	...	4647	4713	Commanded by general Spencer; embarked at Cadiz; landed at Mondego, August 3d
712	563	10,049	11,324	Commanded first by sir John Moore, secondly by sir Harry Burrard; embarked at Portsmouth, April, 1808; sailed to the Baltic; returned and sailed to Portugal, July 31st; landed at Maceira, August 29th.

Artil.	Caval.	Infantry.	Total.	
...	672	.....	672	Landed at Lisbon, Dec. 31st, 1808.
186	...	943	1129	Embarked at Gibraltar; sailed Aug. 14th; landed at the Tagus in September.
94	...	929	1023	Commanded by gen. Beresford; embarked at Madeira; sailed Aug. 17th; landed at the Tagus in September.
...	672	.....	672	Commanded by general C. Stewart; embarked at Gravesend; landed at Lisbon, September 1st.
798	...	10,271	11,069	Commanded by sir D. Baird; embarked at Falmouth; sailed Oct. 9th; arrived at Coruña, 13th Oct.; landed 29th ditto.
...	...	1622	.....	Two regiments sent round to Lisbon from sir D. Baird's force.
...	2021	.....	2021	Commanded by lord Paget; embarked at Portsmouth; landed at Coruña, October 30th.
2592	4277	41,472	46,719	
			1622	Add two regiments sent to Lisbon from Coruña.
			48,341	Grand total, of which 800 were artificers, waggon train, and commissariat.

No. XIX

RETURNS OF KILLED, WOUNDED, AND MISSING, OF THE ARMY UNDER THE COMMAND OF SIR A. WELLESLEY.

1808. August.	Officers.			Men.			
	Killed.	Wound^d.	Missing.	Killed.	Wound^d.	Missing.	Total.
15th. Brillos	1	1	0	1	5	21	29
17th. Roriça	4	19	4	66	316	70	479
21st. Vimiero	4	35	2	131	499	49	720
Grand total for the campaign.	9	55	6	198	820	140	1228

No. XX

BRITISH ORDER OF BATTLE. RORIÇA, 17th AUG. 1808.

Extracted from the adjutant-general's states.

Regiments.

	1st brigade, maj.-gen. Hill,	5th / 9th / 38th	2780	
Right wing.	3d ditto, maj.-gen. Nightingale,	29th / 82d	1722	7246
	5th ditto, C. Crawfurd,	45th / 50th / 91st	2744	
	4th brigade, brig.-gen. Bowes,	6th / 32d	1829	
Left wing.	2d ditto, maj.-gen. Ferguson,	36th / 40th / 71st	2681	5846
	6th ditto (light), brig.-gen. Fane,	95th, 2d bn. / 60th, 5th, bn.	1336	
Artillery, 18 guns, 6 and 9 lbs.			660	660
Cavalry			240	240

Total British   13,992

Portuguese, col. Trant,	Infantry of the line,	1000	1,650
	Light Troops,	400	
	Cavalry,	250	

Grand total, British and Portuguese, including sick men, &c. &c.   15,642

No. XXI

BRITISH ORDER OF BATTLE. VIMIERO, 21st AUG. 1808.

Extracted from the adjutant-general's states.

		Regiments.		
Right wing.	1st brigade, gen. Hill,	5th 9th 38th	2780	2780
Centre.	6th ditto, brig.-gen. Fane,	50th 60th 95th, 2d bn	2293	4953
	7th ditto, brig.-gen. Anstruther,	9th 43d, 2d bn 52d, 2d bn 97th	2660	
Left wing.	2d brigade, maj.-gen. Ferguson,	36th 40th 71st	2681	7612
	3d ditto, maj.-gen. Nightingale,	29th 82d	1722	
	4th ditto, brig.-gen Bowes,	6th 32d	1829	
	8th ditto, maj.-gen. Ackland,	2d 20th	1380	
Reserve.	5th brigade, brig.-gen. C. Crawfurd,	45th 50th 91st	2744	2744
	Artillery, 18 guns, 6 and 9lbs.		660	660
	Cavalry, 20th light dragoons,		240	240

		Total British		18,989
	Portuguese, col. Trant,	Infantry,	1400	1,650
		Cavalry,	250	
	Grand total, including sick, wounded, and missing,			20,639

No. XXII

RETURN OF SIR HEW DALRYMPLE'S ARMY, OCT. 1, 1808.

Head-quarters, Bemfica.

	Fit for duty.	Hospital.	Detached.	Total.
Cavalry	1402	128	28	1558
Artillery	2091	146	6	2243
Infantry	25,678	3196	454	29,328
Total	29,171	3470	488	

Grand total, including artificers, waggon train, &c. &c. — 33,129

No. XXIII

EMBARKATION RETURN OF THE FRENCH ARMY UNDER GENERAL JUNOT.

Key: Of=Officers.; Hor=Horses.; Hosp.=Hospital.;

Pris.=Prisons; Cr.=Criminals.

	Present under arms.			Detached.			Absent without pay.				Total.			Cr.
							Hosp.		Pris.					
	Of	Men	Hor	Of	Men	Hor	Of	Men	Of	Men	Of	Men	Hor	Men
Infantry	273	15,860	....	52	2078	0	46	3281	17	895	..	22,635	..	13
Cavalry	48	1722	1176	..	1	1	..	195	1	...	..	1974	..	..
Artillery	21	1015	472	..	6	..	..	....	..	...	..	1121	..	..
Engineers	14	....	....	..	....	..	..	....	3	...	..	17	..	..

Guns	10	8 lbs.	⎫	
	16	4 lbs.	⎬	35
Howitzers	4	6 inch.	⎭	

Grand total 25,747 men, 1655 horses,
and 35 pieces of artillery.

Note. — On the staff of each division there are

1 General of division.	1 Inspector of reviews.
2 Generals of brigade.	1 Commissary of engineers.
7 Aides-de-camp.	2 Officers of engineers.

Artillery ⎰ 1 General. / 4 Colonels. / 2 Chefs de bataillon.

Engineers ⎱ 1 Colonel. / 2 Captains. ⎰ The remainder in the divisions.

No. XXIV

THE FOLLOWING EXTRACT FROM A MINUTE MADE BY HIS ROYAL HIGHNESS THE DUKE OF YORK IN 1808

Proves that sixty thousand men could have been provided for the campaign of 1808-9 in *Spain*, without detriment to other services.

"There are present in Portugal,

Cavalry		1640	⌉ 31,446
Infantry 34 battalions		29,806	⌋
"Under orders to embark,	⌈ Cavalry	3410	⌉ 14,829
	⌊ Infantry	11,419	⌋
	Total.		46,275

"Of this force the 20th dragoons and 8 battalions should remain in Portugal. The disposeable force would then be

	Cavalry.	Infantry.
From Portugal	1313	23,575
Under orders	3200	11,419
Force to be drawn from Sicily		8000
Total	4513	42,994
"To this may be added four regs of cav[ry]		
And the two brigades of guards	2560	2434
Grand total	7073	45,428

"When to this you add 4 battalions of infantry, which may be spared, and the artillery, it will form a corps of above sixty thousand rank and file."

Note. — The detail of names and strength of the regiments are omitted to save space.

No. XXV

ORDER OF BATTLE OF THE ARMY UNDER THE COMMAND OF SIR JOHN MOORE.

2d Division.	3d Division.	1st Division.
Lt.-gen. Hope.	Lt.-gen. Fraser.	Lt.-gen. Baird.
Brigades.	Brigades.	Brigades.

1st. 2d. 3d.   1st. 2d.   1st. 2d. 3d.

4 batts. 3 batts. 3 batts.   4 batts. 3 batts.   2 batts. 3 batts. 3 batts.

2d Flank Brigade.   *Reserve.*   *1st Flank Brigade.*
German.
Br.-gen. Alten.   M.-gen. Paget.   Col. B. Crawford.

2 Battalions.   Brigades.   3 Battalions.

1st.   2d.

3 batts.   2 batts.

Cavalry.   *Artillery.*
Lord Paget.   Col. Harding.
Brigades.   11 Brigades.

1st.   2d.

66 Pieces.

3 regs.   2 regs.

Return of sir John Moore's army, Dec. 19, 1808, extracted from the adjutant-general's morning state of that day.

	Fit for duty.	Hospital.	Detached.	Total.
Cavalry	2278	182	794	3254
Artillery	1358	97	...	1455
Infantry	22,222	3756	893	26,871
	25,858	4035	1687	31,580
Deduct	2275			
	23,583			

Men composing four battalions, viz.

Total number under arms.

⌐ 3d reg. left in Portugal.
⊣ 76th   ⌐ Between Villa
  51st   ⊢ Franca and
⌐ 59th   ⌐ Lugo.

Note. — Of 66 guns 42 were attached to the divisions, the remainder in reserve, with the exception of one brigade of 3 lbs.

No. XXVI

The following General Return, extracted from especial regimental reports, contains the whole number of non-commissioned officers and men, cavalry and infantry, lost during sir John Moore's campaign:

			Total.
Lost at or previous to the arrival of the army at the position of Lugo,	Cavalry,	95	1397
	Infantry,	1302	

Of this number 200 were left in the wine-vaults of Bembibre, and nearly 500 were stragglers from the troops that marched to Vigo.

			Total.
Lost between the departure of the army from Lugo and the embarkation at Coruña,	Cavalry,	9	2636
	Infantry,	2627	
Grand total			4033

Of the whole number above 800 contrived to escape to Portugal, and being united with the sick left by the regiments in that country, they formed a corps of 1876 men, which being re-embodied under the name of the battalions of detachments, did good service at Oporto and Talavera.

The pieces of artillery abandoned during the retreat were six 3-pounders.

These guns were landed at Coruña without the general's knowledge; they never went beyond Villa Franca, and, not being horsed, were thrown down the rocks when the troops quitted that town.

The guns used in the battle of Coruña were spiked and buried in the sand, but the French discovered them.

N.B.—Some errors may have crept into the regimental states, in consequence of the difficulty of ascertaining exactly where each man was lost, but the inaccuracies could not affect the total amount above fifty men more or less.

No. XXVII

The following states of the Spanish armies are not strictly accurate, because the original reports from whence they have been drawn were generally very loose, and often inconsistent and contradictory. Nevertheless, it is believed that the approximation is sufficiently close for any useful purpose.

STATE I.

Army of Andalusia.

1808.		Armed peasantry.	Regulars.
19th July,	Baylen	Unknown	29,000
1st Sept.	Madrid, La Mancha, Sierra Morena,	–	30,000

STATE II.

Numbers of the Spanish armies in October, 1808, according to the reports transmitted to sir John Moore by the military agents.

	Regulars.	Armed peasantry, incorporated with the regular troops.	
Troops upon the Ebro, and in Biscay,	75,000	70,000	145,000
In Catalonia,	20,000	--	20,000
In march from Aragon to Catalonia,	10,000	--	10,000
Ditto new levies from Grenada,	--	10,000	10,000
In the Asturias,	18,000	--	18,000
Total	123,000	80,000	
Grand total			203,000

STATE III.

Real numbers of the Spanish armies in line of battle, in the months of October, November, and December, 1808.

1st Line.

	Cavalry.	Infantry.	Guns.	
Army of Palafox,	550	17,500	20	Defeated and dispersed at Tudela.
Army of Castaños,	2,200	24,500	48	
Army of Blake,	100	30,000	26	Ditto at the battles of Zornoza and Espinosa.
Army of Romana,	1,404	8,000	25	
Asturians,	–	8,000	–	
Army of count Belvedere,	1,150	11,150	30	Ditto at Gamonal.
Total	5,404	99,150	149	

Deduct Romana's cavalry and guns, which never came into the line of battle	1,404	–	25
Total, brought into 1st line of battle	4,000	99,150	124	103,150

2d Line.

	Infantry.	Cavalry.	
General St Juan's division,	12,000	–	Were beaten at the Somosierra 30th Nov.; murdered their general at Talavera, Dec. 7th, and dispersed.
Fugitives from Gamonal, commanded by general Heredia,	4,000	–	Fled from Segovia and Sepulveda, Dec. 2d, and dispersed at Talavera, 7th.
Fugitives from Blake's army, re-organised by Romana,	6,000	1,400	Beaten at Mancilla, 29th Dec.; retired into Gallicia. Infantry dispersed there.
Asturian levies under Ballesteros,	5,000	–	Were not engaged.
Fugitives assembled by Galluzzo behind the Tagus,	6,000	–	Defeated and dispersed, 24th Dec., by the 4th corps, at Almaraz.
Total, brought into 2d line,	33,000	1,400	

To cover Moore's advance there were on the Ebro, in Biscay, and in the Asturias, according to the Spanish and the military agents reports	173,000
The real number brought into the field was	103,150
Exaggeration	69,850

Note. — The real amount includes the sick in the field hospitals.

No. XXVIII

SECTION I.—STATE OF THE FRENCH ARMY CALLED THE FIRST PART OF THE ARMY OF SPAIN, DATED OCT. 1, 1808.

Head-quarters, Vittoria.

King Joseph, commander-in-chief.

General Jourdan, major-general.   General Belliard, chief of the staff.

Recapitulation, extracted from the imperial states, signed by the prince of Neufchatel.

Officers included, present under arms.

		Men.	Horses.
Division imperial guard, commanded by gen. Dorsenne		2423	786
Do. reserve cavalry, imperial gendarmes, and other troops	Gen. Saligny	5417	944
Corps of marshal Bessieres		15,595	2923
Do. marshal Ney		13,756	2417
Do. marshal Moncey	16,636	22,640	3132
Garrison of Pampeluna	6004		
Garrisons of Vittoria, Bilbao, St. Sebastian, Tolosa, Montdragon, Salinas, Bergara, Villa Real, Yrun, and other places of less note	Gen. Lagrange	8479	1458
Troops disposeable at Bayonne and the vicinity, or in march upon that place	Gen. Drouet commanding 11th military division.	20,005	5196
Do. employed as moveable columns in the defence of the frontier from Bayonne to Belgarde		6042	261
In Catalonia, gen. Duhesme		10,142	1638
Fort of Fernando Figueras, gen. Reille		4027	557
Division of gen. Chabot		1434	—
Total		110,660	19,312

Note.—At this period the Spaniards and the military agents always asserted that the French had only from 35 to 45,000 men of all weapons.

STATE OF THE FRENCH ARMY, CALLED "THE SECOND PART OF THE ARMY OF SPAIN," OCTOBER 1, 1808.

This army, composed of the troops coming from the grand army and from Italy, was by an imperial decree, dated 7th September, divided into six corps and a reserve.

	Present under arms.	
	Men.	Horses.
1st corps, marshal Victor, duke of Belluno	29,547	5552
5th Do. Mortier, duke of Treviso	24,405	3495
6th Do. destined for Ney, duke of Elchingen	22,694	3945
Infantry of the viceroy of Spain's guards	1213	...
Cavalry ditto	456	551
1st division of dragoons	3695	3994
2d ditto	2940	3069
3d ditto	2020	2238
4th ditto	3101	3316
5th ditto	2903	3068
Division of general Sebastiani	5808	185
5th regiment of dragoons	556	531
German division	6067	381
Polish ditto	6818	...
Dutch brigade	2280	751
Westphalian light horse	522	559
General Souham's division	7259	...
Ditto Pino's ditto	6803	...
24th regiment of dragoons	664	731
Regiment of royal Italian chasseurs	560	512
Regiment of Napoleon's dragoons	500	474
Artillery and engineers in march for Perpignan	1706	1430
Total of 2d part	132,530	34,786
Total of 1st part	110,660	19,312
	243,190	54,098

Grand total 243,190 men and 54,098 horses.

SECTION II. – GENERAL STATE OF THE FRENCH ARMY IN SPAIN, OCTOBER 10th, 1808.

KEY:

Hosp.	=	Hospital.
Pr.	=	Prisoners.
Hor.	=	Horses.
CH	=	Cav. Hors. (Cavalry Horses)
AH	=	Art. Hors. (Artillery Horses)
Inf.	=	Infantry.

	Present under arms.		Detached.		Hosp.	Pr.	Effective.		
	Men.	Hor.	Men.	Hor.	Men.	Men.	Men.	CH	AH
1st corps, duke of Belluno,	28,797	5615	2201	219	2939	..	33,937	3329	2501
2d do. – Istria,	20,093	3219	7394	1199	5536	30	33,054	3616	802
3d do. – Cornegliano,	18,867	3186	11,082	2472	7522	219	37,690	4537	821
4th do. – Dantzic,	22,859	2410	955	40	2170	..	25,984	1791	659
5th do. – Treviso,	24,552	3833	188	6	1971	2	26,713	1805	2034
6th do. – Elchingen,	29,568	4304	3381	257	5051	33	38,033	2465	2096
7th do. general St. Cyr,	35,657	5254	1302	198	4948	200	42,107	4045	1404
8th do. duke of Abrantes,	19,059	2247	2137	1	3528	1006	25,730	1776	472
Reserve,	34,924	23,604	3533	733	3553	392	42,382	21,225	3112
1st hussars and 27th chasseurs,	1,424	1463	256	208	74	..	1,754	1675	..
Artillery and engineers in march, coming from Germany,	3,446	958	107	..	..	..	3,446	..	958
Moveable columns for the defence of the frontiers of France,	8,588	477	107	..	146	19	8,860	268	209
Total	247,834	56,567	32,536	5329	37,419	1901	319,690	46,828	15,068

	Under arms.					Detached.		Hosp.
	Artillery.		Cavalry.		Inf.			
Of this number	Men.	Hor.	Men.	Hor.	Men.	Men.	Hor.	Men.
{French,	17,868	15,107	34,172	35,761	152,770	29,647	5052	31,401
{Auxiliaries	1,503	968	4,782	4,831	36,739	2,889	277	6,018
Total	19,371	16,075	38,954	40,592	189,509	32,536	5329	37,419

	Pr.	Effective.		
Of this number	Men.	Men.	CH	AH
{French,	1771	267,629	41,565	14,253
{Auxiliaries	130	52,061	5,261	819
Total	1901	319,690	46,828	15,068

Grand total   319,690 men and 61,896 horses.

SECTION III.—STATE OF THE FRENCH ARMY OF SPAIN, THE EMPEROR NAPOLEON COMMANDING IN PERSON, 25th OCTOBER, 1808.

1148 Officers of the staff.   298 Battalions.   184 Squadrons.

Present under arms. Total,		Detached.		Hospl.	Prisons.	Grand total.		
							Cavalry	Artil.
Men.	Horses.	Men.	Horses.	Men.	Men.	Men.	horses.	horses.
249,046	55,759	33,438	4943	34,558	1892	318,934	45,242	15,498

Grand total   318,934 men and 60,740 horses.

STATE OF THE FRENCH ARMY IN SPAIN, THE EMPEROR NAPOLEON COMMANDING, 15th NOVEMBER, 1808.

Officers of the staff, 1064.   Battalions, 290.   Squadrons, 181.

Present under arms. Total,		Detached.		Hospl.	Prisons.	Grand total.		
							Cavalry	Artil.
Men.	Horses.	Men.	Horses.	Men.	Men.	Men.	horses.	horses.
255,876	52,430	32,245	8295	4517	1995	335,223	43,920	16,808

Grand total   335,223 men,   and 60,728 horses.

SECTION IV. — THE STATE OF THE FRENCH ARMY IN PORTUGAL, JANUARY 1st, 1808.

Extracted from the imperial returns.

General Junot, commander-in-chief.

General Thiebault, chief of the staff.

1st division,	general De Laborde,	⎤	
2d ditto,	general Loison,	⎬	26 battalions, 7 squadrons.
3d ditto,	general Travot,	⎪	
Cavalry,	general Kellerman,	⎦	

10 guns of	8 lbs.	⎤	
22 ditto	4 lbs.	⎬	36 pieces.
4	6 inch howitzers.	⎦	

	Present under arms.		Effective.	
	Men.	Horses.	Men.	Horses.
	16,190	1,114	24,735	1,377
At Salamanca, or in march to join the army in Portugal.	4,795	1,296	4,795	1,296
Total	20,985	2,310	29,530	2,673

STATE OF THE FRENCH ARMY IN PORTUGAL, 23d MAY, 1808.

	Under arms.		Detached.		Hosp.	Effective.		
	Men.	Horses.	Men.	Horses.	Men.	Men.	Horses.	Art.
French,	24,446	2789	—	—	2449	29,684	3586	629
Spanish division of gen. Quesnel,	9281	101	1087	—	651	11,019	—	—
Do. gen. Caraffa,	6309	844	174	13	141	6,624	13	—
Portuguese troops,	4621	483	570	234	116	5,307	234	—
Total	38,657	4217	1831	247	3357	52,634	3835	629

Grand total   52,634 men, 4454 horses, and 36 guns.

SECTION V.—STATE OF THE "2d ARMY OF OBSERVATION OF THE GIRONDE," 1st FEB. 1808, SPAIN.

General Dupont, commanding.

20 battalions, and 1 division of cavalry.

Head-quarters Valladolid.

Present under arms.		Detached.		Hospital.	Effective.	
Men.	Horses.	Men.	Horses.	Men.	Men.	Horses.
20,729	2884	1303	334	2277	24,309	3218

Total   24,309 men, and 3218 horses.

SECTION VI.—STATE OF THE "ARMY OF OBSERVATION DE COTÉ D'OCEAN," 1st FEB. 1808, SPAIN.

Marshal Moncey, commanding.

Head-quarters, Vittoria.

Present under arms.		Detached.		Hospital.	Effective.	
Men.	Horses.	Men.	Horses.	Men.	Men.	Horses.
21,878	2547	2144	—	4464	28,486	2547
Train of the guard					225	509

Grand total   28,711 men, and 3301 horses.

No. XXIX

The following letters from lord Collingwood did not come into my possession before the present volume was in the press. It will be seen that they corroborate many of the opinions and some of the facts that I have stated, and they will doubtless be read with the attention due to the observations of such an honourable and able man.

TO SIR HEW DALRYMPLE.

Ocean, Gibraltar, 30th August, 1808.

MY DEAR SIR,

I have been in great expectation of hearing of your progress with the army, and hope the first account will be of your success whenever you move. I have heard nothing lately of Junot at Cadiz; but there have been accounts not very well authenticated, that Joseph Buonaparte, in his retiring to France, was stopped by the mass rising in Biscay, to the amount of 14,000 well-armed men, which obliged him to return to Burgos, where the body of the French army was stationed.

At Saragossa the French, in making their fourteenth attack upon the town, were defeated, repulsed with great loss, and had retired from it. There is a deputy here from that city with a commission from the marquis de Palafox to request supplies. The first aid upon their list is for 10 or 15,000 troops. The deputy states they have few regulars in the province, and the war has hitherto been carried on by all being armed. In this gentleman's conversation I observe, what I had before remarked in others, that he had no view of Spain beyond the kingdom of Aragon; and in reply to the observations I made on the necessity of a central government, he had little to say, as if that had not yet been a subject of much consideration. I have great hope that general Castaños, Cuesta, and those captains-general who will now meet at Madrid will do something effectual in simplifying the government. In a conversation I had with Morla on the necessity of this, he seemed to think the juntas would make many difficulties, and retain their present power as long as they could.

I hope, my dear sir, you will give some directions about this puzzling island (*Perexil*), which it appears to me will not be of any future use; but the people who are on it will suffer much in the winter, without habitations, except tents; I conceive the purpose for which it was occupied is past, and will probably never return; whenever they quit it, they should bring the stores away as quietly as possible; for if I am not mistaken, the emperor has an intention to keep them, and will remonstrate against them going. I hope you have received good accounts from lady Dalrymple, &c.

I am to sail to-day for Toulon, where every thing indicates an intention in the French to sail. Mr. Duff brought a million of dollars to Seville, and has instructions to communicate with the junta; but he appears to me to be too old to do it as major Cox has done: he is still there, and I conclude will wait for your instructions. Mr. Markland would accept with great thankfulness the proposal you made to him to go to Valencia.

I beg my kind regards, &c.
Collingwood.

P. S. Prince Leopold is still here, and I understand intends to stay until he hears from England. I have given passports for Dupont and a number of French officers to go to France on parole, ninety-three in number. General Morla was impatient to get them out of the country. The Spaniards were much irritated against them; they were not safe from their revenge, except in St. Sebastian's castle.

TO SIR HEW DALRYMPLE.

Ocean, off Toulon, October 18, 1808.

MY DEAR SIR,

I have received the favour of your letters of the 27th August and 5th September, and beg to offer you my sincere congratulations on the success of the British army in Portugal, which I hope will have satisfied the French that they are not those invincible creatures which Buonaparte had endeavoured to persuade them they were.

It is a happy event to have rescued Portugal from the government of France, and their carrying off a little plunder is a matter of very secondary consideration; perhaps it may have the good effect of keeping up the animosity of the Portuguese who suffer, and incite them to more resistance in future.

The great business now is to endeavour to establish that sort of government, and organise that sort of military force, which may give security to the country; and the great difficulty in Portugal will be to find men who are of ability to place at the head of the several departments, who have patriotism to devote themselves to its service, and vigour to maintain its independence. In a country exhausted like Portugal, it will require much ingenious expedient to supply the want of wealth and of every thing military. If it is not found in the breasts of those to whom the people look up, Portugal will remain in a hapless and uncertain state still.

I have not heard from sir Charles Cotton how he settled his terms with the Russian admiral; but as he has got possession of the ships to be sent to England, they cannot but be good: the hoisting the English flag on the fort which surrendered to our troops, I conclude, would be explained to the Portuguese as not to be understood as taking possession by England for other purpose than to be restored to its prince, as was done at Madeira; but in this instance it ought to have been thought necessary to deprive Siniavin of the argument he would have used of the neutrality of the Portuguese flag, with whom his nation was not at *war*.

I left Cadiz the moment every thing in that quarter was pacific; and Mr. Duff arrived there with a million of dollars for their use: this money was sent to the junta of Seville, where I am afraid there are many members unworthy of the trust.

I have only heard once from Cox since I left that quarter. After getting the money, father Gil seemed to have dropt his communications with major C., and their discussions were not of a nature to excite much public interest;

they consisted more in private bickerings than of grave consult for the public weal. Tilly seems to have been entirely disappointed in his project, both in respect to the annexation of southern Portugal to Andalusia and the pension of 12,000 dollars for his service in the supreme council: of those you will be informed by major Cox. I am afraid I related the proceedings to his majesty's ministers of events which were passing almost under my eye, and gave my opinion on them with too great freedom; I mean with a freedom that is not usual; but they were facts of which, without being possessed, his majesty's ministers could not have a knowledge of the real state of affairs in Spain; and the sentiments those facts inspired were necessary to explain my motives and the rule of conduct which I pursued. And still I consider the great and only danger to which Spain is now exposed is the supposition that the whole nation is possessed of the same patriotism which, in Andalusia, Aragon, and Valencia, led to such glorious results. It is far otherwise: there are not many Castaños, nor Cuestas, nor Palafox's; and take from Spain the influence of the clergy, and its best source of power would be lost: wherever this influence is least, the war is languid.

I wrote to you some time since to represent the state of Catalonia. Nothing can be more indifferent to the cause than they appear to be; yet the common peasantry have not less spirit nor less desire to repel their enemy. They have no leaders. Palacio, the captain-general, stays at Villa Franca, west of Barcelona, talking of what he intends to do; and the people speak of him as either wanting zeal in their cause or ability to direct them; while the French from Barcelona and Figueras do just what they please. When the French attacked Gerona he did nothing to succour it. The greatest discomfiture they suffered was from lord Cochrane, who, while they were employed at the siege, blew up the road, making deep trenches in a part where the fire of his ships could be brought upon; and when they came there he drove them from their guns, killed many, and took some cannon.

The French fleet is here quite ready for sea, and I am doing all that is in my power to meet them when they do come out. It is an arduous service: the last ten days we have had gales of wind incessantly: the difficulty of keeping a sufficient squadron is very great. I think the storms from those Alpine mountains are harder than in England, and of more duration.

I beg my best regards to captain Dalrymple, and my sincerest wishes for every success to attend you.

I am, my dear sir Hew,

Your obedient and most humble servant,

Collingwood.

P. S. In the letter which I wrote to you on the state of Catalonia I represented the necessity of sending a body of British troops to Catalonia. There is no other prospect of the French being kept in any bounds. The avenues to France are as open now as at any time they have been. I have kept a ship always at Rosas Bay; her marines have garrisoned the castle, and her company assisted in repairing the works. The French appear to have designs on that place. The presence of the English alone prevents them. If 18,000 men were here of our army I think they would make Mr. Palacio come forward and put the whole country into activity, which till then I don't think they ever will be.

Collingwood.

They want an English resident at Gerona, that they may have somebody to apply to for succour....

[The rest torn off in the original.]

TO SIR HEW DALRYMPLE.

Ocean, off Minorca, April 8, 1809.

MY DEAR SIR,

I received the favour of your letter a few days ago, which gave me great pleasure, after all the trouble and vexations you have had, to hear you were all well.

I was exceedingly sorry when I saw the angry mood in which the convention in Portugal was taken up, even before the circumstances which led to it were at all known. Before our army landed in Portugal the French force was reported to be very small. I remember its being said that a body of 5000 troops were all that was necessary to dispossess Junot. I conclude the same sort of report went to England; and this, with the victory that was obtained, led people to expect the extermination of the few French which were supposed to be there; and when once the idea is entertained people shut their eyes to difficulties.

I remember what you told me, the last time I saw you off Cadiz, of the communications which might be made to you by an officer who possessed the entire confidence of ministers. I thought then, that whatever ministers had to communicate to a commander-in-chief, could not be done better than by themselves; for intermediate communications are always in danger of being misunderstood, and never fail to cause doubts and disturb the judgment. I hope now it is all over, and your uneasiness on that subject at an end.

My labours I think will never cease. I am worn down by fatigue of my mind; with anxiety and sorrow; my health is very much impaired; and while our affairs require an increased energy, I find myself less able to conduct them, from natural causes. I give all my thoughts and time, but have interruptions, from my weak state of body, which the service will scarcely admit of. I never felt the severity of winter more than this last. They were not gales of wind, but hurricanes; and the consequence is, that the fleet has suffered very much, and many of the ships very infirm. I would not have kept the sea so long, because I know the system of blockading must be ruinous to our fleet at last; and in no instance that I can recollect has prevented the enemy from sailing. In the spring we are found all rags, while they, nursed through the tempest, are all trim. I would not have done it; but what would have become of me if, in my preserving the ships, the French had sailed and effected any thing in any quarter? The clamour would have been loud, and they would have sought only for the cause in my treachery or folly, for none can understand that there is any bad weather in the Mediterranean. The system of blockade is ruinous; but it has continued so long, and so much to the advantage of the mercantile part of the nation, that I fear no minister will be found bold enough to discontinue it. We undertake nothing against the enemy, but seem to think it enough to prevent him taking our brigs: his fleet is growing to a monstrous force, while ours every day gives more proof of its increasing decrepitude.

Of the Spaniards I would not say much; I was never sanguine in the prospect of success, and have no reason to change my opinion: the lower class of people, those who are under the influence of priests, would do any thing were they under proper direction; but directors are difficult to be found. There is a canker in the state: none of the superior orders are serious in their resistance to the French, and have only taken a part against them thus far from the apprehension of the resentment of the people. I believe the junta is not free from the taint of the infection, or would they have continued Vives Don Miguel in high and important command after such evident proofs as he gave of want of loyalty? I do not know what is thought of Infantado in England; but in my mind, the man, the duke (for his rank has a great deal to do with it), who would seat himself in Buonaparte's council at Bayonne, sign his decrees, which were distributed in Spain, and then say he was forced to do it, is not the man who will do much in maintaining the glory or the independence of any country, no such man should be trusted now. The French troops are mostly withdrawn from Spain, except such as are necessary to hold certain strong posts, and enable them to return without impediment. Figueras, Barcelona, and Rosas, are held here in Catalonia, and of course the country quite open to them. Will the Spaniards dispossess them? The junta does not seem to know any thing of the provinces at a distance from them. At Tarragona the troops are ill clothed, and without pay; on one occasion they could not march against the enemy, having no shoes; and yet at Cadiz they have 51 millions of dollars. Cadiz seems to be a general depôt of every thing they can get from England. If they are not active the next two months Spain is lost.

I hope lady Dalrymple, &c. &c.

I ever am, my dear sir,

Your very faithful and obedient servant,

Collingwood.

FOOTNOTES:

[1] For a description of this organization, the reader is referred to the "Precis des Evénemens Militaires, par Mathieu Dumas;" a work of infinite labour and research, in which the military story of ten years is told with unrivalled simplicity and elegance.

[2]

Viz.:— about	30,000	Cavalry,
	6,000	Foot Guards,
	170,000	Infantry of the line,
	14,000	Artillery.
	— — —	
Total,	220,000	

Of these, between 50 and 60,000 were employed in the Colonies and in India; the remainder were disposable, because from 80 to 100,000 militia, differing from the regular troops in nothing but the name, were sufficient for the home duties. If to this force we add 30,000 marines, the military power of England must be considered prodigious.

[3] The anagram of Llorente.

[4] I think it necessary to state, in addition to the authorities quoted in the margin, that I have derived my information from officers, some French, some Italian, who were present in the tumult of the 2d of May. On the veracity of my informants I have the firmest reliance; their accounts agreed well, and the principal facts were confirmed by the result of my personal inquiries at Madrid in the year 1812.

[5] Five sail of the line and one frigate.

[6] Forty-two thousand dollars.

[7] Tio Jorge and Tio Marin, which may be rendered goodman Jorge, and goodman Marin, were two of the real chiefs whose energy saved Zaragoza in the first siege.

[8] The late Lord Melville.

[9] This transaction furnishes an example of the imprudence of being precipitate in granting public honours. Lord Strangford's despatch relative to the emigration was written (as it is confidently asserted) not at Lisbon, but at Salt Hill, in the presence of sir James Yeo. His lordship (unintentionally of course) impressed the ministers with an idea that to his personal exertions the emigration should be attributed; whereas the prince regent of Portugal, yielding to the vigorous negotiations of sir Sydney Smith, not only embarked on the 27th, before lord Strangford arrived at Lisbon, but actually sailed without his lordship's having had any official interview with his royal highness, and consequently without having had any opportunity to advance or retard the emigration. The English ministers, eager to testify their satisfaction at that event, conferred the red riband, not upon sir Sydney Smith, who had succeeded, but upon lord Strangford, who had failed! a result that his lordship could not have anticipated, or he would undoubtedly have written his despatch at Lisbon when the facts were fresh on his mind, and when he could have more forcibly described the admiral's share in the transaction.

[10] The coast of Portugal.

[11] This is a remarkable instance of ministerial confusion; the despatch from sir Hew Dalrymple referred to as giving this "assurance," not only made no mention of a promise to the junta of Seville, but the junta itself was not in existence at the time his despatch was written.

[12] The occupation of Cadiz was a favourite project with the English government at this period. They were not discouraged by Spencer's unsuccessful efforts to gain admittance, nor by the representations of sir Hew Dalrymple, who had grounds for believing that any attempt to introduce British troops there, would bring down the greater part of Castaños' army to oppose it by force; nor by the consideration that in a political view such a measure would give a subject for misrepresentation to the enemy's emissaries, and that, in a military view, the burthen of Cadiz would clog all general operations in Portugal.

[13] The ministers were so intent upon occupying Cadiz, and so little acquainted with the state of public feeling in Andalusia, that one of those generals carried with him his appointment as governor of that city.

[14] Yet lord Byron has gravely asserted in prose and verse that the convention was signed at the marquis of Marialva's house at

Cintra; and the author of "The Diary of an Invalid," improving upon the poet's discovery, detected the stains of the ink spilt by Junot upon the occasion.

[15] There is good reason to believe, that a silly intrigue carried on through the medium of the princess of Tour and Taxis with Talleyrand, and some others, who were even then ready to betray Napoleon, was the real cause of the negotiation having been broken off by Mr. Canning.

[16] Sir Walter Scott, in his Life of Napoleon, inaccurately asserts, that sir John Moore, "sent ten thousand men, under sir David Baird, by sea, to Coruña," and that "the general science of war, upon the most extended scale, seems to have been so little understood or practised by the English generals at this time, that instead of the country being carefully reconnoitred by officers of skill, the march of the army was arranged by such hasty and inaccurate information as could be collected from the peasants. By their reports general Moore was induced to divide his army" — — What "the general science of war upon an extended scale" may mean, I cannot pretend to say; but that sir David Baird was sent by the government from England direct to Coruña, and that sir John Moore was not induced by the reports of the peasants to divide his army, may be ascertained by a reference to the Appendix, No. 13, section 2.

[17] Navarre and Biscay being within the French line of defence, the inhabitants were, according to the civilians, de facto French subjects.

[18] In the winter of 1812, captain Hill, of the royal navy, was sent to Cronstadt to receive Spanish prisoners who had been taken by the Russians. Of five thousand Spaniards that were delivered to him, above four thousand were men who had escaped with Romana from the Danish isles in 1808. Captives at Espinosa, they had entered the French ranks, served in Napoleon's continental wars, and being made prisoners by the Russians in the retreat from Moscow, were once more brought back to Spain in English vessels. This is a curious commentary upon the silly stories that have been promulgated relative to the desperate fighting of Blake's army, and the devoted courage with which, Spartan-like, Romana's soldiers died to a man upon the field of battle.

	MEN.
Landed at Gihon, 9th October, 1808	9,404
Deduct cavalry, which never joined Blake's army	1,404
	— —
	8,000
Prisoners delivered to captain Hill	4,500
	— —
	3,500

Now, if we make allowance, 1°. For natural and violent deaths during four years of service under Napoleon, 2°. For those who might not have been taken by the Russians, and if we believe that some *might possibly have escaped from Espinosa alive,* the number of Spartans will probably be thought not to have exceeded the classical number of 300.

[19] Dukes of Infantado, of Hijar, Medina Celi, and Ossuna; marquis Santa Cruz; counts Fernan, Miñez, and Altamira; prince of Castello Franco, Pedro Cevallos, and the bishop of St. Ander, were proscribed, body and goods, as traitors to France and Spain.

[20] The following remarkable instance of courage and discipline deserves to be recorded. John Walton, a native of the south of Ireland, and Richard Jackson, an Englishman, were posted in a hollow road on the plain beyond the bridge, and at a distance from their piquet. If the enemy approached, one was to fire, run back to the brow of the hill, and give notice if there were many or few; the other was to maintain his ground. A party of cavalry following a hay cart stole up close to these men, and suddenly galloped in, with a view to kill them and surprise the post. Jackson fired, but was overtaken, and received twelve or fourteen severe wounds in an instant; he came staggering on, notwithstanding his mangled state, and gave the signal. Walton, with equal resolution and more fortune, defended himself with his bayonet, and wounded several of the assailants, who retreated, leaving him unhurt; but his cap, his knapsack, his belts, and his musket were cut in above twenty places, and his bayonet was bent double, his musket covered with blood, and notched like a saw from the muzzle to the lock. Jackson escaped death during the retreat, and finally recovered of his wounds.

[21] Several thousand infantry slept in the long galleries of an immense convent built round a square; the lower corridors

were filled with the horses of the cavalry and artillery, so thickly stowed that it was scarcely possible for a single man to pass them, and there was but one entrance. Two officers returning from the bridge, being desirous to find shelter for their men, entered the convent, and with horror perceived that a large window shutter being on fire, and the flame spreading to the rafters above, in a few moments the straw under the horses would ignite, and six thousand men and animals would inevitably perish in the flames. One of the officers, (captain Lloyd, of the forty-third,) a man of great activity, strength, and presence of mind, made a sign to his companions to keep silence, and springing on to the nearest horse, run along the backs of the others until he reached the flaming shutter, which he tore off its hinges and cast out of the window; then returning quietly, awakened some of the soldiers, and cleared the passage without creating any alarm, which in such a case would have been as destructive as the flames. Captain Lloyd was a man of more than ordinary talents; his character has been forcibly and justly depicted in that excellent little work called the "Life of a Sergeant."

[22]

Lorges's dragoons	1,400
La Houpaye's ditto	1,450
Franceschi's light cavalry	1,350
	— —
Total	4,200

[23] Ninety-fifth regiment.

[24] I am aware that the returns laid before Parliament in 1809 make the sum 60,000l., and the whole loss during the campaign nearly 77,000l.; but it is easier to make an entry of one sum for a treasury return, than to state the details accurately. The money agents were, like the military agents, acting independently, and all losses went down under the head of abandoned treasure. My information is derived from officers actually present, and who all agree that the only treasure abandoned was that at Nogales, and that the sum was 25,000l. When it was ordered to be rolled over the brink of the hill, two guns, and a battalion of infantry, were actually engaged with the enemy to protect it, and some person in whose charge the treasure was, exclaiming, "it is money!" the general replied, "so are shot and shells." The following anecdote will show how such accidents may happen in war. An officer had charge of the cars that drew this

treasure; in passing a village, a lieutenant of the fourth regiment observing that the bullocks were exhausted, took the pains to point out where fresh and strong animals were to be found, and advised that the tired ones should be exchanged for others more vigorous, which were close at hand; but the escorting officer, either ignorant of, or indifferent to his duty, took no notice of this recommendation, and continued his march with the exhausted cattle.

[25] The author's eldest brother. He was returned amongst the killed. When the French renewed the attack at Elvina he was, with a few men, somewhat in advance of the village, for the troops were broken into small parties by the vineyard walls and narrow lanes. Being hurt, he endeavoured to return, but the enemy coming down, he was stabbed, and thrown to the ground with five wounds; and death appeared inevitable, when a French drummer rescued him from his assailants, and placed him behind a wall. A soldier with whom he had been struggling, irritated to ferocity, returned to kill him, but was prevented by the drummer. The morning after the battle the duke of Dalmatia being apprised of major Napier's situation, had him conveyed to good quarters, and with a kindness and consideration very uncommon, wrote to Napoleon, desiring that his prisoner might not be sent to France, which (from the system of refusing exchanges) would have been destruction to his professional prospects. The marshal also obtained for the drummer the decoration of the legion of honour. The events of the war obliged Soult to depart in a few days from Coruña, but he recommended major Napier to the attention of marshal Ney; and that marshal also treated his prisoner with the kindness of a friend rather than the rigour of an enemy, for he quartered him with the French consul, supplied him with money, gave him a general invitation to his house on all public occasions, and refrained from sending him to France. Nor did marshal Ney's kindness stop there; for when the flag of truce arrived, and that he became acquainted with the situation of major Napier's family, he suddenly waved all forms, and instead of answering the inquiry by a cold intimation of his captive's existence, sent him, and with him the few English prisoners taken in the battle, at once to England, merely demanding that none should serve until regularly exchanged. I should not have dwelt thus long upon the private adventures of an officer, but that gratitude

demands a public acknowledgment of such generosity, and the demand is rendered imperative by the after misfortunes of marshal Ney. The fate of that brave and noble-minded man is well known. He who had fought five hundred battles for France, not one against her, was shot as a traitor!

[26] The loss of the English army was never officially returned, but was estimated by sir John Hope at about eight hundred. The French loss I have no accurate account of. I have heard from French officers that it was above three thousand men; this number, I confess, appears to me exaggerated; but that it was very great I can readily believe. The arms of the British were all new, the ammunition quite fresh, and it is well known that, whether from the peculiarity of our musquets, the physical strength and coolness of the men, or both combined, the fire of an English line is at all times the most destructive known. The nature of the ground also prevented any movement of the artillery on either side; hence the French columns in their attacks were exposed to a fire of grape which they could not return, because of the distance of their batteries.

[27] Sir John Moore's sentiments upon this occasion are expressed in the following letter, which displays the pure and elevated patriotism that distinguished him through life, and rendered his death heroic.

"Portsmouth, 23d July, 1808.

"MY LORD,

"I am this instant honoured with your lordship's letter (by messenger) of yesterday's date. As I have already had the honour to express my sentiments to your lordship fully at my last interview, it is, I think, unnecessary to trouble you with a repetition of them now.

"I am about to proceed on the service on which I have been ordered, and it shall be my endeavour to acquit myself with the same zeal by which I have ever been actuated when employed in the service of my country. The communication which it has been thought proper to make to his majesty cannot fail to give me pleasure; I have the most perfect reliance on his majesty's justice, and shall never feel greater security than when my conduct, my character, and my honour, are under his majesty's protection.

"I have the honour to be, &c. &c.
(Signed) "JOHN MOORE.

"To the Right Honourable Viscount Castlereagh."

[28] Note.—These two words are added in Napoleon's own hand-writing.

[29] Note by the author.—This calculation was made under the supposition that general Avril had joined Dupont.

[30] On ne comprend pas dans ces celculs les garnisons de Pampelune, St. Sebastien, Vittoria, Tolosa, Bilbao, &c.: il n'est pas question non plus de l'armée de Catalogne.

[31] The extract which follows this letter furnishes a curious comment on this passage.